# PERSPECTIVES ON AMERICAN METHODISM:

## INTERPRETIVE ESSAYS

# PERSPECTIVES ON AMERICAN METHODISM

## INTERPRETIVE ESSAYS

Edited by

## Russell E. Richey
## Kenneth E. Rowe
## Jean Miller Schmidt

KINGSWOOD BOOKS
An Imprint of Abingdon Press
Nashville, Tennessee

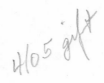

PERSPECTIVES ON AMERICAN METHODISM
INTERPRETIVE ESSAYS

*Copyright © 1993 by Abingdon Press*

93  94  95  96  97  98  99  00  01  02 — 10  9  8  7  6  5  4  3  2  1

---

**Library of Congress Cataloging-in-Publication Data**

Perspectives on American Methodism: interpretive essays    /
    edited by Russell E. Richey, Kenneth E. Rowe, and Jean Miller Schmidt.
        p.    cm.
    **ISBN  0-687-30782-1**
        1. Methodist Church—United States—History.    I. Richey, Russell E.  II. Rowe,
    Kenneth E.  III. Schmidt, Jean Miller.
    BX8235.P478    1993                                                    93-14843
    287'.673—dc20                                                          CIP

---

Printed in the United States of America on recycled, acid-free paper.

# ACKNOWLEDGMENTS

Reprinted from *Rethinking Methodist History*, ed. Russell E. Richey and Kenneth E. Rowe (Nashville: Kingswood Books, 1985), with the permission of the individual authors:

"Evangelical America—The Methodist Ideology," by Donald G. Mathews.

"The Attraction of Methodism: The Delmarva Peninsula as a Case Study, 1769–1820," by William H. Williams.

"African Methodisms and the Rise of Black Denominationalism," by Will B. Gravely.

"Methodist Ministers and the Second Party System," by Richard Carwardine.

"Reexamining the Public/Private Split: Reforming the Continent and Spreading Scriptural Holiness," by Jean Miller Schmidt.

"The Emerging Voice of the Methodist Woman: The Ladies' Repository, 1841–61," by Joanna Brown Gillespie.

"Rich Methodists: The Rise and Consequences of Lay Philanthropy in the Mid-19th Century," by Donald B. Marti.

"The United Methodist System of Itinerant Ministry," by E. Dale Dunlap.

Reprinted with permission of the author:

"A Critical Analysis of the Ministry Studies since 1944," by Richard P. Heitzenrater. Originally published as *Occasional Paper* (76, Sept. 1988), by the United Methodist General Board of Higher Education and Ministry.

"From Christian Perfection to the 'Baptism of the Holy Ghost,'" by Donald Dayton, *Aspects of Pentecostal-Charismatic Origins,* ed. Vinson Synan (Plainfield: Logos International, 1975), 39–54.

Reprinted with the permission of the author and the Community for Religious Research and Education, Inc.:

"Pioneering Social Gospel Radicalism," by George McClain, *Radical Religion* 5 (1980): 10–20.

Published with permission of the author:

"'That Language Might Be Given Me': Women's Experience in Early Methodism," by Diane H. Lobody.

Reprinted with permission from Indiana University Press:

"Nineteenth-Century Black Women's Spiritual Autobiographies: Religious Faith and Self-Empowerment," by Nellie Y. McKay; *Interpreting Women's Lives,* ed. Joy W. Barbre, et al. (Bloomington: Indiana University Press, 1989), 139–54.

Reprinted with the permission of *Methodist History*:

"A Comparison of the Doctrines of Ministry of Francis Asbury and Philip William Otterbein," by Jeffrey P. Mickle; *Methodist History* 19 (July 1981), 187–205.

"And Obey God, Etc.: Methodism and American Indians," by Bruce David Forbes, *Methodist History* 23 (Oct. 1984), 3–24.

"Ordination of Women, Round One, Anna Oliver and the Methodist General Conference of 1880," by Kenneth E. Rowe; *Methodist History* 12 (April 1974), 60–72.

"Denominational Modernization and Religious Identity: The Case of the Methodist Episcopal Church," by William McGuire King; *Methodist History* 20 (Jan. 1982), 75–89.

"The Social Creed and Methodism through Eighty Years," by Donald K. Gorrell; *Methodist History* 26 (July 1988), 213–28.

"The Revival of Stewardship and the Creation of the World Service Commission in the Methodist Episcopal Church 1912–1924," by Stephen Perry; *Methodist History* 23 (July 1985), 223–39.

Reprinted with permission from *Quarterly Review: A Journal of Theological Resources for Ministry*:

"At Full Liberty: Doctrinal Standards in Early American Methodism," by Richard P. Heitzenrater; *Quarterly Review* 5 (Fall 1985): 6–27. Copyright 1985 by The United Methodist Publishing House and the United Methodist Board of Higher Education and Ministry.

"United Methodism's Basic Ecumenical Policy," by John Deschner; *Quarterly Review* 11 (Fall 1991): 41–57. Copyright 1991 by The United Methodist Publishing House and the United Methodist Board of Higher Education and Ministry.

Reprinted with permission from Abingdon Press:

"The Concern for Systematic Theology, 1840–70," by Leland Scott; *History of American Methodism*, ed. Emory S. Bucke, II (Nashville: Abingdon Press, 1964), 380–90.

"For God and Home and Native Land: The W.C.T.U.'s Image of Woman in the Late Nineteenth Century," by Carolyn DeSwarte Gifford; *Women in New Worlds*, ed. Hilah F. Thomas and Rosemary Skinner Keller (Nashville: Abingdon Press, 1981), 1:310–27.

"'A New Impulse': Progress in Lay Leadership and Service by Women of the United Brethren in Christ and the Evangelical Association, 1870–1910," by Donald K. Gorrell, *Women in New Worlds* 1:233–45.

"Creating a Sphere for Women: The Methodist Episcopal Church, 1869–1906," by Rosemary Skinner Keller; *Women in New Worlds* 1:246–60.

"The Social Gospel According to Phoebe: Methodist Deaconesses in the Metropolis, 1885–1918" by Mary Agnes Dougherty; *Women in New Worlds* 1:200–16.

Reprinted with the permission of *Church History*:

"The Sacraments in Early American Methodism," by Paul S. Sanders; *Church History* 26 (1957): 355–71.

Reprinted with the permission of the Society for Historians of the Early American Republic, *Journal of the Early Republic*:

"Social Religion, the Christian Home, and Republican Spirituality in Antebellum Methodism," by A. Gregory Schneider; *Journal of the Early Republic* 10 (Summer 1990): 163–89.

# CONTENTS

## NINETEENTH-CENTURY PATTERNS

## REFORMS

## THE TWENTIETH-CENTURY VIEW

# PREFACE

The essays in this volume sample the best in recent historical scholarship on Methodism. Exhibited as well are a few classic items which serve to round out the collection. The accent falls on U.S. United Methodism and the traditions contributory to it. The collection should serve the serious student of Methodist history and can best be used along with a standard narrative. Although organized in roughly chronological fashion, it cannot and does not pretend to suffice as a coherent presentation. Instead, it provides new perspectives and fresh readings on important Methodist topics; it opens new topics for Methodist self-understanding; it takes in-depth or case-study attention to subjects that overviews must slight.

All the essays have appeared elsewhere but many in useful collections now out of print, notably our *Rethinking Methodist History*[1] and Rosemary Skinner Keller, *et al., Women in New Worlds,*[2] from both of which we sample liberally. *Methodist History* and *Quarterly Review* contribute significantly as well and we appreciate the willingness of the editors of these and other publishers and of the authors to permit us to reprint at modest or no cost. We hope that those intrigued by items included here will track them to their source and discover the other riches therein contained. We encourage the serious student of Methodism to subscribe to these journals.

Of assistance in further exploration are several superb new bibliographies, notably, *United Methodist Studies: Basic Bibliographies,*[3] compiled and edited by Kenneth E. Rowe, *Women in the Wesleyan and United Methodist Traditions: A Bibliography,* edited by Susan M. Eltscher and *The Racial and Ethnic Presence in American Methodism: A Bibliography,*[4] compiled by C. Jarrett Gray, Jr. Also invaluable is *Methodist Reviews Index 1818–1985,*[5] compiled by Elmer J. O'Brien, which covers five scholarly journals in the

Methodist traditions. Such resources guide the reader to aspects of the Methodist saga to which this collection cannot give major attention. For new and important scholarship in Methodist and Wesleyan scholarship, the reader will want to consult other Kingswood Books,[6] a series which achieves with full volumes what this collection attempts with essays.

Several of these essays look at standard themes in Methodist historiography and do so in classic intellectual history style. A number exhibit relatively new methods and/or attend to topics previously unexplored or underexplored. Several, for instance, belong to that amorphous subfield called social history. They draw our attention away from elites, from doctrine, from the hierarchy, from the clergy. Instead, they examine how and in what ways Methodism appealed to the common folk and how it configured itself as a folk movement. Similar findings derive from the number of essays that explore gender, women's roles, the family, women's organizations. Less novel, perhaps, are the topics of race and ethnicity, scarcely new issues for Methodism, but nevertheless always deserving fresh insight. Here also are new readings of spirituality, worship, the diaconate, stewardship, organization, ecumenism, reform, ordination (male and female, black and white). Less conventional subjects include the relation of Methodism to the American party system and Methodist accumulation of wealth and the wealthy. Several authors apply recent theory concerning narrative to the Methodist saga. Here, then, the reader will find some fresh perspectives on the Methodist past.

The attentive reader will note that we have republished essays as they originally appeared, with revisions in only a couple of instances, notably those by Richey and Lobody. We have also reproduced the notes, though taking the liberty to collect them for convenience sake as endnotes (they will all be found at the end of the volume). That produces some divergence in style and in citation of standard items and, of course, continued full references instead of a standardized short form. These patterns seemed to us acceptable, perhaps even desirable, in a volume that features its parts, the individual essays, these interesting re-estimations of the Methodist past.

Russell E. Richey
*The Divinity School*
*Duke University*

# The Founding Period

## CHAPTER 1

# Evangelical America— The Methodist Ideology

## Donald G. Mathews

The Methodist Bicentennial celebrates an institution; but Methodism was first of all a movement. And movements begin beyond public action in the inner life of people who are ill at ease with the way in which institutions and elites have affected their lives. Movements begin when uneasiness becomes a subjective revolution that cuts ties to the past and sets people free to create selves and institutions anew. This is what Methodism did for the Revolutionary generation of Americans. Relying on preachers whose credentials were an ability to elicit intense emotion and to inspire religious commitment, Methodists became so effective at recruitment and mobilization that the post-Revolutionary generation would be called by religious historians "the Methodist Age." It was not that all Protestants had become Methodists, but that most Protestants had become so very much like Methodists in certain significant ways. This transformation was not so much the direct result of Methodism as it was of a larger process at work also with the Calvinist churches, a process that came to be called Evangelicalism.

Calvinist Evangelicals of the nineteenth century were to look back at revivals of religion in eighteenth-century New England for their antecedents. There in Jonathan Edwards' Northampton, in Connecticut, Long Island, and areas scattered broadly enough to suggest a widespread phenomenon, there seemed to have been a Great (religious) Awakening. George Whitefield's tour of New England in 1739–40 was remembered as more than a metaphor for a blazing nova of New Light; it became in the memories of Evangelical historians a widespread, swift revolution in religious life throughout the colonies. But the memory had been inflated by romanticism, sentimentality, and time. Recent scholarship—the enemy of all illusions—has suggested that the awakening was not quite the tidal wave of emotion and transformation that Evangelicals remember. Scholarly skeptics could then conclude that the limited, sporadic, and scattered awakenings still conceded as actual events, could not have had any significant impact on the way in which men and women were prepared for the American Revolution and the Republicanism that pervaded political life thereafter. But here skepticism denied too much. If there was no one event, there had nonetheless been a process of many events changing the moods and forms of American religion. The result was an audience that repudiated deferential assumptions and habits, aristocratic display and waste, and rationalist skepticism repudiating these things not as a matter of principle (from outside the self) but as a matter of self-definition, a projection of the self into public discourse. If Evangelicalism did not cause the Revolution or create Republicanism, it was nevertheless a pervasive language for scrutinizing "authority," establishing "legitimacy," assuming "personal responsibility" and expressing "liberty."

The words were political words as well as religious words, words expressing a continuum of experience in which distinctions between politics and religion could be sustained perhaps during elections and revivals, but not necessarily all the time. When Methodist preachers rode into the American countryside to preach "liberty to the captives" "empowered" by the Holy Spirit, they were in a sense declaring the "politics of God" to people who were bound by race, sex, or social condition as well as personal predicament. Already ahead of them were New Light Baptists and New School Presbyterians. Divided by theologies of church and ministry, these Evangelicals shared emphasis upon the experience of the New Birth, a transformation worked by the Holy Spirit within the believer who had been convicted of sin, but graciously justified through God's intercession in Christ Jesus. One did not need to know how to read scripture or prayer book or to recite the creed. One did not need to explain the experience of grace in careful theological language. One needed only testify as to what was felt when receiving the Spirit within an "amazing grace" (once blind, now seeing; once dumb, now testifying; once fragmented, now whole).

Evangelicalism grew through its various manifestations to become the dominant mood of American Protestantism. Over the course of two centuries the processual transformation of volatile movement into orderly institution contained a logic at odds with the genius of early Evangelicalism. Any formalism that set ministers (authority) apart from most believers and regularized reception of the New Birth would be targeted as increasing the distance between the faithful and God. In response to such apostasy there were recurrent surges of radical supernaturalism. In the 1830s and 40s there were the Millerites; in the post-Civil War generation there was the elaboration of Evangelical motivation and vision in Bible conferences and holiness movements. In the twentieth century came fundamentalists and the current resurgence of "neo"-evangelicalism. Evangelical America, then, has been a movement, a series of movements, institutions, moods, and motivations that have affected our culture in a variety of ways that have yet to be fully understood. Within this persistent cultural form, Methodist ideology has been a significant force.

Ideology has been understood as a belief system serving the interests of those who propagate it as a mask or weapon in the universal struggle for advantage. For others, ideology has been explained as a symptom of and remedy for an imbalance in the social system. The problem with these conceptions of ideology, argues anthropologist Clifford Geertz, is that they do not deal analytically with symbolic forms and the search for meaning in ideologies which are essentially the creative attempts by people to understand social situations that have become incomprehensible to them. Ideology is an achievement of mind, making it possible for people to act purposefully—it is not only a map *of* a problematic social reality, but also a model *for* a more meaningful and new reality.[1] The attitude evoked is not that of scientific detachment, but of commitment; it is an investment of self in a transformation that is promised in vivid and evocative language, stretching the imagination beyond the known present and propelling it into an unknown and only partially charted future.

Methodist ideology was certainly that, and more. It was also a collage of sound, symbol, and act. It was style and mood evinced in oral communication. Some people called it noise. On February 11, 1807 a man in New Bern, North Carolina, reported such noise to a friend:

> About a week past there was a methodist conference in this place which lasted 7 or 8 days & nights with very little intermission, during which there was a large concourse of people of various colors, classes & such, assembled for various purposes. Confusion, shouting, praying, singing, laughing, talking, amorous engagements, falling down, kicking, squealing and a thousand other ludicrous things prevailed most of the time and frequently of nights, all at once—In short, it was the most detestible farcical scene that ever I beheld.[2]

This report—so similar to other reports of Methodist conferences by non-Methodists—reminds us that American Wesleyans relied much less on the written word than that which was spoken. For all the tracts and treatises and sermons that Methodist preachers published and read, they were remembered first of all for their preaching and for the spontaneous verbal responses of their congregations—the shouts, the groans, the sobs of persons brought together to express their most interior and private thoughts. These acts and this noise were at the core of the movement. It is a fact often overlooked by historians who have read journals of circuit riders and come away disappointed because they were all too often merely reports of places visited, texts preached, and appointments kept. In such stark accounts there seems to be no substance because substance is assumed by scholars of the written word to be the written word. Substance for early Methodists, however, was the spoken word, the event and act of preaching and responding, the fusing together of individuals who poured their interior life out into a sharing community through testimony, song, shout, and laughter. The preachers could recall a "melting time" as the result of feeling such "liberty."

The psychodynamics of orality, as described by one of its most distinguished scholars, suggests the significance of early Methodist preaching. The "sounded word," he writes, is power and action in itself characterized by constructing through sound an event in which an audience becomes a community.[3] The often obsessive wrestling of self with self was to be prevented from turning into self-absorption in early Methodism through preaching that actually brought the interior life of each person out into a communal sharing of the drama of salvation and commitment. The religious experience of the one was to be more than the metaphor for the religious experience of the many; it was to be a common *bond* through which public discourse became a communally creative event. The preaching of early Methodism, therefore—the sound of the Holy Spirit—was at the heart of Methodist ideology precisely because it made the gospel an event.

If Methodist orality expressed the interior life of individuals becoming community, it also established, for awhile at least, the authority of the preachers. That authority was not resident in the office of itinerant but in the action that he made possible. If the words he spoke or chanted did not elicit communal response and regeneration, his authority was diminished for the moment, although expectation of the return of "power" through "liberty" in preaching could sustain the relationship between him and the people. The itinerants were, like the words they spoke, transitory, restlessly moving through the lives of their people, personifying a church beyond the isolated houses and little rooms within which they preached at pulpits made from kitchen chairs. Like the words they spoke, they were authoritative so long as they brought the interior life of their people into contact with the Spirit and through the Spirit, with their fellow believers in Christ. Thus the ordained preachers were not so much creatures of the local sacred community as were the ministers of the reformed tradition who were set aside to serve a single, gathered church for a long period of time. To be sure, itinerants achieved their position through recommendations from class meetings and quarterly conferences, but these existed within a larger conception of the church as a network of believers beyond any one place. The circuit rider did not belong to the locality after he had once left it, for he then belonged to the church above the stations, appointments, quarterly conferences and class meetings—the Church Militant, the annual conference. The Methodist movement was thus a dialectic between locality and universality. Cut as free of place as the early Apostles, the preachers came into the lives of the faithful from the outside, underscoring the societal, universal character of their ministry. Their universal relevance and the urgency of their message was also evident in the place and size of their audiences. They preached to persons of all faiths or none, to a congregation of "5 adults and 2 children" or to hundreds, in chapels, meeting houses, brush arbors, barns, cabins, taverns, jails, or court houses, in the homes of masters and in the quarters of slaves. If one had the stamina for such a life, a sense of the dramatic, a vivid experience of grace and the gift for making people feel God's presence and forgiveness, he could become the personification of the universal mission of Christianity and therefore a romantic figure in the eyes of the faithful.

Consistent with their orality and itineracy, Methodists made the entry-way into sacred community the compelling, inner sense of transformation—the New Birth. The immediate result of this conversion was commitment to the continuous struggle to live a holy life. There were two things happening in this in which *act* and *process* are both involved. The *act* is realization, through the oral dialectic of interior privacy and external community, of one's importance. The result was commitment to a process of Christian maturation; the convert was not yet whole in perfect love, but he or she would know from experience itself that he or she could be: that God was making it possible for each person to win in the persistent struggle for life. All Evangelicals shared emphasis on such an experience, but unlike consistently Calvinist Evangelicals, the event in Methodism was no guarantee of final perseverance. The Methodist could not say "I have been saved!" and leave the sacred event at that. The Methodist had to say: "I have been saved, I am saved, I may be saved, I shall one day be saved." Both act and anticipation sustained the believer; but experience was a promise and not a final contract.

A basic characteristic of this New Birth was its openness, an openness to all those who professed to have experienced the presence of Spirit flowing from the Word. The radical nature of this openness in a racist and slaveholding society was revealed in the response by itinerants to the religious experience and exercises of the "poor Africans." The latter seemed to express more vividly than anyone else the power of the Spirit and the love of God who could thus exalt those who had been cast so low. Presbyterians responded warily and timorously to the expressiveness of Africans; but white Methodists—at least in the Revolutionary generation—approached stricken blacks prepared to acknowledge the experience of this exotic people as a manifestation of God's universal love, and evidence of a universal "spiritual sense." The blacks' response to the Methodists' orality was a concrete event, just as preaching had been an event; just as Christ and Moses had been events—not principles and not abstractions, but events. When frustrated and disappointed preachers felt no liberty in preaching to whites, their sense of failure was alleviated by the religious exercises of blacks because, as Frederick Dreyer points out in a recent article on John Wesley, what was important was "not what but how the Christian ought to believe." This emphasis meant, as Dreyer writes, "the believer's powers of self-consciousness" were the means through which the believer knew justification. He or she did not have to prove spiritual authenticity to skeptical ritual elders through affirmation of correct doctrine or citation of Biblical verses. But one could express the interior self's sensation of the spirit. As Dreyer points out, for Wesley—and one could add: for his preachers—faith was a "sensible experience."[4]

Orality . . . Itineracy . . . Sensible faith. These were the means of recruitment, each reinforcing the others, each flowing from the others, *all* creating an appeal to individuals that created a movement . . . Why? The answers to the question are familiar. The surge of Evangelicalism came from a counterattack by the clergy against infidelity. It came from a theological transformation soon expressed in popular terms. It came from a sense of guilt induced by a transformation of social relationships. It came from the translation into religious language of a sense of loss resulting from migrations, and changes within the vertical structure of society. It came as an organizing process parallel to that in government, politics, and commerce. These explanations all emphasize Evangelicalism as order without taking account of the very obvious but often ignored fact that Evangelicalism was first of all DIS-order. Orality, itineracy, and sensible faith were subversive of order. Orality repudiated the rationalist order of the written word that kept the illiterate out of political consideration save as the dangerous class. Methodist preachers could be understood as transforming into virtues what some considered to be disabling impediments to the exercise of power: illiteracy and passion. The itineracy also threatened order—or at least subverted it—by providing an alternative model for what constituted the legitimate relationship between clergy and laity, a relationship that was a metaphor for all power relationships. And the conversion experience or New Birth—a sensible faith—was especially disorderly in Methodism because it rejected or ignored those elements so crucial to good order in religion: the Creed, the Covenant, the Confession. Authenticity of the conversion experience, and therefore the legitimacy of the Christian's faith, was essentially established by the individual who had been drawn into a serious consideration of his or her personal destiny by first hearing that race, sex, and wealth did not dictate the worth of a person.

The full significance of this changed perception of self is clear when we understand the order that Evangelical Methodism rejected. It was an order in which wealth, prestige, race, and sex dictated who were powerful: relatively wealthy white men. The next stage in the argument, however, is not to conclude that the spread of Methodism had political implications that could make Evangelicalism into the Jeffersonian Republicans at camp meeting. The issue is not quite so simple because what is political is not limited to elections or parties. Power is exercised in many subtle ways, forming matrices of relationships, habits, values, and rules that can become so indelibly impressed in the consciousness of people who held little or no power as to be virtually legitimized by tacit acknowledgement that the way things are is the way things probably have to be. . . . Any change in the way in which people think about themselves, what they should value, and how they should act can be a political change to the extent that the values of the ruling elites are challenged or repudiated and the sinews of social deference frayed. In some societies it has been a political act to drink water from a certain water fountain or sit down in a certain seat or pray in a certain pew. In the Evangelical movements of the early Republic, it could be a political act to meet at night to pray: blacks could be beaten for doing so, as many of them discovered. " 'This' cried one black Methodist with blood rolling down his face from a club wielded by a sheriff, 'This is what I have got for praising of my dear Jesus.' "[5]

To be clear in this, reconsider for a moment the slave's words. He had been physically attacked for "praising of my dear Jesus." The important word is "praising," because "praising" is an act and an event as befitted the response of an illiterate slave to the chanting orality of a Methodist preacher—James Meacham—himself obsessed by the demonic and pervasive power of the masters. "Blood!" he shouted at the whites: the *blood* of Calvary, the *blood* of oppression, the *blood* on the black man's face. All could be fused together in a free association of words in the homiletic chant of an itinerant feeling "liberty." In the meeting, demeanor and self-concept had been transformed in the slave— he was a new self that could not be contained in the ascribed status: black-and-slave. He had to shout to praise Him who had broken the shackles of slavery. If the skeptical insist that this was simply the self-delusion of religious fanaticism, they should consider the act of the sheriff who knew—if historians sometimes forget—that power suffuses all human life. Its expression occurs in all its aspects of dominance and subordination, in what Raymond Williams calls "the *whole* body of practices and expectations, the *whole* of living: our senses and assignments of energy, our shaping perceptions of ourselves and our world. It is a lived system of meanings and values which, as they are experienced as practices appear as reciprocally confirming."[6] The New Birth broke into the system of traditional power relationships—sexual as well as racial and electoral—and announced that the traditional rules of the world no longer applied to the new person in Christ.

The New Birth was a *liminal* event. The concept of the liminal comes from the work of Victor Turner and underscores the significance of the disorderliness of Methodist revival. The liminal is that aspect of life in which the ordinary rules of the world do not apply. They have been suspended, ignored, or declared void. Liminality characterizes *rituals through which persons move* from *one status* to *another* as in rites of passage. In them, the subjects are neither children nor adults; they are literally without social rank of any kind, neither dominant nor subordinate. In this situation one feels the essential equality of all human beings (distinctions are personal or individual and not social). As Turner points

23

out, this egalitarian perception or experience can—if allowed to dictate life outside the liminal passage or situation—be dangerous to social order because it suspends all social distinctions. The New Birth as liminal event conveyed something quite significant, therefore, to those whose lives were most rigidly confined by the ordinary rules of the world.[7]

The liminal event was supposed to create a liminal people. The word that Methodists used to name this process was "holiness." The Methodists' goal was to preach "holiness throughout the land," and holiness was an order of life either in opposition to or alternative to worldly values. The difference between oppositional and alternative values was the difference between trying to replace values that sustained traditional patterns of dominance and subordination and trying merely to establish as binding for only a segment of the population values and behaviors different from those that dominated the larger society. Methodism in neither Great Britain nor the New World ever successfully developed an oppositional ethic even though the language of moral struggle was often expressed as opposition to the world. It was a language that Methodists shared with other Evangelicals, all of whom sought to fight or fend off the world. But they each did it within different intellectual contexts.

The context of Calvinist evangelicals embraced and explained the New Birth through ideologies grounded in theological understanding of the social dimensions of human life. Congregationalists, Presbyterians, and Baptists came from traditions tempered in the 17th century English revolution in which the structure of social life—not merely authenticity of the religious experience— was a major concern. Debate in that traumatized generation had ranged from establishing the only significant community as the gathered church to revolutionizing English society and establishing the Kingdom of God on earth—the Millennium. To say that the social structure of Christian life was of intense interest in the tradition of non-Methodist evangelicals would be an understatement. In that tradition, there was a demand for a holistic system, one that was as logical and internally consistent as human thought could develop. The New England way was merely one of the earliest American elaborations of a holistic view of what social life should be like. Later, heirs of that fusion of faith and social context would spin their own holistic systems in Oneida, Brook Farm, the local Baptist church, or the social gospel. Although Methodists might later appropriate a practical system of thought such as social science to analyze a system (a social system), Methodism itself would not inspire the kind of total, systemic speculation that explained what the good society would be like. Methodism was more comfortable with the interior knowledge of the Holy Spirit, which the individual could know, than with trying to understand what only God could know.

Methodists, whose style and mood was often thought to betray fanaticism, sometimes found brother and sister Evangelicals too precise and insistent about

24

matters that were really not very important from the Methodists' point of view (save as matters perhaps of taste). Methodists, for example, would baptize anyone anyway preferred, ranging from the application of a moist hand to total submersion in a creek; their latitudinarianism scandalized Baptists. Baptist particularism in insisting on closed communion was just as offensive to Methodists who opened their table to all those professing faith in Christ. Closed communion and insistence on immersion as the only form of baptism represented bigotry to Methodists who were also offended by the hyper-Calvinist insistence that once a person was converted he or she could not fall from grace. The rationale seemed to be imbedded in a theology more interested in maintaining the consistency of a highly speculative system of thought than in the healing and salvation of souls. Moreover, an assumption of the perseverance of saints seemed to encourage a rigidity and a sense of absolute righteousness that far surpassed what Methodists believed was supported by empirical experience. That is, the moral and religious failures of persons who had once had an experience of grace seemed to be obvious to Methodists. That such persons had lapsed after exemplifying the fruits of the Spirit demonstrated that they needed once more to throw themselves on the mercy of Christ. The Christian life was a struggle, a going on to perfection, the goal was ever ahead.

The point of setting up this contrast—inadequate though it may be in some respects—is to understand the openness of Methodist ideology. The conventional way of making the same point is to mention Arminianism, John Locke, and free will. But this litany does not quite convey the full meaning. Methodism struck at all forms and restrictions that prevented individuals from realizing a full life in Christ, whether conceived in formal theological systems or expressed in the one-and-only-church or limited to the orderliness of certain rituals. The Methodist goal was to make such forms irrelevant on matters that really counted in allowing each individual full access to the Spirit. "Liberty" was the word that Methodist itinerants used to express what they felt in a particularly effective preaching experience; and liberty was to be released from whatever bound the self to reach above the self. Liberty, John Wesley had written, was the "power of self-determination"; it was an experience open to "all human kind," he added, but it seemed to be understood most readily in its celebration by his preachers in the oral rituals of Methodist revival.[8]

But the question still remains as to how Methodist "liberty" or liminality could create Evangelical order out of Evangelical disorder. Personal holiness meant to show forth the fruits of faith. The faith that was sensed empirically (in one's feelings) was to be expressed in demeanor, mood, and self-discipline. The world was repudiated; friends who remained within it were to be left behind; the fiddles that invited dancing were put away; the ruffles on one's shirt were cut off; the strength of spirituous liquors resisted; the advances of worldly men rejected; and the winsome wiles of careless, frivolous young women withstood.

The sexual repression demanded is suggested in this statement by a Methodist bishop:

> Therefore avoid the allurements of Voluptuousness, and fly every temptation that leads to her banquet as you would the devil himself. Oh how she spreads her board with delicacies. Her wine sparkles, her dainties invite, her Mirth charms. . . . Lascivious love stands in her bower. She spreads her temptations & begins to court their regard. Her limbs are soft and delicate; her attire loose & inviting, wantonness sparkles in her eyes. She woos with her looks and by the smoothness of her tongue endeavors to deceive.[9]

This description of voluptuousness when contrasted to the world one left behind in accepting Methodist discipline presents us with a problem. Why would anyone want to resist such allurement?

The question is that of the "world" that sees in sexual repression a misdirection of personal responsibility. Or it could be that of the skeptic who surrenders seriousness to a thoughtless wit. But it is also one that fails to see self-discipline within the personal and social context in which it occurred. Methodist holiness provided a way for individuals to feel the self-determination that Wesley called liberty—which may appear to be self-contradictory. It should seem ludicrous for the repressed, sober, serious, humorless caricature of Methodist holiness to feel liberty—unless of course the pejorative words are translated into "responsible," "sensible," "gracious." More important—even with the pejorative connotations—the power to establish a new order for oneself is a way of taking that power from someone else—masters, husbands, parents, or the worldly elites whose extravagant display and skeptical levity the Methodists joined other Evangelicals in repudiating. Persons who felt that the predominant values of the world did not assign them much honor, prestige, or importance— persons who felt unloved and rootless—could find haven and meaning through joining Methodist classes and societies. Not a few young women could be attracted to religion that specifically denounced the flirtatious silliness of giggly girls and elevated personal integrity, gentleness, reliability, and piety above good looks and fantasy. In Methodism was a pattern of relating to people that received public approval without deferring to the established customs and behavior of the aristocracy which only the wealthy could afford. In all of these situations and motives there is the persistent strain of self-discipline that enhances the self-esteem of persons who have the power of making themselves new, and it was this that was so attractive in Methodist order.

The aspect of practical Christianity that was MOST radical, that was most CLEARLY in opposition to the hegemonic values of early American society was the early Methodist assault upon slavery. It was an attempt to transform the liminal experience of basic human equality, *communitas*, into permanent form. From the very first, however, there was a schizophrenic quality to the move. After a few desultory discussions about slaveholding, the Christmas conference in a burst of liminal enthusiasm ordered all Methodists holding slaves to free them within two years. Francis Asbury had been uncomfortable with slaveholding since he had arrived in the New World over ten years earlier. But if the language adopted by the Methodists in justifying their excommunication of slaveholders is an appropriate guide, Methodist ideology had received a jolt from the politics of the American Revolution. Republican ideology apparently made the new rule possible.[10]

From the first attack on slaveholding, it was obvious that a radical, liminal demand of emancipation would not be effective. The itinerants had to rescind their edict within a few months because of intractable refusal by the slaveholding laity and a general "public outcry." The Methodist itinerants had assumed that the vision of *communitas* that has been elicited through the liminal sounds of the preaching event had the power to call forth the transformation of religious experience into the rules of everyday life. The preachers had themselves felt "liberty" to proclaim "liberty" to slaves as well as masters; but they had been betrayed by their own eloquence to believe it possible for slave and master both to return to the world of structure and rank with the same vision of *communitas*. For a few thousand slaves thus liberated, the hope was fulfilled. For the vast majority of course it failed. In response, antislavery Methodists turned to tactics which they hoped would re-capture the sense of spontaneous *communitas*: preaching and persuasion. In sermons, pamphlets, and animated discussions they tried to formulate an Evangelical-Republican ideology that could link the emotional transformation of conversion with a commitment to Republican equality. The tone of discourse varied with personal style and public place, but those defending slavery or holding slaves could find themselves condemned as "rogues," "oppressors," and "devils incarnate" with such vivid descriptions of their fate as to make one woman shout, "They will be slaves to the devil in Hell" just before she fainted.[11] That woman's personal vision of judgment and her immediate loss of consciousness are nice metaphors for the fate of the Methodist antislavery impulse. That impulse was more a moral judgment than a plan of action, a spontaneous exclamation rather than a reordering of structure. Denunciations of slaveholding and slavery became increasingly erratic and volatile, characterizing the idiosyncratic and eccentric; gradually the westward movement and death claimed antislavery Methodists and resistance to slavery remained in only a few pockets of the southern mountains or a few communities such as those of the Quakers.

Reasons for Methodist surrender to structure are so familiar as to constitute a Pavlovian response: economics and racism. But these were not *new* factors which eventually became strong enough to overpower revolutionary ideology; rather: they were the *context* within which the Methodist debate about slaveholding had taken place. And during that debate (between 1770 and 1810— more than a generation) both society and Methodism were changing. The exodus of non-slaveholding whites to the west—Kentucky, Tennessee, the Old Northwest—meant fewer dissenters in the Atlantic seaboard states. The movement of slaveholding whites into the southwest meant the further development of slavery. The volatility and movement of population required local religious and civic organizations to provide stability through regulation of social relations and the distribution of property. It is not surprising therefore that Methodist membership in the south should have jumped in geometric progression between 1770 and 1820. In the newer areas of the south and west this meant relatively large numbers of strangers present in each Methodist church that popped up as the result of sufficient population density. Thus, each new church, conference, or class had to decide, without reliance on ties of kinship, upon the rules governing decorum, public order, and social relations. This social role thrust upon Methodists responsibility for structure defining "distinctive arrangements" of social position and authority, emphasizing differences, constraining action, creating boundaries, establishing social distance.

The inability of whites to create a consistently liminal place for black-white interaction has traditionally been the measure of early American Methodism. Focus, however, has been on Methodists of the wrong race. The full social meaning of Methodist ideology, the full implications of the liminal experience of the New Birth, are to be found in the process through which blacks in both sections of the new America developed in their own social lives the liminal experience of *communitas*.[12] Liminality of white—those of high estate—has meant participation with those of low estate (blacks) in a ritual process expressing the essential humanity of those bonded by act, perception, and emotion. Suspension of the rules of slavery took place when white and black together heard preachers of both races, experienced conversion together, and came to camp meeting together. The camp became liminal space as both sexes and races mixed. The character of the experience there was recalled by one Methodist in this way:[13]

> To see a bold and courageous Kentuckian (undaunted by the horrors of war) turn pale and tremble at the reproof of a weak woman, a little boy, or a poor African; to see him sink down in deep remorse, roll, and toss, and gnash his teeth . . . and return in the possession of a meek and gentle spirit, which he set out to oppose—who could say the change was not supernatural?

The "poor African," like those who had preached and prayed in Methodist churches for a generation, was not a liminal person simply because of his prayer in that Kentucky camp. He represented the fact of an Afro-Methodist faith which was itself a persistent statement of the liminal and *communitas*. The collective achievement of the blacks' religious experience, because of their social interaction with whites and their own cultural creativity, was to develop between the tensions of white structure and black liminality a community in which the logic of slavery and racism did not apply—that of black Methodists.

In that Kentucky camp meeting lay the metaphor for the Methodist ideology. There and in the conversion of blacks who first formulated Methodism in Charleston, and Wilmington, and Fayetteville, and Old St. George is the liminal insight, the fusion of orality, new birth (and liminal self), practical holiness and *communitas*. The innovation of the first itinerants' coming out of a universal mission into specific locality brought a psychological revolution—the source of all revolutions. The general illiteracy of blacks and the semi-literacy of many whites meant that the orality of Methodism was a revolution in perceptions of authority. Authority was to be thought not aloof from humankind but inherent within it. The metaphor is in the interaction of preacher and people and does not mean that the people are authority in themselves. Only the response *from* the congregation reveals the presence of authority: authority is the prevenient presence of the Spirit called forth from within the people, released in the ritual interaction of preaching.

A message sent to the audience—*to* them—from the aloofness of literacy, form, and reason, creates distance; a message developed from an outpouring of the Spirit within the holy community in a call and response cadence of a people expressing themselves in the preacher creates solidarity. That sense of human solidarity, of human equality—of essential humanness was what the Kentucky frontiersman found in campmeeting from an African. Thus, out of the liminal process of preaching is the liminal self revealed—a new birth.

The sense of the liminal self removed blacks from their slavery and the subordination of race. That this was a function not simply of their social condition is suggested by the fact that some slaveholders also understood the radical implications of the new birth. But the full implications of the Methodist ideology are in the blacks' experience. From their conversion they were cast free of all ties that bound them, and through the practice of holiness brought into being a community in which the ordinary rules of the world did not apply. In concrete terms, black Methodists received at least four things: (1) a language, (2) acknowledged legitimacy in a world where they had not been previously legitimate, (3) a personal discipline that authenticated the psychological revolution and broke the power of slavery, (4) a concrete institution in which *communitas* was acknowledged.

The language was a new means of communication between blacks and whites. Without a common language that acknowledged a common experience and a common obligation, the means of communication between white and black were that of power—work, sex, violence. A language of common religious experience—or failing that, of a common acknowledgement of obligation to the same moral authority—provided a way for blacks to celebrate their humanity in a public way. Whites—especially those professing Christianity—

were now placed in a position of dealing with Christian blacks, knowing that the blacks understood the meaning of Christian obligation. The knowledge within black Methodists of that mutual obligation meant that their willingness to share the vision of *communitas* was the measure of the whites' Christian commitment professed in the new birth. To the extent that whites were themselves unable to embrace the full meaning of that vision they had failed to be truly Christian. The measure of Christianity, then, was reversed—it changed from white to black.

The legitimacy was that of the white world, not the black. Black conversion meant that within the world of structure—society—even the whites had to acknowledge that the blacks now, too, had a public institution—the church. The acknowledgement meant conceding—morally at least—a public claim of blacks to legitimacy outside their own culture and their own souls.

The personal discipline of holiness—the daily struggle to achieve the perfection of humanity in Christ—removed blacks from the power of whites to the extent that blacks now could wrest from whites the power to name themselves, to define themselves not with respect to white power but to the divine— the source of power. The new birth revealed to each black convert the incredible worth of self. The meaningful discipline was not white; the meaningful discipline was to answer to God for self, to act according to an inwardly developed sense of one's obligation and integrity. The achievement and limitations of this discipline are understood in a statement made by Uncle Tom to Simon Legree. He could not have Tom's soul; all he could do was to kill him.[14]

The concrete place in which *communitas* was acknowledged was of course the black Methodist class or society. It was the achievement and nurturer of the Methodist ideology—the model for all Methodists of any race and both sexes that conveyed the liminal insights of *communitas* in which the ordinary rules of the world did not apply. *Communitas* and holiness both underscored the transcendent legitimacy that was repeated over and over again in the religious sensibility of early Methodist ideology. The orality and itineracy that began the Methodist movement brought a dramatic disorderliness to the worldly order of the early Republic even as the liminal vision of community suggested an ideal orderliness. That a few emancipating white Methodists and the community of black Methodists could achieve "perfection" of the Methodist ideology was of course a function of social position and the individual moral heroism that transcends class. It was an ideology that denied the rules of class and exploitation; it was an abrupt, oral, radical intrusion into a world of rank, invidious distinctions, and careless convention. And it is this historic fusion of concrete reality and spiritual sensibility that we honor in celebrating the Methodist Bicentennial.

# The Attraction of Methodism: The Delmarva Peninsula as a Case Study, 1769–1820

## William H. Williams

In 1800, apprentice cabinetmaker William Morgan of Lewes, Delaware, was about to make a momentous decision. Only nineteen, Morgan was very concerned about his future and was convinced that a religious affiliation would give needed direction to his life. Shopping around for a suitable faith, he finally narrowed his choice to Episcopalianism or Methodism.

Cornelius Wiltbank, an elderly Episcopalian, advised young Morgan to join with the Episcopalians so that he could have religion and still enjoy himself. Wiltbank assured Morgan that "God did not require so much strictness as the Methodists said he did." Moreover, Christ's yoke, " . . . is easy and his burden is light. I am sure there is no harm in civil mirth, in going to balls and taking a civil dance; enjoying one's self among young people, hearing the fiddle; it revives one's spirits."[1]

Wiltbank's entreaties were appealing and his logic convincing. How could anyone choose the dour, strict world of Methodism over the enjoyments of Episcopalianism? And yet Morgan and thousands of other Delmarvans chose "strictness" over "enjoyment," causing Methodism to become the dominant faith on the Delmarva Peninsula.

## THE PENINSULA

The Delmarva Peninsula begins about fifteen miles south of Philadelphia and pushes southward for more than two hundred miles. Bounded on the west by the mouth of the Susquehanna River and the Chesapeake Bay, and on the east by the Delaware River, Bay and the Atlantic Ocean, it includes all of Delaware and the Eastern Shore of Maryland and Virginia. Taking its name from these three states, the Delmarva Peninsula gradually widens as it proceeds south, reaching a width of almost seventy miles before receding to a long, narrow neck that finally ends at the confluence of bay and ocean. In the extreme north, Piedmont meets coastal plain. South of the fall line, only an occasional hill or swale interrupts the flatness of the land. The western edge of the peninsula is serrated by hundreds of marshes, creeks, and rivers, producing a waterman's paradise. In 1790, except for the extreme north where the Scotch-Irish predominated, the white population was overwhelmingly of English ancestry. Blacks made up about 35 percent of the peninsula's population, and slightly more than 80 percent of the blacks were slaves.[2]

A few years prior to the American Revolution, the first Methodist itinerants visited Delmarva and planted spiritual seeds on extraordinarily fertile soil. By the end of the American Revolution almost one in three American Methodists lived on the Delmarva Peninsula. By 1820, approximately one in five adults— sixteen and over—Delmarvans was a Methodist, which is an astonishing figure considering the low percentage of Americans of that era belonging to any church. This unusually high concentration of Methodists makes the Delmarva Peninsula an ideal region for the study of why people became Methodists.[3]

## THE ETHNIC FACTOR

During the colonial period, white Delmarvans were drawn to Anglicanism because it was their ancestral faith. Although the American Revolution brought an end to the colonial Anglican Church, the rise of the Protestant Episcopal Church from Anglican ashes continued to provide Peninsula Anglo-Saxons with an "English" church. After all, Episcopalianism was really colonial Anglicanism minus direct ties with England and the troublesome Anglican evangelists called Methodists. Although fresh from declaring their independence from the Church of England in 1784, Methodists also pointed to Anglican roots and, by doing so, offered Delmarvans a second "English" church.

The contest between Episcopalians and Methodists for the hearts and minds of the Peninsula's predominantly Anglo-Saxon population was decisively won by the Methodists for a number of reasons. But of considerable importance was the fact that the Methodists could claim a faith every bit as "English" as Episcopalianism and, therefore, a faith that descendants of Englishmen could feel comfortable with. William Morgan's mother had been of English stock and Anglican. When her son finally narrowed his choice to two churches, predictably they were both "English." It was no accident that Methodism on the Peninsula, as elsewhere, had its greatest success in areas previously dominated by the Church of England and the descendants of Englishmen.[4]

The movement of Delmarvans from Anglicanism to Methodism is amply chronicled in a number of biographies and autobiographies. At times, the sequential pattern included an Episcopalian interlude prior to Methodist conversion. The latter pattern was particularly true on Virginia's Eastern Shore, some scattered regions of Maryland's lower Eastern Shore, and some of the islands in the Chesapeake, because those areas were the last to be visited by Methodist itinerants.

Predictably, Methodism's opponents tried to discredit the "English" nature of Methodism. They would call attention to circuit riders of non-English extraction to make their point. When Joshua Thomas of Somerset County, announced in 1807 that he was going to a camp meeting, his uncle tried to dissuade him by declaring that Methodist preachers were "nothing but a parcel of Irishmen who ran away from their country to keep from being hanged." Asbury was sensitive to this issue and hesitated to assign to the Peninsula preachers of non-English background, particularly if they had heavy accents.[5]

## THE DEMOGRAPHIC FACTOR

Peninsula Methodism received its greatest support in the countryside. Wesley's itinerancy system seemed ideally suited for reaching the isolated farmers and watermen who worked the flat land, and the creeks and sounds of the Chesapeake and Delaware bays. Riding his horse over fields, through forests, around marshes, and across rivers, the circuit rider made himself available to most of the rural folk of Delmarva. Where his horse wouldn't carry him, a waterman's log canoe would.

The location of Methodist chapels reflected Methodism's rural strength. By 1784, Methodists had built twenty chapels on the peninsula, and eighteen were in the countryside. Chestertown, Maryland, and Dover, Delaware, had the only in-town chapels, and even in Dover, the Methodist house of worship was "somewhat out of town." Many well-established communities didn't construct Methodist meetinghouses until well into the nineteenth century. Indeed, future Methodist Bishop, Levi Scott, noted the lack of an in-town Methodist church during his entire childhood in Odessa, Delaware, in the early nineteenth century.

Like most rural based movements, Peninsula Methodism was suspicious of towns and town dwellers. Wilmington, New Castle, and Dover, Delaware, and Elkton, Maryland, were subjected to Methodist criticism, but some of the strongest negative comments were reserved for Chestertown, Maryland. In 1776, one Methodist found the grain port on the Chester River "famous for wickedness," and nine years later Francis Asbury called it a "very wicked place."[6]

The cultural antipathy between the Methodist countryside and Delmarva's profligate towns came to a head in a bizarre controversy, sometimes called the "Great Pig Issue," in Georgetown, Delaware. In 1791, Georgetown was created by legislative fiat to be the new county seat for Sussex. From the beginning, the new county seat was governed by the Delaware General Assembly causing most serious town problems to be settled by legislative enactment in Dover.

As the newly founded community began to rise on former swamp and farm lands, two distinct visions emerged concerning Georgetown's future. On the one hand, in-town Episcopalians, drawn in part from judges, lawyers, and county officials, wanted Georgetown to become an aesthetically attractive and sophisticated county seat. By contrast, Georgetown's Methodists, drawn from residents with rural roots and including some farmers from the edge of town, wanted a community amenable to the less restrictive rural life-style.

The Wesleyans were less concerned with Georgetown's cosmetic appearance than they were with the right to turn loose their livestock to roam through its streets. Consequently, Methodist-owned pigs destroyed Episcopalian flower gardens, and irate Episcopalians demanded legislative action. Reflecting political pressures brought to bear by Methodists as well as Episcopalians, Delaware's General Assembly banned "swine running at large in Georgetown" in 1795, and subsequently stiffened, repealed, and finally in 1821, reenacted restrictions against free-roaming swine. The "Great Pig Issue" is just one example of the identification of Peninsula Methodism with the rural perspective.[7]

## INACTIVITY OF OTHER FAITHS

Methodism's domination of all but the extreme north of the Peninsula was assured by the failure of other denominations to mount effective counteroffensives.

Lacking a clergy that was either numerous or energetic, Episcopalianism seemed capable of only verbal invective to stem the Methodist tide. Rectors focused their verbal attacks on John Wesley, calling him "a fallen Judas," and incorrectly insisting that Methodism's founder had been "disrobed by his [Anglican] Bishop and deprived of all ecclesiastical powers."

34

But beyond invective, Episcopalianism, offered little resistance. Up and down the Peninsula, parishes lacking rectors waited to "be entirely eaten up by the Methodists." Typical was the scene in 1816 at St. Stephen's Parish, Cecil County, where parishioners were joining the Methodists because there was no Episcopal rector.[8] That year, on the entire peninsula, there were no more than twelve Episcopal clergy to compete with approximately thirty Methodist itinerants and more than two hundred local preachers. By 1820, Episcopalians were lamenting that there wasn't an Episcopal Church remaining in all of Caroline County, Maryland.

Lacking the energy of their Methodist counterparts, the few remaining Episcopal clergy demonstrated a general lassitude, particularly in inclement weather. In Accomack County, right after the American Revolution, English Methodist Thomas Coke was told that the Episcopal clergy "never stir out to church, even on Sunday's if it rains." A weakness for alcohol also seemed to hinder the performance of Episcopal clerics. In Lewes, Delaware, in 1799, the local rector often got so drunk at a local tavern that he had to be helped home by parishioners.[9]

In the early nineteenth century, Presbyterians were most numerous in New Castle and Cecil, the northernmost of Delmarva's counties, because it was here that the Scotch-Irish and their descendants were most heavily concentrated. There were some pockets of Presbyterians all the way south to the Virginia border, but insistence on an educated ministry limited the number of available Presbyterian clergy. The shortage of ministers was reflected in an urgent request in 1803 from the New Castle Presbytery that missionaries be sent into all of Delaware south of northern New Castle County, and into every county of Maryland's Eastern Shore. No effective response was made and signs of Presbyterian decline were evident throughout most of the peninsula. By 1813, four Presbyterian congregations in lower Delaware and one in Dorchester County, Maryland, had disappeared.[10]

Unlike other regions south of Pennsylvania, the Baptists never mounted a serious challenge in most areas of the peninsula. By 1812, for example, there were eleven times as many Methodists as Baptists in Delaware. On Maryland's Eastern Shore, Baptists were even less evident.

The only serious Baptist challenge came from Virginia's Eastern Shore. In 1776, Baptist preacher Elijah Baker left Virginia's Western Shore and crossed the Chesapeake to Northampton County, on the southern tip of the peninsula. Two years later, the Lower Northampton Baptist Church was formed, probably the first non-Anglican church on Virginia's Eastern Shore. Despite wartime persecution, similar to what Methodist preachers were facing further north, Baker and fellow preacher George Layfield organized fifteen Baptist churches on the peninsula. Six were in Virginia, five in Maryland, and four in Delaware. By 1785, Virginia's Eastern Shore seemed ripe for a Baptist takeover. At the end of the eighteenth century, however, Baptist leader Elijah Baker died and the Baptist offensive came to a halt. By 1809, Methodists on Virginia's Eastern Shore outnumbered Baptists by 1,515 to 890.[11]

By the end of the eighteenth century other rivals to Methodism on the peninsula, such as the Quakers and their cousins the Nicholites, had long since lost their proselytizing zeal. The few Roman Catholics and Deists raised some concern, but it was more on account of their alien ideas than from the threat of their numbers.[12]

## AN ALTERNATIVE VALUE SYSTEM

During the late eighteenth century, a worship service at an Episcopal church in Dorchester County was disturbed by a loud voice crying out, "choose ye this day whom ye will serve." The challenge came from the lips of a Methodist itinerant as he stood outside the sanctuary. After complaints from the parson, the Methodist remained silent until the congregation filed out. Then he repeated his stirring challenge with considerable effect, and one old lady responded, "I will serve the living God." Subsequently, the Methodist preacher converted so many of those present that the Episcopal church ceased to have a congregation.[13]

On the surface, this seems a straightforward account of Methodist success in converting Episcopalians. But on a deeper level it draws our attention to a compelling aspect of Methodism. The Methodist itinerant was making plain to that Episcopal congregation that one could not serve two masters. Simply put, Methodism maintained that to serve God and His ways required a rejection of the ways of men.

In the Chesapeake world of the eighteenth century, the ways of men were forged and shaped by the gentry and then emulated by the "middling and lower sorts." The same dancing, drinking, card playing, gambling, horse racing, cock fighting, and general revelling that marked the gentry's leisure moments also occupied the free time of those lower on the social scale. The "middling and lower sorts" showed their approval of another aspect of the gentry's value system by dreaming of the day when they too would be masters of black slaves.

But there were many who were increasingly uncomfortable with the dominant culture and its underlying value system. They found little that was attractive in a life-style that emphasized frivolity, competition, brutality, and deference to those of a higher social rank. Moreover, to the ambitious, it was self-evident that many of the ways of men were self-destructive and that adopting those ways, on a personal level, spelled nothing but disaster.

A few evangelists such as George Whitefield and Joseph Nichols, the founder of the Nicholites, had spoken earlier to some of this discomfort with the region's dominant mores. But it wasn't until the arrival of the circuit rider that the entire peninsula was offered a way to deal with this discomfort. The Methodist prescription called for a revolution in values. In order to move from the ways of men to the ways of God, the Methodist message demanded the substitution of seriousness for frivolity, cooperation for competition, compassion for brutality, and egalitarianism for deference.

To those seeking deeper human relationships than found in the surface camaraderie and the boozy haze surrounding the card game, horse race, or gala party, Methodist societies offered a supportive community. To a people facing a life time of long, harsh days that drained youth and high spirits from its young and prematurely aged its adults, Wesleyan societies offered far more than just a way to fight the boredom and loneliness of farm life. They provided a real sense of psychological security as Methodist brothers and sisters offered physical and financial help, or lent a sympathetic ear in time of tribulation. Moreover, while the Methodist class meeting kept its members on the road to perfection, it also encouraged each member to bare the innermost depths of his or her soul. What a wonderful catharsis! This type of activity could not go on in the outside world, dominated as it was by the competitive, self-assertive values of the gentry, which regarded self-revelation, particularly among males, as a sign of weakness.[14]

## THE BETTER SORT

That the Methodist challenge to the mores established by the peninsula's gentry excited and attracted members of the "lower orders" is understandable. More surprising was the willingness of some of the "better sort" to become Methodist, to adopt a serious, pious air and to abandon revelry, gambling, sports, frivolity, and slavery. Evidently, many of the region's planters and their social peers were also searching for a new set of values to live by.[15]

On the peninsula, probably a higher percentage of the gentry and their peers became Methodists than anywhere else in the United States.[16] In part, the unusual number of Methodists among the "better sort" of the peninsula can be credited to the strength of "old Methodism."

During the American Revolution, American Methodists south of the Potomac moved to cut their ties with Anglicanism and set up an independent church. This schismatic movement came to a head in the Fluvanna Conference held in Virginia in 1779. Asbury was able to head off this schism by insisting that American Wesleyans adhere to "old Methodism," which maintained that Methodism was no more than a supportive, evangelistic movement within the Church of England and must remain so. Asbury won his battle against the Fluvanna schismatics because of his own strong leadership and because he fashioned for "old Methodism" a strong support base on the Peninsula while living there from December, 1777, to April, 1780.[17]

Because of their commitment to "old Methodism," Peninsula Wesleyans regarded themselves as Anglicans and worked in relative harmony with the Church of England. For this reason local Anglican gentry found Peninsula Methodism quite congenial and could comfortably support and even join Wesleyan societies while simultaneously remaining loyal to the Church of England. With the collapse of the Anglican Church during the American Revolution, some gentry simply continued their Methodist connection while others joined Methodist societies because, in many areas, that was all that remained of Peninsula Anglicanism.

By the end of the American Revolution, the Methodist seed had taken root among the gentry and even the Methodist declaration of independence from the Church of England in 1784 couldn't halt further germination and growth. The enthusiasm with which many of the wealthy and influential embraced Peninsula Methodism wasn't lost on "the middling and lower sorts." Accustomed as the latter two groups were to trying to mimic the activities of their betters, many followed the gentry into the Methodist camp. By contrast, the schismatic nature of Methodism elsewhere during the American Revolution probably so alienated Anglican gentry that they couldn't, in good conscience, become Methodists.[18]

## THE MIDDLING SORT

Primarily made up of landed farmers but also including successful crafts-men, most merchants, attorneys, and physicians, was the peninsula's "middling sort." Although they might even have a few slaves, the "middling sort" fell far short of the gentry in number of slaves owned, acres possessed, and deference commanded. But falling short was hardly part of the ambitions of many of the "middling sort." They dreamed of upward mobility, worked at upward mobility, and a few were even confident that some day they, too, might be called "squire" or be deferred to in other ways. To reach those heights, the "middling sort" found Methodism very congenial because the Methodist faith reinforced the very assumptions that ambitious young men recognized as crucial to improving their own socio-economic status.

Isaac Davis is a case in point. Born in 1765 to a landed southern Delaware family in "the middle circumstances of life," at an early age he adopted the "habit of Labor, and [the] constant pursuit of activity and temperance . . . " By joining the Methodists as a young adult and by taking seriously the Methodist approach to work and temperance, Davis reinforced previously adopted living and working attitudes which, ultimately, led to the presidency of the Bank of Smyrna, appointment to the Delaware Supreme Court, and considerable wealth.

Moreover, ambitious young men like Isaac Davis found that the Methodist God provided "all things needful" for this world as well as "for eternity." Looking back from old age, Davis credited much of his worldly success to God's intercessions on his behalf. Not only did Methodism attract the "middling sort" because it reinforced the work ethic, it also drew energetic young men to its ranks because it provided them with the confidence that God would be on their side.[19]

In business it was also important to have Methodists on your side. A natural inclination to favor brothers in the faith while engaging in commercial activity was strengthened by specific directives in the Methodist *Discipline*, which admonished Methodists to buy from each other and to employ other Wesleyans when practical. Because, by 1810, approximately 21 percent of the peninsula's adult population—sixteen and over—were Methodists, Wesleyans represented a very significant sector of the buying and employing public. In short, there was considerable economic pressure on craftsmen, merchants, attorneys, and physicians to find truth in the Wesleyan persuasion. At the end of the eighteenth century, a Talbot County, critic of Methodism pointed out that businessmen and professionals "are apt to join in with those amongst whom they are most likely to succeed best."[20]

## POOR WHITES

To be poor—that is, to be a tenant farmer, laborer, or owner of a few acres—left one particularly receptive to "true religion." Francis Asbury shared this rather quixotic view with evangelists of many faiths. The acquisition of wealth, by contrast, sometimes caused men to "forget that they are Methodists."

On a nostalgic trip through the peninsula in 1810, Asbury admitted that the houses of some of the rich were open to him, but "O God, give us the poor." Lack of worldly success characterized many Methodists, but was not limited to just the rank and file of Peninsula Methodism. At Brown's Chapel on the Sussex-Caroline border, even some of the society's principal leaders "had not been successful." But then again, "had they prospered in their pursuits, perhaps they never would have sought God."

Without extant class records, it is impossible to give a precise estimate of the number and percentage of peninsula Methodists who were of "the better sort," the "middling sort," or the "lower sort." But there is no doubt that on the peninsula as elsewhere, poor whites made up a significant percentage of the Methodist membership. On the Eastern Shore of Virginia in 1789, a concerned Francis Asbury lamented the difficulty Methodists had in raising money. "We have the poor but they have no money, and the worldly wicked rich we do not choose to ask."[21]

39

Asbury urged some of the peninsula's poor whites to move west where opportunities were greater. For those poor who remained behind, however, Methodism offered a value system and life-style that was a means for escaping economic destitution. The Methodist regimen called for rising before the sun, working hard and long, and showing little patience with idle conversation, amusements, drunkenness, and other forms of self-indulgence. The type of family that needed Methodism most to set its economic house in order was similar to the one found by Asbury in Delaware in 1781, "lying in bed until sunrise, and drinking a dram after they are up."

George Morgan lived in poverty in Northwest Fork Hundred, western Sussex County. His son, William Morgan, who later moved to Lewes, realized early on that his father's weakness for alcohol "made him poor and kept him poor indeed." Determined not to follow his father's path, young Morgan decided to avoid intemperance and gambling and to work hard at learning a trade. But to avoid his father's vices and thus his father's fate, William Morgan realized that he needed the support of a local Methodist society.[22]

Sometimes, the Methodist way wasn't enough to escape poverty. Illness or accident might kill or cripple breadwinners, leaving poor white families facing economic catastrophe. In such circumstances, belonging to a Methodist class meeting could be crucial economic insurance. In the class meeting, members aired their most private thoughts, and material concerns of an urgent nature were bound to surface. In the process, material sharing became a natural extension of spiritual sharing. At times, critical economic help might come from Methodists outside the local society. In 1796, for example, a sick member of the Georgetown, Delaware, society received donations from Methodists in other societies on the circuit.

Poor whites must have also valued the egalitarian way in which Methodists addressed each other. Certainly French revolutionaries were no more democratic in their demand that all Frenchmen be addressed as "citizen" than were Methodists who cheerfully called each other "brother" and "sister." Although most lay leadership positions were filled on the peninsula by the "middling" and "better sort," this still didn't detract from the heady feeling produced when a poor farmer heard himself called "brother" by a wealthy and esteemed member of the gentry.[23]

## WHITE WOMEN

Like other institutions of that era, Peninsula Methodism was male dominated. All clerical and lay leadership positions were reserved for men. Women weren't even allowed to vote for church trustees and were segregated from men at Methodist worship services. While there is evidence that elsewhere a few

Methodist women may have been exhorters, there is no evidence of this on the peninsula. Perhaps the closest was Mary White, wife of Judge Thomas White of Sussex County, Delaware, who occasionally led class meetings, religious exercises, and probably would have preached if Asbury had been more encouraging. Paradoxically, the same white women who had so little overt power probably represented a clear majority of Delmarva's white Methodists.[24]

In the face of their second-class status, it is difficult to explain why Methodism was particularly attractive to peninsula females. Of course there is the traditional explanation that women have a greater disposition than men for piety. Moreover, the very real threat of death in childbirth must have increased the religious sensibilities of many women.

A second explanation rests on the socio-biological argument that genetic inheritance considerably influences the human personality. The father of socio-biology, Edward O. Wilson, maintains that females are predisposed, by modest genetic differences, to be more intimately sociable than men. The one institution that could meet these female social needs was the Methodist Church. Indeed, the propensity of women to gather at their segregated entrance for a bit of socializing after Sunday service brought such complaints from impatient husbands that the trustees at Asbury Church, Wilmington, did away with segregated entrances in 1832.[25] But like the greater disposition of women for piety, this explanation is impossible to substantiate.

A third explanation rests on the expectations of peninsula families for their daughters. While sons were trained to be breadwinners, daughters were groomed to be good mothers and wives. In many peninsula houses, an education in spiritual values was considered every bit as important as learning to cook and sew. Although Nancy Mitchell of Worcester County was from a family of some means, her father decided against the frivolous education of a boarding school and for an education at home which included instruction on how to "behave herself in the house of God." Far to the northwest in Chestertown, Anna Matilda Moore was brought up "with a strict and scrupulous regard for her spiritual and eternal interests." A case in point was the first wife of Isaac Davis of Kent County, Delaware, who had a religious education, "wanted religion," and subsequently became a Methodist.[26]

But probably the most compelling reason why Methodism attracted more peninsula women than men was that Methodism met the female need for independence, self-esteem, and power. For men, this need could be fulfilled by simply playing out traditional male roles at home or in the commercial and political arena provided by the outside community. To most peninsula women, however, only the local Methodist society offered the same opportunity.

Unlike other decisions that concerned self and family, peninsula women— as the sexual imbalance in Wesleyan societies indicates—often acted independently of their husbands in deciding to become Methodists. This independent step and the resulting deep attachment to a movement beyond the control of non-Methodist husbands must have seemed a bit threatening to some men. Perhaps it was to keep an eye on this threat that some non-Methodist husbands accompanied their wives to chapel services.

Not surprisingly, some men objected to the greater religious intensity of their wives and, on at least one occasion, these objections led to a bizarre scene. In 1802 during a service at Green's Chapel, not far from Dover, a woman cried out for mercy and her enraged husband ordered her out of the chapel. Defiantly she insisted that first she would make her peace with her Maker. Although the irate husband quickly seized his wife and physically removed her from the chapel, she continued her monologue with God even while being dragged down the aisle and out the door. Despite meeting some resistance from their menfolk, women found that attendance at religious services and, particularly, at all-female class meetings not only conjured up a sense of female solidarity, but to some it also offered a respite from their husbands' direct control.

Although the Methodist sermon was delivered by men, it praised such idealized feminine traits as patience, love, gentleness, sensitivity, humility, and submissiveness, and rejected the competitive values of the male-dominated spheres of commerce, politics, and sport. One had only to look to the behavior of Freeborn Garrettson and other itinerants in the face of brutal persecution on the peninsula during the American Revolution for a compelling demonstration of the personality traits that Methodists considered Christlike.[27] By lifting up these so-called feminine traits for praise, circuit riders affirmed female self-esteem. In doing so the itinerants must also have softened resentment over the lack of overt female power in the Methodist polity.

But women did exercise considerable covert power, particularly over the itinerants. Because circuit riders were dependent on Methodist women for their room and board, quite naturally circuit riders did what they could to please their hostesses. Since the itinerants were usually young and single, older matrons often became surrogate mothers who provided circuit riders with sympathetic understanding, advice, and encouragement to go along with a bed and meals. While serving in Dorchester County, in 1800, a young and discouraged Henry Boehm considered abandoning the itinerancy after less than a year in the saddle. Sarah Ennalls, wife of Henry Ennalls, put an end to these thoughts by reminding Boehm that his eternal salvation might depend on the course he was about to take. Two years earlier, a second circuit rider's doubts about remaining in the itinerancy were also ended by Sarah Ennalls' counsel. Even the few older itinerants relied on feminine advice and encouragement. One example was Benjamin Abbott who was substituting on the Dover circuit for his son, when he reported that Mary White, wife of judge Thomas White, "took me by the hand, exhorting me for some time. I felt very happy under her wholesome admonitions."[28]

Certainly women, who could exercise such influence over the itinerants, were a formidable force to contend with when displeased. Not only could Methodist women show their displeasure by refusing their moral support and by closing their homes to hard-pressed itinerants, they could also cut back on their financial contributions and persuade those husbands who were Methodists to do the same. This wouldn't be the first nor the last time that the power of the purse was used to drive home a message to a basically authoritarian institution.

# BLACKS

Free and enslaved blacks joined with white females in presenting, on the peninsula, the same interesting paradox. Despite being segregated and being denied voting rights and leadership roles in the Methodist polity, both groups were inordinately drawn to Methodism.

For the years 1787–1820, more than a third of all peninsula Methodists were black. Moreover, a higher percentage of blacks than whites became Methodists. In 1810, for example, about 25 percent of Delmarva's adult blacks were Methodists, while the figure for whites was slightly less than 20 percent.[29]

Although treated as third-class citizens, blacks were drawn to peninsula Methodism because with the possible exception of the Quakers and Nicholites, no other religious body treated them better. The early Methodist itinerants on the peninsula were generally vigorous opponents of slavery. At first the English-born preachers such as Asbury led the anti-slavery struggle, but shortly peninsula-born itinerants such as Joseph Everett were leading the abolitionist charge. Everett not only preached against slavery, he also refused to eat with slaveholders until they freed their slaves. In 1797, an Episcopal rector in Talbot County observed that the Methodist preachers "relish the manumitting subject as highly as the Quaker preachers and spread the evil far and wide." In Somerset County in 1801, a circuit rider told his congregation to assume that "the clouds of vengeance are collecting over the heads of the inhabitants of this country for their cruelty to the poor distressed Africans."[30] During the early nineteenth century, peninsula Methodism began to back away from its clear stand against slavery. The gradual erosion of black membership after 1810 probably reflected the fact that peninsula blacks no longer viewed Methodism as a vigorous enemy of slavery.

The emotional dimension of early Methodism seemed particularly compelling to blacks. While whites, including even "the better sort," demonstrated their commitment to religious emotionalism, it was often a black outburst from the galleries or from the back of the meeting that proved a godsend to peninsula preachers unable to stir lethargic whites. Indeed, at times black religious enthusiasm made many white Methodist uncomfortable.[31]

But it would be a mistake to see black Methodism as just a highly emotional variant of white Methodism. Some of the peninsula's blacks had been born in Africa while many, if not most of the rest, remembered or heard stories of parents, grandparents, and great-grandparents who had crossed the Atlantic in the holds of slave ships. Over the years most of the culture and language of Africa was lost, but some remnants of the African heritage did survive. It is easy to see, for example, a strong residue of African behavior patterns in the happy, unrestrained actions of blacks at religious services. Perhaps foremost was the positive celebration of life that characterized blacks in worship and led them to reject the sense of guilt which seemed to pervade white Methodism.

To be more specific, the black style of joyful, demonstrative responses during religious services—which seemed so alien and therefore, so threatening to many peninsula whites—had its roots in the religious practices of the African village. As Albert J. Raboteau's study of slave religion has shown, among American slaves the gods of Africa soon gave way to the God of White Christianity, but the African style of worship didn't die. Rather, it found a home in Methodism and in some of the other evangelical faiths. And so it was that peninsula Methodism, as refracted by black sensibilities, preserved in its services the cultural shards of the African past. Put another way, peninsula Methodism provided a theater in which the sons and daughters of Africa could reaffirm, through joyful, emotional participation, just who they were.[32]

## THE PROMISE OF SALVATION

In Talbot County, Maryland, in 1782, Freeborn Garrettson found blacks "in vassalage" but happy in the consolations of Christianity. The central consolation offered by Methodism was the promise of a better life to come. Salvation was the primary focus of itinerants' sermons on the peninsula, and the subject of greatest interest to their listeners, black or white, rich or poor.[33]

In 1773, Samuel Keene, rector of St. Luke's Parish, Queen Anne's County, summed up the Anglican position on life after death. Keene said that he and other Christians only had "the hope" that they were saved, but no certainty. But Delmarvans wanted more than just "hope." They wanted "certainty" and the Methodists not only preached "certainty," they practiced it.

Typical was the way four Methodists met death. Sarah Coulter of Lewes, Delaware, had been delivered from "the bondage of sin and its consequences, the fear of Death and Hell . . . " soon after joining the Wesleyans. On her deathbed in 1789, she "cried out with a strong and distinct voice, 'Oh death where is thy sting, o grave where is thy victory.'" In the early nineteenth century, the wife of Isaac Davis of Smyrna, Delaware, just before dying, "audibly and distinctly said 'Here I go to Heaven' and died without a struggle or a groan."

In 1813 in Queen Anne's County on Spaniard's Neck, west of Centerville, planter Robert Emory was on his deathbed. The dying man was asked by his son John, a circuit rider and future bishop, "Do you see your way clear to heaven?" Robert Emory answered, "Yes, I am as sure of it as that two and two make four." A few minutes later he "tranquilly breathed his last." The confidence with which these and other Methodists faced death caused non-Methodists to stand up and take notice.

But probably no death excited the interest of the general populace as did the death and funeral of John Laws. As a young man living in the St. Johnstown area just east of Greenwood in northwestern Sussex, Laws contracted a terminal illness and was subsequently visited and converted to Methodism by Asbury. Prior to dying in 1779, Laws spoke persuasively to his family and acquaintances of his newfound faith and how it enabled him to face death with confidence. A large number who heard Laws were moved "to reform their own lives and seek the Lord." Approximately a thousand people gathered at Law's funeral and heard a sermon preached by Asbury. That same year a Methodist society, inspired by Laws' words and example, was formed in St. Johnstown.[34]

Peninsula Methodism attracted gentry and slaves, yeomen cultivators and tenant farmers, storekeepers and watermen, men and women. Part of its message appealed to the sensibilities of particular socio-economic, racial, or sexual groups. But its central message, calling for a moral revolution and promising salvation, simultaneously appealed to the needs of all classes, both races and sexes. Because of the compelling nature of its message and the lack of serious competition from other religious groups, in the late eighteenth and early nineteenth centuries Methodism on the Delmarva Peninsula had a greater and more diverse following than in any other region of the United States.

# CHAPTER 3

# The Doctrines in the *Discipline*

Frank Baker

The hastily summoned Methodist preachers who huddled together in a wintry Baltimore that Christmas of 1784 issued their own declaration of independence. For all the thousands of miles of ocean separating them from England they had so far followed the precedents and accepted the oversight of Mr. Wesley. So it had been for more than a decade. Now, apparently with Wesley's agreement, and even on his suggestion, as transmitted by Dr. Thomas Coke, they made a deliberate attempt to erect a new American Methodist church, fraternally linked with British Methodism but quite independent of its control. Now at last they had their own spiritual leaders in Coke and Asbury—technically equal in authority, but far from equal in the allegiance of their colleagues. In 1784 the Methodist Episcopal Church secured its own national leadership, its own power to perpetuate a ministry, its own ecclesiastical organization, and also took an immense step forward in creating its own ethos.

A few of the preachers doubted whether the throwing off of parental restraints (and support) by this eager Methodist adolescent was wise and timely. Thomas Haskins spoke for others when he confided to his journal: "Oh, how tottering I see Methodism now!"[1] Their two bishops managed to hold a precarious balance on the ecclesiastical fence without falling off either on the one side of retaining full theoretical control of American Methodism for Wesley, or on the other of denying him any voice at all. At the very least they insisted that the decencies should be preserved, and that having successfully thrown Mr. Wesley to the ground they should not kick him in the stomach. He was therefore indulged with an occasional kindly reference, but no actual power. Not until 1787 did the preachers explicitly reject their 1784 agreement "in matters belonging to Church government to obey [Wesley's] commands." Perhaps,

46

however, this original agreement should rather have been described as a courteous gesture than a firm commitment.

## A FORM OF DISCIPLINE

The first official document embodying the organization of the new church used the title, followed the pattern, and reproduced three quarters of the contents of its British equivalent, though with the names of Coke and Asbury replacing those of the Wesleys. It was published in 1785 as *Minutes of several conversations between the Rev. Thomas Coke, LL.D., the Rev. Francis Asbury and others.* The extent to which this depended upon Wesley's so-called "Large Minutes" is convincingly demonstrated by the parallel arrangement of the two documents in the appendix to Bishop Tigert's *Constitutional History of American Episcopal Methodism.*[2] The ferment of independence was strongly at work, however, in what was omitted, what was altered, and in what was introduced, including especially the subtitle—"composing a Form of Discipline." The second edition appeared in 1786 as an appendix to the "American" edition of Wesley's *Sunday Service.*[3] This version also retained some reminiscence of the British prototype, but experimented with a different title, which retained little of Wesley's apart from the word "Minutes"—"The General Minutes of the Conference of the Methodist Episcopal Church in America, forming the constitution of the said Church." Thereafter for the remainder of Wesley's lifetime his example was completely forsaken, and the following five editions of the American Methodist preachers' ecclesiastical handbook discarded Wesley's title for their own subtitle, being published as *A Form of Discipline for the Ministers, Preachers, and Members of the Methodist Episcopal Church in America.*[4]

All this time the administrative discipline of American Methodism was evolving, and echoes of Wesley in new regulations steadily and inevitably diminished. The one area where his influence persisted was that of doctrine. Here conditions in America were not markedly different from those in England, and indeed some of the theological battles of the parent society were later re-enacted by her daughter church, when the old weapons forged by Wesley proved to have retained their cutting edge. The dependence of American Methodism upon Wesley's theology has been both deliberately obscured and strangely forgotten by succeeding generations, and only in our own day is it once more receiving careful attention. The extent of this dependence is somewhat difficult to trace, but one of the most interesting clues is to be found in the history of the Discipline.

We have seen that the founding fathers of the Methodist Episcopal Church transformed Wesley's *Minutes* into their *Discipline.* At the American Conference next but one after his death another significant change was made in the title. Instead of *A Form of Discipline* the eighth edition of 1792 introduced the one that became the standard or model for most branches of American Methodism until our own day—*The Doctrines and Discipline of the Methodist Episcopal Church in America*. The operative word in this change, of course, is "doctrines." The dead founder of Methodism is rarely mentioned in the volume, but in its doctrines, thus emphasized by the altered title, we become aware of his dominating though unseen influence, a ghost walking the *Discipline* for all succeeding generations, his teaching enshrined though his identity almost forgotten. Even when in 1812 Wesley's theological bones were disinterred from the *Discipline* and buried in a grassed-over grave exceedingly difficult for later Methodists to discover, his spirit could not fully be exorcised. Here, however, I suspect that my analogy is somewhat hard to follow for those who have not shared with me the excitement of searching out Wesley's doctrinal resting place in a mysterious publication entitled accurately but inadequately *A Collection of Interesting Tracts*. I will therefore return from the realms of fantasy to the prosaic task of the historian, endeavoring to trace the thread of Wesley's theology through the maze of the successive issues of the Methodist *Discipline*.

## THE DOCTRINAL SECTIONS IN THE *DISCIPLINES*

The *Minutes* of 1785 contained no formal outline of belief, but the document did echo most of the doctrinal passages of Wesley's large *Minutes*. Three sections in particular call for mention. A verbatim reprint of Wesley's statement about the rise of Methodism, published originally in the annual *Minutes* for 1765 and incorporated with some minor changes into the large *Minutes* from 1770 onwards, appeared thus: "In 1729, two young men, reading the Bible, saw they could not be saved without holiness, followed after it, and incited others so to do. In 1737 they saw holiness comes by faith. They saw likewise, that men are justified before they are sanctified: but still holiness was their point. God then thrust them out, utterly against their will, to raise an holy people. When Satan could no otherwise hinder this, he threw *Calvinism* in the way; and then *Antinomianism*, which strikes directly at the root of all holiness." At the very least this makes clear the double Methodist emphasis upon evangelical theology and the pursuit of holiness, as well as drawing attention to some of the snares waiting to entangle the feet of unwary Protestant pilgrims who believe that salvation comes and stays by faith alone. Certainly it offers no encouragement to those Methodists who would banish theology from the pew and even from the pulpit to languish only in the rarefied atmosphere of the seminary. The sentence about Calvinism and Antinomianism was omitted from the *Disci-*

*plines* of 1787, 1788, and 1789—presumably to remove an additional snare from the path of the unlearned rather than because Satan no longer wielded those weapons. In the 1790 *Discipline* this section was transferred to the opening address "To the Members of the Methodist Societies in the United States," though it was not made clear that the American Methodist bishops who signed that address were not in fact the authors of the statement, but had employed the services of a ghost-writer. Not until 1796 were quotation marks added, together with a footnote which stated, "These are the words of Messrs. Wesleys themselves." And not until 1948 was this "historical statement" replaced by one, emphasizing Wesley's Aldersgate experience.[5]

Other unacknowledged statements from Wesley's publications, similarly stressing points of doctrine, were carried over from the 1785 *Minutes* into the later *Disciplines*. The two most important were deemed worthy of publication as separate sections in the volume revised by Asbury in 1787 and its successors. "Of the Rise of Methodism" formed Section I of the 1787 *Discipline*, "Against Antinomianism" Section XVI, and "On Perfection" Section XXII. Of these latter doctrinal sections the first emphasized the need for good works as at least a condition of entering into and remaining in a state of salvation. The second urged: "Let us strongly and explicitly exhort all believers to go on to Perfection." Both were taken almost word for word from Wesley's large *Minutes* by way of the 1785 American *Discipline*. Strangely enough, although these two important statements formed an integral element of the official constitution of American Methodism from 1784 until after the epochal General Conference of 1808, their existence was completely overlooked by the classic historians of the *Discipline*, Robert Emory and David Sherman, and only partly realized in the masterly work of John J. Tigert, who incorrectly speaks of them as having been introduced in 1792 and omitted before the passage of the restrictive rules by the General Conference of 1808.[6]

The *Discipline* of 1792 reorganized the numerous small sections of previous editions into three chapters, the third containing miscellaneous matter, mainly doctrinal, of which the retitled "Of Christian Perfection" was section 4, and "Against Antinomianism" section 5. This arrangement was continued in the *Disciplines* of 1797 and 1798. To that of 1798 were added "explanatory notes" by Bishops Asbury and Coke.[7] Those to these particular sections were very brief: "In respect to the doctrine of Christian perfection, we must refer the reader to Mr. Wesley's excellent treatise on that subject," and "The subject of antinomianism has been so fully handled by that great writer, Mr. Fletcher, that we need not enlarge on it, when it has been so completely considered by him." With the removal of the section on education in 1801 they moved up to become sections 3 and 4, and in 1804 were promoted to the head of Chapter 3, which was limited to doctrine and liturgy.

Again contrary to Bishop Tigert's statement,[8] this matter was still retained in the *Discipline* of 1808, when almost plenary powers were secured for General Conferences, subject only to a handful of restrictive rules. The first of these ran: "The General Conference shall not revoke, alter, or change our articles of religion, nor establish any new standards or rules of doctrine contrary to our present existing and established standards of doctrine."[9] This well-meant attempt to petrify the theological *status quo* left a heritage of uncertainty.

## THE DOCTRINAL STANDARDS: THEIR NATURE AND IDENTITY

For one thing, the Articles appear by this time to have gained central importance, so that they alone must not be revoked or altered whereas the other unspecified doctrinal standards must not receive contradictory additions.[10] Is the subtle ambiguity in wording deliberate—as we suspect—or merely careless? Surely it was not the intention of the drafting committee to imply that the Articles were in fact the only standards, with the mention of "Our present and existing and established standards of doctrine" merely a legal device to cover all possible contingencies, with nothing concrete in mind? If not, what are these "existing and established standards" of Methodist doctrine which, like the laws of the Medes and the Persians, may not be altered? They are apparently like the common law, taken for granted by all, yet capable of accurate and complete definition by no one, and never summarized in any authoritative document.

At the present time the candidate for full connection in the United Methodist ministry undergoes an examination modeled on that given by John Wesley to his preachers. Questions 8–10 of the nineteen asked on this occasion run thus:

(8) Have you studied the doctrines of The United Methodist Church?
(9) After full examination do you believe that our doctrines are in harmony with the Holy Scriptures?
(10) Will you preach and maintain them?[11]

Similarly the British Methodist minister is challenged every year of his ministry with this question, asked at the May Synod: "Does he believe and preach our doctrines?" This sounds exemplary, but it does not answer the question, "What *are* these doctrines which we must believe and preach?"

The accepted practice of the Methodist Church was to treat the Articles of Religion as "our doctrines," though with a vague suspicion that something additional was implied, or ought to be implied. With the formation of the United Methodist Church in 1968 a Theological Study Commission on Doctrine and Doctrinal Standards was appointed to clarify the situation, and (if it seemed desirable) to prepare "a contemporary formulation of doctrine and belief, in

50

supplementation to all antecedent formulations."[12] Their report was presented to the 1972 General Conference, with the results noted below. The Methodist Church in Britain has continued to maintain a radically different approach, refusing to make a credal statement, taking general orthodoxy of Christian belief for granted, and regarding "our doctrines" as that something else implied but not stated in American Methodism. What is this "something else," then? Perhaps a closer look at the present position in British Methodism, clinging so much more tenaciously to ancient traditions, will enable us to visualize more clearly the doctrinal standards of our Methodist forefathers in this country, standards bequeathed to us, indeed forced upon us, by the first restrictive rule of the 1808 General Conference, and loyally accepted by the Uniting Conferences of 1939 and 1968.[13]

The doctrinal standards of British Methodism are set out in the Deed of Union adopted by the three uniting churches in 1932, and unlike everything else in that deed may never be altered by the Conference, though the Conference is the final authority in their interpretation. This is much the same as the position of the General Conference in the United States of America. Yet in this British Deed of Union the doctrines are never listed nor defined, no more than they were in any of Wesley's legislation—though he several times had the advice of capable lawyers. They are concerned with the spirit rather than with the letter of the law of God. It is taken for granted that the British Methodist preacher accepts "the fundamental principles of the historic creeds and of the Protestant Reformation," and he is expected to emphasize especially "the doctrines of the evangelical faith . . . based upon the Divine revelation recorded in the Holy Scriptures." Though these are never strictly *defined*, they are *illustrated*, in Wesley's manner, and from Wesley's writings: "These evangelical doctrines to which the preachers of the Methodist Church both ministers and laymen are pledged are contained in Wesley's *Notes on the New Testament* and the first four volumes of his sermons." The Model Deed of the British Methodist Church stipulates that no doctrines contrary to these standards may be preached in any Methodist church. The significance of this lack of precision is thus spelled out in the Deed of Union:

> The *Notes on the New Testament* and the *Forty-Four Sermons* are not intended to impose a system of formal or speculative theology on Methodist Preachers, but to set up standards of preaching and belief which should secure loyalty to the fundamental truths of the Gospel of redemption, and secure the continued witness of the Church to the realities of the Christian experience of salvation.[14]

The voice is indeed Wesley's voice, though the words are those of his followers. For this was the principle on which he tried to ensure the loyalty of Methodism to its evangelical calling, and these were the very documents which he legally established as exemplars of evangelical doctrine.

Exactly this pattern was followed at first in American Methodism. Gradually, however, the Articles of Religion came to occupy a distinctive place as a formal and specific doctrinal standard, and eventually were regarded by many as the *only* genuine standard.[15] As a statement of the theological emphases of Wesley and his American followers, however, the Articles are clearly defective, for where is Christian Perfection to be found? The Methodist Protestant Church tried to remedy this defect by a twenty-sixth Article on Sanctification, but although this has been printed in recent *Disciplines* its status has been left deliberately vague, though clearly it does not have the same authority as the original twenty-five. In addition, from 1968 onwards the omission has been rectified by the adoption also of the Confession of Faith of the Evangelical United Brethren, whose Article XI, "Sanctification and Christian Perfection," is a careful and lengthy statement based solidly on Wesley's teaching.[16] Neither in the Articles nor elsewhere in the *Discipline*, however, were Wesley's *Notes* and *Sermons* mentioned until the 1968 *Discipline* at last reintroduced them by way of a reference to the British Deed of Union.[17] Eventually the 1972 *Discipline*, in adapting the report of the Theological Study Commission on Doctrine and Doctrinal Standards, inserted a careful discussion of the *Notes* and *Sermons* in a section on "Wesleyan Doctrinal Standards."[18]

The early neglect of these two "standards" does not seem to have been deliberate, but the result of the hasty preparation of the 1785 *Discipline* from Wesley's large *Minutes* of 1780—the reference to them was buried in a clause in the lengthy Model Deed, which was not reproduced.[19] This clause is finally included in the 1972 *Discipline*, with comments on its interpretation, along the same lines as the British Deed of Union quoted above, together with an evaluation of this unusual method of securing doctrinal orthodoxy: "The aim here was not to impose an inflexible system of doctrine or to inhibit responsible intellectual freedom, but rather to provide a broad and flexible framework of doctrine which would define the outside limits for public teaching in the societies, in disputed cases. These standards were more flexible than any of the classical creeds or confessions or articles, they gave the Methodists a measure of protection from doctrinal eccentricity, and they gave Methodist laymen a new role in the assessment of doctrinal standards. This particular collegial formula for doctrinal guidance was unique in Christendom. It committed the Methodist people to the biblical revelation as primary without proposing a literal summary of that revelation in any single propositional form. It anchored Methodist theology to a stable core, but allowed it freedom of movement in the further unfoldings of history."[20] Although the statement on the "historical background," including this clause and comment, is not itself either "part of the Constitution nor under the Restrictive Rules,"[21] it is of key importance in defining the doctrinal significance of the general phrase in trust clauses for United Methodist property, namely that the premises are "held in trust for the

United Methodist Church and subject to the provisions of its *Discipline*."[22] Now at length Wesley is no longer present upon Methodist premises in conceal- ment, a dusty skeleton in a dark cupboard.

To visualize the early American situation fully we need to go back behind 1784 to 1773, to the first Methodist Conference held on American soil. The preachers present agreed that "the doctrine and discipline of the Methodists, as contained in the *Minutes*," should be the sole rule of their conduct.[23] In thus accepting the *Minutes*, i.e., Wesley's *Minutes*, they knew that they were accepting the principle that the trust deeds of Methodist "preaching-houses" should contain a clause restricting those conducting worship therein from preaching any other doctrines than those "contained in Mr. Wesley's *Notes upon the New Testament*, and four volumes of *Sermons*." This, indeed, was there for those who wished to see it in the deed for the New York chapel.[24] To make sure that all the preachers knew what this implied Wesley presented a three-volume set of the 1760 edition of his *Explanatory Notes upon the New Testament* to all those present at the 1775 Conference, including the fourteen native preachers: William Duke's set, at least, has survived.[25] Their expected doctrinal loyalties were made slightly more specific in the challenging opening question of the 1781 Conference: "What preachers are now determined . . . to preach the old Methodist doctrine, and strictly enforce the discipline, as con- tained in the notes, sermons, and minutes published by Mr. Wesley?"[26] This same pledge was demanded by the Conference of April-May, 1784, as an essential prerequisite before any European preacher could be accepted into the American work.[27]

Unfortunately the *Minutes* of the American Conferences during the eight- eenth century are little more than statistical bones with only an occasional shred of historical flesh clinging to them, so that they do not enable us to reconstruct the body of the primitive church. It is to the *Disciplines* that we must turn for fuller information. Even here, however, we find the merest crumbs of theologi- cal leaven scattered in the disciplinary lump. The Christmas Conference of 1784 asserted the virtual independence of American Methodism, instituting episcopal government and several modifications of Wesley's original discipline. But his theology remained untouched, almost unmentioned. A few incidental scraps of doctrinal teaching were specifically noted, such as the somewhat inadequate summary in a brief section on pastoral duties of "our doctrine" as "repentance toward God, and faith in our Lord Jesus Christ."[28] In general, however, Wesley's doctrines seem to have been regarded as almost inviolable; the main thing was to give close attention to the discipline.

Both doctrine and discipline, however, were vulnerable. That this was realized may be seen from the wording of a caution against elaborate building plans for new chapels, which might give rich men undue influence—"and then farewell to the Methodist discipline, if not doctrine too."[29] One important omission from the 1785 *Discipline*, as we have seen, was the stipulation about naming Wesley's *Notes* and *Sermons* in trust deeds as the Methodist doctrinal standards, although there survived several incidental references to Wesley's publications both for the preachers' own study and for dispersal among the people.[30] To these was added in 1787 a recommendation that when preachers were not available, as during the sessions of the Annual Conference, "some person of ability . . . in every society should sing, pray, and read one of Mr. Wesley's sermons."[31] For a time, however, the Methodist Episcopal Church had no explicit doctrinal guidance apart from the three doctrinal sections carried over from the 1780 *Minutes*—"Of the Rise of Methodism," "Against Antinomianism," and "Of Perfection."

## THE DOCTRINAL TRACTS INCORPORATED WITH THE DISCIPLINE, 1788–1808

This deficiency was in part remedied by the greatly enlarged fourth edition of the *Discipline*, published in 1788. The title page drew attention to "some other useful pieces annexed"—which in fact comprised two-thirds of the volume. These five "useful pieces" illustrated characteristic Methodist teaching from the writings of Wesley. The first addition was mainly historical and disciplinary in function—*The Nature, Design, and General Rules of the United Societies of the* Methodist Episcopal Church in America—an almost exact reprint of Wesleys' *General Rules* of 1743, though their signatures are replaced by "Thomas Coke, Francis Asbury. May 28, 1787."[32] In 1789 this document was moved up into the general body of disciplinary regulations, and has remained there ever since, forming the subject of the fourth restrictive rule of the 1808 General Conference: "They shall not revoke or change the General Rules of the United Society."

The second tract appended in 1788 was "The Articles of Religion, as received and taught in the Methodist Episcopal Church throughout the United States of America." Once again this was in substance John Wesley's work, his abridgment of the Thirty-Nine Articles of the Church of England into the twenty-five appended to the *Sunday Service of the Methodists*. Once again this was incorporated into the general body of the *Discipline*, though not until 1790, along with other doctrinal tracts. Once again it was named as an inviolable part of the Methodist constitution by the restrictive rule of 1808.

The third tract dealt with Cokesbury College, and does not here concern us. The fourth was *The Scripture Doctrine of Predestination, Election, and Reprobation. By the Rev. John Wesley, M.A.*[33]—an antidote against some of the dangers of Calvinism noted in the statement on the rise of Methodism. Like the Articles, this was incorporated into the body of the *Discipline* in 1790, and was presumably part of the doctrinal standards set up in 1808 as inviolable. The same is true of the fifth tract. Once more it is Wesley, though Wesley in disguise. His original treatise had been entitled *Serious Thoughts upon the Perseverance of the Saints*,[34] but his editors apparently found it necessary for American consumption to expound the word "perseverance" and to expunge the word "saints." The resultant title appeared as "Serious Thoughts on the Infallible, Unconditional Perseverance of all that have once experienced Faith in Christ." (They nevertheless allowed the word "saints" to stand in the second paragraph, where Wesley defined the term.)

To the 1789 *Discipline* a most important addition was made, augmenting generously the tiny section on sanctification. This was no other than that spiritual classic, *A Plain Account of Christian Perfection, as believed and taught by the Rev. Mr. John Wesley, from the year 1725 to the year 1765,* which filled nearly ninety pages.[35]

The year 1790 saw an important change of policy. All the doctrinal tracts were included as numbered sections of the official constitution and to signalize the change a parenthetical phrase was added to the title, which thus became, *A Form of Discipline . . . (now comprehending the Principles and Doctrines) of the Methodist Episcopal Church in America.* Once more an addition was made to these tracts, though this time it was not from the pen of Wesley. It was entitled *A Treatise on the Nature and Subjects of Christian Baptism. Extracted from a late Author.* This had in fact been published in Philadelphia two years earlier by Moses Hemmenway (1735–1811) as *A Discourse on the nature and subjects of Christian baptism.* John Dickins printed about half the contents as a separate work of 71 pages in 1790, and it seems quite possible that the perusal of Dickins' extract led to its official adoption by his colleagues as a doctrinal standard in this insufficiently covered area.[36]

The *Discipline* of 1791 continued to proclaim itself as "comprehending the Principles and Doctrines" of Methodism, but added nothing further to the doctrinal sections. In 1792 the parenthetical subtitle became a part of the main title, and from that year to 1964 the volume remained *The Doctrines and Discipline* of the church—on the title page at least. This same General Conference of 1792 re-arranged the material in its newly designated *Doctrines and Discipline.* The formal statement of doctrine in the twenty-five articles was promoted to first place in Chapter I, after the description of the origin of the church, while the lengthier doctrinal commentary contained in the tracts was relegated to the closing sections of Chapter III. A further addition was made to these, in the shape of what we now know as the Ritual, but which was then described as "Section X. Sacramental Services, &c." For some reason a few copies appeared without the bulky doctrinal tracts, so that "The End" could be printed on p. 72, though the full work contained 264 pages.

In their preface to the 1792 *Discipline* Bishops Asbury and Coke differentiated between the two parts of their doctrinal standards, though insisting on the importance of both, in what amounts to a recital of the titles of the Tracts:

> "We wish to see this little publication in the house of every Methodist, and the more so as it contains our plan of Collegiate and Christian education, and the articles of religion maintained, more or less, in part or in the whole, by every reformed church in the world. We would likewise declare our real sentiments on the scripture doctrine of election and reprobation; on the infallible, unconditional perseverance of all that[37] ever have believed, or ever shall; on the doctrine of Christian perfection and, lastly, on the nature and subjects of Christian Baptism."

Nevertheless they were not prepared to treat this supplementary matter as sacrosanct. Early in 1797 Asbury wrote about a task apparently entrusted to him and Coke by the 1796 General Conference: "We have struck out many to us exceptional [i.e., exceptionable] parts of the tracts. These we did not hold as sacred as the discipline, which we did not alter a word."[38] In fact, however, the bishops' bark was worse than their bite. However vigorously they wielded the blue pencil the published results remained the same through subsequent editions, with the one exception that Hemmenway's treatise on baptism was removed from the 1797 *Discipline*.

The 1798 edition was unique in furnishing "explanatory notes" by Coke and Asbury, who estimated that the discipline proper occupied seventy pages and their notes one hundred pages, so that even with the removal of Hemmenway's treatise and the ordination services from the tracts the resultant volume would contain three hundred pages.[39] In the event, however, it was decided to publish the notes in very tiny print, and to omit the tracts from at least this edition, so that the 1798 *Discipline* turned out to have slightly fewer pages than that of 1797. Not everyone was happy about the changes, and at the General Conference of 1800 "Brother J. Stoneman moved that the explanatory notes be left out of the next edition of the form of Discipline, except the notes upon the articles of religion."[40] After pondering the matter for a weekend the Conference reached a compromise—that the *Discipline* and the notes should each be printed separately, so that preachers could have the *Discipline* alone, or bound together with the notes if they so wished. In the following eleventh edition of the *Discipline* (1801) the notes were accordingly omitted and the tracts restored, and so it remained for the editions of 1804, 1805, and 1808. Nor do the notes appear to have been printed separately, in accordance with the Conference resolution; they simply disappeared without being missed.[41]

# THE *DOCTRINAL TRACTS* SEPARATED FROM THE *DISCIPLINE*

Another major change was ordered by the General Conference of 1812, its manner apparently dictated by the first restrictive rule of the preceding General Conference of 1808. As we have seen, this rule sought to fix for all time the "present existing and established standards of doctrine." These clearly included the articles, and apparently also—though not quite so clearly—the doctrinal principles relating to *Notes* and *Sermons*, the doctrinal sections, and the doctrinal tracts—possibly even the Ritual. All these had been incorporated in the *Discipline* at the time of the restrictive rule. The mass of day-to-day legislation, however, was becoming embarrassingly large. (If only they could have seen the tightly packed little *Discipline* of a century and a half later!) To continue to publish these lengthy tracts in the *Discipline* was difficult, to add to them impracticable, to do away with them henceforth illegal. The delegates who met during May 1–22, 1812, eventually arrived at a neat solution for their dilemma, one foreshadowed and possibly suggested by the treatment of the bishops' "explanatory notes." They would publish their authoritative doctrinal commentary in a volume separate from their doctrinal creed. On the very last day of the protracted Conference Jesse Lee moved and Conference approved this resolution: "That the tracts on doctrine be left out of the future edition[s] of our form of *Discipline*, and that the following tracts be printed and bound in a separate volume, viz.,: 'Predestination Calmly Considered,' 'Scripture Doctrines on Election and Reprobation,' 'On Final Perseverance,' 'A Predestinarian and his Friend,' 'Christian Perfection,' and 'An Antinomian and his Friend.'"[42] In effect it might be said that the *Doctrines and Discipline* was henceforth to be published in two volumes, Volume 1 dealing mainly with Discipline and Volume 2 with Doctrine.

Bishop Tigert did not seem unduly surprised to discover (as he thought) that at least the latter half of this Conference direction had been overlooked for twenty years[43]—and the neglect of the 1800 Conference's injunction to publish the bishops' explanatory notes in a separate volume would lend some color to this belief. (Indeed I understand that even in these enlightened and efficient days it is not unknown for a General Conference to pass resolutions which are immediately forgotten, even by their promoters.) In this particular instance, however, fairly prompt action was taken. The first thing was to issue the revised fifteenth edition of the *Discipline* without the tracts, and this was done that very year of 1812, followed up by a sixteenth edition in 1813. The unwary student tracing these volumes in a card catalogue, however, would hardly realize that extensive cuts had been made, for the volumes retained almost exactly the same number of pages, by the simple expedients of reducing the size of the paper and increasing the size of the type. With these two diminished *Disciplines* under his belt the Conference printer, John C. Totten, turned to the supplementary volume, which one hopes was eagerly awaited.

In 1814 there duly appeared the first edition of the "Doctrinal Tracts," and subsequent editions continued to be given that designation on their leather labels, though never on their title pages. The title remained constant (with minor variations in the second sentence) through at least fifteen editions covering the best part of a century: *A Collection of Interesting Tracts, explaining several important points of Scripture Doctrine. Published by order of the General Conference.*[44] The preface pointed out that these tracts had been omitted so that the quadrennial issue of the *Discipline* "might be small and cheap"—an unfortunate phrase which was amended in 1825 to "might still be within the reach of every reader."

This volume was almost twice the size of its companion *Discipline*, and contained 360 pages. The reason was that Jesse Lee's resolution had been followed not strictly but generously, even to the end of the second mile and beyond. In addition to the original three doctrinal tracts added by 1789, Lee had requested and been granted three more of Wesley's smaller publications (the dialogue between a Predestinarian and his friend, and the two between an Antinomian and his friend), and another of his major works, *Predestination Calmly Considered.*[45] So now there were seven—or would have been had not the two Antinomian tracts been forgotten, or deliberately omitted. Already there was matter here for a volume slightly larger than the *Discipline*. As if to atone for the omission with a work of supererogation, no fewer than nine other items were added, almost doubling the size of the volume. Like all those originally named by Lee, six of these were by Wesley, including his controverted sermon on *Free Grace*, his satire on Toplady's predestinarianism entitled *The Consequence Proved*, and a pinch-hitter for the tract on antinomianism (a word carefully avoided with the somewhat fanciful title *A Blow at the Root, or Christ stabbed in the house of his friends*).[46] The most considerable of the non-Wesleyan items was "A Short Method with the Baptists, by Peter Edwards, several years Pastor of a Baptist Church, at Portsea, Hants.," which filled over thirty pages, and had originally appeared in England in 1793 as *Candid Reasons for renouncing the principles of Antipaedobaptism.* (Possibly a change in title was indeed called for!)

There must have been a reasonably good sale for this volume, because an unaltered second edition appeared in 1817. Eight years later yet another edition was needed. This time there was a general revision. The Methodists were still seeking an antidote to the pernicious doctrines and annoying success of the Baptists. Hemmenway's *Discourse* had been discarded. Now Edwards' *Short Method* was shed. Maybe Mr. Wesley could do as well; at least they would give him a try. And so the preface announced: "In the present edition some new

58

Tracts are added, and Mr. Wesley's short Treatise on Baptism is substituted in the place of the extract from Mr. Edwards on that subject." As always, the preface was unsigned, though it was dated "New-York, October 5th, 1825." This volume was remarkable for the fact that each of the thirteen tracts was presented as a distinct entity, its pages numbered and its gatherings printed separately from its companions, though the gatherings were signed consecutively—with figures instead of with letters. Probably many of the items were in fact sold separately. This was certainly true of the last, Wesley's *Plain Account of Christian Perfection*, which was described on the title page as "Tract No. XXXVI of the New-York Methodist Tract Society." Any surplus pages at the ends of the tracts were filled with appropriate (though little-known) poems by Charles Wesley, or with additional prose material. Even more was added to Wesley's *Treatise on Baptism* (which is in fact mainly the work of his father); this was supplemented by another tract, an extract from William Wall's *History of Infant Baptism* which Wesley had published in 1751 under the title of *Thoughts on Infant Baptism*,[47] and by "Remarks on Infant Baptism, by H. S. Boyd, Esq."—an English patristic scholar.

The demand for these doctrinal tracts continued, and in 1831 this same collection appeared in consolidated form, the gapfilling Charles Wesley hymns omitted, and the other material printed consecutively on 388 pages. Strangely enough even the 1825 preface is reproduced exactly as in the original, complete with the earlier date and the statement that "two editions have been published and sold"—a statement which now contained the truth, but not the whole truth.

The following year the lasting need for such a collection was recognized by the provision of a stereotyped edition. This followed the somewhat condensed pattern of 1831, still more compressed into 378 pages. The editor deserves a hearty pat on the back for at last restoring the original title of Wesley's *Serious Thoughts upon the Perseverance of the Saints*. The preface was almost unchanged except for the rewriting of two sentences, one about the two former editions, the other about "several new tracts" (a phrase replaced by "some new tracts") and the alteration of the date to "New-York, July 5, 1832." Indeed this change of date is the only evidence we so far possess that an 1832 edition was in fact published, no copy of the volume itself having been discovered. This preface appears in a reprint, presumably from the stereotypes, after a title page dated 1834. Copies are also known dated 1836, 1847, 1850, 1854, 1856, and one undated.

In 1861 the volume was once more revised, and the new preface closed somewhat optimistically: "We hope the circulation of the book will be extended until the errors it so ably explodes shall be fully banished from the Church. The Publishers. New York, January 1, 1861." This revision included a caustic defense of Wesley against an attack by a Presbyterian who had been misled by a misprint and his own ignorance. The main alteration, however, was once more in the area of infant baptism. Even Mr. Wesley had not won the day, and he in his turn was dismissed for an anonymous modern writer, apparently a Methodist, who cited not only a liberal Calvinist like Dr. Leonard Woods of Andover, but also long-discarded Peter Edwards. There were at least two reprints of this revised edition, one in the 1870's and another about 1892.

## THE DISAPPEARANCE OF THE *DOCTRINAL TRACTS*

In the face of at least fifteen editions of the *Collection of Interesting Tracts* it is somewhat amazing that Bishop Tigert, writing his *Constitutional History of American Episcopal Methodism* in 1894, had never seen a copy, and in his revised issue of 1904 expressed surprise at meeting with even one edition. This contained the 1832 preface, from which he incorrectly deduced that the book agents had waited twenty years to carry out the Conference injunction—a somewhat excessive delay even in those unenlightened days. He decided to supply the supposed lack of early initiative by himself reissuing the original tracts in two small volumes of what he could then describe as the "well known series of 'Little Books on Doctrine,' entitling the volumes, *The Doctrines of the Methodist Episcopal Church in America*. This was published in 1902.[48]

Methodism constantly needs Bishop Tigerts to reawaken us to our heritage. Our own generation seems at length to have realized that the methods of Methodism are far from being her only glory, that the *Discipline* may have more affinities with Leviticus than with Luke and that the real secret of an effective Methodism is spiritual and theological. It is indeed a healthy sign that under the leadership of Dr. Albert C. Outler we have been summoned once more to study our evangelical foundations, so much taken for granted (until questions of church union force them upon our attention) that they have too often been neglected. As this has been done we have surely realized that John Wesley's gospel as well as his creed, not only in its spirit but even in its literary expression, long remained and apparently still remains an integral though frequently overlooked element in the "present existing and established standards of doctrine" which form an essential legal element in the constitution of The United Methodist Church. True, at first glance "present existing" might seem to refer to 1972, or 1968, or possibly 1939. In fact, however, these are the more recent successors in an unbroken line of exact quotations, all General Conferences having vowed to maintain the "present existing" standards of their predecessors, and thus in effect having vowed to maintain the doctrinal standards existing in 1808. Nor does any change seem likely in the foreseeable future. The report of the Theological Study Commission on Doctrine and Doctrinal Standards presented by Dr. Outler to the General Conference of 1972 pointed out that "despite continued and quite variegated theological development, there has been no significant project in formal doctrinal re-formulation in Methodism since 1808."[49] The Commission, however, suggested neither repeal nor revision, nor reformulation, because our doctrinal standards must not be regarded as inflexible legal instruments, but as a precious and inspiring heirloom, a heritage to be interpreted and reinterpreted in the light of Scripture, tradition, experience, and reason, so as to be kept continuously relevant to current needs and opportunities. To this the General Conference agreed.[50] In this heritage we should include, not only Wesley's *Sermons* and his *Explanatory Notes upon the New Testament*, but those other writings of his incorporated in the "Doctrinal Tracts," not only because a strong legal case could be made that these indeed formed a part of the "present existing . . . standards" named in the first restrictive rule of 1808, but because they were singled out by our forefathers as important illustrations of the essential spiritual and theological heritage of Methodism. In theory at least Methodist theology did not change its eighteenth-century oil lamps for gaslight in the mid-nineteenth century, nor for electricity in the twentieth. Like the Olympic runners, through the quadrennia it has handed on the torch kindled at John Wesley's warmed heart and theology of salvation. Nor need this cause us any impatience or distress. Methods may change, interpretations may vary, but the message of God's eternal saving love in Jesus Christ is the same yesterday, today, and forever.

## CHAPTER 4

# At Full Liberty: Doctrinal Standards in Early American Methodism[1]

Richard P. Heitzenrater

The distinction between doctrines and the standards used to enforce them can be understood as a tension between the weight of tradition and the force of law.

American Methodism has never been characterized by a strong inclination toward careful doctrinal definition. That is not to say that Methodism has had no concern at all for matters of doctrine. From the beginning, the Methodist preachers referred to "our doctrines" with a sense of pride; they likewise expressed concern about the dissemination of erroneous doctrines in their midst. As American Methodism shifted from a movement to an institution (from a society to a church), it quite naturally developed structures and procedures to protect and perpetuate its traditional identity. Such a process included not only the establishment of legal and constitutional means by which to guard the "standards of doctrine," but also the preservation of traditional doctrinal emphases to perpetuate the distinctive, if not well-defined, Methodist proclamation of the gospel which lay at the heart of the movement. The growing desire for order and discipline, in tension with a seeming ambivalence toward doctrinal formulation, provided the setting for a unique development in the constitutional history of Methodism in America that to this day has not received an interpretation that commands a consensus.

The General Conference in 1808 passed a set of rules for "regulating and perpetuating" the conference. Among the provisions that became recognized as constitutionally binding upon Methodism was the stipulation that the General Conference have "full powers to make rules and regulations for our Church," subject only to a list of six "restrictions" subsequently called the "Restrictive

Rules." The First Restrictive Rule, still in effect in the Methodist Church today, states that

> the General Conference shall not revoke, alter, or change our articles of religion, nor establish any new standards or rules of doctrine contrary to our present existing and established standards of doctrine.[2]

Questions of doctrinal standards[3] in Methodism are determined in large part by the interpretation of this rule. The issue of interpretation is often focused on the meaning of the last phrase ("our present existing and established standards of doctrine"), giving rise to no small amount of debate among Methodist theologians during the past hundred years or so.

The interpretation that has prevailed over the last century has been incorporated into the official documents of the United Methodist Church. The *Plan of Union*, approved in 1966–67, noted that, although the last phrase of the First Restrictive Rule had never been formally defined, the "original reference" would include, "as a minimum," Wesley's "forty-four *Sermons on Several Occasions* and his *Explanatory Notes Upon the New Testament*."[4] That assumption provided the basis for subsequent interpretive statements passed by the General Conference in 1972. The "Historical Background" statement, still contained in Part II of the 1984 Book of Discipline, reiterates the claim that Wesley's *Sermons* and *Notes* were "by plain historical inference" among the "present existing and established standards of doctrine" specified by the framers of the First Restrictive Rule in 1808.[5] This view, however, like nearly every comment on the question during the last century, overlooks two key sources of evidence: the Discipline's own historical stipulations for enforcing doctrinal standards (beginning in 1788) and the manuscript journal of the General Conference of 1808 that passed the first constitutional rules. Careful consideration of this evidence challenges the current view and calls for a reconsideration of the assumptions that have prevailed regarding doctrinal standards.

The question of doctrinal standards in early American Methodism has taken on added significance with the decision of the 1984 General Conference to establish a study committee on "Our Theological Task." The committee's charge is "to prepare a new statement [Book of Discipline, ¶69] that will reflect the needs of the church [and] define the scope of our Wesleyan tradition in the context of our contemporary world." The First Restrictive Rule, of course, remains in force, and therefore a clear understanding of the intent of its framers (and thereby the meaning of its language regarding doctrinal standards) is crucial to the constitutionality of any updating of disciplinary statements concerning United Methodist doctrine. Of particular concern in this paper is the relationship between matters that bear the force of law and those that rely on the weight of tradition.

The matter of ascertaining the meaning of the phrase "our present existing and established standards of doctrine" in the 1808 document hinges upon two questions: What do the official documents of the Methodist Episcopal Church from 1785 to 1808 stipulate (legally *establish* by definition or implication) as the doctrinal standards of the denomination at that time? and What did the persons who drew up those documents intend by their language? Two related, but different, questions are, What are the distinctive doctrinal *emphases* of early Methodist preaching? and What documents best exhibited those distinctive doctrines? The developments during the period from 1785 to 1808 are of primary interest in answering these questions regarding law and tradition, but the ideas and actions of the generations of American Methodists before and after that period also help illuminate the issues.

The constitutional developments at the turn of the nineteenth century have never been fully outlined or adequately examined in the light of material now available. These events are crucial to a full understanding of the issues today, however, and deserve our careful attention. We will therefore look at the constitutional activities of early American Methodism step by step with an eye toward discerning the tension and interplay between the force of law and the weight of tradition, in an attempt to contribute to a better understanding of the scope of the Wesleyan tradition in relation to doctrinal standards in The United Methodist Church.

## WESLEY AND THE CHRISTMAS CONFERENCE

The organizing conference of the Methodist Episcopal Church met in Baltimore in December, 1784, to consider the scheme of organization proposed by Wesley, as filtered through Francis Asbury and Thomas Coke. Its main concern was to establish a workable polity for American Methodists, *separate* from their former British connections yet still to some extent reliant upon Wesley, during his lifetime.

The question of doctrine remained largely in the shadows during those days of rewriting the *Minutes* of the British Methodist Conference (also known as the "Large Minutes") into a form of discipline for the American Methodist connection. In fact, the official minutes of the Christmas Conference do not refer at all to any action concerning doctrine as such. One oblique reference appears in a letter from Wesley "To Dr. Coke, Mr. Asbury, and our brethren in North America" that is prefixed to those minutes. The letter spells out Wesley's rationale for allowing the organization of a separate church in the American states in the light of the "uncommon train of providences" by which they had become independent. Wesley concludes by proclaiming that the American

Methodists, being totally disentangled from the English state and church, "are now at full liberty, simply to follow the scriptures and the primitive church."[6]

Lest anyone think, however, that he was casting his American followers adrift in a sea of doctrinal tumult, Wesley sent to the new world, with Dr. Coke, a document that provided the liturgical and doctrinal framework for American Methodism. *The Sunday Service for the Methodists in North America*, received and adopted by the Christmas Conference, contained Wesley's abridgement of the *Book of Common Prayer* and his distillation of the Thirty-Nine Articles. Wesley may very well have conceived of these materials, along with the "Large Minutes," as providing the basic design for the organization of a Methodist church in America, much as John Fletcher and Joseph Benson had proposed to him in a nearly identical scheme for England in 1775.[7] The Methodist preachers in America not only adopted Wesley's revision of the Articles, but also apparently assumed that these materials from Wesley's hand furnished the necessary official doctrinal framework for an ecclesiastical organization, similar to the way the Thirty-Nine Articles provided doctrinal standards for the Church of England.[8] The acceptance of these documents *per se* did not diminish the American Methodists' regard at that time for Wesley's continuing leadership in matters of government or for his other writings as a traditional source of doctrine.[9] In fact, their high regard for Wesley's scheme seems to have convinced them that the specific documents he had drawn up and sent over were deliberately conceived for the purposes of establishing the new church, which now stood in a new and separate constitutional relationship to both the Church of England and British Methodism.[10]

The preachers meeting in Baltimore clearly understood themselves to be establishing an independent organization that *superseded* any previous arrangements that had existed. The minutes of the Christmas Conference point out that "at this conference we formed ourselves into an Independent Church." Also, the answer to Question 3 in their first Discipline, which they drew up in Baltimore, makes this point very clearly:

> We will form ourselves into an Episcopal Church under the direction of Superintendents, Elders, Deacons and Helpers, according to the Forms of Ordination annexed to our Liturgy, and the Form of Discipline *set forth in these Minutes.*" [italics mine][11]

The British "Large Minutes," which formed the basis for these American "Minutes" as revised at the Christmas Conference were thus superseded and no longer had any binding effect on the American Methodists after January, 1785.[12]

There is no reason to suspect that the traditional distinctive doctrines preached by Methodists in America would have changed as a result of any action of the organizing conference. The preachers in the newly organized Methodist Episcopal Church would certainly be expected to preach the same message that had given life to their movement over the previous decade. No one would expect that Wesley's *Sermons* and *Notes* would suddenly be discarded by the Americans; they had long been an important resource for solid Methodist doctrinal preaching.

After 1784, however, a new legal situation had been established in which the *Sermons* and *Notes* would appear to function quite differently than previously. During the decade prior to the Christmas Conference, the American Methodist conference had on several occasions pledged itself to the Wesleyan scheme in both doctrine and polity. It had followed the stipulations of the British *Minutes* to the letter, as was appropriate, given their status as part of British Methodism, under leaders appointed by Wesley. Their chapels were secured by the "model deed" contained in those *Minutes*, which, among other things, (1) required that the preachers be appointed by Mr. Wesley, (2) "Provided always, that such persons preach no other Doctrine than is contained in Mr. Wesley's *Notes Upon the New Testament*, and four Volumes of Sermons."[13] These guidelines for measuring the doctrinal soundness of Methodist preaching were certainly, by any definition, "doctrinal standards." As such, they applied equally in America up through 1784 and were reinforced by specific actions of the conferences of Methodist preachers in America.[14] But the Christmas Conference had established American Methodism as a separate organization with its own set of constitutive documents, similar in form but significantly different in content from the British counterparts. The differences in the legal situation and the tensions with the traditional understandings became evident in the development of American Methodism subsequent to 1784.

# FROM THE CHRISTMAS CONFERENCE
# TO THE GENERAL CONFERENCE OF 1808

After 1784, the Methodist preachers in America no doubt remained committed to their traditional doctrines. But the question remains, what did the Methodist Episcopal Church understand their "established *standards* of doctrine" to be? The fate of the "model deed," which stipulated those standards in Britain, helps answer that question. As noted previously, the Christmas Conference spent a large part of its time revising the "Large Minutes" into the new American form of discipline, published as the *Minutes* of 1785. A comparison of the two documents indicates that, although some sections were altered, many sections were either omitted totally or adopted without change, depending on their applicability to the American scene. The section which contained the "model deed" was omitted.[15] The new Discipline in America therefore specified no doctrinal *standards*, as the British "Large Minutes" had, although it did have many references to specific doctrines and doctrinal writings.

The conference had, however, received and adopted another document, *The Sunday Service*, that did contain a specifically designed formulation of doctrinal standards, the Articles of Religion (printed at the end, in the same manner that the Anglican Thirty-Nine Articles appeared at the end of the *Book of Common Prayer*). These "rectified" Articles, as we have said, had been drawn up specifically by Wesley for the American Methodists. There seems to have been no need in the minds of the American preachers, given Wesley's intentional provision of these Articles, to specify any other *standards* of doctrine by which to measure American Methodist preaching and teaching. This assumption is further supported by the fact that the "model deed," which the Methodist Episcopal Church did insert into its Discipline beginning in 1796, not only (1) designated a new source of authorization for the preachers (the American conferences instead of Wesley), but also (2) specifically deleted the proviso concerning the *Sermons* and *Notes*, thus consciously deleting their force as legally binding standards of doctrine.[16]

A more direct clue to the Methodist Episcopal Church's understanding of its doctrinal standards can be found in the disciplinary provisions for maintaining and enforcing those standards. The *Form of Discipline* for 1788 introduces a section on the trial of "immoral ministers and preachers," in which Question 2 is "What shall be done in cases of improper tempers, words or actions, or a breach of the articles, and discipline of the church?"[17] (This same edition of the Discipline, coincidentally, also has "some other useful pieces annexed,"[18] one of which contains the Articles of Religion.) The first General Conference of the Methodist Episcopal Church, meeting in 1792, divided that question (the second in the section on trials of ministers) into two questions that distinguish between matters of discipline and matters of doctrine. The new Question 3 dealing with doctrine, reads, "What shall be done with those Ministers or Preachers who hold and preach doctrines which are *contrary to* our *Articles of Religion*?" (emphasis mine).[19] It is clear from this question that the only official measure or test of doctrinal orthodoxy (the function of doctrinal *standards*) within the Methodist Episcopal Church at that time were the Articles of Religion. In the same Discipline (1792) which contains this new question, the Articles were moved to a more prominent position at the front of the book, section II. The sacramental services were added to the volume and the title was changed to *The Doctrines and Discipline of the Methodist Episcopal Church in America*.

At no point in the early history of American Methodism were the Articles of Religion designated as standards that demanded positive subscription. Although not a creedal formula in that sense, they did function like the creeds of the primitive church in another way—they were used as standards by which to protect orthodoxy by determining heresy or erroneous doctrines, i.e, those doctrines that were "contrary to" the standards as found in the Articles.[20] No American Methodist candidate for ministry was required to make any positive doctrinal subscription, either to the Articles, to Wesley's *Sermons* and *Notes*, or to any other documents. The Articles served the purpose, then, of providing minimal norms or standards by which to measure the orthodoxy (not necessarily the adequacy) of doctrine held and preached by the Methodists.[21] The Wesleyan Articles of Religion provided a churchly doctrinal foundation for the new American Methodist ecclesiastical organization. They also presented an explicit doctrinal tie to the church universal and as such were a more appropriate standard of doctrine for such a church than the earlier British Methodist standards, Wesley's *Notes* and *Sermons*. In their original context, those British Wesleyan standards outlined what might be seen as a sectarian emphasis (for a movement rather than a church) under the larger umbrella of the Articles of Religion of the Church of England.

So far we have been looking at *standards* of doctrine as found in the Articles. That is not to say that good Methodist or Wesleyan *doctrines* were not to be found in other places. The Discipline itself, beginning with the first edition, contained two sections on doctrine (on perfection and against antinomianism) and explicitly recommended several other writings for specific purposes.[22] Beginning with the edition of 1788 (the "useful pieces annexed"), the Discipline contained several doctrinal tracts in addition to the two doctrinal sections already mentioned.[23] These were apparently not considered to be *standards* of doctrine in the same sense as the Articles since the provisions for the trial of a preacher on matters of doctrine were not altered in any way so as to take these doctrinal writings into account. These treatises certainly contained sound Methodist (if not always, strictly speaking, Wesleyan) doctrine, as did many other writings, but they were clearly never considered to be standards of doctrine.[24] The same can be said of the *Sermons* and *Notes*. Whether or not the American Methodists understood all the ecclesial implications of their separate establishment, they apparently did accept Wesley's intention that their organization be grounded upon a doctrinal statement (the Articles of Religion) that provided basic doctrinal standards and had obvious ties to the larger church universal in both form and content (see note 7). In this context, nevertheless, other Wesleyan writings continued to provide the distinctive shape of Methodist doctrinal teaching and preaching in America, fleshing out the basic Protestant norms provided in the Articles.

# THE GENERAL CONFERENCE OF 1808

Twenty-three years after the Christmas Conference, only a dozen or so of the preachers from 1785 remained active in the Methodist connection in America. At about the same time, the passing of the earlier generations had led the British Methodist Conference in 1806 to ask, "Can anything be done for the security of our doctrines?" The answer in their *Minutes* was that Adam Clarke, Joseph Benson, and Thomas Coke were to "draw up a Digest or Form, expressive of the Methodist Doctrines." Their efforts resulted in two documents, both entitled *Articles of Religion*.[25] In America, a similar desire to protect and perpetuate the established doctrines and discipline of the church was apparently on the minds of Asbury and some of the other preachers at the General Conference in Baltimore in 1808.

On the fourth day of the conference, a committee was established to set rules for "regulating and perpetuating General Conferences in the future."[26] This "committee of fourteen," formed by two members elected by each conference, included all seven of the preachers in attendance (excepting Asbury) who had been in active connection since 1785: Philip Bruce, Ezekiel Cooper, Jesse Lee, John M'Claskey, William Phoebus, Nelson Reed, and Thomas Ware. The subcommittee designated to write the proposal was made up of three persons: Bruce, Cooper, and Joshua Soule, a young preacher who would soon make his mark on Methodism. Their report to the conference came from the hand of Soule, and proposed the following as the first "restrictive rule": "The General Conference shall not revoke, alter, or change our Articles of Religion, nor establish any new standards of doctrine, contrary to our present existing and established standards of doctrine."[27]

The report of the "committee of fourteen" also contained, as its first item, a controversial proposal to establish a delegated General Conference. The defeat of that part of the report, over the question of how the delegates would be selected (largely because Jesse Lee opposed the committee's proposal of seniority as a basis), seemed to doom the whole report, which was then laid aside. As the conference drew to a close, however, the question of designating a time and place for the next conference allowed for the reintroduction of the question of delegation, and Soule's motion that delegates be selected by the annual conferences "either by seniority or choice" broke the logjam and allowed for the rest of the report to be brought up and carried, item by item.

Along with the other rules for governing the conference, the First Restrictive Rule was then passed, including the important phrase in question, "nor establish any new standards or rules of doctrine, contrary to our present existing and established standards of doctrine."[28] The primary impact of that second part of the statement seems to be to allow for new standards or rules of doctrine so long as they are *not contrary to* the existing ones ("present existing and

69

established"). The main intention, then, of the conference's adoption of the phrase seems not to have been to incorporate an additional body of material, such as Wesley's *Sermons* and *Notes*, to their "present and existing standards," the Articles. The primary intent was rather to protect the present standards, the Articles, and to stipulate narrow restrictions under which new standards could be developed.

The intention of the conference in the face of the tension between the force of legal standards and the weight of traditional ideas is made more evident in the actions taken almost immediately after the passage of the Restrictive Rules on the morning of May 24. The first action of the afternoon session was an attempt to clarify any ambiguity caused by the phrasing of the first rule. Francis Ward moved

> that it shall be considered as the sentiment of this Conference, that Mr. Wesley's Notes on the New Testament, his four first Volumes of Sermons and Mr. Fletcher's Checks, in their general tenor, contain the principal doctrines of Methodism, and a good explanation of our articles of religion; and that this sentiment be recorded on our Journal without being incorporated in the Discipline.[29]

Three things are significant about this motion: first, it indicates a willingness among some preachers to specify particular writings that "contain" the core of traditional Methodist doctrine and exposit the "standards" found in the Articles; second, that such sentiment was not inclined to rely solely upon Wesley's *Sermons* and *Notes* but to include also John Fletcher's *Checks Against Antinomianism*; and third, that this sentiment was somewhat hesitant, resulting in a desire for a "memorandum of understanding" only, that would be recorded in the journal of the proceedings but not explicitly stated in the Discipline. The most startling thing about this guarded and carefully worded motion is that it lost. The General Conference was *not* willing to go on record defining its standards of doctrine in terms of documents other than the Articles, not even Wesley's *Sermons* and *Notes*.

The rationale for the conference's negative vote on this motion is nowhere explicitly indicated. Nevertheless, in the light of the wording of the motion as well as the action taken, it seems obvious that the majority of the members present did not consider Wesley's writings to be "rules or standards of doctrine" in the same sense as the Articles of Religion. If the members of the conference had generally assumed such a correlation, the motion would not have been made in the first place, much less defeated. But what is confusing to the present observer is the conference's reticence to specify that the writings of Wesley and Fletcher "contain the principal doctrines of Methodism." This vote seems to be continuing evidence of a spirit of independence among the American Methodists that was more than simply anti-British sentiment, although that spirit can be seen flaring up at several points during the early years of the new denomination, including this period leading up to the hostilities of 1812. The tension between dependence upon and independence from Wesley had long been a mark of the Methodists in America, as illustrated clearly in the life and thought of Francis Asbury himself, who played a major leadership role in the conference of 1808. Asbury was apparently satisfied that the conference had sufficiently protected its Methodist heritage. Three days after passage of the Restrictive Rules he reflected upon the actions of that conference in a letter to Thomas Rankin, noting in particular that "we have . . . perpetuated in words the good old Methodist doctrine and discipline." Although this phrasing echoes the minutes of 1781, when the colonial conference reiterated its allegiance to the British Wesleyan standards, this comment by the bishop can be seen as an indication on his part that the actions of the conference had, without a literal return to their pre-1785 legal condition, preserved the original Methodist spirit in the face of new challenges from both heresy and sloth. Although the Articles of Religion seem to bypass some distinctively Wesleyan ideas, it appears that the Methodists in America accepted Wesley's design for protecting doctrinal orthodoxy through a brief and basic symbol of catholic doctrine, purged of Calvinist and Roman errors.

The intent of the 1808 General Conference thus seems to be clear. The majority desired to restrict Methodism's "established standards of doctrine" to the Articles of Religion that Wesley had provided in 1784 and to avoid even implying, by association or otherwise, that there were other specific writings that were authoritative *in the same manner*. The motion itself is, of course, an expression of the weight of the Wesleyan tradition coming to the fore, howbeit in a form considered inappropriate by most of those present and voting at the conference. The defeat of the motion seems to be conclusive evidence that the General Conference did not understand its standards of doctrine to include Wesley's *Sermons* and *Notes*. The Methodist Episcopal Church was left with a constitutional statement in the wording of the First Restrictive Rule, which refers specifically only to the Articles of Religion, and reiterates and reinforces the crucial importance of the Articles by referring to them as "our present existing and established standards of doctrine."

In the light of those actions of the 1808 General Conference, it is by no means strange that for two successive generations no one ever seems to have raised the question as to what the "present existing and established standards of doctrine" were. The Articles of Religion were the only standards of doctrine that had been "established" by the Methodist Episcopal Church, that is, adopted between 1785 and 1808 with provisions for enforcement as a measure of Methodist doctrine in America. The fact that writers in the last half of the century began to raise the question, and in fact make inaccurate speculations about the intentions of the framers of the First Restrictive Rule, can be partially explained by the absence of any mention of this motion (or attempted "memorandum of understanding") from the published version of the manuscript journal of the conference. A note in the margin of the manuscript journal explains the omission: "N.B. It was voted that this motion be struck out of the Journal." The whole paragraph mentioning the defeated motion regarding the *Notes, Sermons,* and *Checks* is struck through with a huge "X" and consequently deleted from the printed version of the journal. That entry is the only instance of such an action in the whole manuscript volume, which covers the general conferences from 1800 to 1828. The conference did not want to specify its Wesleyan measures for orthodoxy beyond the Articles, but it also did not want the public to know that it had been unwilling to go on record in that matter. The General Conference of 1808 manifested in its actions the continuing tension between dependence and independence, and, in its careful maneuvering, highlighted the distinction that is occasionally evident between the force of law and the weight of tradition.

## THE GENERAL CONFERENCES OF 1816 AND 1828

The evidence outlined above would seem to be adequate to make the point that the doctrinal standards of early American Methodism were understood from a legal and constitutional point of view to be located solely in the Articles of Religion (though perhaps traditionally understood to be illustrated in other Wesleyan writings as well). However, further evidence to corroborate that view can be found in the actions of the General Conference during the two decades following the establishment of the Restrictive Rules of 1808. Two incidents in particular relate to this question, and both are coincidentally connected with Joshua Soule.

In the first case, the General Conference of 1816 decided to appoint a "Committee of Safety," which was assigned the task of inquiring "whether our doctrines have been maintained, discipline faithfully and impartially enforced, and the stations and circuits duly attended."[30] This committee consisted of Enoch George, Samuel Parker, and Soule (a most appropriate person to be in this group, providing continuity from the conference of 1808). The report of the Committee of Safety, apparently drawn up by the chairman, Soule,[31] was approved two weeks later. It begins with the following statement:

> After due examination, your committee are of opinion that, in some parts of the connexion, doctrines contrary to our established articles of faith, and of dangerous tendency, have made their appearance among us, especially the ancient doctrines of *Arianism, Socinianism,* and *Pelagianism,* under certain new and obscure modifications.[32]

The term "established articles of faith" is not precisely the same as "articles of religion," but the committee seems to have had those articles in mind, since the three erroneous doctrines listed are specifically contradictory of Articles II, I and IX respectively of the Articles of Religion.

In the second incident, the General Conference of 1828 exhibited again the relationship that some persons within Methodism saw between the Articles as doctrinal standards and other doctrinal writings accepted and used by the preachers as containing good Methodist doctrine. The conference heard the appeal of Joshua Randall, a preacher from the New England Conference, who, according to the wording of the *Journal*, "had been expelled from the Church, upon a charge of holding and disseminating doctrines contrary to our articles of religion." The charges were upheld by an overwhelming majority of 164 votes to 1. Encouraged by the tone of the conference, Lawrence M'Combs introduced a proposal that accused Bishop Soule (who was presiding at that session!) of preaching erroneous doctrine the previous year in a sermon at the South Carolina Conference. The motion claimed that in the sermon there was "in the opinion of some an apparent departure from several points of doctrine held by the Methodist Episcopal Church."[33] The matter was referred to the Committee on the Episcopacy, on which M'Combs sat. The committee's report was brought to the floor the following day by its chairman, Stephen Roszel, the only member of the group who had been at the General Conference of 1808. The report, adopted by the conference, cleared the bishop of the charges. It concluded by saying, "There is nothing in the sermon, fairly construed, inconsistent with our articles of religion, as illustrated in the writings of Messrs. Wesley and Fletcher."[34]

The conference thus stated its understanding of the relationship between the legal standards of doctrine and the traditionally accepted doctrinal writings. This statement is particularly illuminating in four ways: (1) it demonstrates the position of the Articles of Religion as *the* standards of doctrine; (2) it shows that the doctrinal material found in certain other writings in the Methodist tradition did actually function at that time in a supplemental and illustrative role in relation to the doctrinal standards in the Articles of Religion, similar to the manner expressed by the defeated motion of 1808; (3) it reveals that, among these other writings, the broad range of Wesley's work was considered useful in illuminating matters of doctrine, rather than just the *Sermons* and *Notes*; and (4) it clearly indicates that materials other than the writings of Wesley, in this case (again) the writings of Fletcher, were also considered to be important in this illustrative role. While the Articles of Religion functioned as juridical standards of doctrine, these other doctrinal writings, traditionally accepted as containing sound Methodist doctrine, were seen as exemplary illustrations of the Methodist doctrinal heritage.

73

## CONCLUDING OBSERVATIONS

The developments within early American Methodism indicate very clearly that the "historical inferences" that are "apparent" from the available evidence all tend to confirm the Articles of Religion alone as the "present existing and established standards of doctrine" that the "committee of fourteen" had in mind when it drew up the First Restrictive Rule. The founders of the Methodist Episcopal Church were not legally bound by any action previous to the Christmas Conference (1785) and seem to have taken Wesley's words to heart in considering themselves "at full liberty." At every point where the Methodist Episcopal Church had an opportunity to reiterate and reaffirm its allegiance to Wesley's *Sermons* and *Notes* specifically as doctrinal standards after 1785, it either consciously deleted the references, failed to mention them, or voted to the contrary. At every point where doctrinal *standards* are referred to, it is the Articles of Religion that are specified as the basic measure of proper Methodist doctrine.

That American Methodism was firmly grounded in the broader Wesleyan doctrinal heritage, however, can hardly be denied. Wesley had not only provided the new church with its Articles of Religion; even after 1808 his writings continued to provide the traditional exposition of the principal doctrines of Methodism, despite the General Conference's reticence to make that relationship explicit. The *Sermons* and *Notes* were quite likely alongside the Bible in the saddlebags of many preachers in America, along with *Primitive Physick*, the *Doctrines and Discipline*, and other basic resources of the circuit rider. Just as likely, Fletcher's *Checks* could be found in those same saddlebags, and, shortly, even Watson's *Institutes* and *Apology* would be considered appropriate baggage for a Methodist preacher. The relationship between these traditional doctrinal *statements* (accepted patterns of doctrinal *exposition*) and the established doctrinal *standards* (minimal measures of doctrinal *orthodoxy*) soon became confused as the constitutional distinctions became blurred in the minds of later generations.

By the middle of the nineteenth century, commentators began to read mysterious inferences into that phrase, "present existing and established standards of doctrine," and shortly began to alter the Discipline to conform to their new readings. Bishop Osmond Baker, in his 1855 manual of church administration,[35] was one of the first to claim that the Articles of Religion "do not embrace all that is included in 'our present existing and established standards of doctrine.'" His rationale was quite simple: "Many of the characteristic doctrines of our Church are not even referred to directly in those articles." He therefore suggested that "usage and general consent would probably designate Mr. Wesley's Sermons, and his Notes on the New Testament, and Watson's Theological Institutes" as "established standards of doctrine."

This line of reasoning, confusing traditionally accepted doctrinal statements with officially established doctrinal standards, was continued in southern Methodism by Bishop Holland N. McTyeire, who comments in his manual on the Discipline that "the phrase, 'doctrines which are contrary to our Articles of Religion,' is evidently elliptical." He goes on to mention those works which "usage and general consent" would include in the "established standards of doctrine," and adds to Bishop Baker's list the Wesleyan Methodist Catechisms and the Hymnbook.[36]

In the 1880s, this broadened reading of the meaning of "established standards" was incorporated into the Discipline of the northern church in the section on the "Trial of a Preacher." The charge of disseminating "doctrines contrary to our Articles of Religion" was amended to add the phrase "or established standards of doctrine," thereby referring to a separate body of material.[37] The Ecclesiastical Code Commission that proposed this change to the 1880 General Conference was chaired by James M. Buckley. Buckley's published explanations of doctrinal standards confuses the clear distinctions of legal establishment and traditional acceptance, resulting in continual references to "*other* established standards of doctrine" (my italics).[38] Buckley, along with others who used this frame of reference, was forced into making distinctions between the way the Articles could be enforced and the manner in which these "other" standards functioned. He noted, for instance, that such a range of material provides for "substantial unity" while allowing "circumstantial variety" within Wesleyan Methodism.

The incorrect assumptions (as well as the new wording) of these constitutional historians became explicitly implanted in the 1912 Discipline of the northern church, which referred to "doctrines which are contrary to our Articles of Religion, or our *other* existing and established standards of doctrine" (¶ 245; my italics). This wording was subsequently carried over into the *Discipline of The Methodist Church* after 1939. In the meantime, the First Restrictive Rule had remained unchanged, though by now its original context and intent were fully misunderstood.[39]

The terminology for the section on trials in the present Book of Discipline (1984) is less precise, though perhaps more accurate (if understood properly) in its simple reference to "the established standards of doctrine of the Church" (¶ 2621.g). The phrase should be understood historically and constitutionally as referring to the Confession of Faith (from the Evangelical United Brethren tradition) and the Articles of Religion (from the Methodist tradition). These are the standards of doctrine that have been established as juridical standards and carry the force of law within the church. Any attempt to enumerate *other* "standards of doctrine" confuses the distinction between the constitutional history of the church and the development of its doctrinal heritage. To say that our doctrinal standards are not "legal or juridical instruments" (1984 Discipline,

p. 72) is to ignore our own provisions for enforcing those standards. To say that a particular list of other historic doctrinal statements should in some way be considered "established standards of doctrine" is to confuse the weight of tradition with the force of law.

The task of defining "the scope of our Wesleyan tradition in the context of our contemporary world" includes much more than defining or redefining legal standards of doctrine, although that is also involved. Minimal legal standards of orthodoxy have never been the measure of an adequate witness to the tradition, be it Christian or United Methodist. The heart of our task is to discover how seriously we take our distinctive doctrinal heritage and how creatively we appropriate the fullness of that heritage in the life and mission of the church today.

## CHAPTER 5

# The Sacraments in Early American Methodism

## Paul S. Sanders

In an essay written in 1929[1] Professor Tillich concluded that the sacraments continue to exist in modern Protestantism largely through historical impetus. The conservatism of custom and a vague awareness that their observance is somehow due to our Lord are apparently sufficient to prevent their total extinction. The last generation has of course witnessed a liturgical revival in our churches; but this new interest is by no means universal and appears on the whole to be superficial. It is less devoted to an understanding of Christian faith which might require liturgical expression than to the ornamentation of the places and procedures of worship. Its activity is rooted less in theology than in aesthetics and psychology, being perhaps more often an expression of cultural sophistication than of any serious appreciation of the sacramental quality of Christian life.

Contemporary theological reconstruction would benefit from an historical study of the place of the sacraments in the evolution of Protestantism. How, for instance, has it come about that Presbyterians so little know and appreciate the sacramental teaching of Calvin? The concern of this paper, a modest inquiry into one small part of the large question, may be posed as follows: How does it happen, considering its Wesleyan roots, that American Methodism places so little value upon the sacraments?

As thus phrased the question implies two statements which if true will simply describe matters of fact, and it seeks a connecting link between them. It implies that Wesley practiced a sacramental Christianity. It implies that contemporary American Methodism is typically non-sacramentalist, not to say anti-sacramentalist. Without seeking to establish it further, the latter point may be referred to Tillich's discussion, to my comment on the so-called liturgical revival, and to your own assessment of the temper of American Methodism. The former point will be dealt with immediately.

The remainder of the paper will suggest one area in which the causal connections are to be looked for. Our study will be limited to the period from Methodist beginnings here in 1766 to the division of the Methodist Episcopal Church in 1844, a date which adequately delimits the first period of internal development.

# WESLEY'S SYNTHESIS OF EVANGELICALISM
# AND SACRAMENTALISM

However inevitable the eventual separation of Methodism from the Church of England may now appear to have been, Wesley's own estimate of the relationship is clear. The worship of Methodism, he once wrote, is deliberately defective; like the sermons at the University it presupposes as its proper context the whole complex of corporate worship which is found only in the larger Christian community.[2] His missionary endeavors presupposed the same matrix; as he often said, Wesley was only preaching the "plain old religion of the Church" which people insisted on calling by the "new name of Methodism."[3] His life-long attachment to the English Church was no mere sentiment, but derived from his profoundly soteriological evaluation of the Christian community.[4]

Wesley's conversion at Aldersgate in May 1738 did not, as is frequently claimed, result in an evangelicalism which depreciated the Christian tradition as the objective bearer of redemptive Love. His earliest biographers were content to describe what on occasion seemed to them contrary emphases in Wesley's thought and practice.[5] The issue was first seriously confused in the later nineteenth century when certain Anglo-Catholics, stressing his sacramentalism apart from his evangelicalism, tried to claim Wesley as their own.[6] The Methodists replied by perpetrating the same error in reverse: they accented his evangelicalism apart from his sacramentalism.[7] Most importantly, that aspect of Wesley which was emphasized was reinterpreted in terms dictated by the respective concerns of each of the warring factions.

Wesley was never a high churchman in the Tractarian sense; yet so obvious a fact has seldom been rightly considered. Nor was he one of those "high and dry" eighteenth-century churchmen recently described by George Every.[8] That he may have been to a degree before Aldersgate; but he could slough off the several characteristics of ritualism, asceticism and legalism without its affecting his fundamental stance. He was, most characteristically, a holdover (as

Abbey and Overton have said) of a type of churchman standing in lineal descent from Richard Hooker, Lancelot Andrewes, George Herbert and Jeremy Taylor.[9] And this he was before and after his conversion.

Wesley did not become a revivalist as the nineteenth century would later use that term. Those who have glorified the importance of Wesley's conversion and those who have disparaged it are equally wrong; in George Croft Cell's graphic phrase, "tarred with the same fallacious pitch."[10] The error lies in their all having interpreted the conversion in subjectivistic terms.

Aldersgate gave to Wesley a sense of acceptance before God through no merit of his own but through Christ's atoning blood. What God had done for him he felt constrained to tell all men that God wanted to do for them also. It was not in his own experience but in the Love of God which effectuated that experience that the origin and power of the Revival lay. Wesley's stress on the initiative of divine grace led him to declare that "the true Gospel touches the very edge of Calvinism."[11] The means of congress between God and man were seen as divinely appointed: the Word and sacraments, mediated through the historic church, instruments for the use of the Holy Spirit. Certainly he was accustomed to describe vital religion as "experimental"; but, as Sydney Dimond has said, "Assurance . . . was saved from subjectivism by a larger conception of the grace whereby we are saved."[12] Those interpreters are surely wrong who see in Wesley a proto-Schleiermacher.

Wesley's mature theology—though he may not have used either term—was both Catholic and Evangelical, a synthesis holding together in uneasy but fruitful tension polarities which cannot be pulled together neatly, yet each of which is necessary to its opposite number, as both are to the whole.[13]

In his realization that man of himself can do nothing to save himself, his belief in God's universal love and prevenient grace, and his stress on the necessity of personal acceptance of God's offer of salvation, Wesley was deeply evangelical. In his insistence that genuine religion is social, his demand for "fruits of righteousness," his careful system of nurture, his stress upon corporate worship, his delight in the communion of saints, and his appeal to reason and Christian history, he was genuinely Catholic.

The role of his conversion—which was of course profoundly important—must be carefully assessed. What it did, precisely, was to put God at the center of his life rather than himself. It is exactly this which precludes his being read in terms of nineteenth century revivalism (or twentieth-century liberalism) fully as much as it precludes his being read in terms of ecclesiasticism of whatever sort. Wesley preached no new Gospel but rather the Reformed Catholicism of classical Anglicanism. If it seemed new it was only because personal conviction and the needs of the times had given it a new urgency.

In the light of such an interpretation of Wesley's theological orientation his specific teachings on the sacraments must be studied. A careful survey of the sources for ascertaining his baptismal theology leaves one not altogether sure of his meaning. Since, in any event, Baptism quite naturally played no role in the progress of English Methodism in his lifetime, what can be said may be deferred to the study of American Methodism.

With the Lord's Supper the case is entirely different. Allowing for Miss Underhill's Anglo-Catholic bias one may yet agree that the Wesleyan Revival was as much a sacramental as an evangelical revival;[14] to the dry religiosity of the eighteenth century the one was as much a stranger as the other. Wesley's understanding of the Lord's Supper is chiefly expressed in the 166 Eucharistic hymns based upon Dean Brevint's treatise *The Christian Sacrament and Sacrifice.*[15] Issued over the names of both brothers, the hymns went through nine editions in Wesley's lifetime and the abridged tract was issued besides in separate editions. The doctrine set forth there is consistent and clear, and is reinforced by many other references adduced from Wesley's works.[16]

As a memorial of the death of Christ the sacrament is no mere reminder of that event, but a true *anamnesis*; the eternal meaning of the event is made here and now operative for faith.[17] As symbols the bread and wine re-present the body and blood of Christ as spiritual nourishment with which the Living Christ feeds His people now. The elements are signs; not bare signs, but efficacious signs of the grace they signify. The Eucharist does not itself confer grace, but the Holy Spirit through the sacrament does confer grace; a Christian will not despise the means. Through expectant use of the means ordained by our Lord, faithful communicants are vouchsafed His Real Presence. That Christ is really present as both Host and Food Wesley had no doubt. It would be gratuitous to add that by this Wesley meant no form of *impanation*. His doctrine is most clearly related to that of Calvin mediated through the seventeenth-century divines.

The Holy Supper is a communion feast in which Christians share in Christ and in each other, not only those present but the whole community of saints, in heaven as on earth. It is both anticipation and pledge of the Messianic Banquet when Christ shall have secured His Kingdom. The Wesleyan Eucharistic hymns supplementing the Anglican liturgy revived the eschatological note that had been missing in Western liturgies from earliest centuries.

The Eucharist, moreover, is a sacrifice. Each celebration re-presents the "one oblation, once offered," as also Christ's eternal Sacrifice in heaven. Nowhere is the synthetic character of Wesley's theology more clear than here. In the Eucharist man cannot offer Christ again, nor at all; least of all, instead of himself. Christ eternally offers Himself. Through faith man may claim Christ's self-oblation re-presented in the sacrament. In receiving man offers himself in the sacrament to God. To be able to claim Christ's sacrifice he must give himself; to be able to give himself he must claim Christ's sacrifice. The

Eucharist is at once a call to utter consecration and a means of following the call to the utmost.

Actual reception of the Living Christ depends on faith, in the sense that an unbeliever does not receive Him, but not in the sense that it is the faith of the communicant which effects Christ's Presence. He is present by the Word and Holy Spirit; He is appropriated by faith. The Eucharist bestows grace not only on the justified but on earnest seekers as well. No preparation is required other than a willingness to receive what God offers and to do what God requires to be done. The promises of God are to all; the sacrament is both a converting and sustaining ordinance, symbolizing, witnessing to, and effectuating all that is in the Gospel promised to him who accepts. And since so great benefits flow from the faithful use of the sacrament, it should be received—in Wesley's word— constantly, as often as possible. To do so shows a spirit receptive to the promise of grace and thankful for grace bestowed.

If it is true that Christian faith is defined by action as well as words, then Wesley's own constant reception of the Holy Supper, his frequent admonition to his people to communicate, his evident joy in the large numbers who flocked to celebrations, his instruction to hesitating Methodists that the character of an unworthy celebrant in no way vitiates the efficacy of the sacrament, his observance of great festivals with a daily celebration throughout the octave, his explicit instruction to the Americans that the Eucharist be celebrated every Sunday, and finally, that most bitterly debated of his actions, the irregular ordinations to provide a sacramental ministry for America—all these witness to an understanding of the Gospel in which sacramentalism is so intimately related to evangelicalism as to be put asunder only at the peril of the wholeness of the faith.

## THE ORGANIZATION OF AMERICAN METHODISM

Arising through the efforts of private members and occasional lay preachers who had come to America for reasons of their own, Methodism from its beginnings here was nearly autonomous. Wesley sent over only eight official missionaries. Francis Asbury, the only one who stayed to make a lasting impression, was only 27 years old when he arrived, had had little experience, and was no thoroughgoing Anglican—hardly a man to have been able to interpret the mind of Wesley to the Societies on this side. Yet it was Asbury who must be accounted the founder of American Methodism, even when one allows for his sincere efforts to keep the Americans under Wesley's control.

In any case the remove to America must have exerted influences further tending to remold Methodism, for it could not but be touched by the cultural spirit. Individualism and voluntarism were fundamental values, in religion as in politics and in society at large. Nourished in a society largely unchurched, most active in colonies where Anglicanism represented social, political, and cultural values not shared by the dissenting churches around them, the American Methodists were from the beginning not only autonomous but indigenous.

The early center of the movement was in Virginia, where its beginnings had coincided with the Southern phase of the Great Awakening. Aside from Asbury and Shadford, the most successful preachers were ones such as Strawbridge and Williams, suspect to Wesley because of their attitude toward the Church. Native preachers recruited from the ranks of the newly converted came to share the leadership. Lacking familiarity with the mind of Wesley, as indeed with any larger frame of reference in which to interpret their own conversion or that of any one else, they pursued their preaching not as an adjunct of the English Church but as an isolated revivalistic movement. To equate their position with even the evangelical side of Wesley's synthesis is unwarrantable.

While in 1776 some Virginia Methodists refused to join with Baptists and Presbyterians in the fight for religious liberty, averring that they wished to be considered Anglicans, not dissenters,[18] yet the opposite is more nearly the case. Actual contact between Anglicans and Methodists was slight, even in Virginia. The Methodist people by no means all considered themselves Anglicans. Some belonged to other churches; perhaps most had no church affiliation at all, finding in the Societies whatever spiritual nourishment they had. Some of the preachers were friendly toward the Church, some hostile; most were indifferent. The Anglican parsons who interested themselves in Methodism were few enough to be counted on one hand. Since the origin of their sympathies lay precisely in a feeling that Anglicanism as practiced here was lacking in evangelical fervor, they would not have been effective in acquainting the preachers with the Church's finest claims.

The Sacramental Controversy which racked the movement from 1772 through 1781 revealed the lack of any effective relationship between Methodism and its putative parent together with a growing sectarian spirit among the Methodists. A number of preachers and members had insisted on having the sacraments in their Societies; some of the preachers, having engaged in mutual ordination, began to baptize and celebrate the Lord's Supper. The controversy was finally halted by a tentative decision to stay by the Church until more direct advice might be had from Wesley. Meanwhile the Revolution came to an end and the Anglican establishment was ended. Wesley was but putting the best face on the situation when in September 1784 he wrote: "They are now at full liberty simply to follow the Scriptures and the Primitive Church. And we judge it best that they should stand fast in that liberty wherewith God has so strangely made them free."[19]

Organized during Christmastide, 1784, the Methodist Episcopal Church was now clearly intended to be a church, no longer a preaching mission ambiguously related to Anglicanism. It was furnished an ecclesiastical order: general superintendents, elders and deacons, together with lay preachers and private members, under a centralized system of discipline. It was furnished a standard of doctrine: the Thirty-Nine Articles revised to accord more nearly with the doctrinal needs of the situation and express more clearly an Arminianism already found in them by Anglican theologians. It was furnished forms of worship, together with an Ordinal, in a slightly revised and abridged Prayer Book called *The Sunday Service*; as also a hymn book, significantly a collection of Psalm paraphrases such as were commonly sung in the English Church. Wesley's recommendations had furnished the basis of organization; but Asbury had refused to comply with Wesley's directive that he serve as joint superintendent with Coke, until they should have been elected by the American preachers. These two facts may serve to illustrate the tension between the native bent of American Methodism and the Anglican cast of its Wesleyan legacy, a tension which would run as a *leitmotiv* through its subsequent history.

## THE SACRAMENTS IN EARLY AMERICAN METHODISM

The sixty years from 1784 to 1844 include the Second Awakenings, the Finney era, and the period of most rapid and extensive westward movement. Antedating the rise of any native Methodist theologian, they constitute the new church's first period of internal development and external adjustment. The first decade suffices to show what would prove the main trend.

The Psalm paraphrases were simply ignored. There came into general use a collection of evangelistic hymns, first issued in England in a pirated edition by a preacher Robert Spence, who had been roundly belabored by Wesley for his pains. This was published in Philadelphia in 1799 over the names of Coke and Asbury.[20] Containing many Wesleyan hymns, and covering nearly every aspect of "heart religion," it was admirably suited to its original intended purpose. But it was not adequate, nor had it been intended, to cover all the occasions of faith, life and worship about which a church needs to sing. Augmented from time to time, it remained until 1836 the recommended hymnal. Not until 1849 was a hymnal published which presented in comprehensive fashion hymns on the whole round of Christian life.

The *Sunday Service*, as Jesse Lee wrote with scarcely concealed satisfaction, was soon laid aside.[21] In 1792 the forms for administering the sacraments, the Ordinal, and the occasional services were revised and taken over into the Discipline; the rest disappeared. It had been the prayer book which marked out the form of the new church at its organization in 1784. The next year when the first Discipline was printed it was appended to the Prayer Book. In 1786 a new edition of both was issued under one cover. Six years later only the Discipline was printed, with one section including all that was left of the prayer book.

It is clear what was happening. Wesley had tried to produce a church by decree; he had succeeded in surrounding a preaching movement with the appurtenances of a church. And the new church went on behaving much as it had behaved as a missionary campaign. Under other circumstances Methodism might have been comprehended as a preaching order within Anglicanism. It was in fact erected in America into an independent ecclesiastical body, having the form of a church but not the self-awareness thereof. Unselfconsciously it identified the ecclesia with itself and proceeded to evaluate doctrine, worship and discipline in terms derived from its own parochial understanding of Christian experience. American Methodism showed itself more and more a sect. What was the place of the sacraments in this evolution?

## BAPTISM

Wesley's revision of the Article on Baptism, adopted in 1784 and never changed, read as follows.[22]

> Baptism is not only a sign of profession and mark of difference whereby Christians are distinguished from others that are not baptized; but it is also a sign of regeneration or the new birth. The baptism of young children is to be retained in the church.

The crucial phrase would seem to be "a sign of regeneration or the new birth." Evidence in the sermons and the *Treatise on Baptism*[23] indicates that Wesley held to the Anglican view that infants are in Baptism cleansed from the guilt of original sin; Wesley's Arminianism was not the latitudinarian sort which refused to take original sin seriously. Yet his Arminanism insisted upon a universal objective atonement wrought in the death of Christ; and this Wesley seems never to have related to the teaching of baptismal regeneration.

It is plain, in any case, that whatever regeneration is wrought in Baptism he did not take to be moral regeneration.[24] Man grows up inevitably to sin; to be saved he must be brought to a conviction of sinfulness and an acceptance of pardoning grace. Forensic justification may have taken place in principle in the death of Christ, or mediately in infant baptism; but moral regeneration takes place only in a conscious experience of justification continued in a conscious pursuit of holiness.

As the English Church did, so Wesley distinguished between a sign and the thing signified. Baptism did not confer grace *ex opere operato*. Was it then simply a "badge of profession"? But something must have been meant separable from a profession of faith; for Wesley directed the Americans to retain infant baptism, omitted any reference to sponsors who might be thought to make such an affirmation on the child's part, and omitted the rite of confirmation through which the baptizand might later make the affirmation his own. His meaning is to be sought in a view which preserves the objectivity of grace without compromising the responsibility of free response.

Such a view may be found in Wesley. Indeed, his strongest arguments concern Baptism as a means of incorporation within the covenant community, and the least ambiguous teaching of the revised offices is the same.[25] Yet Wesley omitted from the Article that portion which had described the sacrament as an instrument whereby

> they that receive [it] rightly are grafted into the church; the promises of forgiveness of sin and of our adoption to be sons of God by the Holy Ghost, are visibly signed and sealed; faith is confirmed, and grace increased by virtue of prayer unto God.

Part of American Methodism's confusion regarding Baptism must be laid to Wesley.

The Article on Baptism must be interpreted in the light of that on sacraments generally. Wesley's revision reads thus:

> Sacraments ordained of Christ are not only badges or tokens of Christian men's profession; but rather they are certain signs of grace, and God's good will toward us, by the which he doth work invisibly in us, and doth not only quicken, but also strengthen and confirm our faith in him.

Framed originally to establish against Roman Catholics on the one hand and radical Protestants on the other the view that sacraments are sacred actions in which God and man play mutually interrelated roles, such that, as the Methodist expositor Wheeler says, in them "God embraces us and offers himself to be embraced by us," [26] this Article had been changed slightly. Where the second clause had read, "but rather they be certain sure witnesses and effectual signs of grace," Wesley's revision read, "but rather they are certain signs of grace." The Article still insists that sacraments are "not only badges or tokens of Christian men's profession"; by his omission Wesley may have thought to lessen the danger of an *ex opere operato* interpretation, but he retained the phrase "by which he doth work invisibly in us." It is unlikely that he meant sacraments to be reduced to the barrenness suggested by the modern connotation of the word "sign."

The baptismal offices as revised by Wesley were free of the more obvious expressions of baptismal regeneration. Yet the rites were still capable of teaching it, as is shown by the fact that subsequent revisions were chiefly concerned to whittle away one or another instance of such language. They had been framed to express that doctrine, and short of completely overhauling them—which would be done in the twentieth century—it was impossible to express through them a view altogether devoid of the teaching that Baptism is an effectual instrument of grace.

The American revision of the offices in 1792 further omitted the several elements which most clearly defined Baptism as adoption, possibly influenced by what appeared to be the intent of the Article as revised by Wesley. It is impossible to say on the basis of the offices as they existed after that what Methodism intended by Baptism.

Changes in 1792 in the office for adult baptism opened the way for viewing that rite as believer's baptism. In a largely unchurched society and in a church whose primary aim was the conversion of adults, increased attention to adult baptism and a consequent deflection toward the Anabaptist position would not be unexpected. Indeed, for a two year period it was allowed that one baptized in infancy might be baptized again upon conversion.[27] But a disciplinary provision continued unchanged through the entire period under survey specifically enjoined infant baptism; memoirs of preachers are full of passages noting their defense of the practice. Moreover, a treatise on Baptism appearing as an appendix to the same 1792 Discipline, after fourteen pages defending "sprinkling" against "dipping," spent its remaining fifty-four pages defending infant baptism; of the strictly theological meaning of the sacrament there was however no indication.

The average Methodist, member or preacher, would not have derived his understanding of the sacrament from the Articles or offices alone, or even primarily. From what, then? The first American edition of Wesley appeared in 1826, though surely he had been read in English editions earlier. Watson's *Institutes* was published in New York in 1825, Adam Clarke's *Christian Theology* in 1840. The hymnal meanwhile had been augmented with baptismal hymns by Charles Wesley, Doddridge and Watts. From all these sources a meaningful doctrine could have been derived. Baptism stands witness to the grace of God seeking the salvation of every man. It furnishes the means of incorporation into the covenant fellowship where redemption through grace is normally expected to be found. It binds those baptized to trust in Christ alone for salvation and seals the promises of God that such trust is all that is required. In Baptism there is a spiritual transaction whereby a person's status vis à vis the realm of redemption is changed; to view this mechanically was termed "excess," but to depreciate its reality was no less vigorously termed "defect."

But Wesley, Watson and Clarke were not the most powerful influences upon the preachers. It was not until 1828 that any standard course of reading was prescribed for the preachers; theological education was wholly lacking. There was no parochial system of pastoral care. Baptisms would have been performed sporadically whenever one of the elders or rather larger number of deacons happened on the scene. That large percentage of the preachers who were ordained were debarred from administering Baptism. How significant can the sacrament have been in the absence of any developed sense of the church?

So we have been led finally to that context in which its explication is most significant: the relation of Baptism to church membership. The usual view of the church among revivalistic Protestants in the period under consideration was in terms of voluntary association of like-minded believers. Baptists were consistently sectarian. The Halfway Covenant had of course mitigated the stringency of voluntarism among Congregationalists; the Presbyterians had generally managed to keep their covenant theology relatively intact. The Methodists were in a particular case. On the one hand sectarian patterns abounded. Despite Wesley's dictum that the only requirement for being a Methodist was a desire to be saved, the Americans tended more and more to make conversion a prerequisite. To become a member one must go through a period of probation; he might be admitted or not, and if admitted might later be suspended. Admission and suspension and readmittance depended on meeting certain demands centering in a specific sort of experience and consequent conformity to specific moralistic criteria.

Yet there were always elements working against complete sectarianization. The centralized episcopacy and the itinerancy both provided for Methodists a sense of being an inclusive whole. Hardly less important than conversion was the nurture provided in the bands and classes; derived probably from Wesley's knowledge of the catechumenate in the primitive church, they represented that element of instruction and discipline which has been a constant element in the definition of the Christian *ecclesia*.

Nonetheless, through most of this period Methodism showed remarkably little church consciousness. The early Disciplines often have the word "society" where one expects the word "church." Communicant members of other churches were explicitly allowed to be Methodists, remaining at the same time Presbyterians or whatever. Though both instances are traceable to the peculiar origins of Methodism, they comport strangely with the self-awareness of an autonomous church.

It was not until 1836 that any recognizable concept of church membership was put into the Discipline, not until 1856 that the relation of baptized children to the church was spelled out in the Discipline, and not until 1864 that a form for receiving members into the church was inserted into the Ritual.[28] By then Wesley's Arminianism was being replaced by Daniel Whedon's "Freedomism;" what in Wesley had been "gracious ability" became simply "ability."[29] This example of the way in which American Methodism misconstrued Wesley by dissolving his synthesis indicates also the direction in which it would finally move to delineate the meaning of Baptism; but that would not be until later in the century.

For the early period it may be concluded that Baptism must have meant less than official definitions and systematic treatises suggest. The most noticeable aspect of the question is its ambiguity. Through lack of interest, lack of theological ability, and preoccupation with what no doubt seemed a more pressing task, the church failed to arrive at any view of Baptism clear and profound enough to withstand the corrosive effect of that emasculation of evangelicalism which would be the end product of a hundred years of revivalism.

## THE LORD'S SUPPER

Of the several Articles of Religion concerning the Eucharist the crucial one is No. XVIII, of which the most pertinent section reads as follows:

> The supper of the Lord is not only a sign of the love that Christians ought to have among themselves one to another, but rather is a sacrament of our redemption by Christ's death: insomuch, that to such as rightly, worthily, and with faith receive the same, the bread which we break is a partaking of the body of Christ; and likewise the cup of blessing is a partaking of the blood of Christ.

Originally framed to refute both the Roman doctrine of transubstantiation and left-wing Protestant teaching which a later Methodist described as "but a partial and inadequate statement of the nature and purpose of the Eucharist,"[30] the Article was adopted by the Americans unchanged.

The changes Wesley had made in the liturgy served either to make the office a more explicit expression of evangelical doctrine, as he understood it, or to adapt it to the needs of the American situation, as he understood that. In the former category are only two changes of consequence: the absolution became a prayer for pardon, the word "priest" became "elder." Changes in the latter category were more numerous: the *Sanctus* and *Gloria in excelsis* were to be said, not chanted; the service was shortened by the omission of the long exhortations—which were needless, since the class meetings were a more stringent means of discipline; and rubrics pertinent only to the Anglican situation were excised. No change (save for the omission of one redundant word) was made in the Prayer of Consecration. The effort sometimes made to characterize Wesley's revision as Puritan surely breaks down here; if it had been so, he would have substituted for the Consecration a prayer of thanksgiving and the Words of Institution.

In 1792 the Americans deleted the entire Ante-Communion—all the service preceding the Offertory—and with it the concept of the Christian Year. Other changes were required by the assumption that now the Eucharist would follow a usual preaching service: e.g. the Intercessions were omitted, doubtless because they would have been included in the long extemporaneous prayer earlier. Still others were reflective of the more informal worship prevalent here: the *Sursum Corda* was omitted, along with the Proper Prefaces, and extemporaneous prayer was allowed in the liturgy itself. A rubric at the end authorized the omission of any or all of the ritual *except the Consecration*. The exact form of Eucharistic observance was evidently thought to be a matter of indifference; but a prayer expressive of an undefined but real relationship between the material elements and their spiritual use was retained as the indispensable minimum.

Drastic as the 1792 revision of Wesley's prayer book was, the forms which were preserved were not touched for another sixty years; and these the years during which the influence of revivalism and the frontier should have been most insistent. At the expense of completeness the core of the liturgy was transferred to the Discipline, the one book sure to be available. The requirement that the forms be used was doubtless not heeded literally; in 1824 the Discipline contained a special admonition on their faithful use, doubtless a reflection of a freedom approaching license. Yet the fact that they were retained and used at all indicates some attitude of conservatism toward the Wesleyan heritage.

There is no evidence of an American edition of the Eucharistic hymns, though a few were included in the *Pocket Hymn Book* and a few others added as that collection gradually evolved into a church hymnal. The one best source of Wesley's Eucharistic doctrine was therefore largely lacking.

There was no hymn on the eschatological aspect of the sacrament. It is certain these Methodists were interested in "last things." One recalls further that the great camp meetings began as Eucharistic celebrations, and this remained a normal part of most Methodist meetings. Whether any conscious relation between communion and eschatology was made, there is no evidence.

There was only one hymn on the sacrament as sacrifice. Again, it is certain these Methodists talked and sang about the sacrifice of Christ. The greater number of hymns on the Lord's Supper, whether by Wesley or others, dealt with it as a memorial of the death. But that was the least profound meaning of Wesley's teaching; rather it was the pleading of the eternal sacrifice joined with the Real Presence of the Risen Christ which made Wesley's doctrine potent. Of that particular understanding of the matter among the Americans there is no evidence at all.

Clarke's *Discourse on the Nature and Design of the Eucharist* was published in New York in 1842, having been first published in London in 1812. The teaching of such a work, taken together with that of Wesley and Watson, the Articles of Religion, the liturgy, and such Eucharistic hymns as were available, presented (even more so than in the case of Baptism) a consistent and meaningful doctrine. All alike held the Supper to be both genuine sign and seal of the mercies of God revealed in the death of Christ, as it is also both sign and seal of man's answering self-oblation. Christ is present in His Supper to be received in faith. Like Baptism the Eucharist was seen as a federal rite; participating in it through faith was believed in very fact to assure one's continuance within the covenant of grace. In the sacrament questing grace calls forth answering faith and questing faith meets answering grace.

But how widely are we to suppose that this teaching was known and understood? How often was it expounded? How frequently was the Eucharist celebrated? It remained the rule that only elders could administer the Lord's Supper. It would have been expedient to allow at least every preacher in charge of a circuit to do so; it may be argued that the failure to do this shows that Methodism was not seriously concerned to maintain a regular program of Eucharistic celebration. It could just as well be argued that the refusal to allow lay preachers, even though in charge of circuits, to celebrate constitutes another of those examples of conservatism we have encountered. In any event, communions must have been infrequent, since deacons and unordained preachers constituted the larger number of all the itinerants.

Moreover, there was a growing tendency to "fence the Table." In Notes appended to the Discipline of 1796 the two bishops had admonished the elders to be "very cautious how they admit . . . persons who are not in our society."[31] Although non-members might be admitted after examination, in their case as in that of members the right to communicate appears to have rested upon being adjudged worthy. Nothing was said any more of Wesley's insistence that "honest seekers" be admitted, nor of the converting power of the Eucharist.

Certainly the Lord's Supper was not central to Methodist worship. The Love Feast may at first have been as important; it was more frequently held, and in a revivalistic atmosphere the fervent testimonies of awakened believers may have caused it to seem more vital. Still, the Eucharist would have been celebrated at every quarterly visitation by the presiding elder riding his rounds; the people may have exerted more effort to be present at those quarterly meetings than it would occur to modern Methodists to suspect.

In 1812 a curious move was taken which has ever since further complicated the effort to understand the meaning of Methodist orders: it was allowed that local preachers might be ordained. Local preachers were men in secular occupations licensed to preach and perform some functions of pastoral oversight. In the absence of a parochial system their contribution was immense; but they were (and still are) strictly differentiated from "travelling preachers"—i.e., what we should call the professional ministry. The anomalous situation was created in which a "lay" preacher might be ordained elder and yet be a member of a charge committed to an itinerant who was only a deacon or not ordained at all. The church's answer to infrequent Communion was not to allow unordained men to celebrate but to extend ordination to men who were not itinerants. But it may be supposed that after this the societies had the Communion more often.

As evangelical doctrine became stereotyped within the narrow confines of a particular anthropology and soteriology, so the Eucharist would appear to have lost its fullness of meaning. If the whole significance of justification could be thought to be satisfactorily expressed in the phrase "saved by the blood"; if the whole meaning of sanctification could be thought to be summed up in a moralistic legalism; if the richly varied theology of Wesley could be acceptably reduced to the one word "Aldersgate"; then the Eucharist could presumably be satisfactorily characterized as a memorial rite. It was not sacramentalism alone which suffered. By the end of our period Protestant theology in America, where it had come under sustained revivalistic influence, had become curiously truncated, resulting in a vast oversimplification of the problems of Christian faith and life.[32]

It may be concluded that the Eucharist doubtless meant less than official definitions and systematic treatises suggest; but perhaps more than any overt evidence adduced here shows. The tenacity with which the Methodists clung to infant baptism, apparently finding in it a grace which their logic was never rightly able to assess, is indicative of their attitude. Without being articulate about it, they may have found in the Supper a means through which their gracious Lord designed to feed their hungry souls.

Early Methodism in America was insufficiently acquainted with the mind of Wesley to have been able to sympathize with his insistence that Methodism was understandable only within an Anglican structure, or to appreciate his high regard for the corporate Christian body, or to penetrate his carefully instructed theological synthesis of sacramentalism and evangelicalism. Unprepared to take its place as a church, the movement was suddenly thrust into autonomy; through sixty years, unused to its churchly institutions, untutored in classical Christian doctrine, fumblingly learning what it meant to be a church, at one turn and another it revealed through its actions the effects of its initial orphanage. Further deflected from a full-orbed Christianity by pressures from the American scene, both secular and religious, Methodism most readily aligned itself with pietistic sectarianism and thus reinforced that strain of its constitution which leaned toward moralistic and emotionalistic individualism. Constantly pursuing its missionary labors and but little given to attempts at self-definition, it came all but unconsciously to define itself—and thus to redefine its institutions—in terms of its own narrow understanding of that one primary concern.

Early Methodism in America had failed to achieve sufficient coherence to enable it to preserve the marrow of its legacy while at the same time adapting it to the demands of a new time and a new land. Although maintaining a halting loyalty to its Wesleyan heritage, the church was clearly more concerned with evangelism than with sacramentalism. Wesley's synthesis was dissolved. As revivalism was not the same as Wesley's evangelical ministry, so the confused sacramental teaching and erratic sacramental practice of the Americans was not

91

the same as Wesley's own. The loss of the fertilizing vitality which results from keeping each close to the other was serious enough; but the loss was finally more serious. The church had been rendered peculiarly vulnerable to the infiltration of alien ideologies, and would find itself unable to maintain either evangelicalism or sacramentalism under the impact of the rise of rational idealism.

# A Comparison of the Doctrines of Ministry of Francis Asbury and Philip William Otterbein

Jeffrey P. Mickle

When one inquires these days as to the roots of "United" Methodism, it is not unusual for the answer to ignore the heritage of the Evangelical United Brethren, from whence the "United" arises. If any mention is made of this branch of the church, it is often described as "the same thing as Methodism, except it developed among the Germans." The point of distinction between the Methodists, on the one hand, and the Evangelicals and United Brethren, on the other hand, almost inevitably, in popular explanations, is attributed to the difference in national origins: "They believed the same thing, but could not get together because they spoke different languages; but, when everyone came to speak English, there was no reason to remain separate; therefore, we now have merged our two heritages into one church."[1] These popular sentiments are not merely the ill-founded opinions of misinformed pastors and Sunday school teachers. Similar conclusions have been expressed and supported among ecclesiastical and academic scholars:[2]

> These two churches, similar in doctrinal outlook as well as in matters of organization, may well have come together years ago if it had not been for a language difference—the Evangelical United Brethren doing their work among the German-speaking people, while the Methodists worked among the English-speaking population. With these language barriers now gone, all real reasons for continuing separation ceased to exist.

The problem is that such explanations are simplistic and misleading. They give several wrong impressions, including the notion that the Germans were merely copying what the English had already introduced, and the mistaken idea that there were basically no differences in beliefs or polity between the Germans and the English. To the contrary, however, there were significant differences between the two groups at the time of union in 1968—both theological and governmental—which were set aside in the belief that "the ideal of unity and the advantages of union were worth fighting for." [3]

This paper will address one aspect of the differences between the former Evangelical United Brethren Church and the former Methodist Church: the doctrine of ministry. [4] It is necessary, then, to turn to two of the pioneers of these churches, Francis Asbury and Philip William Otterbein, who shaped the distinctive understandings of ministry in the Methodist Episcopal Church and the Church of the United Brethren in Christ. [5] Beginning with an historical approach to the interactions between these two men and the respective constituencies, and proceeding to a more systematic exposition of each man's doctrine of ministry, we will compare and contrast the two views and draw some brief conclusions about the impact which they made on the future directions of their communions, particularly as they surfaced at the time of unification in the 1960's.

Many of the denominational historians of the nineteenth century reflect a tendency to emphasize the distinctiveness of one denomination as over against another. Recently, the tendency has shifted to a defense of the ecumenicity of the early denominational leaders. [6] In fact, both approaches can be supported from the historical evidence concerning Otterbein and Asbury.

Otterbein arrived in America as an ordained minister of the German Reformed Church in 1752, at the age of 26. He was educated at Herborn University and instilled with an evangelical pietism which changed his understanding of the pastor's role from "being exclusively 'men of the word of God' to also being a 'personally accountable representative witness, and an example of the spiritual life of godliness'." He served Reformed churches in Lancaster (1752–58), Tulpehocken (1758–60), Frederick (1760–65), and York (1763–70, 1771–74), supplying pulpits in nearby congregations as much as he could while retaining full pastoral responsibility for the larger congregations. [7] In 1774, he moved to Baltimore where he became the pastor of the German *Evangelical* Reformed Church, whose name indicates the reputation that Otterbein had acquired. Here he remained until his death in 1813.

Francis Asbury arrived in America in 1771, also at age 26, as one of John Wesley's helpers. In his journal, he claimed his motivation for being in America: "to live to God, and bring others so to do." He, too, was part of the eighteenth-century awakening in the evangelical, pietistic spirit. He moved from his point of arrival in Philadelphia to New York and soon became dissatisfied with the laid-back attitude of his superiors in regard to the itinerancy [8]—an indication of his early commitment to this style of ministry. He also made early objections to the lax discipline which he perceived among the Methodist societies and put forward a plan to rectify the situation.[9] It should not surprise us to learn, therefore, that the earliest verifiable dealings which Asbury had regarding Otterbein—even before they had met—concerned the matter of organization. Along with Benedict Schwope, a German Reformed minister in Baltimore, Asbury decided "to promote his [Otterbein's] settling here [in Baltimore] and laid a plan nearly similar to ours [the Methodist's].[10] A. W. Drury, the United Brethren historian, is quick to point out that Otterbein had gotten along fine without "a plan" before he had come to Baltimore.[11] Furthermore, as we shall see presently, Otterbein may have done just as well without Asbury's advice at this time.

Asbury's *Journal* entry from May 3, 1774, records a meeting he held with Otterbein and Schwope shortly after Otterbein's arrival in Baltimore. It indicates that Asbury talked with them about "the plan of Church discipline on which they intended to proceed." Asbury came away thinking that "they agreed to imitate our methods as nearly as possible."[12] This expectation undoubtedly refers to the establishment of small groups or classes as a means of spiritual discipline among the women and men of the church. In fact, Otterbein had already used such gatherings in several of his previous ministries. In Baltimore he likewise organized a cluster of prayer groups and classes among the congregations of the Reformed in the area.[13] Whether the 48-year-old Otterbein took the advice of the 29-year-old Asbury, or was planning to establish the classes before the meeting with Asbury, we cannot know, although the former seems unlikely.[14] Nevertheless, the Baltimore connection—as the center of early Methodism and the home of Otterbein—was to yield a lasting friendship between the two men as they gradually wielded more and more influence in their respective ecclesiastical circles and in the culture at large.

Over the next decade (1774–84), Asbury and Otterbein met several times. According to Asbury's *Journal*, they met again on March 28, 1775, when Asbury reflected, "They both [Otterbein and Schwope] appear to be sincerely religious, and intend to make proposals to the German synod this year, to lay a plan for the reformation of the Dutch congregations."[15] Unfortunately, there is no evidence that the proposal was ever presented to the German synod. Several other meetings are recorded by Asbury during this period, signaling the continued association of the two men. One tradition even tells of Otterbein protecting Asbury when the latter was arrested in Baltimore during the American Revolution.[16] The climax of this first stage in the Otterbein-Asbury relationship came at the Christmas Conference of 1784, when Otterbein assisted in the ordination of Asbury as bishop, at Asbury's request.[17] In this early stage of interaction, Otterbein and Asbury became friends, as symbolized in the Christmas Conference ordination. They agreed on the evangelical awakening as the foundation for the church's mission. Yet, there were some signs of disagreement on matters of organization and discipline even at this date, which were to be intensified as institutionalization occurred.

The Christmas Conference marks a most significant turning point among the Methodists, from "society" to "church." The next decade (1784–94) was marked by efforts to clarify that identity change and to secure a structure for the church polity. In 1786, there was a symbolic break from Wesley's power over the American church. In 1789, presiding elders came on the scene, officially. The first general conference was held in 1792, at which time the first major schism in American Methodism was triggered by James O'Kelly over the authority of the episcopacy. Let these examples suffice to the informed reader as evidence for the emerging shape of the Methodist Episcopal Church: methodical, organized, disciplined.[18]

With whatever word one may choose to describe the growing Methodist Episcopal Church, several emphases come to the fore as points of distinction for a doctrine of ministry. The bishop, who was elected by the conference and assisted by presiding elders, exercised power which was established as finally authoritative over the itinerancy. The function of this itinerancy was to preach the gospel to both the faithful and the faithless, and to administer general oversight over the discipline of church members through a highly organized system, centralized in the conference and the episcopacy. Primary ministerial identity was derived from membership in the annual conference. Local preachers, who did not travel on a circuit, were not members of the conference (even if ordained); nor were they entitled to an appointment by the bishop. The two norms were itinerancy and conference membership. The motivation for these norms was the desire for a disciplined and adaptable ministry—modeled, according to Asbury, on the apostolic example. The understanding of ordination was taken largely from the Anglican church, with three levels of ordination: deacon, elder, and bishop. The first two orders functioned hierarchically with the deacons seen as a step below elders, but above traveling lay preachers. The episcopacy was understood as a general superintendency, shaped by Asbury into an itinerant office as well. Authority to administer the sacraments, which first became ecclesiastically proper with the ordination of elders, was not the primary means of distinction in Methodist ministry. Indeed, unordained preachers could be members of annual conferences and, thereby, part of the itinerancy. At the same time, ordained clergy who were located did not exercise vote in the conference, although they could administer the sacraments.[19] If we were to characterize this emerging scheme, we would have to say that the *potesta iurisdictionis* (the power of jurisdiction, centered in the various conferences) took priority over the *potesta ordinis* (the power of ordination, traditionally understood as Word and Sacrament.)[20] In fact, the two powers were somewhat disjoined insofar as some ministers only exercised their prerogatives under one of the two, instead of under the authority of both.

In the midst of this formative period, there was a meeting which is significant for this investigation. On June 4, 1786, Asbury met Otterbein and expressed his concern about organizing the evangelical revival among the Germans. Asbury writes in his *Journal*: "I called on Mr. Otterbein: we had some free conversation on the necessity of forming a church among the Dutch, holding conferences, the order of its government, etc." [21] Obviously, there already was a church among the Germans. Clearly, Asbury was not talking about just any church. He wanted to start a Methodist church among the Germans, and evidently tried to recruit the help of an old friend and, furthermore, an eminent German minister. Although there is no literary evidence for an explicit response from Otterbein, one can deduce his reaction from what happened after the meeting.

Three years after Asbury presented his proposals to him, Otterbein called the first regular meeting of the leaders of the German evangelical revival. There were seven ministers present at this meeting, held in Baltimore. Seven others were unable to attend the meeting, yet still were recognized as members of the group. Among these preachers were persons from the Reformed, Mennonite, Amish, and Moravian traditions. In 1791, another meeting was called in York, Pennsylvania, with a slight increase in membership. [22] No minutes were kept at either of these meetings, but there is no sign of following Asbury's design for forming a German Methodist Church. Basically, the group was not ecclesiastical; rather, it was a loosely organized group of preachers sharing a common interest in the growing revivalistic work. [23]

Over the next decade, several emerging forms developed that lend some insight into the doctrine of ministry among the men who were, in 1800, to become the United Brethren in Christ. A volunteer itinerancy took shape. Quarterly meetings were held locally among the followers of these German evangelicals, for preaching and administration of the Lord's Supper. Great meetings or big meetings became an important part of the movement. At these gatherings, people would come from relatively long distances, and all of the preachers would gather for a general revival. At such time, the preachers would usually stay around for a brief conference after the preaching services ended. Thus, business sessions of all of the preachers—itinerant and residential—were conducted in connection with revival meetings. [24] To this point, however, the organization of German revivalistic ministers was for the purpose of cooperating in the spreading evangelistic fervor, rather than for organizing a church. They respected one another's denominational affiliations and recognized each other's ordinations so that they could "preach untrammeled by sect." Ability to preach and zeal for the evangelical revival were evidently the primary qualifications for admission to this group's ministry. Authority to administer the sacraments was reserved for those who had been ordained or specially approved for such functions by the other preachers. [25] There is a clear disdain for excessive discipline beyond biblical guidelines. The personal guidance of Otterbein and, perhaps, some of the Baltimore Church Rules which he wrote for his congregation in 1785, were understood to be sufficient for order among these "united brethren." Certainly nothing of the Methodist style of discipline was adopted, or even desired.[26]

A milestone in the history of the United Brethren in Christ came on September 25, 1800, when a group of fourteen German ministers gathered at the home of Peter Kemp, near Frederick, Maryland, and decided that "yearly a day shall be appointed when the unsectarian preachers shall assemble and counsel how they may conduct their office more and more according to the will of God."[27] In effect, the meeting was the first annual conference. Here, the name, "United Brethren in Christ," was adopted, and two of the preachers were formally elected as superintendents, or bishops: Philip William Otterbein and Martin Boehm.[28]

Before that time, Otterbein had performed the superintending function on the basis of his natural leadership ability, without any formal election:

> All eyes had been directed to him to lead in counsel; the preachers, not one excepted, paid this *deference* to him; the care of all the Churches had been resting upon him, and such was the love of obedience to him, that if he said to one go, he went; if to another come, he came.[29]

It should be noted that there was no ordination or consecration to the position of superintendent; indeed, there was to be no division of rank, but only of duty. Elder, presbyter, and bishop were all references to the same office, set aside by one ordination. Whereas Asbury took the title of "bishop," and was referred to as such in contemporary documents, Otterbein was commonly called "Father," or sometimes "Reverend," or even "Brother" the latter term being the form of address among all the other preachers. Clearly, Otterbein and his fellow ministers were not operating from the same ecclesiological framework as were Asbury and his ministers.[30]

The minutes of the next five conferences (1801–1805) bring to light several important features for Otterbein's doctrine of ministry.[31] In 1801, we find, "The preachers were examined as to whether they are willing according to their ability to labor in the work of the lord." At each conference thereafter, the individual condition of each preacher and his work was among the first orders of business for the conference. Also in 1801, we read the following: "It was *asked* who are willing to take charge of a circuit and preach at the appointed places. Then the following preachers *offered themselves.* . . ." That passage indicates a voluntary itinerancy. In 1803, there was a slight modification of this practice in some locations. In Pennsylvania, for example, two of the leading brethren were named to "*place* the preachers in order . . . as may tend most to the honor of God and the benefit of the hearers and the bettering of the church of God." In other places, such as Maryland, the work was "left to the preachers in Maryland themselves to arrange."[32] Evidently, the norm was to allow preachers as much individual prerogative as possible. If there were some obstacles or special circumstances, however, the conference could appoint special overseers for the good of the general church and its mission. The loosely organized gathering was gradually becoming more structured and centralized in the annual conference. Still, when compared to the authoritarian style of Asbury and his insistence on obedience to the Methodist ecclesiastical hierarchy (especially, the bishop), the United Brethren structure of voluntary cooperation among equals of various ecclesiastical background seemed loose and ungoverned. Asbury's assessment in 1803 was fair: "There are now upwards of twenty German preachers somehow connected with Mr. Philip Otterbein and Martin Boehm; but they want authority, and the Church wants discipline."[33]

One final item of ecclesiology should be noted about the United Brethren during their early days under Otterbein. Unlike the disjunction between *potesta iurildictionis* and *potesta ordinis* found in Methodism, the United Brethren maintained a unity between the two. All preachers were members of the annual conference, whether traveling or not. Thus, all members of the conference had the authority to preach, and all preachers in conference authorized individuals to preach, and/or baptize, and/or administer the Lord's Supper, and/or solemnize marriages. Sometimes all of the sacramental prerogatives were granted; sometimes, only baptism was authorized; other times, an individual was allowed only to preach.[34] No ordinations were performed until October 2, 1813, when Otterbein ordained three of the long-time preachers as elders, six weeks before he died.[35] Administration of the Sacraments and preaching of the Word were responsibilities delegated by the gathered preachers. They did not coincide with ordination or episcopal appointment. In a sense, then, one could say that the *potesta ordinis* became a function of the *potesta iurisdictionis*: the conference authorized the power of Word and Sacrament; that power did not rest on its own authority (i.e., it was not only for ordained clergy). Thus, the two powers were not disjoined.

Before we turn to a systematic exposition of the doctrines of ministry of Asbury and Otterbein, we must briefly consider one final historical matter. From 1809 until 1814, there were serious negotiations between the Methodists and the United Brethren concerning some form of union. Considerable correspondence took place, with the active participation of Asbury and the indirect influence of Otterbein through Christian Newcomer.[36] Agreements were reached to allow mutual recognition of members at the Lord's Supper and in class meetings, as well as free interchange of pulpits among licensed preachers of both denominations. Preaching style and doctrine were almost identical between the two bodies.

Still, there were some significant differences. The Methodists suggested the adoption of their *Discipline* among the United Brethren. In reply to this proposal, the latter characterized the Methodist system of order as "some external church regulations."[37] Here is the crux of the difference: the Methodists regarded church "discipline" as an essential part of their faith, but the United Brethren saw it as a cumbersome externality. More specifically, this issue can be localized in the issue of class meetings. The Methodist plan required such gatherings, but the United Brethren said, "our preachers are at *liberty* to keep class meetings . . . at any place they think proper or to be useful."[38] The irreconcilable difference concerning church organization eventually led to the breakdown of negotiations. Paul Blankenship summarizes the differences as they finally emerged with the adoption of a United Brethren *Discipline* in 1817:

> The organization which emerged was distinctly different from that of the Methodists at several points in spite of many similarities. United Brethren bishops were to be elected for a term of four years instead of for life, pastors were given a large measure of discretion and authority in their work, and the churches were given control of their local affairs. This loose connectional system which leaned strongly toward congregationalism stood in sharp contrast to the Methodist practice of electing bishops for life and giving them almost absolute authority while allowing laymen and local churches very little if any voice in Methodist affairs.[39]

In practice, the United Brethren consisted of mostly local preachers—who had equality in vote with itinerants in the annual conference. To the contrary, of course, Asbury relied on unmarried itinerant preachers and looked down on located preachers, who did not have a vote in the annual conference.[40]

Asbury's funeral sermon for Martin Boehm, preached on April 23, 1812, reflects the same conclusions:

> I pause here to indulge in reflections upon the past. Why was the German reformation in the middle States, that sprang up with Boehm, Otterbein, and their helpers, not more perfect? . . . There was no master-spirit to rise up and organize and lead them. Some of the ministers located, and only added to their charge partial traveling labors; and all were independent. It remains to be proved whether a reformation, in any country, or under any circumstances, can be perpetuated without a well-directed itinerancy.[41]

Here, then, lies the difference between the Methodist Episcopal Church of Francis Asbury and the Church of the United Brethren in Christ of Philip William Otterbein. Language was not the barrier; rather, the barrier was a difference in understanding of church discipline and government. John Robertson surmises, "Had not the difference over discipline stood in the way, the United Brethren would probably have been absorbed by the Methodist Church, as the former gradually adopted the English language."[42]

Let us turn, now, to a more systematic exposition of the doctrines of ministry of Asbury and Otterbein, the two men whose influence in their respective denominations contributed greatly to the differing understandings of church discipline and government. For Asbury, we have an abundance of documentary material with which to work. His *Journal* and letters are filled with many allusions to the doctrine of ministry. From these, we shall focus on his most elaborate exposition on the topic, "A Valedictory Address to William McKendree," written on August 5, 1813.[43] When we turn to Otterbein, however, we find very little material from his own hand, and not much more from his contemporaries on the topic of the doctrine of ministry. Evidently, Otterbein also made at least one major address on the subject in a sermon based on Jude 14–25, delivered before the 1801 annual conference. What remains is the following outline: "I. The Sanctity of the Ministerial Office; II. The Servants of this Office to Be Men of Faith, of Prayer, and of the Holy Ghost; III. The Duties of the Office; IV. Its Great Responsibilities."[44] For Newcomer, the address was powerful; he records, "The force with which he pointed out the greatness, the importance, and responsibility of the ministerial office will never be forgotten by me."[45] Unfortunately, we cannot extrapolate far with that material. Instead, we shall use bits from several sources to piece together Otterbein's doctrine of ministry, with primary attention given to "The Constitution and Ordinances of the Evangelical Reformed Church of Baltimore, Maryland, 1785," which he wrote.[46]

Systematically, there are two questions: first, what is the form of ministry; second, what is the style of ministry? The form of ministry will be analyzed in terms of orders of offices of ministry, and in terms of administration or government of the ministers. The style of ministry will be concerned with the expectations that the church has of the ministers in their official functions.

In his "Valedictory Address to William McKendree," Francis Asbury tries to establish the Methodist Episcopal doctrine of ministry as the recovery of the apostolic model of the New Testament, which has been lost since the second century. In his outline of the apostolic authority of the "primitive order," Asbury relies on Thomas Haweis' *History of the Church of Christ* and here finds a scholarly defense for his doctrine of ministry as grounded in the New Testament. Of course, he also borrows heavily from Wesley.

The form of ministry, according to Asbury, is a three-fold pattern of bishops, elders, and deacons under the governmental scheme of a modified episcopacy. The three-fold ministry is, for Asbury, imperative to restore the order of the apostolic church. Regardless of the Presbyterian denial or the Anglican abuse, the episcopacy, presbytery, and diaconate are all found in the New Testament. Asbury quotes Haweis in defense of this assertion regarding the episcopacy:

> All united in one Church fellowship [so the Methodists] under the superintendency of apostolic men at first and on their decease, the most distinguished for zeal, wisdom, sufferings, influence, or respectability of any kind, was called by the suffrage of the elders and people to be their superintendent, president, *praeses; hegoumenos*, a leader; and thus the name of bishop (*kat' exochen*), on account of preeminence, became very early appropriate to one who was *primus inter pares*; and, as Archbishop Usher says, differed only in degree of advantagement and not in order.[47]

Concerning elders, he cites Haweis as concluding:

> I can only observe here that I find in all these widely dispersed and numerous congregations no mention made of any appointment but that of presbyters, all cemented in one bond of union under the supervisal of the great *itinerant evangelists*.[48]

And, for the diaconate, Asbury, through Haweis, writes:

> The care of the poor widows led to the institution of the order of deacons. . . . These were accordingly chosen by general suffrage, not for each separate congregation, but for the whole body, and were set apart by the apostles after solemn prayer and imposition of hands, to this service. Though the care of the widows was immediately intrusted to them, it prevented them not from being employed in other labors of love. . . . They were village preachers, . . . and were not ashamed of the gospel of Christ. Paul (Acts xxiv, 23), in revisiting the Churches which had been planted principally by himself, edifies, comforts, and establishes them by ordaining elders in every Church with prayers and fasting.[49]

Thus, the three-fold ministry is grounded in the New Testament, as is the hierarchical understanding of deacons becoming elders, from whose number bishops are chosen.

Bishops "examined the chosen candidates for the ministry, and, with the presbyter, ordained them by imposition of hands." Bishops also "preside in the deliberations of their several Churches, with the presbyters, their assessors." Among the ministers, the bishop is the permanent president:

> Though James was not superior to Peter or the other apostles at Jerusalem . . . he had been evidently appointed to fill the place of president, or *primus inter pares*. Yet neither he nor any of his apostolic associates assumed to themselves authority to decide but by the suffrage of the whole body of the Church under immediate divine direction.[50]

Thus Asbury concludes that the conference system has its roots at the Council of Jerusalem. But, the notion of first among equals meant, in practice, a distinctly higher status for bishops in the exercise of disciplinary authority. Asbury honestly states, "There is not—nor indeed, in my mind, can there be—a perfect equality between a constant president, and those over whom he always presides."[51] The bishop, then, is ordained to the permanent status of president of the conference, perpetual overseer of the Church and its ministers, and the one who exercises highest disciplinary authority. Still, the bishop was not the sole authority. The government of the church was in the hands of the traveling ministry. Unlike the Anglican episcopal system, the bishop did not ordain the elders on his own authority. He did so on the authority of the conference. Thus, the form of ministerial government can be described as a modified episcopacy, with authority delegated to the bishop by the conference (or, presbyterate).[52]

Asbury says less in his *Journal* about elders and deacons than he says about bishops. For this data, we must turn primarily to the early Methodist Episcopal *Disciplines*. Here we discover that elders and deacons are on the same level as bishops concerning the preaching of the Word—as are lay preachers. Elders share equally with bishops in the ministry of the Sacraments (both Lord's Supper and Baptism). Deacons share partially in this ministry (Baptism in the absence of an elder and assistance of the elder in the Lord's Supper). Ordination is done by the bishop as a function delegated by the elders. Bishops alone ordain deacons; bishops are assisted by elders in the ordination of elders; and bishops ordain bishops unless there are no bishops, in which case three elders ordain the person elected to the episcopacy.[53] Indeed, the ordination prerogative of elders is an important key to the justification of any Methodist ordinations in the first place.[54] Thus, bishops are different from elders solely in that they are ordained to a higher administrative authority. The governing authority of elders and deacons depended on their conference membership. If they were not itinerants, then they could not share in the governing of the church. If a lay person wanted to share in the church's governing, that person would have to become a traveling preacher.[55]

For Otterbein, whose inheritance comes from the Reformed tradition, the form of ministry is that of a single order of ordained clergy (elders) shared with the laity under the government of a modified presbyterian system. In the Rules which Otterbein drew up for the Evangelical Reformed Church of Baltimore in 1785, he outlines a three-fold pattern of ministry, two of which are lay offices. There is the "preacher," elected by the male members of the congregation to perform pastoral duties, to administer the Sacraments, and to preach and teach the Word. The three lay elders are selected by the preacher for the life-long office (or, until they can no longer serve due to immorality or debility) to exercise discipline among church members and to govern the affairs of the church. Three lay deacons are elected annually by the congregation to share, for one year, the duties of the elders and any others which the preacher may assign to them.[56] It is hard to know if these rules were practiced precisely among the early United Brethren in Christ. According to Spayth, the earliest United Brethren historian, the rules which the church operated under until 1815 were the unwritten rules of Otterbein. Spayth prints these rules and rightly points out that they lack any specific forms or governing rules for preachers. Yet, says

Spayth, "these rules Mr. Otterbein preferred to the general rules of the Methodists."[57]

Furthermore, it should be noted that the 1785 Baltimore rules provide for a connection of preachers among the churches in Pennsylvania, Maryland, and Virginia that "stand in fraternal unity with us."[58] Thus, there is a presbyterate of clergy among the brethren of Otterbein. But the primary governing power lies, according to Otterbein, in the local church. The assembly of ministers is for general review of the various churches' states of affairs, and, perhaps, to discern where leadership needs are to be filled.[59] When Otterbein and Boehm are elected to be superintendents, or bishops, of the United Brethren, there is no ordination to that office. It is understood that such superintendents are not different from ordained preachers in order, but only in the functions of oversight and presiding at conferences. Indeed, the superintendents are elected for four-year terms, rather than life.[60] They do not appoint preachers; preachers usually volunteer for certain assignments or are appointed by the conference of preachers. Still, there is a superintendent among the clergy; thus, the government that Otterbein supports is that of a modified presbyterian system.

As an ordained elder, Otterbein ordains other elders in the Reformed Church.[61] Indeed, the function of ordaining seems to be the only prerogative uniquely reserved for the ordained clergy in the early United Brethren in Christ. Authority to exercise the ministries of Word and Sacrament is delegated by the conference according to the circumstances of the churches and the qualifications of the preacher. It is not tied to the laying on of hands, although Otterbein almost certainly would have regarded the ministry of Word and Sacrament as reserved for ordained clergy in his earlier doctrine of ministry in the Reformed Church. It is significant to note that Christian Newcomer is elected bishop before he is ordained by Otterbein.[62] Indeed, the reason that Otterbein is asked to ordain other people is so that they "may perform the like office for others."[63]

The actual ordination is performed by Otterbein, with the assistance of William Ryland, an elder of the Methodist Episcopal Church. Two elders ordain other people to be elders. Furthermore, the officers of Otterbein's Baltimore congregation gather in Otterbein's home for the occasion, and the ordination certificate is issued in the name of the church vestry, not the United Brethren conference.[64] This is an important sign of Otterbein's doctrine of ministry. When something as important as ordination occurs, he goes to special effort to be sure it is done in the context of the local church. Clearly the ordination is not for the episcopal function (Newcomer was already bishop) or for the administration of Word and Sacrament. Rather, it is for the continuation of the line of ordained clergy among the Church of the United Brethren in Christ. Elders are ordained in order to ordain. The concern is for ecclesiastical succession. The remaining functions of Word, Sacrament and Order reside in, and are distributed by, the conference which approves its own members.[65]

The difference between Asbury and Otterbein regarding the form of ministry is their basic point of orientation. Both men employ the conference of preachers as the main governing body of the connection. But, Asbury's basic orientation is from the episcopacy down; Otterbein's basic orientation is from the local congregation up. Thus, for Asbury bishops function as itinerant evangelists and chief administrators of a distinct order. For Otterbein bishops are pastors of a local congregation who take on added duties as overseers of other ministers for the sake of making sure that each local congregation is being served adequately.[66] For Asbury, there is a two-fold order of ordained ministry, sent by the conference to the local congregation, in addition to lay preachers. For Otterbein, there is one order of ministry which arises from the congregation and is regulated by the conference; the minister-in-charge is related first to the needs of the congregation, not to the conference. Thus, the seeming similarity of the conference structure cannot be used as an argument for the congruency of these two early founders of United Methodism. For Asbury, the conference modified a fundamental episcopalian orientation; for Otterbein, the conference modified a presbyterian foundation. It is quite natural, therefore, that Asbury's concern with centralized discipline would be unappealing to Otterbein, and that Otterbein's loosely-organized structure would be a source of criticism by Asbury.

The same division exists in the style of ministry. For Asbury, again attempting to recover apostolic purity, the style of ministry is necessarily itinerant for bishops, and preferably so for the other ministers. Celibacy, in turn, is a desirable feature for an effective itinerancy.[67] The norm for Asbury is the traveling, single, young man who goes from place to place on his circuit, preaching, visiting the sick, meeting with the societies after the preaching service, keeping close records of membership, exercising supervision and discipline over local leaders, teaching young people, giving a personal example of piety and holiness, and, if ordained, administering the Sacrament, marrying, burying, and conducting the divine liturgy—all according to the detailed specifications in the *Discipline*, even to the detail of naming the hour for morning preaching. Monetary income is sparse; educational attainment, while being encouraged, is not nearly as important as personal enthusiasm, loyalty, and fruits appropriate to the task given.[68] Superintendents, whether presiding elders or bishops, have basically the same functions, only on a broader scale. More than one historian has noted that Asbury himself was the model *par excellence* of this style of ministry.

Otterbein, on the other hand, was a residential pastor, who traveled to other churches occasionally, and at times even had a regular circuit; he, therefore, understood something of the itinerancy, but preferred the residential pastorate for himself. The Baltimore Rules of 1785 presuppose the residential style of. ministry. The preacher is to visit all worshipers, in health and in sickness, and on all occasions. He shall admonish them, baptize their children, attend to their funerals, impart instruction to their youth; and, should they have any children, the Church shall interest herself for their religious education.[69]

Likewise, the preacher is to attend, along with the lay officials, to "all the affairs of the church." He is to lead the weekly class meetings, one for men and one for women, if he is available.[70] He is a pastor who lives among the people through the week. For Otterbein, in the United Brethren, itinerancy becomes an optional form of ministry; but it is certainly not expected. More than half of the early United Brethren are family persons, associated with a particular parish. The ministerial style, then, is largely left to the circumstantial needs which a given minister perceives among the people. There are no rules handed down from above, except a few biblical guidelines. Otterbein's prescriptions for church discipline are fundamentally rooted in Matthew 18:15–17.[71] Of course, Otterbein, like Asbury, expected ministers to be holy persons, exercising exemplary personal discipline and piety. But, unlike Asbury, Otterbein allows the minister freedom to serve as the servant of a particular congregation or circuit, with a relatively small number of restraints or prescribed duties, when compared to the Methodists. As noted earlier, the earliest system of itinerancy is voluntary, and, later, is selectively administered according to regional needs. Roll-taking and membership records are regarded with disdain, particularly with the increasing Mennonite influence. Foot-washing is permitted on the basis of local practice.[72] Briefly, the possibility for a minister to have a more direct or sustained relationship with a local church is viable without loss of standing.

Once again, the basic difference between Asbury and Otterbein regarding style of ministry lies in their basic orientation. For both men, the conference is the primary governing body for ministers. But, for Asbury, the ministry is most effective when the preacher follows the lead of the bishop as a celibate itinerant, bound by rules set forth by the conference. In effect, the traveling preacher is responsible to see that the local church follows the conference rules. For Otterbein, the primary focus shifts from a centralized operation to one based on circumstantial needs, with few specific guidelines being set by the conference, and no discouragement from settling at a particular church. Preacher-pastors are just as acceptable as preacher-itinerants, depending on local needs. Thus, Asbury's Wesleyan background clashes with Otterbein's Reformed background. These two distinctive traditions largely account for the differences between the doctrines of ministry of Asbury and Otterbein, as well as the differences in polity between the Methodists and the United Brethren.

In the following generations, certain changes occurred to bring the two churches closer together. The United Brethren adopted a *Discipline* and the itinerancy; the Methodists became more pastoral in style, and gave the local

106

congregation more voice in church government. Still, at the time of merger between the Methodist Church and the Evangelical United Brethren Church in 1968, several differences in the understandings of ministry existed. Four, in particular, are clearly related to the early roots we have just discussed. First, in the Evangelical United Brethren Church, the minister was a member of the annual conference, but not a member of the charge conference.[73] Perhaps, in practice, this difference made little difference in the function of pastoral ministry, but the difference points to a clear divergence of views concerning the clergy person's relationship to a local congregation. Although the itinerancy was, by now, an essential part of the Evangelical United Brethren, Otterbein's residential character was still reflected in this practice of charge conference membership. Second, the Methodists maintained a two-fold order of ordained ministry (elders and deacons) with bishops as consecrated elders. Among the Evangelical United Brethren, there was a one-fold order (elders) with bishops elected from them. This is a clear reflection of the difference between Otterbein and Asbury concerning the forms of ministry. Third, Methodist bishops were elected to life terms while Evangelical United Brethren bishops were elected to four-year terms, being eligible for re-election. This, too, is a direct reflection of the difference as it existed between Asbury and Otterbein. Finally, Methodist bishops appointed their district superintendents, but Otterbein's descendants elected their superintendents at annual conference. This also reflects a basic difference in understanding of the office of superintendency: is it an office amenable to the conference or the bishop? The Methodist position reflects Asbury's relatively high episcopal notions, while the Evangelical United Brethren position is in keeping with Otterbein's preference for presbyterial rather than episcopal power.[74]

In conclusion, therefore, we make the following observations: First, although Francis Asbury and Philip William Otterbein were contemporaries who shared a great many beliefs, commitments and goals in common, they were not part of the same immediate background. Rather, they emerged from two distinct traditions which led to significant differences between them. Second, cultural differences were not as significant as ecclesiastical differences in explaining the failure to cooperate more closely during the early years of the Church of the United Brethren and the Methodist Episcopal Church. Third, the issue of church government and, particularly, of the doctrine of ministry kept the Otterbein group separated from the Asbury group. Otterbein's modified presbyterianism and Asbury's modified episcopalianism could not be reconciled on either side at that point in history. Finally, several of the significant issues that separated the modern descendants of these two men can be traced directly back to the differences between their doctrines of ministry.

## CHAPTER 7

# African Methodisms and the Rise of Black Denominationalism

## Will B. Gravely

At least since 1921, when Carter G. Woodson published his classic survey, *History of the Negro Church*, it has been commonplace to refer to religious separatism in the free black communities of the post-Revolutionary generation as "the independent church movement."[1] A quarter-century earlier, Bishop James W. Hood of the African Methodist Episcopal, Zion Church used a similar idiom to describe the origins of northern black congregations. Discounting denominational differences among antebellum black Protestants, Hood argued that a common racial bond made for "a general, grand united and simultaneous Negro movement." Regretting the scarcity of early sources and the absence of comprehensive histories, the bishop declared, "there was more in it than what appears on the surface," for "it was a general exodus of colored members out of white churches."[2]

Contemporary historians have reinforced the implications of Woodson and Hood by treating the earliest institutionalization of black religion in the United States, as distinct from the "invisible institution" of slave religion, in terms of an incipient black nationalism.[3] Their interpretive perspective emphasizes the natural evolution of separate churches within the expanding Afro-American community life of northern urban centers in the late eighteenth century. The social forces that account for their emergence lie in the demography of black communities, the effects of migration and economic change on their composition, the presence of intra-religious competition and social dissent within them. Pre-eminently black religious independence arose from communal initiative and a corporate ethnic consciousness that expressed "nationalist aspirations" at a pre-theoretical but practical institutional level.[4] Simply put, black churches, as the first public institutions which black people controlled, provided the original context for what E. Franklin Frazier called "a nation within a nation"— the institutional equivalent to W. E. B. DuBois' insight about the dialectic of double-consciousness in black American experience and identity.[5]

Much of the proto-national orientation of the earliest black churches, to return to Bishop Hood's analogy, existed beneath the surface. Obviously, separate black churches served the needs of the black communities in which they resided. Insofar as these communities formed a separate culture, an implied "black nationality" was present from the beginning. By the 1830's, with a black press, an annual convention system and numerous voluntary associations along-side the churches, such an argument has strong force. But there were interlocking relationships between free African benevolent societies in Boston, Providence, Newport, New York, and Philadelphia as far back as the 1780's, with a coordinated effort to sponsor emigration.[6] Within the independent church movement, however, local developments with differing connections to biracial denominational structures were primary for a generation. Not until the appearance of separate black denominations with itinerating ministers was there a coordinated effort to create networks across and between black communities. Denominationalism, however, brought not only connections to other congregations elsewhere. It also meant schism and competition within black communities.

The nearest equivalent of a corporate linkage between the first separated congregations appears in Daniel Coker's pamphlet against slavery, published in 1810. In his appendix, the black Methodist preacher and schoolmaster used the early Christian images of "chosen generation," "royal priesthood," "holy nation" and "peculiar people" to demonstrate "what God [was] doing for Ethiopia's sons in the United States of America." His evidence was the African church movement, contained in a compilation of four lists, naming thirteen ordained black clergy (excluding himself), another eleven licensed Methodist local preachers, eight "descendants of the African race, who [had] given proofs of their talents" in public, and fifteen separated congregations. The churches represented four denominational traditions, all biracial at this date, and ten cities, including Charleston, South Carolina's ill-fated African Methodist congregation to which Denmark Vesey would belong. But Coker saw them all as "African churches," whose common characteristic lay in their nearly simultaneous emergence in less than two decades.[7]

Over the next twelve years following the appearance of Coker's booklet, a new institutional structure, black denominationalism evolved within the African church movement. In that development, Coker was himself instrumental, becoming a separatist leader among black Methodists in Baltimore and merging his followers with other dissidents in the region, centering in Philadelphia, to form in 1816 the second of three African Methodist denominations. Three years earlier, in 1813, black Methodists in Wilmington, Delaware made the first denominational break with the Methodist Episcopal Church to create the African Union Church. In 1822, a third African Methodist denomination arose in New York City, culminating more than two decades of separate congregational existence of the Zion church.

This paper, as a retelling of a familiar history, has been motivated by three concerns. First, the renaissance of black history over the past two decades has surfaced new or forgotten sources which flesh out the basic story and make possible comparative analysis across denominational and community boundaries. Methodist developments in Philadelphia, Baltimore, Wilmington, and New York can be seen in a larger context of the independent church movement.[8]

Second, this study concentrates on the expansion, in the independent church movement, from congregational autonomy within patterns of interdependence with biracial denominational judicatories, to denominational autonomy. Since the three African Methodist denominations pioneered in this process, my question has been to ask how and why they took religious separatism to its fullest conclusion. In this way an assessment can begin of the implications of denominationalism within American church history generally.[9]

Finally, there are several pragmatic issues which white and black Methodists contested in the evolution of congregational autonomy and in the shift to Afro-American denominationalism. I draw particular attention to five factors indigenous to the organizational life of Christian churches: access to ordination, representation in denominational governance, consultation about pastoral appointments and services, the ownership and use of church property, and participation in congregational discipline. These same factors are present in Baptist, Presbyterian, and Protestant Episcopal settings where, as with Methodists, the maintenance of white control and the refusal to share power with black members triggered the rise of independent congregations. Black churchfolk refused to contain or segregate the sacred power which they experienced in Christian faith from these more mundane forms of power. They wanted to elect and to be elected to office, to ordain and be ordained, to discipline as well as be disciplined, to preach, exhort, pray, and administer sacraments—in sum, to have their gifts and graces acknowledged by the whole community. Where that acknowledgement was withheld, black Christians resisted and protested, organized and created new institutional alternatives for themselves.

I

"Our only design is to secure to our selves our rights and privileges, to regulate our affairs, temporal and spiritual, the same as if we were white people. "—Richard Allen and the trustees of Bethel Church to the Philadelphia Conference of the Methodist Episcopal Church, April 8, 1807[10]

When Bishop Francis Asbury preached the dedicatory sermon on June 29, 1794, the first African Methodist church building, named Bethel, was available for black Methodists in Philadelphia.[11] That event ended eight years of struggle for Richard Allen, ex-slave and a local preacher in the Methodist society who formed a class of forty-two black members in 1786 and first proposed that a separate "place of worship" be erected "for the colored people." He was met with opposition both from the Methodist elder that year, Caleb Boyer, and by "the most respectable people of color in this city."[12] In November, 1787, Allen convened black members of "the Methodist Society of Philadelphia" to consider "the evils under which they laboured, arising from the unkind treatment of their white brethren." The meeting, apparently, followed the incident, told without date in Allen's autobiography, at St. George's church when white trustees pulled black worshippers from their knees during prayer.[13]

Between 1788 and 1791 Allen endured the threats of Richard Whatcoat and Lemuel Green, elders in Philadelphia, who tried, he recalled later, to "prevent us from going on" with an "African church" project.[14] During the same period he was censured and finally excluded from the Free African society, which organization he helped found in April, 1787. As they banished Allen in June, 1789, his colleagues charged him with "attempting to sow division among us" and with "rashly calling or convening the members together." He had, according to his own account, continued to support the ideas of an African church, even though the Free African Association took upon itself in 1791 the major responsibility to construct a building and work out "a plan of church government." When that plan turned out to be Protestant Episcopal in polity, due to Dr. Benjamin Rush's influence, Allen cooperated with the project but refused an invitation to be the church's first pastor. Intent on remaining Methodist, despite the difficulties he had experienced in the denomination, Allen, with a committee of ten others, turned to the community for subscriptions to his Bethel church. The campaign began in the spring of 1794, after the St. Thomas African Episcopal Church was under way. By summer a remodelled blacksmith shop frame had become a suitable building.[15]

If the dedication of the first Bethel building in June, 1794, closed one struggle for Richard Allen, his model for the congregation and its relationship with the Methodist Episcopal denomination insured that further difficulties awaited him. Officially Allen was unordained but licensed as a local preacher with responsibilities under white elders assigned to St. George's church. His initiative had solved the first problem confronting black Methodists whose memories were still fresh of "many inconveniences" that resulted "from white people and people of color mixing together in public assemblys." Issuing a "public statement" in November, 1794, Allen and the Bethel trustees justified their need for "a convenient house to assemble in separate from our white brethren."

The Bethel proclamation contained ten articles and regulations that confirmed the intent to abide by "the Methodist Episcopal Church for our Church government and discipline and with her creeds and articles for our faith." Since the black congregation held the deed for the church property, however, a disclaimer was necessary to protect the "right and proprietary of our house" from denominational ownership. Moreover, the document asserted the goal of the Bethel founders to push for ordination of black "persons endowed with gifts and graces to speak for God." It also declared the "right" of the majority of voting (males in close communion) members of the congregation "to call any brother that appears to us adequate to the task to preach or exhort as a local preacher, without the interference of the Conference or any other person or persons whatsoever." Beyond that, the statement defined provisions for elections, limited membership to "descendants of the African race" while retaining "mutual fellowship" with "white brethren" as visitors "in Bands, classes and Love Feasts," empowered trustees with "temporal concerns," and retained "matters of a spiritual nature concerning discipline" as "now in use in the Church."[16]

The "public statement" was an assertion of black religious independence, not a negotiated agreement with the Methodist Episcopal denomination. The posture of Allen and the Bethel trustees, who insisted on remaining Methodist while holding property for blacks to use and while refusing to go any more to St. George's church, must have been enigmatic to many whites. Allen was publicly committed to the denomination, had its bishop behind him, and opened the building to sympathetic white ministers in the Methodist conference. Yet he did not turn over the property to the denominational officials, and his congregation claimed an autonomy disallowable under Methodist standards. It was not surprising, therefore, in 1795 that "our warfare and troubles," Allen remembered later, "now began afresh." That year John McClaskey, whom Allen had faced down in 1792 over the fund-raising project for the first African church, returned to the St. George's appointment. Determined to respond vigorously to Bethel's autonomy, McClaskey found that it was necessary to turn to Ezekiel Cooper, on leave from the itinerant ministry and trustworthy to blacks because of a strong antislavery commitment, and request him to negotiate a compromise.[17]

It encompassed a charter of incorporation, dated September 12, 1796 and entitled "Articles of Association of the African Methodist Episcopal Church" in Philadelphia. The articles required loyalty to the denomination, but placed the Bethel property under a board of black trustees "for the religious use of the ministers and preachers of the Methodist Episcopal Church" and "likewise for our African brethren." They retained the stipulation from the "public statement" that members would always be "coloured persons." A similar provision protected defendants in cases of congregational discipline, allowing appeal beyond the white elder to a jury from Bethel church. At the same time, the black congregation conceded the right of the white elder to license and assign local preachers and to officiate sacramentally. It added, however, the qualification, "for the time being," after the recognition of the elder's authority over "spiritual concerns." Reiterating the forceful assertion of 1794, the leaders of Bethel anticipated a time when white supervision would end, when "coloured brethren shall graduate into holy orders," as the articles expressed it. Such expectations were established on reasonable grounds of comparison with another denomination since Absalom Jones, former Methodist and leader in the Free African Society, had already been consecrated deacon in the Protestant Episcopal ministry.[18]

Three years after the incorporation, the articles were made public and Bishop Asbury ordained Allen the first black deacon in the Methodist Episcopal Church. A few months later, the General Conference of 1800 approved Asbury's innovation and provided for other such ordinations, but there were still difficulties to be faced. The legislation was left out of the *Discipline*, thus making the office of black local deacon an anomaly in the Methodist system.[19] As it stood, Allen was not a member of the annual conference of travelling ministers, but remained under the supervision of the elder for Philadelphia. The unprecedented local nature of the office prevented him from celebrating the Lord's Supper or officiating otherwise at baptisms and weddings outside the appointment, or when the elder was available.[20]

The curb on Allen's ministerial authority did not hamper the growth of the Bethel congregation. Moreover, Allen's varied business activities kept him active beyond his pastoral duties. Black membership at Bethel, and at another black mission established in 1794 called Zoar, grew spectacularly, from 211 in 1799 to 738 in 1805.[21] In 1801, Allen published a hymnal for use in the church.[22] He maintained good relations with several of the white Methodist clergy who came to the city and who often stayed with him and Sarah Allen when they officiated at Bethel.[23]

The accommodation of 1796, however, only worked when the white elder in Philadelphia conceded a large measure of autonomy to Allen and the black trustees—an autonomy assumed in the public statement of 1794 and effectively guarded in the Articles of Agreement. When the Virginian, James Smith, came to St. George's in 1805, old controversies flared up over congregational discipline and the limits and powers of the white elder. After Smith threatened to lay claim to the Bethel property in behalf of the denomination, Allen was forced to admit how vulnerable the trustees were, depending on how the Articles were construed. Consulting a lawyer, he found a way to secure Bethel's interest. As a civil corporation, the congregation amended its charter by two-thirds vote of the members. The state supreme court approved such a document—"The African Supplement"—on March 16, 1807.[24]

The new legal measure addressed the perennial irritants—the ownership and use of property, the powers of the trustees, and the absence of ordained black elders to function in the congregational life of Bethel church. In place of "the consent of the elder," its first article substituted a two-thirds ratification by the adult male members of "one year's standing" on all property transactions by the trustees. Three other major changes aimed at the power of the elder completed the revisions. The trustees could appoint "any other person, duly qualified" according to the Methodist *Discipline* to "preach and exhort" whenever the elder did preach, as was his right, "once every Sunday, and once during the course of the week." The alteration made the right into a demand and moved the power of determination fully into the hands of the trustees. Amendments also empowered the black local preachers at Bethel to hold quarterly meetings, love feasts, and trials of "disorderly members," when the elder neglected or refused to do so. Disciplinary cases where former members of Bethel who had been expelled had "been received as members of the Methodist Episcopal Church elsewhere" made another change imperative. Having vested the trustees with the right to open buildings to meetings, the Supplement backed them in maintaining excommunication by barring any who had been dismissed from Bethel church.[25]

The Supplement extended the autonomous authority of the Bethel congregation and challenged, again, the usual requirements of Methodist structure. It would not have been necessary, of course, had Allen or other black deacons been advanced to elder's orders or become members of the annual conference. As it was, the Philadelphia conference accepted Allen's notification, signed as "Pastor," that the Supplement had been legally obtained denying independence or separation as a goal, the statement, nonetheless, reasserted black autonomy. "Our only design," it read, "is to secure to our selves our rights and privileges, to regulate our affairs, temporal and spiritual, the same as if we were white people." On behalf of the conference, Bishop Asbury accepted the memorial, expressing confidence "that our African brethren" remained "Methodists according to our Discipline." The carefully worded response did not approve the Supplement, but received it insofar as it was "not contrary to the allowed usages, customs, and privileges of the Methodist Episcopal Church."[26] The two contradictory positions were fated to come face to face before some third party. Meanwhile, Allen had weathered another challenge to an African Methodism, while he remained, however tenuously, within the denominational structure.

The Supplement did not end Bethel's problems, but it did insure the congregation's ultimate protection and pave the way to denominational separation. Its passage went relatively unnoticed for four years, but in 1811 the

Methodist conference went on the offensive. First, the trustees at St. George's church claimed that the Supplement was void because they had not approved it. The contention accompanied a move to reconnect Bethel to the appointment at St. George's. Second, the elder, Stephen G. Roszel, sought unsuccessfully to have the Bethel membership repeal the Supplement by the same means that it had been obtained in the first place. Neither tactic succeeded. In 1812, Bethel was made a stationed church and placed, with two other congregations, under Thomas G. Sergeant. When that plan was discontinued the next year, the old question, rooted in the refusal of Methodists to sanction black elders, emerged again. The Bethel congregation appealed to Bishop Asbury for assistance, but he refused to intervene.[27]

As an effort to curb Bethel's independence financially, a controversy smoldered during the next two years over the fee structure for sacramental services. When Bethel came under St. George's church, its elder and the black trustees disagreed over money. From his point of view, the black congregation ought to contribute funds to support the larger ministry of which it was a part. The issue was not fees charged for services performed, except in cases of conducting marriages.[28] From the point of view of Allen and the Bethel trustees, the one remaining limitation to autonomy was access to elder's orders and the sacramental authority it conferred. Until that could be had, they would pay for the necessary services. Their resistive position was calculated to force the denomination to become inclusive in its clerical orders or face continued aggravation from its black members.[29]

By this time blacks numbered more than 1300, or about two-fifths of the Methodist membership in Philadelphia. By far one of the largest congregations in the denomination, Bethel's success was viewed ambivalently by white officials. Moreover, within the denomination, significant changes had accompanied its rapid growth. Consistently from 1800, it backed away from its original antislavery standards for church membership and ordination. Had Allen been ordained elder, he would have had slaveowning ministerial colleagues in conferences on the border and in the South. Accommodation to proslavery sentiment was so necessary that Bishop Asbury and the General Conferences of 1804 and 1808 approved expurgated versions of the *Discipline* with the chapter on slavery omitted. Following the abortive effort to petition state legislatures in behalf of emancipation in 1800, the denomination withdrew from taking any official position on the social and political question of human bondage.[30] While these developments occurred without Allen's participation or direct comment, he could hardly have failed to notice them.

As a further complication, there may have been a breach between Allen and Bishop Asbury. Although he had sponsored the black diaconate and had earlier been a staunch opponent of slavery, Asbury had finally compromised about emancipation. His journal, in 1809, reflected the denomination's concessions, fatefully conceding that saving the souls of the Africans was more important than freeing their bodies. There is no direct evidence of an overt break with Allen, only Lorenzo Dow's retrospective suggestion, but Asbury made no mention of the black leader or Bethel church in his journal or letters during the last five years of his life. And, after ordaining eight additional black local deacons for New York and Philadelphia between 1806 and 1809, Asbury ceased the procedure.[31]

Two events in the summer of 1814 set in motion the actions that led in the next year and a half to a final break between Allen's Bethel congregation and Asbury's denomination. On July 7, the pastor of the Academy church in Philadelphia and future bishop, John Emory, issued a public letter disowning the Bethel membership as Methodist because the black trustees were exercising the spiritual discipline as outlined in the African Supplement. Later the same month, a legal challenge to their authority forced a showdown. In 1812, Robert Green was excommunicated by a disciplinary committee of ten officials at Bethel church for breach of rules. As a trustee himself, Green complained to the white elder, and then took the case to the state supreme court. His suit was argued on July 30, 1814. The following January, the judges overturned the church's action on procedural defects in the "manner this Committee was selected or appointed" for the disciplinary trial of Green.[32]

A few weeks later, just before the Philadelphia conference met in the spring, Robert R. Roberts, pastor at St. George's church, tested whether the court's action had discredited Allen's leadership or the power of the trustees. He announced his intention to preach at Bethel, as was his right by the original Articles of Agreement, but the trustees, not to be outdone, stood on the authority of the Supplement that it was their prerogative to choose preachers. When Roberts arrived, he found Jacob Tapisco in the pulpit. Rebuffed, he left the building, but further strife was predictable.[33] In a new effort to thwart Bethel's autonomy, the annual conference tried again to include the black church in the regular appointments. The new elder at St. George's, an Irishman named Robert Burch, would add Bethel to his pastorate for 1815.[34]

Green's lawsuit forced another challenge to the Supplement—the issue of local control of property. His victory forced a sheriff's sale of the land and building on June 12, 1815, at which Allen, as highest bidder, successfully retained possession.[35] But the tug-of-war was still not over. In December, Burch, following the example of Roberts, sought to preach at Bethel, using Green, the disaffected trustee, as his host. On this occasion, the congregation blocked the aisles at the New Year's Eve service, preventing Burch from going to the front. That collective symbolic gesture brought the developments of nearly thirty years to full circle. In the early years of incipient black independence, white trustees and black members clashed in St. George's church. Now the shoe was on the other foot, when Bethel trustees and congregation physically prevented the St. George's minister from officiating in their building.[36]

Immediately, Burch petitioned the state supreme court for access to the pulpit as his legal right, but the judges refused to grant his claim. Instead, Bethel church, standing on the legality of the African Supplement, gained its independent status. Four months after the announcement of the court's decision, it joined representations from Baltimore, Salem (New Jersey), and Attleborough (Pennsylvania) to form the African Methodist Episcopal denomination. After waiting seventeen years, Allen was ordained elder, and made, after Daniel Coker became ineligible, the bishop of the new organization, serving in that capacity until his death in 1831.[37]

## II

"Gone with Coker," the designation used in the membership records for the black Methodist societies of Baltimore to indicate those who had withdrawn to form Bethel church and join the African Methodist Episcopal denomination.

The beginning of an independent African Methodist church in Baltimore is difficult to substantiate with primary evidence, limited as are the early sources in specifying the stages that led to a final break for more than two hundred members, exhorters, and local preachers in the black classes in 1815. Secondary sources, in the form of autobiographical recollections and undocumented histories, refer back to the roots of a separatist movement in 1787, the second year that the annual minutes of the Methodist Episcopal Church recorded membership by race. The tradition recounts black objections to seating arrangements in the gallery of the Light Street church, leading to separate classes and prayer meetings in houses and businesses like Caleb Hyland's boot-blacking cellar.[38] The degree of racial separation over the next decade, besides dividing black members into their own classes, which was apparent as early as 1786, is impossible to establish. Black Methodist membership in the city did grow from 111 in that year to 269 in 1788. The numbers seven years later were not substantially higher, with 282 members in the societies of the city and a separate circuit.[39]

In 1795, there was sufficient interest in forming "a distinct African, yet Methodist Church" that negotiations began with white officials like Bishop Asbury. No documents, like the Articles of Association used in Philadelphia and in revised form in New York, survive, but Asbury made clear that the same assertive posture that characterized the Bethel movement under Allen reappeared in Baltimore. In October, 1795, the proposals which had come to him asked that "in temporals" the African Methodists would be "under their own direction." Taken by surprise at the full implications of the plan, Asbury regarded the blacks as asking "greater privileges than the white stewards and trustees ever had a right to claim." [40] Twenty months later, he was still "trying to organize the African church," but by that time the project to obtain a building had already advanced. [41]

It is not clear whether Asbury's reference in 1797 was to a building which the African Academy first leased for black education by the American Convention for Promoting the Abolition of Slavery, or a short-lived effort to establish a second African church on Fish Street in rented quarters. [42] The Academy building, which became by deed in 1802 the Sharp Street church, was the single African meetinghouse listed in Baltimore's city directory that year and on a map in 1804. [43]

During the decade from 1801–1811, there were black trustees holding and selling land and obtaining title to the Academy building in behalf of the African Methodist Episcopal classes in Baltimore. A Bethel congregation, which traced its origins to the abortive Fish Street organization in 1797, may have continued to meet separately from other black Methodists in the Academy, since Daniel Coker's pamphlet of 1810 refers to two African Methodist churches in the city. If that were the case, however, there was still a common identity between all the black Methodist classes of Baltimore until 1815. By 1812, a separate Asbury African church was an additional meeting place for these classes, but it was not until there was a formal break, led by Coker, that the buildings can be said to have spawned identifiable congregations. The Sharp Street and Asbury congregations after 1813 remained loyal to the Methodist Episcopal Church, thus inheriting the property rights of the original African church of Baltimore even though they did not incorporate until 1832. The separatists, on the other hand, were forced to find new quarters, as Coker first rented a former Presbyterian building and then purchased the Fish Street property originally used in 1797. [44]

The date is not clear when white Methodists in Baltimore licensed the first black local preachers and exhorters, but in 1810 Coker, whom Asbury had ordained a local deacon in 1808, listed seven men in those roles. That pattern of leadership, to which black class leaders should be added, remained normative until the secession of 1815. Black classes met in locations, over the city, worshipped in two African churches and depended on white elders for sacramental function and final disciplinary authority. There was a modicum of black independence in the system, for black trustees owned and controlled property, Coker was a local deacon, black local preachers gave congregational leadership, and black exhorters and class leaders functioned in customary fashion. The city's black population responded to the religious energies of the African Methodists, producing significant numerical growth from 637 in 1808 to 973 in 1813. [45] By March, 1814, the totals were indeed impressive: forty-one classes with 1552 members, eight black local preachers and ten black exhorters. [46]

Seeds of dissension were also present, however, as a negotiated agreement between the white elder and "the African Church in Baltimore" in 1814 recognized. The document, designed "to preserve the peace and union" of the black classes with the denomination, spelled out the pastoral expectations of the white elder. The black membership unquestionably felt slighted, so that it had to request that special attention be given to the visitation of the sick, the baptism of children, a regular pastoral conference with the classes at least quarterly, and the performance of funeral services, with sermons "if the deceased have been an aged upright official member, who died tryumphant [sic] in the Lord." In exchange, "the African Society" agreed "to bear their part of the expense of the preacher." [47]

The agreement of 1814, as viewed by the more recent members and by the younger leaders, did not settle the real needs for black independence.[48] With Coker at the center, a group of dissidents met weekly, according to David Smith who belonged in the circle, preparing for full separation. By this time, developments in Philadelphia were well known to the Baltimore organizers, and Coker was coordinating his plans with Richard Allen. The "club," as Smith termed the group, agreed to make the break late in 1815, a few weeks prior to the final round of controversy in Philadelphia. More than two hundred members of the black classes kept to the agreement, leaving Methodist Episcopal authorities to strike their names from the rolls with the comment, "gone with Coker."[49] Over the next four years, the new Bethel congregation worked out problems of incorporation and obtained new property. In 1818, when the first session of the Baltimore annual conference of the new African Methodist Episcopal denomination convened, the number at Bethel church had jumped to 1096, and nine former local preachers and exhorters were ordained by Bishop Allen.[50]

The connection between Allen and Coker, the Philadelphia and the Baltimore movements for independence, was forcefully dramatized on January 23, 1816, when the Maryland African Methodists celebrated the Pennsylvania court decision which freed Bethel church. Preaching to a jubilant audience, Coker claimed that the court had vindicated religious liberty in the United States. The biblical archetype for the victory was the Jewish story of freedom from exile where the chosen people "were held against their will." Black Methodists had experienced ecclesiastical caste like the Jews had known Babylonian captivity. "Those Jews . . . had not equal privileges with the Babylonians," Coker asserted, "although they were governed by the same laws, and suffered the same penalties." The legal decision cleared the way for African Methodists to embrace "the opportunity that is now offered us of being free," as Coker put it in biblical idiom, "to sit down under our own vine to worship, and none shall make us afraid."[51]

If freedom was the major motif of Coker's sermon, his title insisted that the black seceders had "withdrawn from under the charge of Methodist Bishops and Conference, (BUT ARE STILL METHODISTS)." The convention of April, 1816, and the subsequent *Discipline* of the new denomination which appeared in 1817 proved as much. Virtually all features of Methodist Episcopal doctrine and polity were carried over to the new church, which added, appropriately, a strong condemnation of slavery to its standards. With ordination in the hands of the independent denomination and with black churchmen representing their own congregations, the last obstacles to equal power and full autonomy had been overcome.[52]

## III

"Then that body of us who built the meeting house, could not see our way clear to give up all say." Peter Spencer and William Anderson describe the African independent church movement in Wilmington.[53]

An observer at the organizing convention of the Bethel Methodist connection, Peter Spencer of Wilmington had, with William Anderson, anticipated by three years the result of the movements for independence and denominational separation in Philadelphia and Baltimore. Failing to join with Allen, the African Union Church subsequently remained the smallest of the three black Methodist denominations, with a regional base in Delaware and Pennsylvania. Its route to independence, abbreviated to less than a decade, moved through two stages toward congregational, then denominational autonomy.

There were black members of the Asbury Methodist Episcopal Church in Wilmington from its founding in 1789, when nineteen of the original sixty-two persons in the church were classed as "colored." Between 1800 and 1802, these numbers climbed dramatically increasing two and a half times to reach 117, or eight less than the white total for the latter year. Even though black classes met separately, white officials began to complain of overcrowding and of damages to the main floor of the building. Hence, in June, 1805, they acted to force all black classes to meet in the gallery. The resolution instructed black class leaders to "govern themselves accordingly."[54]

Prior to these demands, there was already some interest, dating back to January, in building an "African Church."[55] An appeal for assistance to the general public became the more necessary when, in late June, Spencer and Anderson rebelled against the command of the trustees and led forty-one other secessionists from Asbury church. They met in private homes until the African Chapel, or Ezion Methodist Episcopal Church (named for the port of Ezion-geber where King Solomon kept a fleet of ships, I Kings 9.26), was dedicated.[56]

From the beginning, difficulties paralleling the conflicts in Philadelphia and Baltimore threatened the harmony of the black congregation. It had no local ordained deacons and was, thus, even more dependent on the white Methodist elder for pastoral attention. The founders of Ezion believed they could "refuse any that were not thought proper to preach," but they ran into stiff opposition in 1812 from white elder, James Bateman. When the charter members of Ezion resisted him that winter, Bateman summarily "turned out all the Trustees and class-leaders." The two sides ended in court, but Spencer's protesters lost the case. A minority of black members, siding with the white elder, retained the church property for the denomination, while the remainder followed Spencer in a second schism within eight years in Wilmington Methodism.[57]

The separatists moved rapidly. Forming a board of seven trustees (four of whom were listed as "labourers" and two as blacksmiths in the city directory), they purchased a lot in July, 1813, and opened their building by fall. Incorporating under the Delaware law of 1787 which *authorized* religious bodies, the African Union Church drew up "articles of association" for itself, dated September 18, 1813. Forty charter members, six of whom were women, signed the document.[58]

By the end of the first year, the Wilmington church had linked up with a congregation in Pennsylvania and another in New York to begin denominational connections. In 1815 new churches began in Christiana and New Castle, Delaware. Following the death of "Father" Spencer in 1843, the church suffered fragmentation, but it survived to lay claim to the first black denominational break with the Methodist Episcopal Church.[59]

The African Union movement represented the sharpest fracture with the biracial denomination from which it withdrew. In contrast with both other African Methodist communions, the Unionists simplified their polity. They elected five laymen as ruling elders in each congregation, where power was vested for licensing local preachers and ordaining ministers. Rejecting both the presiding eldership and the episcopacy, the African Union church retained ordination of deacons, who could preach and baptize but not celebrate the Lord's Supper or administer church discipline, and of elder ministers who had full authority in these matters.[60]

The struggle for independence in Wilmington was essentially a lay movement, since neither Spencer nor Anderson were ordained clergy. It emphasized local autonomy more than connectionalism. By providing a skeletal structure as a small denomination, however, the African Union church made it possible for other congregations to organize, to own their own property, and to participate in every level of church government in a congregational or "associated" polity. Insuring black control of local churches, the Unionists gained what had been prohibited them in the Methodist Episcopal Church.[61]

## IV

"So long as we remain in that situation our Preachers would never be able to enjoy these privileges which the Discipline of the white Church holds out to all its members that are called to preach, in consequence of the limited access our brethren had to those privileges, and particularly in consequence of the difference of color." Abraham Thompson, James Varick and William Miller state the source of the separation of Zion Methodism in their "Founder's Address" of 1820.[62]

A third black Methodist denomination began in an independent congregation which was originally part of the John Street church of New York City. Six black classes under white leaders existed as early as 1793, when there were 143 members.[63] In August, 1796, some of that number conferred with Bishop Asbury to request permission to meet separately with their own class leaders. In October, that group rented a house on Cross Street, where they gathered during the next four years for prayer meetings and preaching services. Three of their number, James Varick, Abraham Thompson, and June Scott were licensed by the John Street quarterly conference, which still maintained formal authority over the black society in behalf of the denomination.[64]

In 1799, the Zion society, as it was called, selected trustees and announced a "subscription" before the public to erect "an African church in the city." By July of the next year, the cornerstone was laid at a site on Leonard and Church streets. In September the structure was dedicated. During the next six months the trustees obtained a charter for the church and worked out, as instructed by the General Conference of 1800 to which they had appealed, "Articles of Agreement" with the denomination. Appropriately, John McClaskey, fresh from participating in the same process in Philadelphia, was pastor of the John Street church who acted as formal agent for the New York conference.[65]

There were two significant differences between what had been negotiated in Philadelphia and what transpired with the trustees of Zion church, led by Peter Williams, Sr. The document signed in 1801 in New York formed a board of black trustees, but limited their function to maintaining property for the denomination. In contrast to Philadelphia, these trustees had no authority in matters of church discipline. That restriction kept the Zion society more dependent on the denomination than the Bethel church was. Secondly, the agreement in New York defined the process by which local preachers could be granted ordination as local black deacons. Such authorization both promised a new level of inclusion and simultaneously restricted ordination to the ambiguous legislation of 1800. Any further advancement to elder's orders would require new general conference legislation, a procedure limited to the quadrennial sessions of that body.[66]

Over the next two decades, the Zion church avoided some of the bitter controversy with denominational officials which had erupted in Philadelphia, but it faced internal dissension over matters which remained unsettled in the Articles of Agreement. First, blacks had to wait five years before the first three of their local preachers were ordained local deacons by Asbury. In 1808 William Miller and Daniel Coker joined Varick, Thompson, and Scott, who had been made deacons in 1806, in that rank. Without a plan for rotating black preachers who did not belong to the conference's itinerant ministry, there was inevitable competition among five ordained deacons in one congregation. By 1810, Coker moved to Baltimore. In 1812 Thompson and Scott joined the African Free Methodist Society, led by a former Quaker, John Edwards, but it soon disbanded. Thompson kept his standing in Zion church by returning apologetically, but Scott left for good. Two years later, in February, 1814, Miller founded, with Thomas Sipkins (a former trustee of Zion), a new black Methodist church named African Asbury. By the process of elimination, Varick became the central leader of Zion church, with Thompson as his assistant.[67]

Beginning in 1808, Zion church had become a community center for free blacks in New York City. It hosted five of the next six annual New Year's Day celebrations of the end of the African slave trade. The occasion was marked by parades which featured the city's black benevolent associations and by religious services with choral music and orations. The black preachers connected to Zion congregation figured prominently in the festivities. For 1810, William Miller was the orator, for example, while James Varick was the evening preacher for the first commemoration in 1808. George White, a local preacher, prayed in the ceremonies of 1810, as did Miller and Varick the next year. Abraham Thompson was the preacher on January 1, 1811.[68]

Proclaiming their public convictions about the evil of slavery and celebrating their own freedom, these Zion churchmen provoked the taunts and vandalism of white mobs, but their response was not passive acceptance. Rather they complained formally to the Common Council of New York on at least four occasions between 1807 and 1817, charging that the watchmen of the city were neglecting their duties. They asserted their rights to protection of church property and of religious assembly without interruption.[69]

The perennial goal of the Zionite movement, as it had been for the Bethel congregation in Philadelphia, was access to the regular ministry and conference membership for black preachers. For the entire period of its autonomous existence, from 1796 through 1822, the Zion church had white elders as senior pastors who rotated preaching and pastoral assignments throughout the city. Local black deacons, from 1806, and licensed preachers served under white direction. At the time the congregation began a new building to meet the demands of increased membership in 1818, that practice became a liability, especially after Richard Allen's denomination came to town to form new churches for this connection.[70]

Over the next four years, Zion's leaders petitioned and negotiated, waited and planned, all the while hoping to find a way to remain within or attached to the Methodist Episcopal Church. That possibility required what the General Conference since 1800 and the episcopal leaders of the denomination persistently refused to do—ordain blacks as elders and accept both deacons and elders into conference membership, or, create an "African conference" as part of the connection.

After deciding not to join the Bethel movement, the Zion congregation began to move on its own in the summer of 1820. With the backing of the white elder, William Stillwell, who was leaving the Methodist Episcopal ministry over differences of polity, the members printed a *Discipline* for themselves. In November, Varick and Thompson served their first communion on their own.[71] Meanwhile, they kept pressing for a way to obtain full ordination. Twenty-one months later, after being refused by three Methodist bishops, two annual conferences, and the Protestant Episcopal bishop of New York, the two deacons, with Leven Smith, were consecrated elder by three sympathetic white elders from the parent denomination.[72] A month afterward, Varick became the first superintendent of the Zion denomination, which quickly attracted congregations on Long Island, New Haven, and Philadelphia.[73]

Some adherents to the new movement still hoped that sympathetic white Methodists would be able to convince the General Conference of 1824 to set up "an annual conference for our coloured preachers." That conference dashed those expectations, and continued the exclusive precedent until the Washington and Delaware colored conferences were formed in 1864.[74] Left to go its own way, the African Methodist Episcopal, Zion denomination, which rarely used the appendage "Zion" for much of the antebellum period, completed the institutionalization of racial separation by denomination among Methodists until these were renewed during the era of Reconstruction.[75]

## V

"Your committee feel well satisfied from good authority, that it is not yet time to set off an annual conference, for our coloured preachers; and that such an act, would not at this time, be useful to them, or us; but dangerous to thiers [sic], and our common good." Report of the Committee to whom was referred the affairs of the people of colour, Methodist Episcopal General Conference, 1824.[76]

Though there were differences between the four case studies in this essay, black Methodists in each city faced a set of common circumstances. Their routes to congregational autonomy carried them through the processes of property ownership, church building and maintenance, black trusteeism, access to local preacher, exhorter and diaconal ranks of ministry, the control of congregational discipline and the question of denominational representation. In Philadelphia, where the refusal to grant full ordination was the most blatant, the Bethel congregation took the overwhelming majority of black Methodists into a new separated denomination. In Baltimore, the Bethel secessionists had no separate property claims, which remained with black loyalists who were in the majority and who remained the largest black congregations in episcopal Methodism until after the Civil War. Denial of elder's orders and hence of denominational representation lay behind the dissatisfaction of the separatists who refused to be pacified by the agreement of 1814 seeking to receive more attention from white pastors. In Wilmington, the Baltimore story had been foreshadowed when the loyalists at Ezion church maintained property for the Methodist Episcopal denomination. The African Union church was unable to protect any of its resources which its founder had possessed when active in the Asbury and Ezion congregations. Once again, conflicts with white elders triggered a schism. In New York the Zion church riveted its attention on the issue of ordination, remaining patient beyond any realistic expectation that the Methodist Episcopal Church would budge from its policies of the previous twenty years. When the plan for an African conference within the biracial denomination failed, a third denominational break was inevitable.

The anomaly of the black local deacon as episcopal Methodism's limit to black ministerial standing had no comparable precedent in the early African Baptist and African Presbyterian organizations in Boston (1805), New York (1808) and Philadelphia (1809, 1811). Biracial Baptist associations and presbyteries ordained blacks to the ministry and accepted them and their congregations into regular status in their judicatories. In contrast, the Methodist Episcopal legislation on the black diaconate was kept private, and all ordinations performed by Asbury were conducted apart from regular conference procedures. Without full ordination, there was no chance for direct denominational representation and participation in governance. Episcopal Methodism upheld that prohibition throughout the pre-Civil War period, symbolizing the same denial of political participation by blacks in civil government at national, state, and local levels. Only the Protestant Episcopal Church practiced a comparable discrimination. It granted priestly orders to its first African candidates, but diocesan leaders denied, first in Pennsylvania and then in New York, congregational representation to black churches and their ministers.[77]

The African Methodisms illustrate an important application of lay trusteeism, a movement pervasive in both white Protestant and Roman Catholic churches of the same period. If the black membership in the four Methodist societies considered in this paper had been unable to have black trustees, the economic basis for owning property and erecting church buildings would have been undermined. The St. Thomas African Episcopal Church pioneered the movement, and Allen and his Methodist associates were quick to emulate it.

The Zion society in New York did not have as much power vested with the trustees, but their presence insured the grounds for a separate establishment. In Baltimore and Wilmington, where independence meant the loss of property, black trustees loyal to the Methodist Episcopal Church retained their power and forced new options upon those who seceded.

The Bethel congregation in Philadelphia made the most effective use of trusteeism for controlling pastoral assignments and for exercising congregational discipline and authority. In Baltimore and New York, the thrust for independence came from the ministerial leadership, black deacons, local preachers and exhorters, while in Wilmington the movement was based entirely in lay leadership. Pastoral and disciplinary issues did not hamper the independent developments among black Baptists and Presbyterians since their pastors had full ordination and equal ministerial standing and since matters of church discipline had no been racially divisive. The trustees and vestry of St. Thomas Episcopal church had comparable power to the trustees of Bethel church in Philadelphia, but they did not exercise it in ways that provoked controversy or forced decisions about denominational separation and reorganization.

Interpreters of black church history have often claimed that the evangelical fervor of the Second Great Awakening accounts for the fact that blacks gravitated to Methodist and Baptist churches rather than to more ritualistic or confessional denominations. Following Donald Mathews' revisionist interpretation of the early nineteenth century revivals, our study of the origins of three African Methodisms demonstrates that black Methodists participated in distinctive ways in the organizational revolution of American Protestantism which is the social meaning of the second awakening. They worked with the institutional innovations of the Methodist system to promote local, then connectional autonomy. They moved into lay roles as trustees and class leaders. They became local preachers and exhorters. They sought ordination and got a partial resolution. They purchased property and built churches. When the logic of their developing autonomy failed to include conference membership for ministers, direct representation in the denomination and full ordination, the biracial association which existed for a generation broke down and complete independence brought black denominationalism.[78]

## CHAPTER 8

# "That Language Might Be Given Me": Women's Experience in Early Methodism

Diane H. Lobody

## ON LANGUAGES, SILENCE, VOICES, AND RUCKUS

> A word after a word
> after a word is power.
> -Margaret Atwood[1]

Scholars and poets, like Lord Peter Wimsey, find it so easy to get drunk on words that they are seldom perfectly sober. We live on language, souse ourselves in literature, and, tipsy with the heady brew of ideas, reel happily from one intoxicating text to another. "I wonder how many," Margaret Atwood muses about women like herself, "closed themselves in rooms, drew the curtains, so they could mainline words."[2]

Over the past few years, this inebriation has begun to betray itself most notably within the ordinarily sober (although not altogether temperate) realms of Methodist historiography and feminist scholarship. With slightly dizzying artistry, some of our most interesting thinkers are generating page after page of words about words. Creatively and compellingly, writers are exploring issues of language, narrative, silence, and voice in the texts of history and in the texts of individual lives, suggesting that these rich linguistic and verbal structures are appropriate devices for interpreting contemporary and historical experience.

Russell E. Richey, for instance, has discerned a variety of distinctive languages in early American Methodism, and has constructed an elegant hermeneutic that invites us to penetrate Methodist controversies and communities through careful attention to these ofttimes competing vocabularies. Nathan O. Hatch has alerted us to the power of republican rhetoric—a "grammar of liberty"—in the political discourse of the early republic, and argues persuasively that this language, which found expression in the widely diverse religious movements of the period, may well be construed as the lingua franca uniting such otherwise disparate belief systems as Mormonism and Methodism. Donald G. Mathews, with his comfortable blend of sensitivity and common sense, reminds us of the profoundly oral dynamic operating in early Methodist experience, whose substance was "the spoken word, the event and act of preaching and responding, the fusing together of individuals who poured their interior life into a sharing community through testimony, song, shout, and laughter." Each of these historians, with differing emphasis, lifts up for us the deeply verbal character of early Methodist life; this was a religious faith whose scaffolding was narrative and whose foundation was the transforming word.[3]

Carving out a parallel channel, feminist scholars in a variety of disciplines have noticed that metaphors of voice and silence are central, defining, and organizing principles for women seeking to understand and describe their own lives. Maria Harris observes that "in innumerable conversations as well as in essays and books, women studying women use as the starting point the experience of women's silence and the accompanying and complementary work of finding a voice."[4] Evocative book titles bespeak the prominence of this motif: In a Different Voice; Nobody Speaks for Me; Silences; The Sound of Our Own Voices; Talking Back.[5] Feminist theologians—male and female—have been particularly attuned to the intricate relationship of language, identity, empowerment, and religion; they have noted with ruthless clarity that the position of women in Christianity has often been both unspoken and literally unspeakable, that silence and oppression are closely interwoven, and that cultural transformation is notoriously accompanied by the din and roar of disorderly persons claiming their voices.

Noisy believers certainly populated the Methodist Episcopal Church in its infancy; woods and barns trembled with the shouts and praises of women and men, slave and free, the old and the poor and the disenfranchised. Recent studies in the history of early Methodism have begun to rummage about for clues that might explain why so many persons who were culturally marginalized—and canonically silenced—were drawn to unite with Methodist societies. Again, the work of Mathews is luminous; William H. Williams and Doris E. Andrews have also brought formidable insight to bear on this issue.[6] All three historians point to the notable presence of white women in early Methodism, and each ponders the ideologies of church and society that might explain Methodism's attractiveness to such women.

In related ways, these three scholars describe the explicitly counter-cultural value system owned by early Methodists and explore its empowering impact upon white women. Andrews remarks upon the egalitarian impulse in Methodism and its congruent support of the ideology of republican virtue, arguing that women found in class meetings and societies the very structures that supported women's development as widely admired republican mothers. Williams identifies the Wesleyan theological and ethical message that formed a revolutionary environment in which women found independence, self-esteem, and power not accessible to them in the dominant culture. Mathews conceives early Methodism as a liminal region, a fundamentally disorderly movement whose preaching and practice both mandated and enabled women to challenge or fracture relationships of social and sexual deference.

This egregiously prolonged foray into contemporary historiographical currents is not merely (although it is deservedly) a courtesy on the part of an historian who owes a great deal to the collective insights of this community of scholars. Rather, something very striking happens to our understanding of women's experience in early Methodist culture when we line up these three scholarly trajectories—translating the languages of early Methodism, listening for the silences and voices of women, catching the echoes of the Methodist appeal—and adjust those trajectories ever so slightly, allowing them to converge and cross and redirect one another.

With new subtlety, these perspectives inform the way we might hear the narrative legacy of male preachers and white laywomen. They suggest to us that women's experience within early Methodism was not least a matter of women finding voice, that the disciplines and spirituality of Methodist life and practice nourished and supported women in the process of "speaking themselves," that the Wesleyan theology and ecclesiastical structure of the Methodist Episcopal Church served (to borrow Nelle Morton's familiar and memorable image) to hear women into speech.[7]

In a very real sense, it is well nigh impossible to climb into the lives of long-dead people and root out their understandings of religious meaning and personal identity. The prospect becomes more disheartening when the long-dead are women of the eighteenth century. Many literate women did indeed record their thoughts, feelings, observations, and experiences in diaries and letters. But the words of many women crumbled ineluctably into oblivion; women's personal writings were all too often considered to be of such little consequence that they were discarded or left to molder in attics.

There are, though, some significant extant sources. The journals and memoirs of circuit riders offer captivating glimpses of women in this period. More important, these writings evoke the ethos of early Methodism so vividly that we are able sympathetically to feel our way into their world and capture several visions of what this experience meant for women. In addition, the writings of some women have also been fortuitously preserved. In particular, because of their breadth and intimacy, the two thousand pages of Catherine Livingston Garrettson's diaries and correspondence provide an exceptional window on the interior life of an early Methodist woman. This essay will treat Garrettson's writings and the journals of selected Methodist preachers as a complicated (and not always dust-free) lens through which we might see and attend to the experiences of white Methodist women in the early American republic.[8]

Catherine Garrettson (1752–1849) was a daughter of the New York branch of the preposterously wealthy and politically prominent Livingston family. She converted to Methodism at the age of thirty-five (to the utter mortification of her family) and compounded her unfortunate social faux pas by promptly falling in love and marrying the Reverend Freeborn Garrettson, an upstart Methodist preacher who had evangelized the Livingston territory. The Livingstons were appalled by Catherine's shockingly bad taste in religion and husband, and much of her writing needs to be read within the framework of both the Livingston hostility and Catherine's urgent compulsion to convince and convert her relatives.

Within weeks of her conversion, Garrettson began to keep a diary in which she assiduously recorded her progress in the Christian life, her battles with sin and Satan, her movement toward holiness of heart, her providential messages from God in dreams, and her visions and ecstasies in experiencing the blessing of perfection. The narrative of her early pilgrimage in this new life in Christ throbs with rhythms of speech and silence. These writings are laced with her struggles to find language, to give utterance, to yank the inaccessible words from her willing heart, to speak freely, eloquently, and adequately:

> I had nothing to wish but to be more worthy, and that language might be given me from above, to express my most grateful thanks. . . . Wrote to my sisters, and endeavored to make them sensible of the goodness of my Divine Redeemer: but Eloquence here must fail; tis to be enjoyed not described![9]

Her patterns of speech and silence, her initiation into a new language and vocabulary, and her emergence into her own (and distinctively Methodist) voice all beckon us to listen to the complicated interplay of women's self-definition and early Methodist spirituality.

# REVOLUTION, REPUBLICANISM, AND THE DAUGHTERS OF LIBERTY

"I'm *serious*, Nate! I want to be a Minuteperson!"
-Amy Harris, Revolutionary foremother of Doonesbury's Zonker[10]

The Revolutionary War and the subsequent national conversations about democracy and liberty stretched and pulled at the hopes and identities of all persons in the new republic. The Methodist appeal to women is scarcely comprehensible if we slight the impact and consequences of revolutionary and republican sensibilities on the lives of women. The malleable new social order offered only partial fulfillment of the whispered possibilities and tentative dreams entertained by women in the new nation. The Methodist environment, however, created opportunities for a considerably expanded public role and voice. Our understanding of women's need to claim that voice must begin with consideration of the wider social and political context.

Hatch and Richey have discovered some of the unexpected twists that democratic rhetoric could take in shaping the behavior and thinking of male religious leaders. A number of more secularly inclined historians remind us that the same language of liberty was avidly appreciated by a vast audience of American women.[11] The women who united with Methodist societies in the late eighteenth century had been irrevocably transformed and reconstituted in the crucible of war. The very circumstances of this war forced women out of the private and domestic realm and demanded that they take public and political stances. Wartime economy depended on women who boycotted English goods, concocted herbal teas, wove and wore homespun, and ran farms and businesses in the absence of their male relatives. Throughout the conflict, nearly every domestic decision was also a political one. The novelty of women claiming public voices—in writings, in mob demonstrations, in fundraising, in spinning bees—did not go unnoticed by men or by the women themselves. While women perfunctorily apologized for moving into the political sphere, they also readily marshalled democratic arguments and adopted, for their own as well as national concerns, the language of liberty.

Women were especially cognizant of their vulnerability and of the human cost of war. Battles were fought in their front yards; women were raped, their homes invaded, their property seized, their relatives slaughtered. Garrettson's own family was in the thick of patriot activity; a gunpowder mill was constructed on the Livingston property, and early in the conflict she and the other women of her household watched as their home was torched by the British. "I join with you my dear Madam in wishing that the tumults of War was no more," she wrote to Mercy Otis Warren in 1781. "The inhabitants of our frontier are flying down in droves before an Enemy we are too weak to oppose. A few days since, a large tract of country was laid waste. Men, Women, and Children wantonly murdered, and the few unfortunates that escaped, exchanged affluence and ease, for unsheltered poverty and wretchedness."[12]

When peace was declared in 1783, it was clear to the victors that the principles of liberty had triumphed. It was evident as well that political structures, social hierarchies, and familiar relationships had been irrevocably altered and would continue to undergo considerable negotiation and reevaluation. In ways both obvious and invisible, gender became an agenda. Politicized women who had been shoved out of their domestic borders and who had paid a huge price for democratic ideals positioned themselves for participation in the new republic.

But their status was hauntingly ambiguous. Having participated actively in the war, women found themselves constitutionally and legally still silenced, although few had even imagined that they would be given full rights of citizenship. Expected to be virtuous mothers training their children in the arts of republican virtue, women nonetheless heard virtue almost exclusively defined in terms of virility and masculinity, while vice was decried as effeminacy and weakness. Enlightenment philosophes had exercised their psychological adroitness by positing the "perfectibility of man," but barely conceived the extension of that vision to include the perfectibility of woman. Liberty was symbolically portrayed as the Goddess, but some women took a jaundiced view of her power to change their circumstances. "I confess I have not such romantic notions of the Goddess," commented one of Catherine's distant cousins. "You know that our sex are *doomed* to be obedient in every stage of life so that *we* shant be great gainers by this contest."[13] America itself had consistently been imaged as "a fragile woman in the wilderness beset by the 'malignant rages' of the red dragon," but the fragile woman had conquered.[14] The culture, as Linda Kerber has noted, had to devise a notion of women's citizenship and develop a new understanding of the civic role of women in the republic, one that took women seriously as competent, rational, independent persons and politicized their traditional roles.[15]

Garrettson's few existing pre-conversion letters, which date from this early post-war period, manifest the shifting and ambivalent opinions that women held about gender and their own sex. While she castigated her own sex for its duplicity, artifice, credulity and weakness, she also dismissed the misogynist letters of the Earl of Chesterfield (a wildly popular book) and worried about her brother's propensity to fritter away his time in such frivolous (and unvirtuous) pursuits as the theatre and dancing.[16]

Garrettson's sense of the chaos swirling around gender relationships was rendered even more uneasy by personal interactions. She loved her four brothers deeply, and deemed her parents' marriage a model of mutual devotion and respect. And yet she and her mother were obliged to provide sanctuary for

Nancy Shippen Livingston when Nancy fled her abusive husband Henry, Catherine's brother. Despite the support of the Livingston women, Nancy found herself with no legal right to sue for divorce and no legal right, within or outside marriage, to retain custody of their daughter. Catherine herself was not about to abdicate her own rights to a mutually affirming relationship in marriage, and the pliant cultural discussions were raising pointed questions about older patterns of deference of wives to husbands. Fending off the unendurable and emotionally extortionate advances of one of Mercy Warren's brothers, Catherine wrote a firm letter of rejection. Her merciless dismissal of Mr. Otis hinged on her unwillingness to compromise her sense of self-worth: "I have frequently asserted to you sir, that I should forever forfeit my own esteem were I capable of giving my hand to any who had not the most indisputable [hold] over my Heart also."[17]

The troubling dynamics in Garrettson's personal life were not and are not unusual for any woman or man. But in this era, as people discerned the cultural confusion reflected in their private relationships, women like Garrettson began to long for satisfying resolution. They found themselves dismayed by prevailing moral values, disturbed by destructive social behaviors, and distressed by their truncated freedom to govern their own lives. In a time of debates over individual rights and republican obligations, faced with a precarious future and crumbling social structures, cacophony reigned. Finding the dissonance increasingly harsh, Garrettson turned to evangelical religion in a quest for harmony, meaning, and spiritual peace. In the Methodist Episcopal Church, she and many women like herself found a compassionate and stern community engaged in the business of reconfiguring values, relationships, and conceptions of personhood. Early Methodism provided a structure—a grammar and a rhythm—by which believers could order and organize their worlds in a new way. A significant evidence of the power of that remarkable grammar and rhythm was the unsilencing of women.

## OPENING THE GRAMMAR AND ENTERING THE RHYTHMS

> When I am a woman—O, when I am
> a woman,
> my wells of salt brim and brim,
> poems force the lock of my throat.
> -Denise Levertov[18]

Liberty as symbol and as event was freighted with powerful meanings for Americans in the early republic. Even the most political constructions on this word carried extraordinarily mythic overtones; one Revolutionary preacher had

133

depicted liberty as "the daughter of God, and excepting his Son, the first born of heaven."[19] Methodists—both preachers and laypersons—readily claimed the idea of liberty and vested it with a particularly evangelical authority. The word itself pulsates in the preachers' journals with rhythmic, almost formulaic, regularity: preachers preached with liberty, prayed with liberty, set their listeners at liberty. Liberty in this kerygmatic context was always connected with the spoken word. The speaking of the word in liberty was an undeniable manifestation of God's presence; the word spoken in liberty had a supernatural power to convert—that is, to set listeners at liberty from sin; the liberated believer was then given liberty by God to speak the saving word to those who were still in captivity.

Women were the hearers, the receivers, and the bearers of liberty, just as the preachers were. An incident recorded by Benjamin Lakin is instructive. In succinct fashion, Lakin describes the complete cycle of liberty for women:

> Had liberty in preaching, and the Lord was with us in class. One woman got so happy that she hung upon her husband in raptures of joy. Then she ran through the house. But the house could not hold her she rushed out at the door to invite others to come to Jesus. All the time her countenance bore the most solemn appearance. Others some were shouting and some in tears, God was with us of a truth.[20]

The images in this vignette are provocative. The freeing word in preaching and in community brought profound joy to this unnamed woman whose first instinct was to cling to her husband. She then moved out of his orbit, and raced through the house. *But the house could not hold her.* That sentence alone could stand as a distillation of Methodist women's experience. The liberating word and the liberating community rocketed women out into wider and wider circles over the generations. Even in this early period, Lakin's anonymous woman moved from husband to house and then out the door, where she found her voice and invited others to come to Jesus. In all of this, she was affirmed and supported by her shouting, weeping, praying companions in the glorious liberty of the children of God.

The ritual, institutional, and disciplining structures of early Methodism provided unprecedented opportunity for huge numbers of women to experience liberty and to begin, in poet Marge Piercy's words, "unlearning to not speak."[21] As Mathews has noted, the preaching in early Methodism was predicated on the interactive call and response between preacher and people. The power of God might at any moment open the mouths of the community and unleash the groans, the sobs, the shouts, the praises, the songs, the prayers, the testimonies of any of the people. Silence in the context of preaching was in fact a sign of the presence of tenacious sin. Hardhearted, recalcitrant, obstinate hearers who refused to permit the word of God to enter and transform their hearts manifested their willful attachment to sin by their deadly and unresponsive silence.

This ritual expectation that the preached word called for response injected some women with a winsome gutsiness, a zest for confronting non-Methodist clergymen on their own turf. Thomas Ware describes the unexpected reception given to an Episcopal priest by a congregation who had been infected by Methodist preaching:

> 'John Wesley,' [the priest] continued, 'was the prince of enthusiasts. He, with his babbles, as Rowland Hill calls them, has filled England with enthusiasts. And mark! no stream can rise higher than its source; consequently the preaching of the Methodists can only kindle an enthusiastic flame—a mere ignis fatuus—in any one.' As he thus expressed himself, a very interesting, pious female cried out, 'Glory to God! If what I now feel be enthusiasm, let me always be an enthusiast!' This was a quietus, and threw the clergyman into serious embarrassment, as it was too evident not to be perceived by all that this rebuke from a lady highly esteemed for her accomplishments and piety, was approved by the congregation generally as justly merited.[22]

Episcopal, Baptist, and Calvinist clergymen found themselves frequently at the mercy of vocal and disorderly Methodist women. In finding voice, women were also supported by a fundamental evangelical conviction that no human authority could be permitted to stand between the believer and God. If her experience and her reading of scripture revealed a truth to a Methodist woman, then no ecclesiastical convention or theological etiquette would stand in the way of her speaking her mind.

Clergymen were therefore besieged by strong-minded Methodist women arguing doctrine and talking back. Catherine Garrettson, for instance, was staying with her sister when the Dutch Reformed pastor came to invite the family to attend holy communion:

> I told him if he would admit a Methodist, I should be glad to come also; but he refused me bluntly. We entered into some arguments on the doctrines of the Methodist Church. The fear of man was taken from me, and I was taught to defend the innocent with zeal and love. Alas! how does prejudice transform. This dear man told absolute falsehoods of the Arminian Creed, and then said he did not believe any one of that sect would ever go to heaven. I told him we did not say such harsh things. We believed that many Calvinists would go there.

Uppity women do get their rewards. Although barred from the dominie's table, Catherine received an immediate consolation from Jesus Christ himself:

> Glory be to his dear and ever blessed name He gave me a lively hope, that tho' I was refused by man to be a partaker of his Broken Body and shed Blood, yet spiritually I might partake of without the outward means.[23]

The love feasts celebrated at quarterly meetings provided a more structured and profoundly emotional environment in which women could and did find voice. The sacramental character of shared bread and water received sacred language in the sharing of word and testimony. The love feast was the deep meeting place of private and public experiences of God. All persons were invited to testify to their most intimate experiences of God's love. In the intensity of this environment, women and men often felt themselves overwhelmed by the knowledge of God's love and grace, and were compelled as if by God's power to speak publicly of this witness. William Watters delicately etches the emotional power of the love feast:

> Our love feast was one of the best I ever was in. We sat together in heavenly places; and to express myself in the words which I immediately wrote down, I was as in a little Heaven below, and believe Heaven above will differ more in quantity than in quality. Never did I hear such experiences before. Our eyes overflowed with tears, and our hearts with love to God, and each other. The holy fire, the heavenly flame, spread wider and wider, and rose higher and higher.[24]

Swept away by the rush of communal emotions, women could transcend their inclination toward public reticence and speak with authority and eloquence before large groups of men and women.

The sinews of Methodism, though, were its classes, and these more intimate ritual settings consistently served to structure women's speaking. It was here that women became fluent in the grammar of public discourse. Every person who united with a Methodist society became a member of a class, and some also belonged to bands. At every stage of one's pilgrimage—from awakening through perfection—the believer participated in an ordered rhythm of community life. Within the context of the class meeting, the class leader counseled with each member about the state of her or his soul, and all members were invited, encouraged, and expected to pray aloud and to narrate publicly their struggles, problems, and hopes.

Women and men alike related the ongoing stories of their lives, and class knew no rank. In these egalitarian relationships, women found invigorating support and bracing nurture as they revealed their deepest feelings. Within this fertile environment, women also discovered their power to speak publicly in love, advising, critiquing, and confronting the other members of the community.

The narrative structure of Wesleyan spirituality demanded that women tell their stories; these stories were heard with acute attention, for they were laden with implications for the narrator's salvation. They had cosmic significance— eternity depended on detailed self-disclosure. Women hauled out their most private thoughts, laid them on a public altar, and saw them treated with the utmost respect and tender solicitude. William Watters describes an emotionally exhilarating class meeting, in which the interplay of eternity, community, and individual importance are forcefully conveyed:

> On that day four weeks, I had been peculiarly stirred up to seek the Lord, to deepen his work in my heart, and at the same place as brother D___d was speaking to the class, just after I had been preaching, many were groaning for a deeper work of grace, while our hearts melted before the Lord as wax before the fire, and the Spirit and the bride said, come, O! come and accomplish thy gracious promises in our souls. Come and destroy the man of sin, and make us complete in thy image. He spoke to each one in particular, and earnestly pressed them to look up by faith, and to look up now just as they were.[25]

That gentle invitation addressed to "each one in particular" took seriously the individual circumstances of all the women present and heard women "just as they were." In class meetings, women could expose their shattered and wounded selves. They could and did speak of the unspeakable pains of isolation, abuse, poverty, loneliness. When Catherine Garrettson found herself cut off from support of other Methodists, she felt choked by silence: "I feel at times as if alone in the world, far from the society of those who [are] truly united to Jesus. My griefs and my joys are all shut up in my own bosom."[26]

By speaking their realities women discovered and gave to one another healing and integrity. "Openness," writes feminist bell hooks, "is about how to be well and telling the truth is about how to put the broken bits and pieces of the heart back together again. It is about being whole—being wholehearted."[27] Methodism opened a grammar of liberty for women, and that opening worked as a balm in Gilead, making the wounded whole.

## BECOMING FLUENT IN A SUBVERSIVE SPIRITUALITY

> But even with masculine dominance,
>     we mares and mistresses
> Produced some sleek saboteuses.
>                     -Carolyn Kizer[28]

The demands of early Methodism, reinforced by its disciplined spirituality, unintentionally gave women permission and authority to project their voices beyond the bounds of the class meeting. Methodism was a community of accountability, and John Wesley had provided a convenient yardstick of behavior in his "Nature, Design, and general Rules of the United Societies." Rules and expectations can have an inadvertently subversive effect. If one is part of a community whose regulations require members to act in socially unacceptable ways, then loyalty to the community gives one license to do so with impunity. The community code can confer justification to be as disorderly and improper as one may wish, and the burden of responsibility is borne only minimally by the believer. Wesley's rules were few but explicit, and one section was the catalyst for an explosion of women's voices:

> It is expected of all who continue in these societies, that they should continue to evidence their desire of salvation, Secondly, by doing good, by being in every kind merciful after their power, as they have opportunity, doing good of every possible sort, and as far as possible, to all men. . . .to their souls, by instructing, reproving, or exhorting all we have any intercourse with.[29]

Now here was one glorious opportunity for women. In the name of God and for the sake of the eternal destiny of perilously endangered souls, every Methodist—male or female—had been given the mandate to instruct, reprove, and exhort everybody in the entire world. Furthermore, according to Methodist discipline, every Methodist—male or female—was publicly accountable for his or her actions in honoring that obligation. When nervousness or timidity assailed women, the impetus to press on with this (potentially public) work of speaking was provided by the institutional structure.

That authority was also at the heart of the Wesleyan order of salvation. Progress in holiness was both bolstered and manifested by showing love and doing good to neighbors. It did not go unremarked by women that this expectation to instruct, reprove, and exhort fell under the category of "doing good." Women discovered that speaking was a good work, and that their growth toward perfection (itself a stunningly revolutionary notion for women to assimilate) could be advanced or impeded by their willingness and ability to speak to "all we have any intercourse with," no matter how public the circumstance.

In Catherine Garrettson's diaries, the themes of sanctification, voice, and usefulness are woven into a seamless cloth. Early in her new Methodist life, this articulate woman found herself mute, absolutely unable to express her experiences of God. "I experienced so much of the love of God that I wept for Joy. . . .my only grief was that I could not express the feelings of my heart, nor make any returns to my God for all his benefits conferred upon me but He who form'd the Heart, can read what he has written there." "O! that Language was given me adequate to the Sublimity of the Subject, that I might acknowledge how gracious, how tender, how like a God He acts with his Servants." "O! that I was able to speak to the tenderness of His love and bounty."[30]

Nor could she speak easily to other persons about these deep and important spiritual matters. "I had the pleasure of seeing a Mr. Dean, who I believe is on the road to *Zion*. I would have entered into conversation with him but I have not the power of conversing on religious subjects, tho' I may with sincerity say there is none that engages my affections, or interests my feelings, equal to them. But Lord my Master I submit; when thou shalt need my testimony, thou wilt open my Mouth."[31] Indeed, speaking tended all too often to be a dangerous opportunity for sin. Throughout the diaries she castigates herself for the sins of voice: speaking too frankly, laughing too freely, arguing too warmly, criticizing too bluntly.

Even as she wrestled with her incapacity to speak, Garrettson also lamented her inability to serve. She yearned fervently to be useful in God's work: "My path tis true, is a retir'd one; but in my little sphere can I do nothing?—quicken me O my God Teach me heavenly wisdom! Oh let me not pass thro' life and be of no service to my Fellow Creatures. Shew me in what manner I may be useful. And enlarge my Capacity."[32]

As she advanced in holiness, Catherine widened her "little sphere", found a career of usefulness in the prospect of marriage to Freeborn, and claimed a public voice. In 1792 she began to experience the blessings of perfect love. Those ecstatic visions and consummating hours of union with God unleashed the power of language: "The Lord has condescended to shew me in a wonderful manner that he has shut my mouth, and none should open it, that he would open, and none should shut it."[33]

The experience of perfect holiness issued forth in intercessory prayer, in shared testimony, and in evangelical exhortation. Writing to her friend Kitty Rutsen in 1793, Garrettson described in eloquent terms God's self-revelation of unifying love. She concluded her letter with instructions to share her words:

> Give my love to Br. Marretta you may if you please show him this letter; but you know my dear, there is not many who could hear it. I leave this to your discretion. If any one soul might be edified by what the Lord has condescended to do for his unworthy worm, I have no right to withhold what was freely given. O may I live the Servant of Christ's Church and ever hold myself bound to do all in my little sphere of action to promote its spiritual welfare.[34]

Garrettson, like many women, struggled mightily with her conflicting sentiments about public speaking and exhortation. "I hope you do not think I have any desire to be a public speaker," she wrote to Rutsen. "Ah! No. I want to do all the good I possibly can before I go hence, and am no more seen, both to the souls and bodies of men."[35] That, of course, was the rub. According to the Methodist community, doing all the good *included* public speaking when the circumstances demanded it. Garrettson cast the burden upon the Lord, praying "that he would give me strength and ability for any work he would be pleased to honor me with—particularly that he would be graciously pleased to 'Open my mouth, that my lips may show forth his praise.' That the fear of Fellow Worms may be removed, and that I may be bold as a Lion in the cause of my Lord. May the gentleness of the Lamb be added to this intrepidity."[36]

Garrettson found as she progressed in holiness that God compensated for her diffidence and weakness: "Was called upon to pray with the Family, would have evaded it; but could not. Glory be to God he was with me and taught me to speak."[37] Here and in every situation that required her to teach, criticize, and evangelize, God carried the responsibility and God received the glory, but Catherine did the speaking.

At times the cultural censure and her own internal conflicts became particularly stressful, and her desire to be a responsible speaking Methodist was nearly drowned out by these antagonistic public and private messages. In a theologically deft move, Garrettson translated those contrary noises as temptations from Satan. After one spectacular vision, she was beset by insecurities about the experience. She felt that Satan was responsible for these doubts, telling her that God would not bother to pay such attention to so worthless a creature as Catherine. Garrettson recognized a snare when she saw one: "I determined to go to my Class leader and speak to him on the subject, fain would my Adversary have kept me from this, by suggesting that these were the Secret Things of God, that I must not reveal. . . . I would not give way. I fulfilled my intentions, and found that the fiend was again stripped and stood confessed the Father of Lies."[38]

When smitten with doubt and uncertainty, it was immensely liberating to interpret those murmuring worries as demonic attacks. It was even more freeing to argue that God had put the words into her mouth and empowered her to speak. But she also openly acknowledged that she could not live with her own silence. "I know unless the Spirit of the Lord shall pour conviction on your mind," she wrote to an unconverted sister, "I shall only give offense by this letter. But this is far from my intention. Tho' if it were to have this effect I could write no otherwise; because I could not answer it to my conscience."[39]

Throughout subsequent generations Methodist women would anguish over their conflicting feelings about public speaking, and would use similar arguments to justify their deep desires to preach and debate in church and society. In early Methodism, the structures of spiritual discipline and the premises of Wesleyan theology were essential parts of the framework of support for women. They nurtured women's self-esteem by soliciting and celebrating their stories. That framework taught women to value their thoughts and their feelings. Women learned quickly that it was a responsible act to pay close attention and listen intently to themselves, and having done so then to speak with candor and courage. The very subversive spirituality of Methodism coaxed women into speech.

# OWNING A LANGUAGE AND SPEAKING IN TONGUES

> We are volcanoes. When we women offer our experience as our truth,
> as human truth, all the maps change. There are new mountains.
> —Ursula LeGuin[40]

Methodism embraces an episcopal polity, and in the early republic this ecclesiastical structure was cast in overtly patriarchal terms. We might well wonder about the effect upon women of what appears at a distance to be an overwhelmingly male institution. All the clergy were men, and, by the early nineteenth century, all the class leaders were men as well. Preachers bonded closely with one another as brothers, and the vehemently paternal character of the bishops can scarcely go unobserved.[41] Women appear to have been entirely excluded, and the ecclesiastical riots that ensued in later eras over the rights of women in the church indicate how tightly the fraternal bands were tied.

But the journals of these early Methodist clergy swell with the irrepressible presence of women. Women are everywhere in these writings: they provide meeting places, they house preachers, they exhort sinners, they argue with Baptists, they embarrass their husbands, they walk miles to come to preaching. Women are continually lifted up as mentors and models and mothers in Israel. Their presence was compelling, and in sheer numbers they always constituted the majority of members. Much of the appeal of Methodism was ignited by the structures of spirituality discussed earlier. But lurking in the diaries are hints of another source of Methodism's allure. This was a women's church because it spoke a women's language.

Like any culture, the early republic held incontrovertible assumptions about men and women. While questions about women's roles might still be up for negotiation, everybody was very clear about the fundamental qualities of womanliness. Certain basic characteristics defined excellent femininity: sentiment, tenderness, mercy, gentleness, submissiveness, self-sacrifice. Even some qualities that were classically understood to be masculine could be given over to women and redefined for feminine application: virtue translated into social responsibility, reason was feminine when it served family and republic. In all, it was evident to any rational person that most of the softer qualities were rightly the purview of women.

Richey has identified an entire popular language that dominated descriptions of Methodist community.[42] Within the context of early republican culture this language was suspiciously feminine; within the context of Methodist culture these loaded feminine words conveyed the personal and corporate experiences of men and women alike. Over and again, with almost ritual intonation, we hear the language of tender and uncontrollable emotionalism—the language of women's nature and behavior. Preachers and believers felt and wept, trembled and groaned; persons melted and softened and sank into God; hearts were "tendered" and filled and comforted. The power of God evidenced itself in the "quickening amongst the members," like the first stirring of life in the womb, and the passive voice dominates.[43]

Early Methodism *was* a stunningly emotional movement, and it is important to acknowledge how difficult it was to search out a language adequate to express the depths of feeling that this movement tapped. Garrettson once lamented, "that which ought to make the dumb Eloquent, makes me dumb!"[44] And men, who may well have been acculturated to express their feelings in more reasonable or perhaps antisocial ways (or indeed not at all), might have turned instinctively to this stereotypically feminine imagery in their attempt to find their own voices. The point here though, and this is simply suggestive, is that this vocabulary must have felt natural and comfortable for women. Affective and emotional language was their mother tongue. With little difficulty, women could resonate with a language and a community that understood tears, that melted with tenderness, that felt the presence of God as a mother feels the quickening of her child. This was familiar language expressing familiar feelings. Just as important, by elevating these feelings and adopting this language, the community validated and celebrated the experiences and perceptions of women. Here was a religious language that women could instantly embrace.

Women could also resonate with the theology of self-deprecation preached by the clergy. As Williams has observed, the characteristically feminine virtues of meekness, patience, self-sacrifice, love, and so forth were lifted up as praiseworthy, and in so doing "circuit riders affirmed female self-esteem."[45] That is no doubt true. But women in orthodox Christian churches had been hearing these virtues preached for generations without much apparent gain in feelings of self-worth.

Several dynamics seem to have operated in redeeming this theological language for women. First, not only were these virtues antithetical to the values often admired by the wider culture, but they were also antithetical to the nastier cultural depictions of female character. Lord Chesterton, whose letters had drawn Garrettson's ire, was typical in his estimation of women as gossipy, vain, unreasonable, frivolous, unforgiving, stupid "children of a larger growth."[46] The Methodist definitions of vice were not gender specific. Men as well as women could, if still in sin, be stupid and vain and so forth. Further, as cultural conceptions of virtue were inflated to make room for women's contributions to the republic, Methodist preaching served to reinforce those grander visions of useful womanly qualities.

More significant, though, was the extent to which the male preachers themselves incarnated the very feminine virtues they preached. They lived intentionally in imitation of the merciful, self-sacrificing, submissive Christ. This is particularly noticeable in their expressions of eagerness to live a Christ-like life in the midst of hardship and persecution. William Watters is exemplary in his explicit identification with his Lord:

> Tho' I was deprived of many conveniences, yet he made all up unto me in spirituals, and I was contented to sleep in cabins—to eat a dry morsel—and frequently to retire into the woods to read—to pray and meditate. My Lord and Master on earth had no place whereon to lay his head, and shall not I be thankful

for the meanest place? He was hated—spit upon—condemned—and crucified—and shall such a poor worm as I am look for anything better?[47]

And women too discerned their identity with Christ in equally dramatic fashion. Catherine recorded many versions of radical imitation, often in narratives of visions or dreams sent to her during periods of great suffering:

> I dreamed once since I came home that I was going to be crucified that they were raising the cross upon which I was stretched and I was in expectation of great sufferings.[48]

Preaching these Christ-like and feminine attributes carried great authority when the preachers themselves embodied those qualities, and that embodiment in turn may well have deepened their value to women who were already easily identified with those qualities. If men could willingly embrace feminine behaviors, then women could delight in those traits and more easily cherish themselves.

They could also cherish the preachers. In discussing the fraternal affection that bound the preachers together, Richey traces the subtle shifts of language that mark those relationships, charting in particular the use of the appellation "brother."[49] Interestingly, women also employed that language when addressing or referring to Methodist preachers.[50] Women appear to have found in their "brothers in the Ministry" a radical respect and a deep admiration for women as persons; certainly the preachers' journals radiate that affection and appreciation.

It is no wonder that Catherine Garrettson was perplexed by the decision of an evangelical friend to marry an unconverted man: "I heard a Woman yesterday mourning over her misfortune who was unequally yoked. O with what regret did she recall those happy days when she had none to molest her in the service of God. . . . Let others do as they please, for my part was I free from every engagement, I would sooner wed my coffin than a man that was not converted."[51] Note the language here: evangelical marriage is identified with equality; an unequal, unconverted partner is a molester; a coffin would be a preferable husband. These highly charged images crackle and spit. Women drew upon a vibrantly liberating force in their relationships with Methodist preachers. These men took seriously the needs, the gifts, and the identities of women as individual persons.[52]

Laywomen and clergymen resonated with one another on a level that lay very deep in their respective psyches. Their sense of mutual harmony was not merely a matter of men respecting and listening to women. In this liminal and chaotic Methodist culture, some of the rigid boundaries of gender were blurred. With unconscious grace, male preachers described themselves in evocatively feminine symbols, and Methodist women described themselves with provocatively masculine imagery.

143

William Watters, in a passage earlier quoted, portrays himself as one of the brides of Christ. Benjamin Lakin characterizes his affectionate attachment to his circuit as "an uncommon degree of effeminacy." Freeborn Garrettson sees himself as a mother whose children cling to her. Watters, also drawing upon maternal metaphors, envisions himself as gathering the people and feeding them with milk. In a more subtle link with a specific woman, Thomas Ware speaks of "the eloquence of tears" as a sign of his call to ministry, and later, in a thickly textured passage, identifies the converting power of a woman with her "eloquence of tears."[53]

Catherine Garrettson, in turn, seizes for herself martial and militant imagery. Her readiness to claim the language of battle and warfare, naming herself as a soldier of Christ, is one of the governing structures of her diary. Further, in dream narratives she colorfully experiences herself in priestly, pastoral, and kerygmatic roles.[54]

It is, of course, important not to read too much into the shadings of language. Neither men nor women ever own exclusive rights to so-called "masculine" or "feminine" qualities. But it is also vital that we not underrate the significance of such gender-crossing imagery, where men are feminized and women claim masculine qualities. As Linda Mercadante has persuasively demonstrated, a shift in gender imagery betrays a profound transformation in gender roles as they are lived out in the community.[55] Language reflects practice; language is political.

In early American Methodist culture, women's voices blended felicitously with the ecclesiastical men's chorus. Women's license to speak was legitimized by the sustained affirmation of men who honored, integrated, and incarnated feminine qualities. Women belonged in this community—they inhered, they fit. In an exquisite description of her place with these beloved companions, Catherine Garrettson narrated a dream:

> I now found myself in the region of the Blessed, and more happy than human frailty can tell. I was with a number of beauteous creatures, and inferior to none. One heart, one will seemed to unite us all.[56]

In early Methodism, as in few other cultures, women's voices were not discordant, their language was not dissonant, and their experiences were not off key. Here women were not the alien and mysterious "other", but sisters and friends, and—at least in the eyes of God and of themselves—inferior to none.

## CHAPTER 9

# The African Methodists
# of Philadelphia, 1794–1802

Doris Andrews

The story of the exodus of the black Methodists from St. George's Church in Philadelphia in the late eighteenth century and the subsequent founding of Bethel African Methodist Church was first told by Richard Allen in a memoir written late in his life.[1] Allen's story, famous as a symbol of black independence in the Revolutionary era, illustrates the extent to which interracial dynamics characterized social life and popular religion in post-Revolutionary Philadelphia. The birth of Allen's congregation in the city was not an accident: Philadelphia's free black population had grown rapidly with the migration of ex-slaves attracted by Pennsylvania's anti-slavery laws and jobs afforded by the city's expanding commercial economy. The founding of the church also highlights the malleable character of American religion at this time; the ways religious groups became rallying points for the disenfranchised, the poor, and the upwardly mobile; and the speed and confidence with which Americans created and re-created ecclesiastical structures and enterprises.

Despite the significance of this early black church, historians have not known the identities of the many black Philadelphians who became Methodists in the late eighteenth century, either those joining Allen's church or those remaining at St. George's.[2] The names of these African Methodists were in fact recorded in a register entitled "The Names of the Officers, and Members of the Methodist Church in Philadelphia," located among the records at the St. George's United Methodist Church at 4th and New Streets.[3]

N.B. I want to thank Richard Dunn, Gary Hash, and Jean Soderlund for their thoughtful comments, and Brian McCloskey, St. George's United Methodist Church, Philadelphia.

The itinerant preachers stationed at local churches or societies (the terms were used interchangeably) kept the Methodist membership registers which were usually of two types. One gives the names of individuals received on trial into a society, listed chronologically by date of admittance. The other type, usually taken down annually, records the "classes," or evangelical conscious- ness-raising groups into which Methodist societies were customarily divided. Probationers were assigned to a class as soon as they entered the church, and the name of the leader, the layman or woman in charge of the group's weekly sessions, follows each name in a register of probationers, or heads each class list in a register of classes. Methodist membership records thus illuminate the divisions within individual churches as well as lines of authority among the laity.

Reproduced here are the earliest surviving registers for the black classes at St. George's Methodist Episcopal Church, the class lists for Allen's African Methodist Episcopal Church, as well as the lists of probationers admitted into Zoar, a black Methodist society under the charge of St. George's. St. George's lists were not dated, but they were written by itinerant Thomas Morrell, who was stationed in Philadelphia from April 29, 1794, through April 21, 1795.[4] Morrell almost certainly took down the names of Blair, Smith, and York's classes in the period from May to July 1794. John Burkib, a member of York's class, did not join St. George's until May 26; the next black members, admitted on July 12 and 13, do not appear on the class lists, suggesting that Morrell had completed the record for the Philadelphia Society by this date.[5]

These records show that the classes at St. George's, like Methodist societies throughout the Middle Atlantic, were segregated by race. The registers are specifically identified as comprised of "black" members, distinct from the other eighteen white Methodist classes meeting in the city in 1794. Two were headed by white artisans, William Blair and Hugh Smith.[6] What is notable is that the third class leader, Jonathan York, was a black laborer, resident in Southwark where many Afro-American immigrants settled in the 1780s and 1790s. Thus in the early stages of Methodism in America, a black man of relatively low social status held a position of importance.[7]

In Philadelphia after the Revolution some blacks, like Richard Allen, also became prominent in the Afro-American community at large. Allen was born in the city in 1760 and spent most of his young adulthood working on a plantation in Delaware, where his master Benjamin Chew had sold Allen's family. He converted to Methodism when still a teenager and returned to Philadelphia in 1786 after six years of traveling as a day laborer and informal preacher in Delaware, New Jersey, and Philadelphia's western hinterlands. He quickly developed the idea of organizing a separate congregation for the city's black population, suggested it to "the most respectable people of color," but their reception was lukewarm. As an alternative measure, Allen and a number of other black Philadelphians in 1787 founded a mutual aid society, called the Free African Society, to assist free blacks "without regard to religious tenets, provided, the persons lived an orderly, and sober life, in order to support one another in sickness, and for the benefit of their widows and fatherless children." The group was religiously mixed and in addition to Allen included Methodists Absalom Jones, Dorus Jennings, and William White; Quaker Cyrus Bustill; and probably many black Anglicans.[8]

After the founding of the society a number of the black Methodists, the Free Africans prominent among them, left St. George's in a dispute over the segregation of seating within the chapel. At the beginning of a Sunday service following the construction of the church's galleries, the sexton directed Allen, Absalom Jones, William White, and other black members to sit in this new part of the building. They did so, expecting, as Allen writes in his memoir, to take seats above those they normally sat in on the ground floor. "We had not been long upon our knees," Allen continues, "before I heard considerable scuffling and low talking." What he was overhearing were two of the chapel's trustees attempting forcibly to remove Jones and White from their places. The black members, deeply offended by the behavior of their fellow church members, responded with group decorum and, as Allen writes, "we all went out of the church in a body."[9]

By the telescoping of events in his memoir, Allen appears to suggest that the confrontation at St. George's took place not long after the founding of the Free African Society, in the late 1780s, and that the decision to establish some kind of separate church immediately followed the incident. According to the financial accounts at St. George's, however, and a remark in Methodist bishop Francis Asbury's journal, the chapel's galleries were not completed until the late spring or early summer of 1792, dating the conflict at St. George's to several years after the founding of the Free African Society.[10]

By this date the Society, with the assistance of a public subscription and several influential white Philadelphians, Benjamin Rush among them, had already begun to carry out plans for constructing an African church on the second of two lots purchased in the New Market Ward the previous winter. These plans, furthermore, had been in the making since the summer of 1791. Opposing the project were a number of the city's white ecclesiastical leaders, including the Episcopalian bishop William White, several of the Quakers upon whom the Free Africans had been relying for meeting rooms, and the Methodist itinerant stationed at St. George's.[11] Judging by this sequence of events and the reaction of the religious establishment to the possibility that black Christians might move beyond their control, the aggressiveness of the trustees at St. George's can be seen as having stemmed at least in part from their resentment of the black Methodists' rising independence. In the long run, the Free Africans decided to affiliate themselves with the Protestant Episcopal rather than Methodist Episcopal Church and their chapel opened under the name "St. Thomas's" in July 1794. A number of the Methodists among the original members of the Free African Society, including Jones, White and Dorus Jennings, chose to join the new church; thus their names do not appear on St. George's register of classes in 1794.[12]

Allen, in the meanwhile, stayed with the Methodists, "Notwithstanding we had been so violently persecuted," he wrote in his memoir, "by the elder [the preacher stationed at St. George's]." Nevertheless, a number of the black Methodists preferred to remain a part of the Methodist Episcopal Church: "for the plain and simple gospel suits best for any people; for the unlearned can understand, and the learned are sure to understand; and the reason that the Methodist is so successful in the awakening and conversion of the colored people, the plain doctrine and having a good discipline." In May 1794 he and a group of other black Methodists held the first of several organizing meetings to set up an exclusively African Methodist congregation.[13] Allen does not explain why the Methodist conference changed its mind about an African church, but with the example of St. Thomas's, or by *fait accompli*, by the early summer of 1794 he had succeeded in putting his idea of an African Methodist Church, an official society of the Methodist Episcopal Church, into effect. He writes, "I bought an old frame that had been formerly occupied as a blacksmith shop, . . . and hauled it on the lot in Sixth near Lombard street, that had formerly been taken for the Church of England [St. Thomas's]. I employed carpenters to repair the old frame, and fit it for a place of worship." Francis Asbury and John Dickins, a located itinerant at St. George's, opened the church in late June 1794. "The house was called Bethel, agreeable to the prayer that was made. Mr. Dickins prayed that it might be a bethel to the gathering in of thousands of souls."[14]

The "List of the members of the African Methodist Episcopal Church in the City of Philadelphia" reproduced here is a record of the two classes that comprised the congregation of this new church. Like the class lists for St. George's, those for Bethel are not dated, but since they too are written in Thomas Morrell's readily identifiable hand, their approximate date can be ascertained. Morrell probably did not take down the names of Bethel's members any earlier than July 13, 1794, when one of Bethel's members, James Gibbs, first joined St. George's, and may not have done so until September when he ceased to include either black probationers or classes in St. George's register. Benjamin Tanner, historian of the African Methodist Episcopal Church, notes from a lost record that 108 members belonged to Bethel in November 1794. From the relatively small size of the two classes recorded here, comprising a total of 32 members, it appears likely that these are the original members of Allen's church, meeting at Bethel for the first time in the mid summer of 1794.[15]

Bethel's class lists show, as Allen suggests in his memoir, that the African congregation subscribed to the Methodist church polity, or Discipline, and both of its first class leaders, Blades Wildgoose and John Clinton, were white local preachers from St. George's.[16] Within two years, it was incorporated as a Methodist church under articles of association that reserved certain powers to the Methodist stationed preacher, including the right to preach at the church twice weekly, a stipulation that was to provoke tensions between the African Methodists and the white ministers at St. George's in the following years.[17]

At the same time, however, the articles assured that the church was legally owned by a board of black members, both by placing nearly all the control of temporal affairs in the hands of its trustees and by specifying that "none but coloured persons shall be chosen as trustees of the said African Episcopal Bethell Church." The articles further provided that these trustees were to be chosen from among the church's members who were themselves to be exclusively "Africans and descendants of the African race." The Methodist stationed preacher was also directed to license African exhorters and preachers; to defer to the opinion of black local preachers, exhorters, and class leaders in the church's disciplinary affairs; and to recommend qualified members for ordination in the Methodist Episcopal Church.[18] The "African" identity of the church could not have been more explicitly expressed.

The last five lists reproduced here are comprised of members admitted into the African Methodist Society called Zoar. This church opened on August 4, 1796, in a neighborhood called Campington in the Northern Liberties. Asbury remarked on the racially heterogeneous character of the group of members and bystanders who came to hear him inaugurate the new chapel: "I was called upon by the African society in Campington to open their new house, which I did, on Rom. i, 16–18, and had an unwieldy congregation of white and black. Brother Dickins gave a lively exhortation on the new birth." Unlike the registers for St. George's and Bethel, Zoar's lists of admissions can be dated specifically to the month and day by the date of admittance noted beside the name of each probationer.[19] It is also evident from the records that Zoar was supervised by the itinerants stationed at St. George's between 1800 and 1802; these preachers' names appear at the top of each list. Lawrence McCombs was replaced by Richard Sneath after a falling out with the Philadelphia conference's presiding elder in the autumn of 1800. Sneath was replaced as a matter of course by itinerants Samuel Coate and Daniel Higby in 1801, and Higby by William Penn Chandler in 1802.[20]

Zoar's class lists are not extant (or may never have been recorded), so it is uncertain how many of the black members of St. George's switched their allegiance to this new congregation in the late 1790s. At least one African Methodist, Solomon Britanham, belonged at one point or another to all three congregations. Like the classes at St. George's and Bethel in 1794, Zoar's class leaders were all white members of St. George's.[21] Perhaps for this reason, or because of the other advantages Afro-Americans might gain from membership in an incorporated African church, black Philadelphians tended to join Bethel rather than Zoar. Both churches appear to have profited by the impressive revivals that took place among the Philadelphia Methodists at the turn of the century, but Bethel most of all. Philadelphia's black membership, as officially recorded each spring in the Minutes of the Methodist Episcopal Church, rose from 257 in 1800 to 448 in 1801, an increase of 191 members. According to the registers reproduced here, 38 of these new African members joined Zoar. The balance of 153 members probably joined Bethel.[22] Nevertheless, Zoar must have been at least moderately sized at this time, consisting of old members loyal to St. George's and probably the majority of the African Methodists resident in the northern sections of the city. The congregation donated \$57.50 to the Methodist Church's Philadelphia conference in 1803, a sum that equalled a little more than half of what Bethel donated, and more than a fifth of that donated by the white members at St. George's.[23]

The African Methodists represented the greater black population described by Benjamin Rush in a letter to Granville Sharp in 1791. "In Pennsylvania our laws have exterminated domestic slavery'," he wrote to his fellow abolitionist, "and in Philadelphia the free blacks now compose 3,000 souls. Their men are chiefly waiters, day laborers, and traders in a small way. Their women are chiefly cooks and washer-women." The majority of black residents in Philadelphia after the Revolution were women, many of them working as domestic servants in the city's white households. Likewise, most African Methodists in the 1790s and early 1800s were women. Bethel is an exception to many Methodist societies, both black and white, in that its membership included more men than women. At St. George's and Zoar, however, women outnumbered men by about two to one and four to three respectively. The registers for these groups seem also to indicate that many female members were unmarried, or at least that they joined the Methodist society independently of their husbands. Twenty of the 30 women at St. George's in 1794 appear without men of the same last name. Even more striking, 29 of the 34 women joining Zoar during and after the revivals of 1800–1801 joined without a spouse.[24]

Few women or men at St. George's and Bethel, furthermore, appear in the 1795 City Directory that identified the "African" residents among its entries, suggesting that African Methodists were generally of humble social status or not yet established in their occupations. Of seventy-three members, the only ones appearing in the Directory were: Richard Allen, as a master chimney sweep, at 150 Spruce Street; Jane Gray, a washerwoman; Hester Vanderill, a cook; William Hooper, a carter; David Solomon, a carpenter; and John Morris, another chimney sweeper.[25] The greatest number of African Methodist men can be identified, not in the city directories, but in the maritime records of the Port of Philadelphia as mariners aboard the numerous ships and brigs that sailed from the city in the late 1790s and early 1800s. Of the twenty-six men who joined Zoar from 1800 to 1802, as many as seven appear to have been mariners, including Ignatious Cooper, John Farroon, Benjamin Jackson, Francis James, Nero Luff, Henry Williams, and George Yorker. In the nineteenth century the name "Zoar" came to refer specifically to a chapel for seamen.[26] This association may have been particularly strengthened by the numbers of black mariners who became evangelicals.

The male members at all three societies tended to be newcomers to the public arena. Only Allen and John Morris had been members of the Free African Society. Few Methodists, furthermore, seem to have opted for the Protestant Episcopal Church that the Free African Society was transformed into in 1794. Twenty Free Africans appear on St. Thomas's original membership register, making this church more socially and politically formidable than the black classes at St. George's and Bethel combined. And so far as the record shows just two Methodists, both of them women in Blair's class, left for St. Thomas's after the latter was dedicated in July 1794.[27]

There are indications, however, that the social status of the African Methodists was changing in the 1790s. Compared with the living standards of recently emancipated slaves, most of whom relied upon domestic service and day labor for their livelihood, a number of African Methodists were becoming men of relatively prosperous means including Allen and Morris. Allen had garnered notable wealth in the 1790s through his chimney-sweeping business but also through a shoemaking venture and investment in real estate. In 1794 he was assessed £250 for a dwelling in the city's New Market Ward and £40 for his team of five horses. In 1796 the dwelling was valued at $550.[28] Morris owned a house in the South Mulberry Ward valued at £85 in 1794, and £100 in 1795.[29] Three members of Jonathan York's class in 1794, Robert Green, Jacob Gibbs and John Burkib, were each householders in the New Market Ward in 1796, with frame residences valued at $80, $100 and $200 respectively.[30] Jonathan York was assessed $450 in 1799 for his two-story brick house in Southwark.[31]

Perhaps more typical, however, was the career of Benjamin Jackson, one of the members of Zoar's congregation in the early 1800s. Jackson was born in Maryland in about 1773 and, like many other blacks in this region, moved to Philadelphia before the end of the century. Here he became a mariner, styling himself as "Capt Jackson" for the tax assessor in 1798 and appearing in the 1800 Directory as a resident in German Street in the Northern Liberties, not far from Zoar's chapel. He is also named in maritime records as a crew member aboard two different brigs sailing from Philadelphia in 1798 and 1800. Jackson first appears in Methodist records in February 1799 when he married Phillis Bryan. In January 1801 he joined Zoar and became member of a class run by

William Sturges from St. George's. Two years later, in 1803, he can be found among the crew of the Ship Amsterdam, bound for Bordeaux. He is described as a 30-year old free black man standing 5′5″ tall with black woolly hair. This time, however, he was on board as the ship's steward rather than just another seaman.[32]

Despite the historical obscurity behind which most of the other African Methodists are hidden, both they and their more prominent companions had times of personal heroism and public achievement. Sarah Bass, a "poor black widow," served as a nurse along with many other blacks in Philadelphia during the devastating yellow fever epidemic of 1793. She and Allen were married by anti-slavery preacher Ezekiel Cooper in 1801.[33] The names of many African Methodists, furthermore, appear on a petition against the slave trade that Philadelphia's black community sent to Congress in 1799. Among the petition's seventy-one supporters were Allen, Morris, Jacob Gibbs, Robert Green, and Bethel trustee Prince Pruine. Names of less well-to-do members appear as well: the mariner, Benjamin Jackson, along with Lunar Brown, Ignatious Cooper, David Jackson, Stephen Miller, Thomas Watson, and Henry Williams.[34] And of course Allen was one of the outstanding Afro-Americans of his time, becoming a major anti-slavery publicist and spokesman for black rights, as well as the most prominent leader of African Methodism in America, a founder and the first bishop of the independent African Methodist Episcopal Church, and the head of the Negro Convention Movement before his death in 1831.

## ST. GEORGE'S

(I.) Black Class. William Blair. Leader Meets on Monday Night
William Blair Leader

[c. May-July 1794]

| | |
|---|---|
| Hester Vanderill | Violet York |
| Susannah Blandford | Ann Palmer |
| Phillis Starling | Phebe Parker |
| June Watson | Jane Gray |
| Hester Thompson | Servina Miller |
| Rhoda Slaser | Jane Vanderiff* |
| Ann Yorker | Polly Posey |
| Barnhart Johnson | Mary Spiser |
| Phillis Johnson | Samuel Spicer |
| Hester Norton | Benjamin Ellis |

*"excluded"

(II.) Hugh Smith Leader. a black Class. Meets on Wednesday night

[c. May-July 1794]

John Smith* Morris

Philis Morris

Tho⁵ Barbury

William Hooper

Peter Louk

Tho⁵ Watson

Stephen Miller

*"Smith" lined out

Sabinah Miller

Thomas Little

David Solomon

James Roy

Lydia Solomon

Solomon Britinham

(III.) Black Class Meets at Jonathan Yorks. Leader

[c. May-July 1794]

Jonathan York

Mary d°

Edeth Manning

Patience Lux

Peter Lux

Favorite Bush

Rob' Green

Hester d°

Jacob Gibbs

Hannah d°

Phebe Boss

Cyntha Bell

Zediah Mills

Rachel Eyres

John Burkib

Hester Thompson

## AFRICAN METHODIST EPISCOPAL CHURCH

(IV.) List of the members of the African Methodist Episcopal Church in the city of Philadelphia

[c. July-September 1794]

N° 1.

Blades Wildgoose. Leader.

Meets on Monday evening

Richard Allen

Benjamin Clark

William Hogen

Flora Allen

Eli Sans

Sarah Bass

Jonathan Trusty

Esther Trusty

Daniel Smith

John [ ]en*

Ro[ ]e Ford*

Dieleh Johnson

Charles Wansley

Elihu Sammons

Jane Anderson

N° 2

John Clinton Leader. meets on Sunday evening.

| | |
|---|---|
| James Gibbs | Priscilla Petekin |
| David Jackson | Cynthia Bell |
| Peter Petekin | Esther Freeman |
| Jupiter White | Sabina Miller |
| Hill** | Lucy White |
| Solomon Brittenham | Jane Gebron |
| Stephen Miller | Mary Spires |
| Francis Spires | *letters illegible |
| Eliz<sup>th</sup> Claypoole | **no first name listed |
| Saborah Morris | |

## ZOAR

(V.) A list of Members received upon trial at Zoar. by Lawrence M'Combs 1800

[June]

| | |
|---|---|
| Lunar Broon | Elizabeth Farier |
| Phebe Clouds | Rachel Cook |
| Hagate Necolson | |

(VI.) A list of persons recievd on trial at Zoar by Rich.d Sneath

[November-December 1800]

| | |
|---|---|
| Francis James | Lurana Dobson |
| Rachel Miller | Rebekah Jones |
| John Farroon | Polly Porter |
| Margaret Williams | Rebekah Henry |
| Dinah Wansling | Will<sup>m</sup> Porter |
| Flora Wheler | Cambridg Nickson* |
| Grace Young | George Yorker |
| Peter Gray | Solomon Britanham |
| *"rejected" | |

(VII.) Coulard people recieved on trial by Rich<sup>d</sup> Sneath

[January—May 1801]

| | |
|---|---|
| Rachel Barns | Nancey Evans |
| Daniel Furah | Philis Hatten |
| Rebekah Johnson | Betsey Williams |
| Benj<sup>n</sup> Jackson | Polly Williams |
| George Laws | Faney Johnson |

Judith Griffith
Mary Mathews
Nancey Petterson
Thomas Poke

Samuel Posey
Henry Williams
Abigail Laws

(VIII.) A Lit [sic] of the Coulard people taken in at Zoar by Samuel Coate and D. Higbee

[October-December 1801]

Jacob Cooper
W$^m$ Short*
Samuel Green
Hannah Turner
Solomon Alexander
*"from Burlington"

Jesse Armstrong
Ellener Lewis
Salley Mason
Adam Waterford

(IX.) a list of coulard people taken in at Zoar [by Samuel Coate and William P. Chandler]

[February-April 1802]

David Gardiner
Charles Gardiner
Hanneble Summers
Richard Oglebee
Ignatious Cooper
Rachel Bryan*
Nancy W$^r$ite
*"From Conte [country]"

Rachel Rogers
Silence Siddons
Pricilla Swan
Nero Luff
Eliz$^{th}$ Luff
Mary Summers

# Nineteenth-century Patterns

## CHAPTER 10

# Methodist Ministers and the Second Party System

Richard Carwardine

Amongst the most far-reaching of the many profound developments that marked American society in the first half of the nineteenth century was the establishment of a democratic political system, based on universal white manhood suffrage, tending towards two-party polarisation and recognisably the forerunner of the country's modern political forms. During the 1820s and 1830s a new breed of professional politician and party manager, typified by the "Little Magician," Martin Van Buren, experimented with conventions and other forms of elaborate party discipline and machinery as a means of coming to terms with the broadened suffrage; by 1840 two competing and almost equally balanced parties, Whigs and Democrats, whose popular strength extended into virtually every corner of the union, dominated the political landscape. In the early and mid-1850s, with the disintegration of the Whig party, this so-called "second party system" collapsed but its characteristic political practices survived into the new party alignments that superseded it.[1]

Contemporaneous with the emergence and maturing of this party system was a second process of profound importance for the shaping of America, the phenomenal growth of Methodism. Numbering only 73,000 members in 1800, the Methodist Episcopal Church [MEC] grew at a rate that terrified other religious bodies, reached a membership of a quarter of a million by 1820, doubled its members in the following decade, penetrated into every quarter of the country, including traditionally hostile New England, and became the largest denomination in America.[2]

Methodist advance and the emergence of mass political parties were not causally related, but neither were they wholly unconnected processes. Both were sustained by and helped foster a mood of growing egalitarianism in American society and a faith in the ability of the ordinary American to speak and act for himself. Methodist Arminianism, inclusive, democratic and optimistic, was just the faith for a society where traditional patterns of political deference were no longer secure. Methodist practices, too, contributed to the political forms and culture of the second party system. The style and fervour of Methodist camp meetings and revival singing, for example, found their way explicitly into the often frenzied election meetings of the period, and party activists were quite capable of adopting the terminology of the Church. Whig campaigners in Tennessee in 1840 planned "political Camp-meetings" in every county of the state, described their political hierarchy in ecclesiastical terms ("Bishops" for senators, "presiding elders" for electors, "local preachers" for party activists) and aimed "to make war upon the heathern (sic)" through the "preaching" of "political salvation."[3]

Curiously, we lack any sustained study of the political role of the Methodists in an era when they were increasing in social prominence and when political culture was changing so dramatically. This gap is all the more serious in view of the writings of the "ethnocultural" school of political historians. These not only argue that in this period religious preference and ethnic attachment were of primary significance in determining voting behaviours, but seem to suggest a pivotal role for Methodists: Ronald Formisano concludes that it was a shift in Methodist partisan attachment that contributed to the political confusion and realignment of the 1850s.[4] This paper aims to help fill this historiographical hole by exploring the response of Methodist ministers to the new forms and practices of the second party system. What political and moral responsibilities did they consider themselves to lie under? What was their proper mode of political action? What partisan preferences did they hold? How did those preferences shift? And what political influence, if any, did they wield?

# I

The early Methodist preachers were preeminently soul-savers and revivalists for whom election and other forms of political activity were subordinate and largely irrelevant to their primary purpose. "From pure motives I have ignored politics, so far as parties are concerned," Heman Bangs reflected during the highly-charged campaign of 1860. "Since I became a minister of Christ, my only business has been to save souls." As a young circuit-rider in Kentucky, Thomas Eddy found no difficulty in dismissing the Clay-Polk struggle of 1844 and in focusing on his own advance towards entire sanctification and on the cultivation of a general revival: "I could scarcely bear to labour all year, & see no outpouring of God's spirit." Whether pursuing their own or the country's spiritual needs, ministers at times of high political excitement were swift to show that the language and themes of political discourse were more appropriately employed in a higher cause. Leonidas Hamline, attending the General Conference of 1840 in Baltimore during the great Log Cabin rallies in the city, protested that he scarcely gave politics a thought: "I am myself a candidate, but it is for *eternal life*. I aspire to a throne, but I must have one which will not perish." When later in the year the electorate went to the polls the editor of the *Pittsburgh Christian Advocate* reminded his readers that there could be only one successful candidate for the presidency "but we may all be successful aspirants after the honor that comes from God . . . and all make our election sure . . . Our *souls* are at stake." Daniel De Vinne succinctly summarized the views of his generation when he concluded that "if I had another life to live over again, I had rather it should be that of a Methodist preacher, than that of the President of this Great Republic."[5]

More to the point, political activity, especially electioneering, was regarded as positively harmful, since it hampered the individual's spiritual growth. Matthew Simpson, attempting to stiffen his moral resolve in the face of the distractions of the Log Cabin campaign, drafted a private memorandum enjoining tougher spiritual exercises: "Converse no more on politics, unless in answer to a question propounded." Many lacked Simpson's discipline. In Missouri William Patton concluded that during that election Christians "suffered considerable loss in their own personal enjoyments," and echoed the words of a Pennsylvania colleague that "in nine cases out of ten . . . religious politicians are generally the most inattentive to the means of grace." Election campaigns were widely believed to extinguish, interrupt or delay revivals. Peter Cartwright's complaint that "great *declensions* and many *backslidings*" resulted from the political "tornado" of 1840 were reiterated across the country, and similar complaints of religious "havoc" followed the later presidential elections, particularly the "hurrah" campaigns of 1844 and 1856.[6] Local church revivals did not disappear entirely during election campaigns, as many ministers were anxious to explain: "Never perhaps were more Camp M[eetings] held in this region," Robert Emory wrote from Churchville, Maryland, in September 1840, "& never, perhaps, in spite of the political excitement were they more successful"; Joseph Fort recalled that despite the counter-attractions of the presidential election of 1852 "such was the general interest . . . shops, and stores, and even the hotel was closed at night" in New Providence, during one of the greatest revivals of his ministry.[7] Nonetheless the consensus amongst ministers was that political excitement when unchecked tended towards limiting church growth.

Scrutiny of the features and implications of the second party system served to reinforce Methodist disquiet. The church's spokesmen, sympathetic to the view widely held in the early years of the new republic that political parties were factional and unhealthy, regularly denounced what Bishop James Andrew described as "the wild, blind, reckless partisanship" of the times. Parties had "an awful tendency to engender strife, discord, division"—"denounced in the holy Book as crimes of no small import." They could divide congregations, "arraying father against son, and neighbor against neighbor, and alienating the affections of brethren from each other." They artificially divided the wider community, whose natural unity, inspired by republicanism and Christian sentiment, was only able to blossom in brief moments of national tragedy, as after the deaths of William H. Harrison and Andrew Jackson, when political conflict momentarily ceased. Party antagonisms obstructed millennial advance, for only a "nation of freemen, united in common support of a government established by common consent" could provide the necessary unity of effort that would spread "true holiness in their own happy land, and abroad over the face of the whole earth." Internal denominational acrimony over the slavery question, of course, heightened Methodists' sensitivity to the evils of party. The secessions from the church of abolitionist Methodists (regarded by regulars as shameless "partisans" who set brother against brother) and the sectional schism of the 1840s, dramatically demonstrated what "party spirit" could do.[8]

Parties were not necessarily evil, for as Francis Hemenway remarked, "We know there may be an honest difference of principles." But in the hands of party managers and professional politicians, for the great majority of whom politics were no longer a trust but a trade, political parties were used to promote individual self-interest and narrowly defined group interest, ahead of the needs of the nation as a whole: "The government is administered, now by this party and now by that, for party purposes, and not for the good of the country. Laws are enacted not to promote justice, so much as to secure political power." Such self-interest was but a step away from "dishonesty, corruption, vice, chicanery, and political artifice and intrigue," "Jesuitism in politics," "sleight of hand measures." To win and retain power unscrupulous demagogues manipulated the gullible amongst the native population and more especially amongst the ever-growing hordes of immigrants who, "uncultivated in morals and mind" and "intoxicated by a few inspirations of the air of liberty . . . gather around our ballot boxes . . . the inviting dupes of the designing."[9] Consequently "infidel, swearing, drunken black-legs," "duelists, Sabbath-breakers, [and] profane persons" secured office by trampling down reason and free discussion in emotional election campaigns that degenerated into little more than "bear shows," a sequence of "disgraceful scenes" that endangered the morals of the community. The heated abuse and sharp invective of stump orators and propaganda sheets ensured the "scalping and roasting alive" of political opponents; political friends were idolised and eulogised—Alfred Brunson grumpily dismissed Andrew Jackson's reception after his election to the presidency in 1828 as "man worship"; flamboyant parades, and rallies of unprecedented size and passion discouraged careful private assessment of political issues; candidates and their supporters travelled and canvassed on the sabbath; the hard cider campaign was by no means the only one to witness the "treating" of a liquor-loving electorate. Even tobacco consumption reached distressing levels, for as Robert Emory reported from Baltimore during the 1844 campaign animated groups of election-minded tobacco-chewers spat their juice "in such quantities, that Market St. for several days, could not be promenaded with any safety to [the ladies'] dresses—the pavement was so flooded."[10]

Such corruption of American democratic republicanism prompted a number of Methodists to follow Bishop Andrew's advice to "avoid politics." "There has been an unusual degree of political excitement & and parading here, but it is all nothing to me, & really looks like vanity . . . to see human beings intoxicating themselves with delusive hopes and vain aspirings," Enoch Mudge reported from Massachusetts in 1844. "I have not exchanged a word with . . . anyone here on the subject of politicks. I am not a voter." Mudge's attitude and that of like-minded colleagues was not a prelude to a Garrisonian-style, anarchist crusade against all political institutions: the worst human government was better than none at all, since society could not exist without government. Nonetheless, Mudge's thinking was erected on a providentialist premise that ultimately only God could rescue American society from its ills, that undue faith in the political process represented an over-reliance on human instrumentality. "I . . . abide the decisions of Providence, reposing on the arm that overrules & directs the storms in church & state, as in our physical world." As James Bontecou of the Ohio Conference remarked, reflecting on the decline of moral standards in political life, "if God don't come to our rescue, we are gone, I fear."[11] For such men the death of William Henry Harrison in 1841, the first president to die in office, and that of Zachary Taylor a decade later served to confirm the folly of trusting in the political process: if men put too much faith in their leaders, God would remove them to teach the nation to trust in him alone.

The vast majority of Methodist ministers, however, for two broad reasons, did not opt out of political life, but instead sought to fashion their own code of proper political activity, often very different from the code of the non-devout, and often showing considerable variation from one minister to another. First, total political withdrawal would have set them swimming against the tide of American popular culture in an era when in so many other ways they found themselves flowing with it. Public interest in politics reached a new intensity in these years; turnout in the presidential elections of 1840, 1844 and 1856 far exceeded earlier levels and was rarely to be equalled in later contests. Methodist ministers found it difficult to resist the pressures brought directly to bear on them. H. H. Green recalled at the end of his life that in the 1840s and 1850s "politics was the very breath of life, every man was a politician. They talked politics in the morning, they thought politics through the day, and they drank politics and fought politics around the corner grocery at night . . . The preacher was systematically scolded by one party because he preached politics and by the other party because he did not preach politics." An exasperated correspondent of the New York *Christian Advocate and Journal* complained that "[p]ublic meetings teem with censure upon the preacher who will not enlist for" this party or that, a lament viewed with sympathy by the editor, Thomas Bond, who for a period in the 1840s refused to publish political news in consequence of the abuse he received alternately from Whigs and Democrats for alleged partisan bias.[12]

Second, it was argued that Methodist abstinence from politics left American democracy and republicanism vulnerable to the powers of darkness. Christians had a duty to God and their country to protect a system of government sanctioned by scripture, founded on Christian principles, defensive of religious liberties and designed by the Almighty to be a beacon to the rest of the world. Typically, Rezin Sapp of Michigan, for whom the Bible was a "purely democratical" textbook, reminded Christians that God would "hold them responsible for the non-performance of the duties which they owe as citizens of an elective government" destined to spread "the principles of liberty and virtue in their highest forms throughout the globe." Without Christian guardianship, republicanism—as in the classical world—would fail: "A republic is the body, Christianity is the soul."[13] The overturning of "the purest and best of all human governments," democratic republicanism, made more likely by the recent political abuses of the second party system, could only be prevented by "Christian patriotism," by members of the religious community vigorously exercising their political rights.[14] The sheer numerical strength of Methodism gave to both its lay members and its ministers a particular responsibility to throw their political influence "on the side of good morals, equal rights, [the] Constitution, law and peace." In Ohio, for example, where in the 1840s Charles Elliott calculated that about half the population were members or adherents of the MEC, the thousand or so local and travelling preachers were regarded, together with the rest of the membership, as particularly "responsible to the state, the United States, and the world, for good government."[15]

Those who shared in this attitude towards Methodist political activity were generally agreed that their principal political obligation was to engage in prayer for the country's rulers. Scriptural and other historical examples indicated that the Almighty was "intimately concerned with the passing events of time" and would not hesitate to intervene to reward those who diligently sought him. As Abraham had interceded for the cities of the Plain, and Moses for the Jews, so God had graciously rewarded the prayers of the Pilgrim Fathers, the rebellious American colonies and the founders of the new nation. He would continue to assist the good and correct the wicked in response to Christian pleading.[16]

Yet prayer alone was insufficient. Just as their theology of revivals encouraged the use of a range of means extending beyond prayer—protracted meetings, sustained preaching, the call to the altar, and so on—so Methodists advocated various additional "instrumentalities" in pursuit of Christian political ends, the most essential being "a regular and conscientious exercise of the elective franchise." "Every man should feel himself *bound* to vote," every vote counts, "Heaven has provided the ballot-box" were common pulpit refrains. Ministers practised what they preached, even though itinerants, and particularly bishops, complained that their travels tended practically to disfranchise them. David Lewis recalled how the business of the Ohio Annual Conference was hurried to a close in 1840 to allow members to get home in time to vote; writing to Bishop Simpson in 1860 Aaron Wood asked for a day's postponement of the Northwestern Conference to prevent a clash with the state election.[17] A confirmed voter, George Coles described his perseverance in a very close New York election in 1844: "I tried three or four times to get a chance to put in my vote but the press was so great that I could not get to the door till between 3 & 4 P.M."[18]

In preparation for voting, ministers recognised their obligation to scrutinise the issues and the candidates with great care; for instance, James Gilruth, as presiding elder in the Detroit district in the mid-1830s considered it his duty to chew over a mixed diet of Whig circulars and a biography of Andrew Jackson. Their aim in voting should be "the glory of God" and, as James Finley urged, to promote "the general good, . . . the good of [the] country" and not "Individual or party purposes." William Winans explained that consistency was not a virtue when it meant voting for a man solely because of his party attachment. The Methodist's priority in an era when standards of public morality appeared annually to be declining had to be "to prevent improper incumbents from getting into office." According to Leonidas Hamline, "A Christian citizen ought sooner to thrust his hand into a burning furnace, than suffer it to place in the ballot box a ticket blurred with the name of an infidel, vicious candidate." A contributor to the *Western Christian Advocate* began with a disclaimer—"We do not ask that those who claim our votes, should belong to this denomination or that, nor even that they should be *pious* men"—but continued: "we fear that . . . wrath will come upon us . . . if we vote for those who treat with open scorn the Christian religion, whose characters are stained with *drunkenness, Sabbath-breaking, profaneness, gambling*, or *murder, (dueling)*." Public scrutiny of the private lives of political candidates—particularly unmarried men, notoriously the most vulnerable to moral decay—would eventually teach the political parties to nominate only moral men for office. Voting, then, was indisputably a moral act and "bad voting," as Calvin Fairbanks termed it, a sin. "I as much expect to give an account to God for the manner in which I *vote* as for the manner in which I pray," explained Thomas Eddy, echoing Samuel Lewis' view that at the day of judgement men would have to answer individually for their votes and would not be able to hide behind the skirts of party.[19]

In their discussions to establish the boundaries of legitimate political activity, many ministers concluded that their active political responsibilities ceased after casting their votes and accepting the election result with equanimity. The American who said in the 1830s that clergymen were "a sort of people between men and women" nicely represented their position, which fell short of the adult white male's unquestioned freedom to air his political opinions and participate fully in the processes of party politics, but which exceeded that of the unfranchised woman. It was widely agreed that ministers should not attend political meetings, preach on party political questions, stand for office, or in any way attempt to convert their congregations to their own political opinions. It would only encourage church members to "speak evil of magistrates or ministers," expressly forbidden by the Methodist *Discipline*. It would also, as Charles Browne of Port Republic, Virginia, explained, "lose [us] considerable influence with our people." The provision of his state's constitution excluding clergymen from membership of the state legislature pleased those who argued that both scripture and good sense enjoined their ministers to stick to their task of spreading the gospel. Joshua Soule was all too aware of the problems that ministerial association with a particular party could cause when in 1840 he found his private eulogy of William Harrison incorporated into Whig propaganda; he consumed considerable time, energy and embarrassment attempting to explain away his gaffe. At Indiana Asbury University, where it was said on the eve of the 1844 election that William Larrabee "spends at least half his hour in the recitation room in teaching Locofocoism," Lucien Berry was terrified that the charge would weaken the institution's public standing at a critical period in its history.[20]

Similar concerns led the editors of Methodist newspapers to steer clear of party politics. Reflecting on a list of about fifty thousand subscribers to the four major publications, representing an estimated readership of a quarter of a million, Thomas Morris reminded Matthew Simpson, as he took over the editorship of one of them, the *Western Christian Advocate*, that his paper could "accomplish more than the entire episcopal board" provided it took a conciliatory, non-controversial approach.[21] The New York *Christian Advocate* and its Pittsburgh namesake customarily disclaimed any desire to discuss the bank or tariff questions, deliberately avoided the issue of Texas annexation, and apologised for mischievous partisans who slipped separately printed political speeches into the paper at the point of distribution. "There is not a vestige of party politics in our paper, on one side or the other," protested the editor of the *Pittsburgh Christian Advocate*, worried by those who had discontinued their subscriptions on the grounds that it had failed to carry the occasional messages of the state governor. Political self-denial equally characterised the formal proceedings of the Methodist annual and general conferences for the reason that many members would be alienated, and that any attempted control of Methodists' political action would be the first step towards turning the MEC into the established church of the United States: "All political parties would pay court to our ministers, and from a spiritual Church we should be degraded to a mere government machine."[22]

It nonetheless proved impossible in practice to purify the ministry of its compulsive partisans. Some, like David R. McAnally, edited campaign newspapers, or lent their moral authority to a particular candidate, as did William Barnes and Arthur Elliott to Harrison in 1840 by officiating at his meetings. Others, like Peter Cartwright and Alfred Brunson, even stood successfully for political office, as Illinois Democrat and Wisconsin Whig respectively. Colleagues might raise their eyebrows and even their voices at such goings-on but there was a clear logic to this public commitment to party, implicit in John Inskip's recognition that "all political questions have a connection, more or less direct, with both morality and religion."[23] If Methodists had a duty to God to promote righteousness and eliminate national sins—a principal theme of Methodist and other evangelical Protestant literature of the period—and if one particular party appeared to be more clearly identified than the other with those sins, then the public embracing of the lesser of two political evils had a clear moral justification. Of course, ministers often saw little morally to choose between the contending parties, whose divisions they regarded as factitious and unrelated to religious issues. But not all saw matters in this light, and as political questions of undoubted moral and religious significance began not only to intrude into but to dominate party politics in the 1840s and 1850s, so more and more Methodists saw no conflict between their religious profession and a highly visible political posture. They found it increasingly difficult to remain silent on matters relating to temperance, Roman Catholicism, the Mexican War, the spread of slavery and the future of the Union itself, despite the continuing opposition of "non-political," "quietest" Methodists, particularly in the South. This increasingly public political activity of Methodist ministers was closely related to significant shifts in their party attachments in the 1840s and 1850s. Both developments deserve a careful analysis not simply for what they reveal about the history of Methodism but as a means towards a fuller appreciation of the second party system and the process of its collapse.

## II

The persecution of the early Methodists by the defenders of the ecclesiastical and social establishment, most particularly in New England, is a well-told story. Methodists were obliged to pay taxes to support the churches established by law; poor ministers incurred heavy fines for performing marriage ceremonies for their own members; hostile mobs destroyed meeting houses, intimidated worshippers and attacked itinerant preachers, whom they regarded as "incarnate demons" and "intruders into the land of steady habits." Even where the early Methodists suffered no legal disabilities they experienced discrimination at the hands of socially entrenched Calvinists, as in the Western Reserve of Ohio where the informal Standing Order of Presbyterians and Congregationalists worked to deny them access to preaching places.[24] Part of Methodism's strategy of self-defence had been to take political refuge in the Jeffersonian Democratic-Republican party, whose ideas on religious freedom and on the separation of church and state drew succour from the Federal Constitution and stood in sharp contrast to those of the Federalists, generally regarded as the party of the Calvinist establishment and the socially well-to-do. Although Jefferson himself was perceived as at best a deist and by his Federalist enemies as an atheist of doubtful morals, Methodists very generally rallied to his party's standard. Many ministers could have described themselves, as did William Winans, as "rather enthusiastic" Jeffersonians; a few, like Jeremiah Stocking of Connecticut and Dan Young of New Hampshire, even sought state political office as Republicans in order to fight for full disestablishment and for Methodist equality under the law.[25]

The forces that made most Methodists Jeffersonian Democrats under the first party system lured many of them into the ranks of Jacksonian Democracy during the second, particularly in its early years. Jacksonians were committed to a philosophy of *laissez-faire* not only in political economy and social legislation, but also in the area of religion and the legal enforcement of moral behaviour.[26] They seemed to offer a home to those Arminian Methodists who continued instinctively to define themselves politically as anti-Federalist, and who feared that John Quincy Adams' National Republicans and then nascent Whiggery represented the Calvinist establishment in new clothing. It was no accident that Solon Stocking adopted Democratic principles, as had his Jeffersonian father, when he found the full social weight of Connecticut's Standing Order pressing down on him as he tried to conduct Methodist revival services in the 1820s; Calvinist arrogance and bigotry, or the enduring memory of them, drove a number into the welcoming arms of the Jacksonians. Herein undoubtedly lies part of the reason for Methodist resistance to the charms of a Whig party which made markedly successful overtures to the membership of other evangelical denominations. Hugh McCulloch certainly exaggerated when he argued that up to the 1850s there were few exceptions to the rule of general Methodist identification with the Democratic party, but the evidence produced by Lee Benson, Ronald Formisano and other historians who have attempted to correlate party strength and church attachment makes it clear that in the heyday of the second party system Methodists maintained a considerable Jacksonian attachment, symbolised by the assertive loyalty of such luminaries as Edward R. Ames, Edmund S. Janes and Peter Cartwright.[27]

Yet, without necessarily calling into question the findings of the ethno-cultural historians in regard to the political loyalties of the mass of Methodists, it is clear from a careful reading of their published autobiographies and private papers that Methodist preachers were disproportionately Whig, not Democrat, during the second party system. Some showed their colours early on. George Peck might keep his hostility to Jackson private in the 1828 election, but William Winans, who had followed Henry Clay in his pilgrimage from anti-Federalism *via* National Republicanism to Whiggery, made no secret of his antipathy to Jackson. Winans' political sermons were a model of discretion, however, when compared with the prayers of "a violent Anti-Jackson preacher" in the Baltimore Conference who, when visiting the White House in 1831 along with thirty or so of his colleagues, knelt and prayed that the Gen[eral] might be converted', "which he did so loud, that he could be heard at the Presidents gate." By the 1840s Whiggery had a firm grip on the Methodist leadership: Henry Bascom, James Andrew and John Emory upheld it in the South; Matthew Simpson and Chauncey Hobart, who had to swallow hard before preaching his sermon on Jackson's death, typified the party's ministerial supporters in the west, where it was claimed that most of the Indiana Conference was Whig in 1840; John Inskip, George Crooks, John McClintock and George Coles spoke for many in northeastern Methodism. When the English Wesleyan James Dixon visited America in 1848 to attend the General Conference, it was his clear impression that the vast majority of the Methodist ministers that he met on his extensive travels were firmly in that political camp.[28]

In a few instances Methodist ministers gravitated towards the Whigs out of despair over those Jacksonian economic policies that had helped give definition to the parties in the 1830s, particularly the attack on the Bank of the United States. Lorenzo Dow's admiration for Jackson evaporated, while George Brown held the Democrats morally responsible for the financial panic of 1837 and the economic distress that followed.[29] Most Methodists, however, did not move in a Whiggish direction for reasons of specific economic policy. They did so rather because the Democrats unabashedly embraced social groups and sub-cultures which increasingly appeared to threaten the influence and status of evangelical Protestantism in the culture as a whole, and because Whiggery seemed to offer the best means of sustaining Christian influence in public life.

The same liberal Jacksonian philosophy that attracted Methodist enemies of the informal Calvinist establishment also offered equality of treatment to Mormons, freethinkers and others out of step with the dominant Protestantism around them.[30] Most threatening of all the groups sheltered by the Democrats was the burgeoning Roman Catholic community—German and Irish immigrants whose alleged hard-drinking habits, disrespect for the Sabbath and obedience to dissolute priests not only offended evangelical sensibilities but undermined the Christian purpose of the nation. The full evangelical indictment of the Catholic Church needs no recapitulation here. What does deserve emphasis is the close identification of that church with the Democratic party—by 1844 some 95 percent of New York's Irish Catholics were loyal Jacksonians—and the recognition of this alignment by fearful Methodists. If William Gannaway Brownlow was the most vitriolic of Methodist critics, charging Catholic immigrants with almost unanimous support for the Locofocos, denouncing Van Buren as a sycophantic flatterer of the Pope, and portraying Bishop John England as a Jacksonian propagandist, his was not the only pen to denounce the Democrats' furthering of Catholic ends. The *Christian Advocate and Journal* grew ever more angry at the efforts of the Catholic hierarchy in the early 1840s to secure state funding for their schools in New York and other cities: "The school question is now made a political one in the city of New York with the Romanists claiming the aid of the Democrats, and the Whigs asking the help of Protestants . . . . The Protestants have not done this; . . . the Romanists are the aggressors." Methodists grew similarly embittered—particularly those of Irish extraction like Charles Elliott—by the Democratic party's complicity in the efforts of the Irish Catholic community to secure the repeal of the Anglo-Irish Union of 1800.[31]

Although the Whigs did not adopt an unequivocally anti-Catholic posture, as William Seward's attempted wooing of the Catholic hierarchy in New York in the early 1840s made clear, they were nevertheless able to establish themselves as the best hope of thwarting Catholic political influence and on a number of occasions in the 1830s and 1840s successfully annexed embryonic nativist movements.[32] More generally, they worked with great energy to cultivate their image as the Christian party in politics, a mantle they took over from the Antimasonic party, whose members they had largely managed to absorb. Freemasonry was a sensitive issue for Methodists, both at the time of its emergence as a political issue in the 1820s and throughout the antebellum period: it was hated and feared by many individual Methodists and regarded with disfavour by some conferences, although the Church as a whole did not pass judgment, since too many Methodists were prominent in this and other secret societies. Whiggery undoubtedly benefited from Methodist animus against the order. It was also helped by its "Christian" and paternalist stand on the Indian question, as compared with the "sordid cupidity" of the Jacksonians' policy, which Methodists regarded as "crooked and disgraceful," a distinct break with the traditional Republican policy from Jefferson to Adams. Whig anti-partyism, with its implications for the return of a cohesive Christian community, helped sustain their Puritan image, as did their much emphasised sympathy for sustaining overt Christian influence in government, symbolised by William Henry Harrison's invoking of religion in an inaugural address for the first time since

Washington and in President John Tyler's reversing Jacksonian policy by calling for a day of national humiliation and prayer.[33]

Democrats, fearing a convergence of Methodism and evangelically-oriented Whiggery, stressed in their propaganda the "Federalist" roots of the Whig party, and its threat to the separation of church and state, but to little avail. Whereas in the early years of the century the fear of Federalism and state-supported Calvinism had been powerful enough to hold within the Republican party both Methodism and, as Alfred Brunson recalled, "the infidel portion of the community, though these classes were antipodes in all things pertaining to religion," by the 1830s very many Methodists were quite prepared to take their place in a party ideologically shaped in part by Calvinists. Concerned by the decline of religion in the public life of the nation—financial corruption and the evils of the "spoils system," the threat to chaplaincies in Congress and the state legislatures, congressmen's continued resort to duelling to settle disputes, Sabbath-breaking and intemperance amongst public figures, for example— many Methodist ministers appear to have concluded that the Whigs, sympathetic to legislation to defend moral standards, offered a surer hope of a remedy than the Democrats and their principle of moral *laissez-faire*. During the 1830s and 1840s many Methodists abandoned their faith in moral suasion alone as a means of preserving a Christian social order and turned to the government for legislative support, whether to outlaw duelling, prohibit the liquor trade, forbid gambling, sustain the traditional Protestant Sabbath or protect camp meetings from the disturbances of liquor sellers and scoffers. For the benefit of those within and outside Methodism who worried that such measures represented a threat to the separation of church and state, Methodist spokesmen sought to distinguish between an improper sectarian establishment and an entirely proper exercising of Christian influence over legislation: "No enlightened Christian wishes to see Church and State united in government; but if men [are] to do all things to the glory of God, they must be constantly governed by the moral law of God; and hence religious principle must be made the basis of political action." [34]

Methodists' growing readiness to sit alongside Calvinist evangelicals in the same political party was encouraged by a developing harmony between the two groups as theological and socio-economic gaps narrowed. In the first place, the enormous popular appeal of democratic Arminianism during the Second Great Awakening imposed irresistible pressures on the Calvinist churches to modify their doctrines of human inability, election and limited atonement. Many Calvinist ministers either responded to pressure from below, as their congregations revolted against a strict creed, or were themselves the popularizers of a "new divinity," the Arminianized Calvinism associated with Nathaniel Taylor, and practitioners of the "new measures" adapted by Charles Finney from Methodist revivalism.[35] As the Second Great Awakening drew to a close both

171

Methodists and Calvinists came to reassess their theological position and to recognise their near agreement on evangelical fundamentals in the face of threatening heterodoxies: Mormonism, Universalism and, most seriously, Roman Catholicism. "[T]he times call for unity of spirit and effort among the evangelical churches," announced the *Christian Advocate and Journal* in 1842, at the very time when all orthodox Protestant denominations were already involved in defending themselves against Catholic intrusions, through the American Protestant Union. At the Evangelical Alliance meetings in London in 1846, much applauded by American Methodists, George Peck, carried away by the occasion, could demand: "Perish the Calvinistic and the Arminian controversy." During the 1840s and 1850s many evangelical ministers took him at his word as they co-operated in interdenominational efforts for revival, often spurred by a common attachment to perfectionist doctrine.[36]

Second, some of the antipathy between Arminian and Calvinist melted as Methodists progressed from being a socially despised sect of the poor, "the offscouring of all things," into a respected denomination of some power and influence in the community, able to throw off its inferiority complex and forget much of the suffering experienced at the hands of snobbish Presbyterians and Congregationalists. As Methodists grew wealthier and built larger, more ornate churches with organs, rented pews and steeples, as they demanded and secured a college-bred, more sophisticated and urbane ministry, as they preached before Presidents and respected statesmen and officiated as chaplains of the Senate and the House of Representatives, so they left their persecuted past behind.[37] When Selah Stocking transferred from the New England to the Oneida Conference in the 1830s he discovered that "his church members were among the leading citizens of the place; and he soon found himself associated with families of wealth and refinement." Similar reflections emanated from southern and western Methodists in that and later decades, and even in New England significant improvements in their wealth and social status occurred during the antebellum period. Methodist representation amongst the wealthiest and most influential in the community was the exception and not the rule, but by the 1850s Methodists were to be found in state governorships, in the United States Senate and in the Supreme Court.[38] By no means all Calvinists accepted Methodists' new status: a senior Ohio preacher complained to Matthew Simpson in 1850 of the Presbyterians continued "vauntings and . . . thrusts at Methodism" and in Galesburg, Illinois, a few years later Milton Haney experienced "persistent and bitter" opposition from a transplanted colony of New England Congregationalists. Yet, more tellingly, in the same decade George Coles could look back over his thirty years in America and conclude that "[o]ne thing is certain, the evangelical sects are more harmonious in their feelings toward each other than they were formerly"; while the elderly Nathan Bangs, addressing an interdenominational prayer meeting after the revival of 1857–58 confessed: "I have been a man of war all my days almost. I have fought the Calvinists, the Hopkinsians, and the Protestant Episcopalians . . . but I have laid aside the polemic armour long since, and I felt it my duty to preach . . . upon brotherly love"; and the New Hampshire Congregationalist Nathaniel Bouton confirmed that "[t]here is now more liberality and charity among different denominations than formerly. If our fathers erred in being too exclusive and bigoted, we are in danger of the other extreme." [39]

In 1840, at the very moment that Whigs were demonstrating that they had come of age, that they had an ideology and organisation sufficiently coherent to win them a national election, two issues that were eventually to destroy the party were already raising their heads: slavery and nativism. Methodists could ignore neither. Indeed, they and other evangelical Protestant denominations did much to force public discussion of issues whose moral implications they believed justified their active involvement in the political arena. As the leaders of Methodism came to define their positions and reconsider their Whiggery, they made their own particular contribution to the complex political configurations of the early and mid 1850s and to the collapse of the second party system.

A small minority of northern Methodist ministers of strong antislavery principles deserted the Whigs near the time of the election of 1840, most particularly the Ohio local preacher, Samuel Lewis, who was later to stand variously for state and national office as candidate of the Liberty party and the Free Soilers. Lewis' departure from a party whose position on economic issues he much admired was the result of what he regarded as its succumbing like the Democrats to the control of apologists for slavery, particularly once John Tyler had entered the White House. But most northern Methodists were not then ready to take his radical step of supporting "independent nominations"—abolitionism in a political context, as it seemed. Typical of mainstream ministerial attitudes was that of the Pittsburgh Conference, which in 1841 according to Charles Elliott regarded abolitionism as "a system of agitation—a political faction—a slandering of their Church—an injury to the colored race—a schism in the Church—an appeal to revolutionizing sentiments and feelings." "Ultras" like Lewis were regarded warily, sometimes excluded from churches, their status as preachers even in jeopardy at times. Abolitionist and third-party action threatened Methodist unity and the integrity of the Union, both of them essential to the fulfilment of America's religious destiny.[40]

However, during the 1840s antislavery sentiment deepened within the northern branch of the church at the same time that the vast majority of its members remained resistant to militant abolitionism. Already convinced that slavery was a great moral and social evil, they were increasingly persuaded that they faced an arrogant and aggressive southern leadership in both church and state anxious to strengthen the place of slavery not just in the south but in the nation as a whole. Despite the Plan of Separation established after the church schism, MEC ministers in the border conferences of Ohio, Baltimore and Philadelphia later in the 1840s suffered physical violence at the hands of mobs encouraged by Methodist editors and lay sympathisers. Moreover, southern magistrates regularly suppressed or burnt copies of the supposedly seditious *Christian Advocate and Journal* and the *Western Christian Advocate.* Some southern ministers were said to have engineered the breach in Methodism to encourage southern secession, the break up of the Union and an eventual civil war: Thomas Bond likened William A. Smith, president of Randolph Macon College, to Marat and Robespierre for his disunionist demagoguery. Against such a background it was little wonder that many northern Methodists who considered themselves moderates on the slavery question came to regard the annexation of Texas and the Mexican War as the product of a Slave Power bent on spreading its social and political influence within the Union. "That 250,000 slaveholders should rule this great empire is a thing not to be endured," John McClintock told Stephen Olin, adding ominously: "it can't be endured much longer." [41]

By the time of the political crisis and settlement of 1850 many northern Methodists had taken up a free-soil stance of opposition to the expansion of slavery into all territories. Francis Hemenway, in his Independence Day celebration of American liberty and prosperity in 1851, could not avoid dwelling on the "great moloch" of slavery: only the slave states had the power to challenge slavery within their borders, "but we do claim," he said, "that this odious God-defying . . . institution shall be divested of its nationality . . . and that our Federal Government—our nation shall cease to patronize & uphold it." Thanks also to the demands of the new Fugitive Slave Law, men like Asa Kent, transformed from a harsh critic of antislavery Methodists into a moral and financial supporter of passengers on the underground railroad, were either drawn into the Free Soil party or sought free-soil commitments from the Whigs and Democrats. "Think not that I am a 'naked abolishionist '[sic] for I have always heretofore 'went the regular nominee,' but I now wish it distinctly understood that I'll do so no more, unless that nominee is an out & out Wilmot Proviso man," wrote a Methodist from Eaton, Ohio, to Matthew Simpson at the time when Simpson's free-soil editorials in the *Western Christian Advocate* had been causing a major political stir: "Our preacher Bro. White is commending your course & articles *very highly*." [42]

Antislavery Methodists were only prepared to go on voting Whig for as long as the party evidenced sympathy for free soil; in the early 1850s northern Whiggery appeared sufficiently true to the cause for its Methodist supporters to remain generally loyal. A number of southern Methodists, of course, were growing increasingly suspicious of the free-soil elements in Whiggery, their concern well epitomised by William G. Brownlow's desertion in 1852 of his party's regular presidential nominee, Winfield Scott, who it was feared would fall under the sway of Seward and northern radicals. But what most seriously threatened to cut the ties joining Methodism to Whiggery were the problems relating to immigration. The three million immigrants who entered the United States between the mid-1840s and the mid-1830s inevitably intensified existing Protestant fears over Catholic influence, its threat to common-school education and democratic republicanism, and its encouragement of Sabbath-breaking, intemperance, crime, and pauperism. Yet at the time when anti-Catholics and nativists turned for solutions to these problems towards their most natural political allies, the Whigs, a combination of tolerance, anti-nativism, and careful political calculation was pushing that party into wooing the immigrants and Catholic community. William Seward's overtures to the Catholic hierarchy in New York state had been a straw in the wind: many Whig leaders, including Scott in 1852, spoke flatteringly to Catholic audiences, eulogising Daniel O'Connell, praising the Pope, and even commending their Irish brogue. Despite pressure on them to support temperance measures along the lines of the Maine Law, many Whigs sought to fudge the issue and to avoid a commitment for or against prohibition that would in one way or another lose them votes.[43]

In growing anger Methodist ministers, disgusted by the way the politicians of all parties temporised, spoke of igniting what Thomas Goodwin described as "a flame of righteous indignation that will burn till all party bonds are consumed, and freemen will vote for good men who will not give the reins of power to the lawless and unprincipled." William Simmons declared that he would never "vote for any man, Whig or Democrat, for the legislature of Ohio, who is not a friend to the temperance cause." If the regular parties would not put up sound candidates then Methodists, as Goodwin and his Indiana colleague B.F. Crary argued early in 1853, "being now free from the yoke of party," would simply amputate the "gangrened members on the body politic" and elect non-aligned and decent men. Francis Hemenway of Massachusetts and George Coles of New York were just two whose practice matched the prescriptions of their ministerial colleagues by voting the Maine Law ticket in state and local elections that year.[44] At the same time very many Methodist ministers, hypnotised by the glorious prospects held out to them by the nativist and anti-Catholic Know-Nothing party, cast off their traditional ties. A few like Mark Trafton of Massachusetts and W. H. Goodwin of New York even stood successfully for political office; very many more offered their votes, most dramatically in Indiana, where Joseph Wright, the state governor and himself a Methodist, complained that at least two-thirds of MEC ministers were connected with the secret organisation. By no means all Methodists approved of the intolerance, secrecy and proscription encouraged by the new party, but it drew quite enough support to destroy the informal alliance between the church's ministers and Whiggery.[45]

During these years, then, and particularly in 1854—when the repeal of the Missouri Compromise and the bursting forth of Know-Nothingism shattered political loyalties—disillusioned southern, pro-slavery Methodist preachers like Brownlow, northern free-soil ministers like Simpson and northern prohibitionists and anti-Catholics like Coles moved from Whiggery to new political attachments by a variety of routes. By the election of 1856, however, their destinations were becoming clear: the majority of northern Methodist ministers, if not their members, had moved into the Republican party, noisily anti-slavery, silently anti-Catholic, while southern Methodists either found their way into the Democratic party (from which not all had strayed anyway) or into Millard Fillmore's American party, Whiggish, anti-Democratic and mildly nativist. The alignments of the second party system were dead.

## III

Methodist ministers, then, took their political duties seriously during the era of the second party system—so seriously that increasingly during the 1840s and 1850s they were attacked for interfering in political matters supposedly beyond their proper concern. When John Inskip publicly attacked the Polk administration for its involving America in a war with Mexico he was himself denounced as "reverend stumper"; Matthew Simpson's editorial stand in the *Western Christian Advocate* on free soil and the "higher law" during the crisis of 1850 called down the fury of hostile politicians; B. F. Crary's involvement in the politics of temperance evoked cries of "meddling with politics" from what he regarded as canting, "whiffling demagogues." Whether or not Methodist ministers really were meddling in politics—and it could be argued that what increased was not simply their outspokenness, but the level of sensitivity of the issues raised, and the fragility of political parties—it is clear that their critics had a considerable respect for their potential political influence. Why else should they worry about what Methodist leaders said in their pulpits and wrote in their denominational newspapers? Why else were the eyes of the political world fixed on the quadrennial General Conferences of the church? Why else should politicians court her ministers and leading laymen? Typically, in 1840 Andrew Jackson encouraged Van Buren to offer a Tennessee postmastership to a Methodist minister who wielded considerable local influence, on the grounds that if he were deprived of the post on President Harrison's taking office, the county would swing to the Democrats in protest. As Francis Hodgson complained in 1856, "now that the church was so strong each political party was eager to make her its tool."[46]

In fact, critics of Methodism in some ways worried too much about ministerial political influence. Methodist congregations were often so clearly divided on political issues that ministers hesitated to offer clear partisan directives: Joshua Soule explained that as an officer of a church that embraced "citizens of different opinions in political matters, I conscientiously decline any interference . . . in the recommendation of my friends who are applicants for office." Charles Browne was clear that "[a]s ministers, if we warmly espouse either side of [a] great political question, we will lose considerable influence with our people." It was not unknown for church members to walk out of services—as sometimes happened when Samuel Lewis preached—or to join another congregation, to escape "political preaching" of one kind or another. Ministers were less reluctant to exert partisan influence in private, however. Lucien Berry, confirmed Whig, wrote jubilantly to Matthew Simpson of the defeat of an Indiana opponent: "The preachers done [sic] all they could privately & nearly the entire Methodist vote went against him."[47]

Where Methodist ministers wielded greatest political influence, however, was less in demanding particular partisan allegiances, as in helping to sharpen the sensibilities of their church members on the moral issues that came to dominate political discourse in the 1840s and 1850s. By encouraging a public debate on the correct moral response to slavery, to the possibility of its expansion into new territories, to the Catholic influence in politics and education, to the social and moral threats posed by immigration, they encouraged their members to adopt positions that forced the major parties to respond. Thomas Bond, editor of the *Christian Advocate and Journal*, thought it was improper for him to consider the political aspects of the slavery question; yet he did remind his readers that "as individual citizens we are bound by Christian duty to determine the moral obligations which our religious professions enjoin, in respect to it, and to act upon the sober conviction to which we may come in the exercise of our political rights and privileges." He continued: "no well-intentioned Christian can be justified before God in withholding whatever of political influence he may have, from the effort to ameliorate, and ultimately to abolish the whole system of slavery as it exists in the United States."[48] By such means ordinary Methodists were encouraged, not to support a particular party, but to see slavery, intemperance, Catholic intrusions and so on as national sins whose elimination was essential for the moral and religious growth of God's chosen country and for the avoidance of God's wrath. The implications for party politics were profound. Moral absolutism challenged compromise and consensus as the controlling forces of political thought and action. Politics became sectionalized, and by April 1861 compromise and consensus had collapsed.

# Nineteenth-century Black Women's Spiritual Autobiographies: Religious Faith and Self-Empowerment

### Nellie Y. McKay

Acknowledgment of the significance of black women to all aspects of the life of the Afro-American community, and recognition of the role of the spiritual or conversion narratives of the ante- and postbellum periods are among landmark advances in recent Afro-American scholarship. Little need be said here of the part that feminist scholarship and black feminist scholars have played in facilitating this new awareness of the importance of gender in the making and interpretation of a people's history. On the other hand, it is more difficult to understand why, in spite of the pervasiveness of the cultural influence of the Afro-American religious tradition, early studies of the black autobiographical narrative tended to focus mainly on the heroic and political dimensions of slave

N.B. The original essay was dedicated "For My Students at the Harvard Divinity School, Fall 1986." I owe special thanks to Deborah McDowell, who first suggested that I explore the lives of Jarena Lee and Rebecca Cox Jackson for this essay. In addition, many people read or listened to this paper in its early drafts and offered encouragement and/or helpful suggestions for its improvement. I specially thank Constance Buchanan, director of the Women's Studies in Religion Program at the Harvard Divinity School, Carol Christ, Riffat Hassan, Alexandra Owen, and Chava Weisler, Research Associates at the Divinity School 1986–87, who read, listened, and gave me positive and supportive criticism. I also thank Warner Berthoff, Randall Burkett, St. Clare Drake, Nathan Huggins, and Werner Sollors for their sensitive and helpful comments. Especially for encouragement and fellowship I am grateful to Victoria Byerly, Katie Cannon, Marion Kilson, Deborah McDowell, Marilyn Richardson, and Mary Helen Washington.

narratives (male), to the exclusion of the dynamic power of the spiritual or conversion narratives. Fortunately, the new scholarship, in quest of a more fully developed intellectual understanding of Afro-American life, recognizes and has begun to explore the spiritual and secular importance of black religious faith in eighteenth- and nineteenth-century black men's and women's narratives.[1] Such study has more than historical implications, and the narratives of twentieth-century black women and men continue to reflect the profound impact that the early religious traditions of the nineteenth century have had on their individual and collective lives. Using autobiographical writings of two black women of the nineteenth century, I shall examine in this essay the roots of the tradition of black women's engagement with the spiritual life of the community, the roles they assumed within that religious framework, and the extent to which faith in the "divine" gave expanded meaning to their lived experiences.

The current flowering of Afro-American autobiography and autobiographical criticism is not undeserved. Afro-American prose writings began with autobiography: the slave, conversion or spiritual, and confessional narratives, preeminent from the middle of the eighteenth century through the middle of the nineteenth. In spite of major changes and developments, the form continues to hold a central position within the twentieth-century black American literary tradition.[2] Scholars of the evolution of black traditions in writing point to a number of reasons for the popularity of the personal narrative over other literary forms among Afro-American writers in the early years. Not the least of these were indeed the other politics and propaganda it directed toward the outside world and the internal sense of order and control it bestowed on a group whose external world demanded subservience and dependence on others. For as Pamela S. Bromberg notes in another context, the "self-generated and self-motivated [narrative] . . . tends . . . toward a unity of point of view and coherence that makes it . . . patterned and meaningful," not disordered and purposeless, in conflict with "coincidence—the unforeseen, random, [and] unpredictable"—in human experience.[3] Moreover, the appeal of the personal narrative for blacks also lies in the challenge of critic Albert Stone's theory of autobiography as literary convention and cultural activity: imagination and history.[4] As Andrews notes, the nineteenth-century black writer, in telling his or her story, had to be sufficiently imaginative to avoid the pitfall of boring "facts," even while he remained true to the personal history.[5] In the final analysis, autobiography connects the writer to her or his individual self as well as to collective human existence. In black autobiography, to a greater degree than in white, author and white reader, with separate racial identities within the same culture, are forced toward a common reading of experience.

In this respect, eighteenth- and nineteenth-century blacks who told their own stories forced a different relationship between Afro-Americans and the dominant culture. Escaped slaves who condemned the "peculiar" institution by indicting its atrocities in writing, and spiritual narrators who claimed equal access to the love and forgiveness of a black-appropriated Christian God could not be nonpersons in the eyes of the white world. Their narratives compelled a revisionary reading of the collective American experience, as specific situations and individual acts of memory and imagination yielded to identifiable patterns within the larger cultural context. And while the centrality and importance of the individual life initially motivates all autobiographical impulse, in black autobiography this "act of consciousness" in the present bears the weight of transcending the history of race, caste, and/or gender oppression for an entire group.[6]

The spiritual and slave narratives, one religious and addressed mainly to the black community, the other secular and intended for a white readership, offer profound second readings of the American and Afro-American experiences against prevailing white American views in their time. Clearly, the authors of these narratives wanted more than to create and recreate the self-in-experience in literature. In establishing their claims to full humanity, they wanted their words to change the hearts of the men and the women whom they reached. Robert Stepto reminds us that in the Afro-American slave narrative these claims sought validity in the "moral voice of the former slave recounting, exposing, appealing, apostrophising, and above all *remembering* his ordeal in bondage.[7] Similarly, in his argument for the significance of the spiritual narratives, Andrews maintains that they are "models of the act and impact of biblical appropriation on the consciousness of the black narrator as bearer of the Word."[8]

Other scholars have ably demonstrated that the rhetorical aims of early Afro-American autobiographical narrative focused on the authentication of the black self in a world that had denied that self humanity. As the form evolved through the mid-1800s, it revealed more clearly the nature of creative tensions between the black self and white cultural assumptions of that self in relationship to the dominant white society, and between the black individual and his or her psychological needs beyond survival.[9] In the slave narrative, the writer's concrete quest was physical freedom, while literacy—the ability to articulate that quest through writing—intimated a less restricted self, socially and otherwise. For spiritual autobiographers, the escape from sinfulness and ignorance of a worthwhile self and the achievement of salvation and knowledge of God's saving grace bestowed a fundamentally positive identity.

Much has been made of narrative differences and meanings in early black autobiography based on severe antebellum legal and extralegal strictures against black literacy. Critics of black narrative and autobiography have fully discussed the loss of authorial authority to the amanuensis-editor and the use of authenticating documents by whites, such as appended prefaces, letters, and the like, to give historical validity to the narrator. Historians, anthropologists, and literary critics, among others, agree that the narrative written by the subject of the text has a higher "discursive status" than the dictated narrative, edited and shaped by another, especially one outside of the experience. Consider, then, the significance of the fact that the first relatively autonomous black narrative was a spiritual narrative, published in 1810.[10] In addition, almost all of the spiritual narratives published through the 1860s were relatively autonomous documents. Their largest distribution appears to have been within the perimeters of the black church and at revival meetings. While most lacked the immediate overt political value of the slave narratives (i.e., they seldom clamored for abolition), they presented readers with a radical revision of prevailing white myths and ideals of black American life. Spiritual narratives were written by ex-slaves as well as freeborn blacks and provide a valuable cross-sectional view of nineteenth-century Afro-American intellectual thought.

As noted earlier, critical evaluation of black women's autobiographical narratives, past and contemporary, is rapidly becoming a substantial part of new Afro-American scholarship.[11] While the major concern for all black people in America has always been the issue of race, the narratives of black women present a more complicated dilemma than those of their male counterparts. In the search for self, issues of gender are equally as important as those of race for the black female, a matter black men usually overlooked. Consequently, as male slave and spiritual narrators sought autonomy in a world dominated by racist white male views, black women writers demonstrated that sexism, inside and outside of the black community, was an equal threat to their quest for a positive identity. Black women use the personal narrative to document their differences in self-perception as well as their concerns for themselves and others, their sense of themselves as part of a distinct women's and racial community, and the complexities of the combined forces of race and gender for the only group beleaguered by both.

In all categories of writing, considerably fewer nineteenth-century texts by black women than men survive. Most of these are spiritual narratives. While the majority of women who wrote were Northern and freeborn, all—former slaves or free women—felt "called" to a mission that transcended the mundane activities of their daily lives and manifested their first loyalties to a being more powerful than humans. Most were itinerant preachers and/or missionaries who traveled extensively in America and abroad, with or without the sanction of the established black church. Their stories focus on their religious convictions, on their willingness to respond to a calling that demanded they overcome formidable personal and societal hindrances in the process, and on a consciousness of the authority that came to them in the service they carried out. Nor is it surprising that religious black women of great personal power and authority emerged from their communities. Often referred to as the glue that has held the black church together, black women within this institution developed the "independence, self-reliance, strength, and autonomy" that the dominant culture little suspected they possessed.[12] Nineteenth-century black female spiritual autobiographies vividly demonstrate this claim in their delineation of women's participation in the ideological conflicts of their religious communities—in their insistence on the validity of the doctrine of ecstatic experience and the rights of women to the clergy.

This essay focuses on two representative spiritual narratives by Northern antebellum black women who claimed authority largely on the basis of their ecstatic religious experience and the fundamental right of women to self-determination: Jarena Lee and Rebecca Cox Jackson. Lee never mentions the latter, but Jackson notes one meeting between them in Philadelphia in 1857. Apparently, the women had disagreed vigorously at earlier times, most likely over religious matters, and Jackson claims that Lee had been "one of her bitterest persecutors." In 1857, however, the meeting was amicable. Jackson attributes this to the "Lord's doing," and the "answer to her prayer." According to Jackson, Lee "spoke lovingly" to her, read from the Scriptures, sang, prayed, bestowed a blessing on Jackson's house, and left her "with love."[13]

Lee was an itinerant preacher with affiliations to the AME church. She claimed fame for her astonishing record of traveling thousands of miles—many of them on foot—across the border states, Ohio, and Canada, to dispense her message. In 1835, for instance, she covered more than seven hundred miles and preached almost as many sermons. Jackson, on the other hand, began her religious career independently of approval from organized religion and traveled only moderately within the North Atlantic states. Both women claimed gifts of vision as one confirmation of their faith. In their journals, kept over several years, they wrote of their experiences of faith and mission. These narratives illuminate the differences that a strong religious faith made in their lives and their perceptions of the freedom they achieved through that faith. Both emphasize the women's search for Christian perfection, the highest state of salvation in life; the process of their development as leaders; their challenges to male authority; and their unfaltering belief in the authenticity of their special gifts of power through vision.

The black female autobiographical tradition begins with Lee's narrative: *The Life and Religious Experience of Jarena Lee, a Coloured Lady, Giving an Account of Her Call to Preach the Gospel. Revised and Corrected from the Original Manuscript, Written by Herself* (24 pages), published in 1836.[14] Lee printed a thousand copies of her text, paying the cost of thirty dollars herself, and sold them at camp meetings and other church gatherings. She believed that her story, a record of God's work through her, would be a useful tool to lead others to him. In 1839 she printed another thousand copies, and presumably dispersed them in the same way. In 1844 she tried without success to convince the book committee of the AME church to publish an expanded version of the narrative. Against the church's rule forbidding traveling preachers to publish books or pamphlets without its approval, *Religious experience and journal of Mrs. Jarena Lee, giving an account of her call to preach the gospel* (97 pages) appeared in 1849.

Rebecca Cox Jackson, twelve years younger than Jarena Lee, kept journals of her religious experiences from 1830 to 1864. She died in 1871, and her words remained unpublished for more than a hundred years. *Gifts of Power: The Writings of Rebecca Jackson, Black Visionary, Shaker Eldress*, edited by Jean McMahon Humez, appeared for the first time in 1981. The existence of Lee's and Jackson's works, an immediate record of the women's experiences, demonstrates that black women felt it was vital that they preserve documentation of their personal convictions and spiritual leadership. Both Lee and Jackson had almost no formal education and no social privilege. Although she could read from the Bible by the time of her conversion, Lee claims to have been to school for approximately three months. On the other hand, Jackson purports to have been wholly illiterate but to have prayed for and received the "gift" of literacy in her search for autonomy after her conversion. This was an extraordinary blessing, since it not only enabled her to read the Bible for herself but freed her from what Humez calls the "editorial tyranny of her more [literate] privileged" preacher-brother (*Gifts*, p. 19).

Following their conversions, Jarena Lee and Rebecca Cox Jackson began their ministries as members of Holiness groups within the Methodist faith.[15] These groups, which also existed outside of Methodism, held firmly to a belief in justification—the recognition and acceptance of the power of God to forgive sins. Beyond that, they reinforced the women's commitment to seek sanctification, the controversial doctrine of "the blessing of perfect love," the ability to strive constantly for a higher "experience of divine grace" (*Gifts*, p. 5): to be in harmony with the will of God. Largely female in composition, the "praying bands" met in each others' homes. In these "relatively intimate, highly participatory, democratic religious gatherings in the familiar world of women friends," the members were encouraged to develop their "spiritual talents and speaking skills" within a safe and protective community (*Gifts*, p. 6). In describing a group of which she was a member, Jackson comments on the presence of women who were "gifted either in prayer or in speaking" and notes that meetings were conducted "as the Spirit of God directed," with members having "[equal] liberty to move as they felt" (*Gifts*, p. 102). Initially refused permission to preach by the church, Jarena Lee held prayer meetings in such groups, at which she spoke as the spirit moved her and exhorted before more public audiences. Around 1821, requests for her to preach came from far and near and transformed her into an itinerant preacher. By then, Bishop Allen approved her activities, although she was never ordained.

Rebecca Jackson belonged to no formal religious groups until she joined the Shakers. Before that, rather than seek the approbation of the Christian church, she disapproved of much that it did: "I saw that these churches were not the Lord's, and neither were these people serving the Lord in the way which was acceptable to him. Therefore I labored among them for the good of souls" (*Gifts*, p. 103). On the other hand, she struggled within herself for confirmation of the authority to preach, for a long time not trusting the "inner voice" prompting her in that direction. She feared that Satan was leading her into the sin of presumptuousness. Her narrative suggests that she regularly attended weekly prayer group meetings of women (the Covenant Meeting), and in 1831 she became a leader. In time, she assumed voice and authority beyond the prayer group.

While Jarena Lee's life was outer-directed, Rebecca Jackson's was inner-directed and depended heavily on her reliance on the efficacy of her dreams, the gift of foresight, waking visions, and an inner voice. Lee's motivation to print her journals—giving herself voice and authority within the established religious community—does not apply to Jackson. Although her narrative implies a reader, we have no indication that Jackson attempted to publish the materials during her lifetime.[16] Why then, keep a journal of these experiences? One might surmise that as a black leader in a predominantly white religious group, she intended her record to confirm her racial presence and leadership among the Shakers, except that the preciseness with which she records the dates and events in her life in the 1830s indicates that she began to keep journals several years before she knew of the Shakers, and more than a decade before she joined them. Unresolved (and perhaps ultimately unresolvable) issues such as this emphasize Marilyn Richardson's astute observation of how little we know of the intellectual thought of black women in the nineteenth century—to say nothing of whether still-undiscovered black women's journals and other writings exist from that period.[17]

What is certain, however, is that the desire to read and interpret the Bible on their own was one that propelled women such as Lee and Jackson toward the competence that made it possible for them to keep records of their civic and religious activities. On this level, literacy was power bestowed on the self by the self. Philosophically, their achievements in writing are further proof that for black women as well as men, there was a close relationship between freedom and literacy in the minds of eighteenth- and nineteenth-century Afro-Americans. Spiritual narrators participated in the quest for literacy and gained the freedom to assert their relationship to God by their ability to read and expound on the Bible through their own powers of understanding. In this and other ways, their literacy negated some of the most debilitating effects of race and/or gender oppression and enhanced their self-respect and sense of autonomy.

Although she was not a slave, Jarena Lee, born in Cape May, New Jersey, in 1783, was the child of very poor parents. At age seven she was sent out to "service." Her parents, she tells us, were "ignorant of the knowledge of God" and gave her no religious instruction. No doubt she, and other black women like her, were deeply affected by the general wave of religious revivals that swept New England in the late 1700s and early 1800s after the American Revolution. This places Lee's consideration of her preconversion self as a "wretched sinner" within the larger context of women's religious conversions in the nineteenth century. Much like white women caught up in the fervor of such awakenings in this period, black women were more convinced of their membership in the collective sinfulness of the human condition than of their guilt in having committed particular sins.[18] Thus Lee, a young, poor black woman, more sinned against by the conditions of her life than guilty of sins of her own, could bypass feelings of alienation and estrangement that her race, class, gender, and social circumstances dictated and feel joined to the fallen state of all humankind, as needful and worthy of divine forgiveness and salvation as all others, no matter how outwardly different their life situations were from hers. Once converted, black women (and men), as members of the community of believers, felt themselves equal before divine authority, for, as Lee later noted, citing St. Paul's letter to the Romans, and including herself among the blessed, "as many as are led by the Spirit of God are the sons of God" (*Sisters*, p. 48).

In a dramatic moment in 1804, when the Reverend Richard Allen, later the bishop of the AME church, was preaching in Philadelphia, Lee was converted:

> My soul was gloriously converted to God. . . . it appeared to me, as if a garment, which had entirely enveloped my whole person . . . split at the crown or my head, and stripped away from me, passing like a shadow, from my sight—when the glory of God seemed to cover me in its stead. (*Sisters*, p. 29)

Four years later she received the gift of sanctification. Some four or five years beyond that, an inner "voice" called her to preach. Lee's response (common among black women evangelists of the nineteenth century) to the "call" was to deny her ability to carry out such a mission. But like the Old Testament Moses, who hesitated to assume responsibility to deliver the Children of Israel out of Pharaoh's Egypt, she was assured by the "voice" that words would be put into her mouth and that her enemies would become her friends (*Sisters*, p. 35). Still not obeying the call, she married a minister in 1811 and moved to an outlying township of Philadelphia, where she supported his ministry until his death six years later. Then, convinced of the authenticity of her call to the great work of preaching to save souls, she left her two young children and began her public career. She traveled extensively through the country, addressing black and white audiences, condemning slavery, preaching the gospel, and saving souls. Initially, she met with opposition from black male church leaders who disapproved of women as preachers, but she eventually gained the support of many of them. For a number of years she enjoyed a successful evangelistic career. In spite of her lack of formal education, she mastered the Scriptures and was an intelligent, effective carrier of her message. Sustained largely by unfaltering faith, she later wrote:

> I have been fed by his bounty, clothed by his mercy, comforted and healed when sick, succored when tempted, and everywhere upheld by his hand. (*Sisters*, p. 41 )

Rebecca Cox Jackson, also a free black woman, was born outside of Philadelphia in 1795. Jackson's journals reveal almost nothing about her life before 1830, when, she says, she became a "new creature" to carry out the will of God. Her father, it seems, died around the time of her birth. Until age thirteen, when her mother also died, she lived alternately with a grandmother and her mother. Subsequently, she went to live with a brother eighteen years her senior. He was a minister, a prominent figure in one of Philadelphia's most well known black churches, and a widower with six children. When she married, Jackson and her husband lived under her brother's roof. She was housekeeper for her brother, his children, and her husband and also earned her living as a seamstress. She appears to have had no children of her own.

Between her mother's death and her conversion, Jackson's external situation appears relatively safe and comfortable. Although there was a good deal of racial unrest in the city between 1829 and 1849, Philadelphia had a growing free black community with its own religious and social institutions. Even before she married, because she lived with her brother and had a respectable trade, Jackson, no doubt, escaped many of the indignities that black women who lived with white employers suffered. Like Lee, she felt in her youth that her life was full of sin and that the religion she was familiar with offered no salvation. In 1830, during a severe thunderstorm, Jackson, who until then had feared thunder and lightning, experienced conversion. Like Lee, she described the event as well as the contrasts between the sinful and redeemed selves in dramatic language. Of the former state she wrote:

> My sins like a mountain reached to the skies, black as sack cloth of hair and the heavens was as brass against my prayers and everything above my head was of one solid blackness. Then, the old gave way to the new: . . . the cloud bursted, the heavens was clear, and the mountain was gone. My spirit was light, my heart was filled with love for God and all mankind. And the lightning, which was a moment ago the messenger of death, was now the messenger of peace, joy, and consolation. (*Gifts*, p. 72)

Not only did she feel that her sins were forgiven, and that the peril of the moment, "the expect[ation] of every clap of thunder to launch [her] soul at the bar of God," had passed, but she immediately lost her phobia, and thunder and lightning became sources of God's redemptive power.

During a revival the following year, Jackson received the gift of sanctification and began her preaching career in the homes of fellow believers. As a result of her conversion, she felt called to practice celibacy, although she was married. "I saw clearly," she wrote, "what the sin of the fall of man was." She claimed that at the moment of that recognition, had she owned the earth, she would have willingly given it all away to once again become "a single woman" (*Gifts*, pp. 76–77). Jackson's decision to reject sexual love occurred several years before she knew of Shaker doctrine on the subject. She made claims for sexual abstinence on the basis of her implicit belief that after conversion her body was no longer her own but had become a vessel dedicated to a higher-than-human will. To maintain its consecrated state it was necessary, she said, to free it from the desires of physical lust. Yet the decision is a powerful manifestation of self-assured empowerment. It is reasonable to think, as Jean Humez does, that by invoking her religious conviction, Jackson (consciously or unconsciously) used that conviction (the only one she had) to reclaim control of her body (*Gifts*, p. 17).

Although closely associated with the AME church as a child, and later through her brother and the "believers" whom she knew, Rebecca Cox Jackson never joined the church. Her religious life continued through direct personal intercourse with the Holy Spirit, with whom she made a pact at the time of her conversion to "obey in all things, in all places, and under all conditions" (*Gifts*, p. 85). This communication continued immediate through "secret and continual prayer," which she called her "wall of defense" (*Gifts*, p. 82). Focusing intently on interior reality, she was able to use the power of God to her best advantage when she sat still and waited for instructions from her inner voice. Listening within herself became the most active and demanding process of her life. Her "gifts of power," her wisdom, knowledge, foresight, and the power to heal, came to her not from human sources but "by faith and humble prayer and holy living and . . . being led by the Spirit of the true God" (*Gifts*, p. 99). She noted that she would "inquire of the Lord from day to day to know His will" required of her, adding: then, "'I put my hands to work and my heart to the Lord' with a double resolution to do His will" (*Gifts*, p. 85).

Although outside of the church, Jackson had major confrontations with it from the beginning of her ministry. These, she said, separated her "further from the professed Christian world" even as she came "closer to the Lord." Her insistence that humans could attain salvation through grace and deliberate resistance to sin met opposition from laity and clergy. Most church members felt they could be saved only by the "merits of Christ," and not by their deeds. She disputed this as an evasion of personal responsibility to struggle for individual righteousness. As a result of her opposing doctrinal position, her refusal to join the church, her criticism of its laxities, her insistence on her immediate access to God, the validity of her leadership, and her position on celibacy, ministers and leaders saw her as a divisive force within the religious community. In 1837, church leaders, all male, accused her of heresy but denied her request for an interdenominational trial on those charges. While this event seems to mark the end of her relations with her family and the church, she interpreted the refusal of the leaders to confront her, in a forum in which she could defend herself, as a personal victory over them. In the early 1840s she belonged to a small group of religious Perfectionists who lived near Albany. Although these people had separated themselves from their churches in search of the holy life, Jackson found that "they lived in the flesh, like all the churches . . . and were all unjust, to God, to Christ, to His Spirit, and to His Holy cause" (*Gifts*, p. 184). She stayed with and admonished them for a short time; then in 1843 she committed herself to the faith of the Shakers, the people whom she believed "to be the true people of God on earth" (*Gifts*, p. 171). As a group, their way of life and religious beliefs were compatible with her own. Jackson took up residence with them in 1847 and lived in their community in New York State until 1851, when she returned to Philadelphia to organize a mostly black, mostly female Shaker society there. That small community lasted forty years beyond her death.

Jarena Lee and Rebecca Cox Jackson, women of different dispositions, conducted very different ministries. Lee concentrated on her external life and struggled with the male hierarchy of the black church, choosing to work within its structure. Both women's narratives record ecstatic experiences, but Lee's are more illustrations to prove spiritual authority. Her text is impressive for its overt feminist qualities: her rejection of the traditional woman's place as wife and mother, her determination to defy gender biases against women's spiritual leadership, and her physical ability to carry out the ministry she did.

Jackson, on the other hand, believed that the most important aspects of her experiences were connected to her visionary abilities. The strength of her text resides in the rich details of its descriptions of spiritual experiences. Although her public career was important to her as an example of the truly redeemed, Jackson's main priority was the continual searching out and verification of the sacred force which guided her actions, which she was determined to obey in all things. Throughout her religious life, she made frequent use of such traditional ascetic methods as fasting, weeping, praying, and going without sleep for long periods of time as ways of altering and heightening her consciousness, of sharpening her visionary gifts.

Free black women in the nineteenth century were not cut off from each other or other people in the world, and they were not silent. Supportive communities enabled them to know that external, oppressive authorities were not all-powerful, and that they were not completely powerless. The small prayer groups afforded women like Lee and Jackson an opportunity to display their "gifts" of speech and thought, and gave them the encouragement of their peers and the confidence to move beyond their intimate circles. In these woman-centered groups, women living in a male-dominated world, aware of the disadvantages of race and their lack of education, did not restrain their speech or apologize for their feelings. They explored the power of words and used them to express developing thoughts. For those who could read, even in rudimentary ways, language and literacy came together for them in the reflection that occurs when the oral and written traditions meet and mingle. They spoke and listened to each other and shared and expanded their perspectives on experience.

Lee and Jackson are joined as black women in the nineteenth century whose religious faith enabled them to achieve a sense of autonomy and selfhood that otherwise would have been impossible for them. Other women, such as Sojourner Truth, Maria Stewart, and Frances Harper, were able to combine the religious and secular gospels, and to leave other kinds of powerful imprints on the pages of history as well.[19] One important aspect of these writings that survive is what they teach us about major differences between three groups of nineteenth-century black women. Sojourner Truth stands virtually alone in her accomplishments. Perhaps one of the most powerful orators of her day, she never achieved literacy, so others had to record the intellectual legacy of this extraordinary woman. On the other hand, women such as Stewart and Harper had the advantages of formal education, which gave them additional options and their own peculiar vision of life and freedom.[20] Jarena Lee, Rebecca Cox Jackson, Amanda Smith, and others, denied education or other opportunities for public life, fought the battle for selfhood and independent black womanhood on the only grounds available to them—the religious frontier, where they challenged the boundaries of race and gender in nineteenth-century white America.[21] Religious faith meant self-empowerment; and in their hands, the spiritual narrative turned the genre of autobiography into a forceful weapon to express and record another chapter in the history of black women's liberation.

Striking aspects of these narratives include the challenge they mount to conventional women's roles and male authority in their time. Their faith gave them the self-assurance they needed to search out the positive identity that other circumstances in their lives denied. In their quest they ran headlong into the opposition of men and social customs at home and in the church. Lee was a widow with two small children, one only six months old when her husband died. Her behavior shatters the stereotype of the selfless black mother. Her itinerant evangelistic career lasted more than thirty years, and her absences from home took place during some of the important early years of her children's lives. Yet, she makes it clear that she had no maternal anxieties about leaving them for extended periods of time, and this and her struggle against the church fathers for affirmation of her ministry, on the basis of gender equality, place her in the forefront of women's struggle over fundamental issues of female autonomy.

In Jackson's case, even without children of her own, she had traditional household responsibilities to her husband, her brother, and four of his children. Her conflicts with her family began shortly after her conversion. Predictably, her husband responded with open hostility to her decision to be celibate; but for her gift of foresight, his attempts to do her bodily harm on this account would probably have been successful. On the other hand, the intensity with which she gave herself to her spiritual inclinations and yearnings was equally a source of family disruption. Of early in this period, when she tried to fulfill her obligations to herself and her household, she wrote:

> I sewed all day, . . . [saw] that the house was kept in good order, done all their sewing, keep them neat and clean and took in sewing for my living, held meeting every night in some part of the city, then came home. And after Samuel would lay down, I would labor oft times till two or three o'clock in the morning, then lay down, and at the break of day, rise and wait on the Lord. . . . And fasting the three days, Monday, Tuesday, Wednesday—at evening of each day I would take a little bread and water. This brought my system low, yet I had strength to do my daily duty. (*Gifts*, p. 86)

Only her conviction of a divine calling enabled Jackson to stand up to the opposition of her brother and her husband at home, and of the church on the outside. In her own defense against black male authority, she claimed, like Lee and others, that God was the authority and power behind her actions. But as both Jean Humez and Alice Walker conclude, Jackson's narrative is a study in conscious self-control, "an assertion of the power and reality of her inner sources of strength and knowledge" (*Gifts*, p. 2). Walker describes her as "a woman whose inner spirit directed her to live her own life, creating it from scratch, leaving husband, home, family, and friends, to do so." [22] Seen in this light, Jackson's ability to concentrate on her interior reality was the source of her inner authority. Her constant intense periods of prayer and contemplation as she awaited instructions to act were dialogues with self: an assertion of the power of her inner reality. Not surprisingly, before coming to Shakerism, she believed implicitly in a four-person Godhead: God the Father, God the Mother, Christ the Bridegroom, and his Bride, each having equal power and authority.

My argument for the significance of these texts rests on premises that black spiritual autobiographies were one vehicle through which nineteenth-century black writers sought spiritual healing from oppressive social conditions and gained literacy and power in the language of the dominant culture. For men and women, the genre permitted black people the freedom to "elaborate" on the Book of Books, "the white text, in a black voice, and through a black perspective." [23] To a certain degree, the political and economic freedom sought by the fugitive slave was grounded in the black spiritual autobiographer's claim that black people were fully human, with as much right to spiritual salvation as white people. Black spiritual autobiographers recorded the process by which they were saved from sin, and recognized and celebrated the new empowered selves who emerged out of their conversions. Like the slave narrative, the spiritual autobiography gave black women in nineteenth-century American life an opportunity to expand the genre beyond the boundaries set by black men. They used it to express female identity through the religious faith that gave them direct access to God in the Self—the highest authority; this knowledge imbued them with pride, self-respect, and control over their intellectual lives. In the face of other inhumane circumstances, they believed that in the "democracy of saved souls" all "were on an equal spiritual standing *with them* before the Lord" (italics mine; *Sisters*, p. 19). In bypassing and defying the place that white people and black men allotted them by asserting their right to control their perceptions of themselves and their assumptions of full selfhood, they declared an independence of spirit that made them outspoken feminists of their time. In the words of Alice Walker, we need to receive them as gifts of power in themselves.

# Social Religion, the Christian Home, and Republican Spirituality in Antebellum Methodism

### A. Gregory Schneider

James B. Finley, a Methodist traveling preacher, was meeting one of he many classes on his Kentucky circuit. He had been warned that a prominent distiller in the neighborhood had gathered a gang and was going to break up the meeting. Methodism, evidently, was bad for the liquor merchant's business. Finley posted a sentry at the door of the cabin to keep the gang out. As the preacher inquired into the religious experience and practice of member after member, the class responded to each stirring testimony with murmured "Amens," then with shouts of "Glory!" Soon their spiritual enjoyment grew loud enough to be heard a mile distant. The sentry at the door was so enraptured that he neglected his post just long enough for the distiller to break in.

Quickly the sentry came to himself and slammed the door on the rest of the gang. In this way the local servant of Demon Rum found himself standing spiritually alone, an island of depravity in a sea of frenetic devotion. Finley stepped up to him and poured on "a warm exhortation." The sinner was furious but his rage could not withstand the ocean of divine love that roared around him. He fell to the floor in conviction of sin just as the devotional excitement billowed to its peak. To Finley, "it seemed as if heaven and earth had come

N.B. An earlier version of this article was presented to the American Academy of Religion at its national convention in Boston in 1987. The author wishes to thank Stephen Stein, Jan Shipps, and the North American Religions Section of the academy for the discussion and criticism they provided. Thanks are due also to the National Endowment for the Humanities for a fellowship in 1985–86 during which much of the research for this article was done.

together." The sentry at the door shouted the news to the gang outside, "H. is down! H. is down!" They all rushed to see the awful sight, and many of them fell upon one another in the doorway—some, presumably, under conviction of sin as well as under the weight of their comrades. The rest, observed Finley, "ran to their horses and fled with the greatest precipitancy and consternation to their homes." The distiller joined the church and never again harassed a meeting.[1]

The documents of antebellum Methodism in the Ohio Valley are full of stories of this sort, stories in which the saints meet apart from "the world," experience significant spiritual blessings together, and exert influences which either transform or repel the watching worldlings. It may seem a long leap from such stories to claims for the existence of a republican spirituality. This essay, however, will build a case for the following assertion: Methodist rituals of "social religion," like Finley's class meeting, laid foundations in experience for a transformation of the meaning of republicanism among an important segment of American evangelicals in the first half of the nineteenth century.[2] This transformation of meaning, moreover, created an evangelical Christian version of republican ideology in which three basic republican themes—liberty, unity, and virtue—facilitated a rhetorical identification of religion, family, and nation, or, more flippantly, God, Mother, and the Flag.[3]

The case for these claims will rest on historiographic foundation stones which stress the significance of ritual, rhetoric, and ethnocultural diversity in the interpretation of republicanism. One such foundation stone comes from the work of Rhys Isaac and others who have discovered a cultural conflict between the more traditional "ethos of honor" characteristic of colonial Virginia and the evangelical ethos of the popular Protestant denominations.[4] Circuit rider Finley's frenetic class meeting was an instance of such conflict as it was carried west with the tide of migration. A second stone comes from historians of ethnocultural and class divisions in early American politics who have discovered several different sorts of republicanism in different regions and among different groups in the new nation.[5] A third basis, perhaps most fundamental of all, is the literature on republican ideology provided by historians such as Bernard Bailyn and Gordon Wood.[6] These works alerted us to a constellation of concepts with which people of the early American nation illuminated their social and political experience: power intruding against liberty, unity of the people for the sake of the common good as the effective defense against power, virtue and simplicity in the people as the means to such unity and as the foundation of good republican government. More recent historiography has demonstrated the diverse ways in which various peoples of the new republic bent these concepts to their particular experience and interests, but the central importance of these concepts to political rhetoric in the early republic is well established.[7]

The way the upper South bent republicanism to its experience and interests is evident in the way it construed these themes: liberty, unity, and virtue. The images of the traditional South that emerge from recent social and cultural historiography suggest a rhythm of events like court days, militia musters, Sunday services, horse races, dances, cock fights, and legislative election contests, all of which served to maintain a precariously established traditional community of southern planters. It was a deferential order, dominated by patriarchs of the white gentry. The gentry demonstrated their honor, manliness, wealth, and generosity in these events, many of which had the character of a contest or a treat provided for the lower orders. As they played the part of fascinated observers in these ritual dramas, or directly participated in their own more rustic imitations, they experienced a "continuous socialization" into the outlook and interests of the gentry. This traditional ritual economy exuded what Isaac and others have termed the "ethos of honor." This implied an understanding of self in which external appearance and performance and the judgments of others constituted the center of personal identity and self-worth. The central questions of social order were those of sovereignty and deference. Who was to defer to whom? Who was the superior, who the inferior? In this context, the republican concepts of liberty, unity, and virtue had particular meanings.

Liberty, to the southerners, was not an abstract principle, but a concrete experience of personal and community independence in the management of local affairs, free from outside interference. A man's self-regard depended upon certain visible marks of independence: a wife, children, property on which to support them, and clearly visible patterns of action which made it clear that he was master of events that pertained to his sphere of society. Some spheres, of course, were more extensive than others. Liberty, therefore implied a subtle and precarious balancing act: on one hand, an individual or community needed to preserve a socially recognized and respected sphere of control over personal or local affairs; on the other hand, cultural norms and economic necessity required deference and loyalty to those whose greater wealth and privilege gave them patriarchal power to govern the commonwealth and paternalistic obligation to care for its several members. The American struggle for independence was a major moment in a long process that tipped this balance toward individual and local liberty and undermined patriarchy as the organizing metaphor for the life of the commonwealth and its constituent communities.[8]

The overthrow of patriarchy as metaphor for the integration of the commonwealth, however, did not immediately destroy it as metaphor for the family. Family, in the traditional social order that supported the ethos of honor, meant a patriarchal household or estate, an economic and political entity made up of all those dependent upon the order and productivity of the estate and defined by the sovereignty of the patriarch. This view of family as the basic unit of social and political order, and as the foundation of an adult male's rights, liberties, and selfhood, persisted well beyond the founding of the nation. The great migration westward expressed, at first, men's traditional quest for the grounds of honor in the eyes of the community more than it did a rationally calculated, individually self-interested economic individualism. Through at least the first half of the nineteenth century, this traditional quest animated what Robert Kelley finds to be the South's characteristically libertarian version of republican ideology.[9]

The concrete association of the idea of liberty with one's household involved a configuration of perception and feeling that conferred great motive power upon republican rhetoric. Men of honor asserted themselves in trade, in the management of servants or slaves, in horse races, or in war, not simply for themselves, but also for their families, especially their women. They pictured a moral cosmos constructed of an interior space, which was soft and vulnerable, surrounded by an exterior boundary that had to be hard and strong in order to protect the vulnerable interior from the encroachments of a threatening world. This configuration shaped the identities of both men and women. Men belonged in the world, but they were there for the sake of patrolling and building up the boundary that protected that inner space of household, hearth, and home which grounded their claim to an independent manhood. Women, by statute, were hidden in the persons of their husbands, charged with sanctifying the soft interior space and making it appropriately receptive and productive of progeny. To threaten a man's wife, or mother, or sister, or children, or home was to threaten the most vulnerable part of himself. Nothing could evoke greater fury. The fundamental opposition in republican ideology between aggressive, masculine power and vulnerable, feminine liberty reflected and exploited this archaic configuration of sentiments.[10]

Liberty in the ethos of honor had nothing to do with freedom to defy established conventions. Liberty was self-determination in one's appropriate ethical sphere, not license or anarchy or lack of obligation to enforce and promote the cohesion and prosperity of the social whole. Liberty, then, far from scattering the community of honor into isolated individuals, walked hand-in-hand with unity.

The unity in question was a moral consensus of the respectable citizens of a community. Such consensus might be demonstrated at the boundaries of acceptable behavior by rituals of detestation like lynching, the milder charivari, or various movements of vigilantism modeled on the example of the colonial South Carolina "Regulators." These actions were generally conservative efforts on the part of the propertied citizens to secure their lives, families, and property against what they perceived to be lawless elements. Similar actions were perpetrated by American Whigs against persons who failed in one way or another properly to support the patriot cause. Early versions of republicanism conceived of liberty and rights as belonging to the people taken as a whole in

195

opposition to the power and interests of rulers. Liberty was, first of all, public and political not private and individual. Hence, there could be no legitimate opposition between individual liberties and the common good of the people in a republic. Those who placed their private interests above the common good were diseased tissue in the body politic, and might be subjected to harsh remedies. Unity in the cause of the common good, then, sometimes required an oppressive conformity.[11]

Another manifestation of the required unity of this sort in consensual democracy was in the competitive pastimes, social drinking, and especially the carnival atmosphere of election days. In frontier agricultural communities, these events fostered the camaraderie necessary to essential social cooperation and mutual aid in large-scale projects or in the face of threats by enemies or natural catastrophes. In more established communities, the drinking and gambling bouts associated with court days, militia musters, or election days continued to provide that aggressive sociability whereby men isolated by the geography of agriculture might come together to escape solitude and lay claim to pride, place, and power in fellowship. The cultivation of personal privacy was not a generally recognized virtue. To refuse to participate in these face-to-face events that created society was, at best, to court charges of believing oneself too good for the democratic fellowship of sturdy republican yeomen; at worst, it invited the stigma of cowardice or treason.[12]

Virtue, the most essential trait of republican citizens, was absent in cowards and traitors. They placed their own welfare above that of the common good. The essential meaning of virtue in republican ideology was the setting aside of such private interests. This selfless dedication to the commonweal was termed "public virtue." Its widely and deeply felt expression in the ethos of honor was martial virtue, the readiness to lay down one's life in defense of hearth and home, kin and community. The requirement and respect for military prowess and courage in men was part of the cultural logic that underlay the compulsive attractions of drinking and gambling. These contest pastimes were substitutes for war, settings in which men tested each other's fortitude and ferocity in order that they might know and trust them as comrades in battle.[13]

Public virtue, however, depended upon private virtue. According to republican ideologues, men beset by selfish lusts had no sense of order or benevolence and were, therefore, incapable of serving the public interest. A republic, in the final analysis, rested upon the private industry, frugality, temperance, and charity of its citizens. The ideal republican was spartan patriot, Protestant saint, and sturdy yeoman rolled into one.[14] Such a paragon was fully capable of resisting the seductions of the monarchical style of government and social life that seemed to rely on luxury and conspicuous consumption for its influence. The emulation inspired by luxury and its display led to a train of vices: dependency, debauchery, dissipation, idleness, extravagance, and effeminacy.[15]

Industry and frugality, then, secured autonomous manhood, and only such manly virtue could undergird the republic.

It is important to note also the feminine connotations of the idea of virtue. The ideological abstractions about public virtue for the sake of preserving liberty in the republic took their concrete meanings from honor's hallowed vision of a feminine inner space to be protected from a hostile world's intrusions. The rich ambiguity of the term, "virtue," allowed republican ideologues to appeal implicitly to the sentiments and motives surrounding feminine virginity even while they discoursed explicitly on the theory of liberty. The archaic meaning of virtue in woman was to keep other men out of that anatomical life-giving space that belonged to her husband alone and that was indispensable to the continuity and purity of his family line. Virtue in man was the capacity to keep other men out of the affairs of his household, that social and psychological sphere containing and corresponding to his woman's inner space. This household space and the actions required to keep it sacrosanct constituted the ethical sphere of an honorable man's autonomy. Expanded by analogy to comprise the community and the commonwealth, this sphere was the heart of republican liberties, patriotic unity, and public virtue.

Themes similar to those wrapped in republican ideology resided in Methodist spirituality. Rather than an ethos of honor, however evangelicals aspired to a community of spiritual equality based on personal disciplines that led to and sustained the "new birth" and on the shared sentiments that resulted from it. At the heart of the evangelical sense of community were the rituals of "social religion," or "social means of grace." By these terms evangelicals referred to a variety of meetings in which laity were the major performers and that were characterized by extemporaneous prayer, singing, inquiry, exhortation, and, above all, testimony. The essential element of social religion was the creation of a community of intense feeling. This atmosphere of spiritual intimacy was a powerful context that taught participants to experience the divine intimacy of God in the new birth.[16]

Two structures in particular characterized Methodism's cultivation of social religion. Class meeting, according to the ideal laid down in the *Discipline*, was a weekly meeting of twelve persons required of all members. The class leader, appointed by the circuit preacher, was to inquire into each member's outward practice and inward experience of religion. Inquiry in class meeting, while often an effort to keep people faithful to Methodist rules for conduct and piety, was always an invitation to tell fellow believers what the Lord had done for one's soul. The extemporaneous testimonies that flowed from the formal "religious conversations" with the class leader were free speech that frequently elicited shouts and tears of joy from fellow believers, or cries of conviction and contrition from those still seeking religion. Love feast, the second of the distinctive Methodist forms of social religion, was generally held at the quarterly meeting of a given circuit or station, usually early on a Sunday morning before the sacrament of the Lord's Supper. Only church members in good standing in the various classes within the circuit or station were to attend. After partaking of a meal of bread and water symbolic of fellowship, members were free to speak of their religious experience as the spirit moved them.[17]

Three themes in the ritual practice of social religion ought to be of particular interest to the student of republicanism; liberty in religious expression which symbolized freedom from sin; unity of the family of God set against the world, yet also transforming the world; and a self-mortifying piety, "the way of the cross," as the condition for and result of liberty and unity.

Liberty, in the context of Methodist ritual, meant a spontaneity, extemporaneity, and emotional power in speech which elicited similar responses from the speaker's hearers. Methodist preachers often noted in their diaries and journals whether or not they had such liberty in preaching. People who testified in class might have similar liberty, their testimonies eliciting the sort of holy noise described in the above account of the Reverend James B. Finley's class meeting. This ecstatic shouting and weeping was a response to the deliverance from temptation, guilt, and sin that occurred at the new birth and which recurred at various points in the religious careers of the faithful. Methodist preaching and testimony were evidence of and models for this experience of liberation from sin. They reminded believers of the anxiety and suffering leading to joy and peace that they had undergone in their quest for religion and reinforced them in their experience. They also convinced nonbelievers of their need for such religion, showed seekers of religion the way, and gave them hope of finding it.[18]

Evangelical liberation from sin implied also a certain liberation from some forms of social control in the ethos of honor. The sense of self characteristic of this ethos was sensitive to shame, the horror of being seen and exposed as ridiculous, cowardly, or simply weak and "lowdown."[19] Evangelicals played upon and transformed this "public" sense of self. They required every believer to engage in highly visible avowals of cosmic weakness and lowliness, the weakness and lowliness of a repentant sinner before God. The acts of faithfully attending the meetings of the despised Methodists in the face of mocking worldlings, of coming forward for all to see at the altar or "mourners' bench," or of braving the intimate exposure of one's life and feelings in class meeting, required believers and seekers of religion to suffer and rise above the constraints of shame. These public actions and avowals symbolized inner psychic states which became the focus of new self-understandings for the religious. A central implication of these new inner feelings was that ridicule and rejection from the public or even from family did not matter so long as one had the inner assurance of acceptance by God. Out of such understandings might come a sort of holy shamelessness that set at defiance the ethos of honor. Thus did one James

Henthorn write to his preacher friend Daniel Hitt that at a recent quarterly meeting, "We had a very considerable shout to the praise of God, while others stood laughing, scoffing and mocking, but the devil fights best on his own ground, he with all his forces gained but little by coming on ours that day; because we faced them man to man: O that we still may grow in holy zeal and boldness. . . ." [20]

Finley's distiller and his gang, on this understanding, were probably concerned about more than lost whiskey sales in the neighborhood. The refusal of local Methodists to enter into traditional convivial drinking symbolized their general determination to defy certain conventions of the community and judge them deficient. Such defiance and judgment likely violated the gang's sense of life, liberty, and pursuit of happiness. Their raid on Finley's class, in this view, was an attempt to reassert the consensual unity of their neighborhood and override the spiritual liberty of the saints.

Spiritual liberty implied spiritual unity, a unity that overwhelmed the distiller when he found himself alone in the midst of it. The shared testimonies, shouts of praise, cries of conviction and contrition, and tears of "mournful joy" that occurred repeatedly in rituals of social religion made for a "bond of union." Finley, years after the class meeting that had floored the liquor merchant, remembered wistfully the classes of older, experienced Methodists who taught him the deeper spiritual life during his early years as a green itinerant. Those were times, he reminisced, when "love filled every heart" and so bound the believers together that "persecution" only moved them to greater faithfulness. [21] What obtained for frontier days might also occur for a later generation, according to a contributor to the *Western Christian Advocate*. This writer observed that in Methodist societies where class meetings were neglected, members grew languid in their religious enjoyments and the devil sowed discord and confusion. In contrast, where believers met regularly in class there reigned peace, harmony, and love: "There are no feuds, nor envying, nor rankling prejudices, but CHARITY." [22]

A precondition of this unity of the believers in social religion was some separation from the world. Only members in good standing were to attend; the early Methodist bishops noted that the frequent admission of worldly or "unawakened" persons to class and love feast meetings tended to stifle "that liberty of speech" that made the meetings such a blessing. A later preacher echoed the bishops as he justified this aloofness to an acquaintance of his who was critical of Methodist discipline. The critic asserted that because class meeting and love feast were the church's best meetings, they ought to be open to sinners and all others. The preacher replied, "It is the peculiar manner in which these meetings are held, by those united in Christian fellowship apart from the world, that makes them better than other meetings: if they were held like other meetings, then truly they would be like other meetings." As another apologist put it, "no worldly motive, no temporal purposes can have any influence here: shut out from the world with its anxious cares, they then speak only of the concerns of their souls."[23]

The Methodists, like other evangelical groups, readily adopted the language and gestures of family as a metaphor for the community of feeling created and sustained by their social religious practices.[24] The family metaphor not only captured the loving sentiments felt in social religious contexts, but also helped to ritualize the interactions of members outside of specifically religious events. The vitality and pervasiveness in the way early Methodists used the titles of Brother, Sister, Mother, or Father in addressing each other forbids the supposition that they were observing empty convention. It was a language of spiritual kinship whereby believers identified themselves as belonging to one another and fostered among themselves the moods and motivations appropriate to their membership in the family of God.[25]

Like the natural families of the ethos of honor, the family of God needed to have its boundaries patrolled, a fact most visible in the enforcement of closed doors for class meeting and love feast. Beyond such highly symbolic acts, however, members of classes and circuits exercised oversight and "solicitude" to see that no brother or sister acted contrary to family principles. Jacob Young remembered how his class leader intervened to have Young dissolve a contract he had made to serve as an overseer on a slave plantation. Such association with one of the leading exemplars of the ethos of honor would have been, as the class leader put it, Young's "final ruin." [26] This concern to sustain the boundaries around the family of God echoed the imperatives of honor to keep one's household sacrosanct. The sacredness of the family's inner space was the foundation of liberty for both the literal family of republican honor and the metaphorical family of evangelical religion.

Methodist evangelicals, however, sustained the boundaries of their family not simply for the sake of preserving their spiritual liberty and unity, but also for the sake of propagating it. Enforcement of discipline in and through class meeting, for example, often purged delinquent members and stirred up piety among the remaining faithful, increasing feelings of love and unity that, in turn, typically led to revivals and new accessions to the church.[27] The pattern of maintaining closed doors in class meeting and love feast also aided in the propagation of the Methodist gospel. Benjamin Webb, for example, went to a Methodist preaching service with some of what he called his "companions in wickedness." After the sermon, the preacher announced the customary class meeting and asked all non-Methodists to leave the house. Being excluded from the house made the wicked young men feel all the more keenly the point of the preacher's text: "Set thine house in order: for thou shalt die and not live." Rather than consent to total banishment, they remained on the porch and tried to hear as much as possible of what went on inside. Their lingering and listening led to conviction of sin, and the noise of their penitence caused the saints to interrupt their class meeting in order to minister to the mourners outside. Four of them joined the church that night. Events like this one, multiplied many times, demonstrated the rhetorical power of Methodist ritual. Through their disciplined practice of social religion, early American Methodists were able to persuade many that they were at the center of something vital, something worth the sacrifices demanded.[28]

Sacrifices were certainly in store for believers in the ethos of honor, especially white males, who became Methodists. According to the code of honor, "A man ought to fear God and mind his business. He should be respectful and courteous to all women; he should love his friends and hate his enemies . . . eat when . . . hungry, drink when . . . thirsty, dance when . . . merry . . . and knock down any man who questioned his right to these privileges."[29] Methodist evangelicals were likely candidates for knock-downs because they did question a man's right to dance. They also condemned his drinking habits, and, worst of all, tried to intrude into his domestic life by converting his wife and children.[30]

To the evangelical way of thinking, the selfhood of the man of honor was based on attachments to his own physical prowess and its fruits in family, wealth, status, and power; his central motives were self-willed sensuality, pride, and violence. Prohibitions, like those found in the Methodist *Discipline*, against drinking, brawling, wearing of "gold or costly apparel," dancing, "needless self-indulgence, sharp or dishonest business practices," and a variety of other evils "most generally practised," became tactics in a comprehensive strategy for confronting and rooting out the worldly attachments and motives at the center of the ethos of honor.[31] Sacrificing worldly practices only foreshadowed the deeper spiritual sacrifice that led to the new birth.

The new birth, or conversion experience, required a deeply felt conviction of sin and of God's rejection, a metaphorical death, before rebirth. Conversion began in an uneasy awareness of sin and judgment that led to terror and despair at the conviction of one's own sinfulness and of God's direct and personal condemnation. The very intensity of this negative emotional state cried out for a transformation into a positive state in which an ecstasy of joy led to peace, hope, and love. The same Bible that spoke of the depravity of humankind and the wrath of God also spoke of God's mercy and love in the sacrifice of Jesus Christ. Faith was an action of the heart that personally claimed the grace of Christ and led to a personal assurance of pardon for one's sin. The painful emotions were swept away and "a new class of affections, principles, and emotions is brought into the heart of a most pleasurable kind." Most significant among these was a lasting feeling that, in accord with Romans 8:16, one had been adopted into the family of God: "The Spirit beareth witness with our spirit that we are the children of God."[32]

Christ's crucifixion and resurrection were the model for the emotions of the new birth. Dying and rising with Christ, however, was never done once and for all. The conversion experience inaugurated a dying life, in which the conversion struggle was a sort of narrative pattern for the ongoing skirmishes of the soul. Evangelicals called this pattern "the way of the cross." It consisted of a habit of self-denial linked to a tenacious disposition to expect affliction to yield comfort, sorrow to bring joy, pain to lead to spiritual pleasure, depression to give way to exultation, discouragement to redound to renewed courage, just as Christ's death resulted in the resurrection. "Strange as it is, it is very true," marveled James Henthorn, "the lower we sink, the higher we rise." The love of Jesus, he declared, led to this fountain of meekness and joy.[33]

The way of the cross established inner harmony in the soul of each believer and in the family of God. Taken together this personal and social religious harmony constituted the full realization of the love of God in Christ. "Christ," observed Henthorn, "is the cement of union, so that while we abide in Him, we shall be one in heart." Divine love, he rhapsodized, was "the misterious [sic] cement of the soul, sweetener of life, and consolidater [sic] of Society." Only when the saints got to heaven and were bathed in the immensity of love at the Father's right hand, would they be able to tell what love in all its branches and channels had done for the fallen children of Adam. "It is enough," Henthorn sighed, "to dissolve the most flinty soul into tears of deep contrition."[34] Devout Methodists passed through tears of contrition to join the family of God. Many referred to their fellow believers as "the friends." In their rhetoric, heaven, the church, friendship, and family were all identified with one another through the common denominator of sentimental love. The order of heaven was a harmony of sentiment.[35]

The rituals of social religion were designed to foster this order by inculcating the disciplines of the way of the cross and celebrating its pleasures. By extension, the harmony of sentiment experienced so powerfully in social religion also became the Methodists' criterion of order, unity, and liberty in the home and in the nation.

By the 1830s, Methodism's protest against an impious ethos turned more and more into a proclamation of the respectability of evangelical values and ideals that had become widespread, if not dominant, in middle-class culture. A vast popular literature of apology and exhortation accompanied this change, as Methodists articulated for themselves and others the sort of culture they were creating and to which they were accommodating. This literature borrowed heavily from two strands of thought: the ideology of domesticity or "woman's sphere," and the ideology of republicanism.[36] This borrowing was not mere cultural diffusion, but an assimilation guided by basic ways of organizing experience learned in the evangelical family of God and its rituals of social religion.

202

Those basic ways of organizing experience centered in a configuration that pitted an inner space of harmonious sentiment against an outer world full of forces hostile to the love within, but also susceptible to it. The Methodist faithful identified this secluded but contagious space with the religious society, with the soul of the believer, and, eventually, with home and family. Its dual quality of seclusion and contagion defined what might be called the dialectic of evangelical identity. In its seclusion from the world, the sacred inner space of the evangelical family of God was an icon of holiness, the home of a spiritual liberty deeply affecting to behold and a delight in which to participate. In its evangelistic power over the world, this inner holiness was an instrument of morality, generating activities and virtues that would prosper religion and preserve the republic. As Methodists appropriated republican ideology, they transformed the meaning of key republican themes in accord with this dialectic of iconic and instrumental moments.

The evangelicals' most obvious point of contact with republicanism was the concept of virtue. An untitled poem in the Methodists' popular monthly, *The Ladies Repository and Gatherings of the West*, encapsulated their understanding of virtue as consisting of an inner harmony set against a disorderly world:

> What, what is virtue, but repose of mind
> A pure ethereal calm, that knows no storm;
> Above the reach of wild ambitions wind,
> Above those passions that this world deform.[37]

Such virtue, because of its distance from the world, had salutary effects on the republic.

Methodists evinced this pattern of thought in conceiving of the place of institutional religion in the republic. American Methodists came late to the campaign for the separation of church and state. The shape of politics in the early republic, however, led them to see such separation in terms of holy distance. The wild, blind, reckless partisanship, the clamorous hurrahs, and the vociferous denunciations manifest at political gatherings seemed destined to destroy rather than serve the public good. Such party spirit was inimical to moral duty and to the harmony of Christian character. Alongside the stormy passions of politics was the frenzy of speculation, a misuse of liberty in the worship of mammon that threatened both the temporal and the spiritual prosperity of the nation. The licentiousness and drunken debauchery evident in Fourth of July celebrations was an affront to God and a disgrace to the country. All these things were signs that large numbers of the American people lacked the virtue necessary to the preservation of the republic.[38] Only a free, enterprising Christianity untrammeled by political establishment and unpolluted by state policy could remedy this state of affairs. Through a sort of strategic retreat from the worldly realm of politics, Christians might exert the exemplary influence necessary to redeem the nation from its perilous course. Church members and ministers were to stand aloof from party wrangles. The Christian patriot served the nation by his knowledgeable vote, his prayers, his temperate conversation, and his pure example—modes of influence critically dependent upon his ability to stand above the factional storms of politics. The only reason, in fact, that licentiousness was not more widespread in American society was that religion had lifted the standard of public sentiment and marshaled a "standing army of well-trained consciences" against it. Religion, as an icon of patriotic holiness, was instrumental as a moral leaven for the mass of American citizens even though most were not professed Christians.[39]

At the heart of religion's leavening influence on the national culture was the unity of the believers. Just as unity of feeling among the brothers and sisters in any given religious society on a circuit was a contagion leading to evangelism, revival, and moral reformation in its neighborhood, Methodist publicists believed the national unity of evangelical believers undergirded the millennial mission of the republic. "Every sect that is actuated by a supreme love to God," declared a contributor to the Pittsburgh *Conference Journal*, ". . . is contributing its quota toward the civil and political salvation of the country." This united love to God, furthermore, would do much to enable the American republic to spread the blessings of civil and religious liberty over the earth.[40]

As they grew into the middle decades of the nineteenth century, Methodists adapted their ritual events to realize palpably their unity of sentiment in political religion. Methodist editors and contributors in the 1830s and 1840s rejoiced in the changes in Fourth of July ceremonies, occasions that had, in earlier years, been evidence of the vicious character of the American people. No longer beset by drunkenness and revelry, Independence Day celebrations were now times for great Sabbath School jubilees, family gatherings, and pious sociability. "The Christian community . . . ," rejoiced one writer, "assemble on that day . . . with their families and youth, to sing praises, and to worship and praise God, and to call upon him to continue our national, social, and family blessings, and to teach our children the history of, and duty to their country and their God." It was a day to pray for a union of hearts that would secure the union of states, a day that kindled hope for a time when Christ's perfect law of liberty would become the law of the land, and a day to rededicate oneself and one's children to the sacred trust of bringing civil and religious liberty to all the nations of the earth.[41]

Republican unity in the ethos of honor occurred chiefly away from home in the midst of the world: on the courthouse green, on the muster field or battlefield. It was both foreshadowed and realized in the good sportsmanship and conviviality of contest pastimes, in the shared moral indignation of charivaris, and in the blood brotherhood of soldiers dedicated to fighting a common foe. Republican unity in the evangelical ethos originated in the family of God apart from the world. It was foreshadowed in the rituals of social religion and in the spiritual fellowship of common efforts to evangelize the worldly. It was realized in pious patriotic festivals of exemplary sentiment and propriety. It was also realized, according to another body of popular literature, in the private patterns and public influence of Christian domestic life.

The Methodist family of God had, from its earliest beginnings, aimed at recruiting literal families, a recruitment that also meant transformation. Where the traditional view saw relations of sovereignty and deference as the defining characteristic of family, evangelicals saw the shared affections and sentiments of the members as most significant. The family became a crucible of moral influence, analogous to the rituals of social religion. This crucible mirrored the felicities of heaven, modeled the fellowship of the saints, and molded the motives of family members in ways that fitted them for that fellowship here and hereafter.[42] It also forged them into frugal, industrious, and self-denying republicans.

The Methodist ideology of the family reflected basic themes of the rituals of social religion. Just as those moments of fellowship were to be separated from the world, so was domestic life to be separated and protected from worldly influences. Indeed, one of the chief functions of class meeting inquiry was to see that heads of families regularly held family prayer, a ritual that extended the spirit of sentimental community to the family circle and prompted Methodist leaders to exhort their fellow believers against any social contacts that might distract from the regular practice and persistent influence of family religion.[43] "Evil communications corrupt good manners," went an oft-repeated maxim, and writers attempted to persuade parents to keep children home and careless company out of the home. "Labor to make your children understand," counseled the author of the *Methodist Family Manual*, "that they are a community of themselves, and that they are to depend upon possessions within themselves for happiness here, and not on the outward excitement of receiving and paying visits, and hearing and sending news. . . ."[44]

The separation of the family from the world, like the separation of the family of God from the world, went hand-in-hand with claims for the heavenliness of the affections that members of *Christian* families held for one another. The modifier received special emphasis; evangelical moralists insisted that even natural family feelings must be subjected to the discipline of Christ, to the way of the cross.[45]

These principles of separation and self-denial were at work in a variety of counsels to husbands and wives that urged mutual respect for each other's spheres and issued constant warnings against selfish passion. An even more abundant literature on children urged the governing of their passions early, by precept and example when possible, by the rod when necessary. Never was correction to be done in anger or vengeance, for the child had to learn self-control from the parent or from no one. On the other hand, indulging a child's willfulness because of an undisciplined affection in the parent would ruin family government and blight the eternal prospects of the child. Fellowship in the family, like fellowship in social religion, was founded upon the mortifications inherent in the way of the cross.[46]

The significance to the republic of such family government was in the cultivation of virtue and in the consequent creation of domestic harmony in the home and in the nation. Just as Methodist evangelicals thought that proper attention to the ritual forms of their community promoted revivals of religion and general prosperity, peace, and harmony within the family of God, so they believed that families ordered on the principles of religion would also insure the virtue and harmony of society as a whole. Only a people who could govern their passions could be trusted to respect one another's liberty. Civilization itself depended on the well-governed evangelical domestic fellowship. Parents, asserted the Methodist author of *A Discourse on Domestic Piety*, were the republic's alternative to the standing armies that oppressed the other nations of the earth. If parents proved unfaithful in family government their children would be unable to govern themselves, and they would betray and murder "social, civil, and religious liberty."[47]

The specific private virtues of industry and frugality were touted as a basic product of this sort of family government. These virtues were essential to the republic because they enabled citizens to enjoy a moderate prosperity without being seduced into excess, corruption, and dependence. The outlet for the energies of children reared in circumscribed evangelical retreat was to be work. Not for them were the frivolous excesses of visiting and public amusements. By early training in diligent work they would acquire the skills and the habits of industry necessary for a virtuous independence in society. Such habits and skills combined with a proper Christian avoidance of popular vices and dissipation would assure also a slow but certain ascent up the ladder of personal prosperity.[48]

The nineteenth-century home, of course, was in the "woman's sphere," and Methodists readily adopted the doctrine as their own. By 1841 they were making their own major contribution to the elaboration and propagation of it in the Cincinnati-based *Ladies Repository*. The "official" version of women's nature promoted by the male editors of the *Repository* is familiar to students of nineteenth-century women's history. Women were more inclined to piety than men, more given to the self-sacrifice that religion required. They were made for a position of retreat in society, eschewing the honor and recognition that men craved and sought in the realms of politics and business. This selfless piety fit them for the all-important labor of rearing virtuous children for responsible citizenship and eternal bliss, a rearing accomplished not by force but by wounded love. They also stabilized the morality and mitigated the trials of their husbands who labored in the heartless world. All the qualities of self-sacrifice, affection, purity, and retreat that characterized the best moments of fellowship in the family of God seem to have inhered "naturally" in the female character. These spiritual qualities, furthermore, allowed a woman to exude a transforming moral influence that drew people to religion and virtue almost in spite of themselves. Even as Christ, by his self-emptying servanthood unto death, was exalted to lordship over all creation, so woman, by her self-denying retreat to a domestic sphere at the margins of society, attained a pervasive moral sovereignty that was, claimed one author, "more absolute than that possessed by the conquering hero or the sceptered monarch."[49]

This official view was largely the perspective of the *Repository's* male editors, who projected onto women primarily the iconic moment in the dialectic of evangelical identity. Woman in woman's sphere was an angelic icon of holiness who evoked exclamations of moral admiration from her largely male promoters. Her instrumental power, though exaggerated in rhetoric, was restricted to her roles as companion to men and mother to children. Neither could woman's power be exercised directly, but only as that paradoxical "female influence" that was effective because it demanded nothing.

Other writers, more women than men, sensed and articulated a more active instrumental role for woman. Claims to attention women made in correspondence submitted to the *Repository* were evidence of this more active stance.[50] Also, in the content of some articles, there were calls to women to engage in mission work to improve the world, minister to the sick, care for the widow and orphan, convert the sinner, and, if God opened the way, evangelize the heathen in foreign lands.[51] Although women remained formally identified with domestic space, these lines of thought and activity expanded the definition of woman's sphere and contributed some small steps to the process of liberating women from the narrow confines of traditional social roles.[52]

These early steps toward the liberation of women began not primarily with freedom from Britain or from the threat of social and economic dependence upon Britain's monarch. They did not arise out of any sort of sustained or sophisticated social or political analysis. They began, instead, with the intensely personal experience of freedom from sin and a total spiritual dependence upon God. In 1808 William McKendree had melted the Methodist General Conference into tears when he noted the "shouts of applause" so often heard at celebrations of American liberation from slavery to Britain and her king, and then thundered, "How much more cause has an immortal soul to rejoice and give glory to God for its spiritual deliverance from the bondage of sin!" The sermon was instrumental in his election as bishop. A generation later, children in Methodist Sunday Schools were singing songs that pled for "a Liberty more blest, more high" than mere civil liberty, an independence from sin that would clear their path to heaven.[53] Methodists became staunch republicans, but they continued to believe their spiritual liberty transcended the temporal liberty of republican political culture.

Their highly personal experience of spiritual liberty was far from socially or politically irrelevant. One reason spiritual liberty was greater than temporal liberty was that the essential fruit of spiritual liberty was self-control rather than mere absence of social control by other human beings.[54] Without such self-control, Methodist evangelicals claimed, temporal liberty was a danger to families, communities, and the whole nation. Both evangelical republicans and republicans of the ethos of honor identified their liberty with an inner space of feminine sacredness to be defended from the incursions of worldly power. The inner space of evangelical religion, however, possessed the power of the Holy Spirit to transform the forces which threatened it. Christian holiness, therefore, made the pious mothers and praying families of the evangelical churches a collective wellspring of eternal life and liberty, which flowed out to create a national community of virtuous sentiment. Only by such a community might the merely temporal life and liberty of the nation be preserved and the republican vision redeemed.

## CHAPTER 13

# "And Obey God, Etc.":
# Methodism and American Indians

## Bruce David Forbes

In reminiscences about his brief missionary work among the Ojibwa people, Methodist minister Thomas Fullerton recalled the advice he gave to one potential convert: "I required him, if he would be one of us to have his hair cut off, dress as near as he could in civilized garb, keep himself clean, and obey God &c."[1] As the admonition reveals, historical Methodist relationships with Native Americans involved much more than the simple proclamation of the gospel. Missionaries also functioned as carriers of white Americans culture, which often was linked to the Christianity they sought to promote. Evangelical efforts were influenced by encroaching white settlement, and the missionary ventures were complicated by twists and turns of federal Indian policy. Native responses to all of this cannot be seen simply as spiritual decisions but must be viewed also as responses to wide-ranging cultural conflict and disruption.

The following somewhat impressionistic survey is intended to provide an interpretive overview of historical relationships between Methodism and American Indians. More detailed discussions of virtually every subject raised here are available elsewhere, but this article hopes to contribute by drawing an outline of the story in broad strokes. Those unfamiliar with the subject may find it a helpful introduction, and specialists may be stimulated by some bold generalizations they can test or challenge. This overview inclines more toward offering interpretations or generalizations, both standard and provocative, than to detailing the names and dates associated with various efforts, but a bit of both is attempted. Finally, even distillation has its limits; this summary focuses on the nineteenth century. The twentieth century, with its greater appreciation for cultural pluralism and self-determination, deserves its own discussion.

# METHODIST MISSIONS BEFORE THE CIVIL WAR

One might expect Methodism to be exceptional in the amount of effort it gave to Indian missions, because even its founder was interested in being a missionary to Native Americans. John Wesley's venture in Georgia (1736–37) was a fiasco, for well-known personal reasons, but he entered into it with great enthusiasm, naive about American Indians and hopeful that his work among a simple and innocent people would help his own soul.[2] Instead he was appointed as a minister to the colonists, and when he expressed desires to leave the settlements and work among Indians he was refused permission. Governor Oglethorpe wanted his settlers provided for, and the Chickasaws said that warfare made the timing inappropriate.[3] Wesley's contacts with Indians were brief, limited to a few delegations that visited Savannah. On his return to England, disheartened by his romantic and other misfortunes, Wesley recorded in his journal some general descriptions of Native Americans that were simply vicious. All of the Georgian Indians, except perhaps the Choctaws, were "gluttons drunkards, thieves, dissemblers, liars . . . implacable, unmerciful murderers . . . Whoredom they account no crime, and few instances appear of a young Indian woman's refusing any one." The Chickasaws were "extremely indolent and lazy, except in war."[4] Wesley did not claim that these descriptions were based upon personal observation. They were, instead, a consensus of the descriptions he had heard from traders and others, but Wesley reported them without a hint of a disclaimer. He had traveled far from his earlier impression of American Indians as uncorrupted.[5] Later, removed from the Georgia experience and established as the leader of a growing religious movement, Wesley wrote to Francis Asbury (1787):

> one thing has often given me concern . . . the progeny of Shem [Indians] seem to be quite forgotten. How few of these have seen the light of the glory of God since the English first settled among them! And now scarce one in fifty among whom we settled, perhaps scarce one in an hundred of them are left alive? Does it not seem as if God had designated all the Indian nations not for reformation, but destruction? How many millions of them have already died in their sins! Will neither God nor man have compassion upon these outcasts of men? Undoubtedly with man it is impossible to help them. But is it too hard for God? . . . Pray ye likewise the Lord of the harvest, and he will send out more labourers into His harvest . . . .[6]

Neither Asbury nor Thomas Coke responded with any burst of attention to Indian missions. Historian Wade Barclay cites this casual remark in Coke's journal as an indication of attitudes: "We have in this state [North Carolina] got up to the Cherokee Indians, who are in general a peaceable people. I trust the grace of God will in time get into some of their hearts."[7] Journals and conference minutes provide a few passing references to two or three Indian converts or to an intention to start a mission among Indians, but nothing verifiable resulted. As Barclay has summarized,

> It cannot be said that the missionary zeal of the earliest Methodist pioneers expressed itself in extensive efforts for the conversion of the Indians. Wherever their labors extended they must have come in contact with them but evidence is lacking that, at any time during the closing years of the eighteenth century and the beginning of the nineteenth, organized effort was made by Methodists for their evangelization.[8]

Methodist societies were organized in America by 1766, and a national church was officially established in 1784, but Methodists cannot claim the beginning of an "official" continuing Indian mission until 1819. From that beginning through the Civil War, Methodist Indian missions might be summarized principally in four clusters: the "first mission" among the Wyandots, missions in the southeast that followed natives when they were removed to Oklahoma, efforts by Canadian and United States Methodists in the Great Lakes region, and the fabled mission of Jason Lee and others in the northwest.

The efforts of John Stewart among the Wyandots in what is now northern Ohio are generally acknowledged as the first Methodist mission to American Indians. Stewart, a "mulatto," part black and part Indian, joined the Methodist church as the result of a camp meeting, probably in 1814.[9] Some time later while praying in the fields Stewart heard voices that seemed to come from the northwest, saying "Thou shalt declare my counsel faithfully."[10] Without church sponsorship, he responded to his call to preach by literally traveling northwest, eventually settling among the Wyandots at Upper Sandusky. He recruited Jonathan Pointer, a black, as his interpreter. Preaching, singing, and praying, Stewart converted Pointer and several native leaders, including Between-the-Logs, Mononcue, and Squire Grey Eyes. Stewart also encountered problems with church authorities, because he had administered baptism and performed a marriage ceremony without appropriate credentials. In 1819 he applied to a Quarterly Conference held near Urbana for a Local Preacher's license and received it. The Methodists thereby became more fully aware of Stewart's efforts, and the 1819 session of the Ohio Annual Conference took the mission under its wing, appointing local preacher James Montgomery as missionary "to the northern Indians," chiefly the Wyandots, with Stewart as an assistant. This was "the first appointment by the Methodists of a missionary officially designated as such, to the American Indians."[11] Several other missionaries followed, the most noted being James B. Finley. Stewart continued with the mission but struggled with ill health, dying in 1823 at the age of thirty-seven.

The Wyandot mission included not only a worshiping congregation but also a farm and a school. By 1826 the mission reported three hundred church members, fifteen Class Leaders, four native preachers, and seventy Indian children in the school.[12] The school boarded students through the week, but most returned home on weekends. As many as half of the Wyandot people were associated with Methodism, and many adapted considerably to white American culture. They erected a church, school, and housing similar to that owned by whites, and they established their own tribal store. They divided their land among families, introducing notions akin to private property, although the land was still considered part of the Wyandot nation and individuals had no authority to sell plots outside of the tribe.

In spite of these adaptations, the Wyandots were unsuccessful in resisting the federal policy of removing eastern Indians to the west. For almost fifteen years the Wyandots, especially the Christian faction, repeatedly voted down proposals to emigrate. Missionary James Finley vigorously defended their right to remain on their lands.[13] Yet pressures continued, and increasing murder and robbery by white neighbors eventually convinced a succeeding missionary, James Wheeler, that removal "might be for the best."[14] He continued to support Wyandot resistance, but a removal treaty was signed finally in 1842, and the Wyandots were relocated to Kansas a year later. Methodist missionaries followed. Christian Indians in their new location then became caught in the crossfire of the slavery issue, which divided the church as well as the nation, weakening the Methodist Wyandot community. By 1860 Wyandot tribal relations were dissolved, making individuals citizens of the United States. Some who wanted to retain tribal relations later accepted land in Oklahoma, further scattering the people. Cultural adaptation encouraged by sincere missionaries finally did not prevent disruption of the people.

Within a year after the Ohio Conference took responsibility for the Wyandot mission (1819), the general church chartered a Missionary Society. Methodists prided themselves on the missionary character of their entire church and previously had seen a special society as unnecessary, but in 1820 the Missionary Society of the Methodist Episcopal Church was approved by General Conference "to enable the several Annual Conferences more effectually to extend their Missionary labours throughout the United states and elsewhere."[15] At the beginning it was essentially a funding organization that assisted annual conference initiatives. With business conducted by a volunteer Board, it had no administrative budget and no paid staff officer for seventeen years. It had no power to approve or send out missionaries or to make direct appropriations of funds. Bishops and annual conferences drew on funds as needed.[16] Thus, it was a weak Society in terms of centralized authority or direction, but its financial assistance enabled many annual conferences to undertake missions they could not otherwise afford.

Missions in southern states began only a few years thereafter. William Capers, later to become a bishop, is considered not only the "founder of missions among the slaves" but also "the pioneer of Methodist missions among the Indians of the Southern States."[17] In 1821 he was authorized by Bishop McKendree to raise funds for Indian missions, and in 1822 he visited the Creeks to propose a mission. Missionaries were soon assigned, under Capers' superintendency, and the Creek mission eventually was the location for the Asbury Manual Labor School, attended by several natives who became strong Methodist leaders, most notably Samuel Checote.

Methodist initiatives among other southern tribes followed. Richard Neely's Tennessee circuit bordered Cherokee villages, and in 1822 he began preaching among them. In 1825 the Mississippi Conference organized missions among the Choctaws and Chickasaws. Alexander Talley, celebrated as the "Apostle to the Choctaws," was appointed a missionary to Indians in northern Mississippi in 1827. This flurry of Methodist activity in the 1820s claimed an estimated four thousand "Methodist Indians," including native leaders such as Checote, James McHenry, John Page, Greenwood LeFlore, and John Boot.[18]

Creeks, Cherokees, Choctaws, Chickasaws, and Seminoles, all located in the southeast, have been popularly designated as the "Five Civilized Tribes" because of their agricultural subsistence pattern and their considerable adaptation to white American culture. Far more than the Wyandots just discussed, these tribes, (especially the Cherokees) developed governmental systems similar to that of the United States, established an extensive free public educational system, their own press, and more. Yet, as with the Wyandots, such acculturation made little difference when the federal government determined to remove Indians from eastern lands. With missions among four of the five "civilized" tribes, Methodists were just beginning in the 1820s when the disruption of removal came in 1829 and the following decade. The tragic "Trail of Tears" wrenched natives out of their homelands and relocated them in the dramatically different geography of what is now Oklahoma.

The most dramatic resistance to removal was offered by the Cherokees. When missionaries who supported the Cherokees were imprisoned, legal action began which eventually went to the Supreme Court in the famous case of *Worcester v. Georgia*. Samuel Worcester was a missionary for the American Board of Commissioners for Foreign Missions, a Presbyterian-Congregational agency, and the American Board was the most activist of Christian groups in attempting to defend Cherokee rights. Methodists were divided among themselves, with missionaries in the field taking strong political stands against removal but with conference bodies urging neutrality. Local or regional control of missions in the Methodist system worked in this case against courageous protests. As historian William McLaughlin has written, "although the Methodist circuit riders were sympathetic to Cherokee interests, those who appointed and supervised them spoke primarily for the interests of the white frontier settlers on the borders of the Cherokee Nation who raised the funds for the missions."[19]

Removal brought understandable bitterness, and many natives "lost faith in the white man and in the white man's religion."[20] Although relocation and reaction erected obstacles, Mississippi, Missouri, and Tennessee conferences continued to send missionaries into Oklahoma. By 1844 they organized their own Indian Mission Conference, with 85 white, 33 "colored," and 2,992 Indian members.[21] In that same year the Methodist church divided into northern and southern bodies over the issue of slavery, and the Indian Mission Conference became part of the southern church. Leland Clegg and William Oden, historians of Oklahoma Methodism, suggest that "from 1848 until the Civil War, the primary work of the Indian Mission conference was educational."[22] Federal policy was a major reason for the emphasis, because in that period the United States government permitted churches and missionaries to administer schools federally funded through Indian agencies and Indian National Councils. With such financial encouragement, Methodists established thirteen Indian schools in Oklahoma in the late 1840s and 1850s. Much of this was decimated by the Civil War, and church membership was cut by more than half.

Methodist missions in Kansas might be included in the Oklahoma story, because most of them constituted the Kansas District of the Indian Mission Conference. Efforts of varying size and duration were attempted among the Kansas, Shawnee, Delaware, Kickapoo, Peoria, and Potawatomi, along with a continuation of the Wyandot mission. Most of these Native Americans had been displaced from their homelands in the east, in the removal story that now becomes repetitious. Of all these ventures the most noted has been the Shawnee Mission Manual Labor School. Reverend and Mrs. Thomas Johnson arrived in 1830 to establish a mission, and by 1839 they had added a school, assisted by a 2,240 acre land grant from the government. The school's farm included acres of corn, oats, Irish potatoes, garden vegetables, and Kansas' first apple orchard. Buildings included a mission house, a dining hall capable of seating two to three hundred people, dormitories, blacksmith shops, barns, cribs, granaries, toolhouses, a sawmill, and a steam flour mill. The establishment was so substantial that the first territorial legislature met in its buildings. At its height in 1854–55, the school enrolled two to three hundred students. The twelve hour school day was divided evenly between the classroom and manual employment. Like the Oklahoma missions, the school was disrupted by the Civil War. At least two major battles were fought in the vicinity of the Shawnee Mission, with the school's buildings serving as hospitals. In 1864 the Johnsons gave up the mission and moved to a farm where, a year later, he was shot and killed by one of Quantrill's guerrillas.[23]

A third cluster of Methodist Indian missions arose in the Great Lakes area, including Canada, New York state, Illinois, Michigan, Wisconsin, and Minnesota. In the recording of "firsts," Canadian Indian missions would claim the preaching of Joseph Sawyer to Indians of the Credit River in 1801 and the preaching of a single sermon by Nathan Bangs to Canadian Indians when Bangs stayed overnight with a trader in 1803. Sustained efforts in Upper Canada, however, began when the Genesee Conference in 1822 appointed Alvin Torry to the Grand River Mission (now southern Ontario), under Presiding Elder William Case. Ojibwa native leaders converted there became crucial for other Great Lakes area missions. Canadians formed their own Annual Conference in 1824 and a separate Methodist Episcopal Church of Canada in 1828, but the United States church continued to offer some assistance until 1832.[24]

On the United States side mission beginnings were slower. In 1823 and 1824 James Finley, with two Wyandot chiefs, Monomcue and Squire Grey Eyes, and Jonathan Pointer as interpreter, made an extensive missionary journey to the Michigan Territory and Canada, but nothing lasting resulted.[25] Sustained Methodist missionary efforts in the United States portion of the Great Lakes region did not really begin until the late 1820s and early 1830s, a decade after the rise of Wyandot and southeastern missions. The one exception was a short-lived mission among the Potawatomies; established by Jesse Walker in 1824, under sponsorship of the Missouri Conference, the Salem Mission was discontinued in 1829 because of removal to Kansas.

Beginning in 1829, several annual conferences sponsored a variety of initiatives. In 1829 Daniel Barnes was appointed superintendent of Oneida missions in New York state, but "the most effective evangelistic work was done by Daniel Adams, a young Christian Mohawk from Upper Canada."[26] Efforts were barely begun when many Oneidas began to move to the vicinity of Green Bay, Wisconsin, where John Clark came from New York City to superintend missions in 1832. Clark also helped establish missions in Michigan and at Sault Ste. Marie, although he had been preceded about two years in the region by the preaching of John Sunday, an Ojibwa leader converted in Canada. As new conferences were formed nearer the locations of Indian missions, they in turn would take responsibility for the work. Thus, in 1835 and 1836 John Clark was appointed to the Chicago District of the Illinois Conference and Alfred Brunson took charge of Wisconsin missions, also initiating new ones in Minnesota. In 1843 John H. Pitezel was appointed to Sault Ste. Marie and the surrounding area.

This list becomes dizzying, but the point to be made here is that most of the standard, well-known names cited above are not the ones who really spent their daily lives with Native Americans. Torry, Brunson, and Pitezel all published autobiographical reminiscences, and their books naturally help give them prominence, but in most cases they were busy traveling from mission to mission, to conference meetings, and to the east soliciting support.[27] Often the real laborers in the field were unheralded, such as David King in Minnesota, one of the few non-Indian missionaries who made a substantial effort to learn a native language, or Electa Quinney among the Oneida, who like many other forgotten women served as a teacher in mission schools.[28]

Most important were native leaders, and in the Great Lakes area four names arise again and again. John Sunday, an Ojibwa chief already mentioned, was the "first generation" among the four. Canadian missions then helped bring three other important leaders into the church: John Johnson, George Copway, and Peter Marksman. In the fall of 1837 the Illinois Conference approved funding for an interesting experiment in leadership training. They wanted to send the three Ojibwas to Ebenezer Manual Labor School near Jacksonville, Illinois, to be students alongside three non-Indian youth who had committed themselves to missionary service: Samuel Spates, Allen Huddleston, and "One Weatherford" (first name unknown). The Ojibwa youths were to gain knowledge of Christianity and "civilization," while the non-Indians were to gain knowledge of native language and culture through acquaintance with their Ojibwa fellow students. After two years at the school, all except Weatherford emerged to provide substantial leadership in the Great Lakes area. The three Ojibwas became quite renowned. Copway, although criticized by some fellow workers and historians, published a widely distributed autobiography.[29] Peter Marksman has been called by one historian "the outstanding Michigan Methodist Indian preacher of the nineteenth century"; John Pitezel published a book-length account of Marksman's life.[30] Johnson was an active Methodist missionary until an unhappy dispute caused him to leave in 1848; thereafter he achieved greater prominence as an Episcopal priest (Enmegahbowh) and an associate of the noted Bishop Henry B. Whipple. Huddleston died of illness in December, 1839. Spates worked among the Ojibwa until the general unrest surrounding the Dakota War of 1862 (also known as the Great Sioux Uprising), when he began serving non-Indian parishes in the Minnesota Conference.

In spite of the many names and scattered mission locations, the Great Lakes missions never gathered great numbers, especially when compared with the Indian Mission Conference encompassing Oklahoma and Kansas. On the eve of the division of the Methodist Episcopal Church into northern and southern bodies (1844–45), Indian church membership was reported to be 4,339, with 3,557 in the Indian Mission Conference. When the church divided, the northern body was left with nine missions, fourteen missionaries, and an Indian membership of 778.[31]

The fourth cluster of missions, in the Pacific northwest, relates tangentially to the first Methodist mission among the Wyandots. When John Stewart arrived among the Wyandots he was encouraged and assisted by the government Indian subagent there, William Walker Sr., and his wife Catherine Rankin Walker. He, a non-Indian, had been captured by the Delawares as a child and was eventually adopted by the Wyandots; she was the daughter of an Irish Indian trader and a mixed-blood mother. Thus, although their blood-relatedness to the Wyandots was not strong, they were considered a part of the Wyandot community. Their son, William Walker, Jr., active in the Methodist mission, was in St. Louis in 1831, making arrangements for the transfer of his people to Kansas, when he encountered a delegation of four Nez Perce and Flathead leaders who were also visiting the city. Fourteen months later Walker wrote a letter which was soon published in the New York *Christian Advocate and Journal*, recounting the story of how the four Indians had traveled over 2,000 miles to plead for the white man's "Book of Heaven" and some missionaries. Such a delegation did indeed visit St. Louis, but it is doubtful that their major purpose was religious. Walker's letter drew "on his own piety and a fertile imagination" (in historian Ray Billington's words), but the results were spectacular. Money poured into the Missionary Society, and Jason Lee with four companions arrived in the northwest in 1834 to commence the Methodists' Oregon Mission. Within two years Presbyterians had also begun two missions under Marcus Whitman and Henry Spalding.[32]

Lee was a persuasive promoter and the mission expanded rapidly, in both personnel and locations. Six stations were founded, with a missionary staff of seventy. Lee envisioned a full cultural program, with manual labor schools, farms, the erection of Euroamerican-style houses, mills, and more. Unfortunately there were not as many Native Americans in the area as Lee had estimated, and many were disturbed by the influx of non-Indians, who threatened to take over their land. Daniel Lee, Jason's nephew and a missionary, wrote in 1843: "Of the mass [of the Indians] it may be said that three-fourths and more appeared careless and indifferent about the teachings of the gospel, and many of these were even against hearing it preached, that they might go on in their heathenish practices, and in direct opposition to its commands, unrestrained."[33]

Other missions had been sponsored by various annual conferences, augmented by financial assistance from the Missionary Society, but this venture, so far removed geographically from settled annual conferences, was more directly dependent upon the Missionary Society. In the 1840s the Society began to shrink back from the great cost of the Oregon Mission, and when they began to hear complaints from other missionaries about Lee's management, he was replaced in 1843. Lee traveled east, defended himself, and was exonerated by the Society's Board, but the mission was now in other hands. The Board wanted the Oregon Mission reduced, and in 1844 all but two of the mission stations were abandoned. In 1845 another was liquidated, and in 1847 the last was handed over to the American Board (Presbyterian-Congregationalist) free of charge, on the condition that they would continue the mission. Thirteen years after the venture had begun in great excitement, the Methodist Oregon Mission was terminated.[34]

Jason Lee and his Methodist mission have been the subject of much writing, a disproportionate amount if measured by the mission's lack of success in converting Indians. The episode is colorful, from beginning to end, which helps draw attention, but the major reason is Lee's role in the settlement of Oregon. The area was jointly occupied by England and the United States, and U.S. hopes for a final claim of the land rested upon its ability to fill the region with its own settlers. Excitement about rich, fertile valleys, helped turn a trickle into a flow of settlement. In fact, historians love to debate Lee's true motivations. Was he sincerely interested in missionary work among Indians, or was it a cloak for purely materialistic colonizing ambitions? Whatever his motivation, the significance of Lee's work rests more with his role in the annexation of Oregon than it does in providing a model for Indian missions.[35]

## EVALUATIONS OF METHODIST MISSIONS

The cumulative impression left by all of this is not one of overwhelming success. Sacrificial labors notwithstanding, Methodist missions were hindered by several features of missionary history and strategy. Although Methodists saw their whole system as missionary in character and prided themselves on the circuit riders' effective work in following the westward flow of white settlers, Methodist missionary efforts were preoccupied with the white frontier. Aside from experience with American blacks, the church was relatively late in gaining experience in cross-cultural situations, both foreign and Native American. American Methodism's first, limited "foreign" experiences did not come until the late 1830s, beginning in the independent nation of Texas, among black American colonists in Liberia (neither of which were radically cross-cultural situations) and in South America.[36] The American Board of Commissioners for Foreign Missions, in contrast, was involved in both foreign and Native American missions within a few years after its founding in 1810, and lessons they learned abroad about cross-cultural missions (the importance of the use of native languages, for example) could be applied promptly to efforts among Indians. The Roman Catholic Church, because of its international scope, had cultural diversity imbedded within it. Compared to many other denominations, Methodists were late in obtaining cross-cultural experience upon which to base missionary strategies.

Further, the Methodist system also made it difficult to share the experiences once obtained, because of a decentralized mission system. Annual conferences rather than a central mission board took most responsibility for Indian missions within their borders or in neighboring lands, as is illustrated in the foregoing narrative. Thus, personnel were generally recruited from white ministries, given local responsibilities with little or no special training, and with almost no benefit of contact with other missionaries to Indians around the nation. Because mission boards were primarily funding organizations, not given to considerable development of mission theologies, strategies, or training, early Methodist missionaries each had to "reinvent the wheel" until more centralized and powerful mission organizations developed, primarily in the twentieth century, or until missions clustered sufficiently in one region, as they did in the Indian Mission Conference.

In addition, the circuit riding system, built on the principle of itinerancy, worked poorly for Indian missions. The appointment system treated circuit riders almost as interchangeable chess pieces, moved from one appointment to another at least every three or four years. It was not unusual to take a minister from a white circuit, appoint him to an Indian circuit, and then a few years later appoint him once again among whites. Such mobility obviously made it difficult to adequately understand a culture or learn a language. M. A. Clark, an Oklahoma minister, complained in 1907 about this very hindrance. "Previous to this time," he noted, "our church authorities would not allow a missionary to stay on a charge longer than four years. Imagine a missionary being changed from China to Japan and from Japan to Africa every four years. What could the church expect of him?"[37]

In essence, the Methodists took an itinerant style of ministry that had served them well on the white frontier and attempted to apply it to Indian missions, where it was less appropriate. The difference was a cross-cultural situation, which required preparation for cultural understanding, more patience and sensitivity in communication, and more stable, long-term support. On the white frontier, rough-hewn preachers might communicate with the "common people" more effectively than would seminary educated clergy, but in Indian missions unprepared white preachers had no such automatic advantage. The mobility of wide circuits and frequent shifts in personnel might be efficient in extending ministry among people of somewhat similar Euroamerican backgrounds. However, it was a mistake to assign circuit riders interchangeably when they had to move among tribal cultures so dissimilar that they spoke mutually unintelligible languages and held markedly contrasting cultural assumptions.

A factor which helped compensate for these hindrances in Methodist policy was the development of native leadership. Indeed, the early Methodist system in England and America relied heavily on local leadership while the circuit rider traveled a large circuit, sometimes returning to a specific point only after a month or two. Missions of all denominations found native leadership helpful. Among the Methodists it was especially crucial when missionaries had little facility with native languages and understood little of tribal cultures. Perhaps the weaknesses of Methodist mission strategy unintentionally fostered more Native American leadership and made it more difficult for missionaries to take the place of native leaders in mission communities than was the case in missions of some other denominations.

Another feature of Methodist missions may have been an advantage among Native Americans, although it has seldom been discussed by historians. Methodist evangelism was based upon revivalism and camp meetings, and this approach naturally carried over into Indian missions. In many tribes, traditional religious ceremonies extended over several days and were social as well as religious events, with much peripheral activity. The sun dance and the green corn ceremony among several tribes might serve as examples. Extended, somewhat free-form camp meetings would seem more akin to such traditional events than would a brief one or two hour liturgical service. However, other denominations have offered similar arguments for their worship styles. Catholics and Episcopalians claim that the ceremonialism of their worship was more appealing to American Indians because it was congruous with the pageantry of native ceremonies.

The latter comments hint at a shift in attention in the study of Indian missions. It is no longer satisfactory to focus exclusively on the names of missionaries, the construction of buildings, and the examination of missionary intentions. Invisible in such accounts are Native Americans themselves, who were much more than passive pawns in the process. Calls for "new Indian history" in the past two decades remind us that Native Americans have histories of their own, involving developments within and between tribes and not always centering upon Euroamericans.[38] When contact with whites enters the story, "new Indian history" emphasizes that natives brought their own viable cultures to the exchange and were capable of initiatives and critical responses. With its institutional focus, this survey does not purport to be such a history, but the emphases of "new Indian history" help all of us become more sensitive to the cultural role of missions.[39]

Missionaries of all denominations were not only evangelists for their particular forms of Christianity; they were carriers of Euroamerican culture which they encouraged American Indians to adopt. Mission literature is filled with repeated references to a twofold task: to "Christianize and civilize" the Indians. From one perspective the missionaries' cultural program was a humanitarian attempt to improve the lives of fellow human beings. From another perspective it was ethnocentric, with missionaries unable to distinguish between Christianity and white American culture. In yet another view, it was simply cultural imperialism. From the perspective of many Native Americans, it brought religious and cultural division to previously unified communities and functioned as the vanguard of a disruptive foreign presence.

Viewed in terms of cultural systems, many missionary intentions that sound simple actually had far-reaching cultural implications. The effort to "teach Indians to farm" serves as an example. The very phrase is misleading, for most tribes had pre-contact subsistence patterns which relied on domestic agriculture in varying degrees; it is more accurate to say that missionaries were trying to

220

introduce European agricultural practices and technology and were encouraging a more total reliance on domestic agriculture. When they urged mission Indians to farm more and to hunt or gather wild foods less, they were encouraging a less diversified subsistence pattern which sometimes proved disastrous when crops failed. In tribes where women had responsibility for domestic crops, attempts to get male mission Indians to farm asked them, in effect, to become women, altering native cultural understandings of sexual roles. Hidden behind some advocacy of agriculture was an assumption about the value of industriousness. If hunting appeared to be sport, while agriculture involved proper labor, even commanded by God in Genesis, any Indian who resisted missionary encouragement to farm could be judged lazy, by definition. The farming program also involved introduction of private property, for missionaries doubted that anyone would work in a communal field if one could harvest what another had worked hard to produce. Thus, if mission Indians were to "get ahead," missionaries felt, land needed to be allotted to individuals or families, and then a whole new legal system would be required to protect the private property. Finally, when missionaries attempted to introduce their farming programs in nomadic or semi-nomadic tribes, it was often with the ulterior motive of locating the natives in one place so that they would be more accessible to preaching and teaching. Mission farms had many implications.[40]

Schools could be examined in a similar fashion. Boarding schools were more culturally coercive than day schools, for they clearly attempted to isolate children from their native cultural settings and to surround them with white American culture in microcosm. Children were given new names (often those of mission donors), new clothing, new haircuts, and a curriculum intended to introduce not only information but the values and worldview of the dominant culture.[41] Literacy programs, which seem so evidently helpful, had their own cultural implications, especially if English was emphasized rather than native languages. The 1851 *Annual Report of the Missionary Society of the Methodist Episcopal Church* declared: "With the English language, the Indian will acquire the elements of English literature, and the forms of thought, and the feelings which it represents, both social and religious. We doubt whether the Indians will ever be raised to a good state of civilization and religion, without the use of the English language. The influence of a language upon the principles, feelings, and habits of a people, is not appreciated as it ought to be."[42] In retrospect, Christians wonder whether some of the cultural program did not contradict Christianity's own teachings, making people more greedy, less attuned to creation, and so on.

Such cultural discussion easily becomes tangled with value judgments. Condemnation of any and all change encouraged by missionaries runs the risk of freezing Native Americans into a sort of anthropological zoo, forgetting that native cultures adapted and developed as the result of intertribal contact long before they encountered Europeans. The ethical issue is whether change is forced or freely chosen, not the mere fact of change itself. From the opposite direction, some people justify the missionary cultural programs by easily referring to the inevitability of Euroamerican control of the continent; adaptation, it is argued, was important for American Indian survival. Yet the historical story tells of many who adapted but who lost land or encountered racist rejection nevertheless.

However one deals with the ethical issues, the cultural discussion helps non-Indians understand more fully the variety of responses to Methodist and other Christian missions by Native Americans. First of all, when missionaries encountered native resistance, other explanations are possible besides the work of the devil and the agitation of whiskey traders. John Hicks, a Wyandot chief, reportedly replied to an early sermon by John Stewart with these words:

> I, for one, feel myself called upon to rise in the defense of the religion of my fathers . . . No, my friend, your disclaiming so violently against the modes of worshipping the Great Spirit, is in my opinion, not calculated to benefit us as a nation; we are willing to receive good advice from you, but we are not willing to have the customs and institutions which have been kept sacred by our fathers, thus assailed and abused.[43]

Native Americans might be willing to dialogue with missionaries, mutually sharing and learning, but when Euroamericans totally condemned native culture and spirituality, although also claiming an intention to help, it was an affront. When this arrogance threatened to divide a native community or contribute to the loss of a homeland, the missionaries appeared dangerous. Fon du Lac chiefs said to an American Board missionary: "Those who sent you here want our country. You are their forerunner. They will come and ask for a little and then take a great deal." [44]

Few conversions came while tribes lived in relative autonomy, able to relate to Euroamericans on fairly equal terms. When the encroaching white presence interfered more and more with traditional ways, and when military defeats crushed some native communities, conversions came more quickly. If Euroamericans had shown themselves to be more powerful, perhaps adopting their religion would give American Indians access to some of that power. Yet conversion was not merely capitulation. Christianity helped provide a new organizing center for disrupted lives. Even then, many Native Americans practiced selective adoption, retaining features of their native heritage while embracing some aspects of Christianity. Missionaries tended to offer their religion and their culture as a total package, but it was not always received that way. Oklahoma missionary John Jasper Methvin quoted Stumbling Bear as saying, "White man's road heap good, better than Indian road. But not *all* of the ways of the white man better than *all* the Indian ways. Some Indian ways best."[45]

## METHODISTS AND FEDERAL INDIAN POLICY

Even prior to the beginning of the nineteenth century, the "civilizing" goals of Christian Indian missions were shared by the United States Government, and from the enactment of a Civilization Bill in 1819 onward, the federal role in Indian life increased. However, until the Civil War, one could argue that missionaries usually spearheaded the drive for acculturation. After the war the initiative seemed to shift into federal hands. Native Americans were increasingly confined to reservations; Grant's Peace Policy enlisted church workers as Indian Agents but under federal control; after the demise of that program's church-state cooperation, government schools and federal allotment programs shaped the scene. Missions remained, but they were no longer the vanguard or the focal point of Indian-white relations, and frequently they served the government's purposes.

Thus, while one could continue tracing the development of mission institutions following the Civil War, including the founding of women's home mission societies, north and south, and the diffusion of missionary efforts among additional tribes, in a brief survey like this attention might properly move to Methodist roles in federal Indian policy. A general history of Methodism and Native Americans should include more than missions; Methodist attempts to influence federal policy, or a tendency to avoid such issues because they were "too political," are part of the story as well. Methodist attitudes toward federal policy could be shaped by people who had never met an Indian, and sometimes they ran contrary to the views of missionaries in the field. Much room remains for systematic study of Methodist views on public policy issues pertaining to Native Americans. What follow are some introductory impressions.

Three major features of federal policy in the nineteenth century were removal, Grant's Peace Policy, and the "Allotment Act" of 1887. The first, removal, has been prominent in the mission narratives already provided. Between 1816 and 1848 twelve states entered the Union, and in the process "scores of treaties were negotiated by which the tribes relinquished the bulk of their holdings east of the Mississippi and consented to removal west," immediately or eventually.[46] Frequently accomplished through enticements or coercion (both subtle and not), the removal policy was based on the assumption that Indians had no right to block "progress." Governor William Henry Harrison asked, "Is one of the fairest portions of the globe to remain in a state of nature, the haunt of a few wretched savages, when it seems destined by the Creator to give support to a large population and to be the seat of civilization?"[47] Others rationalized that removal also would be better for American Indians, because they would be isolated from the less elevating features of frontier contact, such as the availability of alcohol.

Missionaries and mission organizations were divided on the issue. Isaac McCoy, a Baptist, has become the best-known missionary proponent of removal, arguing that it would protect Indians from exploitation. Methodist missionary Alexander Talley also supported removal. Most missionaries among the tribes protested the federal policy, although historians can argue whether the opposition was based upon concern for native rights, self-interest in protecting from disruption the missions they had worked so hard to establish, or both. In the Cherokee case, although the American Board of Commissioners for Foreign Missions was in the forefront of protest, two Methodist missionaries (James Trott and Dickson McLeod) were imprisoned for their support of Cherokees, along with their better-known ABCFM colleagues. In 1830 eight Methodist circuit riders signed a resolution expressing firm support for the Cherokee Nation, which served as a model for resolutions signed by missionaries of other denominations. The eight also wanted their denomination to issue "a public and official expression of sentiment" against oppression of the Cherokees, but it did not come.[48] Later, James Finley among the Wyandots also opposed removal. His reminiscences include the frequently quoted statement: "I have always been opposed to the removing plan, and have honestly told my sentiments to Indians and others. I used my influence to persuade the Indians not to sell, but to remain where they were; for if they were removed to the base of the Rocky Mountains, or beyond them, the white population would follow them . . . This was, and still is, the honest conviction of my mind."[49]

Although missionaries who worked directly with Indians usually opposed removal, they received little support from denominational bodies. Circuit riders among the Cherokees were members of the Tennessee conference. The 1830 Tennessee Annual Conference not only refused to join the missionaries in protesting removal policies; they rebuked the missionaries for trying to push the conference into politics. The officer who arrested Trott described him as a preacher "who had been discountenanced by his own Conference for his officious and over-zealous interference in Indian politics."[50] Much of the church at large seemed to share a view published in the New York *Christian Advocate* in 1835: "With these matters it is not our providence to meddle. Our business is to 'preach Christ crucified'; and this, by the grace of God, we are resolved to do"[51]

In spite of the hesitation to speak out on political issues, Methodist periodicals did issue some editorial statements about removal. The New York *Christian Advocate*, for instance, objected to the forcible ejection of the people against their will, but it expressed "no opinion" on the justification of the removal program in general.[52] Regarding many of these editorial statements the generalization of historian William T. Hagan applies. "As usual," he wrote, "moral indignation over the plight of the red men varied with the distance from him. Those whites avid for Indian land or fearful for their scalps were ever inclined to classify him as subhuman and devoid of rights. Those far removed from the frontier detected great potential in the Indian."[53]

The relation of churches to federal Indian policy took a decisive turn after the Civil War. In 1869 President Grant surprised most observers by announcing a church-related reform program to eliminate corruption and reduce violent conflict in federal-Indian relations. Commonly called his "Peace Policy," the program included church nomination and influence upon Indian agents, creation of the Board of Indian Commissioners, and expanded federal aid for Indian education and missions.[54]

With long-standing charges that Indian Agents were corrupt and making fortunes at the expense of Native Americans, Grant asked Quakers and then other denominations for nominations of more suitable agents. While the agents would be legally responsible to the government, denominational organizations also were expected to exert oversight, making the precise responsibilities of both unclear. Linked to the nomination of agents was the allocation of agencies among denominations. On their assigned agencies, Grant explained, "the societies are allowed to name their own agents, subject to the approval of the Executive, and are expected to watch over them and aid them as missionaries, to Christianize and civilize the Indian, and to train him in the arts of peace."[55]

The criteria for the allocation of agencies were not carefully defined, but it was generally assumed that previous activity on a reservation should have some bearing. If so, it was frequently disregarded. Of seventy-one agencies assigned in 1871, Hicksite and Orthodox Friends (Quakers) controlled sixteen, having been the first group invited to participate, on the basis of their legendary reputation for just dealings with Indians. Methodists were a close second, with fourteen agencies. Presbyterians received nine, Episcopalians eight, Roman Catholics seven, and a variety of other denominations received less. Catholics, who supported the most widespread and vigorous Indian missions at the time, felt cheated. Southern Methodists were also slighted, although the situation has been less often noted by historians. At least three-fourths of Methodist Indian mission activity was in southern hands in the 1860s and 1870s, but the northern church received all of the agencies in the post-Civil War context. Historian Robert Keller, Jr., exaggerates when he says that "the Methodist Church [northern] had virtually no Indian missions in 1870," but in comparative terms he is close to the truth.[56] Robert Whitner is a bit more careful in stating: "During the period in which the peace policy was in effect, the Methodist Episcopal Church had long since lost the great interest it once had in Indian mission work, and it made little effort and spent little money to implement or extend it."[57] The

Peace Policy, then, allowed Methodists to undertake efforts they did not choose to finance themselves. "More than any other church under the Peace Policy," says Keller, "Methodists allowed the federal government to sustain their entire Indian mission program."[58]

When Methodists received almost twenty percent of the agencies, critics charged religious favoritism. Grant had been raised in a Methodist home and associated with Methodism throughout his life, although he never joined the church. Catholics charged that in allotting agencies Grant had been duped as a "tool in the exaltation and propagandism of the Methodist Church." One member of the Board of Indian Commissioners declared that the BIC had been nothing but a Methodist Kitchen Cabinet. Robert Keller's assessment is that

> although no direct evidence supports the specific charges against it, the Methodist Church did enjoy unusual power in Washington during the 1870s. Grant himself once remarked that there were three political parties in the United States: the Republicans, the Democrats, and the Methodists.[59]

The Peace Policy did not seem to improve Indian Agents appreciably or bring much to Native Americans besides further pressure for assimilation. Its major result was interdenominational squabbling, with considerable evidence of anti-Catholic prejudice. Although it did not occur to people at the time, it was a "flagrant violation of the First Amendment."[60] Religious division and growing government disenchantment brought a gradual withdrawal from the policy, finally terminated in 1882. Historian Whitner concludes that the record of the Methodist Episcopal Church in the Peace Policy was "largely a failure. It did little to improve the service or the condition of the Indian. It did much to perpetuate sectarianism and intolerance and bigotry in America."[61]

A third major phase of federal Indian policy was enacted in 1887 with the adoption of the Dawes Act. Missionaries and other non-Indians had long advocated the elimination of tribal communalism and the introduction of private property, so that Indians might "advance in civilization" and melt into American culture. The first Methodist mission among the Wyandots encouraged division of lands. In 1855 George Smith wrote about a Michigan mission, claiming that nothing would "prevent this mission from becoming self-supporting at an early day" if Indians could learn their hardest lesson, "economy in proper provision for the future." That would be accomplished by a division of land among individuals and families. "Their community principles make it absolutely impracticable—reducing the industrious and saving to the condition of the thriftless . . . ."[62]

In the late 1800s a crescendo of voices advocated the elimination of reservations. Reformers who viewed themselves as friends of the Indian, including the Indian Rights Association, the Women's National Indian Association, and the Lake Mohonk Conferences, joined unknowingly with others who saw an opportunity for land acquisition in the dispersal of reservations. As a result, Congress passed the Dawes Severalty Act of 1887 which "enshrined as general policy what had been taking place piecemeal for years." [63] At his discretion the President could allot reservation land to Indians, conferring U. S. citizenship at the same time. Although land titles were to be held in trust by the government for twenty-five years, "surplus" reservation land was offered for sale immediately, and much allotted land passed out of Indian hands over time. The Dawes Act was a culmination of century-long pressures for acculturation.

Support for this policy was so widespread that it would be misleading to claim a special role for Methodists, but they were actively involved. The President of the Board of Indian Commissioners from 1881 to 1890 was Clinton B. Fisk, "a devoted Methodist who played an active role in the Methodist Publishing House and in General Conferences of the Church." Daniel Dorchester, a Methodist minister, was appointed Superintendent of Indian Education just as the allotment plan was being implemented. [64]

Led by missions in early years, and eventually dominated by the federal government, nineteenth century Indian-white relations included persistent efforts to eliminate native cultures. Frederick Norwood notes that "the only ultimate solutions of the Indian problem, it was finally believed," were (1) extermination and (2) assimilation. "The churches may at least take credit for almost universally rejecting the first of these." [65] At times Methodists courageously stood for justice, against broken treaties, physical coercion, and predatory traders. In organization and education they were ill-prepared for cross-cultural encounters, but that worked serendipitously to promote the importance of native leadership. Yet whatever the helpful intentions and the particulars of mission strategy, the missions participated in the century-long push for assimilation. In doing so, non-Indian Methodists simply reflected common assumptions of their day, believing in the self-evident superiority of Euroamerican civilization and preparing American Indians for what seemed to be inevitable domination. The twentieth century has witnessed some revision of these assumptions, with the Wheeler-Howard (Indian Reorganization) Act of 1934 and with heightened appreciation of cultural pluralism and self-determination. It is unfair to judge people of one century by the cultural standards of the next, but Native Americans experienced the results regardless.

227

# Reexamining the Public/Private Split: Reforming the Continent and Spreading Scriptural Holiness

Jean Miller Schmidt

When the Methodist Episcopal Church was formally organized in 1784, the preachers assembled there in Baltimore followed John Wesley's example forty years earlier in asking: "What may we reasonably believe to be God's Design in raising up the Preachers called *Methodists*?" The answer of course was a reaffirmation of Wesley's earlier one: "To reform the Continent, and to spread scriptural Holiness over these Lands." [1] In this address I want to explore what these terms, "reforming the Continent" and "spreading scriptural holiness" (roughly equivalent to "public" and "private") have meant in American Methodist history, especially during the period from 1840 to 1939. Before turning to this history, however, I want to explain briefly what I mean by "the public/private split" and why I think it merits our attention as we look at our own Methodist past for the sake of the future.

During the turbulent decade of the 1960s, when many graduate students tried to assuage consciences burdened with the luxury of the academic enterprise in such troubled times by writing a "relevant" dissertation, I completed my graduate work at the University of Chicago Divinity School with a thesis entitled, "Souls or the Social Order: Polemic in American Protestantism." Concerned by the painful and sometimes bitter division between social activist and conservative evangelical Christians in the 1960s, I tried to discover how two parties which obviously laid claim to the same tradition of evangelical Protestantism in mid-nineteenth century America could have arrived at such different convictions about the appropriate role of the church in relation to society. Because my research indicated that the same evangelical Protestants were likely to be involved in saving souls *and* social reform in the 1830s to 1850s, I surveyed the period from 1857 to the 1920s in an effort to discover how and why a split of such consequence had occurred.

If this sounds familiar, it is probably because you are acquainted with Martin E. Marty's prize-winning historical essay entitled *Righteous Empire: The Protestant Experience in America*, in which (as Marty himself indicated clearly in the footnotes) my dissertation formed the basis for chapter 17.[2] In that book, Marty described the fateful "public/private split" which developed in American Protestantism, claiming that without an understanding of that "two-party system" twentieth-century Protestantism was incomprehensible.

Marty's book was published in 1970. Since then the two-party thesis has been subjected to sociological research, and some writing has explored possible approaches toward overcoming the split. Evangelical scholars like George Marsden and Donald Dayton have questioned the adequacy of the label "private" as a description of their own tradition, reminding us of the social concern of evangelicals and holiness groups prior to the "Great Reversal" which began about 1900.[3] There has also been much more sophisticated reflection upon the meaning of the term "public."[4] Perhaps most surprising of all has been the way in which the so-called "private party" of the 1960s has gone public in the 1980s as the Moral Majority or new religious right, seeking to impose its private vision on the public realm.

If I had been asked to write an article for the recent *Christian Century* series on "How My Mind Has Changed" (covering the decade 1969–79),[5] there is much I would have had to confess or take into account as well as bring up to date. There was the strong trend toward private religion in the 1970s, but at the same time, the rediscovery by "young evangelicals" of a prophetic social witness (Sojourners, for example). My 1969 dissertation had almost no mention of black religious history during this period, nor of women's history, nor the relationship between denominational religion and "civil religion" in America. Clearly the contribution of social historical studies in the past twenty years has had a tremendous impact on the way historians now interpret the American religious past. Finally, perhaps in an effort to avoid doing denominational history (with its attendant dangers of parochialism and triumphalism), I paid little attention in my dissertation to the Methodists, concentrating on those who were first to develop a social gospel (Congregationalists and Episcopalians) and those who were most involved in the Fundamentalist-Modernist struggle of the 1920s (Presbyterians and Baptists).

For a number of reasons, I decided that this issue needed to be addressed in our Bicentennial Consultation. First, because the phenomenon which the two-party system attempted to explain is far from being resolved in contemporary American religion. Many Americans have yet to be convinced that religion should be anything but private. Second, because the split, however it be described, has had destructive and damaging consequences to the churches as well as to the quality and health of American public life. Most important of all, I believe that the Wesleyan denominations in America (including all those groups which regard the Christmas Conference of 1784 as in some way a part of their founding history) have within our traditions resources for nurturing a vision that moves beyond the public/private split.[6] It is especially for this last reason that I think the issue demands our attention here.

In quest of such a vision, which moves beyond the split to embrace both personal and social transformation, I want to lift up examples of Methodists who combined conspicuously well the spiritual and social dimensions of their faith. As a group they represent a Methodist tradition, true (I believe) to the thought and example of their mentor John Wesley, and worthy of our exploration. Because of time limitations, I intend to use aspects of their stories to illuminate public/private issues at certain revelatory moments in our common past as Methodists. Here symbolic dates will serve as windows on a larger period: the dates I have selected are 1840, 1866, 1884, and 1919.

I am suggesting here one possible approach to a new history for our times. While by no means claiming to have done prophetic history, I have intentionally concentrated on stories of women and black Methodists that were missing from the histories to which Kenneth Rowe referred.[7] I am convinced that the figures I have chosen are important for us precisely because they were able to relate private faith to public order in a way not typical for their historical moment.

## 1840

The account of the American Methodist struggle to establish an antislavery norm is important background for an exploration of this first period.[8] By the General Conference of 1804, the mood was clearly one of retreat in the face of public outcry, especially with the approval of an expurgated edition of the Discipline for use in conferences south of Virginia.

Francis Asbury's moral anguish over this defeat was reflected in a journal entry of 1809. In it, he conceded that if Methodist preachers were to have access to the souls of slaves, they might have to settle for amelioration of their condition within the system, rather than continuing to work for their emancipation.[9] By 1816, Methodist accommodation to the system of slavery was marked by a sense of futility that "little can be done to abolish a practice so contrary to the principles of moral justice." This disillusionment over the failure to enforce an antislavery norm, and the shift in early Methodism from attacking the institution of slavery to a religious concern for slaves within the system, helped establish the pattern of overcoming social evils by changing individuals.

Bishop McKendree seemed to articulate this orientation when he told the preachers at the General Conference of 1816 that God's design in raising up the preachers called Methodists was "to reform the continent by spreading scriptural holiness over these lands." [10]

While Southern preachers engaged in a vigorous evangelizing mission to the slaves, most Northerners managed to avoid endorsing either slavery or abolition by supporting the new scheme of African colonization. The recovery of the earlier emphasis on social reform with regard to slavery would have to await the Christian abolitionism of the 1830s. [11]

In 1837–38, preachers in the South Carolina and Georgia Conferences declared that slavery was not a "moral evil" but merely "a social and domestic institution with which, as Ministers of Christ, we have nothing to do." [12] By the time the General Conference met in 1840, Southerners and Northern anti-abolitionists alike were determined to defeat the troublesome abolitionist minority in the church. That conference commended the work of the American Colonization Society, and in the infamous Silas Comfort case resolved to prohibit the testimony of black church members in church trials in any state where blacks were denied that privilege by law. Declaring that "the simple holding of slaves constitutes no legal barrier to the election or ordination of ministers," the conference asserted that it would be "a sore evil to divert Methodism from her proper work of 'spreading Scripture holiness over these lands.'" [13]

By the early 1840s, the Methodists had become the largest Protestant denomination in America. Thus at the very time when American Methodists were rejoicing at God's approbation, evidenced in their remarkable success in evangelizing the nation, they also succeeded in silencing the radical antislavery minority in their midst. These Christian abolitionists took the uncompromising position that slavery was a sin regardless of circumstances and that good people could be the bulwarks of an evil system. Orange Scott had been a key figure in the debates on slavery in the 1836 and 1840 General Conferences. Although he was deeply troubled by the possibility of secession, by 1842 he was convinced that the Methodist Episcopal Church would never take action against slavery, and he did withdraw. In 1843 Scott and La Roy Sunderland led in forming the Wesleyan Methodist Connection on the basis of abolitionism and John Wesley's doctrine of Christian perfection. As the pastoral address at the organizing conference explained: "It is holiness of heart and life that will give you moral power to oppose the evils and corruption in the world, against which we have lifted up a standard." [14]

For 1840 then, we would point to the examples of Orange Scott and Scott's successor in leadership of the Wesleyan Methodists after his early death in 1847, Luther Lee. Both men were born in 1800, they grew up in impoverished homes in Vermont and upstate New York, received little education, and gave themselves to the Methodist ministry after conversion experiences in their young adult years. Both rose to prominence among the Methodists because of their powerful preaching and leadership abilities. Both became converted to abolitionism in the 1830s. As Orange Scott later described it, "being wholly devoted to the one idea of saving souls, I omitted to examine, faithfully and critically as I should, the condition of the country in respect to great moral evils. My eyes, however, were at length opened." For the rest of his life, Scott would insist on the conjunction of "piety and radicalism." [15]

After Scott's death, the mantle of leadership passed to his cohort Luther Lee, who presided over three of the first six general conferences of the new denomination and became editor of its paper, *The True Wesleyan*. While serving pastorates in upstate New York and Ohio, he was active in the Underground Railroad, and in 1864 became professor of theology at Wesleyan Adrian College before returning to the M. E. Church after the Civil War. In a sermon entitled "The Radicalism of the Gospel," Lee argued that "the Gospel is so radically reformatory, that to preach it fully and clearly, is to attack and condemn all wrong, and to assert and defend all righteousness." [16] He understood that religion must not be divorced from political responsibility and in 1840 had helped to organize the antislavery Liberty party. In 1853, Luther Lee preached the ordination sermon for Antoinette Brown, the first woman to be fully ordained to the Christian ministry in an American denomination. As one historian said of leaders like Scott and Lee: "The implication of the abolitionist preaching was a new kind of society much different from the old—an implication only gradually being realized in the 20th century." [17]

# 1866

By 1861, each of the two Methodist bodies that had separated in 1844 had become the largest Protestant church in its geographical area. The two churches were separated not only by sectional interests, but by different understandings of the appropriate role of the church in society. The Southern church in its defense of slaveholding claimed to be faithful to the only Scriptural mission for the church, namely preaching repentance, faith, and holiness, and leaving the affairs of state to those competent to deal with them. It accused Northern Methodism of being a "political" church, intent on subjugating the South. To the end of the struggle, Southern Methodists insisted that their church had appropriately avoided political involvement. [18]

The view of many Methodists in the North that the church must influence political action on the slavery issue (particularly after the passage of the Fugitive Slave Law in 1850), reflected the growing sense of responsibility for shaping the national conscience associated with the denomination's new institutional prominence. The antislavery stance of the Methodist Episcopal Church, however, was considerably qualified by its concern over the possible loss of the border conferences. It was not, therefore, until 1864 (more than a year after the Emancipation Proclamation) that the General Conference acted to alter the General Rule and exclude all slaveholders from church fellowship.

The preeminent symbol of Northern Methodism's new status in the 1860s was Bishop Matthew Simpson, whose popular War Speech concluded with the affirmation (made, he said, with all due reverence) that God "cannot afford to do without America." [19] The Methodist bishop believed about equally in the triumph of Christianity, the peculiar destiny of the American nation, and the greatness of the Methodist Episcopal Church.

That church had "come of age" when *Harper's Weekly* could comment, during the centennial observance of 1866, that Methodism had become "for good or ill . . . the predominant ecclesiastical fact of the nation." [20] Methodist celebration of that centennial was marked by Abel Stevens' historical volumes, by the raising of over $8.5 million for the Centenary Educational Fund and the opening of Drew Theological Seminary in 1867, and by the American Methodist Ladies' Centenary Association's raising money to erect Heck Hall on the campus of Garrett Biblical Institute in honor of founding mother Barbara Heck.[21]

Northern Methodists made the centennial of American Methodism a time for a great push forward, particularly in the areas of church extension into the West, and missionary, educational, and social work among the freed people in the South.[22] Some Methodist Protestants participated in this centennial observance. The Methodist Episcopal Church, South, preoccupied with its own struggle to survive as a separate church, noted that it would hold no formal centennial celebration until 1884.[23] As northern black Methodists engaged in their own mission to the southern freed people, the A.M.E. Church celebrated its own semi-centennial in 1866, commemorating its first general conference.

At least one important voice was missing from the Methodist scene for most of 1866. Gilbert Haven, the New England Methodist preacher, noted abolitionist, and outspoken defender of racial equality in church and society was in semi-retirement most of that year recovering from what was then called "nervous prostration." [24] Raised in a religious home in which Puritan and Methodist influences were equally strong, Haven's abolitionism and the New England insistence on the church's role as the conscience of the social order were already evident in his sermon of 1850 entitled "The Higher Law." During the decade from 1851–61, Haven held five pastorates in the New England Conference and identified with the radical antislavery contingent in the church. Like the evangelical abolitionists of the 1830s, Haven was openly critical of reformers like William Lloyd Garrison who had abandoned evangelical faith and declared the fundamental immorality of American society. Haven retained his basic confidence in both American politics and evangelical religion. He also declared himself to be a loyal abolitionist; that is, he would stay in the Methodist Episcopal Church, to which he was devoted. His ministry, however, must be one of social reform. In Haven's view, it was the task of preachers to preach "salvation from all sin personal, social, and national."[25]

In the 1860s, Gilbert Haven shared the views of many northern Methodists that the Divine purpose was being worked out in the Civil War, that God's millennium was coming, and that American evangelical Protestants in general, and the Methodists in particular, had a special mission. There were, however, crucial differences in the way he interpreted these matters.[26] Even before the outbreak of the war, he emphasized the complicity of both North and South in the sins of slavery and racism, and urged the necessity for national repentance. As he reflected on the Civil War in 1862, he was more than ever convinced that through it God was working out his sovereign purpose of purging the "model republic" from the evil of slavery and inaugurating an era of interracial harmony. After the Emancipation Proclamation, Haven was optimistic about the coming of God's kingdom, seeing it as "God's bringing all into subjection to him."[27]

The new order would be characterized by liberty, equality, and unity. While confident of America's destiny in relation to the millennium, Haven was aware of the contradiction of racism. His view of America's chosenness was conditional: "If we cooperate with Him [by inaugurating this interracial brotherhood], He will make us his vanguard. If we refuse, He will . . . cast us off, and raise up another people who shall follow his guidance."[28] It was the church's role to become a racially inclusive community in order to prod the nation toward "a racially integrated and just society."[29] This insistence that the church take "the more excellent way" and "entirely ignore the idea of color in the organization of our Churches and conferences throughout the whole land"[30] earned Haven little support. He was widely criticized in the church when he refused to accept an appointment as missionary to black people in Vicksburg, Mississippi, because he objected to the segregationist policy of the missions. The basic cause of Haven's breakdown in 1866 was his agonizing realization that so few of his contemporaries shared his vision of the transracial character of America's national mission.[31]

He described this vision in a sermon explaining why colonization could never solve America's race problem:

"They [American blacks] will never leave us or forsake us . . . They must abide with us till we acknowledge by word and act that they are one with us . . . God will keep them with us till He has cured us of our sins. Then shall we rejoice to abide with them always and to build up a grand nationality of one humanity, of one language, having one Redeemer, and one future on earth, and, if in Christ, forever."[32]

In March 1867, Haven (having recuperated from his illness) was elected editor of *Zion's Herald*. From this post, he resumed the crusade for racial equality in church and state, advocating civil rights, social equality and racial assimilation. In addition, he was a zealous advocate of prohibition and women's rights, including both suffrage and ordination.[33] Haven campaigned unsuccessfully for the merger of the A.M.E. and A.M.E. Zion Churches with the M.E. Church. In spite of some opposition he was elected bishop in 1872, and assigned to Atlanta. His outspoken protests notwithstanding, in 1876 the General Conference of the M.E. Church approved the segregationist policy of separating all the annual conferences according to race. Most northern Methodists accepted this new segregationist policy and the accompanying spirit of cooperation with the Southern church called "Methodist fraternity." Haven could not welcome it because of the price that had been paid in terms of racial attitudes and commitments.

When he died in January of 1880, a somewhat lonely man, it was the black Methodists who understood best the convictions that had motivated his entire career. As Benjamin Tanner put it in the *Christian Recorder*:

> "He was one of the few that *made* public opinion instead of following it; and happily for mankind, like the great Master he loved, he made it on the side of the poor, the bond, and the ostracized. We have spoken of him as the finest type of our American religion—a religion that, to a large extent, sanctioned slavery in the past and both sanctions and practices caste in the present. But the great soul of Gilbert Haven was against both." [34]

## 1884

Classic accounts of the rise of the social gospel in American protestantism (like those of Henry May and C.H. Hopkins)[35], tended to focus on the formation of the Methodist Federation for Social Service in 1907, and the adoption of the Social Creed by the General Conference of 1908, and therefore to stress the "lateness" of a Methodist social gospel. Scholars who looked elsewhere than to episcopal pronouncements and General Conference decisions could discern signs of a social awakening in the 1890s in the Methodist press, in the city missionary work of people like Frank Mason North, and in memorials to General Conference from the New York East and Rock River annual conferences.[36] For the most part, the story prior to the 1890s, however, was one of neglect, inattention, and complacency with regard to urban and industrial problems.[37] Yet during the 1880s, Methodist women initiated a whole range of activities that not only would constitute a pragmatic social gospel in its own right, but would result in a greatly enlarged sphere of influence for the women themselves, in both church and society. As Beverly Harrison pointed out nearly ten years ago, these women were responding to the subtly encroaching split between the interpersonal and the public sphere that industrialism was effecting.[38] They wanted to "feminize" the ever more remote public world. I want to use the stories of three women here, to lift up both their personal example and the cumulative impact of their efforts. As a window into the decade, I've chosen the symbolic date of the Methodist centennial in 1884.

The 1884 celebration appears to have differed in two important respects from the one in 1866: it involved both major branches of episcopal Methodism, as well as smaller Methodist bodies, and it seemed to strike a more sober note, warning of the dangers of neglecting the poor, and of becoming assimilated to the world.[39]

In 1866, Frances Willard was corresponding secretary of the American Methodist Ladies' Centenary Association. By 1884, she had been national president of the W.C.T.U. for five years; in 1888 she would actually be elected a lay-delegate to the M.E. Church General Conference.[40] Although that 1888 General Conference ruled the five women delegates ineligible, the struggle for full laity rights for women in the church had begun. That same General Conference officially recognized the new Methodist deaconess movement, begun the preceding year by Lucy Rider Meyer. In 1886, women of the Southern Methodist Church had gained approval of their General Conference for a Woman's Department of Church Extension which would become the Woman's Home Mission Society. Its outstanding leader was Belle Harris Bennett, who would lead the fight in her church for full lay rights for women. As women moved into these expanded roles, it is no wonder that James M. Buckley as historian and guarantor of the old order saw Methodism deteriorating![41]

The movement of middle-class Protestant women in America beyond the world of home and church into larger spheres of influence and "usefulness" came primarily through their creation of organizations "for women only."[42] The New York Ladies' Home Missionary Society was organized as early as the 1840s, and in 1850, at the instigation of holiness evangelist Phoebe Palmer, women undertook support of the Five Points Mission in one of New York City's bleakest neighborhoods. The greatest impetus to women's activities came, however, with the Civil War and the important role women played in nursing and relief efforts. After the war, American Protestant women perceived other needs calling them from their homes into the world.

Frances E. Willard (1839–98) was the means by which countless Victorian "ladies" left the sanctuary of their homes to support the causes of temperance and woman suffrage for the sake of "home protection."[43] Intrepid leader of the W.C.T.U. for nearly two decades, her story is almost too familiar to be fully appreciated by an age less enthusiastic about teetotalism than was her own. Recent research on her life and thought has made clear both the extent of her involvement in a wide range of social reform issues, and the early social gospel character of her mature religious convictions.[44] On the Wisconsin frontier where she spent much of her childhood, Frances was able to escape many of the limitations of prescribed roles for young women, but she early envied her brother's rights to an education, the vote, and a ministerial career. After a decade of teaching and administration, Willard was converted in the 1870s to the two causes to which she would give the rest of her life—women and temperance.[45]

Proclaiming itself "organized mother-love," the W.C.T.U. began with a commitment to prohibition, and under Willard's "Do-Everything Policy" moved into active participation in a wide range of issues, including woman suffrage, social purity, concerns of labor, peace and arbitration, welfare work among blacks and immigrants, temperance education, health and hygiene.[46] Frances Willard challenged women to redefine the ideal of womanhood, rejecting the notion that women's nature and virtues were inherently different from men's, requiring different spheres of existence and influence.[47] Under her leadership, women gained an increased sense of their own power and a new self-assurance. She raised women's consciousness on important public issues, and instructed them in the rudiments of what she called "Gospel politics," which included petitioning legislative bodies and participating in political parties such as the National Prohibition Party. As the motto "for God and home and native land" suggests, W.C.T.U. women were urged to develop their gifts for the sake of the christianization of their nation. "To help forward the coming of Christ into all departments of life," Willard said, "is, in the last analysis, the purpose and aim of the WCTU." [48]

Compared with the progress of the social gospel, Willard's own commitments in the 1880s and 1890s were remarkable. She became a member of the Knights of Labor in 1887, wrote articles for the Christian Socialist journal the *Dawn*, and joined the Fabian Socialists in England in 1893. During these years, there is no question that she increasingly perceived the relationship between poverty and alcoholism in such a way as to understand the latter as a social evil, and not simply a personal vice.[49]

Like Orange Scott, Luther Lee, and Gilbert Haven, Frances Willard's social reform was motivated by a deep Methodist piety. Had she been a man, she would very likely have become a Methodist minister.[50] Having become a full member of the Methodist Episcopal Church in Evanston at age twenty-two, she later consecrated herself completely to God during holiness meetings led by Phoebe Palmer and her husband. For a time during the 1870s, she led inquiry meetings and Bible studies in Moody's revivals. After the unsuccessful attempt of Anna Oliver and Anna Howard Shaw to be ordained in the M.E. Church in 1880, she wrote *Woman In the Pulpit* to urge the cause of women's ordination and to claim its biblical basis. Her concern for health was reminiscent of Wesley's, and she urged women to care about diet and exercise (especially recommending riding a bicycle as excellent exercise for women!). She saw Christian commitment and social reform as fundamentally connected. As she put it, "When the spirit of God has been generated in a human being, it must not be shut up in the prayer-meeting or the church building, but turned on the saloons, the gambling houses, the haunts of shame." [51]

This same phenomenon of women's beginning with the simple intention of extending the influences of the home and gradually increasing their involvement in the public sphere occurred in both the deaconess movement and the women's missionary movements.[52] The woman chiefly responsible for founding the deaconess order in the Methodist Episcopal Church was Lucy Rider Meyer (1849–1922).[53] Born in Vermont to parents of Puritan stock, she was raised in a strongly religious home where she "came to Jesus" at age thirteen in a Methodist revival and subsequently joined the church. She graduated from Oberlin College and Cook County Normal school, was Professor of Chemistry at McKendree College for a time, and later completed a medical degree. While serving as field secretary of the Illinois State Sunday School Association, she met many young women whose lack of preparation kept them from lives of usefulness.

After her marriage in 1885 to Josiah Meyer, the couple opened the Chicago Training School for City, Home, and Foreign Missions. The course of study was comprehensive, including Bible classes, but also studies in "hygiene, in citizenship, in social and family relationships, in everything that could help or hinder in the establishment of the Kingdom of Heaven on earth." [54] An important aspect of the program was the provision for field work in the city, since most of the students came from rural or small town homes. In the summer of 1887, Lucy Meyer enlisted several of her trainees in a program of visiting and assisting the immigrant poor and needy in Chicago. It was the beginning of the Methodist deaconess movement, which spread rapidly to other cities like Cincinnati.

Methodist deaconesses were determined to transform the city. They began by "visiting," canvassing tenement neighborhoods to discover those in need of help. While ministering to people's basic needs and demonstrating neighborly concern, they also gathered important information on prevailing social conditions. As literature like the *Deaconess Advocate* reveals, they came increasingly to look for the underlying causes of the misery they found, and then to attack the evil social structures responsible. (The same might also be said about holiness social work among the poor in the 1880s and 1890s.)[55]

These women were activists rather than theorists. They saw what they were doing as "pure practical Christianity." They responded to Christ's call with the resolve to become *useful*, to further God's purpose for the world. Methodist deaconesses formed a new breed of church women. Trained for and consecrated to the order, they became experts in the field of Christian social service.[56]

Women in the Methodist Episcopal Church, South, were like their northern sisters in developing a sense of responsibility for Christian work that reached beyond the local congregation.[57] The Woman's Department of Church Extension was originally established to raise funds for building and repairing parsonages in the West. In spite of considerable opposition, the women continued to expand their home mission work. By the early 1890s, they had become convinced of the need for organized city mission work among the poor in cities like St. Louis, Nashville, Atlanta, and New Orleans. The Woman's Home Mission journal, begun in 1892, was significantly entitled *Our Homes.*

In 1884, a young woman named Belle Harris Bennett (1852–1922), from a prominent Kentucky family, gave her life wholly to God at a summer conference at Lake Chautauqua, New York.[58] A few years later while attending a missionary meeting, she became concerned about the evident lack of preparation of missionaries and wrote to Lucy Rider Meyer for information about her training school. Feeling called by God to establish a training school for missionaries, she presented her idea to the Woman's Board of Foreign Missions in 1889, and was promptly appointed "agent" of the Board to raise funds and promote the idea. As a result of her efforts, the Scarritt Bible and Training School was opened in Kansas City in 1892.

In 1897, she established the Sue Bennett School for poor children in the mountains of Kentucky in honor of her sister who had died several years earlier. As president of the Woman's Home Mission Society from 1896, and of its governing board from 1898, she urged the establishment of church settlement houses (judiciously calling them "Wesley Community Houses"). The first was begun in Nashville in 1901. In 1902 she persuaded the General Conference of the Southern Methodist Church to authorize deaconesses. She led the home missions women in educational work among blacks, supported woman suffrage, and worked for more restrictive child labor laws.

When in 1910 the Southern Methodist women's home and foreign mission boards were merged into a single Woman's Missionary Council under a largely male Board of Missions, Bennett had the difficult job of serving as president. Although the change resulted in a significant loss of autonomy for the women's work, they had not been consulted, nor were their protests heeded. Belle Bennett immediately launched the struggle for full laity rights for women in her church. With the vote of the General Conference in 1918 and ratification by the annual conferences in 1919, women were finally seated as delegates in the General Conference of 1922. Although elected by the Kentucky Annual Conference as its first woman delegate, Belle Bennett was too ill to attend; she died of cancer that July.[59]

The standard biographies of Lucy Rider Meyer and Belle Harris Bennett, written by women who were also deeply involved in deaconess and home mission work, make clear how deeply spiritual these women were, and how untroubled by any distinction between spiritual and social spheres. As Belle Bennett's biographer Tochie MacDonell explained: "The motive of Miss Bennett's missionary zeal was the building of God's victorious kingdom on earth. She sought to show the way of regeneration through Christ to the individual and fought to conquer the evil that clogs the salvation of society. 'Eternal life for the individual, the kingdom of God for humanity,' was the slogan of her life. For this reason she led the women of the Church in much endeavor for human betterment, not then classed as religious work."[60]

As Southern Methodist missions women came face to face with "the ugly realities of industrializing society," they gradually came to embrace a more public role and to engage in a more active political program to achieve social change. They were willing to say of themselves, "Grow we must, even if we outgrow all that we love."[61]

# 1919

Black Methodists in the 1880s and 1890s had to deal with two sets of challenges: those facing Christian America, and those confronting black America.[62] A central theme in Afro-American religious thought had always been the interpretation of black suffering, the conviction that God would soon bring a slaveholding society to judgment. A primary issue for black Christians after the failure of Reconstruction, therefore, was the death of hope, the question of meaning.[63] In 1883, the Civil Rights Act of 1875 was struck down by the Supreme Court. With the approval of the legality of racial segregation in the 1890s, private discrimination became public policy. There were 2500 lynchings of black Americans in the years from 1884 to 1900. Thus black Christians had to cope with both a racial and a religious crisis.

In addition, black Methodists were experiencing a lack of leadership in the 1890s.[64] Between 1890 and 1895, for example, all five of the bishops of the A.M.E. Church who had been elected before 1880 died. Chief of these was Bishop Daniel Alexander Payne, who died in 1893. From the time he joined the A.M.E. Church in 1841, his vision of a black Christian culture and of what the A.M.E. Church should be had become increasingly dominant. He had a central role in launching the A.M.E. effort to reach the freed people in the South as early as 1863. His belief in the traditional Wesleyan values of education, disciplined living, and service was formative for his church. Wilberforce University, of which he was president, was the "black Athens," the *A.M.E Church Review* was the leading black journal. After Bishop Payne's death, it was Bishop Henry McNeal Turner who was the next great leader of the A.M.E. Church. Bishop Turner's disillusionment with America after the reverses of the 1880s was so strong that he became an outspoken advocate of African colonization. In late nineteenth- and early twentieth-century America there was also the beginning of an autonomous black culture no longer under the tutelage of the A.M.E. or any other Protestant church, and the massive movement of blacks into the cities. The A.M.E. Church, in short, was overwhelmed by the combined forces of industrialism, urbanization, and racism.[65]

In 1919, Methodists were celebrating yet another centenary, this a $100 million drive commemorating the beginning of the Methodist missionary enterprise and closely associated with the interdenominational Protestant missionary effort called the Interchurch World Movement. That year was also important for Methodists since the Joint Committee of Reference was appointed in 1919 to draw up a proposed constitution for a unified Methodist Church.[66] In the country as a whole, 1919 saw the passage of both the Volstead Act to enforce Prohibition and the amendment for woman suffrage; these went into effect in 1920 as the Eighteenth and Nineteenth Amendments. Later that summer of 1919, the first widespread radical urban black resistance broke out in cities like Chicago and Washington, D.C. Black Americans, "in sackcloth and ashes" commemorated the official anniversary of the coming of the first Africans to Virginia as slaves three hundred years earlier.[67]

For 1919, it seemed appropriate to look at two figures, one the man most responsible for providing the A.M.E. Church with a new vision of what its place might be in the modern city, Reverdy Ransom, editor of the *A.M.E. Church Review* and pastor of the mission Church of Simon of Cyrene in New York City.[68] The other is Francis McConnell, bishop of the Methodist Episcopal Church since 1912, and also president of the Methodist Federation for Social Service since that same year. In 1919, he was forty-eight years old and had already earned an outstanding reputation both as a presiding officer and as a prominent churchman vitally concerned about the industrial order in America.[69]

Unlike his predecessors in leadership of the A.M.E. Church, Reverdy Ransom was a man of the city. Born in 1861 in Ohio, educated at Oberlin and Wilberforce, Ransom had entered the A.M.E. ministry in 1886. After serving in small mission churches in Pennsylvania for four years, he was moved by Bishop Payne in 1890 to the prestigious North Church in Springfield, Ohio. From there he was moved to Cleveland, and in 1896 to Bethel Church in Chicago. In 1900, he left Bethel to launch the Institutional Church and Settlement House, "the only colored Social Settlement in the world."[70] In 1905, he began a two-year pastorate in Boston and was actively engaged in the Niagara Movement. From 1907 until his election as editor in 1912, he was pastor of Bethel Church in Harlem. He was elected bishop in 1924 at age 63, and lived to be 98, serving as bishop until 1952!

After the death of Bishop Turner in 1915, it was Reverdy Ransom who was most responsible for carrying forward under changed circumstances the A.M.E. Church's traditional concern with forming a black Christian culture. Ransom's vision differed significantly from that of Payne in terms of theology, worship, and his view of the Christian life. Although he wrote no extended theological works, his was clearly a "liberal, social gospel theology." While sharing some of Payne's sense of propriety in worship, he believed black churches should know and own their own tradition of "spontaneous enthusiasm." For him, the heart of the Christian life lay in "active concern and forgiving love for the downtrodden and outcast." He was thus a good deal less stringent than Payne about the "weaknesses of the flesh," and "greatly softened" the authoritarian cast of Payne's "strictly ordered" vision of what African Methodism should be.[71]

Ransom encouraged an expanded role for women in the A.M.E. Church, supporting deaconesses and woman suffrage. From the time of his 1896 article on "The Negro and Socialism," he worked for the amelioration of the working class in contemporary society. In that article he said, "The present social order with its poverty and vast reserve army of the unemployed cannot be accepted as final, as the ultimate goal for which the ages have been in travail. If man is the child of God, the present social order is not divine. God has never sanctioned, as by divine right, a social order into which the vast majority must be born only to find, 'no trespass' posted upon every portion of the domain of nature, which is their heritage, and to lead a life of privation and suffering in a struggle to maintain an existence."[72]

He looked to democratic socialism as the movement which could transform this situation, and he dreamed of the day when black and white workers would join in a common movement, and when a new civilization would arise, recognizing the solidarity of the human race, and allowing all to share the blessings of their common heritage.

Ransom's chief service to the A.M.E. Church was offering it a way into the future. In his sermon before the General Conference of 1936, he described the "church that shall survive" as a church that knows "neither race, color, nor nationality." Yet he was concerned for the totality of black Christians in America. He believed that the A.M.E. Church must be enlisted in the struggle for social justice and unafraid to bring prophetic judgment to bear on the evils of American society. "I see little hope for the survival of the A.M.E. Church," he warned, "if we do not so apply the Gospel of Christ as to make it a vital force in the life of society."[73] Ransom's vision "rested upon a deep personal commitment to the Christian faith, a preoccupation with remoulding the surrounding world under the impetus of that faith, and a conviction that the A.M.E. Church could be a place where that commitment and that preoccupation significantly affected the life of black America."[74] The church from whose service he retired in 1952 was not the activist community he wished it to be, but it was far better prepared for the civil rights struggles of the 1960s than it would have been without him.[75]

In 1919, Bishop McConnell was chosen to chair the commission of inquiry investigating the strike against U.S. Steel (under the auspices of the newly-organized Department of Industrial Relations within the Interchurch World Movement). Before 1912 it would have been difficult to predict such a role for McConnell. Born in rural Ohio, the son of a Methodist preacher and an intensely devout mother, he graduated from Ohio Wesleyan, studied for the ministry at Boston University, and went on to complete a Ph.D. under Borden Parker Bowne. He served four appointments in Massachusetts and one in Brooklyn, New York, before becoming president of DePauw University. At heart a philosopher and theologian, he apparently became interested in the social movement only in 1912. He was, in fact, the first of Bowne's students to demonstrate the theoretical significance of Boston personalism for social reform.[76]

The special commission of inquiry for the steel strike included both prominent church people and experts in industrial research who were competent to handle the technical investigations. The strike itself, which involved half of the nation's steel workers in a fight for union recognition, has been regarded in labor history as a pivotal struggle. (It was made even more interesting to Methodists by the fact that the chairman of U.S. Steel was Judge Elbert Gary, a devout Methodist!)[77]

In spite of the collapse of the strike, the commission completed and published its report in January 1920. The report corroborated the grievances of labor and helped to end the twelve-hour day and seven-day work week in the steel industry. It also revealed an extensive "spy network" operated by the steel management and the systematic denial of the workers' civil liberties. The report therefore explicitly requested the intervention of the federal government in the regulation of industry and the protection of the civil liberties of the workers. That the report was finally adopted by the Interchurch World Movement in spite of attempts to suppress it was largely due to Bishop McConnell's determination and courage. He himself admitted that the report might have caused the demise of the movement's financial campaign "if the movement had not already been dead when the report was published." [78]

As chair of the commission of inquiry, McConnell came under intense pressure, including sometimes vicious personal attacks. Associates who knew him well credited his profound faith in God as the foundation for his courage and social hope. As one of them put it, "the quiet courage of Bishop McConnell, the relative indifference to immediate results, a certain half-humorous detachment which often marks him, roots here." [79] In his autobiography *By the Way* (1952), McConnell warned oversensitive souls to find something else to do for the kingdom than to attempt to be socially radical preachers.[80] For his work in the steel strike investigation, the University of Colorado awarded Bishop McConnell the LL.D. degree. A New York rabbi, probably Stephen S. Wise, wrote to him, "I feel you are my bishop. You are bishop of my people." [81] Recent scholarship on this period suggests that the steel strike investigation was a decisive factor in causing the dissolution of the older social gospel coalition and the emergence of social gospel radicalism.[82] During the 1920s, McConnell's example served as a "prophetic symbol" for many younger radicals, to whom he gave new faith in the church. Reinhold Niebuhr said of him even after his own disillusionment with social gospel liberalism, he is "one of the most honest, courageous, and prophetic voices of American church history." [83]

Bishop McConnell's commitments were deeply theological and pastoral as well as social. He warned against an activism that was not thoroughly grounded in the intellectual pursuit of truth. In a little book he wrote in 1916 entitled *The Essentials of Methodism*, McConnell listed the new birth, entire sanctification, and the witness of the Spirit as essentials of the theological tradition to which he believed himself faithful.[84] He described conversion as a gift of God, as passage into new life through surrender to the Divine Will, as transformation so radical that it must manifest itself in one's life. Sanctification meant bringing all of life under subjection to God's Kingdom. Clearly personal salvation was fundamental for him, and engaging in a penetrating critique of American culture was not to be divorced from one's deep religious faith.

There are striking similarities between Ransom and McConnell in terms of personal faith. "Though reared in an atmosphere of prayer by a devout Christian mother" and nurtured in the piety of the A.M.E. Church, Ransom had neither been converted nor joined the church before he went off to Wilberforce. Part of the problem, as he himself recognized, was his unwillingness to submit to the "spectacle" of the mourners bench. At Wilberforce, he experienced "one of those rapturing moments . . . when earth and heaven meet and blend in the happy consciousness that God has entered into our life making Himself known." He never ceased to testify to the importance of this life-changing experience. Similarly, Francis McConnell's mother was known for her profound Wesleyan piety (which he always honored). Yet when he became a member of the church of which his father was pastor, he simply "went forward and shook hands at the altar rail" with his father; "that was all there was to it." [85]

Both Ransom and McConnell were theological liberals and social gospel figures. It would be a serious mistake, however, to underestimate the depth of their personal faith, which was basic to all of their efforts for social transformation. Their inclusion in this address is in part to urge that the power to transform the world must be rooted in profound spirituality, biblical faith, and theological reflection (and not simply human effort), while insisting equally that this must *not* mean conforming to a particular type of piety.

I claimed at the outset that the individuals at whom we would look were faithful to the thought and example of John Wesley. During the formative years of the Methodist social gospel, there was a spate of research and publication on the "social implications of Methodism." [86] I believe that contemporary Wesleyans seeking a vision which embraces both personal and social transformation can claim to be in the Wesleyan tradition. Although after Aldersgate, John Wesley understood justification to be the indispensable foundation for salvation (never to be superseded), he clearly believed that the divine intention was the actual transformation of both persons and society, bringing them into active conformity to the will of God.[87] The General Rules outlined and the entire Methodist organization served this conception of the Christian life as social holiness, as character organized around a habitual disposition which embraced both spiritual and social concerns. The early Methodist people were taught to feel a personal responsibility for relieving social need.[88]

To sum up and conclude then, what have we said about reforming the nation and spreading scriptural holiness and what they have meant in our two hundred years as a denomination? In this address, we looked at the period from 1840 to 1939 and took "depth soundings" at revelatory moments for Methodists. Such, I have suggested, were 1840, 1866, 1884, and 1919. We wanted to explore the way public and private were related typically for Methodists in each of those moments. Then we looked at individuals who were visionaries, prophets, examples of holiness in the sense of relating their profound personal faith to a way of life that was morally courageous and socially transforming. They were usually also pioneers and innovators, relating private faith to public order in a way not typical for their historical moment.

In the 1960s when I wrote my dissertation, the dominant framework for interpreting the rise of the social gospel was the stimulus-response thesis formulated by Arthur Schlesinger.[89] A major weakness of that framework (as Robert Handy made clear in *A Christian America*)[90] was its inability to account for the dynamic, purposive, and culture-shaping power of the religious traditions which responded to those challenges. For all its diffuseness and apparent imprecision, the concept of modernization has seemed to me since to be a fruitful interpretive framework for looking at the relationship between public and private in American religion. It attempts to describe a process which includes different rates of change within various sectors of society and also counter-modern or re-traditioning trends. It is a concept which embraces the whole range of great cultural changes (social, political, economic, technological, and religious) which have marked modernity in western European and American life over the last four centuries.[91] I want to mention here only three aspects of religion in modernization.

First, all religious traditions in contemporary America are descriptively modern, in the sense that no tradition is immune to modernity. Traditions have to be reaffirmed, consciously kept alive by believers. Thus in this respect, the major difference between conservatives and liberals is one of response. Second, it has generally been assumed that the social gospel was a modern response to social change, while so-called private Protestantism was traditional. Yet I would submit to you that much of the thrust of the social gospel was an attempt to bring traditional values such as the importance of community into a modernizing public world. On the other hand, as many conservative Christian churches reveal, some of the most characteristic features of modern life—such as sophisticated use of media—are to be found there.

Finally, there is in modernization a wedge that compartmentalizes individual and social spheres of existence. One aspect of that split is the higher valuation of the individual than existed in traditional cultures. The ironic consequence, however, of the religious freedom of the individual is the inevitable tendency toward the privatization of religion. All religious traditions in the modern world have to struggle with this problem of how to articulate a credible public theology and ethics. The point of Martin E. Marty's *The Public Church* is that a "convergence of constituencies" of mainline Protestants, evangelicals, and Roman Catholics is needed so that those who share a concern for relating private faith to public order can contribute together to social and public morale.[92]

Perhaps we need a new conception of social ministry. This is the suggestion both of Presbyterian Dieter Hessel in a recent book and of Jane Cary Peck in a *Christian Century* article on ministry.[93] Both assert the need for a whole ministry which will express simultaneous concern for personhood, community, and global society. The relationship between the church and social transformation has usually not been deeply rooted in the local congregation. Hessel urges that we resocialize the private modes of ministry, such as preaching and pastoral care, and personalize the public modes so that they are meaningful to people at the local level.[94] Where the church ought to serve as a bridge between the public and the private, it has all too often been seen primarily as an extension of the private.[95] John Wesley understood well the relationship that Jane Cary Peck is reaffirming between transformed individuals, the nurturing and challenging of people in small groups (not only for personal growth but to enable social ministry), and the vision and power to change the world.

I am convinced that there is no greater need for the church of the 1980s and 1990s than to move beyond the public/private split to a vision which embraces both personal and social transformation. As United Methodists and others in our family of denominations look back on two hundred years of our history for the sake of moving forward, we have magnificent resources in our traditions for just such a vision. We need to encourage people who do not believe that their efforts make a difference by helping to acquaint them with heroes and heroines of their own tradition (as well as other traditions) who combined personal faith and social vision and action in their time. Methodist historians in particular might bring their awareness of history to the task of helping the church spell out the values inherent in the Methodist way of life. I think Earl

Brewer was pointing to this when he urged that we develop and practice "new holistic disciplines of holiness, joining personal and social dimensions." [96]

At the 1884 General Conference of the Methodist Episcopal Church, one of the resolutions of the Committee on the Centennial affirmed: "For a church polity so effective, for doctrines so scriptural, for a ritual so precious, for leaders so heroic, for experience so vital, for a success so unexampled, we give God thanks." [97] What comparable affirmation would we make in 1984? Although surely they can no longer signify for us what they meant for Wesley or even for the Methodists in 1784, perhaps an appropriate way for us to move into our third century is by reflecting on what scriptural holiness and reforming the nation might mean!

## CHAPTER 15

# The Emerging Voice of the Methodist Woman: *The Ladies' Repository*, 1841–61

Joanna Bowen Gillespie

At the end of its first American century, Methodism took time to congratulate itself on its success in using print as an instrument of salvation and evangelization. Paeans of praise flowed from Methodist pens in a volume titled *Methodism and Literature* (1883), published for the Methodist centennial. Methodist clergy lauded their own newspapers, "that great family of *Advocates*"; their own Sunday school literature—instruction books, question books, and Sunday school library books; and their own official literature—theology history, and sermons, "a veritable stream of living waters." They also exalted Christian biography as the Christian's obligation because it "served to embalm the great and the good, perpetuating what otherwise might have passed away." Their once-prestigious magazine, *The Ladies' Repository and Gatherings of the West*, published monthly by the Methodist Publishing House in Cincinnati from 1841–78, was not mentioned in that celebratory volume.[1]

This fact is puzzling, since in its time *The Ladies' Repository (LR)* was an impressive denominational achievement. For thirty-five years a handsome professionally-published octavo-sized magazine, embellished with high-quality steel engravings, was sent out each month to a paid subscription list numbering as many as 40,000 during the 1850s—its numerical peak. Undoubtedly each issue was read by many more than such numbers indicate to us today, thanks to group subscriptions and copies passed from hand to hand. *The Ladies' Repository* intended to be the Methodist *Godey's Lady's Book* and to siphon off some of that emerging women's audience which magazines were helping to create in the second quarter of the 1800s. But *LR*'s numerical inferiority alone would not have daunted Methodist celebrators of publishing successes.[2]

Perhaps the Methodist evaluators of their print achievements did not view a "commercial" women's magazine as "serious" Methodist literature, although they had no trouble seeing their children's literature in that light. Or perhaps the demise of *LR* in the decade just preceding the publication of *Methodism and Literature* excused them from dealing with it. Perhaps it was assumed, if indeed it was consciously debated, that women Methodists would have read the same religious matter men Methodists did.

Whatever the reasons for not celebrating the *Ladies' Repository* in 1883, we in 1983 treasure it as a rich source of Methodist social history in the mid-nineteenth century.

From the vantage point of two hundred years of American Methodism, we can see that the crucial fact about *LR* was its readers; they were *the* educated women of mid-nineteenth century Protestant Christian evangelicalism. Methodist subscribers (many were from other denominations as well) tended to be those women who were ambitious, well-educated for their time, and would-be local leaders. It was these "new American women" that the successful Cincinnati Methodist layman Samuel Williams had in mind when he initiated the *LR* in 1839–40. He wanted to produce a magazine which would be more religiously appropriate for them, "less full of sentimental tales and fashions direct from France" than secular women's journals.[3] And Methodist women themselves eagerly welcomed their *own* Christian publication according to letters in the *Advocates*.[4]

For the better part of two centuries, the only published expression of a woman's interior experience available to Christian women was the genre of pious memoir—since novels were strictly out of bounds and there were relatively few women authors of travel writings or history. From 1830–50, the "modern" American woman's consciousness began to be cultivated by and to surface in a stream of popular magazines. For the first time, ordinary women found their everyday lives visible in print. Even good evangelical Methodist women gave themselves religious permission to use their daily lives as subjects for literary expression. Reflections inspired by the daily routines of a frontier homestead or employment in a bakery shop began to be viewed through a kind of halo, thanks to vehicles such as *LR* in which females could "talk" with each other about such mundane but religiously-hallowed activities.

Up to the 1830s it was extremely rare for the average woman to have any visible public role, even if the rare Methodist woman had been testifying and exhorting along a wilderness circuit with her husband as early as 1815.[5] Large numbers of evangelical girls and women had flocked to teaching in Sabbath schools during the second decade of the nineteenth century, but the mass movement of females into public school teaching was still in the future. Women were simply not welcome in public life, even that of their churches. And while the new phenomenon of a denominational magazine didn't make them any more welcome, it did whet the Methodist female's taste for a somewhat more visible place in the life of her church. *LR* provided a print "bridge" for the woman who wanted to reach beyond her domestic boundaries into some sort of modest public recognition, but also to remain safely within her religiously-prescribed identity.

Thus what *LR* did was to assist educated Methodist women, long before they would have articulated such a culturally-daring thought to themselves, to reach out from their own kitchen tables, to an authority—a public voice—to whom they felt the right of access: the editor of "their" magazine. For many evangelical women, a first entry into the public eye was via print, not directly. This paper traces the emergence of the voices of these ordinary midnineteenth century evangelical women in their initial "public appearances" through letters to *LR*'s editors during its first two decades.

It is the letters themselves (and the readers who wrote them) that reveal the difference between a religious magazine such as *LR* and a popular, secular one such as *Godey's*. The magazines were not so different in their literary tone, although *Godey's* was filled with stories and *LR* eschewed fiction almost entirely until the 1860s.[6] But the topics about which women corresponded with the two magazines were totally contrasting. *Godey's* editorial and exchange department was full of practical household-management information: letters requested recipes, patterns, etiquette, and nutrition facts. *LR*, on the other hand, followed what it considered "the higher path." Articles and essays were never about such prosaic things as food or clothing, only about religion and woman's role, religiously defined. Articles on "concrete" topics were limited to biblical history, nature, religious family life, and various intellectual currents of the time, such as phrenology, spiritualism, or phonography.[7] But in *LR*'s pages, at least, women were allowed to experience and occasionally comment about essays in this male-defined intellectual field. *LR* implicitly encouraged women to "theologize," as well as poeticize, about their own inner experiences.

While other women's magazines of the period published other aspects of the American female's life and thought, *LR* provided a major forum for women's abstract thinking. Evangelical women of the mid-1800s equated religious thought with abstract thought; they had no separate category of secular philosophical thinking, so participating in any kind of discussion about religion in a popular magazine was a significant new step for the average woman. *Godey's* fiction "feminized" its moral instruction, making it more palatable by disguising it, in fictional form. *LR* took an unabashed prescriptive stance for the better part of its first twenty years, and thus engaged its readers in thinking about and reacting to "male" topics of discourse.

By the end of the nineteenth century, a readership such as that nurtured by *LR* had interacted with its own print medium in such a way as to produce an entirely new consciousness. Even by the 1870s, the imaginations of increasingly self-confident Methodist women were no longer enthralled with male-prescriptive religious journalism; women were writing it themselves, as well as moving into other intellectual fields.

From the 1870s on, women authors within the religious community were developing, with their own specialized journals, new areas of Christian women's activism. These newer women's magazines focused specifically on temperance or on foreign missions.[8] But even the least-sophisticated Methodist women in the 1880s, whose daily lives remained very circumscribed, were no longer satisfied with the former didactic style of religious journalism. They too were blossoming into a broader range of interests including some where religion was only an overtone rather than the major tune. It is as if the *Repository's* own well-intentioned "preaching" to women had been subverted by its own success. *LR* readers had so absorbed its messages of women's spiritual autonomy and self-development that they had become able to move outside the mental perimeters of their Methodist subculture. They were thus ready to be "at home" in the wider world where the culture itself was fostering women's interest in themes of discovery, self-management, pragmatism, and achievement.

During its first two decades, the official public authoritative (male) voice of the *Ladies' Repository* was perceptibly weakened, while the female reader's private, increasingly-independent agenda, religiously authorized and encouraged by her own "in-house" print forum, became more and more audible. Pouring this bursting sense of self into letters, articles, and poetry, offering the bright sayings of her children to her own religious community, the "modern" mid-nineteenth century Methodist woman leaps from *LR's* pages. We must wend our way through the same thickets of nineteenth-century religious rhetoric as did these females did in order to discern *LR's* role in their religious, literary, and social-psychological evolution.

# I

Midwestern boosterism was important in the Methodist venture of producing a women's magazine. Easterners who had become Ohio transplants wanted to prove that they were as civilized as their citified cousins, and that there was indeed a full-blown culture out on the banks of the Ohio River.[9] Besides wanting to make Cincinnati "the Athens of the West," midwestern Methodists prided themselves on being less awed by social rank and tradition than Easterners, and on being in the vanguard of education for the people. In spite of a backwoodsy, anti-intellectual stance consciously cultivated by some of their leaders, Methodists were as deeply committed to literacy as to salvation. This alliance had put them in the forefront of the Common School movement—Methodists were involved in founding all types of educational institutions designed to civilize the frontiers,[10] including the first women's college west of the Mississippi, MacMurray College, in Jacksonville, Illinois (founded 1848). And Methodism was, by their reckoning, a special gift to women: "The rise of Methodism, more than any preceding religious uprising since the apostolic days, has contributed to the *solution of the woman question* in its ecclesiastical relations" [11] (emphasis added). Such a grand claim was not generally held by the denomination as a whole, but Methodism was seen as a popular and progressive religious movement, including what it did specifically for women.

Built on John Wesley's systematized religious practice, Methodism offered a useful mode of living in a new expanding nation because it "adapted to crude masses of newcomers congregating in our new states and territories, from all nations. It takes hold of and reduces them to order, imparting life to their hearts and regularity to their conduct," as Bishop Morris wrote in the *LR* (1856).[12] Besides self-discipline and the channeling of ambition, Methodist religious experience gave spiritual self-empowerment to the everyday Christian. In its intensely personal impact, Methodism impelled an instinctive energy in its converts which had to find outlets in action, right there in local situations. This action often set them at odds with other Christians—protesting against a mill owner whose conscience was not troubled about doing business on Sunday, for example. Their activist tendency also fueled their eagerness for their *own* publications.

The Methodist version of Christianity often had a defensive ring, in prose and print: "If we had not our own [publishing house], our young would grow up in complete alienation from Methodism. . . . Our church lives in an atmosphere of polemic hostility.[13] And [in the competition for religious-print supremacy] the kingdom of printing ink must needs be taken by Methodist violence."[14]

Methodist self-definition and Methodist literature may have benefited from Methodist chauvinism, but Methodist numerical success undoubtedly had more to do with the organizing genius of its founder and the personal perfectionist energy created in its adherents. In each of the years between 1840 and 1844, Methodists documented an average gain of 107,724 members. "It is generally conceded that Methodism has been the most energetic religious element in the social development of the continent, if not the mightiest agent." [15]

From an aggregate membership in 1844, the last year before Northern and Southern Methodists divided over the issue of slavery, of 1,170,000 members and 4,600 travelling preachers, Methodism expanded to an astounding centennial count in 1884 of more than seven million members. As Abel Stevens exulted in his centennial history of Methodism, "we are more than one-fifth of this nation." [16]

Stevens named four factors as critical to this denominational success story: "We are a system of spiritual life, of evangelical liberalism, of apostolic propagandism. . . . But above all, we are a stupendous means of popular intelligence." [17] Intelligence for the people, not just the clergy—for women and children, too. Methodism was synonymous with education, the means of self-cultivation, instruction, and learning—due to "our magnificent press system, the admiration of all our sister churches." [18] Wherever Methodist preachers went ("and where did they *not* go?" Stevens trumpeted rhetorically!), they carried glad tidings of salvation on their lips and published the acceptable year of the Lord by means of their press. "What a mighty engine is the press! What an event when this engine was first set in motion! . . . Since then, what a revolution has been effected in the entire civilized world!" [19]

Allowing for centennial hyperbole, it is possible to see at least part of that revolution—that occurring in Methodist women's consciousness—in the fresh, highly individualistic voices of readers which were bubbling up around the edges of the conventional academic essays dominating *LR*'s pages. We can also trace the function of Methodist print as "a stupendous means of popular intelligence" by watching the interplay between the two voices "visible" in *LR*: that of the Methodist ministers who were the officially-appointed editors and writers, plus those few women sounding exactly like them who wrote similarly-didactic religious essays, *and* that of the reader, slowly becoming visible in dialogue with herself, her fellow readers, and the editor. During *LR*'s first two decades, we can almost see the ground slowly being washed away from the foundations of official prescriptive Methodism toward women—until, after the Civil War, the whole superstructure crumbled and was reformulated.

Today we see that the succession of Methodist minister-editors: The Revs. L.L. Hamline, 1841–44; Edward Thomson, 1844–46; B.F. Tefft, 1846–52; William Clark Larrabee, 1852–53; David W. Clark, 1853–63; (and after the scope of this paper, Isaac William Wiley, 1864–72; E. Wentworth, 1872–76; and Daniel Curry 1876), were confronted with an impossible task. They were to shape and direct the minds and aspirations of their readers according to an already-outmoded Second Great Awakening world view. But in order to build a paid constituency they also had to respond to what was becoming an ever-more-independent readership—something their magazine was helping to create. Response to readers may be one explanation for the increasing visibility of letters in *LR*. By printing more and more from the readers, the editors demonstrated their journal's popularity, reduced their own isolation, and unwittingly provided a print platform for the ambitious farm girl or young mother. Small wonder the *LR* editorial voice became less strident during the 1850s; it was being "seduced" into addressing a new type of reader who wanted less hortatory messages and in a different voice.

For *LR* readers, dramatic public activism in a crusade such as suffrage was still many years away. But numbers of them were in training for it, literarily speaking. Even in the modest forum of prayer groups or Sunday school classes, the development of a distinctive voice for women who were spilling across the boundaries of their "sphere" was seriously under way. "The Church today in Indiana, and everywhere owes as much to the patient labors of *women* in their warfare upon sin, as to men, in many cases even more. In the nursery, in departments of charity and benevolence among the poor and lowly, in the aggressive temperance movement, in public schools, around altars of prayer, in the esthetical departments of social and religious society, hers is the creative genius." [20]

The contents of this church journal dedicated to these new women, judged by contemporary conventions of what is good literature, measure up surprisingly well—in spite of our mind-set that most nineteenth-century evangelical literature falls outside our standards of intellectual respectability. Our ear for this type of popular religious writing has been deadened by a din of modern superiority and condescension. We have been unable to read nineteenth-century women's writings with unarched eyebrows because of what we label as the "sentimentality" visible beneath a coating of quaint rhetoric, archaic scholarship, and dated religious concepts.

But if we set aside this cultural conditioning and scholarly bias, we begin to discern the situations from within which these women and their advisors wrote. We begin to empathize with their peculiar combination of civil powerlessness, personal dignity, and religious empowerment. We relinquish the luxury of condemning these midnineteenth century women for not being what we wish they had been, and stop denigrating their religious self-expression as merely "sentimental."

By tracing the ideas and language in the *Repository* to their location in the psyches and social experience of the writers, we begin to see and hear the emerging sense of personal importance, spiritual independence, and self which the mid-nineteenth century Methodist woman was developing, *within* her own subculture. If her writing in her own church magazine seems, at first, as a modern critic writes, "like a cluster of ostensibly private feelings which (unaccountably) attain public, conspicuous expression," we are finally able to see that the remarkable thing about it was its being published at all. [21]

Although it has been easy, in the past, to dismiss the ornate circumlocutions and flowery self-denigration of much nineteenth-century female writing as sentimentalism, that kind of scolding now seems historically inappropriate. For example, "Sentimentalism always and only exists in tandem with a failed political consciousness" and "has no content but exposure, while it invests that exposure with special significance."[22] Such judgment obliterates any awareness that for an ordinary, bright-but-unsophisticated village girl in mid-nineteenth century America, exposure in print was a necessary first step toward the development of what would eventually be called "political consciousness." Unpalatable as the terms of these women's self-discovery may seem to us today, we must realize that even such a minor experience as seeing their thoughts in public print in a church periodical was a crucial landmark in many women's psychological and religious history.

A second stumbling block is that few modern scholars can identify with the psychic strength that *LR* readers would have found in *their* religious experiences—in Methodism's affirmation of self and its assurance of salvation, its gift of an unassailable, inner confidence which was new. It is also doubtful if many historians today can make intuitive connections between evangelicalism in the nineteenth century and the emergence of mid-nineteenth century individualism in women.[23]

What is clear to us through the pages of *LR* is that its readers in the 1840s and 50s, emboldened by a religiously-engendered individualism (resulting from their evangelical conversion experience and given public nurture through a magazine encouraging their "conversation" about this "abstract" part of their lives), were forging an autonomous self and voice. They were allowing themselves to view this self-development as part of their Christian duty, rather than something egotistical or evil. For the educated mid-nineteenth century Methodist woman, expressing opinions in print could be considered almost a requirement in the living out of her own particular Christian calling.

## II

The first issue of *The Ladies' Repository* exuded confidence in the competence and intellectual ability of its readers. (It struck me on first reading, as an 1840s equivalent of a top-flight feminist—non-religious, of course—journal today, such as *Signs*.) The articles were intelligent and demanding, displaying erudition. The initial essay, "Female Education," stated the standard nineteenth-century ambivalence about educated women, putting down "female fanatics" and elevating "the modest mien of true religion." But the magazine's credal statement was found in a long, stylish essay entitled "Female Influence," by the Rev. J. S. Tomlinson of Augusta (Georgia) Academy: "I have long felt that the amount of reading matter included in the Ladies' Departments of our periodicals [presumably he means the weekly newspapers, the various *Advocates* for each region of the country] was altogether inadequate."[24]

This brave beginning, which appeared to be heading toward a critique of the superficiality of much journalism, veers into a tangential argument about

255

quantity (rather than the quality and rigor of articles aimed at women). Tomlinson spares a glance at the "modern fashionables" who would not enjoy his thesis, i.e., that women's major arena for influence is in the nurseries of the nation. Thus he enunciates *LR*'s central theme: religious domesticity. His argument is standard. If either sex is to be stinted in terms of literary nourishment, let it be the male. "There are no great men without strong-minded, sensible, well-informed women as mothers," he concludes with the highest praise he can use.

Forceful adjectives are the surprise in this essay, since they are words not usually associated with Victorian females—mostly portrayed as delicate, shrinking, and ethereal. The women Tomlinson conjures up as mothers of the future are frank, forthright, and strong. Naturally such new women will be free of "slavish" interest in worldly adornment, self-display, and (by implication) egotistical ambition.[25] The wasp-waisted gowns so appealingly pictured in *Godey's* outrage him because they "horribly compel women to pass through torture and agonies [differing from Indian suttee only in that the suffering caused by fashion] is far more protracted, and too often transmitted in all its terrible consequences to an innocent unfolding posterity."[26]

Recalling himself abruptly, Tomlinson admits, "I have wandered from my original point, [which is] the superior place that maternal influence has in the formation of individual and social character." To this Methodists now bring "all the additional aids afforded by periodical publication."[27] Mr. Tomlinson's object is to place before *LR* readers, in the most eloquent style at his command, the ideals for the evangelical woman of 1841. His essay carried the clarion call of authoritativeness right into the parlors and kitchens of *LR* readers—right into their own "sphere."

The editors never doubted their prescriptions for women—Christian mothers first, then as wives or daughters, teachers or missionaries. Any self-doubt expressed in *LR* came more from Ohio-based defensiveness or regional pride. Two contradictory impulses were often side by side in an issue: sophisticated elitist essays promoting "self-elevation," and populist mid-western egalitarianism expressed in blunt, flat-footed prose.

The intention of making the *Repository* a journal of high literary quality was often tempered by demographic as well as religious considerations. Methodists were bound to see that grace was as generously bestowed on the humblest farmer's daughter as on the new graduate of their academies or colleges. In a belief-community where each person's experience of salvation was as valuable as the next one's, on what grounds could an "in-house" editor reject the spiritual musings of a country girl and accept only the more elaborate poetry of a college graduate? A Methodist minister attempting a high-brow literary task risked being thought un-Christian for such decisions. He was a captive of his own Arminianism, and of midnineteenth-century midwest egalitarianism.

By late 1842, at the end of the second volume of *LR,* the editor's struggle to maintain an elevated standard through "good sense in the tone of the articles" and "high literary and artistic merit" had begun to weigh heavily. The year's last editorial contained an aggrieved note: "We have tried to keep the *Ladies' Repository* as pure, and as entertaining as could comport with purity . . . but some readers seem to find the best articles least entertaining. What do they want, *experiences and 'such like?'*"[28] (emphasis in original).

Regional boosterism sometimes evoked regional envy. A Midwesterner's review of a new volume of the *Lowell Offering* in 1844 expressed both:

> Verily New England beats everything. We admire the land of the Pilgrims for its granite hills and its granite intellects, its cold ice and its cold calculations, its scaly fishes and its scaly notions, its stormy oceans and its restless independent spirit. . . . We would like to look at these "factory girls." We shake hands with them in our hearts across the mountains and hope that the *Lowell Offering* will be a blessing both to readers and contributors.[29]

Until the last sentence of the review, the reader is uncertain as to which will prevail, admiration or resentment. Even as late as 1849, the editor (and by extension, Midwestern Methodists generally) could be stung by the Eastern disdain in a letter "marvelling" at the idea of "an elaborate ladies' monthly by the Methodists of the Midwest!" The editor took revenge by characterizing this correspondent "from Yankeedoodledum" as "waxing puffatory" "over the presumption of Porkdom."[30] Eastern condescension was met with an elaborate bumptiousness as close as a Methodist editor could come to verbal fisticuffs.

After five years in publication the second editor, Edward Thomson, was driven to lament: "Within the limited walk assigned to *LR,* it is exceedingly difficult to find attractive themes."[31] This is the first hint at a discrepancy between the official public voice and what people might rather be reading about privately. He added wistfully, "Could we enter the arena of politics or religious warfare . . . it would be much more interesting."[32] Editorializing over the flood of Roman Catholic immigrants into the countryside or beating the drums for abolition would have appealed to many *LR* subscribers and writers, but would definitely have crossed editorial boundaries the official church magazine was constrained to honor.

Although *LR* had been brought into being to compete with *Godey's,* the editor at the end of its first decade cautioned readers not to compare their magazine with commercial ones. Rather the readers should focus on the higher spiritual and intellectual standards adhered to by *LR's* official stance. "It is not the design of this work to descend to the low degree of the world around us, but to bring that world up to the true standards of good sense, sound knowledge, correct taste, and pure religion."[33]

But in bringing the rest of the world up to *LR*'s standards, a first major accommodation to the world was made. In 1853, what would have been a humor column in a secular magazine made its first appearance, titled "The Mirror of Wit, Apothegm, Repartee, and Anecdote." In 1856, editor Clark could proudly report: "We have never believed that only 'light literature' was good for a ladies' magazine. . . . We are happy to report that to the honor and intelligence and *mind* of the ladies of this country, some of the most elaborate and profound articles in the *Repository* last year were among the most popular, that is, elicited the most remarks and attracted the most attention." [34]

Even as he wrote, Clark may have subconsciously realized that this was the apotheosis of the official prescriptive voice for Methodist women. His readers were ready to take those good minds into other, greener pastures. Bright students at the midwestern Methodist MacMurray College, in Illinois, would eagerly greet the *Repository* as it arrived each month—but they would take from it what they liked and ignore the rest. They were no longer looking to their church's magazine for wisdom and authentication, because they were discovering it in other dimensions of self-cultivation.

## III

The readers' voices appear initially in offhand mention only; the first, 1842, is when the editor refers to a letter from a poetry contributor whose latest submission has been delayed due to an injury sustained in a fall from her horse. Next we see a few long letters treated as mini-essays on public issues; e.g., one in 1850 on women's property rights, another on the presumption of visitors who overstay their welcome in ministers' homes. Eventually a column appeared which was totally composed of letters from readers—and they were about the readers' children.

By the 1850s, *LR* readers used two main topics as excuses for seeing their writing in print (other than articles and poems): death and children. "Memorializing" the death of a friend, spouse or child was sufficient sanction; many letters state frankly the writer's hope to preserve the dear one's name in print, thus obtaining print immortality for them. ("Letters are tiny tributes to dead friends . . . and achieve immortality while still here on earth." Vol. VII #3, March 1847.)

But crowding out death as a topic, by 1855, was the reporting of children's bright sayings. Here the newer voice of the Methodist mother becomes apparent. The women who write proudly about their children's amusing way with words have enough sense of self and of language to enjoy a child's verbal mistakes. We also observe the instant blossoming of parental competition. "I have been fond of glancing over your 'Sideboard for Children.' I have been much amused with instances of precocity and early natural genius with which it is sometimes laden. It strikes me that I have a little fellow who in this respect will suffer but little in comparison with any of them . . . he is little beyond his second year." [35]

And another mother writes, "As you occasionally treat your readers to specimens of children's talk, and as the race of *smart* children has not entirely died out, I submit a few scraps." [36]

The noted Hartford, Connecticut poet and author, Lydia Huntley Sigourney may have spoken for the entire class of educated evangelical mid-nineteenth century mothers when she introduced an article titled "Words of the Little people" in August 1856. "It would sometimes seem as if the wit and pathos of the present world were with the children. Their unsophisticated minds and simplicity of heart give such force to every original idea that it is a pity their sayings should so often be forgotten." [37]

Here was a summary of a change in evangelical women's perspective, from the 1840s to near Civil War times. Like other formerly-struggling folk, some Methodist women had achieved an emotional and intellectual perspective which allowed them to appreciate, and even boast about, their children's experiments with language. They also had a religiously sanctioned vehicle in which to experiment with their new literary self-expression. They could unapologetically own their children's forwardness ("I'm tired of always being your child, let's pretend *I'm* the mother") and dignify baby-talk by recording it. For example,

> *Preach Small.* "Mother," said a little seven-year-old, "I could not understand our minister today, he said so many hard words. I wish he would preach so that little girls could understand him. Won't he, mother?" (Mother replies yes, if we ask him.) Soon after, her father saw her tripping away. "Where are you going, Emma?" "I'm going over to the minister's house, to ask him to preach small." [38]

And

> *The Moon and her Babies*, we read this: "Mamma, mamma," cried a little one whose early hour of retirement had not permitted much study of the starry heavens, "here is the moon come, and brought a sight of little babies with her." [39]

The popular exchange of children's "wisdom" became an acceptable topic for the mother who had no other reason to write, women who were perhaps the majority of *LR* readers.

Those women who dared correspond about something more self-centered than children simply poured out personal feelings: "I love the *Repository*; it embalms the memories of loved ones who have joined the song of the redeemed in the upper sanctuary. In this wild west its regular visits are esteemed like those of a familiar friend." [40]

In 1846, a questing voice appeared for the first time, in a letter to the editor written for no reason other than "the prompting of my own heart to send a few lines to the *Repository*." [41] The letter is arresting in its eagerness. The writer uses cliches which she assumes will communicate more than their literal meaning; i.e., describing homesickness for her Missouri homeland, "my spirit as a caged bird longed to soar to its native mountains." [42] At the age of twenty-two, she has had little exposure to the wider world, but she idealizes her "plain little village" as "free of affectation or refinement." Her highest praise is couched in midwestern scorn for "ceremonies of fashion, dress, or manners." "If things are neat and becoming, they have reached the popular standard [prevailed here]; the height of our ambition seems to be to encourage everything calculated to elevate the mind and improve the heart." [43]

But then she reveals that she is a normal young woman after all (instead of a moralizing middle-aged minister): "Many young couples are here, who having plighted their faith in a far distant land and left parents and friends, have cast their lot among us. In the fate of such I always feel intense *interest*." [44]

As is often characteristic of first appearances in print, the writer must append a self-deprecating comment and justification: "I find I must close. I am aware that what I have written is exceedingly desultory; and I would not have written at all had I not noticed that there is seldom if ever anything sent you from Missouri, [signed] Mary." [45]

This letter, printed without comment or explanation by the editor, shows Mary-the-reader striving to be part of a public dialogue, displaying a literate if not altogether accurate vocabulary, and feeling proprietary about *LR*. She felt at ease writing about nothing in particular except her own limited observations of a limited horizon. In effect she was saying, "Look, world, here I am!" This vivid testimony to the private idiosyncratic effect of print (as compared with oral) communication was arming a population of Methodist women all across the land with a means of psychic mobility while they sat at their own kitchen tables.

More often, women wrote the editor to check up on a poem or manuscript, and to obtain some sort of verification of their talents. "Just as two years ago I peeped between your leaves at my neighbor's and espied, with many blushes, my first saucy little note to the editor." [46] Or, as another woman wrote, "Burn it if you like, but do read it first. Criticize it and *me*; poke fun at it if you like, but do *notice* it." [47]

Letters served some women as a preprofessional correspondence school: "I don't send my contributions because I consider them worthy, by any means, but it is something of pleasure to see my rhymes in print. It comes so natural for me to scribble I oft find myself poetizing before I know it." [48]

One correspondent used military metaphor (the only indication of the impending Civil War in *LR*, 1861) to elicit a response from the editor about her manuscript: "In times of war, one feels an aversion to neutrality, to being nowhere, and if my articles do not pass muster, say so and relieve me of my long-endured suspense. I had rather go forth at once to execution . . . than remain in the prison of my anxiety any longer." [49] However, she closed by assuring the editor of her deep loyalty to the *Repository*: "I shall not secede from my valued and well-tried friend, the *Repository*, even for rejection of anything I write." [50]

An example of the new Methodist female voice appears in rather self-assertive images that occasionally surface, as in a poem about a young woman leaving home, titled "Going Forth," by Augusta Moore. The sixth stanza reads (emphasis in original):

> So I strove to strangle fear and sorrow,
> And to nerve my heart for coming strife;
> And I vowed I would not flinch or falter,
> Tho' through *fire* led on my path of life—
> Dare the strife,
> Dash ahead and *force* a way through life.

The final stanza ends with the motto: "Face the danger—it will flee away." [51] These verbs are surprisingly harsh for a women's poetic contribution to a religious journal.

However, the most astonishing example of the new female literary boldness appeared in a response to an earlier letter to the editor by Jesse Brumbler (obviously a pseudonym). He had waxed nostalgic about the "good old days" of Methodism and was judgmental about the current Methodist clergy and their wives. The scorn with which his suggestions were rejected by a woman who was not a clergy wife indicates both the way mid-nineteenth century Methodists had come to view themselves and their place in the scheme of things, and the self-confidence a formerly-submissive Methodist female could now display in arguing for progress. Her letter mandates extensive quoting: "From the religion which produces no liberality of views, no enlargement of heart, Good Lord, deliver us."

> [In answer to his complaint against expensive church edifices] . . . The elegance of our churches has by no means kept pace with our means as a denomination. This is a shame when Christians live in elegance and continue to worship God in unsightly, mean, and repulsive buildings. Nine times out of ten this results not from love of "old-fashioned Methodism" but from lack of refinement or of feeling and manners . . . or from miserliness and meanness. There is no religion or love of God in it!

[Rejecting the correspondent out of hand]
Such persons make religion repulsive, and dishonor Methodism. If we were poor, unable to do otherwise, it would be right that we should worship in log houses.

[About ministers wanting to be settled in one location for a term] Your mean notion that preachers ought to work through the week like other people, on the land, so as not to be a burden to others. . . . You are right, that the minister ought to work—on sermons, study, and visiting his flock. [You are] the type of person who is always first to grumble if [you] find out the minister has a little property. . . . This attitude, meanness and dishonesty will drive the best men out of the itinerancy. . . .

[About ministers' wives taking in sewing or washing to supplement the minister's income, one of his suggestions in the earlier letter] Mr. Grumbler, that is an argument which defies reply. One can only sit in the silent admiration of your lofty views.

Throwing all restraint to the wind, her closing peroration veers into attack and an unfortunate lapse of grammar: "If God don't send leanness into your soul—we fear it is already nothing but leanness now—and if your children are not ruined by the miserable pelf you are robbing God in order to hoard, I shall be greatly mistaken. So farewell!" [52]

The writer was confident that *LR* readers shared her indignation, since most of them would also be in favor of modern, full-time, salaried clergy living in parsonages and conducting a professional ministry rather than itinerating and preaching under the elms. These new ideals were the product of ambitious and educated Methodist Christian women, those poised on the forward edge of Methodist subculture, headed inexorably into the mainstream of middle-class sophistication. Their daughters would undoubtedly become the clubwomen of the 1880s.

Sophronia Naylor Grubb, a member of the first MacMurray College graduating class (1852), was one of those forthright midwestern college women who was far beyond the idea of education for mere survival, even if she was not quite ready to contemplate entering the male profession of medicine, as Mrs. Sarah Josepha Hale (of *Godey's*) had been urging in a letter to college women including students at MacMurray.

We had no dream beyond being homemakers as our mothers had been before us; the girl who wished to prepare herself for a career, who had a definite ambition to do original or creative work in music, art, or literature had not been born . . . but, the acquisition of that . . . education . . . to which we were giving our best energies, was to fit us more perfectly for homemaking, to render us dispensers of a more graceful hospitality, and to add a glory, all its own, to the common life. [53]

Mrs. Hale's phrase, "to add a glory . . . to the common life," epitomized the changed focus of Methodist women's inner experience from 1840 to 1860.

Education and print media such as *LR* had breached the domestic sphere, beckoning them toward more than just basic self-improvement. "Girls from small towns or rural communities with a restricted social and intellectual background who were eager to learn how to add a glory to the common life," wrote Clarissa Keplinger Rinaker, also MacMurray Class of 1852, longed for a mental world more congruent with that of the secular world.[54]

Of course the world outside their Methodist college wouldn't let them choose the avenues they thought they were preparing themselves for, "inspired with the belief that we were expected to accomplish something for ourselves and for humanity. . . ."[55] But education and internal strength, religiously sponsored, had unleashed an energy which was beginning to defy external shaping. Methodist women were ready to run their own foreign mission study and fund-raising programs. No wonder *The Ladies' Repository* was shortly to become irrelevant to them.

## IV

Methodist popular literature, that "stupendous means of popular intelligence" in the mid-nineteenth century, had included a women's religious journal in an effort to sound one voice—official and prescriptive—in the lives of its women. But readers of the *LR* used it to shape an unforeseen expansion of themselves and had in turn been shaped by their interaction with it. The occasional naivete in some of the letters of the first two decades must be seen for what it was: evidence of an emerging independent perception of self in relation to church, community, and the larger world.

A century later, several questions about *LR* remain with us. Why did the Methodists, so eminently practical in every aspect of religion and life, choose to exclude the practical side of women's lives from their magazine? How could the editors avert their gaze from the arena of daily household minutiae to which they were high-mindedly directing women's religious efforts? Also, with their ambition for a "quality publication," why did they eschew illustration and a more readable layout, leaving that to secular journals such as *Godey's*? And why were they so committed to a bland, non-partisan official voice, in contrast to their individual Christian commitment against such evils as slavery? (Similarly, *Godey's* editor for nearly fifty years, Mrs. Sarah Hale, worked privately for abolition but never alluded to it in her editorials.) Apparently, *LR*'s evasion of controversial topics was not unusual in its time, nor is it unknown in ours.

We may thank those hard-pressed *LR* editors for maintaining a print vehicle which became the instrument of self-expression for a mid-nineteenth century population of Christian women, preserving a picture of their thoughts and motives for us. For historical Methodism, *LR* is a revealing record of the commonplace, from time to time brightly illuminating a particular segment of life in its era.

*LR*'s first two decades offer us exemplary cultural data about the mid-nineteenth century evangelical Methodist women who evolved from viewing themselves as part of a subgroup in American culture into claiming part of the mainstream as their location. *LR* was part of the new "information-culture" of the mid-1800s which ushered in and developed the new consciousness of American women, interacting with its readers as a significant factor in the social landscape of their everyday lives. It helped readers understand and articulate their own times and provided a literary bridge from the earlier genre of popular religious literature—pious memoirs—to the specialized women's religious journals of the post-Civil War era.

*The Ladies' Repository* was one of the means by which the religious and social authority in official Methodist literature accommodated to the changing social environment, as it shaped itself to the readers' market it had helped cultivate. That *LR* readers outgrew their own magazine in 35 years or less is one kind of testimony to its effectiveness.

# Rich Methodists: The Rise and Consequences of Lay Philanthropy in the Mid-Nineteenth Century

Donald B. Marti

Silas Lapham had real-life counterparts in the middle and late 19th century. Real Laphams were rising from modest beginnings to great affluence. They made an awkward new elite, sometimes, hardly knowing how to enjoy their fortunes, but they had at least one definite idea about the use of money. Just as Lapham "gave with both hands" to his unspecified church and its charities, so his actual counterparts gave abundantly to churches which, not infrequently, were Methodist Episcopal. Their philanthropies enriched Methodist institutions; their consequent influence with ministers and their rising confidence produced a new kind of lay participation in Methodist polity. The church fully shared the advantages and hazards of their new fortunes.[1]

The idea that Methodists might be rich was novel in the middle third of the 19th century. Methodists had always been characterized, in and out of their fellowship, as very ordinary people. A Maryland Episcopalian, in 1798, described them as "for the most part persons of the lower classes of life, and distinguished by that ignorance upon which the Jacobin" (read Jeffersonian Republican) "chiefs work so successfully." Methodists themselves agreed that their denomination had first grown among poor folk. The Reverend Gilbert Haven of the New England Conference, later a bishop in post-Civil War South Carolina, thought that some of the denominination's special virtue arose from that fact. Poor folk, if they were also decently independent, had a wholesome radical tendency. It was good to be economically and socially unprepossessing. It did no moral harm to be looked down upon by more respectable elements. Francis Asbury made the same point when he criticized Quakers for having become "respectable." He said: "There is death in that word."[2]

After the middle of the 19th century Methodists spoke of their lowly origins with a new kind of pride. They began to congratulate themselves on how far they had risen. William Claflin, for example, told the 1890 Centennial Convention of the New England Conference that only the "common people" had responded when Jesse Lee first brought Methodism to Boston, that the good man had preached standing on a table provided by some anonymous layman because there was no better pulpit for him. But now, Claflin observed, the "conveniences for our meetings are somewhat increased." He did not have to add that laypeople were making better provision for their preachers because some of them were richer and less anonymous than they had been in Jesse Lee's time. Claflin exemplified all of that obviously enough. He was an ex-Governor of Massachusetts, a wealthy manufacturer of boots and leather, and one of the first laymen to serve in the General Conference of the denomination. Several hundred thousand dollars stood between him and his modest origin. He was part of the change that his speech described.[3]

Ministers understood that the rise of some considerable fortunes among the laity was changing the denomination. Matthew Simpson, who became a bishop in 1852, was notably sensitive to its implications. Since 1839, when he became president of Indiana Asbury University (later DePauw), he had been learning to cultivate brethren with money and political influence. Such laymen were distressingly few in Indiana when Simpson first went there, but they became more numerous and really useful as his career flourished and took him to other places. He thought that was the great social change affecting American Methodists. The Lord was rewarding his common people for their diligence, and they were sharing their success with the church. They were also sharing it with ministers, particularly Matthew Simpson. Their hospitality, lecture fees, and business advice gave him some first-hand knowledge of how much better it was to be rich than poor. At the height of his career Bishop Simpson was markedly different from the plain-living circuit rider he had been in his youth.[4]

Rich Methodists changed Simpson. He was delighted to observe that they were also changing the church. In 1855, for example, he encouraged some of the wealthier brethren in Pittsburgh to erect Christ Church, the first American Methodist church built in the Gothic Revival style. Previous Methodist chapels had been deliberately modest, as John Wesley decreed; they made no great show beside the architectural splendors of other denominations. When Christ Church and other grand edifices arose, Methodists discovered that their new churches needed formal pews, rather than the plain benches to which they had been accustomed. They called for liturgical embellishments as well. Simpson welcomed all of that. Certainly men who had earned fine homes and "social refinement" had the right to expect similar graces in their churches. The fact that they were willing to pay for them made their claim all the stronger.[5]

Simpson's appreciation of rich Methodists and the importance that he attributed to their impact on the denomination, had a particularly detailed expression in 1878. He then published the first edition of his *Cyclopaedia of Methodism*, which purported to describe all of the branches of Methodism throughout the world. In fact it concentrated on the Methodist Episcopal Church in the northern United States, with only a little attention to other Methodist bodies there and abroad. Nearly sixteen hundred entries describe individual people, mostly Simpson's contemporaries. They suggest who, and what sorts of people, were most important to Simpson's church.[6]

More than eleven hundred of the entries describe ministers; thirty-two concern women, mostly the wives of ministers. The remainder describe laymen, including 347 members of the Methodist Episcopal Church (North). A few of those laymen were included for achievements in music; one was a reformed drunkard become temperance lecturer. But the vast majority were listed because of their achievements in medicine, law, politics, education, or some kind of business. Twenty-two were physicians or dentists, primarily; thirty-seven were chiefly notable for their political and military attainments; forty-six were primarily attorneys; fifty-two were educators, mostly college professors; and one hundred and forty-eight were businessmen. None were chiefly known as farmers. A few had a little farm experience, usually early in life, but nobody was listed because of his achievements on the land. And only one man, an engraver for the United States Mint, was recognized for craftsmanship. Simpson's lay elite was professional and commercial.[7]

Simpson's capsule biographies are often more fulsome than specifically informative. His descriptions of business careers are only occasionally circumstantial; sometimes they merely note that the subject was a "merchant" or a "skillful businessman." Of Daniel Drew's business life it was enough to say that he had started as a cattle drover and had gone on to steamboats, railroads, and "heavy stock operations in the New York market." Readers of the newly published *Chapters of Erie* might have thought that "heavy," though an appropriate adjective, was not enough. Certainly later writers found Drew a more colorful subject than he appears to be in Simpson's account. Similarly, the bishop swept briefly over other careers that were important in less controversial ways. He reports, for example, that the Harper brothers had a considerable publishing house. The important point, about the Harpers and Drew alike, was that they were successful and Methodist. Simpson had seen enough of snobbish attitudes toward his denomination; he meant to prove that Methodists could be men of mark.[8]

The bishop's descriptions of the rich men's gifts to the church, and their various works on its behalf, range from vague to quantitatively explicit. He reports that Oliver Archer, a railroad man, was a "generous giver" and that Charles Rowland, an "extensive manufacturer in Cincinnati," was "largely identified" with church interests. At the same time, he wrote that Daniel Drew had committed $500,000 for the seminary that bears his name. He also knew that George Jackson Ferry, a trustee of both Drew and of Wesleyan universities, had divided $25,000 between the two institutions. Simpson could be very specific about such numbers. He was also specific about laymen's membership on church boards and societies that were intended to promote Sunday schools, missions, church extension, and other good works.[9]

Simpson's references to particular philanthropies show that laymen had a broad range of interests, but that one kind of benevolence was especially popular. Lewis Miller, an Ohio farm implement manufacturer, was the principal source of money behind the Chautauqua movement; Joseph H. Thornley, a Philadelphia dry goods merchant, was one of several rich men who financed camp meeting associations; Abel Minard, a New York banker, established a home for the daughters of foreign missionaries. But rich Methodists gave most frequently for church buildings, missions, Sunday schools, and—above all-—colleges and seminaries. Seventeen of the good works that Simpson specifies benefited Sunday schools, which were about as popular as church construction and missions. He specifies fifty-seven benefactions to colleges and seminaries.[10]

Of course Simpson himself was especially interested in education. He had been a college president. He was sensitive to the imputation that Methodists were educationally inferior to other denominations. Not surprisingly, gifts to Indiana Asbury, Drew, Wesleyan, Northwestern, Syracuse, and other new Methodist institutions of the period got his particular attention. Colleges and seminaries were also, pretty clearly, of special interest to the rich men he described. The middle of the 19th century was the denomination's great period of college founding; from 1830 to the Civil War various groups of Methodists "founded thirty-four permanent schools of higher learning." A few others, such as Boston University, began immediately after the war. Colleges and seminaries, above all else, were the monuments that rich Methodists left to mark their success and their impact on the church. The pastor who encouraged Drew to found a seminary said that it "will live when you are dead." Many such institutions preserve the memory of Drew's contemporaries, though not usually their names.[11]

Methodist colleges and seminaries drew groups of rich men together in local or regional clusters. John Evans, Orrington Lunt and other rich men in Chicago came together around Northwestern University; prominent New York and New Jersey Methodists focused on Drew; western New Yorkers combined to build Syracuse University; Michigan had Albion; Pittsburgh made originally Presbyterian Allegheny College into a Methodist institution. All over the country clusters of rich men made colleges and seminaries their principal means of embellishing their church.[12]

One such cluster flourished in Boston. Its principal members were Lee Claflin, Isaac Rich, and Jacob Sleeper. All three received substantial notices in Simpson's *Cyclopaedia*, though the bishop is characteristically general about their commercial lives. Considered in more detail, the Bostonians exhibit common characteristics which suggest ways of thinking about rich 19th century Methodists generally.[13]

All three were highly successful businessmen; none left a detailed account of his working life. They were tight-lipped about business. Perhaps, as Edward Chase Kirkland suggests of even richer businessmen in the period, they were diffident about their success, considering that it "occupied a low priority in any absolute scheme of values." The best-documented of the three was Lee Claflin, whose family papers, including some of his own diaries and correspondence, have been preserved.[14]

Lee Claflin was born in 1792, tenth of eleven children in a poor Hopkinton, Massachusetts, family. Orphaned at age five, he spent the next several years in the home of a farmer who took care to exact enough labor to pay for the child's board. Claflin left for an apprenticeship in the tanning trade at the earliest possible moment, probably not long after his tenth birthday. He joined the Methodist Episcopal Church during his apprenticeship, and remained loyal to it until he died in 1872.

Claflin had his own tannery at Milford, close to Hopkinton, by the early 1810s. It was a small business, as tanneries generally were at the time. It grew because of a thousand dollar dowry obtained, with other gifts, from his bride's family, in 1815. Loans from trusting fellow Methodists also helped him to expand the tannery, and begin some modest vertical integration. By 1825 he was putting out leather to neighborhood shoemakers for conversion into heavy men's boots. He first marketed his boots in Providence. Then, in the early 1830s, he began to ship to New Orleans and St. Louis, where he also bought hides for his several tanneries and for others' as well.

Claflin abandoned the putting out system in 1840. He then concentrated his bootmaking in a factory at Hopkinton. He was one of the first entrepreneurs to do that. At the same time, he concentrated his personal attention increasingly on marketing and a complex of investments in land, coal, shipping, and banking. He found it convenient to do all of that from an office in Boston. Country boy made good, he had come to the metropolis. He resembled Silas Lapham in that, but the parallel is not perfect. Hopkinton was near Boston, so he kept his home there, lived plainly in the style of that place, and avoided the social agonies that Lapham had to confront in fashionable Boston.[15]

Less is known about Isaac Rich, but his acquaintances agreed on a few facts and some traditions. He was born on a poor Cape Cod farm in 1801, then came to Boston at age fourteen. After working in an oyster shop, he began to sell fish on his own account from a wheelbarrow. He prospered, admirers believed, because of extraordinary diligence and religious inspiration. The inspiration came to him through Wilbur Fisk, then a minister at Charlestown, later president of Wesleyan University, who met the poor young peddler pushing his wheelbarrow across the Charlestown bridge. Fisk invited Rich to attend his church; Rich came and joined the denomination a few years later. The religion it gave him included assurance that God was good to hard-working young men. That made him fearless. Late in life he said that he had "never doubted . . . that I should succeed, never was discouraged." In fact he did succeed, in both fish and real estate.[16]

Jacob Sleeper also began in a country place, New Castle, Maine, where he was born in 1802. Apparently his family was somewhat more prosperous than the Claflins and Richs; at least it gave him an academy education, but such advantages were abruptly lost when his father died. Then fourteen years old, Sleeper went to work at an uncle's store in Belfast, Maine. He joined the church in his Belfast period, which ended when he left for Boston in 1825. Starting his city career as a bookkeeper, Sleeper formed a partnership with a clothing dealer ten years later. The firm prospered by selling clothes to the navy. Sleeper further increased his fortune by shrewd investments in real estate, banking, and insurance. He rose from more advantageous beginnings than Claflin and Rich could claim, but he certainly rose.[17]

Claflin, Rich, and Sleeper all experienced a great deal of mobility, both economic and geographic. Oscar Handlin suggests that they were uprooted, in their own fortunate way, from their class and local backgrounds. They were "internal immigrants" who could neither identify completely with older elites nor accept an entirely separate identity with the foreign immigrants of the day. Handlin guesses that they resolved that dilemma by "continual emphasis upon their Protestantism and their Yankee heritage," which certified that they were not like the Irish, and by insisting on the special character of their Protestantism, which was evangelical and not some attenuated ghost of Puritanism such as the Brahmins espoused. Being Methodist defined their status in a secure and satisfying way, Handlin thinks.[18]

In any case, being Methodist was obviously important to them. Among other things, it guided their use of money. Money, they said in various ways, was for doing good. While Rich and Sleeper lived well, and studiously plain Lee Claflin enabled his children to live very well indeed, they all reserved large parts of their fortunes for good works, mostly within the church. Sleeper, for example, gave altogether a half million dollars to one Methodist cause, Boston

University. He had retired from active business with less than that, and though he surely increased his estate by later investments, his gifts must have been a substantial proportion of the whole. When he thought that he had enough, he began to give the bulk of his additional income to good works. Similarly, Lee Claflin is estimated to have given as much as a half million dollars to a variety of causes, mostly within the church. When he began to keep a systematic record of his giving, in 1849, he said that he had enough and would devote his "increase" to benevolence. Finally, Rich devoted the great bulk of his estate to the church. What he did not give in life was assigned to Boston and Wesleyan universities in his will. He had little else to do with his money; all seven of his children died before he did.[19]

Claflin, Rich, and Sleeper were serious philanthropists. They gave abundantly and with studied intent. Claflin, especially, made the mindfulness of giving explicit. Usually taciturn, he produced one long, private letter to his son William, on the subject of stewardship, in 1845. It was an important topic, so much so that he asked William to keep the letter and refer to it from time-to-time. Its point was that a real Christian had to practice a kind of asceticism. "If you are a Christian," Lee Claflin wrote, "you have forsaken all for Christ. Our saviour says if any man will be my disciple let him forsake all that he hath and follow me." Clearly Lee did not want William to forsake his boots and leather, but he did want him to do all of his work as Christ's steward. He especially wanted his son to remember the "saying of the great Wesley—I get all I can, I save all I can, I give all I can."[20]

Claflin had obviously read or heard John Wesley's 1744 sermon on "The Use of Money." It was an appropriate text for him. Wesley wrote it at a time when humble English Methodists were rising economically, making him fear that they would become "lovers of the present world." Wesley had to exhort them not to use their money self-indulgently, but to live modestly, preserving a surplus to "do good to them that are of the household of faith." If an "overplus" remained, they ought to do good outside the household. Lee Claflin understood all of that, and acted on it. And if his friends spent more than he did on their own pleasures, they at least honored Wesley's injunction not to "stint" in doing good. They also followed Wesley in concentrating their gifts within "the household of faith."[21]

The results of their philanthropy were impressive, especially for educational institutions. The Wesleyan Academy at Wilbraham, Massachusetts, for example, which was New England's first enduring Methodist school, survived because of their gifts. Begun in 1825, it struggled through a generation with donations as small as ten cents each solicited from the laity in general. In 1850 Lee Claflin enrolled his younger son, Wilbur Fisk Claflin, accepted election to its boards of trustees and examiners, and began to give money. His presence was critically important in 1857, when the academy had a disastrous fire. Then a committee of eleven clergy and laymen, including Claflin, Rich, and Sleeper, more than replaced the losses. A brick boarding house was named for Rich, who gave more than $38,000.

The three also gave substantially to Wesleyan University at Middletown, Connecticut. Begun in 1831, the first Methodist college in New England, it received large donations from Claflin, Rich, and Sleeper, all of whom served on its board of trustees. Rich alone gave $40,000 to the library that bears his name, and $100,000 to the university's endowment. Similarly, all three contributed to the Biblical Institute that began at Concord, New Hampshire, in 1847. The institute was the cornerstone of their largest venture in education.[22]

It assumed that importance in 1867 when its trustees, of whom Lee Claflin was president, decided to move the institute to Boston. That was expected to increase the interest and generosity of Boston Methodists, who had no educational institution belonging to the denomination in their city. Then some individuals began to urge that an ambitious university be organized around the Institute. The Reverend William F. Warren, later president of Boston University, attributed the idea to Lee Claflin; the Reverend J. H. Twombly, later president of the University of Wisconsin, claimed the credit for himself. Twombly thought that a university would improve the "inferior" intellectual and professional status of Boston Methodists. He later recalled that Sleeper was the first important layman to encourage the project, and that Lee Claflin also gave it early support. Sleeper and Claflin together recruited Rich, who felt some initial reluctance to divert any large part of his money from Wesleyan University.[23]

Rich, Sleeper, and Claflin gave to other causes as well, but educational institutions were their clear favorites, just as they were the clear favorites of the men listed in Simpson's *Cyclopaedia*. Handlin suggests that they favored education because they identified it with social advancement; it was a means of assuring their children's status. However that may have been, it is more obvious that they deeply respected education because they revered the clergy. Education, certainly college education, had become the special qualification and perquisite of ministers.

By one account, Isaac Rich wanted to be a minister. But he felt that "God didn't give me a call; I prayed for one, but it didn't come." So he was a businessman who kept a portrait of the Rev. Wilbur Fisk in his office for daily inspiration, and put his money where it would be used to train more such godly men. So, too, Lee Claflin revered Fisk, for whom he named a son, and viewed education as a means of getting more such learned clergymen. Son William was removed from Brown University when it became clear that he had no calling to preach; a man God did not want for a preacher would do better to learn the boot trade than to spend useless years in college.[24]

For Rich and Claflin, at least, support of education was most fundamentally a way of supporting the clergy. Claflin also did that through his contributions to the Preachers' Aid Society, which he served as president, and his gifts to individual ministers and their families. He also had a marked tendency to find his friends among clergymen. Son William showed the same preference; a business associate once complained that William was more attached to "smooth tongued flattering politicians and priests" than he was to his business associates. Rich and Sleeper also enjoyed clerical society. It had a gravity and glamour not to be found among bootmakers and fish venders.[25]

If simple businessmen, painfully modest about their merely commercial accomplishments, revered the clergy, ministers also professed some strong feelings for the businessmen. They were grateful for gifts that improved their personal and professional lives. And they admired the businessmen's sheer practical competence. Ministers had their high callings, and occasionally some learning, but they were not esteemed for their worldly competence. Ann Douglas suggests that some of them—she does not refer to Methodists in particular—were set apart with the ladies, given a vague kind of influence in place of real power. Men in that position respected the businessmen for their practical accomplishments. A writer in *Zion's Herald*, for example, conceded that "we preachers are undeniably not the best financiers in the world," and advised the church to take advantage of businessmen's practical expertise. Similarly, J. H. Twombly argued that the New England Conference could benefit from the "counsels of men of extensive practical business." The ministerial members of the conference presumably lacked practical experience.[26]

Twombly made that point as part of an 1857 report to the New England Conference from a special committee appointed to consider the wisdom of lay representation in the conference. He argued that the church's growing educational and philanthropic enterprises required practical management, something businessmen were best able to provide. Further, he guessed that the laymen would become even more generous when they had a voice in governing church affairs; "men have more interest in an enterprise when they help to control it, than when they do not." Finally, Twombly thought that the "preeminence of the clerical over the lay element" was the one really dangerous source of dissension in the church. Methodists had never fought over doctrine, but they had occasionally experienced divisions about lay representation in conferences.[27]

Twombly was observing some very polite dissension on that point when he wrote his report. All through the 1850's the conference newspaper, *Zion's Herald*, had been reporting innovations favoring lay representation in other places, and creating echoes in New England. It reported, for example, that the Virginia and South Carolina conferences allowed lay members of their boards of stewards to speak on all financial issues that arose in the conference meetings. The *Herald* endorsed that because it was a way of harnessing the laity's practical competence without diluting essential clerical authority. In 1855 the New England Conference tried to achieve the same result by allowing its committees on financial, educational, and philanthropic matters to select lay members. Only the committee on education chose to do that. Lee Claflin, Rich, and Sleeper served with three other laymen and seven ministers.[28]

Lay participation in the New England Conference expanded again in 1858. The previous year's session adopted Twombly's report on lay representation which required the stewards in each of the conference's four districts to choose five lay delegates to the 1858 meeting. The lay delegates were to have voice and vote on benevolent and educational matters; everything else was for ministerial delegates only. Lee Claflin and Jacob Sleeper were among the first twenty lay delegates; Isaac Rich served two years later. They were also among the lay delegates who actually attended conferences. Some of the people selected as lay delegates did not. When the system was allowed to lapse in 1871, it was thought that laymen had lost interest because the conference gave them too little to do.[29]

At the same time, laymen in other places were showing a great deal of interest in being represented in general conferences. In 1852 Philadelphia laymen began an ultimately successful twenty-year campaign for that reform by holding a national lay convention in their city. The convention was less national than its sponsors hoped that it would be; New Englanders, in particular, held back because they suspected the convention organizers of southern sympathies. One of the two delegates from Massachusetts, a minister, gave some credence to that suspicion by arguing that the church would never have been allowed to divide over slavery if only laymen had been represented in the critical general conferences of the previous decade. Despite its limitations, the convention produced a petition to the General Conference of 1852 which was seriously received. The conference even took time to hear laymen sent as spokesmen for the convention.[30]

The convention had some claim to be treated seriously, pro-Southern or not. Its leaders were substantial characters. One of the spokesmen dispatched to the general conference was Francis H. Root, a Buffalo, New York, manufacturer of stoves and iron castings who was a principal mover behind the foundation of Syracuse University. Men of such weight had to be heard. So the conference listened, and formed a special committee to examine the petition. The committee decided that lay representation was "inexpedient" for the time being, but it said nothing to prejudice future discussion of the issue. In fact, its chairman would become the principal advocate among the clergy, of lay representation. He was the newly-elected bishop, and long-time admirer of successful laymen, Matthew Simpson.[31]

Lay representation gathered increasing support over the next decade. The General Conference of 1860 tried to settle the issue by a vote of adult, male church members, but the result was both negative and inconclusive. Lay conventions continued to meet; Bishop Simpson addressed one in New York in 1863, arguing that lay representation would increase lay philanthropy. "Laymen, bring your money," he urged. The assembled laymen cheered: "God bless the Bishop." A year later Lee Claflin chaired a convention in Boston which declared that Methodism without lay representation was undemocratic, and all too nearly Roman. Two weeks later he went with others, including son William, to a national lay convention in Philadelphia. A report of the general conference of that year approvingly noted that the lay convention included "the best business talent in the country." [32]

The campaign for lay representation continued through the General Conference of 1868. Boston, for example, had an 1867 lay convention chaired by William Claflin. Then Lt. Gov. Claflin praised the church for its ready adaptation to change, and made very clear that the next year's general conference should decide the issue. In fact the conference did call for another vote. It was affirmative. Two lay delegates from each annual conference were received in the General Conference of 1872. [33]

It would be all too easy to exaggerate the importance of lay representation in the general conferences. In the long view of Frederick Norwood's general history, the proportion of lay delegates in the general conference was small; equal representation waited for the next century. Arguably laymen were actually losing ground in the denomination because the old offices of lay preacher and class leader were becoming less important as ministers were increasingly available to do the work that had belonged to such officers early in the century. Laymen were not necessarily more important than they had been. But some laymen had assumed a new role in church polity. [34]

Ministers who attended the 1872 General Conference said that those laymen were an impressive sight. Bishop Simpson was predictably approving, and Andrew Endsley of Pittsburgh Conference enthused that the "one hundred and twenty-nine laymen here are in the main men of note in their respective localities." They were successful merchants and manufacturers, leading politicians, and distinguished attorneys. In fact they were all of those things and more. Simpson listed ninety-two of the lay delegates in his *Cyclopaedia*, including five governors, a dozen congressmen, at least fourteen college trustees, and one professor. Almost all of the delegates enjoyed business or professional success, though there were a few men who worked for the Book Concern and one black farmer whose moment of political prominence had ended with Reconstruction. He was exceptional. In 1872 the church was recognizing its "men of note." [35]

That seemed appropriate. After all, the diligent, upwardly mobile laymen had shared their success with the church. They had brought their money, as Simpson and other clerical promoters of education, benevolence, and good architecture had asked. Thanks to the embellishments they provided, Methodists no longer had to feel themselves inferior to Episcopalians, or at least Presbyterians. Whatever Asbury or Wesley might have thought of the fact, they had become respectable.

## CHAPTER 17

# The Concern for Systematic Theology, 1840–70

## Leland Scott

It is to be remembered . . . that the Arminian scheme has yet to be reduced to a systematic and logical form. . . . It has furnished us, indeed, with some detached negations and philosophical theories. . . . It is clear that an exposition of this theology which shall satisfy the logical consciousness is indispensable to its perpetuity, otherwise it cannot take possession of . . . minds, educated by the Word and Spirit of God, and disciplined to exact analysis and argument.[1]

## EARLY ATTEMPTS AT A MORE SYSTEMATIC THEOLOGY

American Methodism in the early nineteenth century—greatly swelled in numbers after two generations of intense evangelical effort—*did* gradually face the problem of introducing its people into the broader, more "systematic" phases of historic Christian understanding and experience. Many agreed with President Stephen Olin of Wesleyan University, who observed (according to B. F. Tefft) that the great lack in the theology of Methodism was "the reduction of its tenets to a scientific system."[2] Actually, many Methodists hoped it would be Olin himself who would commit the Wesleyan motifs to such treatment, but the demands of administration and, more particularly, the desperate instability of his health restricted the ultimate extent of his own writings. Olin died in 1851. There were others, such as William F. Warren, who began anticipating that Methodism's seminaries would gradually provide the opportunity for such a genuinely "scientific exposition" of Methodism's total doctrinal heritage.

This desire to pass beyond mere controversial theology did not, in itself, constitute any deviation from the basic theological attitude of Wesleyan Methodism. Methodist interest had always been simply to emphasize "first principles" of evangelical truth, except where the very possibilities of experimentally appropriating such truth were obscured by what was considered erroneous doctrine. Nevertheless, during this mid-century period there was a noticeable contribution, to the theological literature of American Methodism, of works dealing systematically with the various elements of Christian doctrine.

A common theme runs through the prefaces of such works: There is a need for a summary statement of the fundamental doctrines of the Bible in terms which the laity as well as the younger ministry of the church can understand. For some, this meant an exposition of Methodism's twenty-five Articles of Religion;[3] for others, it meant an independent attempt at dealing summarily with the great evangelical truths;[4] and for still others, it meant an American rewriting of Richard Watson's early-nineteenth-century, British Wesleyan *Theological Institutes.*[5]

It was Watson's systematic treatment of the theological motifs of Wesley and Fletcher (in the style and with some of the content of his own contemporary English "systems") which proved to be the standard theological source in American Methodism for at least three decades following the early 1840's. Watson's treatment of (I) the Evidences, (II) the Doctrines, (III) the Morals, and (IV) the Institutions of Christianity not only provided a norm for subsequent doctrinal studies, but gave direction to the whole theological enterprise within American Methodism—integrating Methodist theology into the polemic categories of contemporary anti-deistic, anti-Calvinistic theology.

The intention of adapting Watson's *Institutes* is quite explicit in Wakefield's *Complete System of Christian Theology*. Besides his abridgment of Watson, Wakefield included certain original matter at various points in the discussion. He also prefixed "a brief Introduction to the Study of Theology, principally derived from the theological writings of Knapp, Dick, and Horne" (Knapp was an early-nineteenth-century pietist theologian at Halle, in Germany; the other two were contemporary British theologians). In 1863 Wakefield's volume received an extended review by Daniel Whedon, then editor, in the January issue of *The Methodist Quarterly Review*. Whedon's remarks are indicative of the concern of many in the church for a genuinely indigenous and wholly independent Methodist systematic theology. The review concludes:

> There are points in which the author bases himself upon Watson, in which we concur with neither. There are points of philosophy in which Mr. Watson followed the prevalent theories of the Locke philosophy which Dr. Wakefield has preserved, and which we should have expunged and replaced with the reverse view. There are some minor points of theology in which we differ from him

[Wakefield]. . . . Yet, as a whole, as to the main outlines of our Arminian
Wesleyan theology . . . the volume before us [is representative].

Whedon himself was to become a major factor in diverting the mind of
nineteenth-century American Methodism away from any unqualified appeal to
the doctrinal positions of Richard Watson. Through his articles and reviews as
editor of *The Methodist Quarterly Review* (1856–84), through his *Freedom
of the Will,* and through his definitive article in the *Bibliotheca Sacra* (1862)
on the "Doctrines of Methodism," Daniel Whedon proved a formative influence
in the emergence of an indigenous theological tradition within American
Methodism. His *Freedom of the Will as a Basis of Human Responsibility*[6]
proved to be a major instance within American Methodism of the influence of
Edwardean Calvinism in substantially revising and delimiting traditional issues
between Calvinistic and Arminian theological orientations.

The writings of William Fairfield Warren are further indicative of the new
theological independence characteristic of American Methodism in this mid-
century period. Warren, who became the first dean of Boston University's
School of Theology (as well as first president of the university itself), published
an introduction to systematic theology[7] in 1865, while serving as theological
professor at the Methodist seminary in Bremen, Germany. In a review of
Warren's work John McClintock writes:

> To state and vindicate the Methodist system of doctrines, with reference to the
> theological and philosophical relations of the time, is a task that must have fallen
> to some one; and we are thankful it has fallen to one so well qualified to
> accomplish it. . . . American Methodism, whose birth was some forty years later
> than that of English Methodism, has waited as many years after the publication
> of Watson's great work for the appearance of its first work of systematic
> theology. Not that she has produced nothing in the field of theological literature;
> on the contrary, the practical and controversial demands of this period of her
> development have been most ably met in the writings of Bangs, Emory, Fisk,
> Olin and others, now among the dead; and of Elliott, Whedon, Peck, Porter,
> Foster, and many others of the living. But an original . . . work on systematic
> theology has not yet been brought out in American Methodism. The work . . .
> by Dr. Warren forms the introduction to such a work; but, as yet, it is only a
> noble beginning.[8]

Unfortunately, the main body of Warren's proposed systematic theology was
never completed; but his supplementary writings in methodology and in soteriology proved to be quite significant.

There were several systematic writings in preparation during this period.
Thomas Summers, dean and first professor in systematic theology at Vanderbilt
University's Biblical Department, prepared his extended lectures on the Articles of Religion during the late 1870's, although they were not published until
1888. L. T. Townsend's *Outline of Theology* and *Elements of General and*

*Christian Theology* were published in the 1870's, while Townsend was professor of practical theology in Boston University's School of Theology. John Miley's *Atonement in Christ*, first published in 1879, was completely incorporated into his later *Systematic Theology*. Actually, the first original and complete system of theology to be published within American Methodism was that of Miner Raymond of Garrett Biblical Institute. Raymond succeeded John Dempster in the chair of systematic theology at Garrett in 1864; his *Systematic Theology* was published in 1877–79.

## METHODISM AND ADVANCED INTELLECTUAL DEVELOPMENTS

"A little before and after the year 1840 we witness the first considerable effects of German philosophy and criticism on American religious thought. This oceanic current reached us by two channels, one direct, the other by way of Great Britain." [9] What were the points of contact between American Methodist thought in this middle period and the dynamic intellectual developments which so characterized nineteenth-century Europe? The first two continental figures to receive significant attention in *The Methodist Quarterly Review* were A. Tholuck (the "conciliatory" theologian at Halle, following 1826), and Victor Cousin (the French romanticist philosopher). In quite broad terms it may be said that the elements of pietism and theological ability in Tholuck, and the emphases on intuitional realism and the voluntary self in Cousin, were factors making these men attractive to their Methodist reviewers. Herder, Schlegel, and Kant also were reviewed—Kant's reviewer being careful to distinguish his transcendental philosophy from "modern transcendentalism."

It was under the editorship of John McClintock (1848–56) that the readers of *The Methodist Quarterly Review* were made most keenly aware of that world of thought which proved so definitive of nineteenth-century intellectual history. Even before McClintock's election as editor, he personally had contributed some of the most significant of the earlier review articles on continental thought. As editor he insisted—even in the face of severe criticism—that Methodism's intellectual horizons be expanded still more. During the eight years of McClintock's editorial supervision he himself contributed or directly solicited articles and reviews on Bushnell, Channing, Morell, Hamilton, Comte, and Coleridge.

One of McClintock's most important contributions to the theological literature and thought of American Methodism was the introduction of regular sections of "Literary Intelligence—Theological." In these pages appeared critical notices of the publications, journals, and major intellectual developments in England, France, and Germany. The October, 1850, issue, for example, included the announcement that Professor J. L. Jacobi of the University of Berlin had been secured as a regular correspondent for the *Review*. Jacobi's initial contribution was a favorable notice of the theological work of Schenkel, Roth, Müller, Neander, Nitzsch, Sack, and Hagenbach, with strong critical remarks directed against David Strauss and Bruno Bauer. William F. Warren served as foreign theological correspondent for the *Review* during the early 1860's. Following 1867, these review notices—especially those regarding German theological publications—were furnished by John Fletcher Hurst.

Daniel Whedon was elected editor of *The Methodist Quarterly Review* in 1856, and continued the tradition of attending editorially to the broad stream of contemporary intellectual and theological developments. For instance, during Whedon's first decade and a half as editor he either contributed or directly solicited reviews on Cousin, Mansel and Hamilton, Maurice, Darwin, Spencer, DeWette, and Schleiermacher, as well as the more conservative such as Knapp, Tholuck, Hagenbach, Hengstenberg, Harms, Lange, Ullmann, and Schenkel. There also were notices of such American theological contemporaries as Theodore Parker, Horace Bushnell, Charles Hodge, George P. Fisher, Laurens P. Hickok, Edwards A. Park, and Henry B. Smith. Whedon encouraged articles by fellow Methodists—Warren, B. F. Cocker, Alexander Winchell, Borden Parker Bowne, *et al.*—dealing with some of the most advanced phases of philosophical, scientific, and theological thought in the nineteenth century. With respect to doctrinal articles more directly involving Methodist standards, Whedon's policy was to exclude only that which was quite clearly contrary to such standards. On articles involving variances he added his own editorial notes and qualifications.

In such an intellectually revolutionary time American Methodism, together with American Protestantism, found itself involved in the concomitant—and sometimes antagonistic—pull of two methodological concerns: (1) a stubborn determination to sustain the essentials of biblical theism and Christian evangelicalism; and (2) a desire to encourage contemporary intellectual relevancy, even if it meant the revision of traditional doctrinal formulations. Actually, the critical period of intellectual-theological adjustment did not come until the 1870's, a period especially marked by the publication of Darwin's *Descent of Man*. In this instance, it may be said that American Methodism's more advanced thinkers defended the reasonableness of biblical theism (in the face of the new evolutionary science and thought) in one or both of the following manners: (1) divorce the evolutionary naturalist of any scientific ground for his atheism; (2) explicate the inevitability of the theistic solution to the question of ultimate causation.

*The Methodist Quarterly Review* was not the only major theological journal in American Methodism during this period. Beginning in 1847 there was a *Quarterly Review* for the newly formed Methodist Episcopal Church, South. Interestingly enough, the great division of 1844 did not determine, in any significant way, the transitions into this important theological middle period. Those characteristics which defined this newer theological period—the concern for a more systematic statement of evangelical belief and the growing awareness of the larger currents of nineteenth-century thought—were quite evident in the Southern Church.

In 1858 Thomas O. Summers was named to succeed D. S. Doggett as editor of the Southern *Quarterly Review*. He continued to edit this journal until late in 1861, when the War Between the States forced its discontinuance.[10] Summers' editorial policy, as he himself expressed it, was to conserve, express, and encourage the truest evangelical orthodoxy of Arminian Methodism. He conceived the province of the *Quarterly Review* to be quite properly a conservative one—"to reflect rather than to direct the thought and opinion of the Southern Methodist Episcopal Church."[11] And yet, Summers was not wholly averse to admitting articles which reflected differences of opinion on biblical, theological, and philosophical matters. He even acknowledged that he could "tolerate a little scientific heresy, however pertinacious he may be in regard to theological orthodoxy."[12] His most succinct statement of his editorial method came in 1880, upon resuming the editorship of the *Quarterly Review*: "Scientific and theological speculations of a vagarious character are not desired—nothing contrary to our recognized standards should appear in its pages, except to be refuted—it is a *Methodist* Review; yet, in keeping with the genius of Methodism, no pragmatic shibboleths will be enforced upon any writer."[13]

During Summers' first editorial term (1858–61), he admitted articles on Comte, Hamilton, German theology, German philosophy, and Kant.[14] He himself contributed reviews of Mansel's Bampton Lectures on the *Limits of Religious Thought*, and of Darwin's *Origin of Species* (which, to his mind, simply did not settle "the vexed question of the origin and variation of species and fertility of hybrids").

## METHODISM'S THEOLOGIANS AND EMERGENT RELIGIOUS PHILOSOPHIES

What, more specifically, were the Methodist reactions to those revisionist religious philosophies which were emerging from Germany and England? Although generally sympathetic with the transcendental revolt against empiricism (or sensationalism), and although themselves broadly influenced by the principles and methods of that intuitional realism which characterized the writings of Reid and Cousin, the American Methodists tended to be quite critical of those efforts at a Christian rationale which characterized the writings of Coleridge, Schleiermacher, the American transcendentalists, Bushnell, and Maurice. The tendency toward philosophical romanticism which characterized the theological writings of this latter group seemed, to the Methodists, to constitute a fundamental capitulation to an ever-encroaching rationalistic age— employing "the formulas of ordinary theology in a sense diverse from their apparent original intention." This was a serious charge, for in the Methodist view the realities of evangelical experience could only be sustained in a context which upheld the essential affirmations of historically orthodox evangelicalism.[15] To interpret Christianity in terms of "the modernly so called *transcendental philosophy*," wrote Miner Raymond in 1854, meant either reducing the central truths of Christianity to nonentities or rendering them wholly inoperative "for any purpose of experimental or practical godliness." [16]

Were the American Methodists opposed to all efforts at dealing intellectually with the fundamentals of evangelical experience? There were many who defended the assertion that Methodism, essentially, was "religion without philosophy"; doctrinal formulation, according to some Methodist interpreters, was an obscuration of the stress on evangelical experience—a stress which belonged uniquely to Methodism. But it is important to note that leaders in American Methodist thought—Bangs, Olin, McClintock, Stevens, Whedon— strongly repudiated any such radical disjunction between experience and theology.[17]

It was at this very point that Methodism's theologians entered a methodological protest against emergent nineteenth-century religious philosophies. Both Whedon and McClintock criticized the tendency in Coleridge, Maurice, and Bushnell to denounce systematic ("scientific") doctrinal statements or historically oriented apologetics. The Methodists generally insisted that the evident character of religious experience had reference value for Christianity only in a context of objective historical testimony, systematically related. "What we most disapprove . . . is . . . setting the conscious experimental evidence of religion in *opposition* to the historical and logical, instead of presenting them as coordinate and harmonious reciprocal conditions to each other. Historical Christianity is largely the basis and body of that religion which evidences itself to the soul." [18] It was this conviction which led Whedon to reject an assertion by Frederic H. Hedge, a Unitarian transcendentalist, that Methodism had proved a practical "corrective" to the evils of the "Paleyan age." The reference here was to William Paley, whose *View of the Evidences of Christianity* (1794) contained the apologetics of Christian faith so characteristic of eighteenth-century English theology—the arguments from prophecy, miracle, and historical-literary vindication to the unique and authoritative fact of the Christian revelation. Whedon, and the greater portion of American

Methodism, remained stanch advocates of the Paleyan method of cumulative historical "Christian evidences."

> We are not . . . to be fascinated out of that firm maintenance of Christian FACTS, for the masterly statement of which William Paley's name is illustriously trite. With all our Methodism [and its appeal to experience], we would not give one ounce of Paley's solid evidential sense for the entire volume of transcendental gas that exhilerates the brains of . . . glowing intuitionalists.[19]

But was there not a certain affinity between Methodism's stress on Christian experience and that religious empiricism which was emerging in the nineteenth century? Although the overly subjective nature of the religious epistemology of Schleiermacher and Coleridge quite generally was stressed, still there were those within American Methodism (e.g., Olin, McClintock, Curry) who saw in such writings a vindication of Methodism's own traditionally unique emphasis on experimental religion. "To Methodism Christianity is primarily a new life in God, mediated to the believer by the Church through the preaching of the word and prayer; so to Schleiermacher."[20] That there was "conscious experimental evidence of religion" was seen to be the testimony "of Augustine, Bernard, Coleridge, Schleiermacher, and others"; but "more effective expositions" of the intrinsically self-evidencing power of Christianity could be found in the writings of Wesley, Fletcher, and Watson.[21]

Perhaps even more significant than the notice of such affinity was the recognition on the part of a few sensitive observers that American Methodism— in its own theological presentations—had failed to integrate that emphasis on experimental evidence which had been such a promising aspect of its earlier heritage. Its academic apologetics were limited almost completely to the methodology of natural theology (the traditional, rational arguments for the existence of God, etc.). J. A. Reubelt, of Indiana Asbury University, concluded his article on Schleiermacher with these penetrating remarks:

> Both Methodism and Schleiermacher's theology deny that the natural man, the unchanged and unsanctified intellect, has any insight into the mysteries of religion; but this identity is only partial. When we go to a revival meeting, to a class meeting, or love-feast, we cannot be mistaken as to the completeness of the identity; but when we go to the recitation-room in our higher institutions of learning, and our theological seminaries, if we examine the course of study prescribed for our young preachers, then this identity is greatly marred; not only the identity of Methodism and Schleiermacher's theology, but also the identity of *Methodist life* and *Methodist theology*. This is the case with nearly all our apologetical literature. Here we meet as highest authority Paley, Butler [Analogy], and other writers from the deistical period. None of these men viewed Christianity *as a new life from and in God, none referred to the testimony of the Spirit*, none makes a change of heart the *conditio sine qua non* of understanding the Bible; but all endeavor, as Supernaturalism did, to construe from

284

miracles and prophecies an argument amounting, if it could have been completed, to a demonstration.[22]

The self-apparent inconsistency (as Reubelt termed it) here was, at best, only partially comprehended by American Methodism. The method of traditional apologetics (set forth, for instance, in Watson's *Theological Institutes*) was followed with care and attention, although some sporadic efforts were made at supplementation in accord with the dimensions of internal evidence and the appeal to experience. There were to be some few attempts at the type of integration urged by Reubelt, but American Methodism generally did not grasp the unique relevance of its methodological heritage to the contemporary discussions in theology.[23] Actually, Methodism's primary attention was drawn to the necessity of sustaining a theological context adequate to the demands of truly Christian experience. Methodism conceived itself to be one of the leading forces in the evangelical "front" against materialistic and rationalistic elements in the contemporary intellectual scene.

# Reforms

## CHAPTER 18

# From "Christian Perfection" to the "Baptism of the Holy Ghost"

## Donald W. Dayton

In spite of extensive recent scholarship devoted to the history of pentecostalism, the origins and background of the movement are still obscure. Earlier history has been combed for occurrences of glossolalia, but there has been little attempt to delineate carefully the development of the complex of theological and religious ideas that culminated in pentecostalism.

Most students of pentecostalism have noticed the holiness movement as an immediate antecedent. This has been defended and developed most extensively by Vinson Synan, whose stance within the holiness-pentecostal tradition has enabled him to see this connection more clearly.[1] But as Synan himself admits,[2] his delineation of the development of the holiness movement is based largely on secondary sources prepared by representatives of Methodism and the classical holiness tradition who have not given particular attention to those features that have led more directly into pentecostalism. Much of this work needs to be redone with new questions in mind. I will offer here only a sample probe into this literature; a close tracing of the development of the doctrine of the Baptism of the Holy Spirit will indicate the lines that need to be followed up.

Some students of pentecostalism have assumed that this doctrine derives ultimately from early Methodism and the Wesleys. Hollenweger comments, for example, that "John Wesley . . . had already made a distinction between the sanctified, or those who had been baptized in the Spirit, and ordinary Christians."[3] But such a statement is at best oversimplified and at worst completely misleading. Wesley taught a doctrine of Christian perfection and not a Baptism of the Holy Spirit. Indeed, if we may trust the recent study of Herbert McGonigle, Wesley seems not even to have put major emphasis on the place of the

Holy Spirit in the work of sanctification. His development of the doctrine in the *Plain Account of Christian Perfection* is almost entirely Christocentric in character. Wesley does use the expression "Baptism of the Holy Spirit" a very few times, but always, McGonigle concludes, in reference to conversion or "justifying grace."[4]

This pattern holds true also for other early British Methodists. Wesley's preachers (whose lives and testimonies are collected in *The Lives of Early Methodist Preachers*) were not inclined to describe their experience in terms of a Baptism of the Holy Spirit. Nor is the expression characteristic of early Methodist hymnody. Adam Clarke does not speak in this manner in either his exegetical or his theological works. John Fletcher, however, does use the expression a very few times, but, according to McGonigle, ambiguously, applying it equally to the new birth and sanctification. Perhaps of more significance is the fact that at one point Wesley found it necessary to reprimand Joseph Benson, who was the editor of Fletcher's works, for speaking of sanctification as a "receiving of the Holy Ghost."[5] But it does seem clear, nonetheless, that there was no developed doctrine of a Baptism of the Holy Spirit in early Methodism.

Further study of these questions needs to be undertaken. There seem to have been developments in England that climaxed by the mid-nineteenth century in William Arthur's *The Tongue of Fire*, which will be discussed below. My study has concentrated on the American scene, and there the situation is much like that described above for early British Methodism. By 1830 or so, American Methodism had begun to neglect its crowning doctrine, and there arose in the following decade forces to reassert it. Particularly important were *The Guide to Christian Perfection* under the editorship of Timothy Merritt, the "Tuesday Meeting" for the "promotion of holiness" under the leadership of Phoebe Palmer and her sister Sarah Lankford, and perhaps most interesting of all, the school of Oberlin perfectionism that arose among Congregationalists and Presbyterians. In all of these, the emphasis was on Christian perfection developed along classical Wesleyan lines. There was occasional reference to a Baptism of the Holy Spirit, but with little precision in its application.

As nearly as I can determine, the first sustained development of this doctrine took place, at least in America, in Oberlin perfectionism. Many students of pentecostalism have noticed this movement and especially its two greatest leaders, evangelist Charles Grandison Finney, who became the first theology professor at Oberlin, and Asa Mahan, the school's first president. But it is very difficult to trace the development of Oberlin theology. Frederick Dale Bruner emphasizes Finney's Baptism of the Holy Spirit language in his *Autobiography*.[6] But Finney uses the term very generally, referring to both his conversion of 1821 and the spiritual unction which he claimed was the *sine qua non* of an effective ministry. The *Autobiography*, moreover, was not published until 1876, when the teaching was relatively common. It plays no part in such earlier statements as his *Views of Sanctification*[7] or his systematic theology (the relevant section was first published in 1847). Though he may well have made earlier statements, the first I have discovered is his address on the "Baptism of the Holy Spirit" before the Oberlin Council of Congregationalism in 1871.[8]

Greater emphasis should perhaps be placed on Asa Mahan, who was in many ways the major architect of Oberlin perfectionism and much closer to Wesleyanism and the growing holiness movement within Methodism.[9] But Mahan reveals a pattern similar to that of Finney. The expression "Baptism of the Holy Ghost" dominates his *Autobiography*[10] and the more spiritually oriented *Out of Darkness into Light*.[11] Mahan himself refers to those "two great doctrines [i.e., "Christian Perfection" and "Baptism of the Holy Ghost"] which have been the theme of my life during the past forty-six years."[12] This statement would date his interest in the subject to at least as early as 1836. But this is the date of his sanctification, and there is no evidence that he described his experience at the time in terms of a Baptism of the Holy Ghost. The expression plays no part in his *Christian Perfection*[13] or other early writings. Mahan's full development of the doctrine was not published until 1870,[14] but we do know from Mahan's correspondence with Phoebe Palmer that the content of this book was first given as lectures at Adrian College six to eight years before publication.[15] Other indications in Mahan's writings would suggest that his thought did not turn to this doctrine until 1855 or so. This period (the late 1850s and early 1860s) seems to coincide, as shall see, with broader interest in the doctrine.

But there does appear to have been at Oberlin an even earlier development of the doctrine among the other two members of the theological faculty. A third figure, Henry Cowles, placed greater emphasis on the place of the Holy Spirit in effecting sanctification, though usually without using the expression "Baptism of the Holy Spirit."[16] But two short sermons by Cowles do make the identification. The second of these concludes that "the plan of salvation contemplates as its prime object, the sanctification of the church; and relies on the baptism of the Holy Spirit as the great efficient power for accomplishing the work."[17]

Even more significant is the work of John Morgan who published in the first volume of the *Oberlin Quarterly Review* (1845—then under the editorship of Mahan) two essays to bolster Oberlin Perfectionism. One of these, "The Holiness Acceptable to God," develops the nature of holiness without identifying it as a work of the Holy Spirit, but the second essay, "The Gift of the Holy Spirit," is a sustained argument that "the baptism of the Holy Ghost, then in its Pentecostal fullness, was not to be confined to the Primitive Church, but is the common privilege of all believers."[18]

These essays are important for several reasons. In the first place, they illustrate the tension that must always exist between a doctrine of Christian perfection and one of the Baptism of the Holy Spirit. (This tension will be spelled out shortly.) The first essay has almost no reference to the Holy Spirit, while in the second, "perfection" and "holiness" fade almost entirely into the background. Asa Mahan was later to attempt to bring the two into more of a synthesis, but even there, one may detect problems. It is difficult, however, to trace any impact of Morgan's essays (though the former was published as a pamphlet in 1848 and the latter was serialized in the *Oberlin Evangelist*) until after the publication of Mahan's book on the subject in 1870. *The Gift of the Holy Spirit* was reprinted in 1875,[19] when it had major impact on A. J. Gordon, identified by Bruner as a major figure on the way to pentecostalism.[20] Gordon found Morgan's essay "a decided advance in the way of thorough scriptural discussion of this important subject."[21]

But Oberlin perfectionism was already by this time taking new directions and losing its earlier impact and influence. Apparently Morgan's works were largely buried in this decline, and one must look elsewhere for the continued development of the doctrine. Our study of Mahan has already drawn attention to the years of the late 1850s and early 1860s. Several other important developments seem to have taken place during this period. Eighteen fifty-six saw the publication of *The Tongue of Fire* by English Methodist William Arthur. This book develops the work of the Holy Spirit in terms of Pentecost and ends with the prayer:

> And now, adorable Spirit, proceeding from the Father and the Son, descend upon all the churches, renew the Pentecost in this our age, and baptize thy people generally—O, baptize them yet again with the tongues of fire! Crown this 19th century with a revival of "pure and undefiled religion" greater than that of the last century, greater than that of the first, greater than any "demonstration of the Spirit" ever yet vouchsafed to men![22]

There is a sense in which this prayer found immediate fulfillment. The next two years (1857–58) saw the "layman's revival" which "spread abroad the ideals of the holiness and perfectionist movements."[23] A cursory overview of this revival reveals that contemporary reports often described it as a new Pentecost and spoke of the Baptism of the Holy Spirit. Phoebe Palmer, who had by this time become the most important advocate of holiness, also played an important part in this revival. She had been engaged in evangelism in Canada where the revival broke out, and she was present at the first stirrings. She also spent several years in the British Isles in the wake of this revival, continuing its spirit in vigorous evangelistic work.[24]

Though the language is not characteristic of her earlier works, Phoebe Palmer was by this time very committed to speaking of the Baptism of the Holy

Spirit. In her letters home, printed in the *Guide to Holiness*,[25] she commented that the importance of this doctrine had just recently been impressed upon her. Perhaps it was William Arthur's book that produced this impact. It had been published in New York (1856), and Phoebe Palmer's terminology seems at times to reflect Arthur's. But whatever the source of the teaching, she sent back from England such reports as "we talked about the endowment of power, the full baptism of the Holy Ghost, as the indispensable, ay, *absolute* necessity of all the disciples of Jesus."[26] By this she meant "holiness," for which she seems to have discovered a new language. And this new language now permeates her work.

But it was still left to an Oberlin theologian to give the doctrine its final formulation. In 1870, Asa Mahan approached Phoebe Palmer about publishing his *Baptism of the Holy Ghost* under the auspices of the *Guide to Holiness* which she now edited. From their correspondence at the time, it is apparent that the doctrine was still controversial (Phoebe Palmer was reluctant to publish the book) but that it was already widely discussed (Mahan was able to argue that such discussion was the major reason that his "non-controversial" and "experiential" treatment was needed). In the end, the book was published and soon both generated and rode the crest of a wave of interest in the Baptism of the Holy Ghost. Within a dozen years, Mahan could report that his book had been "very extensively circulated in America, in Great Britain and in all missionary lands; and has been translated into the Dutch and German languages."[27] Mahan carried the message to the Oxford (1874) and Brighton (1875) meetings from which the Keswick movement emerged. At both conventions, he spoke and led very popular seminars on the subject. Revivalist D. L. Moody had wrestled with the doctrine in 1871, achieving a spiritual resolution that has seemed to a number of his biographers more important than his conversion in launching his evangelistic campaigns. At any rate, the doctrine was picked up by Moody and his followers, and Keswick was introduced back into the United States by Moody's Northfield Conventions.

But our interest lies still more with the impact of the new view on the Methodist and holiness traditions. Within a year, the *Guide to Holiness* could quote rave reviews from Methodist periodicals, while in 1874, Daniel Steele, then of Syracuse and later of Boston University, described his own experience in terms of a Baptism of the Spirit and appealed to his brethren to "cease to discuss the subtleties and endless questions arising from entire sanctification or Christian Perfection and all cry mightily to God for the baptism of the Holy Spirit."[28] The cumulative effect of this doctrine can be traced in the pages of the *Guide* until it climaxed in 1897 with title change. In that year, the words "and Revival Miscellany" (dating from Phoebe Palmer's days) were dropped in favor of "and Pentecostal Life" in response to "signs of the times, which indicate inquiry, research, and ardent pursuit of the gifts, graces and power of the Holy Spirit. 'The Pentecostal idea' is pervading Christian thought and aspirations more than ever before."[29] The same issue includes a testimony to Mahan's continuing impact. The inside front cover announces a new edition of that "Great Pentecostal Gift," the *Baptism of the Holy Ghost*, "this truly magnificent work of Dr. Mahan on the Great Theme of the Period."

By the turn of the century, *everything* from camp meetings to choirs is described in the *Guide* as "pentecostal." Sermons are published under the heading "Pentecostal Pulpit"; women's reports under "Pentecostal Woman-hood"; personal experiences are reported as "Pentecostal Testimonies"; and so on. Even devotional periods take place in the "pentecostal closet." What took place on the pages of the *Guide to Holiness* was typical of what happened in most holiness traditions in the 1880s and 1890s. By 1900, the shift from Christian perfection to Baptism of the Holy Spirit was nearly universal.

The usual holiness interpretations of this shift, where it has even been noticed, have minimized its significance. It has been seen as a valid extension of Wesleyan doctrine and primarily a terminological shift. But it is much more than that. It is a profound transformation of theological ideas and associated concepts. The significance of this theological shift can best be understood by comparing the two books by Asa Mahan. His earlier *Scripture Doctrine of Christian Perfection* stands very much in the classical Wesleyan tradition (though differing in a few nuances) while his Baptism of the Holy Ghost represents later developments and includes most of the seed of what followed. Both books were published under the auspices of the Methodistic holiness movement. The first was published by D. S. King, who soon thereafter became the publisher and then an editor of the *Guide to Christian Perfection*. The later book was published by the Palmers, after Phoebe Palmer had become editor of the same journal, now renamed the *Guide to Holiness*.

The shift in terminology involved, in the first place, a shift from Christo-centrism to an emphasis on the Holy Spirit. Mahan's *Christian Perfection*, like Wesley's *Plain Account*, is basically oriented to Christ for the work of sancti-fication; thus he says, "The Spirit shows not himself, but Christ to our minds."[30] Mahan likewise gave the Spirit no autonomy in guidance and advised ignoring "undefined impressions" to "testify" or follow a particular course of action. But in the *Baptism of the Holy Ghost*, the Spirit becomes primary. Christ Himself was dependent upon the "indwelling, and influence, and baptism of the Holy Spirit, the same in all essential particulars as in us."[31] This shift in emphasis underlined an interesting shift in terminology. In the earlier book, salvation history is divided into two covenants (law/grace) whose line of demarcation is Christ, especially His atonement. But in the later book, the division is into dispensations (the Spirit is "the crowning glory and promise of the New Dispensation")[32] and Pentecost is the new fulcrum.

This shift involves, in the second place, a movement away from the goal and nature of Christian perfection to an emphasis on the event in which it is instantaneously achieved. Wesley was clearest in his statement of the ideal but vacillated somewhat as to whether this was to be achieved in crisis or in process. Mahan's basic definition of perfection was, "a full and perfect discharge of our entire duty, of all existing obligations in respect to God and all other beings. It is perfect obedience to the moral law." [33] In the second book, Mahan emphasizes the method by which this is to be achieved and explicates it in terms of the Baptism of the Holy Ghost. This necessarily involves an emphasis on the "eventness" of the experience, perhaps to the detriment of a concern for ethics, particularly social ethics. It may be that the ground was prepared for this new teaching by the impact of revivalism in reshaping Wesleyanism on the American scene. Particularly with Phoebe Palmer, there was an emphasis on "claiming the blessing *now*" without the struggle sometimes characteristic of early Methodism. [34]

In the third place, there is an almost complete shift in the exegetical foundations of the doctrine. In *Christian Perfection*, Mahan, like Wesley before him, hardly ever appeals to the Book of Acts. Use is made instead of passages that refer to cleansing and perfection (such as Ezek. 36:25; Mat. 5:48; II Cor. 7:1; I Thess. 5:23–24; John 17:20–23, etc.). In the *Baptism of the Holy Ghost*, most of the crucial texts are taken from the Book of Acts. Basic, of course, is the account of Pentecost, but also important is Acts 19, especially verse 2: "Have ye received the Holy Ghost since ye believed?" as well as other passages speaking of a reception of the Holy Spirit. Of particular interest is the appeal to Joel 2:28, "And it shall come to pass in the last days I will pour out my Spirit upon all flesh; and your sons and daughters shall prophesy" (Acts 2:17), Zechariah 13:1, "In that day there shall be a fountain opened to the house of David," and a few other Old Testament prophetic passages.

This exegetical shift involves an intensification of the sense of eschatology and the use of predictive prophecy. Wesley's relative lack of interest in eschatology is well-known. In Oberlin perfectionism this was somewhat altered by American millennialism, though it plays little part in Mahan's *Christian Perfection*. His later book, however, picks up the theme and assigns to Methodism a special place in the divine drama:

> The central article of her creed is the great central Truth of the Gospel. If she will be true to her calling, she will not only enable "the fountain to be opened" in her own midst, but also in other communions. When this takes place, "then is the millennium near, even at the door." [35]

In this quotation, we may also see the seed of an idea that gained importance. Mahan was troubled by the meaning of the expression "in that day" which occurs in a number of the prophecies that he utilized. In *Baptism of the Holy*

*Ghost,* he devotes several pages to this problem and concludes that the "fountain" is to be opened in these *latter days.*[36] But we may see here the hermeneutical problem that resulted in the distinction between the earlier and latter rains of the Spirit's blessing which became so important in later holiness and pentecostal thought. In Mahan this is all, of course, still expressed in terms of the postmillennial framework of his thought, but we can see how these patterns of thought and interest would find much in common with the prophecy conferences which were to begin in America in 1878. And it was not until 1883, for example, that A. T. Pierson capitulated to premillennialism.[37]

This shift in exegetical foundations, finally, turns attention to a new set of ideas and associated contexts. A new emphasis falls on the empowering of the Holy Spirit. Following such passages as Acts 1:8 ("But ye shall receive power, after that the Holy Ghost is come upon you"), Mahan noted that at Pentecost *"power* was one of the most striking characteristics of this baptism."[38] Another emergent emphasis is on prophecy, usually interpreted as "testifying" or "speaking as the Spirit giveth utterance." Mahan finds this now "the common privilege of all believers."[39] It is also very significant that the gifts of the Spirit move into the center of attention. Mahan, like many holiness writers, attempted to emphasize not the gifts but the fruit of the Spirit, and not "the miraculous, but common influence of the Spirit."[40] This concern is, of course, somewhat weakened by the development in the second book. And one can quite easily trace in the latter third of the nineteenth century a rising interest in such things as "divine healing."

One may go on. I am convinced that one can find in late nineteenth century holiness thought and life every significant feature of pentecostalism. The major exception would be the gift of tongues, but even there the ground had been well prepared. Once attention had been focused on the Book of Acts, on Pentecost as an event in the life of each believer, and on the gifts of the Spirit, the question inevitably arose.

Mahan's later book also reveals a strong concern for "assurance." This, of course, has its antecedents in the Wesleyan doctrine of the witness of the Spirit, but appears intensified in the *Baptism of the Holy Ghost.* Mahan was convinced that the Baptism of the Spirit would have a conscious and perhaps even a physical effect. "Where the Holy Ghost is received, such a change is wrought in the subject that he himself will become distinctly conscious of the change . . . a change also observable to others around."[41] Hannah Whitall Smith's posthumously published papers on religious fanaticism also report, from 1871 or so on, several cases of people desperately seeking a "conscious" Baptism of the Holy Spirit that would even result in "physical thrills."[42] It is easy to see how the gift of tongues would fill this longing.

Indeed, in the last quarter of the nineteenth century, one can trace a number of incidents in which tongues did break out. Relying on the work of Stanley

Frodsham (*With Signs Following*), William Menzies mentions several such instances which "occurred principally in Holiness revival and camp meetings," particularly in southeastern United States.[43] I have come across other incidents that could be added to this list. One of them took place in 1881 at a holiness camp and reveals the sort of development that naturally took place.

> One day right in the midst of a great sermon, a woman from Carrol County, a holiness professor, sprawled out at full length in the aisle. This, in itself, was not much to be thought of, for to tumble over now and then was to be expected. But the unexpected happened in this case. It kept some of the sisters busy to keep her with a measurably decent appearance. Directly she began to compose a jargon of words in rhyme and sing them with a weird tune. She persisted till the service was spoiled and the camp was thrown into a hubbub. Strange to say, the camp was divided thereby. Some said it was a wonderful manifestation of divine power, some said it was a repetition of speaking in unknown tongues as at Pentecost. But every preacher on the ground without exception declared it to be of the devil. But the camp was so divided in opinion that it had to be handled with the greatest of care.[44]

We see in this passage how this sort of event could occur, how the interpretation naturally developed, and also an example of the antagonism that characterized the response of holiness people to the practice, particularly in the early part of the twentieth century.

With all of this in the background, the emergence of pentecostalism in the next century may be seen as a natural development of forces that had been set in motion much earlier. And when we turn to those events usually identified as the beginnings of the pentecostal movement, these connections are very apparent. It was a *holiness* evangelist, Charles Fox Parham, who after founding Bethel Bible School near Topeka, suggested that his students during his absence continue a study of Acts 2 to discover the "evidence" of the Baptism of the Holy Spirit. He returned to discover that the students had concluded that the evidence is speaking in tongues. And in 1906, it was W. J. Seymour, a Negro *holiness* evangelist and a student of Parham, who had come to Azusa to speak in a *Nazarene* Negro mission, but found himself locked out when he preached from Acts 2:4 his pentecostal doctrine. The Azusa Street revival that launched pentecostalism was then held in an abandoned Methodist church. It is, therefore, not surprising that pentecostalism swept through many holiness churches, particularly in the south; nor that for a decade most pentecostals claimed to be holiness in theology; nor that a large number of pentecostals today view themselves as standing in the Wesleyan tradition.

# The Ordination of Women: Round One; Anna Oliver and the General Conference of 1880

Edited by Kenneth E. Rowe

The first major "test case" in the ordination of women in the Methodist Episcopal Church occurred at the 1880 General Conference. Anna Oliver's name was repeatedly before the conference and its committees, where there was lively debate over the general question of licensing and ordaining women. The journal of the General Conference reports eleven memorials or petitions from nine annual conferences on the issue, including several specifically on Miss Oliver.[1] Manuscript copies of several of these memorials, and the reports of the various legislative committees upon them, which have become landmark documents have been "discovered" in the General Conference papers in the Drew University Library. None were printed in the journal of the conference and only a few were recorded in the *Daily Christian Advocate* of the conference and thus are not generally available.

From its founding in 1870 Boston University in principle welcomed women to the student body and faculty of all of its schools. Three years later the first woman to enroll in the School of Theology did so without much fanfare under the name of Anna Oliver. Actually that was not her real name. Her distinguished and scholarly family, and especially her brother who was rector of a prestigious Episcopal Church in Brooklyn, were so upset over her determination to study theology and prepare for the ministry that she decided to drop the family name of Snowden and use instead the name of an aunt—Oliver—so as not to embarrass them. After having completed undergraduate studies in Rutgers Female College, Anna first enrolled at Oberlin, but found that, in spite of its official policy of welcoming all educationally qualified students, there still was much discrimination against women in the theological department. So she transferred to Boston and after a three-year course of study, received the Bachelor of Sacred Theology degree in 1876. Among the number of distinguished scholars in her class, including a future bishop and a future theological professor, Anna was chosen to give one of the senior honors orations at Commencement. She chose as her theme, "Christian Enterprise; its Field and Reward." [2]

Obtaining a theological degree was one thing; ordination and appointment to a Methodist parish was quite another! Problems relating to Anna's ordination and appointment would keep Bishops and Presiding Elders, Annual Conferences and General Conferences, pastors and layfolk buzzing for some time to come.

In September of 1876 Miss Oliver, fresh from seminary, began pastoral duties under very difficult circumstances in the newly-reorganized Methodist Episcopal Church in Passaic, New Jersey. In April of that year the three-year-old church, which had become the victim of the stock market crash of 1873 and the hard times which followed, was sold under foreclosure. On August 17, however, a new Methodist church was organized under the name of the First Methodist Church of Passaic, the church building was bought back and a much reduced mortgage was assumed.[3] Her salary was set at $470, whereas her predecessor received $2,000.[4] Her first Sunday's congregation numbered only 15 out of a total membership of 25.[5] The weary young pastor called for assistance from a highly successful itinerant evangelist, Amanda Smith, a black woman. "Between them," reported a local newspaper,

> Passaic is having a lively time; what with stirring up sinners and Christians on the one hand, and on the other, two women in the pulpit, and one black, the buzzing glows apace![6]

Although the youthful pastor could report in April of 1877 a membership increase of more than 500 percent, the Newark Annual Conference refused to recognize her even as a "Supply Pastor" and quickly replaced her with a regularly licensed and ordained male pastor for the next year.[7] Local pastors ignored her when they held their "union" Thanksgiving and Week of Prayer services. Neither Passaic nor the Newark Conference was ready for such an innovation as a lady pastor. A local newspaper commented prophetically;

> A slip of a preacher with curls and petticoats, and equipped with a knowledge of the two inspired tongues, isn't an easy thing to dispose of, for Miss Oliver is no light skirmisher.[8]

The news about a woman in the Passaic pulpit spread widely, for on February 19, 1877, the stuffy New York Methodist Preachers' Meeting, a weekly gathering of Methodist clergy from across the city for lunch and an address by an invited guest, adopted a resolution inviting the pastor from Passaic to deliver a sermon before the preachers on the first Monday in March. At the next weekly meeting, James Monroe Buckley, the articulate pastor of the Hanson Place Methodist Episcopal Church in Brooklyn and an unabashed woman hater, asked that the matter of Miss Oliver's invitation be reconsidered. The motion set off a noisy discussion which made headlines in the *New York Times* and other newspapers.[9] The *Syracuse Sunday Morning Courier* of March 4, 1877, reported the event in detail:

> The subject of permitting women to preach in Methodist pulpits was incidentally, but rather racily, discussed at the Methodist ministers' meeting in New York City a few days since. A Miss Oliver—a more or less reverend lady—had been invited to preach to the ministers at their next meeting, and the question was raised, by what authority she was invited? Thereupon Brother Buckley took the floor and gave expression to his dissent in the following terms:
>
> I am opposed to inviting any woman to preach before this meeting. If the mother of our Lord were on earth I should oppose her preaching here. [Sensation and murmurs of disapproval]. Oh, I do not mind that, I like at the beginning of a speech to find that there are two sides to my question. There is no power in the Methodist Church by which a woman can be licensed to preach; this is history, this is the report made at the last General Conference. It is, therefore, not legal for any quarterly conference to license a woman to preach, nevertheless here is a woman who claims to have such a license, and we are asked to invite her to preach.
>
> A BROTHER: We have the right!
>
> BROTHER BUCKLEY: Oh, you have the right to believe the moon is made of green cheese, but yet have no right to commit the ministers of this city on an unsettled Church question. [Laughter and applause]. The tendency of men—now here is a chance to hiss—the tendency of men to endeavor to force female preachers on the Church, and the desire to run after female preachers, is, as Dr. Finney said to the students at Oberlin, an aberration of amativeness. [Roars of laughter and applause]. When men are [more] moved by women, than by men under the same circumstances it is certainly due to an aberration of amativeness. [Applause and more laughter]. For some time the male and female students at Oberlin used to have their prayer-meetings together, but after a time they divided, and the young men complained to Dr. Finney that the Holy Ghost no longer came with equal force. Dr. Finney said this showed amativeness or that the men were back-sliding.
>
> BROTHER DICKINSON: As to the talk of amativeness, what about our holiness meetings and seaside meetings where we go to hear woman, and to be moved by her words and her personality? It must be amativeness which urges them to go and hear men preach. [Laughter].
>
> DR. ROACH: If this meeting has any dignity, has any Christian intelligence, has any weight of character, it ought not to take this action. [Laughter]. What wildness, what fanaticism, what strange freaks will we not take on next? [Laughter and applause].

Brother McAllister and others took part in the discussion, and finally, amid cries of "Motion," "Question," points of order, and the utmost confusions the question was put, and the meeting refused to invite Miss Oliver to preach by a vote of 46 to 38. The result was received with ejaculations of "Amen" and "Thank God" and "God bless Brother Buckley." The chair announced that Brother Kittrell will preach next Monday on "Entire Satisfaction," and the meeting adjourned.[10]

The details of Anna Oliver's ministry for the next two years are not yet clear, but in the Spring of 1879 we find Miss Oliver taking leadership of another beleaguered Methodist congregation in her native Brooklyn. In March of that year a heavily mortgaged church at the corner of Willoughby and Tompkins Avenues was sold at public auction under a foreclosure by the first mortgagee, the Williamsburgh Savings Bank. Offers were made by the Roman Catholic diocese and by several enterprising businessmen who proposed to convert the elegant gothic premises into a livery stable or a beer garden! A baker's dozen of women and men "of several religious denominations, who desired a certain work to be there carried on," purchased the church in April for $14,000 and requested Miss Oliver to be their pastor and to hold the property in her name. Fearing the worst from the male-dominated New York East Annual Conference in which they were situated, the group drew up the deed without the usual Methodist trust clause, lest the brethren and fathers claim the property and appoint a male pastor.[11] Membership dipped from the original thirteen to eight by August of that year, but by April of 1880 Anna's flock multiplied to 140 and she presided over a Sunday school manned by 36 teachers with an average attendance of 200![12]

In March of 1880 Miss Oliver launched a Spring offensive on the Methodist Episcopal Church, hoping to press a test case on the ordination of women. As a preliminary step she needed a recommendation from a Quarterly Conference. Having given up on getting a sympathetic hearing, let alone a recommendation for Deacons Orders, from her ministerial colleagues like Dr. Buckley of the New York East Conference, she pinned her hopes on old friends in the familiar territory of Boston. A seminary classmate, the Rev. James W. Bashford, a vigorous supporter of women's rights in the church, was then serving the Jamaica Plain Methodist Episcopal Church in Boston. Blessed with a sympathetic Presiding Elder, the Jamaica Plain Quarterly Conference enthusiastically recommended Anna as a suitable candidate for Deacon's Orders.[13] Support came from other quarters as well, which must have cheered her. During the same month the alumni association of Boston University School of Theology passed the following resolution, with one dissenting vote:

*Resolved*, That the Alumni of the Theological School of Boston University memorialize the General Conference to ordain those women who have felt called to the Gospel ministry, and who have taken the thorough preparation of our

301

colleges and theological schools, and who have shown by gifts, grace and usefulness, that they have the essential qualifications for the Methodist ministry.[14]

The next test would come within a few weeks when her recommendation for ministerial orders would reach the floor of the New England Annual Conference. Anna attended the session on Saturday, April 10, 1880, when the candidates for the ministry were presented. When her name was presented by the Rev. Lorenzo R. Thayer, Presiding Elder of the Boston District, the Presiding Bishop Edward G. Andrews interrupted the proceedings with a solemn pronouncement:

> In my judgment [intoned the Bishop] the law of the Church does not authorize the ordination of Women. I therefore am not at liberty to submit to the vote of the Conference the motion to elect Women to orders.[15]

No sooner had Presiding Elder Thayer announced that he would appeal the Bishop's decision to the forthcoming General Conference, than another ministerial colleague rose to a point of personal privilege and proposed that Miss Oliver address the conference on her reasons for seeking ordination.[16] For half an hour, the New York *Christian Advocate* reported, the

> . . . slight, bright attractive-looking lady—held the conference and the great audience with the fascination of her musical voice, her touching pathos, and her very persuasive eloquence.[17]

At the close of her remarks the Rev. George Whitaker offered the following resolution, which was adopted by a large majority;

> Resolved, that our delegates to the next General Conference be and are hereby instructed to use their influence to remove all distinctions of sex in the office and ordination of our ministry.

Whereupon Dr. Daniel Steele, retired Syracuse University Professor, read by permission Romans 16:1–2 as a fitting benediction.[18]

Anna Howard Shaw, another woman B.D. from Boston University, class of 1878, whose name had also been presented that day for ordination, recalled that she and Anna Oliver were both "staggered but not surprise" by the Bishop's decision. Upon adjournment they called on the Bishop and asked for his advice. He told them bluntly that there was no place for women in the ministry of the Methodist Episcopal Church and suggested that if they persisted in their dream, they should leave the church. Anna Howard Shaw decided to leave, and was ordained by the New York Annual Conference of the Methodist Protestant Church later that year. Anna Oliver, however, confided to her colleague that she would rather fight than switch.[19] She returned to Brooklyn disappointed but not disillusioned and within a week her Official Board added another petition on her behalf to the General Conference.

David H. Wheeler, editor of *The Methodist*, an independent Methodist weekly published in New York, born twenty years before out of the struggle for rights for lay *men* in the church, reflected on Anna Oliver's "test case" before the New England Conference. He skirted the real issue at first by questioning the practice of ordaining pastors for churches "not under our control." Finally the editor moved on to the standard Methodist arguments against the ordination of women based on two hallmarks of Methodist polity—connectionalism and itinerancy.

> A minister must be acceptable to a number of churches [he insisted]; and the making of ministers of women depends upon a demand for them. If many churches demand women pastors, or when they demand them, the demand would be swiftly granted—but not till then.

Since the average pastor in a lifetime serves at least twenty churches, Wheeler argued, for every woman admitted to a conference there must be at least twenty churches where she would be an acceptable pastor. Although he believed the day might come, he knew of no demand for women preachers at the moment.[20]

Thus the stage was set for the supreme "test case" on the ordination of women in the highest legislative body of the Methodist Episcopal Church. The 23rd quadrennial General Conference met in Cincinnati beginning May 1, 1880. The brethren and fathers, 399 delegates representing 95 annual conferences, gathered in Pike's Opera House. Although neither a clergy nor a lay delegate, Anna Oliver made the long trip from Brooklyn to Cincinnati in May for the Conference, her suitcase filled with copies of a pamphlet she had prepared for distribution at the proper moment. As the duly elected delegates took their places on the morning of Tuesday, May 17, they discovered the small eight-page pamphlet on each of their desks. It was her appeal from the decision of Bishop Andrews against her ordination and full installment as pastor of Willoughby Avenue Church in Brooklyn. In the pamphlet Miss Oliver asked not for licensing for evangelist work, but for ordination to the pastorate.

> I am sorry to trouble our dear mother Church with any perplexing questions [she writes], but it presses me also, and the Church and myself must decide something. I am so thoroughly convinced that the Lord has laid commands upon me in this direction that it becomes with me really a question of my soul's salvation. If the Lord commands me to just the course I am pursuing as only they that do His commandments have right to the tree of life, I have no alternative.

She went on to give the reasons that led her to believe that she was called to pastoral work:

> I have made almost every conceivable sacrifice to do what I believe God's will. Brought up in a conservative circle in New York city that held it in disgrace for a woman to work, surrounded with the comforts and advantages of ample means, and trained in the Episcopal Church, I gave up home, friends and support,

went counter to prejudices that had become second nature to me, worked for several years to constant exhaustion, and suffered cold, hunger and loneliness. The things hardest for me to bear were laid upon me. For two months my own mother did not speak to me. When I entered the house she turned and walked away. When I sat at the table she did not recognize me. I have passed through tortures to which the flames of martyrdom would be nothing, for they would end in a day; and through all this time and to-day, I could turn off to positions of comparative ease and profit. However, I take no credit to myself for enduring these trials, because at every step it was plain to me, that I had no alternative but to go forward or renounce my Lord.

Claiming to be neither a "fanatic" nor an "enthusiast," but a loyal member of the Methodist Episcopal Church, she concluded,

I have no one under God with whom to advise but the Bishops and Brethren of our Church. Therefore I ask you, Fathers and Brethren, tell me, what would you do, were you in my place? Tell me, what would you wish the Church to do toward you were you in my place? Please only apply the Golden Rule, and vote in Conference accordingly.[21]

Later that same morning two clergy delegates, the Rev. William Butler of the New England Conference and the Rev. Thomas N. Boyle of the Pittsburgh Conference, separately presented the petition from Willoughby Avenue Church asking for ordination of their pastor, Miss Oliver.[22] A brief account of this eventful morning in the life of the General Conference appeared on the front page of the *New York Times* the next morning.[23]

## WILLOUGHBY AVENUE CHURCH PETITION[24]
[April 19, 1880]

Resolved—That we, the Willoughby Avenue M.E. Church of Brooklyn, New York, of which *Miss Anna Oliver is Pastor*, are loyal to the doctrines and disciplines of the Methodist Episcopal Church, and that we will and hereby do *petition* the General Conference of 1880 to make such alteration or alterations in the Discipline as they may consider necessary to remove the disability or disabilities in the way of the *ordination* of our Pastor.

| | |
|---|---|
| Gilbert E. Currie | George P. McClelland |
| Thomas G. Henderson | George H. Hinds |
| Joseph B. Stanton | Cornelia Mitchell |
| Mary P. Tracey | Hester Chasty |
| Charles E. Davis, Trustees | Helen M. Weeks |
| | David Lawson, Stewards |

William Story
Caroline Aspinall
Sarah Seabrook
Wm. M. Parish
John B. Whitney
Martha Dibble
King H. Caddoo
W. J. Caddoo, Class Leaders

The petition, along with others on the subject of the licensing and ordaining of women, was directed to the legislative Committee on the Itinerancy, or ministry.

Five days later the conservative mind of the Conference on the matter became obvious. The first report of the Judiciary Committee took up the appeal of Presiding Elder Thayer of the New England Conference on Bishop Andrews' decision against the ordination of women:

## REPORT OF THE JUDICIARY COMMITTEE, NO. 1[25]

In the matter of the appeal of Rev. L. R. Thayer, of the New England Conference, in the case of Sister Anna Oliver, the Judiciary Committee respectfully report:

That it appears from the record that Sister Oliver had been recommended to orders by a Quarterly Conference, and, upon said recommendation coming before the said Annual Conference, Bishop Edward G. Andrews, then presiding, gave the following decision to wit:

"In my judgment the law of the Church does not authorize the ordination of women; I, therefore, am not at liberty to submit to the vote of the Conference the vote to elect women to orders."

Your committee have come to the conclusion that such ruling was in accordance with the Discipline of the Church as it is, and with the uniform usage of administration under it.

The committee, therefore, report that said appeal should not be sustained.

George G. Reynolds, Chairman
L. C. Queal, Secretary

The ninety-five "man" committee on the Itinerancy neatly rejected the Willoughby Avenue Church petition on a technicality:

## REPORT OF THE COMMITTEE ON ITINERANCY NO. IX[26]

The Committee on Itinerancy, to whom was referred a memorial from a body styling itself "The Willoughby Avenue M.E. Church of Brooklyn, N.Y." and asking the General Conference to change certain regulations of the Methodist Episcopal Church, beg leave to respect-

305

fully report:

That upon due examination and inquiry they find that there is no society in connection with the Methodist Episcopal Church known as "Willoughby Avenue M.E. Church," and that the document is not legitimately presented to the General Conference. The Committee therefore respectfully return the paper to the General Conference without consideration of its subject matter.

D. A. Whedon, Chairman
I. W. Joyce, Secretary

But there were other petitions on the issue too regular to be dispatched on a technicality. The Committee, however, took as uncompromising a position as Bishop Andrews did in Boston a month before:

## REPORT OF THE COMMITTEE ON ITINERANCY NO. X[27]

### Licensing of Women to Preach, &c.

The Committee on Itinerancy beg leave to present the following report:—

They have considered the several papers referred to them in relation to the licensing of women as exhorters and local preachers, their ordination, admission to the traveling connection and eligibility to all offices in the church; and, inasmuch as women are by general consent of the Church accorded *all the privileges which are necessary to their usefulness*, the Committee recommends that in the respects named no change be made in the Discipline as it regards the status of women in our church.

D.[aniel] A. Whedon, Chm. [Providence]
I[saac] W. Joyce, Sec. [N.W. Indiana]

However there was a minority report on the above issue signed by nineteen dissenting clergy and lay committee members:

## MINORITY REPORT ON THE STATUS OF WOMEN IN THE CHURCH[28]

*Whereas*, the Majority Report on The Status of Women, &c., is not according to fact in stating that the right of women to official privileges in the church "is universally recognized among us"; and

*Whereas*, said Majority Report favours the continuance of an unauthorized and irregular granting of official privileges to women by individual Pastors and Presiding Elders; and

*Whereas*, the great and growing work of "The Women's Foreign Missionary Society" devolves hortatory and didactic practices, and imposes official duties upon women, and

*Whereas*, these practices, privileges and duties ought to be authoritatively regulated; therefore

*Resolved*, that this General Conference does hereby interpret the Discipline concerning all offices of the laity as applying to women in the same sense and to the same extent as to men.

P[ark] S. Donelson
  [Central Ohio]
E[zra] F. Hasty
  [North Indiana]
John J. Hight
  [Indiana]
Geo. R. Palmer
  [East Maine]
J[ohn] F. Patty
  [Louisiana—Reserve Lay]
Geo. L. Curtiss
  [S.E. Indiana]
J[onas] W. Brown
  [Wisconsin—lay]
C[hristian] H. Afflerbach
  [California]
Isaac Taylor
  [Michigan]
L[ucius] N. Wheeler
  [Wisconsin]

Emory Miller
  [Upper Iowa]
W[illiam] H. Shier
  [Detroit]
Isaac F. King
  [Ohio]
D[aniel] P. Mitchell
  [S. Kansas]
J[ames] L. Clark
  [West Virginia]
T[heodore] L. Flood
  [Erie]
W[illiam] H. Crogman
  [Savannah—lay]
C[harles] E. Alexander
  [Tennessee—lay]
J[ohn] W. MacDonald
  [Iowa]

Anna Oliver returned to her flock in Brooklyn with little hope of ordination and regular appointment in the near future from her church, but with great hope for her future ministry in Brooklyn. In December of 1880 the church published an impressive 12-page church annual outlining an ambitious program. Anna, recalled Anna Howard Shaw, "was not only the minister and the minister's wife, but she started at least a dozen reforms and undertook to carry them all out." [29] She regularly welcomed women in the temperance and suffrage movement into her pulpit, along with co-laborers in the struggle for women's rights in the church, especially the growing contingent of women graduates from Boston University School of Theology, including Anna Howard Shaw (class of 1878) and Katherine A. Lent (class of 1881). [30] A determined pastor and laity vowed to make ends meet in the fashionable suburb of New York City without

> church fairs, festivals, oyster suppers, necktie socials, leap-year entertainment, charades, tableaux, cantatas, wax-works or any other of the numerous projects gotten up by churches in order to meet their expense. [31]

307

Despite gifts from friends from Kansas to Massachusetts, including a live buffalo from the plains of Kansas, finances finally conquered the pastor and remaining members of the Willoughby Avenue Church experiment.[32] In March of 1883 the church was abandoned and Miss Oliver, her health failing, resigned and went to Europe to recover. Dr. James M. Buckley, now wielding the editorial pen of the weighty New York *Christian Advocate*, editorialized on the whole affair. Miss Oliver, he wrote,

> has had the advantage of being regarded as a martyr for the rights of her sex; appeals have been made for money and sympathy; the Church has been advertised in the papers as the Willoughby Avenue *Methodist Episcopal* Church, contrary to the facts in the case and the wishes to some of her supporters; but it could not survive. The attempt to force the ordination of women upon the Church by buying a church, and making its retransfer to our Denomination conditional upon a change without warrant in Scripture, precedent, necessity, or general desire, did not succeed.[33]

William F. Warren, president of Boston University, remained a loyal supporter of his first theological alumna and personally presented a memorial for her at the 1884 General Conference.[34] But with Dr. Buckley chairing the Legislative Committee on the Itinerancy, it was deemed "inexpedient to take any action on the subject proposed."[35]

Little is known about Anna's ministerial career after 1883, except for the fact of her untimely death in Greensboro, Maryland, November 20, 1892.[36] The Rev. Anna Howard Shaw delivered a moving tribute to Anna Oliver before the Convention of the American Suffrage Association in Washington, D.C., in January of 1893.[37] Thus ended round one of the battle for full clergy rights for women in the Methodist Episcopal Church. Other women would take up the cause, for it would take seventy-five more years before such rights were fully granted by her church.

# "For God and Home and Native Land": The W.C.T.U.'s Image of Woman in the Late Nineteenth Century

Carolyn DeSwarte Gifford

The Woman's Christian Temperance Union (W.C.T.U.) was formed in 1874 when American women responded to the battle cry of the Ohio crusaders: Saloons must go! As the "sober second thought" that followed a spontaneous series of praying demonstrations against liquor dealers, the W.C.T.U. eventually mobilized several hundred thousand women under the motto "For God and Home and Native Land."[1] The organization worked for the prohibition of alcoholic beverages by various methods and in many areas of American life, searching for effective ways to persuade people that drinking was evil. Developing strategies and molding a tight, efficient group to implement them, W.C.T.U. leaders projected the image of a woman equal to the tasks before her in the war for the nation's sobriety.

What sort of person was this W.C.T.U. woman? What qualities did she exhibit? What strengths did she possess? What ideals motivated her to enter what promised to be a long, difficult, even dangerous struggle? What beliefs led her to confront powerful adversaries who controlled wealth, were wiser in the ways of the world, and would stop at nothing to gain their ends?

This essay is addressed to these questions. It seeks to describe the W.C.T.U. woman as some of the union's earliest leaders envisioned her and as they embodied, in their own lives, the woman dedicated to the union's cause. It examines speeches and writings of Annie T. Wittenmyer, first president of the

National W.C.T.U. (1874–79); Frances E. Willard, second president (1879–98); Mary B. Woodbridge, recording secretary of the national union (1878–93) and also president of the Ohio union (1879–86); Mary T. Lathrap, president of the Michigan union (1881–95); and Sarepta I. Henry, national union evangelist during the 1880s. Of these, Wittenmyer, Willard, Lathrap, and Henry (until late in her life) were active Methodist Episcopal laywomen, deeply imbued with the culture of American Methodism and well connected to its clergy. These officers labored to bring women into W.C.T.U. membership and to keep them working actively toward its goals. Through their words, a portrait emerges of the kind of woman they sought to recruit. As they wrote and spoke, exhorting their membership, the officers' own dreams for women led the union toward new possibilities. These dreams and possibilities did not develop without conflicts among W.C.T.U. leaders as to woman's nature and proper sphere, however, and this essay will explore these tensions as well.

Much research has been done in the past decade on the image of woman in the nineteenth-century United States, but historians have concentrated on the first half of the century and on the woman's suffrage movement in the later part. They are just beginning to recover the lives, ideals, and accomplishments of women in the second half of the century. During that period, W.C.T.U. members were a significant force in American history.[2] They envisioned a "new American Christian Woman"—a powerful image, admirable, worthy of emulation, and yet in some ways disturbing. Through this vision, American women, especially churchwomen, have been influenced by their foremothers in the W.C.T.U. more than they may realize. It is time to recall that segment of the past and reclaim it.


## RE-VISIONING THE IMAGE OF WOMAN

In the 1860s and early 1870s, most middle-class Protestant women in the United States were encouraged to be devotees of the "cult of true womanhood" that had developed during the first half of the century. They worshiped at the shrine of domesticity, serving their husbands and children. If they left their homes they were often bound for church, where they were preached at by male clergy who expounded the sacred teachings of this cult. Only in extreme situations did a few bold women venture beyond the confines of home and church. The Civil War was such an emergency. It led many women from the relative security of their accustomed sphere into exciting, risky adventures. With risk-taking and movement into the world came authority, power, and the ability to envision broader roles.

Annie Turner Wittenmyer, the first President of the W.C.T.U., worked for the Christian Commission during the war, overseeing two hundred women who provided relief for sick and wounded northern troops. She witnessed the dedication, the self-denial, and the steadfastness with which these women cared for the soldiers' physical and spiritual needs as they bravely accompanied armies onto the battlefields. In the thick of fighting or in the squalid conditions of army field hospitals and prison camps, women ministered to dying men. They comforted and prayed, wrote letters to mothers, wives, and sweethearts, and on occasion accompanied the caskets back home. They were heroines, "mothering" armies. Wittenmyer became convinced through her war experiences that women, by their very nature, were more spiritual, virtuous, faithful, sober, and sympathetic than men.[3] She believed that the image of "true womanhood"—pious, pure, and domestic—was a valid one, rooted in female nature.

It is well known that men who have experienced battlefields and the roving life of armies often find it difficult to settle into civilian rhythms again. After the Civil War, many American women also found themselves changed. They perceived other "emergencies" that were calling them from their homes into the world. In particular, the cities' poor and suffering humanity, swollen through immigration, seemed to need women's ministry as much as the soldiers had. Woman's natural "heart qualities" suited her for peacetime service in the home mission field, an area of church activity then developing in response to the rapid urbanization and industrialization of the late 1860s.[4]

In 1868 Annie Wittenmyer helped to establish the Ladies and Pastors Christian Union to promote women's evangelizing work among the destitute and unchurched of the cities. The program was modeled on the Lutheran deaconess centers in Germany and sought to create a diaconal ministry parallel to the pastoral ministry, which, in most denominations, was open only to men.[5] Both Wittenmyer and her supporters within the hierarchy of the Methodist Episcopal Church realized that while women made up two-thirds of the church membership, they had very little opportunity for officially recognized ministry. The world was beginning to open up in the face of American women's insistence. Could the church afford to lag behind the world in tapping the enormous potential energy of faithful women for its redemptive work? With the blessings of several male Methodist leaders, among them Bishop Matthew Simpson, Annie Wittenmyer issued a challenge to church members: What can woman do for Christ and humanity? What is "woman's work for Jesus?"[6]

The evangelistic work Wittenmyer proposed, with its home visits to the urban poor and personal witness for Christ, unsettled both the women and the men of the Ladies and Pastors Christian Union. She appeared to threaten the bases of the cult of true womanhood in which they believed so firmly. Churchmen seemed quite satisfied with women in the home and not in the world, typified by the sprawling, noisome cities. Most churchwomen also preferred this division of space. The call for home mission workers, in effect, brought into question the commitment and activities of women who thought themselves pillars of the church, living exemplary Christian lives as wives and mothers. Wittenmyer's call exposed the fastidiousness of churchwomen who would rather not come too close to suffering and poverty. She confronted women too much at ease in their faith; she suggested that their Christianity had not demanded that they witness to others of its saving power. Painting a vivid picture of ladies who were martyrs to fashion rather than for Christ, she blasted middle-class women's idleness, frivolity, and vanity. She insisted that the Scriptures warned against such sinfulness and that instead, they called women to works of charity. In the context of a scathing attack against the snares of fashion, Wittenmyer mentioned the drunkenness of upper-middle-class women who spent their afternoons gossiping in drinking places made attractive and inviting for ladies. Other women, she reported, bought patent medicines, readily available in drugstores, and drank at home. "There are many women in the church who love these things more than they would like to confess. The church must ask: Why this increasing drunkenness among women and what can it do to stay this terrible tide?"[7]

Wittenmyer's description of churchwomen's drinking is one of the few passages by W.C.T.U. leaders that deal with this issue. Usually the leaders preferred to emphasize the plight of woman as victim—the gentle, innocent female, crushed by the evil of drinking men, liquor profiteers, and crooked or spineless politicians. This portrayal, in pointing up women's relative powerlessness, contained an element of truth. Theologically, however, it allowed and encouraged women to identify with Christ "the Sinless Victim," rather than with sinners in need of salvation. In her most prophetic critical moments, Annie Wittenmyer did not allow her followers such an easy identification. She called women's actual behavior into question. Even though she usually glorified women as supremely moral and spiritual beings, Wittenmyer occasionally understood that they, like men, were liable to sin and temptation. When she did, she shook woman's pedestal of virtue. She implied that women and men shared in a particularly awesome equality before God the Judge. However, much of W.C.T.U. rhetoric secured woman on her pedestal, insisting that sinful men would be saved by pure women.

Churchwomen did not rush into the home mission field in the early 1870s as they did into the crusade against liquor dealers. Perhaps part of their reluctance to join Wittenmyer in her evangelistic efforts in the cities could be traced to their unwillingness to see themselves as sinful or as lacking deep commitment. This was not what the cult of true womanhood preached about their nature. Women were not yet quite ready to give up their familiar cultic roles as guardians of piety and purity. Both the crusade of 1873–74 and the early W.C.T.U. remained narrowly within the prevailing ethos of American Protestantism which reinforced the conception of women as servants of men, and ultimately their saviors.

312

The idea of woman as savior was closely linked with the idea of woman as mother. Frances Willard, the outstanding educator and Methodist Episcopal laywoman who succeeded Wittenmyer to the W.C.T.U. presidency, made the connection explicit. "Mother-hearted women," she announced, "are called to be the saviours of the race."[8] Not all biological mothers automatically possessed the quality of mother-heartedness, while many childless women were, nonetheless, mother-hearted. Both Susan B. Anthony and Frances Willard, neither of whom ever married, are notable examples. Proponents argued that the quality manifested itself in an all-embracing sacrificial love for humanity, which had the power to raise the human race to a higher level of life. Thus women's capacity for love became a force for social reform. In revealing the mother-heart of God, mother-hearted women were like Christ the Savior, who by his revelation of God's embracing love lifted humanity out of sin.[9]

Individual women already performed this mother-savior function for fathers, sons, and brothers, union leaders noted. How much more effective they could become if they worked together in the saving task of mothering. Perceiving the advantages in cooperation, the W.C.T.U. proclaimed itself "organized mother-love." This slogan originated by Hannah Whitall Smith captured both the style and strategy of the union;[10] Frances Willard identified its basis of organizational strength: "The great power of organization is that it brings [women] out; it translates them from the passive to the active voice; the dear, modest, clinging things didn't think they could do anything and lo and behold, they found they could."[11]

Willard also supplied a theological justification for organized mother-love: "To my mind, organization is the one great thought of the creator; it is the difference between chaos and order; it is the constant occupation of God, and, next to God, the greatest organizer on this earth is the mother."[12]

Imitating God, then, the "mothers" of the W.C.T.U. prepared to bring order out of the chaos they found rampant in American life—specifically, chaos owing to brains disordered by drink. Here was an emergency situation as threatening to American life as the Civil War, less than two decades earlier. And women, mother-hearted and organized, responded. In the mobilization against "King Alcohol," enormous numbers of women moved, as Willard had said, "from the passive to the active voice." Sarepta I. Henry described this move: "It was as if a great peril had suddenly overtaken the loved ones without. . . . And what was left for woman to do? Nothing but to hasten to the scene of danger, dragging her work with her, maybe, but *going*, true to the strongest instinct of the human soul."[13] "Without" was the world outside the home; the "scene of danger" was the saloon.

Sarepta Henry, a young widow with three children, was speaking autobiographically. She had gone outside her home to argue for Prohibition in the main streets of Rockford, Illinois, where saloons were tempting her son. Henry proceeded from Rockford's business district to its churches; from the town's leading attorneys, to meetings of the city council, to its parade grounds, where she organized the youth of Rockford into the first Loyal Temperance Legion. Eventually she went on to the National W.C.T.U., where she quickly became superintendent of the newly created Department of Evangelism. Once Henry began to move she did not stop, and in her determination she was typical of many W.C.T.U. women.[14] They left their homes on rescue missions and found themselves in a vast new territory, socially, culturally, and politically. Although at first they might experience the public world as dangerous, help was available to conquer their fears and doubts. The fast-developing organizational apparatus of the W.C.T.U. stood ready to aid women in their "translation" from "modest, clinging things" who "didn't think they could do anything" to independent women who firmly believed they could do everything.

The W.C.T.U.'s "Do Everything Policy" became the concrete expression of Frances Willard's boldest vision for women. In her most daring dreams, which appeared in her volumes of counsel for young women, Willard challenged her readers to shape themselves according to a new image. Victor Hugo's prediction that "the nineteenth century is woman's century" became her trademark. In 1871, even before the W.C.T.U. had been formed, she declared that the time had come for women to define themselves and to cease accepting definitions from traditional sources. Willard implied that this process of redefinition should not continue to focus on the image of women as oppressed. It should address instead the self-determining question, "What manner of women ought we to be?"[15]

Frances Willard was confident that this crucial question was in fact being answered by W.C.T.U. women as they pursued their multifaceted activities. The re-visioning of woman underlay their stated goal of Prohibition:

> The W.C.T.U. is doing no work more important than that of reconstructing the ideal of womanhood. . . . In less enlightened days, your ideal woman composed the single grand class for which public prejudice set itself to provide. She was to be the wife and mother, and she was carefully enshrined at home. But happily, this is the world's way no longer. . . . Clearly, to all of you, I am declaring a true and blessed gospel . . . concerning honest independence and brave self-help.[16]

With this feminist "gospel," Willard announced the toppling of woman off the pedestal. The object of veneration for the cult of true womanhood would no longer hold power over W.C.T.U. women.

Furthermore, women must reject the cultic doctrine that men and women possessed inherently different natures and virtues which necessitated different spheres of existence. This was false teaching for Willard. It obscured the deeper truth that men and women should share together in all areas of life. By denying men and women common space and shared actions and labeling some traits male and others female, traditional thinking had robbed both sexes of their greatest potential for good, Willard argued.

> Conservatives say: "Let man have his virtues and woman hers." Progressives answer: "Let each add to those already won the virtues of the other. Man has splendid qualities, courage, intellect, hardihood; who would not like to possess all these? What woman would not be greater and nobler if they were hers? And what man would not be grander, happier, more helpful to humanity if he were more patient, gentle, tender, chaste?" [17]

The view Frances Willard ascribed to "Conservatives" was in fact a belief firmly entrenched in the minds of many W.C.T.U. members. There were many things women ought not to do and many places they must not enter. They definitely were not called by God to cast ballots or to run the institutions of government. They were to labor through the church on behalf of suffering people, employing their particularly female spiritual, intuitive, compassionate natures in this appropriate way. Wittenmyer may have shaken woman's pedestal by questioning whether some women really deserved to be placed there; but she did not ask women to redefine true womanhood as Frances Willard did in her most visionary moments.

## THE NEW W.C.T.U. WOMAN:
## FOR GOD AND HOME AND NATIVE LAND

Religious faith was an integral aspect of the W.C.T.U. woman's self-definition; W.C.T.U. members were, above all, *Christian* women. They thought in the language patterns and framework of nineteenth-century Evangelical Protestant Christianity.[18] Frances Willard was particularly skillful in couching her most radical thoughts in familiar language that would not alarm her audience. Thus she suggested redefining womanhood in terms of "calling." Each woman had received unique gifts which should be cultivated so that she could become what God called her to be. As part of this process of becoming she must realize that others also had received unique gifts—women were called to honor other people's talents and to allow them to flourish.[19] Willard's model for self-development was Christ, "the prophet and priest of individuality." Jesus' life was God-defined, not dictated by the world, and he encouraged humans to discover and use their talents.[20]

In order to heed God's call, women should develop the mind, one of God's gifts they had neglected. Men must allow and encourage this intellectual pursuit. Willard rallied both sexes under the banner of "the New Chivalry," which proclaimed the "liberation of ideas" for women as well as for men. Women must be educated to understand the passwords to the vast cultural heritage from which they heretofore had been excluded.[21] Willard called on women to seize and use direct power in the shaping of American life; therefore, they must be given the key to that power—education through the college level. Furthermore, they should prepare themselves to enter all the professions, the business world, and institutions of government. Woman "is learning the art of the greatness and sacredness of power, that there is nothing noble in desiring not to possess it, but that to evolve the utmost mastership of one's self and the elements around one's self that can be, is to the individual, the highest possible attainment."[22] Willard was careful to warn that power must be used for good. But her central message for those so long excluded, and so often taught the virtue of powerlessness, was that women must no longer shrink from acquiring power.

Mary Lathrap and Mary Woodbridge were two powerful women of the sort that Frances Willard admired. They seemed to epitomize the new image of the W.C.T.U. woman. The introductions to both women's biographies laud them as examples of the "fact that in intellect there is no sex." Lathrap and Woodbridge each presided over strong state unions and were deeply involved in political struggles for Prohibition. The campaign for a Prohibition amendment, managed by Mary Woodbridge in Ohio during the early 1880s, was an astounding feat of grass-roots political organizing. Willard revered Mary Lathrap of Michigan as "Our Queen of Prohibition Orators"; she persuasively combined appeals to reason and to conscience, thus blending "male" and "female" characteristics.[23]

The W.C.T.U. drew upon biblical models of power as well as those within their own leadership as sources of courage in their struggles. Recalling Deborah, the Old Testament heroine, Mary Woodbridge declared, "God's power through woman is no less to-day than in Deborah's time, and His command to each 'to do whatsoever her hand finds to do,' and His promise 'to be with her always' is the same."[24] The women of the W.C.T.U. could surely rely upon God's help in their battles just as had Deborah and the people of Israel. Union speakers were particularly fond of citing the prophecy of Joel that the Spirit would be poured out on both women and men, since this passage confirmed the availability of God's power to all who believe, regardless of gender.

Almost everyone, from secular reporters to the participants themselves, interpreted the original Ohio crusade as a spiritual baptism, a new Pentecost which had filled women with power. The W.C.T.U. women eagerly sought to recapture the early crusade enthusiasm, and the events of that time came to be seen as the union's formative experiences. References to the crusade abounded in W.C.T.U. speeches; rituals were established using biblical texts connected with the crusade days; songs and poems were written; crusade "mothers" graced the platforms of national union meetings; pilgrimages were made to the Ohio towns where the crusade began. With refreshing candor, Mary Lathrap chided a Michigan annual convention about all this glorification:

316

> It is quite the fashion to exhort each other to personal consecration, to earnest evangelism and to prayer for the old Crusade fire, but my sisters, God never repeats himself. . . . Divine power was not exhausted in 1873. God's tomorrows are even greater than his yesterdays. He has gifts and revelations for the temperance hosts they have never yet known.[25]

Her message was that the ladies must stop dwelling on the past and get on with present business; at the same time, she emphasized God's continuing support.

Sarepta I. Henry felt God's persistent call to join the temperance fight and she too believed that God's faithful would be empowered. When news of the crusade of 1873 reached Rockford, Henry felt it was her Christian duty to bring the crusade fire to her city, but she was timid and frightened. As she went about her domestic chores and her writing, she tried to ignore God's challenge; however, she found she could not concentrate on her work, and finally one evening, she fell to the living-room floor and wrestled all night with God's question, "Will you obey or will you not? I saw at once, that this matter involved salvation: that the salvation of my soul was in the balance. If I did not obey I would lose my standing with God. That meant disaster, and I had to say, I will."[26]

Other women reported similar experiences. They were most fearful of speaking before groups, especially from the pulpit, and entering saloons, gambling dens, city council chambers, courtrooms, and halls of state government. They were terrified of becoming public spectacles. The public space was man's space, and women were neither comfortable or welcome in it. But armed with God's might, temperance workers could and did invade that forbidden territory. To persuade their members to move into the public sphere, W.C.T.U. leaders entreated, coaxed, commanded, and shamed them, often using all these rhetorical skills in the same speech. But union women testified that, ultimately, it was the power of the Lord that enabled them to act or speak. What they dared not do by themselves, they would do when God was with them. This interpretation of "calling" was somewhat different from Frances Willard's vision of women's call to self-development. But the similarity of the language, coupled with the women's own experiences of God's call, persuaded them to heed their leader's words. Had God not accompanied them into bars, pulpits, courtrooms, legislatures? Perhaps he also was calling them and their daughters into colleges, professions, and the voting booth. Perhaps they could indeed "Do Everything," since God expected this of them. At least they could try.

This combination of comfortable, familiar language and radical reinterpretation characterized the campaign for the Home Protection Ballot. For many W.C.T.U. members, leaders as well as followers, the idea of woman suffrage was extremely difficult to accept. Annie Wittenmyer could not approve it. Sarepta Henry and Frances Willard disputed the issue for years. Mary Woodbridge prayed about it. Yet Willard, the most radical, kept bringing up the possibility. She insisted that home was "the citadel of everything that is good and pure on earth." [27] It was the place where men as well as women were renewed and strengthened. As such it must be protected against all threats to its stability. But women could not guard their homes effectively by shutting themselves up and keeping the influences of the world out. It was impossible to maintain a barrier between the home and the world, as Henry and others had discovered.

Women must lay claim to the power of the world and use it for their own ends. For many, the phrase "home protection" merely implied that women would petition for men's option to vote for Prohibition and would then persuade men to vote the way they wanted them to. However, Frances Willard did not intend such an indirect exercise of power. She demanded the home protection ballot for women so that they could embark on political housekeeping, to "make the world home-like." [28] The moral influence of the home and of womanhood must be spread abroad in the world. This line of argument seemed, on the surface, to reinforce the traditional understanding of woman's domestic role. That role was no longer to be confined within a limited space, however, and men were urged to share in the "woman's task" of world-home maintenance. "Good men" would see the value of a home-like world and would work alongside women for its establishment, Willard maintained. She was also questioning the rigid division between man's and woman's work, however cautiously. The language of home protection was designed to help women to feel somewhat more at ease in a new environment, and with W.C.T.U. women, it succeeded. If working in the political arena involved housekeeping, surely they knew how to do that.

The term "gospel politics" is still another instance of juxtaposing familiar, reassuring language with a new demand upon women. Mary Lathrap's phrase originally was intended to indicate that the usual gospel methods of prayer, Bible reading, hymn-sing meetings, and pledges were no longer effective in promoting Prohibition and that it was time to take the fight into the political realm.[29] But gospel politics soon came to mean that the union should widen its commitments to include study and action on a vast array of issues besides Prohibition, if it wished to assume a responsible role in national life. After taking a hard look at the United States, the W.C.T.U. leadership became convinced that the country was in even more serious trouble than they originally had perceived. Indeed it was in imminent danger of losing its "national soul" and thus stood sorely in need of redemption. The W.C.T.U. leaders called for rededication to what they believed to be the country's original ideals.

Since the leadership was overwhelmingly white Anglo-Saxon Protestant, it interpreted the nation's ideals from that framework. Union leaders were alarmed by what they felt to be the undermining of such treasured values as Sabbath observance and Bible reading in public schools. They were uneasy about labor disputes that threatened to become violent. The cities' growth and complex problems frightened them, particularly since many of them came from rural and small-town backgrounds. The rising tide of immigration from Catholic areas of Europe also filled them with anxiety. They were convinced that the immigrants valued neither the republican system of government or the public education system that transmitted allegiance to America's governmental forms. Their response to all these issues was to attempt, through gospel politics, to "place the government upon Christ's shoulders"—to "christianize" the nation. Following the slogan that "law and moral suasion go hand in hand" in such efforts, they saw praying and voting as complementary duties of the American woman.[30] This slogan suggested that there should be no division of labor by sexes—no longer would only women pray and only men vote. All who were concerned about the nation's unredeemed spiritual condition were to join together in every aspect of gospel politics.

Some union leaders and members interpreted the redemptive task narrowly in terms of working toward legislation for Sabbath laws and Bible-reading in public schools, cracking down on labor agitators, and converting Catholics to "Christianity" and Prohibition. For Frances Willard, however, the vision of national redemption was much broader in scope. It entailed radical solutions to national problems, but such visions could inspire only those women who were becoming accustomed to thinking and acting beyond the limited sphere of the home.

Through its national and state conventions and its weekly paper *The Union Signal*, the W.C.T.U. provided an "adult education" program in which the membership could participate in discussing issues of national and global importance. The union became a training ground for widening women's horizons. A conscientious W.C.T.U. member was obligated to answer the call to intellectual self-development that Willard had issued. By the early 1890s she was able to state, "I do not know a White Ribbon woman who is not a Prohibitionist, a woman suffragist, a purity worker, and an earnest sympathizer with the Labor movement."[31] This was hyperbole, but it does suggest that from 1880 to 1895, many W.C.T.U. women participated vicariously, yet enthusiastically, as their exceptional president grappled with some of the most thought-provoking questions of the day. In her public addresses, pamphlets, books, and articles, Willard alerted her audiences to an ever-widening range of issues, many raised by other reform groups, political parties, and labor organizations of the period. And through their beloved president, the W.C.T.U. membership also pondered them.

In her vision of the self-defined independent woman, Frances Willard also advocated a fundamental equality between men and women in their most intimate relationships; this would be the foundation of the equality of the sexes in all areas of life. Willard's phrase "The White Life for Two" referred to a whole complex of sexual equality issues, ranging from marriage to the elimination of prostitution. She was convinced that the institution of marriage was degraded by the laws, customs, and structures that made women dependent upon men; as a result, men became potential tyrants and women lost their self-esteem. Ideally, marriage would be a partnership. For genuine equality, it would be necessary for women to enter marriage from a vantage point of independence. If a woman had a way to support herself, she would not rush into marriage, nor could she so easily be enticed into prostitution.

Once married, the wife should retain the right to her own body. Most husbands and the legal system of the time still understood wives as *femmes couvertes*. The expectations implied by that phrase and the laws giving substance to those expectations must be removed, Willard asserted. In an egalitarian marriage, she declared:

> The wife will undoubtedly have custody of herself and . . . she will determine the frequency of the investiture of life with form. My library groans with accumulations of books written by men to teach women the immeasurable inequity of arrested development in the genesis of a new life, but not one of these volumes contains the remotest suggestion that this responsibility should be equally divided between husband and wife. The untold horrors of this injustice dwarf all others out of sight, and the most hopeless feature of it is the utter unconsciousness with which it is perpetrated.[32]

Using the argument that woman should have custody over herself to justify her work through the W.C.T.U., Frances Willard set out to rescue "white slaves" and also to research more deeply the reasons women became prostitutes. Out of these investigations arose union efforts to establish industrial training schools for women, and attempts to provide congenial, safe living arrangements for young working women in the cities.

During the first quarter-century of its existence, the W.C.T.U.'s "important work of reconstructing the ideal of womanhood" went on continually. The reports of departmental superintendents in the minutes of annual meetings and in *The Union Signal* reflect the many different paths union women chose in their "reconstruction" work under the Do Everything Policy. They also reveal that alternative images of the "ideal woman" coexisted in the organization. Women who still felt most comfortable with the earlier image of true womanhood were represented, as well as those who championed the image of the independent, self-defined woman. Probably most W.C.T.U. members held views somewhere between those two poles.

At times, the management of the organization appeared to be somewhat like a large and complicated juggling act, as Frances Willard and the other leaders tossed and twirled a variety of roles and activities for women. If the roles were unfamiliar or controversial, they were sometimes put to one side. At other times, no juggling was even attempted. But the roles inevitably would be tossed up again and eventually some union women would hold onto them throughout their lives. These are the women who should be rediscovered and reclaimed—women who were inspired by the new W.C.T.U. vision of womanhood and who continued to work out their inspiration in concrete forms, well into the twentieth century. The names and reports of these second- and third-generation members are waiting on the shelves of the W.C.T.U. archives at Evanston.

In the 1890s, in the second decade of her presidency, Frances Willard began to sketch out a "new and magnificent profession for women." She strongly urged independent young women of the future to enter philanthropic work, since it was appropriate for Christians and epitomized the ideals of the W.C.T.U. Philanthropy would seem to be traditional "woman's work," but there were novel elements in Willard's definition. Josephine Shaw Lowell of the Charity Organization Society of the City of New York, and others, were developing the concept of "scientific social work." They attempted to expose the real causes of poverty and were calling for systemic changes to fight the conditions and the collusion of interests that kept people poor. Willard predicted that the new woman would enter this new philanthropic profession. "After women have conquered a firm foothold in the trades and professions, [they] will gradually withdraw from mechanized work and devote themselves to the noblest vocations that life affords—namely motherhood, reform work, and philanthropy."[33]

What was novel about this? Was this not exactly what women had been doing? The new notion was that women should choose their work. Formerly, they always had envisioned and pursued these tasks thought of as the "proper roles" for women—those that fit smoothly into the earlier nineteenth-century image of true womanhood. In the future, if women were to dedicate themselves to reform work, or to philanthropy, or to motherhood, they would elect that activity out of all the possibilities opening before them. They would choose their work, knowing that they could enter any profession, confront any task. For the new W.C.T.U. woman, the motto "For God and Home and Native Land" would imply a call answered by informed, independent women, eager to serve their God and their country with every gift they possessed.

# "A New Impulse": Progress in Lay Leadership and Service by Women of the United Brethren in Christ and the Evangelical Association, 1870–1910

Donald K. Gorrell

The emergence of laywomen in leadership levels and visible service in two denominations, the United Brethren in Christ and the Evangelical Association, occurred during the four decades after 1870. By 1910, the basic roles of leadership and service for laywomen had been determined and remained fixed until these two rather dissimilar churches of German background united in 1946.

It is common today to study the Evangelical United Brethren heritage as one tradition in The United Methodist Church. As this study will reveal, however, the Evangelical and the United Brethren branches were far from uniform. While common motivating stimuli can be identified, the responses in each denomination differed markedly and produced divergent results. Consequently, much of this essay will constitute a study in contrasts. It is noteworthy also that for both the Evangelical Association and the United Brethren in Christ, the period in which women sought a larger role in the work and ministry of the church was influenced by internal schismatic difficulties, as well as by general Protestant emphases on missions and lay leadership.

Given these complexities, the scope of lay leadership studied here has been narrowed to exclude consideration of women as deaconesses and lay preachers.

Both these vocations in fact required a full-time commitment to a specialized ministry that was not typical of most laity at the time. Instead, attention has been confined to two areas where women acquired leadership, power, and influence through more typical lay functions—namely, in women's missionary associations and as lay representatives to annual and General conferences, the decision-making levels of both churches beyond the local congregation.

One obvious similarity in the two traditions is the motivation that inspired their women. In both heritages, the terms *a new impulse* or *a new impetus* appeared when the leaders referred to the origins of the women's missionary movement. For instance, recounting the history of the first decade of the United Brethren Woman's Missionary Association, the initial issue of the organization's periodical, *Woman's Evangel*, said in 1882, "Ten short years ago a woman's missionary association was a thing unheard of in our church. . . . About that time a strange awakening occurred, a new impulse was aroused among us." [1] In 1884, Mrs. W. H. Hammer remarked similarly to a convention of Evangelical women, "When our first missionaries to Japan left home and kindred to enter upon this arduous work, this heart-felt desire [to organize for missions] received a new impulse, and Mrs. Dr. Krecker and Miss Hudson carried with them the awakened sympathies of the workers at home." [2] This "new impulse" was the women's keen recognition of the needs for foreign missions—in Japan for the Evangelicals; in West Africa for the United Brethren.

A second similarity is evident in the laywomen's response to this new stimulus: Both denominations soon formed effective all-female organizations. After Lizzie Hoffman, a United Brethren schoolteacher in Dayton, Ohio, had struggled with her soul about going to Africa as a missionary, she found peace finally in the conviction that God would rather that she organize women to support missions, and she was responsible for initiating the United Brethren work in 1872. [3] When Evangelicals such as Emma Yost in Cleveland in 1878 and Minerva Strawman in Lindsey, Ohio, two years later, felt impelled to assist missionaries, they thought immediately of organizing women. [4]

Since women in those days had no channels for such activity, they sought the aid of churchmen involved with denominational mission boards. The support of men, particularly those on the boards, differed greatly in the two churches. Lizzie Hoffman shared her conviction of the need to organize women with John Kemp, a founder and longtime member of the Home, Frontier, and Foreign Missionary Society of the United Brethren in Christ. Kemp counseled her, and together they called a meeting of interested women and ministers in Dayton, Ohio, on May 9, 1872. Those who attended that meeting voted to organize the Woman's Missionary Association of the Miami Conference. When the men of that annual conference met later that year, they adopted the following resolution: "*Resolved*, That we are highly pleased with the interest taken by a number of sisters in the cause of missions in our conference, and gratified to learn of the organization of a Woman's Missionary Society in our midst, and that we will heartily second the efforts of this society in their noble work."[5]

In May 1873, the quadrennial General Conference of the United Brethren heard endorsements of the Woman's Missionary Association in the bishop's address and in the missionary secretary's report, and the delegates commended the "zeal and enterprise" of the women and urged "that all the 'women's missionary associations' be made auxiliary to the branch missionary societies of the conference within whose bounds they are organized."[6]

In contrast, when Emma Yost and friends petitioned the Board of Missions of the Evangelical Association in 1878, they were refused permission to organize.[7] Two years later Minerva Strawman revived the idea, but with a modified form and emphasis. "The propriety of organizing an independent Woman's Missionary Society is questionable," she admitted, "but we find no reason whatever why Woman's Missionary Auxiliaries should not be formed."[8] Men finally recognized the value of having women raise money for missions, but their enabling action stipulated that women's groups could exist only on the local level and must be "under the supervision of the preacher."[9] When the General Conference of the Evangelical Association in 1883 authorized a national Woman's Missionary Society, the wife of one of the delegates explained to the woman who led the campaign for the women's organization: "Mr. Wiest did his utmost to get the petition before the Conference . . . but had much trouble with the German element of the committee . . . as they could not endure the idea of women *usurping so much authority*."[10] The men's attitude is characteristic of the Evangelical tradition in this study.

Another contrast between the Evangelicals and the United Brethren was the difference in organization. Initially, Evangelical women were allowed to organize only at the local level, while United Brethren women first created missionary associations in the annual conferences. This distinction faded in importance, however, as it became clear in both denominations that churchwide organizations were needed. To achieve that goal, Evangelical women followed a predictable pattern of petitioning the Board of Missions for "permission to organize a Woman's Board of Missions" that would be "auxiliary to the Parent Society" and under its supervision and authority.[11] Even that docile relationship was granted begrudgingly, with the requirement that the women submit their proceedings to the Board of Missions annually "for examination and approval."[12]

In a similar process, some United Brethren women decided, in consultation with male leaders of their board, that a national woman's organization was desirable; they prepared a proposed constitution indicating that their society would be an auxiliary to existing missionary boards. A number of women regarded themselves as "co-workers and co-laborers in the great mission field" and saw no need for "a separate and independent existence." In the thinking of the men, women were needed to carry the gospel to women and children in mission areas and to educate women and children in local churches in order to raise money for such ministry.[13] However, in contrast to their Evangelical sisters, when the United Brethren women met in October 1875, they decided that it was necessary to be related only to the General Conference and that they could be otherwise independent in structure and function. Thus on their own initiative, United Brethren women amended their constitution and voted to create a churchwide Woman's Missionary Association.[14] One of the more militant women wrote in defense of this action, "We do not propose to wait for any 'Board' or for any authority, save that of General Conference. If God shall give us the missionaries and the means, we shall find the field, whether the original Board has found it before or not."[15] When the association sent two women to report to General Conference in 1877, those representatives simply requested recognition of an existing group which had already sent its first missionary to Africa. Upon recommendation of its Committee on Missions, this General Conference recognized the Woman's Missionary Association as an official church agency, approved its constitution, and confirmed its officers.[16] Such independence in organization typified the United Brethren Woman's Missionary Association.

This contrast in organization was the consequence of a difference in style of operation. From the outset, Evangelical women were affected by their dependent and auxiliary relationship to the male Board of Missions. Although the 1883 General Conference had approved their society, Evangelical women were forced to wait a year to begin to function, because the board, which needed to approve the constitution and officers of the woman's society, did not meet officially until October 1884. To save time and facilitate plans, the women met at the same time as the board and twice adjourned their sessions to confer with that body. At last, the board ratified the constitution of the Woman's Missionary Society, and the women could finally elect their officers and begin to function.[17] When they wanted to publish a periodical and when they wanted to support a "special field" of work, it was necessary for them to petition the board, which repeatedly rejected their requests. Both finally were approved in 1899, but the woman's society had first requested them fourteen years earlier, in 1885![18] In fairness, it must be recognized that the women's activities were impeded by a denominational division; nevertheless, support for women's missionary endeavors developed slowly among Evangelicals.

By comparison, United Brethren women enjoyed considerable autonomy and were able to do as much mission work as they could afford to support. When they felt the need of a periodical, for example, they solicited subscriptions; when they had secured the necessary 1,000, they began publication of their own monthly, the *Woman's Evangel*, in January 1882.[19] With that degree of independence, the achievements of the United Brethren Woman's Missionary Association were remarkable. At the 1877 General Conference, it was reported that the association had 3 conference branches, 18 local societies, and annual receipts of $325. Thirty-two years later, the association informed the General Conference that they had more than 20,000 members and that during the past quadrennium they had raised $175,000 to support 42 missionaries in the foreign field, in addition to 60 native workers. In their missions in Africa, China, and the Philippines, United Brethren women had established churches, Sunday schools, schools, orphanages, and dispensaries with a property valuation of $98,000. As the men of the Foreign Missionary Society acknowledged, the women were responsible by that time for half the denomination's overseas mission program.[20]

These achievements gave United Brethren women considerable power. When the church reorganized its entire plan for missions, in 1909, the Woman's Missionary Association was asked to combine its resources with the other mission boards; in return, the women would constitute one-third of the membership of the boards and their executive committees.[21] Mrs. L. R. Harford, president of the association, interpreted the meaning of the proposal to the General Conference.

> The plan proposed of joint control is ideal. Men and women, each with their natural characteristics, join in the great work of bringing this lost world to Christ. We firmly believe that this is a great forward movement, and, if it would not seem like egotism, I would say, brethren, that within the last quadrennium you have almost caught up with us, and we are now ready to join with you in the forward work.[22]

Explaining the significance of the action in the *Woman's Evangel*, Mrs. Harford affirmed, "Just as we believe we were divinely called to begin work thirty-four years ago, so we believe we have been led to take the step now in harmony with the spirit of the times." Noting that United Brethren women had received all they had requested and had been elected to the boards, she went on to observe:

> By this arrangement we not only have a voice in the administration of our own funds, but in all the funds of the Church; not only in the appointment of missionaries in the three fields we have in the past, but in the five foreign fields of the Church and in all the work in home missions. We not only have an interest in property in the three mission fields where we invested, but in all the property in all fields.[23]

Furthermore, women were given more opportunity to work with young women and with the Junior Societies of Christian Endeavor. They were to continue to publish the *Evangel* and were convinced that "this action does not change our form of organization in the least."[24]

Through this major reorganization and their larger involvement in the management of the church, the Woman's Missionary Association secured a new status and power for women, described by one officer as "epoch-making."[25] That accomplishment marks a fitting place to end the study of women's rise to leadership and power in the missionary work of the United Brethren in Christ.

By the same year, 1909, the Woman's Missionary Society among the Evangelicals also achieved institutional acceptance, although accompanied by far less power and influence. While consistent with earlier patterns in the denomination, the limited status of women was partially the result of the harrowing effects of schism in the Evangelical Association. Whereas the events that had divided the United Brethren Church in 1889 had had little effect upon its women's missionary activities, the contentions among the Evangelicals directly affected the development of their Woman's society. The impact of denominational division thus has provided another contrast in women's rise to power and leadership in the two churches.[26]

As the 1891 Evangelical General Conference approached, contending factions pushed issues to the breaking point, and the executive committee of the Woman's Missionary Society "saw fit to postpone their annual meeting until after the session" of that deliberative body. Angered by the delay, the Board of Missions condemned the action as a violation of the society's constitution, declared its officers displaced, and called for a reorganization meeting in February 1892. The editor of the denominational weekly of the majority party wrote:

> The circumstance which necessitates this reorganization, is to be deplored, but it is only one of the many sad results of the rebellion in our church. The Woman's Missionary Society has been peculiarly unfortunate in having been planned and manipulated for several years largely in the rebel camp. The male rebel leaders were back of certain women who carried out their schemes as far as possible. Loyal officers were frozen out of the general organization; general officers of the society were sympathizers with the seceders.[27]

As a result, the Evangelical Woman's Missionary Society was split in two and continued separately in each branch of the divided church.

Continuity of leadership in the society went with the schismatic group, which called itself the United Evangelical Church when it organized formally in 1894. During the interim from 1891 to 1894, the woman's organization achieved little and became disheartened. When they met in September 1895, the president poignantly noted, "As an organization we are twelve years old, but as the Woman's Missionary Society of the United Evangelical Church we are holding our first meeting." In the new denominational structure, she reported, women would have a larger influence, with representatives on the quarterly conference of each congregation and on the general Board of Missions. Moreover, they would at last be able to publish their own periodical, *Missionary Tidings*, and to support two women in a foreign mission soon to be established.[28]

The initial elation of the United Evangelical women diminished when they discovered that the constitution they had drafted in 1895 had been drastically modified by the Board of Missions, giving the society less representation than promised. Despite protests by the women, Bishop Rudolph Dubs explained to the 1898 General Conference that the constitutional changes had been necessary in order to avoid "conflicts of authority" and "future friction." The changes also did away with the office of corresponding secretary, which functionally deprived the society of its active leadership and thereby weakened its program.[29] At the 1910 General Conference, the men praised the women for their ability to provide missionary funds, for their efficiency in missionary education, and for their insistence on establishing foreign mission work, which had resulted in the denomination's mission in China.[30] In short, the fact that it was a helpful auxiliary to the Board of Missions was seen as the primary accomplishment of the woman's society in the United Evangelical Church.

It will be remembered that in the mainstream Evangelical Association, the Woman's Missionary Society had been ordered to reorganize itself in the wake of the division of the denomination. At the society's reorganization convention in Cleveland, Ohio, in 1892, new officers were elected. The existing constitution was readopted, but a committee was appointed to revise the document and report to the annual meeting in September. At that meeting, the corresponding secretary of the mission board advised the delegates that they should "gather up the scattered portions of the Woman's Missionary Society of our Church and re-unite them under efficient, faithful management." The women sought to do this by changing the constitution to provide for quadrennial, rather than annual, meetings of the whole society, with only the executive committee meeting annually. They also committed themselves to helping liquidate the mission board's large debt.[31]

Within two years the women were praised for successfully overcoming the difficulties caused by reorganization and for efficiently collecting funds to alleviate the financial crisis.[32] Despite such adulation, however, a request by the society to be given sole use of the *Missionary Messenger* was denied by the Evangelical Association's General Conference and their request that a "special field" be designated for their financial endeavors also was rejected as "superfluous" and "impracticable." Given the mission board's directive that the officers of the woman's society should refer all "important measures and methods" to the board's executive committee for "its investigation and approval," the leaders of the women could not fail to see their limited status in the eyes of the men who governed the Evangelical Association.[33]

At the end of the next quadrennium, however, women's work was more positively evaluated. In 1898 the Evangelical Board of Missions noted that the women were "in prosperous condition" in both money and members, and upon its recommendation, the 1899 General Conference amended the board's constitution to enable a woman representative to become a member. Evangelical women were pleased, too, that this General Conference approved two long desired requests: that the monthly *Missionary Messenger* be designated the "organ of the Woman's Missionary Society," with the society empowered to select its own editor, and that the society be permitted to maintain two of its own missionaries in Japan.[34]

As the Woman's Missionary Society of the Evangelical Association entered the twentieth century, its work had achieved stability. At last it was accorded recognition and assigned expanded responsibilities. Institutional acceptance was evident when the categories "W.M.S. Auxiliaries" and "W.M.S. Members" were officially added to the statistical reports of the church in 1903. An editorial in the *Evangelical Messenger* in September of that year indicated the organization's point of arrival: "The Woman's Missionary Society of our Church had a small and troubled beginning, and a slow growth; it had some opposition and more distrust and disinterest to encounter. But it has clearly won the day. It has shown its fitness to survive and take its place in the family of the church." [35] The direction and pattern of the organization as an auxiliary of the Board of Missions was clearly fixed in the first decade of this century and remained so until its eventual reunion with the United Evangelicals in 1922. There is no doubt that Evangelical women exercised less power and influence in missionary work than did their counterparts in the United Brethren Church.

Lay representation was a second area in which women came to exercise leadership. This area, too, affords a study in contrasts between the two traditions, for the United Brethren in Christ enabled women to be seated as lay delegates in both annual and General conferences in the period from 1870 to 1910 while at no time were women in either branch of the Evangelical tradition accorded that right.

Lay representation was requested by United Brethren men as early as 1861, but that was impossible without amendment of the constitution; this in itself was an issue so controversial that a permanent division occurred in the church in 1889. It was decided in 1877 that while the constitution forbade lay representation at General Conferences, it did not specifically deny it at annual conferences, and the following year, some annual conferences admitted laity to membership for the first time. By 1883 in the Miami Conference, and by 1888 in the East Ohio Conference, women were elected as lay delegates.[36] Liberal legislation enacted under the revised constitution confirmed by the General Conference of 1889 gave United Brethren women even more status and power. After the schismatic minority withdrew, new enactments provided that women could be elected as lay delegates at all levels of the church and that they could be ordained as clergy, as well.[37] Of the fifty-two lay delegates seated for the first time at the 1893 General Conference, two were women, and their presence was resoundingly acknowledged by the bishops.

> Since the world began, until now, it is not probable that in an ecclesiastical body of such functions and proportions as belong to this General Conference have women been recognized on an equality with their brethren. Several conferences have chosen to send as delegates esteemed women from among them. These Christian women are here to-day accorded this highest representative trust in the Church, and are welcomed to sit with us in the highest council of the denomination.[38]

From this historic beginning, women delegates were elected to every succeeding General Conference of the United Brethren Church. Initially the numbers were small—six in 1897 and two in 1901—but their ranks swelled after 1905, when lay people were allowed to be seated in equal numbers with ministers; there were twenty-four women delegates in 1905 and twenty-two in 1909. While laywomen theoretically were granted full powers and rights, it is obvious in the records of United Brethren General Conferences through 1909 that female delegates seldom spoke and never chaired a committee. When the bishops assigned delegates to standing committees, they apparently were influenced by certain images of women's role, for the first women to be assigned were both placed on the Missionary Interests committee.[39] This at least testified to women's influence in that area. In 1897 women continued to serve on Missionary Interests but also were placed on committees on Sabbath Schools and Young People's Christian Union, and in 1901 a woman was assigned to the Educational Institutions committee.[40] When the number of lay delegates to General Conferences was increased in 1905, the twenty-four women present were assigned to thirteen of the twenty-eight committees; consequently, their influence was greatly expanded.[41]

Thus, in lay representation as well as in missionary activities, women shared at least moderately in the full leadership of the United Brethren Church. While it is doubtful that they exercised the power and influence suggested by the editorial "Woman's Rightful Place," in a 1901 issue of *Religious Telescope*, it is clear that by 1910, women's place in that church was considerably more elevated and powerful than in the Evangelical branches.[42]

By contrast, lay delegation itself, apart from the question of gender, was opposed and delayed in the Evangelical Association. Lay representation became a major issue in the schism that split this denomination between 1891 and 1894, though there were both rebel and loyalist conventions of laymen. From the beginning, lay representation was advocated by the minority group which formed the United Evangelical Church. However, an examination of its lists of lay delegates reveals that women were not represented. In the more conservative Evangelical Association, the issue of lay delegation was delayed into the twentieth century, with the first layman being seated at the 1907 General Conference. No women were seated then, or at any succeeding conference, until union with the United Brethren was imminent in the 1940s. Thus, in the

Evangelical tradition, in sharp distinction to the United Brethren, women never had an opportunity to exercise power as lay representatives.

Women in both the Evangelical Association and the United Brethren in Christ felt similar impulses to organize, to assume leadership, and to engage in more visible and recognized service during the years from 1870 to 1910. But the historical evidence contrasts in the implementation of these impulses. The United Brethren were much more appreciative of women's status and role, and much earlier than the Evangelicals; consequently, women were able to exercise increasingly greater power, influence, and leadership in the ranks of that denomination. Finally, this study underscores the fallacy of assuming too easily that the two churches that today comprise the Evangelical United Brethren tradition within The United Methodist Church were alike in origins, practices, and attitudes. In the case of the status and roles of laywomen, the work that began as a study of a single heritage has necessarily developed into an essay tracing women's evolution in two distinct traditions in the four decades from 1870 to 1910.

## CHAPTER 22

# Creating a Sphere for Women: The Methodist Episcopal Church, 1869–1906

Rosemary Skinner Keller

The "woman issue," in a multiplicity of forms, was the most controversial question confronting the General Conferences of the Methodist Episcopal Church from 1869 until shortly after the turn of the century. The action taken by 399 male delegates (248 ordained ministers and 151 laymen) who met in Pike's Opera House, Cincinnati, for the 1880 convention, was symbolic of a trend which was to continue for almost forty years. The report of relevant legislation stated simply:

> An episcopal ruling that the Discipline provides neither for the ordaining nor licensing of women as local preachers was approved; but it was ordered that the masculine pronouns "he," "his," and "him," wherever they occur in the Discipline, shall not be construed as excluding women from the office of Sunday-school superintendent, class leader, or steward.[1]

The decision of that 1880 conference defined, in large measure, the status and role of women in the heritage of The United Methodist Church until the mid-twentieth century. By denying ordination to women and by revoking their rights to local preachers' licenses, the church prohibited them from entering fields of leadership and service in which they could work as colleagues with men and share governing power and clerical functions. However, by sanctioning the service of women as Sunday school superintendents and volunteer workers, the conference determined that females would have an essential, though subordinate role, as "helpers" of men in positions of authority. Finally the delegates tangled, for the first time, with the "language" issue as it related to women in the church. Ironically, because the church could not function as a voluntary organization unless women assumed a variety of service tasks, it disregarded the significance of the male gender when the daily needs of the institution were at stake—when need be, *he, his,* and *him* could apply to women as well as to men.

In the late nineteenth century, another development equally consequential in determining the pattern of female leadership within United Methodist tradition was taking place. The major female service organizations of the Methodist Episcopal denomination—the Woman's Foreign Missionary Society and the Woman's Home Missionary Society—were being formed and given official sanction and support by the same General Conferences which denied women the right to preach, be ordained, or serve as lay delegates in the church's governing councils. These organizations, the first to send unmarried women missionaries throughout the world and deaconesses into the inner-city slums of burgeoning American cities, were forerunners of the present United Methodist Women and its parallel organizations in other denominations.[2]

By the turn of the century, the leadership and the service of women in the Methodist Episcopal Church were simultaneously being constricted and expanded. The legacy from these conflicting trends is complex. Women's activities were channeled into a sphere separate from men's which precluded the possibility that females could share decision-making authority and clerical rights. However, it also resulted in the development of powerful women's organizations, originally designed to be autonomous and to draw the women of the church together in bonds of sisterhood, but which have trained women for broadening positions of leadership both within and outside the church and have enabled the church to function as a voluntary organization.

This heritage is not limited to the United Methodist tradition. Restriction of women's function to a separate sphere determined the pattern of women's leadership and participation in all mainline Protestant traditions of America—Episcopal, Presbyterian, Baptist, Lutheran, and United Church of Christ denominations.

One essential approach in recovering the history of women is to discover and interpret clearly defined movements for freedom and equality—suffrage, education, property, employment, and other concerns within secular society, as well as ordination and laity rights in the church. A second focus is equally essential: to discover the variety of functions females have performed and to analyze the subtle changes in the constriction and expansion of roles that have affected the evolution of women's position in society today.

Using the Methodist Episcopal Church, this paper will combine these two approaches in a study to analyze the patterns of women's leadership in the church. It will focus on two movements which occurred simultaneously, and which resulted in the creation of a sphere for women in the church: the denial to women of the opportunity to lead and work with men on a basis of collegiality, and the founding of the first national women's organization of the denomination, the Woman's Foreign Missionary Society (W.F.M.S.). The W.F.M.S. was an accommodation to the system, the only way possible for women to work within the denomination and at the same time develop their vision and use their talents on behalf of the church. The underlying question for the historian is whether the significance of a separate sphere for women resulted in the containment and isolation of women's activity, or whether its more important aim and consequence was to expand their function and even to liberate them from the constrictions of the church in the late nineteenth century.

A sphere for women in the church resulted both from the denial of equal clergy and lay rights and from the initiative which women took to create their own organizations and to maintain authority in their carefully carved-out domain. Though the struggle for women's rights in the church in the mid-twentieth century has centered on ordination, which was gained in the United Methodist tradition only in 1956, that was not the center of controversy in the late nineteenth century. A sprinkling of women were local preachers in the Methodist Episcopal Church after the highly effective evangelist, Margaret Van Cott, had gained that right in 1869. No woman threatened male domination of clergy rights until the late 1870s, however, when Anna Howard Shaw and Anna Oliver sought to be ordained by the New England Annual Conference, although support for preaching and clerical roles for women was not great enough to arouse much opposition to the strong will of the male majority of the 1880 General Conference.

There was a recurring bone of contention, however. By the 1880s, vigorous support had developed for voting rights for laywomen at the General Conference, which met every four years, and at annual conferences, which covered regional or state areas. The issue involved the election of females as lay delegates to these governing conventions of the denomination. Laity in the Methodist Episcopal Church were usually referred to as lay*men*. The issue took visible and personal form when four duly elected female delegates from the Rock River (Illinois), Nebraska, Minnesota, and Kansas conferences sought to claim seats at the 1888 Convention. The Rock River representative was Frances E. Willard, founder of the Woman's Christian Temperance Union and an ardent advocate of women's suffrage. Seventeen other women had been elected as reserve delegates by their respective conferences.[3]

The minutes stated that "much time was given to the discussion of the 'woman question'." Debate was intense, contention being so strong that the delegates referred the decision to the membership of the entire church. The tally of votes reported at the next quadrennial conference in 1892 indicated that 235,668 members of individual churches voted for the eligibility of women, and 163,843 against, while 5,634 ministers were in favor of women delegates, and 4,717 against. Though a plurality of the membership and ministers affirmed the change the necessary three-fourths majority had not been attained. A ruling by the Committee on Judiciary was designed to clarify the meaning of the vote: "The intent of the lawmakers in using the words 'lay delegates,' 'laymen,' and 'members of the Church in full connection,' in paragraphs 55 to 63 inclusive, in the Discipline, was not to apply them to both sexes, but to men only." [4]

The dissension was not a quibble over words, however, but a question of possession of governing authority and decision-making power in this major Protestant denomination. Once again, the determination was left to the membership and ministers of the entire church. When four more women were elected delegates to the 1896 conference, one male lay representative, deeply fearful of change, alleged that "to seat the claimants would tend to destroy all respect for the constitution of the Church." [5] Conference members, wearied of the challenge, finally agreed that they could not agree and passed a "compromise" plan—that "no formal decision of the question of eligibility be made at this time." Lewis Curts, editor of the conference journal, made a significant commentary on the import of the 1896 decision: "Compromises may sometimes be useful as peacemakers, but more often they end in making more confusion." [6] This lack of clarity and indecisiveness characterized the attitude of the conference until 1906, when the so-called language issue was resolved and women became recognized officially as lay people in the Methodist Episcopal Church.

Failure to grant them lay and clergy rights could have resulted in greater subordination of women and their relegation to increasingly menial tasks, always directed by men. At the same time the General Conferences were constricting their role, however, many women of prominence and capability recognized that opportunities must be developed for leadership and service in the church. They consciously created a sphere for their sex by founding organizations of service to the church and by maintaining their authority within those domains. The Woman's Foreign Missionary Society of the Methodist Episcopal Church was formed in 1869, the year Margaret Van Cott received the denomination's first local preachers' license granted to a woman. Before the society was one year old, it had sent two missionaries to India: Isabella Thoburn, the first unmarried woman missionary of the Methodist Episcopal Church, and Clara Swain, also a single woman and the first female medical missionary to the Orient from the United States. [7] During the next year, the society sent female workers to China and began to develop a broadly based world missionary program.

In 1880, a complementary organization, the Woman's Home Missionary Society, was formed to concentrate on mission priorities within the United States. Five years later, Lucy Rider Meyer founded the Chicago Training School for women missionaries and almost immediately originated the deaconess order, one of the most significant forms of home missionary work in the denomination's history.[8] As prior conferences had sanctioned the Woman's Foreign and Home Missionary societies, so the General Conference of 1888 commended the training school.

A close look at the formation and early development of the Woman's Foreign Missionary Society suggests the far-reaching vision of early missionary-society leaders and missionaries, and points to the significance of a separate sphere in expanding women's role in the church. Founded in March, 1869, by six women who gathered on a stormy day at Tremont Street Church in Boston, three months later the W.F.M.S. began to edit its monthly publication, *The Heathen Woman's Friend*. Directed to all women in the denomination, it began as an eight-page paper, and three years later had doubled in size. The lead article of the first issue stated the purpose of the society concisely and persuasively: "An earnest desire to develop among the ladies of our Church greater interest and activity in our Missions, together with the firm conviction that the pressing needs of our Foreign Missions demand our immediate attention." The founders admitted forthrightly, however, that "apart from all considerations of duty to others, it will be profitable to ourselves to unite together in such associations as are contemplated by this Society."[9] The W.F.M.S. was created not only to liberate women in non-Christian lands from the bondage and insubordination to which custom and religion had subjected them, but to provide outlets for the energy, ability, and leadership of American women in missionary societies, since such avenues were closed to them in the existing structures of the church. Christianity was the faith that promised true womanhood, and the W.F.M.S. was designed to advance the cause of women as well as to meet the needs of the church.

Methodist Episcopal women had participated in antecedent missionary societies such as the Female Missionary Society, founded in 1819, and the Ladies' China Missionary Society of Baltimore, organized in 1847. Both were auxiliaries to the General Missionary and Bible Society of the denomination and were not autonomous women's societies, and both had disbanded several years before. The Woman's Union Missionary Society had been organized in 1860 by women of six denominations, but some of its members felt that societies of separate denominations could better address the needs. Before the end of the decade Congregationalists and Methodists had withdrawn to form their own organizations, and others followed shortly thereafter.[10] When the Woman's Foreign Missionary Society was formed, Jennie Fowler Willing, who was corresponding secretary of the west division and the key leader in the midwestern states, urged women to join this new "avenue of work, that they may think, and plan, and talk, and write, to increase the enthusiasm of the Church, for the salvation of all people everywhere."[11]

The great demand which had called the society into existence was the support of female missionaries abroad. An evangelistic thrust was at the heart of the missionary movement and many missionaries and society leaders stressed that native women must be reached in order to evangelize India and China, the first countries to which the Methodist Episcopal Church sent foreign missionaries. "We know too how inestimable is the value, and how incalculable the influence of a pure Christian home," wrote the editor in the initial appeal of *The Heathen Woman's Friend*.[12] A steady stream of articles presented this goal to missionary society members to gain their support and their identification with the evangelistic cause. The Church need not worry about the conversion of heathen men if it could convert the women. Equally crucial was the influence of the Christian mother over her sons and daughters. The native woman must be taught to order her household and to give her children Christian training.

Because women of India and China were secluded in their homes, they could not be reached by male missionaries. Only female missionaries, sent through the contributions of thousands of members of the Woman's Foreign Missionary Society, could release the 300,000,000 women enslaved in India, wrote the Methodist missionary there, T. J. Scott. Indian women were more superstitious than men and the main support of idolatry. Once enlightened by Christianity, however, the case was reversed, and women were more zealous than men in accepting the gospel. Native opinion recently had turned strongly in favor of female education, missionaries contended in 1869. At that time, 30,000 pupils were being taught in 700 mission schools for girls—one for every 3,000 women. The largest numbers of these women were being reached by the 500 Roman Catholic nuns in heathen India. The Methodists were confronted with a sharp challenge: "Are the women of the Roman Catholic Church to show more zeal, more energy, more self-sacrificing devotedness to the cause of Christ, than the true followers of the Lord Jesus?"[13]

If one purpose in uplifting heathen women was the evangelization of whole dark continents, W.F.M.S. missionaries and leaders also wrote of the education of native women for their own sakes. Christianity was the friend of women, wrote T. J. Scott. Long-held customs of Hinduism and Mohammedism stressed female inferiority and subservience, and where Christianity had not reached, women were ignorant, degraded, and enslaved. These missionaries contended not only that women existed for the sake of advancing Christianity, but that Christ came to save the whole person. The "foundation principle" of the faith, wrote Mrs. E. E. Baldwin, Methodist Episcopal missionary to China, was "the command to give the gospel to every creature." To bring Christ to Indian women meant that they must be given social and mental elevation as well as religious enlightenment.[14]

The education provided Indian girls who attended the orphanage sponsored by the Methodist Episcopal Church at Bareilly indicates that the missionaries were genuinely concerned about the cultural and intellectual development of the natives, as well as about their religious conversion. In supporting the native children, branches of the W.F.M.S. changed the little girls' Indian names to Anglo-American ones. Those adopted by the New England Branch, for instance, were given names such as Susan Hamilton, Hester Poole, Elizabeth Monroe, and Harriet Richardson, for the missionaries' relatives and members of the societies. The assumption that the education of these young women meant their Americanization may be too hasty a response. Isabella Thoburn, the Woman's Foreign Missionary Society's first unmarried woman missionary, describes an eighteen-year-old girl who came to the orphanage with her baby of three months after they had been abandoned by her husband. The young woman wanted to learn English, but the missionaries persuaded her that she must first become fluent in reading and writing her native tongue. Girls were taught to read secular books, as well as the New Testament, in Urdu and Hindu, and were instructed in the geography and history of India. Descriptions of individual students' progress indicate that their course of study which included arithmetic, cooking, sewing, and needlework, was well rounded.[15]

Primarily, the missionaries sought to train the young women to return to their cities and villages, and to aid their native sisters. Many of the girls were members of medical classes taught by Clara Swain, first woman medical missionary from the United States to the Orient, and by various male missionaries. They were educated to be doctors and nurses of practical medicine, and some continued in more advanced work upon graduation. Others were hired to assist the missionaries as Bible readers to women in the zenanas—apartments containing the harems of upperclass Hindus. The goal for students is best described in the progress of Rebecca Pettis, one of the best scholars in the school and a very good teacher herself. After graduation, she married a young native Christian and "went at once with her husband to Nainee Tal, where they both joined Dr. Humphrey's medical class. She is a very useful woman, well fitted in every way to work among the women of this country."[16]

Beyond their vision of evangelizing and educating native women in the mission field, the early missionary-society leaders were equally clear in the goals they sought for their society, and for women generally, in the Methodist Episcopal Church at home. Their effort to create an autonomous women's organization and to manage their own affairs was a sensitive issue from the beginning. Even before the formation of the society, its leaders were urged by John P. Durbin, secretary of the General Missionary Society, or "parent board," to develop their society in light of these restrictions: "(1) To raise funds for a particular portion of our mission work in India, perhaps also in China; (2) Leave the administration of the work to the Board at home and the missions on the field." In short, Durbin wanted the new women's organization to be an auxiliary of the General Missionary Society. The women, however, carefully delineated their understanding of themselves as co-laborers with the general board and pastors. They regarded the W.F.M.S. as an autonomous agency committed to harmonious relations with the General Missionary Society, "seeking its counsel and approval in all its work." [17]

One fear of the general board was that the woman's society would encroach on potential missionary giving. Describing themselves as an educational arm, the women contended that they would expand missionary donations for the entire church "by increasing the missionary intelligence and enthusiasm of the people." [18] Only once—at the 1876 convention—did the General Conference of the Methodist Episcopal Church recommend a closer financial union of the woman's society and the parent board. The women's response was firm and clear: "We regard closer financial union as prejudicial to our interests, in short, a change would be disastrous." Maintaining the delicate balance as a coordinate, but not subordinate, agency, the W.F.M.S. won the commendation of the General Conference and also gained increased freedom in its work. By the 1890s, its members were taking collections for the women's missionary program in regular church services. [19]

In consciously creating a sphere for women's work, the missionary-society leaders hoped also to give women of the church, with their unrecognized and unused abilities and energies, an expanded purpose for their lives. By developing a sense of responsibility for their sisters on the other side of the world, women could be caught up in a Christ-ordained task of immense proportions; only they, as women whose lives also were restricted and limited to the home, could value this task as being consuming significance. The cause was presented graphically in an article entitled "Facts for Christian Women."

> Suppose that these millions of degraded women were to rise up and pass in review before us, their Christian sisters, marching so that we could count sixty persons each minute. They pass by us at this rate all the day for twelve longs hours, and we find that 43,000 have passed us. Days grow to months, and months to years, still the procession moves on. She who started as a pretty, innocent little girl, has grown to womanhood, yet with all that is lovely, noble, and pure in her nature crushed out in her growth. For twenty long years we must stand and count ere we number the last of this sorrowful procession of 300,000,000 heathen women, whom Satan hath bound in such galling chains "lo, these many years." [20]

Not only was it necessary to picture these throngs of women dramatically; it was also necessary to place the burden for their care on the Methodist Episcopal women in an equally intense manner. "It is indeed a fearful sight to see these millions hastening to destruction," the article continued, "but is it not almost as melancholy a sight to see Christian women quietly, carelessly sleeping the while, instead of putting forth the most strenuous efforts to save them?"

The creation of an enlarged purpose for their members' lives was closely tied to the creation of bonds of sisterhood, stretching from the women of the church at home to the native women in the mission field. "Dear sisters! shall we not recognize, in this emergency, God's voice as speaking to us—for who can so well do this work as we?" questioned the executive board in the initial appeal of *The Heathen Woman's Friend.* "Does it not seem as though the responsibility were thus laid directly upon us? And shall we shrink from bearing it?" [21]

Jennie Fowler Willing articulated this theme of sisterhood most persuasively. In articles entitled "Under Bonds to Help Heathen Women" and "Put Yourself in Her Place," Willing challenged members, "If all men are brothers, all women are sisters." She argued that while American women had the opportunity for education, females of Eastern cultures cowered in the gloom of paganism. "We have it in our power to rescue thousands of our Pagan sisters," and, by bringing them Christianity, to insure a better civilization. [22]

The bond of sisterhood which Willing and her colleagues sought to instill in missionary society members included an understanding that they themselves were "missionaries," like those women whom they sent abroad by the contributions of their pennies and dollars. As young ladies nobly qualified to be "Protestant Sisters of the Cross" were waiting to be sent directly to their heathen sisters, so all women of the church must be aroused to organize societies, raise funds, and sponsor orphans in India and China: "Let every lady, who feels that she *would be a missionary,* go to work at home, and she may, by every dollar raised, teach her heathen sisters." [23]

The missionary society urged that a branch be created in every church with a female membership large enough to sustain it. Detailed directions, "How We Formed Our Auxiliary," were given in *The Heathen Woman's Friend,* and resulted in the early success of 130 branches after one year of the society's existence. The whole scheme of fund raising, "based upon a constant and systematic gleaning of small sums," was designed both to raise money for mission projects and to insure that "all women, even the most humble, could have a share in the work." Membership fees in the W.F.M.S. amounted to one dollar a year, attainable by "every Christian woman laying aside two cents a week." Similarly, the price of *The Friend* was only thirty cents a year, designed to be "within the reach of all." [24]

Further, the pages of *The Heathen Woman's Friend* were avenues for companionship and support. Letters to the editor were a means of sharing "most welcome words of encouragement from distant cities and states." One sister wrote from Indiana, "I cannot tell you how delighted I was to hear of the existence of such a Society." From another state, a woman wrote of her long-held desires and prayer for such an organization and the eagerness of three members of her branch to enter foreign mission service. Still another letter, described as "a cheering note from Illinois," symbolized the way the missionary society helped to bridge the loneliness and isolation felt by women in far-flung rural areas and small towns and offered them a unifed purpose for their lives.

Dear Madam:—A Copy of "The Heathen Woman's Friend" has reached me here in my prairie home, and wishing to help forward the work in so good a cause, I here enclose to the "Woman's Foreign Missionary Society" ten dollars ($10.00), with the prayer that it may help some poor, benighted sister to know the truth as it is in Christ Jesus our Saviour. I am but a poor music teacher, the daughter of a poor Methodist minister, and it is but little I can give; but my "mite" is given cheerfully, praying that God will bless the missionary cause in *all* its branches, and convert the heathen from their sins.[25]

In addition to their goals of maintaining an autonomous society and developing purpose and sisterhood among its members, the founders gained personal value from the Women's Foreign Missionary Society, since it was an outlet for their own energies and capabilities. It is crucial to consider the identities of the founders and first officers of the society. Primarily, these women were wives of bishops of the church, wives of secretaries of the General Missionary Society, wives of governors and college presidents, wives of leading pastors and missionaries. The first W.F.M.S. president was married to a bishop, and eight of the original forty-four vice-presidents were wives of bishops. Because of their husbands' positions, these women were concerned with maintaining the society as a middle-of-the-road organization—keeping harmony between the women's society and the larger church and being sure that it did not take independent courses of action which would challenge the constituted authority.

But who were these women in their own right? In the past, they had found identity through their spouses; their basic professional roles had been as their husbands' confidantes, supporting and advising informally in their leadership of the church. But they were highly cultured and well-trained women, who needed a sphere in which to express their own commitment to the church and to develop leadership ability. The Woman's Foreign Missionary Society provided such a channel, and it also opened the way for other women to find avenues for self-expression. This emerging sense of their own identity, and the conflicting emotions it must have produced among the women involved, may have been reflected in the various ways correspondents signed articles in *The Heathen Woman's Friend*. Some continued to refer to themselves as Mrs. Bishop Osman Baker, Mrs. Rev. Dr. Patten, and Mrs. Gov. Wright, while others used their own names—Mrs. Annie R. Gracey, Mrs. Emily C. Page, and Mrs. Jennie Fowler Willing.[26]

The Woman's Foreign Missionary Society had been clear about its goals— to evangelize and educate women of non-Christian countries and to create for themselves an autonomous society which could provide purpose, sisterhood, and avenues for leadership and service to its members. By all measurable standards, the cause flourished. When the society celebrated its twenty-fifth anniversary in 1894, the progress report was impressive. Two hundred thirty-one women missionaries had been sent out by the W.F.M.S., and 161 were still serving actively at that time. Strong mission stations had been established in India, China, Japan, Korea, Burma, South America, Mexico Malaysia, Bulgaria, and Italy. Property holdings in mission countries were valued at $408,666. During the year, 57,000 patients had been cared for at 13 hospitals; 13,000 girls were in day and boarding schools. Almost $3.5 million had been received and spent for missions.[27]

Surely any commentator would have praised the women for their notable service to the church. Bishop Mathew Simpson did so in addressing a public meeting of the New York Branch of the society. He lauded the strides women were making in the late nineteenth century in the attainment of increased rights in education and suffrage. This was a time of culmination for women, he said. "God is intending, evidently, that woman shall do something in this age more than in the past. . . . I think I see in this Society an answer to the great question, 'What shall women do?'"[28]

To Bishop Simpson, the Woman's Foreign Missionary Society appeared to be the fulfillment—even the containment—of women's progress. How would the founders and leaders have evaluated their gains? In looking back, we can conclude that by developing an autonomous organization which opened up expanded purpose, sisterhood, and leadership for women, the founders possessed the enlightened vision and practical know-how to begin a movement which one day would enable women and men together to eliminate a separate sphere for women in church and society.

# Denominational Modernization and Religious Identity: The Case of the Methodist Episcopal Church

## William McGuire King

Historians of religion in America frequently marvel at the resilience of the Protestant denominational structure. Although the denominational idea began in the eighteenth and early nineteenth centuries, the critical period in determining the shape of denominational organizations was the era between the Civil War and the First World War.[1] It was by no means obvious that the major denominations would be able to maintain their popularity in the face of internal tensions caused by the increasing secularity of modern culture, the greater heterogeneity of American society, and the rapid proliferation of sectarian movements, many of which propagated an anti-denominational, anti-bureaucratic point of view. Despite these obstacles, however, the major denominations retained the loyalty of most of their members and even expanded their base of support within society.

Curiously enough, the modernization and rationalization of bureaucratic structures helped—rather than hindered—the denominations to meet the challenges of the new age. To be sure, this conclusion stands in contradiction to the modern predilection to consider bureaucratic structures as necessarily impersonal, and hence as "alienating." Whatever truth there may be to this intellectual predisposition, it nonetheless fails to explain the practical outcome of denominational consolidation between 1865 and 1920. In reality, the bureaucratic revolution of this period was not something arbitrarily imposed on the masses from above. Although much of these changes was surely due to the inner logic of bureaucratic development and to the ambitions of denominational bureaucrats, the success of such changes depended on other factors. The denominations prevailed in this period because they discovered how to use supraparochial structures as vehicles for creating and sustaining denominational identity and loyalty. This process succeeded to the degree that it related organizational consolidation to the desiderata of modern democratic culture and yoked organizational ideals to the aspirations of an ascendant middle-class culture.

The actual course of modernization, of course, differed from denomination to denomination. But a good illustration of the bureaucratic dynamics involved can be derived from the story of a denomination that flourished in this period: the Methodist Episcopal Church. During the first half of the nineteenth century, Methodism had suffered from a series of debilitating internal conflicts and schisms. While aggressive revivalistic techniques had produced numerical growth, they could not provide sufficient ballast against the winds of dissension. The heroic effort of the "holiness movement" to salvage denominational unity proved in itself to be divisive in a society becoming increasingly complex. By 1920, the situation had become reversed. Revivalism had waned as a mark of denominational identity. The denomination had instead evolved into a corporate body, and denominational loyalty was grounded primarily in a sense of corporate identity. Methodists found personal pride in belonging to a far-reaching organization that epitomized middle-class ideals. The rationale of the bureaucracy was that it could articulate and promote these values in the modern world. The relationship between the people and the bureaucratic structure was not supposed to be—although it often was—an impersonal, contractual arrangement. Rather, the denominational corporation saw itself as a working community of interests, whose purpose was to provide a role system in which the members could experience a feeling of mutual loyalty and commitment.[2] Such an organization "provides to each member of the group much of the information, assumptions, goals, and attitudes that enter into his decisions, and provides him also with a set of stable and comprehensible expectations as to what the other members of the group are doing and how they react to what he says and does."[3] In the modern corporate denomination, theological disputes need not terminate in ecclesiastical schism; for denominational engagement, actual or vicarious, not theological integrity, furnishes the cement in the denominational mortar.

The process of corporate consolidation in the Methodist Episcopal Church occurred in two basic stages. Between 1865 and 1872, the denomination as a whole became absorbed in benevolent enterprises and for the first time took direct responsibility for what had previously been voluntary operations. The climax of this phase happened when the General Conference, the governing body of the Methodist Episcopal Church, assumed complete legislative control over all phases of denominational life. The full consolidation and rationalization of the supraparochial agencies, however, did not come about until the progressive period, 1908 to 1920, when the General Conference assumed full executive, as well as legislative, responsibility for denominational operations. Each of these stages involved an expansion of denominational horizons and could not have succeeded without the active support of the Methodist laity.

The most important event during the first stage of the transformation of the Methodist Episcopal denominational structure took place at the 1872 General Conference. This conference adopted the report of the "Special Committee on the Relation of Benevolent Institutions of the Church to the General Conference." The report placed the benevolent institutions of the denomination "under the full control of the General Conference," by stipulating that the boards of managers of the various benevolent agencies were to be elected by the General Conference itself.[4] This decision seemed so sound at the time that the delegates scarcely debated the merits of the report and the religious press virtually ignored it. Yet this simple step was fraught with significance. It represented the culmination of a process that had begun a decade earlier with the General Conference expanding its authority over the operations of the denomination and committing the future of the denomination to the fortunes of an extensive network of executive agencies.

Alpha J. Kynett, who was at the time the corresponding secretary of the Church Extension Society and the person most responsible for the 1872 Report on Benevolent Institutions, knew exactly what the report signified. It meant that the General Conference, "the supreme legislative body of the Church," would now command "all its great interests for the diffusion of Christian civilization" and "have a controlling power in all the missionary operations carried on in the name and behalf of the Church."[5] Kynett acknowledged that the decision also altered the operations of the benevolent institutions. The General Conference had converted the major benevolent enterprises from society-type to board-type agencies. According to Kynett, the "carefully matured plan" of the 1872 General Conference explicitly intended that the society structure "should be superseded by a Board to be elected by the General Conference, and to be placed under its immediate control."[6]

This decision involved a complete transformation of the traditional Wesleyan conception of the ministry of the church.[7] Originally there had been a division of responsibility between the work of the clergy and that of the laity. The preachers constituted a "preaching order," governed completely by the bishop(s) "in conference" with the entire brotherhood of preachers. Clerical duties were mainly evangelical and spiritual in nature. The local congregations, or "societies," were neither parishes nor sects but voluntary communities gathered to edify and care for one another. Temporal matters, including financial obligations, were almost exclusively a lay responsibility. Thus, as late as

1868, a group of conservative laymen, protesting against proposed changes in Methodist polity, could sensibly argue that

> as our Church is now governed there is a most happy separation of the spiritual and secular offices of the body. The ministry, as the servants of the Head of the Church, are at the head of the spiritual offices, while the laity hold and manage all Church property, the ministry having no legal claim even for their own subsistence.[8]

Until 1872, when lay delegates were admitted to the General Conference for the first time, this principle of the separation of responsibilities had operated as a limiting factor on General Conference power. For example, the 1828 General Conference, in rebutting charges of clerical dominion over the church, denied that it could exercise any such control. It unanimously adopted a report, written by Bishop Emory, which stated:

> We claim no strictly legislative powers, although we grant that the terms "legislature" and "legislative" have been sometimes used even among ourselves. In a proper sense, however, they are not strictly applicable to our General Conference.

The General Conference existed solely to regulate spiritual (i.e., clerical) matters: preaching, sacramental life, and moral discipline.[9]

Unfortunately for theory, the formation of Methodist benevolent societies in the 1820s and 1830s complicated the workings of the denomination. These agencies (primarily the Missionary Society [1819], the Sunday School Union [1827], and the Tract Society [1852]) sought and received General Conference approbation. Local pastors were encouraged to support them "by forming [local] societies and making collections for these objects."[10] Annual Conferences were expected to keep meticulous records of the amounts raised in the conference for benevolent purposes. By 1852, the General Conference was applying even more pressure on behalf of these societies. "It will be expected," read the *Discipline*, that "in the examination [of each preacher] in the Annual Conference, reference will be had to the faithful performance of the duty of preachers on this subject in the passage of character."[11]

Nevertheless, the benevolent societies were not organized as arms or agencies of the General Conference. They were purely voluntary and auxiliary institutions, not integral parts of denominational polity. The purpose they served was largely financial: to assist the ministry of the church by facilitating the redistribution of fiscal resources. The Missionary Society, for example, collected funds that were used at the discretion of the bishops and annual conferences of the denomination. The parent society did not decide missionary policy or devise strategy, although it did correspond with missionaries on the field for record-keeping reasons. The intention of the founders of the Missionary Society was simply "to call forth the ability and liberality of the Church."[12]

The relationship between the benevolent societies and the denomination was therefore an ambiguous one. Membership in the Missionary Society, for instance, depended on a two-dollar contribution; and the board of managers, who were laymen living in the vicinity of New York City, were elected at an annual meeting of the society. Yet, in spite of the autonomy of the board of managers, every Methodist preacher was an *ex officio* member of the board (a relatively inconsequential matter except for a handful of New York clergymen), and the General Conference reserved the right to appoint the corresponding secretary. In 1844, the General Conference created a General Missionary Committee, composed of church-wide representatives, to work with the board of managers. But this measure was less an attempt to infringe on the independence of the society than an effort to facilitate communication between the society and the conferences.

By the 1850s, the unsatisfactory nature of these arrangements had become clearer. Increasingly, the societies functioned as important adjuncts to the ministry of the church. Yet they were forced to rely on voluntary support and had no real leverage to exert on local pastors other than exhortation. Moreover, neither the General Conference nor the societies could initiate new policies or set missionary priorities. The societies were forced to work within the constraints of immediate interests and local demands.

This situation changed dramatically in the 1860s. For one thing, throughout the denomination interest in benevolent causes stirred. The expansion of the middle-class base of Methodism meant that attention was ever more directed beyond local concerns to broader interests of a national and idealistic nature. The receipts of the existing societies rose rapidly, as the following reveals:[13]

|  | 1850 | 1855 | 1859 | 1865 |
|---|---|---|---|---|
| Missionary society | $108,000 | 198,000 | 248,000 | 643,000 |
| Sunday School Union | 5,000 | 11,400 | 12,800 | 17,700 |
| Tract Society | —— | 3,400 | 4,100 | 13,600 |

The first thing to notice is that the expansion of receipts began in the early 1850s, before the Civil War, but during a time of heightened national consciousness.[14] The second thing to notice is that the figures for 1865 are not quite so impressive when the Civil War inflation rate of sixty percent or more is taken into account.[15] The figures become significant, however, when one realizes that these older societies had to compete with a host of new charitable agencies and causes, which were generated by war-time needs.[16]

The popular enthusiasm for benevolent causes continued during the reconstruction era, as several new denominational agencies came into existence. In 1865 the Church Extension Society was incorporated at Philadelphia and began its work with considerable fanfare and hope.[17] The Freedmen's Aid Society of the Methodist Episcopal Church appeared in 1866, and in 1868 the General Conference created the Board of Education to invest the money received during the Methodist Centenary campaign of 1866.

This Centenary celebration was itself evidence of the support generated in this period for benevolent purposes. The Centenary Committee had anticipated the collection of two million dollars in donations by October, 1866. Instead, it received over eight million dollars.[18] More than sheer idealism accounts for this outpouring of philanthropy. In part, denominational pride was involved. Abel Stevens, promoting the centenary movement, wrote that since the Methodist Episcopal Church is

> the leading Church of the country, it bears, before God and man, the chief responsibility of the moral welfare of the nation. *The better consecration of its wealth to the public good is therefore one of the principal responsibilities of its future.*[19]

Bishop Matthew Simpson, the most eminent figure in post-bellum Methodism, reminded the denomination that it must cultivate its "social power" if it wishes to stay a step ahead of the other denominations in growth and influence.[20]

The most frequently reiterated reason for promoting benevolence, however, was one that has since been virtually ignored. Lay and clerical spokesmen alike related the educational and charitable enterprises to immediate denominational needs, particularly to the need for denominational unity and identity. Many were beginning to realize that the benevolent work of the church provided church members with a sense of common purpose. The urgent necessity of such a purpose was expressed eloquently during an impromptu convention of clergy and laity at Boston's Tremont Temple in June, 1866. What did the convention hope to achieve?

> We answer, the first and prime object is to revive and strengthen the old connectional bonds of Methodism. All else is subordinate. It is not for division, but harmony. It is not to widen, but lessen breaches. It is that all may see that we are, as a Church, in practice what we are in theory,—a unit.[21]

Revivals alone, the speakers implied, could not produce this unity of spirit. What the church requires is an effort "to expand and intensify certain [benevolent] agencies," for "these are ligaments that unite, and forces that vitalize, the ecclesiastical body."[22] Indeed, Abel Stevens indicated that the organizers of the church-wide Centenary movement wanted "to promote the Connectional spirit of Methodism, and to bind anew, in cords of fraternal love and of devotion to the common cause, the East, the West, the north [sic], and the South." Only by means of a tangible demonstration of harmony, that is, "by the grand unit of our vast societies," could the spirit of secession, both national and denominational, be overcome.[23]

The prospect of directing the idealistic and benevolent impulses of the laity into channels of denominational pride and unity was enticing. In order to put it into effect, the denomination as a whole would need to assume responsibility for benevolent work. Not surprisingly, the General Conference delegates in 1872 were disturbed that "as our benevolent societies are now constituted and governed, they are practically controlled in their election of boards of managers by a few of the members who live near the places of meeting, and they are really irresponsible to the Church through any of its authorities."[24] Basic assumptions had changed. The benevolent enterprises now appeared in an entirely new light, not as auxiliaries of the church, but as executive agencies of the church. Considering the sums of money that these agencies now controlled[25] and the desire to develop coherent policies for the use of that money, one can comprehend why few resisted the actions of the General Conference. Certainly the corresponding secretaries of the benevolent societies did not resist, since they were the ones who had the most to gain from the new state of affairs.

What ultimately insured the success of the report on restructuring the benevolent societies was the decision in 1872 to admit lay delegates into the General Conference. It was no coincidence that Alpha J. Kynett, the report's sponsor, was also an ardent advocate of lay representation. If the General Conference were to assume full responsibility for benevolent operations, then it could no longer justly exclude the laity from General Conference deliberations. The whole church now became the constituency of the benevolent boards, and the whole church would have to play a role in defining the responsibilities and delegating the powers of the boards. The General Conference was the only body that could claim to represent the whole church.[26] So, overnight, the argument against lay representation became an anachronism.

Rather than bemoaning the change in the character of the General Conference, the new generation of Methodists welcomed it. As lay spokesmen told the clergy in 1868, "it is impossible to carry forward Methodism, now that it has grown to be so vast, without the use of large legislative powers."[27] The Episcopal Address of 1876 revelled in the thought that now "under the government and direction of the General Conference as her supreme authority," and by means of "the great agencies of the Church," Methodism had become an army "having unity of purpose and action."[28] The centralization of denominational power in the hands of the General Conference was a *fait accompli*.

By an historical paradox, the expansion of benevolent enterprises peaked in the year 1872. The last quarter of the nineteenth century was a difficult period for the new denominational boards. The corresponding secretaries of the boards had hoped that the change in status of the benevolent agencies would rally the church behind them. Instead, the secretaries discovered that the growth of benevolent giving was slowing, as the following table demonstrates:

|                     | 1870      | 1875    | 1885    | 1890      | 1900      |
|---------------------|-----------|---------|---------|-----------|-----------|
| Missionary Society  | $640,000  | 603,000 | 700,000 | 1,000,000 | 1,200,000 |
| Sunday School Union | 23,000    | 17,500  | 16,000  | 25,000    | 22,000    |
| Tract Society       | 22,000    | 16,600  | 15,000  | 22,600    | 21,000    |
| Church Extension    | 67,000    | 61,300  | 100,500 | 155,500   | 131,000   |
| Freedmen's Aid      | ———       | 44,200  | 77,300  | 109,200   | 125,000   |

The only major increase in benevolent giving occurred during the five-year period between 1885 and 1890. The reasons for this particular rise in charitable contributions needs further investigation. It may be the result of an increase in missionary enthusiasm, especially on college and university campuses; or it may be a reflection of the growing size and affluence of Methodist congregations. Between 1885 and 1890, for example, the value of Methodist Episcopal churches and parsonages soared: the value of churches increased 22%, while the value of parsonages increased 35%.[29]

In any case, the demand for services from the boards surpassed the resources available. Board secretaries were forced to operate cautiously and to devise new strategies to meet financial exigencies. Alpha J. Kynett, who remained corresponding secretary of the Board of Church Extension, was again the one who initiated new policies. Kynett operated his board on modern banking principles. He created a permanent loan fund, to lend money to needy churches, and solicited contributions to the work of the Board by selling life annuities, which he then invested at high interest rates.[30] He was also the first secretary to make effective use of the board's denominational status by organizing a rigorous apportionment system, which prescribed a minimum contribution from every local church, and by reducing appropriations to annual conferences that failed to meet their apportionments.[31] Despite these attempts to rationalize benevolent finances, all of the boards, except the Board of Education, found themselves in serious financial debt in the 1890s.

Part of the difficulty was that the General Conference, despite the 1872 decision, was reluctant to take an active role in the operations of the boards before 1900. This reluctance distanced the work of the boards from the General Conference. The boards remained semi-autonomous agencies in the sense that their policies continued to be set by powerful corresponding secretaries, who guarded their territory zealously. Periodic attempts by delegates to get the General Conference to consolidate and to supervise the work of the benevolent agencies came to naught before 1900.

The General Conference hesitated to act in these matters because its attitude toward benevolent operations was still undergoing transition. The General Conference had assumed full legislative authority over the denomination. It was not yet willing, however, to assume full executive responsibility as well. In fact, it preferred to delegate executive authority to the corresponding secretaries and to the bishops of the church. The bishops were the ones expected to supervise and coordinate the work of the boards. That is why the bishops did not oppose the General Conference's actions in creating denominational boards. The Episcopal Address to the 1876 General Conference, for example, strongly supported the reorganizational measures, while reminding the delegates that

> the General Superintendency has always been, and will continue to be, a strong bond of unity. . . . Owing to the great extent of the connection, we can perceive no other way by which a uniform administration can be maintained; and without uniformity—without oneness of executive authority and administration—we do not see how the unity, the connectional character, of the Church can be preserved. Our profound convictions on this subject have led us to great care and constant effort to secure a uniform administration.[32]

As late as 1896, the bishops resisted General Conference attempts to establish special commissions to study the operations of the boards. They reminded the General Conference that "we superintend the expenditure of millions of dollars; the precise unity of the Church is conserved by our semi-annual meetings for the consideration of the work as a whole."[33]

The progressive period, however, brought about a changed attitude on the part of the lay delegates to the General Conference. They felt more assured of their competence to supervise the work of the denomination and were convinced that the application of progressive business techniques to the work of benevolence would benefit the whole denomination. Moreover, most of the older, authoritarian secretaries and bishops in the denomination had died or retired by 1900, giving the new generation of delegates a freer hand to work its will.

The first indication that the General Conference was prepared to assume executive control of denominational boards came in 1904. The General Conference in that year reduced the number of boards to three: the Board of Foreign Missions, the Board of Home Missions and Church Extension, and the Board of Education, Sunday Schools, and Freedmen's Aid. This effort at reduction was anachronistic, however, for the upswing of interest in benevolent enterprises in the progressive period produced an expansion of benevolent operations. Thus by 1920, there were ten denominational boards in operation, rather than three.

Between 1900 and 1905, the receipts of the benevolent agencies increased about 30% to 50%. In addition, new extra-parochial organizations multiplied: the Epworth League, the deaconess movement, the National City Evangelization Union, the Methodist Federation for Social Service, the Temperance Society of the Methodist Episcopal Church, the Brotherhoods of Men, and others. The drift of the times tended toward greater lay support and participation in the benevolent work of the denomination. The push for expansion came from below, not from above. It is time, said the general secretary of the Methodist

Brotherhood, for a "harnessing of our manhood to the big problems of the Church of Jesus Christ—a putting of our strong manhood back of the program of Jesus Christ." [34]

The fruits of this movement were a more general interest in the work of the boards and a desire to consolidate the power of the General Conference in relation to them. The initiative of the laity, with the concurrence and contrivance of the new generation of socially-minded clergy, produced a complete transformation in the administrative and financial structure of the Methodist Episcopal Church between 1908 and 1920.

The group most responsible for this transformation was the Laymen's Missionary Movement, which organized a strong Methodist auxiliary in 1908. The Laymen's Missionary Movement had two objectives: to increase benevolent giving within the church at large through high-pressure promotional campaigns and to demand greater efficiency and rationality in the operations of the boards. The two goals were interrelated, of course, because efficiency was being touted as the remedy for lackluster denominational performance.

At the 1912 General Conference, the Laymen's Missionary Movement presented what it called "The New Financial Plan." This plan sought to replace the endless rounds of collections for the various benevolent causes with a unified benevolence collection from each congregation. Church members could be relied on to support the principle of benevolence giving in general. Duplex envelopes were to be used for the weekly collection, in which the donor designated a portion of his contribution to local church expenses and gave the rest to denominational enterprises. The advantages of this system were many. Church members would be encouraged to see themselves as participants in the *entire* ministry of the denomination. Stewardship would become systematic and regular. Local churches would find it easier to meet benevolent obligations, and a church-wide apportionment system could be instituted. Boards would now have a relatively guaranteed and predictable source of income, and they could plan future operations with more assurance of success.

The New Financial Plan was adopted in 1912, although everyone knew that it meant a major readjustment of the administrative structure. A central accounting agency would need to be created to determine apportionments and to fix the level of appropriations by the various boards. This function became the responsibility of the newly approved General Conference Commission on Finance. The boards accepted the situation because they had already decided to abandon their autonomy in return for financial stability. As compensation, the corresponding secretaries were assured a vote on the Commission on Finance. The bishops, more and more overwhelmed by executive duties, eagerly turned the supervision of the boards over to the General Conference and the Commission on Finance. As the 1912 Episcopal Address to the General Conference stated, in recommending the adoption of the New Financial Plan:

the church [should] forecast her needs and consolidate her estimates for all connectional demands—not by the uncertain process of five or six boards and committees sitting apart and acting independently, if not competitively, but by a competent connectional board or commission—in which or before which all interests may be represented—and with final authority to fix the aggregate budget and properly apportion the total amount among the Conferences.[35]

The bishops hoped that they could now concentrate on the "spiritual" oversight of the church.

With these steps, denominational identity advanced further in the direction begun in the 1860s Methodists now belonged to an ecclesiastical corporation, which sought to promote church unity by means of the responsiveness of its executive agencies to the religious ideals of the whole constituency. Speeches given at the national convention of Methodist Men, gathered in Indianapolis in 1913, articulated this theme with astonishing regularity. "While Methodism was growing in numbers and expanding her world parish," noted one speaker, "she built up an ecclesiastical organism combining firmness with elasticity, democracy with strong central power, unity of aim and purpose with adaptability to local needs and conditions."[36] The convention's watchword for the denomination was "unification, co-operation, co-ordination."[37]

With this slogan in mind, the Laymen's Missionary Movement asked the 1916 General Conference "to consider the advisability and practicality of unifying the benevolent work of the Church."[38] The General Conference responded by drawing up a plan of unification for the 1920 General Conference. This latter General Conference adopted a report on the "Correlation and Coordination of the Benevolent Boards." A permanent executive agency, the Council of Boards of Benevolence, replaced the Commission on Finance. The mandate of the new agency was to "review and determine the administrative budget of each constituent Board." More importantly, it was empowered to prepare a "Four-Year Plan" that outlined the goals and programs of each board. The overall objective was to fashion "one harmonious and unified world program of missionary, educational, and benevolent activities."[39]

This entire program was designated "The World Service Program of the Methodist Episcopal Church." It held rallies throughout the denomination to generate enthusiasm for the new aspirations of the General Conference and promoted the motto "To Serve the Present Age." There were four elements to the "World Service Program: evangelism, stewardship, "life-service" vocation, and "an adequate, systematic, general financial program that will reach every member."[40] Although the last item was the immediate objective, the more idealistic items were not slighted. The World Service Program organized an active Department on Christian Life Service, which attempted to interest young people in missionary work and social service vocations. The four items were all interrelated. The evangelism that was promoted stressed denominational service, not individual piety. Thus, in the words of the committee, "it is highly important that any church-wide program should so combine these activities that no section and no committee or commission can mistake the unity or can break the correlation." [41] So important was the World Service Program to the interests of the General Conference that its budget in 1922 was $787,000, second in size only to the Board of Foreign Missions, the Board of Home Missions and Church Extension, and the Board of Education. Indeed, the General Conference was investing an extraordinary sum of money in its attempt to integrate the work of the denominational boards with the religious concerns and personal aspirations of the laity.

By the 1920s the General Conference had assumed supremacy over all phases of denominational life. The historical significance of this fact, however, does not lie simply in the degree of bureaucratization and centralization that such a development entailed. More profound was the transformation of denominational self-understanding, a transformation which bestowed a measure of legitimacy on the process of bureaucratization. Methodists had never relied upon doctrinal uniformity to facilitate denominational fellowship, but rather upon evangelistic zeal. The basic difference after the Civil War was that such evangelism was considered not only the responsibility of the individual preacher or the individual society member, but also the responsibility of the denomination in its corporate capacity. Thus Kynett, for example, could defend "organized forms of church-work" by explaining that "the command [of Christ] is 'Go'; and the life-impulse is 'Go,' and the result is organized going—the Church *as a body* obeying the command of its Master and Head, and the impulse of its life." [42] For many Methodists in the twentieth century—although certainly not for all—denominational commitment meant an allegiance to this corporate conception. No longer could a sharp line be drawn between the vocation of the clergy and the vocation of the laity, for both shared in this corporate ministry to the world.

Despite certain peculiarities of the Methodist case, the other major denominational bodies probably underwent a similar reorientation of denominational self-understanding. Every major denomination was affected by the trends of society and culture between 1865 and 1920. These trends—the trend toward participatory democracy, the trend away from absolute distinctions between secular and sacred, the trend toward bureaucratic rationalization, the trend away from theological divisiveness—all produced extensive adjustments in religious thought and ecclesiastical expectations. Such adjustments necessarily put a strain on denominational ties; and few denominational bodies were so secure, or so conservative, that they could ignore the need to reckon with this strain.

Whether this reorientation of denominational self-understanding was ultimately good or bad is a vital question, but one which cannot be answered on historical grounds alone. In yielding to a corporate self-understanding, the denominations may have betrayed their religious mandate. Certainly the dangers of ecclesiastical positivism and theological nihilism are all too evident. Stripped of its spirit of boosterism, however, the corporate redefinition was a sincere effort to translate the Christian ideal of an inclusive, serving community into a modern idiom. If the corporate ideal threatened to erode the transcendent ground of Christianity, it may also have helped to prevent Christianity from becoming merely a sectarian backwater in the floodplains of modernity. In whatever manner one decides to answer this question, one ought at least to be scrupulous enough to acknowledge the ambiguities and paradoxes of the denominational search for religious identity.

# The Social Gospel According to Phoebe: Methodist Deaconesses in the Metropolis, 1885–1918

### Mary Agnes Dougherty

## INTRODUCTION

No specific date, event, or movement clearly marks the birth of the social gospel and social Christianity. Some would agree that these were established in the teachings and ministry of Jesus of Nazareth himself in the first century A.D., and that they have been carried out in every generation since by followers who have heard his word and done it. Most church historians, however, agree with C. Howard Hopkins that in its modern American form, social Christianity originated in "the reaction of Protestantism . . . to the ethics and practices of capitalism as brought to point in the industrial situation" following the Civil War.[1] Henry May, for example, claims that "three earthquakes—the industrial upheavals of 1877, 1886, and 1892–94—awoke Protestant America's slumbering social conscience from a complacency engendered by the alliance between conservative religion and conservative economics.[2] The first church groups to respond to new social conditions were Unitarians, Congregationalists, and Episcopalians, the last inheriting a "state-church tradition of responsibility for public morals." The Methodists and Baptists only awoke to their social duty later, Hopkins argues.[3] Within all the denominations, it has been commonly supposed that clergymen and professors designed the social-gospel response to the "urban impact."[4]

The essence of social Christianity, however, involved carrying out the gospel, not theorizing about it. Histories that credit its origins to theologians, ministers, and lay*men* usually overlook, slight, or ignore the contribution of church*women* to the formulation of the social gospel. Yet nineteenth-century clergymen who saw themselves as leaders in a new Christian endeavor were not ignorant of their indebtedness to women. They understood that they were entering a field of service that previously had belonged to women. For example, John R. Commons, secretary of the American Institute of Christian Sociology in Indiana, was perceptive about churchmen's need to be tutored in the elementary techniques of social work. He noted with unconscious androcentrism that Christian men "have hired someone else to love [their neighbors]. They have left it to the women." In an effort to help church*men* catch up with the women, Commons patiently explained the hows and whys of friendly visiting: "It means to go yourself, to get acquainted with your neighbor, to pick out some hard-worked mechanic, some shiftless pauper, some slave of drink, and love him." [5]

And what of the women? Churchwomen, who throughout the nineteenth century had served as the social arm of Protestantism, are largely absent from the accounts of a movement defined by one scholar as "America's most unique contribution to the great on going stream of Christianity." [6] It seems improbable that women retreated from this work. It is more likely that historians have overlooked or minimized the significance of churchwomen in the rise of social Christianity because they saw nothing unique or unusual in their role as society's servants. Above all else, the social gospel asked its adherents to *love* their neighbors, especially the least among them. Such a demand was considered "natural" to the female personality, making it an improbable source of the new and unforeseen mood in the churches. By contrast, the social gospel demanded a radical change in the attitudes and actions of Protestant men. As a result, for traditional church history, the social gospel was born only when male ministers and professors and lay*men* began to think and behave in ways which nineteenth-century American culture considered characteristic of womanhood. [7]

Much like Victorian fathers who assumed an interested role in rearing their offspring only when the children were well out of infancy, Protestant churchmen assumed full paternal responsibility for the social gospel in 1912, when it already had matured. In that year, the Federal Council of the Churches of Christ in America adopted the "social creed," with each of twelve denominations pledging to promote its sixteen-point program. [8] The years 1911–12 also saw the creation of the Men and Religion Forward Movement, whose purpose was to enlist Protestant "manhood and boyhood" to carry the social-action message to the churches through a combination of "evangelical fervor and method . . . and the techniques of sociology." [9] In 1912, theologian Walter Rauschenbusch concluded that the Men and Religion Forward Movement had "made social Christianity orthodox." [10] The weight of Rauschenbusch's opinion has led one distinguished historian to estimate that "social Christianity reached its popular peak" in this movement for laymen, but we may conclude that by that date it was respectable enough to be institutionalized, as Rauschenbusch's use of "orthodox" suggests.[11] Prominent theologians and ordinary laymen alike now became votaries of the social gospel.

## DEACONESSES IN THE RISE OF SOCIAL CHRISTIANITY

A full quarter-century before the "popular peak," certain Methodist churchwomen began to nurture the social gospel by reviving the office of deaconess within Methodist polity.[12] Although Hopkins claims that "in the absence of a well-developed sociology, the 'eighties became a period of discussion rather than practical application of social Christian principles," it was in 1885 that Lucy Rider Meyer founded the Chicago Training School for City, Home and Foreign Missions (C.T.S.).[13] During five years as field secretary for the Illinois Sunday School Association, Meyer had discovered that, as she phrased it, "among women, there was plenty of general intelligence, and personal qualities, plenty of latent power . . . but not the machinery for developing the power and making it effective."[14] To correct this situation, she established her training school. The house-to-house visiting in Chicago's tenements that was part of the school's curriculum opened her eyes to the need for a new Christian approach to urban problems. Within two years, with the encouragement of Mr. and Mrs. Meyer, two C.T.S. students moved to a rented flat at the corner of Dearborn and Erie Streets, not far from the training school, and the first Methodist Deaconess Home in the United States was opened.[15]

For most of Protestantism, the decade of the 1880s was a time of meditation, yet major contributions to social-gospel literature stimulated thought, discussion, and action on the issue of Protestantism's response to industrialism.[16] The revival of the female diaconate within Methodism in 1887 belies Robert Handy's conclusion that social gospel leaders were "not so much activists as they were preachers, proclaimers, and educators."[17] Female social-gospel leaders *were* activists. The work of the early deaconesses also challenges Henry May's conclusion that "only in the early twentieth century when progressive social reform had become a creed of much of the American middle class, did Methodists contribute to the social gospel in proportion to their number, discipline, and fervency."[18] When Methodist women are considered as serious historical actors, the picture of Methodist contribution changes. Upon discovering the latent potential for social good in the ancient and nearly forgotten office of deaconess, a significant number of Methodist women enlisted for active duty in the ranks of social Christianity; and they worked as ardently as the men then engaged, "to change men's views and attitudes, to win them to a new religio-social faith."[19]

Sentiment among some churchwomen for reestablishment of the diaconate, in fact, predated by twenty years its official revival in 1888, the year the Methodist Episcopal General Conference recognized the office in church polity.[20] In Philadelphia in 1868, Annie Turner Wittenmyer organized the Ladies' and Pastors' Christian Union, an organization which "to a great extent" supplied "the want of the order of Deaconesses."[21] Also in 1872, Susan M.D. Fry attempted to arouse interest in the office through a series of historical articles entitled "Ancient and Modern Sisterhoods," in *The Ladies' Repository*.[22] At the time, neither of these proponents found Methodist women receptive, but by the 1880s, when the urban situation in the United States cried out for attention, the idea of a modern diaconate had gained relevance.

## THE SCRIPTURAL MODEL OF PHOEBE

The Methodist deaconess obtained her license to minister from Scripture—specifically from Romans 16:1–2, in which Phoebe, a wealthy and cultured woman known for her beneficence, is reported to have served in the primitive Christian church as deaconess to a mission in Cenchrea, near Corinth. Phoebe's *diakonia* was a ministry of service—"a ministry distinguished from other vocations . . . such as prophesying, presiding, teaching, or working miracles."[23] Paul tells us that Phoebe's service was freely and lovingly given; it was not service for pay or such as was required of a slave. At Cenchrea, Phoebe "challenged hunger and disease on the doorstep of the perishing and in Christ's name made them retire." This tradition of Phoebe's *diakonia*—her ability to see "the world's pain" and her desire to overcome it through personal service—was just what nineteenth-century Methodist women wanted to revive.[24]

## METHODIST DEACONESSES IN THE METROPOLIS

Phoebe's field of mission work, as well as her active ministry, is relevant to the modern Methodist diaconate. The women from rural America who first attended deaconess training schools like the one at Chicago held fixed and frightening images of the city.[25] Many novices saw parallels between their own work and the work of Paul's Phoebe among the "human flotsam" of the seaport town described by one minister:

> As a suburb of licentious Corinth [Cenchrea] received foul drainage of the city-sloughs; panderers out of favor; wastrels amazed at their own self-created ministries; and victims of cruelty, injustice and luck, each with a story that would make angels weep. To some of these Phoebe was the only haven of kindness they ever knew. She presided over their rehabilitation; or, where she could not

nurse them back to health and hope, she nursed them on to God . . . "a succorer of many." What histories underlie this superb phrase![26]

For rural women, such dark impressions of urban life only reinforced their fear of the city.

As agents of the emerging social gospel, these modern Phoebes were compelled to make friends with the city or fail in their vocation. William N. Brodbeck urged deaconesses to regard the great cities as a "magnificent opportunity" for the church, rather than as impediments in the path of world evangelization. "There would be no . . . achievement marking the first century of the Christian era," had the apostles confined their labors to the countryside, he reminded them.[27] Aware of the rural loyalties of most American Methodists, another supporter of deaconesses spoke to them boldly, evoking the era's optimistic sense of progress.

> While respecting the country and the people who are born there . . . I regard the city as the most moral institution in our Christian civilization, not [as a place] where all the basest passions are developed, but as the theater of the struggle of man to ultimate victory over himself and his surroundings.[28]

This spokesman promised "miracles" to deaconesses who would share his belief in the potential of the city. "He who goes about the city with the vision of the Throne before him will see the city transformed."

Most new students in urban training schools in fact faced a difficult period of adjustment as they adapted to the pulse and rhythm of the city. Provincial impressions of urban life, drawn from rural viewpoints and based on fiction, popular myth, and gossip, predisposed them to distrust the city. The prospect of rubbing shoulders with slum dwellers frightened them. A decision to enter deaconess work was a heroic undertaking for country girls who perceived the city as a "great center of evil," a world of "squalor, ignorance, brutishness," or "an overgrown social and political tumor."[29]

Deaconesses applied their energies to the urban environment more readily than they adjusted their attitudes. In Chicago, Lucy Rider Meyer, principal of C.T.S., helped her students become acclimated by sharing her optimism that the American city had a potential for Christian endeavor equal to that of mission fields in any foreign land. She reminded her students that the religious reformers Martin Luther and John Wesley, the apostle Paul, Augustine, and Jesus himself had worked in cities to bring about the kingdom of God.[30]

In reality, deaconesses accepted the city provisionally; they determined to spend their lives transforming it. They shared their image of a renewed city with the folks back home through their newspapers. For instance, the *Message* of June 1889 described an ideal deaconess home as envisioned by Protestant sisters in Chicago. Located in the city's worst section and surrounded by tenements, their fantasy home was immaculately white and surrounded by a green lawn. The streets in its vicinity were clean and sanitary, free of debris and garbage, thanks to the city fathers. The ideal deaconess home was the center of activity for the people in the neighborhood. This Bit-of-Heaven House, as they named it, suggests the transformation the deaconesses hoped for, as well as betraying their homesickness for a gentler, tidier world. Although settlement houses never became a major arena for their work, the Bit-of-Heaven House indicates that deaconesses considered creating such institutions before they became common agencies of Progressive social reform.[31]

By introducing novice sisters to the city as a "new Jerusalem," offering them hopes and plans for its transformation, the deaconess movement gave rural daughters confidence that the city was not to be feared, but conquered. Thus armed, deaconesses embraced their role as transformers of urban life.

## LEARNING BY VISITING

Before any deaconess could see the city transformed, it was necessary to undertake the difficult, unromantic task of visiting the poor. Work in tenement neighborhoods was initially a shocking experience. No amount of rural charity work done on the behalf of hometown congregations prepared young Methodist women for the sights they confronted in the city.

"Visiting" was the modern Phoebe's means of canvassing neighborhoods to discover those who might want or need help. In the slums, a deaconess did not find the needy in separate houses, but in basement hovels, out-shacks, lean-tos, hallways, and alleys. Welcomed by some residents and rebuffed by others, it required determination to overcome shyness and timidity, to let unkind words pass, to brave personal slights. Her evangelistic purpose and the good she might do needed to outweigh her personal fears and anxieties.

Despite the raw and depressing conditions of tenement life that could be unnerving to a novice, the successful visitor was alert to the least encouragement that would grant her entrance into the dwellings of the poor. There she might find a scene such as this:

> A Bohemian family was found in two rooms, one a mere shed of an old frame building. The father had been sick for five months with rheumatism. A dead child was lying in the back room, a tiny baby, lacking clothes, was tied up in a pillow. Their destitution was shocking. They lacked clothes, bedding, bread, everything.[32]

While deaconesses visited the poor primarily to help meet their elemental human needs and to evangelize by demonstrating practical love for neighbor, many also functioned in part as students and agents of the new field of quantitative sociology. Like the secular social workers, Protestant sisters gathered information on social conditions during their visits of mercy.[33] In these activities they were guided by the prevailing belief that the scientific study of society was essential to the solution of social problems and the establishment of a just order. A Methodist bishop solemnly voiced this view at a service for the consecration of deaconesses in 1890: "The Deaconess while she visits, may investigate, and with scientific carefulness, collate facts for the use of scientific people, who from facts, draw inferences and are thus able to set at work the great forces which touch society at the center and lift it up." [34]

Students at the Chicago Training School also broadened their educational experiences by visiting institutions such as Graham Taylor's settlement, the Commons. It was reported enthusiastically after such a visit in 1895 that "the Commons is a center of life and light to the neighborhood in which it is located and is an exponent of the real Pauline *charity*." [35]

In turn, the deaconesses themselves were studied as part of the urban landscape by the famous photographer Jacob Riis. In 1911, the *Advocate* printed Riis' photograph of a deaconess at work, with this caption: "I have seen a deaconess through quiet and loving ministry in the chaos of a ghetto transform a street which was a jungle into a spot that breathed of heaven's first law. It is the gentle and noiseless influence that makes mightily for the coming of the Kingdom." [36]

## DEACONESSES AS ANALYSTS OF SOCIETY

During home visits, while ministering to people's physical needs, deaconesses also heard their explanations as to why they were depressed, sick, drunk, or despairing. The daily repetition of such tales in neighborhood after neighborhood led these Methodist women to look for the underlying causes of the misery they witnessed. The literature of the deaconess movement reveals observations sympathetic to working people and the dispossessed: "The shutting down of a factory, a fit of sickness—and sickness is always lurking about those sunless rooms with their damp walls and leaky sewer pipes—any little unexpected addition to ordinary expenses entails a debt, and a debt is a vampire sucking the very life blood of a family." [37]

In order to finance their work in the city, modern Phoebes needed the support of Methodists elsewhere. To gain this aid, they relied upon the persuasiveness of their press. As the training schools were established, they produced a variety of newspapers to be circulated to friends, families, and neighbors in small-town America, to spread the social gospel message and enlist material support for their programs. These journals carried vivid accounts, and readers who caught "Glimpses of the City Field" responded by sending canned goods, farm produce, freshly cut garden flowers, and clothing by rail and wagon to stock the shelves of the "poor closet" in the Deaconess Home. Readers also sent money, and gifts were regularly acknowledged in the newspapers.[38]

Deaconesses were not asking fellow Methodists only for expressions of Christian charity, however. As they gained first-hand experience in the slums, Methodist deaconesses raised questions about the causes of urban poverty, decay, and corruption. Since most deaconesses, particularly in the early years of the movement, were not formally educated, it is not surprising that their contributions to social-gospel thinking were more practical than theoretical. Even so, one can be analytical without advancing to theory, and the deaconesses' perceptions of economic injustice were sharp and clear. In probing the sources of poverty and misery, they frequently approached a class analysis. In 1899, one wrote:

> When Mr. Van Court, the wealthy merchant needs a little ready money in his business he goes to the bank, where he is treated with the greatest deference. . . . But, when Mrs. Bilinski, who supports her five children by washing, is forced to raise a loan . . . she betakes her to a shop over whose entrance hangs three gilt balls.[39]

If deaconesses' writings lacked the sophistication of academically trained male social-gospel theorists, they nevertheless rang with authenticity. People back home did not doubt the veracity of their daughters.

Deaconesses tried to help impoverished people overcome immediate difficulties caused by lack of food, clothing, fuel, and medical care. But they soon learned that the family they saved from disaster on Monday could be in the same position again on Tuesday. Their experiences challenged older notions that poverty was the result of individual depravity; they disclosed the complacency of "blaming the victim." Isabelle Horton, one of the movement's most perceptive social critics, expressed her views in the *Deaconess Advocate*:

> These were not born paupers, but have had pauperism thrust upon them. Perhaps it has been years—perhaps but a few weeks or months since the head of the family failed in health, or in business, or "lost his job." But once down, there is scarcely one chance in a thousand to regain his footing.[40]

Many deaconesses looked into the inequities of the nation's economic system for causes. "Have you ever stopped to think that most foreigners are disappointed in America?" one sister asked deaconess supporters. She argued that the immigrants had expected America to be a land of opportunity, but they had discovered instead "a cruel relentless system of labor."[41]

## SOLVING URBAN PROBLEMS THROUGH POLITICS, PREVENTION, AND NEW INSTITUTIONS

Deaconesses were sympathetic to those who had been victimized by the economic system, and they tried in their own ways to find jobs for the unemployed, although the magnitude of the labor problem far exceeded their ability to deal with it. Their decision to use the facilities of deaconess homes as employment offices reveals their acceptance of purely political solutions, however. When the state of Illinois established employment offices in 1899, the *Advocate* welcomed them as "a move in the right direction," and in 1908 the paper reported that this work had been taken up by the newly founded Methodist Federation for Social Service.[42] The deaconess movement did not develop a sophisticated critique of the political and theoretical aspects of the labor problem, as did some of the intellectual leaders of the social gospel, but it did give attention to the working conditions of female domestics, a problem ignored by nearly everyone else.[43]

At the turn of the century, Chicago's deaconesses, in particular, actively supported reforms as the lively Progressive movement gained force in their city.[44] Since they worked principally, although not exclusively, with women and children, deaconesses followed with special interest the work of such reformers as Florence Kelley, whose exposés of child labor were reprinted in deaconess literature. In 1902, editors of the *Deaconess Advocate* pointed an accusing finger at New England manufacturers who were being investigated for exploiting children in textile mills. While praised in their own communities as "philanthropists and public-spirited men," manufacturers worked thousands of children twelve hours a day for daily wages of from ten to twenty-five cents.[45] Deaconesses supported legislation to curb such exploitation.

Imbued with Methodism's strong temperance tradition, deaconesses abhorred drink, and their work among immigrant groups who drank beer as though it were water tested their Christian charity. Deaconesses were shocked to witness the consumption of alcohol by children and women and strenuously tried to win the drunkard from his cup. Yet they did not blame the drunkard as much as the salesman and the saloonkeeper. They enthusiastically supported efforts to close the saloons; they opened coffee houses as substitute gathering places. In 1896 the *Deaconess Advocate* endorsed the Prohibition party as offering the "thousands of church members opposed to the liquor traffic . . . an alternative in exercising their vote." The *Advocate* two months later backed the editor of the Methodist *Epworth Herald* in judging the Republican party's statement on temperance "an empty platitude."[46] However, while endorsing the Prohibition party's stance on liquor, the *Advocate* expressed discontent with its silence on free silver and woman's suffrage, both of which the paper favored.

The deaconess movement also perceived prostitution as primarily a social problem, rather than a question of individual depravity, and sought to combat it through prevention—the solution favored by Progressives. Deaconesses did not establish homes for "fallen women" as gospel welfare workers had done in the past. Instead they stationed themselves in railroad depots, where they kept a watchful eye for young women who appeared new to the city and none too sure of themselves, approached them, and directed them to a respectable boarding house if they did not have friends or relatives in the city.[47] Calling themselves Traveler's Aides, deaconesses often competed in this work with procurers of prostitutes, who frequented depots looking for recruits.[48] The aim of the deaconesses was not only to thwart the procurer, but to encourage churchwomen to show more tolerance and understanding toward prostitutes.

## DEACONESSES AND THE CITY CHURCHES

The failure of established Protestant institutions to accommodate the foreign immigrants flooding into the cities was seriously pondered during the 1880s by early social-gospel theorists. In *Modern Cities and Their Religious Problems,* published in 1887, Samuel Loomis marshaled a volume of statistical evidence to show that urban churches were declining in numbers. In what Hopkins has assessed as "probably the most acute analysis of the urban religious dilemma," Loomis concluded that Protestantism was failing to win the working classes, who saw the churches as tools of capitalism.[49] In addition, the churches were experiencing a condition that in a later, more racially charged context, would be called "white flight."

The decline of the downtown churches aroused concern in every denomination; conferences were called, papers were written, and criticism was meted out generally. Interdenominational rivalry surfaced, with Methodists and Congregationalists contending over which group was comparatively the greater failure.[50]

In their visiting, the deaconesses saw the truth of Loomis' argument, though probably few had read his book. Through a contributor, the *Advocate* warned, "There is a growing estrangement between the poor and destitute classes and the church of God";[51] and in 1890 it published the following attack by one critic of the churches.

> The churches, instead of trying to establish themselves in these strongholds of evil, are removing from them. When asked why they abandon the places, they reply that they want more respectable quarters; there was so much sin in that district they could not stand it any longer. Think of it! The church, pledged to Christ and commissioned of high heaven. Is that not enough to cause angels to weep and devils to laugh?[52]

The deaconesses were seeking to assist "over-taxed city pastors," in the phrase of the C.T.S. catalogue, which pointed out to readers that the female diaconate was thereby contributing to contemporary Methodist Episcopal Church polity.[53]

The Methodist Phoebes came to believe that the church's traditional forms of ministry were simply ineffective with the new city dwellers. They contended that even if the urban churches opened their doors wide, all the immigrants could not be accommodated. In 1888 the *Advocate* reported that in Chicago's thirteenth ward, churches had a combined seating capacity of 1,500 members, while the total population of the ward was 26,000. Mathematics proved, then, that only one in twenty of the ward's residents could find accommodation in the churches.[54]

Deaconesses proposed to create new church institutions in which immigrants could find acceptance and practical assistance. For example, one of the first undertakings of the Chicago Training School was the opening of an industrial school in a room of a downtown church.[55] Over time, the deaconesses developed other institutions to bridge the distance between the church and the unchurched. Thus they not only recognized the weak influence of Protestantism among the growing immigrant population; they took innovative steps to strengthen it.

## MODERATING TENSIONS
## AND CHRISTIANIZING THE SYSTEM

In condemning the churches' departure from the city and in sympathizing with the precarious lot of the poor, the deaconesses did not turn against the rich. Inherent in social-gospel theory was the belief that the prevailing economic system could be Christianized. Deaconesses, like other advocates of the social gospel, accepted this principle. When Walter Rauschenbusch wrote *Christianity and the Social Crisis* in 1907, he asserted that the churches had become servants of "bourgeois culture." [56] Although Rauschenbusch expected chastisement from his ministerial colleagues, his book was highly praised—perhaps because although he had harsh words for Christianity's alliance with capitalism, he nevertheless firmly believed that if the church would repent and rethink, it could Christianize commerce. These hopes were widely held also by deaconesses.

The deaconess movement did not, on the other hand, exonerate the rich. "We have inaugurated missions and movements to reach the *dregs* of society; we ought to inaugurate others to reach the *scums* of society," claimed one *Advocate* writer. "It is not Coxie's deluded crowds that form the greatest menace to society," he added, "it is the idle rich."[57] Social-gospel advocates criticized capitalists, monopolists, usurers, trusts, businessmen, and stony-hearted corporations for their abuse of wealth, and occasionally a deaconess might radically denounce the economic system. Isabelle Horton wrote, in 1899:

> If this be true—if under the present system a "righteous distribution" of profits is impossible, let the "moral forces" be brought to bear, though the system be destroyed. Or if "destroyed" savors too much of revolution and anarchy, let us say replaced by a new system which shall not set a man's best self and his business interest over against each other; one in which one man's success shall not mean the failure of hundreds of his weaker brothers, but in which his gain shall mean the good of all.[58]

In the main, however, deaconesses saw themselves as moderating class antagonisms. Their desire was to bring rich and poor Americans together in a common Christian brotherhood, and they encouraged cooperation, rather than competition in the economic sphere. They believed that the businessman could end "poverty, misery, and crime" by dealing morally with the working man, and they praised businessmen who instituted profit-sharing programs.[59] In practice, of course, Methodist deaconesses had little contact with businessmen. Though their leaders appealed to business for funds, the Protestant sisters worked primarily with women and children of the poorer classes.


## CONCLUSION

The Methodist deaconesses' reasoned approach to the church's urban crisis cannot be dismissed as sentimental charity offered in the lady-bountiful tradition. Trained for and consecrated to the order, Methodist deaconesses formed a new breed of churchwomen. They were significant agents of applied Christianity and early exponents of the social gospel about which Walter Rauschenbusch wrote perceptively in 1917, "We *have* a social gospel. We need a systematic theology large enough to match it and vital enough to back it" [emphasis added].[60] The work of helping the "whole needy man, body, soul, and spirit . . . was scarcely touched before our coming," observed one deaconess of her movement's contribution to Methodism; she thoughtfully recalled, "My great mother, the Church, looked askance at first at me, her latest born."[61] When allowed to speak her own lines, the Methodist deaconess claims her historic place in pioneering the social gospel for a chary church.

Adhesion to the social gospel had a different meaning for churchmen than for churchwomen, as suggested by a personal reminiscence of Rauschenbusch. Recalling his early involvement, he wrote from a male perspective:

367

All whose recollection runs back of 1900 will remember that as a time of lonesomeness. We were few and we shouted in the wilderness. It was always a happy surprise when we found a new man who had seen the light. We used to form a kind of flying wedge to support a man who was preparing to attack a minister's conference with the Social Gospel. Our older friends remonstrated with us for wrecking our careers. We ourselves saw the lion's den plainly before us, and only wondered how the beasts would act this time.[62]

It escaped Rauschenbusch's notice that deaconesses were flourishing at that very time. They were rarely overcome by "lonesomeness" in their work, nor did they worry over "wrecked careers." On the contrary, in their espousal of the social gospel, those venturesome women discovered sisterhood and enough meaningful work for a lifetime. They also achieved significant status in their church, by making themselves trained experts in the field of Christian social service.

# The Twentieth-century View

# Pioneering Social Gospel Radicalism: An Overview of the History of the Methodist Federation for Social Action

George D. McClain

The Methodist Episcopal Church was tardy in coming to support of the social gospel. At the turn of the twentieth century many other denominations were far more social gospel-oriented than the M. E. Church. Though slow to embrace the movement, this denomination nevertheless became, in the words of historian William King, "the social gospel's most ardent advocate." The organization most responsible for this was the Methodist Federation for Social Service, later renamed the Methodist Federation for Social Action.

This issue [of *Radical Religion*] seeks to recover for present day church activists the important story of the Methodist Federation as it extends over almost three-quarters of a century. Present day Christian radicals can receive encouragement and a broadened perspective through acquaintance with the "great cloud of witnesses" who have pioneered radical Christianity through the Methodist Federation.

The contributions included in this issue [of *Radical Religion*] are best understood in the context of an overview of the history of the Methodist Federation.

# 1907–1916: ADVOCATING SOCIAL REFORM AND COMMUNITY SERVICE

The Methodist Federation for Social Service was established in 1907 at the initiative of Frank Mason North, composer of "Where Cross the Crowded Ways of Life" and a New York City mission executive; Worth M. Tippy, pastor of Epworth Memorial Church in Cleveland; Herbert Welch, president of Ohio Wesleyan University; Robb Zaring, an editor of the Western Christian Advocate; and Harry F. Ward, pastor of the Union Avenue M. E. Church in the stockyard district of Chicago.

The organizational meeting was held in December, 1907, in Washington, D.C., where the new Federation pledged itself "to deepen within the church the sense of social obligation and opportunity to study social problems from the Christian point of view, and to promote social service in the spirit of Jesus Christ." Herbert Welch was elected president; John Williams, New York State Commissioner of Labor, first vice-president; and Harry Ward, second vice-president. At the conclusion of the founding meeting, participants were officially presented to President Theodore Roosevelt at the White House.

The first task of MFSS in winning the denomination for the social gospel was to influence the 1908 General Conference. The new organization was remarkably effective; it secured the adoption of the first denominational Social Creed (direct ancestor of the present United Methodist Social Principles) and gained the formal recognition of the General Conference, which requested the Federation to make recommendations about the social application of the Gospel to the next General Conference.

At the 1912 General Conference the Federation was recognized "as the executive agency to rally the forces of the Church in support of (social reform)," with the stipulation that three bishops be designated each quadrennium to sit on the Federation's General Council. Thus was established a unique quasi-official role, combining access to the denominational power structure with independence from strict oversight. To assure this freedom to pursue its prophetic mission, the Federation was established as a membership organization with financial support solely from its own membership rather than official denominational sources.

During this period the Federation was a somewhat uneasy coalition of social gospel adherents whose concepts of the social gospel ranged from promoting local church involvement in community service and social work to identifying the church with the Progressive political views of the day, with some who were beginning to question the inherent morality of a capitalistic economy.[1]

After the initial success in 1908, the Federation experienced several disappointing years. Then in 1911 a most significant step was taken in securing Harry F. Ward as Federation executive. He immediately brought enormous vigor and incisive analytical abilities to the service of the Federation, founding the *Social Service Bulletin* in that initial year. In 1912 the newly elected Bishop Francis J. McConnell was chosen as MFSS president, inaugurating a partnership with Harry Ward that was of enormous historical consequence over the next 32 years of Federation life.

One Federation priority was to set the church's house in order in labor relations by securing hiring preference for union affiliated workers at the denomination publishing concern in Cincinnati, an effort that proved unsuccessful.

The major energy in the 1912–16 period, however, was directed toward social evangelistic missions to encourage local churches to perform community service. To this end, Ward in 1912–13 spoke at 347 meetings and led thirty-six workshops in seventeen different states. This Federation effort was so successful and the community service idea achieved such acceptance that MFSS was able in 1916 to turn over this concern to the Board of Home Missions, with the blessing of the General Conference.

This left the Federation free to devote itself more thoroughly to its mission of "Christianizing the social order," which meant, about all, championing the cause of labor in its struggles for decent wages, humane working conditions, and collective bargaining, and, most basic of all, for the right to have work—a "spiritual necessity."

# 1916–1928: THE EMERGENCE OF SOCIAL GOSPEL RADICALISM[2]

With the coming of World War I, international issues suddenly demanded urgent attention from the social gospel movement and MFSS.

The most controversial issue of the time was the Russian Revolution. In 1919 Ward and his associate, Grace Scribner, issued a *Social Service Bulletin* on "The Russian Question," which, because of the cautious support it gave to the Russian Revolution, became a *cause célèbre* within the denomination. Scribners regular weekly column in the *Sunday School Journal* on the "social interpretation of the lesson," which she had contributed since 1914, was dropped. The editors' section of the *Sunday School Journal* publishers voted to eliminate Ward's books from the lesson series and, vindictively, urged that the plates of his books be destroyed. In this climate of hysteria, Ward was accused by the New York State Committee Investigating Seditious Activities of teaching a "new gospel of Bolshevism," a charge which thoroughly misrepresented his actual orientation as a Fabian socialist, rooted in Christian teaching and the idealist tradition and having basic differences with orthodox Marxism.[3]

During the World War the Federation vigorously defended the rights of conscientious objectors and political dissenters. As the political repression deepened after the war, commitment to civil liberties and opposition to political repression became a central theme in MFSS life. Out of this concern Harry F. Ward helped found the American Civil Liberties Union and served as its president for twenty years.

The steel strike of 1919 found the Federation deeply involved through the Interchurch World Movement's investigating committee, which McConnell chaired. The report, sharply critical of the average work week of 68.7 hours and other steel industry labor practices, generated enormous publicity and helped mold public opinion against industry abuse in a time when support for the cause of labor met with massive resistance.

In 1922 MFSS convened a national conference in Evanston on "Christianity and the Economic Order," considered "the first church gathering in this country to be devoted entirely to the discussion of the ethical aspects of economics." A second Evanston conference four years later on "The Preacher and the Economic Order" launched a movement to make preachers' salaries equitable and "brotherly."

Tragedy entered Federation life in 1922 when Grace Scribner was instantly killed by a hit-and-run driver. Brought in to replace her as Ward's associate was Winifred Chappell, a very astute activist and publicist who was to get deeply involved in the intense labor struggles of the day and was a primary factor in moving the Federation to a more radical advocacy of a new social order. Miriam Crist's article in *Radical Religion*, "Rediscovering Winifred Chappell," constitutes a long overdue recognition of her central importance to the Federation and the social gospel movement.

Divisions of opinion over the Russian Revolution, civil liberties, and the cause of labor helped precipitate the breakup of the old social gospel coalition which constituted MFSS. Some turned toward the temperance movement or the new missionary opportunities that were opening up with the expansion of American power. Others, like Worth Tippy, opted for a moderate reformist position.

But a significant core of Federation adherents, thanks especially to the leadership of George Coe, Winifred Chappell, Harry Ward, and Francis J. McConnell, found themselves in increasingly sharp opposition to the very direction in which American society was moving under industrial capitalism, and they created for the Methodist Federation the role of standard bearer of a fully developed social gospel radicalism. In a far more forthright manner than the earlier social gospel, this "revolutionary idealism" confronted racism, the profit motive, militarism, labor exploitation, and imperialism. Years before the Depression shattered the unbounded optimism of capitalist America, the Federation and its leaders had unmasked the prevailing economic myths and exposed capitalism as resting tenuously on "the cultivation of greed."

Alan Thomson's article, "Prophetic Religion and the Democratic Front: The Mission of Harry F. Ward," describes the roots and qualities of the prophetic religious stance of the central figure in this movement. A close look at Federation life as this period came to a close in 1928 is found in "The Methodist Federation on the Eve of the Great Depression," by George McClain.

# 1929–1936: THE ALL-OUT ATTACK ON CAPITALISM[4]

The Depression era, which suddenly broke upon the nation with the stock market crash of late 1929, found the Federation harboring no illusions either about the soundness or the morality of U.S. capitalism. Just months before the Northeast Ohio Conference had adopted a Federation-inspired statement that declared American capitalism to be a "pagan economic order." Likewise the Pittsburgh Conference had declared: "After all, the real issue in the economic problem is capitalism" with its "enormous waste . . . its undemocratic control . . . its concentration of wealth."

The Federation executives, Winifred Chappell and Harry Ward, sought constantly in this period to educate their constituency and the church regarding the reality of class conflict. As the stock market crashed in October of 1929, members of the Federation were reading in that month's *Social Service Bulletin* about the wave of textile workers' strikes sweeping the South. In the rhetorical questions so typical of the Chappell/Ward style, the message was conveyed that these strikes were clear instances of the class struggle in which the churches of the South were the captives of the mill owners. Repeatedly throughout the Depression, they pointed out how workers were having to bear the biggest brunt of the economic distress.

In 1930 a third Evanston Conference was held, this time on the theme "The Layman and the Economic Order." Honored at a special dinner were three women: Mary McDowell, a pioneer social worker and charter MFSS member; a textile "mill girl"; and a labor organizer among the embattled textile workers. Following the conference Winifred Chappell concluded hopefully, "There is a small band of Methodist preachers who are consciously through with capitalism."

The Federation responded with great urgency as the social crisis of the Great Depression unfolded. There soon developed an unprecedented receptivity in the church to the Federation's critique of the social order. Such criticism was echoed in local preachers' meetings, annual conferences, and even by the 1932

General Conference of the Methodist Episcopal Church, which declared: "The present industrial order is unchristian, unethical, and antisocial." The editors relentlessly pressed this social criticism to the conclusion that capitalism could not save itself. The New Deal rescue measures were seen as "the official recognition of the fact that capitalism can no longer run on its own power," but needed to be propped up by full-scale government support of intervention in the economy, a development labelled "economic fascism."

The Federation in this period was moved by a palpable sense that "an old order is passing and a new one dawning." The important thing was to get involved, whatever the risk, in the shaping of the new age, in the birthing of the new and potentially more just and Christian social order. If it meant being labelled "red," then the label was to be worn proudly. If opposing injustice and unchristian treatment of workers "constitutes what they call a 'red'," the *Bulletin* approvingly quoted one correspondent, "then what intelligent and decent man could be anything else but a red?"

The sense of urgency also derived in part from the financial distress that the Federation itself was experiencing, not because of its members' objections but because of their personal financial distress and consequent inability to contribute at the same level. In 1932 the situation was salvaged by a voluntary salary cut by the paid staff, Winifred Chappell and Gertrude Rutherford. (Ever since 1919, Ward had donated his time.) Still, serious consideration was given to closing the office. The deteriorating situation in the next year was only saved by an emergency foundation grant, reducing by half the number of *Bulletins* (with the name now changed to *Social Questions Bulletin*), and placing the salaried executive Winifred Chappell on a part-time basis.

Out of the soul searching occasioned by the social breakdown without and the financial crisis within, the decision was made to continue, though with a more specific focus than ever on the social crisis of "a dying capitalism" and its attending threats of domestic fascism and international war. The Federation's entire energy was officially thrown into the struggle against the capitalistic order. By vote of the general meeting and ratification by the membership in late 1933 and early 1934, the Federation was henceforth to be identified as "an organization which seeks to abolish the profit system and to develop the classless society based upon the obligation of mutual service."

With this action MFSS launched what historian of the Federation Milton Huber calls the Federation's "all-out attack on capitalism." This attack was inaugurated with the writing and distributing of a series of remarkably effective "crisis leaflets." Designed for wide popular distribution, both within and without the church, the leaflets were issued in three sets, the first dealing with the breakdown of capitalism, the second with the forms of economy to replace capitalism (above all, "people's control") and finally with the method of change to a planned economy.

This attack on capitalism was carried out in a more intellectually rigorous way through a continuous monitoring and analysis of the New Deal. Beginning in late 1933 and for 15 consecutive months the *SQB* measured the New Deal's promises against its performance in the areas of agriculture, the welfare of blacks, unemployment relief, education, labor, war preparations, and "the economics of scarcity." The editors concluded that the New Deal's attempt to prop up our present economy by state aid produces profits and relief lines faster than it does jobs or a rising standard of living" and that there still is "no middle ground between accepting the system and abolishing it." In sum, capitalism under the New Deal was basically "organized poverty."

In 1934 Ward became president of the American League Against War and Fascism (later renamed the American League for Peace and Freedom), the broadest and largest united front organization in U.S. history. Ward's leadership is described in Alan Thomson's contribution to this issue [of *Radical Religion*]. Ward and Chappell, both active in the League, sought to bring the Methodist Federation into League membership as a specific action to bolster the forces resisting fascist tendencies. The recommendation of the 1934 MFSS executive committee meeting to join the League occasioned one of the more serious internal divisions in Federation history. The issue was that of cooperating in an organization in which Communist Party members played an important role. The Federation was the only church group ever to affiliate with the League.

The turbulent times gave rise to a constellation of tensions centering on the leadership of Chappell and Ward, of which the controversy over the united front affiliation was only the most dramatic. On one side were those Federationists gathered around the Chicago-based Christian Action Conference, who expected from MFSS not only a strong educational program, but also a strong action program. Others felt there was insufficient religious orientation in the Federation's public posture, a concern that appears to have some merit in view of the entirely non-theological orientation of the *Bulletin*. Then there were those who have some credence to what the *SQB* called "the widespread gossip throughout the church as to the secretaries' (i.e., Ward and Chappell's) positions regarding violence, Communism, and a united front with Communists." Finally, some felt that the policy-making process gave insufficient opportunity for membership participation. This latter concern was quite justified, for the decision-making process was inordinately concentrated in the staff, with yearly or biennial meetings of a small, New York-based executive committee being the only structure for shared decision making.

These issues were thoroughly aired at special meetings in Pittsburgh, New Haven, Evanston, and Denver between September, 1935, and April, 1936. In effect, the leadership of Ward and Chappell was confirmed.

A position clearly repudiating violence was adopted, but this had always been Ward's position (though he was not a pacifist as such). There was a decision that the secretaries' political views and affiliations were "their own business;" and the leadership was supported on the question of affiliation with the American League Against War and Fascism, the vote in the Midwest meeting being 53–10. The Chappell/Ward description of the economic system that should replace the profit system was adopted—"a planned and planning economy"—understood to "rest upon the social ownership of the resources and plant . . . by the people" and "the continuous extension of the democratic process throughout all its operations." At the same time the leadership had to accept recommendations that "study and action . . . must be tied together" and that certain structural changes were to be instituted to facilitate more "democratic decisions."

These internal strains were to a great extent a reflection of the anti-communist hysteria generated by what Robert Goldstein calls "the abortive red scare of 1934–35."[5] During that period right-wing charges of communist influence in the Roosevelt administration had reached flood-tide proportions, particularly through the William Randolph Hearst newspaper empire. The Hearst press also ran a syndicated series of articles, "Rid the M. E. Church of 'Red' Incubus," in which author Ralph Easley urged the 1936 General Conference to "deal with the McConnell-Ward-Chappell radical aggregation without gloves."

Also at this time Elizabeth Dilling published her infamous "exposé" of communist subversion, *The Red Network*, which listed some 500 organizations and 1300 persons allegedly involved in communist conspiracy, among them Mahatma Gandhi, Chiang Kai-Shek, and Eleanor Roosevelt. Federationists listed included Francis J. McConnell, George Coe, Ernest Fremont Tittle, G. Bromley Oxnam, Halford Luccock, Winifred Chappell, Paul Hutchinson, Charles Webber, Gilbert Cox, Owen Geer, W. B. Waltmire, Harold Case, Stanley High, and Worth Tippy.

Inevitably this red-batting had its champions within the church. Robert Gilman Smith of the Methodist Episcopal Church, South circulated his pamphlet, "Methodist Reds," which suggested MFSS rename itself the "Marxist Federation for Social Strife."

The Conference of Methodist Laymen, headed by two Chicago bankers, and the Methodist Laymen's Committee of Southern California were organized to advocate the return to purely personal religion and to oppose the MFSS and its influence in the church. These groups sought General Conference action to have the Federation investigated and deprived of the use of the title "Methodist." Some also sought the establishment of an official commission on social concerns which could be bound to moderate views and would hopefully eclipse the Federation's radical influence.

These moves failed at General Conference, although the Federation agreed informally always to make clear that it was an unofficial organization. But neither did General Conference accept the Federation recommendations to reject outright a system based on the struggle-for-profit and replace it with one based on social planning.

The Federation experienced one serious casualty of these years of struggle, namely the loss to MFSS of Winifred Chappell, who following General Conference took a leave of absence for reasons of health and exhaustion, probably arising out of the intense financial, ideological, and administrative strains the Federation had been experiencing. Her absence proved to be permanent and represented symbolically the close of an era in Federation history in which its fundamental ethical stance—its opposition to capitalism—came to its clearest articulation and experienced its greatest receptivity across the church. Earlier in the Depression Federation leaders had realistic hopes of heading a majority movement. (A survey conducted in 1934 among some 5,000 Methodists found 39% of them ready to scuttle the system and replace it with socialism, while another 56% favored "drastically reformed capitalism.") But in 1936 it was apparent that these hopes would have to be laid aside for the foreseeable future and the Federation would find its proper role as a prophetic minority.

Federation life during these years was undergirded by a profound devotional life. This dimension, generally neglected in accounts of Federation history, is illuminated by the accompanying article, "Prayer and Class Struggles: Devotional Life Within the Federation." Particular attention is given to a collection of devotional material compiled by Wade Crawford Barclay, a Federation activist and denominational mission education executive who in the 30's led a Federation study group at the denominational headquarters in Chicago and in the 40's edited the *Social Questions Bulletin* for several years.

## 1936–1944: FROM NEW INITIATIVE TO AN UNCERTAIN FUTURE

The Federation came out of the 1934–36 struggles with renewed strength and confidence, vigorously criticizing General Conference for its equivocation and platitudes regarding the economic issue, and tripling its budget with the anticipation of hiring additional staff.

Soon after General Conference the Rev. Charles C. Webber was employed as a field secretary for the purpose of revitalizing the Federation's grass-roots support. Webber had a background as inner city pastor, Union Theological Seminary professor, and labor secretary for the Fellowship of Reconciliation, in which latter capacity he had given personal leadership in a number of labor struggles and strikes, sometimes occasioning arrest. Within a year Helen Grace

Murray, a social worker with editorial experience, came on the staff to replace Winifred Chappell.

The situation required a new strategy for channeling Federation influence into the denominational structures. One effect of the reactionary tendencies that had come out into the open during the 1936 General Conference was that many conference social service commissions, which had earlier served as local units of the Federation, were either turning conservative or being merged with more conservative groups, such as commissions on temperance. The successful strategy developed by Charles Webber was to promote the formation of independent MFSS units, and within two years such units had been formed in twenty conferences and nine colleges.

Another Federation response to the growing reaction within Protestantism was to play a leading role in the creation of the United Christian Council for Democracy, "the first radical religious united front." The UCCD embraced representatives of nine denominations and was dedicated to a platform almost identical to the Federation's. In his field work Webber assisted in the formation of local UCCD units. As he travelled extensively throughout the country, Webber focused Federation attention on the rights of labor, the threat of a U.S. fascism, the insufficient measures of the New Deal, and the evils of racial discrimination.

Throughout the 30's increased attention had been given to the concerns of blacks. The MFSS joined with other groups in sponsoring the defense of the Scottsboro defendants. Several issues of the *Bulletin* [ . . . ] were devoted to countering discrimination against blacks, both in the church and in society. At the close of the decade, the Federation led an effort to persuade the denominational Board of Temperance of The Methodist Church to require the restaurant leasing its facilities to serve blacks without discrimination.

Webber's responsibilities increased as Harry Ward reduced his work load, Helen Grace Murray left Federation employment, and Webber was made the executive secretary. A reprinted page from the June, 1942, *Social Questions Bulletin* contains a comprehensive summary of his extraordinary field work for MFSS during the 1939–42 period when he was the sole paid executive staff.

As the U.S. became involved in the war, the Federation concentrated on civil liberties issues—the rights of women workers, racial discrimination, the rights of conscientious objectors, and the detention of Japanese-Americans in relocation camps.

In spite of the growth in membership stimulated by Webber's fieldwork, the Federation experienced increasing financial difficulty from 1940 on. The overriding sense of urgency about the war effort focused people's attention away from the radical reform issues promoted by the Federation. Furthermore, the Federation was split regarding its position on the war and decided in the interests of harmony to take no position at all. To stave off financial disaster,

Charles Webber went to Virginia in 1943 to do organizing for the Amalgamated Clothing Workers of America while his wife volunteered in the Federation office in New York. In December of that year Webber resigned from his position as executive secretary to work full-time as a national representative for the Clothing Workers.

Just prior to Webber's resignation, Harry Ward too announced his resignation after serving as Federation secretary without remuneration since 1919. His resignation was to be effective with the close of the 1944 General Conference, at which time Bishop McConnell also would be retiring from the MFSS presidency, which he had occupied since 1912. An Ad Interim Administrative Committee, chaired by Wade Crawford Barclay, appropriately acknowledged that "due to them (McConnell and Ward) more than any others the Federation has served well the cause of Christian social interpretation and action in the whole of Protestantism." It then turned to examine the serious question as to whether the Federation would have a future.

## 1945–1953: EXPANSION AND REPRESSION

An intense canvassing of the Federation membership throughout 1944 indicated a broad consensus regarding the need for both an official social action commission and the continued existence of the Federation, with the MFSS to play the role as "advance guard" on social issues and to prevent any official organization from "merely marking time or falling asleep." With this clear affirmation of the need for the Federation, a search was made for new leadership to carry on. New officers were chosen: as president, Bishop Lewis Hartman: as vice-presidents, Bishop James C. Baker and Bishop G. Bromley Oxnam; and as secretary, Thelma Stevens, executive secretary of the Woman's Division Christian social relations department.

Chosen as the new Federation executive secretary was a twenty-seven year old, Georgia-born U.S. Maritime Service chaplain, Jack R. McMichael. He had been the chairperson of the national YMCA-YWCA student association, as well as of a united front organization, the American Youth Congress. Following a year in China as the "Y's" ambassador of goodwill to its Chinese counterpart, McMichael had studied at Union Theological Seminary, where he had been an assistant to Harry Ward.

One reason for selecting McMichael as executive was his background as a southerner. In 1939 the northern and southern branches of the church were reunited after breaking apart during the era of slavery. The Federation had operated wholly within the northern branch, the Methodist Episcopal Church, but now after unification there was concern to expand into the South and create a fully church-wide base for Federation objectives.

381

The Federation exploded with energy under McMichael's leadership. New Federation chapters were organized, many of them in the South; and by the late 40's the Federation could count chapters in some three dozen annual conferences, as well as additional ones in certain colleges and cities. An MFSS "Advisory Committee for Cooperation with Organized Labor in the South" was organized, including in its membership evangelism leader Harry Denman, Methodist women's leader Mrs. M. E. Tilly, and bishop of the Central (black) jurisdiction Robert Brooks. The Federation membership reached an all-time high of some 5,000 members, and under the editorship of Wade Crawford Barclay the *SQB* grew in size from its usual 4–6 pages to 16 pages.

Perhaps due to his background as a southerner, McMichael brought a special sensitivity to issues of racial justice and the racial inclusiveness of the Federation. A deliberate effort was made by McMichael to organize Federation members across the lines of racial segregation that had been adopted as the price for the unification of the northern and southern Methodist denominations. Many members of the Central (black) Jurisdiction joined the Federation and this movement of blacks into the organization was appropriately culminated in 1948 in the election of Central Jurisdiction (black) Bishop Robert N. Brooks, of New Orleans, as president of the Methodist Federation for Social *Action*, as it was renamed that year.

In the international arena, the Federation attacked the Cold War policies of the Truman administration, calling for detente with the U.S.S.R., the recognition of the People's Republic of China, and the boycotting of fascist regimes in Greece and Spain. It also sought the international control of atomic energy, disarmament under United Nations supervision, and an end to peacetime conscription.

This period of Federation history very much deserves detailed, objective study from several perspectives—its pioneering in race relations in the church, its critique of the developing Cold War, and, above all, its experience from 1948 to 1952 when it was again at the center of controversy in the denomination.[6] The Federation was unquestionably a victim—in fact, the chief victim among all religious groups—of the McCarthyite anti-Communist persecution which engulfed the country, evaporating the courage of normally courageous persons and twisting the American "tradition" of civil liberties into a mere caricature of itself.

Congressional committees—the Senate Sub-committee on Internal Security and the House Un-American Activities Committee—led the way in creating a poisonous social climate in the late 1940's and the 1950's.

Committee hearings and published listings were widely employed as devices for condemning persons and groups on the basis of nothing more than hearsay evidence, personal association, espousal of a particular cause, the unreliable testimony of paid informers, or other so-called "evidence," none of which was ever presented for cross-examination by those accused. These committees were thoroughly contemptuous of the constitutional guarantee of due process. Mississippi Senator James Eastland said regarding rules of procedure his Senate subcommittee: "I will decide those as we go along and announce them when I desire."

Thus with total disregard for the reliability of evidence or due process, these committees damaged the reputations, ruined the careers, or caused the firing of thousands of persons who were never convicted of any offense. Hundreds of organizations, such as MFSA, were similarly slandered, again with never a conviction of illegality or even a trial. The result was to create a general climate of fear and intimidation in which persons were afraid to advocate any unpopular opinion, join any liberal organization, or even read a dissenting periodical or think questioning thoughts.

The press in the 1950's collaborated in this denial of basic freedoms and injury to innocent persons and organizations by printing these Congressional committee accusations as though they were reliable and factual and by themselves engaging in similar accusations.

In December of 1947, Frederick Woltman wrote a series of articles in the New York *World-Telegram* characterizing MFSS as a "sounding board" for the Communist party. The United Press picked up the charges and some papers described McMichael as "former chairman" of the Young Communist League. Even *The New York Times* repeated this false accusation; later it published a retraction stating McMichael had never been chairman of the Young Communists, "nor (was) he connected with any other Communist organization." [7]

Then in 1950 Stanley High wrote a *Reader's Digest* article, "Methodism's Pink Fringe," which renewed charges against the MFSA. The result was a concerted campaign to villify and destroy MFSA, headed by a coalition called Circuit Riders, Inc.[8] Through wide circulation of false accusations, innuendo, and guilt-by-association, a bitter attack was waged against the Federation in the months leading up to the 1952 General Conference. This campaign was assisted enormously when HUAC, partly at the urging of the Circuit Riders, published at government expense an 88-page "Review" of MFSA which repeated and appeared to dignify the charges of Woltman and High.[9]

In this atmosphere there was no chance for objectivity and sanity regarding the Federation. The General Conference voted to express disapproval of "many of the statements and policies" of the Federation; it also asked it to "remove the word 'Methodist' from its name" and endorsed the move to evict MFSA from its rented office space in the Methodist Building in New York City.

Ironically the General Conference, as part of its repudiation of the Federation, created an official Board of Christian Social Concerns, which the Federation had sought since 1944. The role of the Federation in the creation of an official social action agency suggests the words of Jesus: "Unless a grain of wheat falls into the earth and dies, it remains alive; but if it dies, it bears much fruit."

The attack upon the Federation was completed the next year when HUAC summoned Jack McMichael to testify regarding accusations of his Communist affiliation. The accompanying excerpts from the official record of that hearing illustrate the tenor of the attack by the Committee and McMichael's spirited resistance, which several times during the two days of hearings led the committee members into bickering with each other.

As historians and social critics have come to understand the diabolical character of McCarthyism, this action against MFSA has been increasingly shown to be a most sorry chapter in the life of American Methodism. Perhaps the profoundest commentary on this episode was the action of that same General Conference to eliminate from the Social Creed any reference to "the subordination of the profit motive to the creative and cooperative spirit."

## 1953–1980: SURVIVING AND REVIVING

After Jack McMichael voluntarily resigned as executive secretary in 1953 to take a local church appointment in California, the Federation was kept in existence only by the valiant effort of volunteers, especially the Rev. Lloyd F. Worley of Connecticut, the president; the Rev. Mark Chamberlin, who devoted practically full-time as a volunteer to administer the Federation office out of his home in Gresham, Oregon, and Jack McMichael himself, who took over as editor of the *Social Questions Bulletin* while also serving in the pastorate.

In 1960 the Federation again employed an executive secretary, the Rev. Lee H. Ball of Ardsley, New York. Lee Ball travelled extensively across the country knocking on the doors of Methodist ministers everywhere. He lent the support of the *Social Questions Bulletin* to dozens of progressive causes, including the elimination of racial prejudice from The Methodist Church and the society as a whole and opposition to the war in Viet Nam. As early as 1962 Ball attacked this war and urged President Kennedy "to withdraw our troops from Thailand and recall our navy from Southeast Asian waters, before we get another Korea, or worse." During this time the MFSA participated in the Religious Freedom Committee, which had been set up to protect progressive clergy from right-wing attack. It also demanded the abolition of HUAC and repeal of the Smith and McCarran Acts.

With organized support from only the two Federation chapters in the Oregon/Idaho and California/Nevada Conferences, Lee Ball, ably assisted by his wife Mae, kept the Federation alive until a time when the Federation experience under McCarthyism would be understood not as a condemnation of the Federation, but as a tribute to its visionary purpose and its courage in resisting the Cold War hysteria.

At the time of Lee Ball's retirement the leadership responsibilities were passed to a new executive secretary, the Rev. George McClain and to a younger generation who had been radicalized through participation in civil rights and anti-war struggles. Building on a long tradition, MFSA hired two seminarians, David and Kathy Munson-Young, as field staff for the 1973–74 year, asking them to provide on-site organizing support for the striking non-professionals at the United Methodist hospital in Pikesville, Kentucky. In 1976 the Federation issued a *Daily SQB* at the General Conference and instituted a study-action program critical of capitalism and oriented around liberation theology.

Between 1975 and 1980 new chapters were organized in ten additional conferences. Other signs of new vitality included the Federation's successful promotion throughout the church of the J. P. Stevens and Nestle boycotts and its organizing of the Coalition for the Whole Gospel to unite progressives at the 1980 General Conference. In January 1979, it published a carefully documented critique of the growing "evangelical" Good News Movement, concluding that its leadership constituted "the presence and influence of the New Far Right" in the United Methodist Church.

When the denominational clergy magazine published an analysis of political forces shaping the approaching 1980 General Conference, cast in the form of a humorous baseball "scouting report," it listed MFSA as playing in "left field." Given the history of the Federation during and since 1952, the significant factor was that for the first time in almost three decades MFSA was once again "in the ball game" and, ideologically speaking, back at its accustomed position.

## CHAPTER 26

# The Social Creed and Methodism Through Eighty Years

## Donald K. Gorrell

In May 1988 The United Methodist Church celebrates the eightieth anniversary of the Social Creed. But most persons know little about the role and function of this distinctive document, or its varied forms. Nor do they appreciate the unique relationship of this literary genre to Methodism. My purpose here is to describe the origin and evolution of the Social Creed, with special attention to its ties to Methodism through eight decades.

American religious historians generally have accepted Harry F. Ward's evaluation that the adoption of the Social Creed in 1908 constituted "a significant fact in the history of religion" because it marked "the deliberate and conscious entrance of the Church upon the field of social action." [1] But few of them have bothered to explain the development of the social pronouncement beyond the acknowledgement that "it stands as one of the great symbols of the Social Gospel." [2]

Typically, the interpretation of most historians emphasizes four essential ingredients: the Social Creed first was adopted by the Methodist Episcopal Church in May 1908; then it was approved in modified form by the Federal Council of Churches in December 1908; four years later it was supplemented, revised, and reaffirmed by the Federal Council; and it remained unchanged for twenty years until the ecumenical organization again revised and enlarged it as the Social Ideals of the Churches in 1932. And then it virtually disappears from history. In most narratives the context of the Social Gospel and of ecumenical Protestantism is the primary emphasis. While its Methodist origin is sometimes noted, the cooperative response of Protestant churches to society's problems has been regarded as more important. Strangely, these interpretations account for less than half of the time the Social Creed has existed and the full story cannot be told without devoting major attention to the relation of Methodism to this social declaration.

In the account that follows I focus on the Social Creed as an official document. Several useful books interpret the Creed, but their primary purpose is to understand and explain the affirmations stated in it. In contrast, I view the Creed as a literary entity containing a number of ideas that was adopted as a unit, and I trace what happened to the total document, not to just one or more issues stated to it. Hence my emphasis is on the social statement as a unique and pliable type of literature.

Another distinct feature of this narrative is its primary orientation to institutions, since officially incorporated organizations authorized the pronouncements. In the account, interaction of three institutions becomes centrally important. The Social Creed was initially created by the efforts of the Methodist Federation for Social Service; it was first officially adopted by the Methodist Episcopal Church; and it was then endorsed by the Federal Council of the Churches of Christ in America. These three bodies existed throughout the eighty years of the Creed's development and they continue to exist, although the names of each have changed along the way. The interaction of these institutions ranges from times of remarkable cooperation to periods of obvious differences and even to stages of open alienation. These shifts in relationships among the organizations directly affected the Creed's development.

The importance of Methodism in this study is explained by the fact that this denomination has the only continuing relationship to the Social Creed throughout its eighty years' existence. Methodists were authors of its major recensions and were leaders who affected the origin and preservation of the document. Moreover, Methodism was the only tradition that consistently used the term Social Creed and that continues to authorize such pronouncements to the present time.

With these distinctive emphases in mind, we turn now to trace the Social Creed through six stages of development.

## ORIGINS OF THE SOCIAL CREED (1907–1912)

Although hindsight shows clearly that the origins of the Social Creed were multiple and derived from forces working inside and outside of the churches, in England and Europe as well as America, those who shaped the document believed they were responding to the immediate needs of their time in the United States.[3]

In an era of unscrupulous business leaders and unprotected laborers, of political corruption and insurance scandals exposed by muckraking journalists and progressive reformers,[4] the Methodist Federation for Social Service was created at Washington, DC, on December 3–4, 1907. Through the leaders and strategy of this organization the Social Creed had its birth.

From its inception the Methodist Federation for Social Service determined that it would "be kept wholly unofficial in its relation to the General Conference and other official societies of Methodism" in order to maintain the freedom to speak prophetically. But that autonomy did not inhibit the organization from seeking to influence its parent church. By a strategy of publicity, planning, and perseverance its leaders worked to arouse the Methodist Episcopal General Conference in May, 1908, to take a stand on the economic problems that troubled the nation. A strategy of petitions that were assigned to a committee with sympathetic leaders enabled Herbert Welch and Harry F. Ward, two Federation officers who were not delegates, to collaborate with the sub-committee that prepared a report on "The Church and Social Problems." Through their informal unofficial participation the two quietly wrote most of the report that was approved by the conference on May 30, 1908. Later Welch acknowledged that Ward was the primary author of the report submitted.[5]

Within the three page report was a list of affirmations that comprised the original Social Creed, which stated:

> The Methodist Episcopal Church stated:
> For equal rights and complete justice for all men in all stations of life.
> For the principles of conciliation and arbitration in industrial dissensions.
> For the protection of the worker from dangerous machinery, occupational diseases, injuries, and mortality.
> For the abolition of child labor.
> For such regulation of the conditions of labor for women as shall safeguard the physical and moral health of the community.
> For the suppression of the 'sweating system'.
> For the gradual and reasonable reduction of the hours of labor to the lowest practical point, with work for all; and for that degree of leisure for all which is the condition of the highest human life.
> For a release for [from] employment one day in seven.
> For a living wage in every industry.
> For the highest wage that each industry can afford, and for the most equitable division of the products of industry that can ultimately be devised.
> For the recognition of the Golden Rule and the mind of Christ as the supreme law of society and the sure remedy for all social ills.[6]

This list of affirmations was recognized immediately as "a Methodist platform on social problems" that enabled the denomination to move "to a front place on questions of labor and capital," but the statement was not originally called the Social Creed. At the time of the General Conference that title was not in use, but by the late summer of 1908, when the Methodist Federation reprinted the report, the section of eleven principles was titled the "Social Creed of Methodism." [7]

Adoption of the full report also recognized the greatness of Methodism's "opportunity in the present crisis and the consequent urgency of its duty." The report went on to summon the denomination "to continue and increase its works of social service" and assigned responsibilities to the Methodist Federation for Social Service during the next quadrennium, thereby granting that organization unofficial recognition. [8]

During the autumn of 1908 Frank Mason North, another of the Federation's leaders, created a second version of the Social Creed. An active ecumenist as well as social activist, North chaired a committee that prepared an eighteen page report on "The Church and Modern Industry" that was presented to the first meeting of the Federal Council of the Churches of Christ in America in December. In that document he included most of the recently adopted Methodist Social Creed but added four additional affirmations that called for more rights for workers and the abatement of poverty. Based on a more elaborate theological rationale and the conviction that it would take the combined efforts of American Protestantism to deal with the social and industrial problems of the nation, North viewed the affirmations as an authoritative declaration by the combined denominations of the new Federal Council of Churches. [9] Without any evident authorization, he shared the Methodist Social Creed with other denominations and transformed the pronouncement into the Social Creed of the Churches. That his goal was achieved was evident when Lyman Abbott's *The Outlook* declared that the "resolutions concerning the relation of the Church to modern industry, in fact, to the whole social order . . . may be said to constitute a charter, a bill of rights, which the Protestant Churches of America recognize on behalf not only those who toil but also of society." [10]

Probably due to the close proximity of these two versions of the Social Creed within a few months, there has been confusion among historians concerning authorship. Harry F. Ward and Frank Mason North have each been designated as the original writer. [11] Both were among the five persons who called the meeting that established the Methodist Federation for Social Service, both worked diligently for the organization and social ministry generally, and both had a rightful claim to authorship. Nevertheless, it seems clear now that Ward composed the original Social Creed of Methodism while North authored the later ecumenical Social Creed of the Churches. But during their lifetimes North received the accolades because he authored a signed report and delivered it publicly while Ward's labors were unofficial and behind the scenes with a sub-committee. A touch of Ward's disappointment is evident in a letter to his wife but he never made the matter public in his books and articles concerning the Social Creed. North never claimed more than his Federal Council contribution and graciously accepted the praise. [12]

For the nascent Council of Churches the Social Creed served as a symbol of both the ecumenical and social commitment of member denominations. But the Council also facilitated social ministry in other ways. It created a Commission on the Church and Social Service, which North chaired, and it formed a Secretarial Council consisting of the executive secretaries for social service chosen by member churches. When Ward became executive secretary of the Methodist Federation for Social Service in 1912, he became a leading figure in the Secretarial Council, which served as a clearing house and coordinating office for social strategy and publication. The first common Council publishing subject was titled *The Social Creed of the Churches* and was edited by Ward.[13]

Upon the recommendation of the Secretarial Council a third revision and expansion of the Social Creed was endorsed by the Federal Council in 1912. As various denominations adopted the 1908 Creed they made additions or alterations and a common text of the statement was threatened. To regain uniformity the social service secretaries worked out "the best form of what has come to be called the Social Creed of the Churches" for the churches to adopt. Evidencing the growing interest in social problems, the delegates not only adopted the revised Creed but added two additional declarations from the floor. Although industrial problems still dominated, the list showed a broadening social perspective that now incorporated statements about the family, child development, health, liquor traffic, and property.[14]

During the four years from 1908 to 1912 the Social Creed emerged first from the efforts of the Methodist Federation for Social Service to be endorsed by one Methodist denomination, and then, second, had been translated to an ecumenical declaration by the vision of a single person, only to become in a third version the product of cooperative ecumenical thinking and planning. This was achieved by close interaction and oneness of purpose among the Methodist Federation, the Methodist Episcopal Church, and the Federal Council of Churches. By 1912 the Social Creed had become a stabilized feature of the institutional Protestantism whose social commitment it symbolized.

## ELABORATIONS OF THE IDEALS (1912–1928)

The sixteen point Social Creed adopted in 1912 served as the basic pronouncement of the Federal Council for twenty years, but the social platform was not actually as stable as that fact implies. Although the text remained unaltered, changing attitudes and circumstances in churches and the nation affected the document.

While there was no modification of the sixteen affirmations approved in December 1912, it was clear that member churches of the Federal Council felt free to make additions to the main platform. In 1916 the Methodist Federation for Social Service recommended the addition of a series of paragraphs on five topics relating to community service and industrial conditions which the General Council approved and added to its Social Creed.[15] Three years later, when the first World War ended, the Federal Council itself urged the addition of "four resolutions supplementary to the Social Creed of the Churches" that related to industrial problems and argued for "full political and economic equality with equal pay for equal work" for women.[16]

Despite this willingness to accept additional statements, four Presbyterian and Reformed denominations questioned the basic premises of social ministry between 1913 and 1915. In the largest of these bodies, the northern Presbyterians, the attack led the secretary of the Bureau of Social Service to resign, compelled the Board of Home Missions to reorganize, and forced the Federal Council of Churches to curtail its social service program and more clearly define its principles for social ministry. Part of this assault condemned the social Creed because the Federal Council had "no authority to draw up a common creed." Since Presbyterians believed that creeds referred to the earlier "ecumenical creeds of Christendom," they preferred to use the term "social ideals."[17] On this issue other denominations concurred, as evidenced by a pamphlet entitled "Social Service Ideals" issued by the social service commission of the Northern Baptist Convention in 1915. In 1920 the term Social Creed still was used in the reports of the Federal Council but by 1928 the dominant term was Social Ideals.[18] It was felt by then that the word "creed" in reference to social concerns suggested that a humanitarian platform was replacing religious convictions, while the word "ideals" conveyed the notion of goals yet to be achieved by institutions in which all members had not reached consensus.

As the trend toward ideals persisted in the twenties, so did the tendency to add large supplementary statements to the Social Creed. Most important of the denominational changes were the paragraphs added to the 1912 basic text by the National Council of the Congregational Churches in 1925. Convinced that new issues of national concern deserved a place in a social platform, Congregationalists adopted a series of statements that translated the Social Creed into five concrete areas: education, industry and economic relationships, agriculture, racial relations, and international relations.[19] By 1928 these additions were also approved by two other denominations.

That one of these bodies was the Methodist Episcopal Church evidenced a change caused by the Methodist Federation for Social Service. Its views had become more radical since World War I but were muted for political reasons. However, Harry Ward refused to take the initiative to again change the Social Creed because he now desired action more than words. Thus delegates at the 1928 General Conference were told that the changed text that they endorsed "is largely taken from the action of the Congregational Council of North America."[20]

At its quadrennial meeting in December 1928 the Federal Council of Churches observed the twentieth anniversary of the Social Creed, which had become a charter for the churches that "served as a guide, as a basis for educational effort, and as an interpretation to society of the church's point of view" even though it had not been fully attained. Nonetheless, it was recognized that new statements had to be added in light of new needs and the delegates authorized a total rewriting of the Social Creed by the Council's next meeting in 1932.[21] The practice of adding supplements to a basic platform was no longer workable. Unlike the Apostles' or Nicene Creeds, whose strength lay in their unchanged wording, a social Creed had to be changed periodically to keep it relevant to changing conditions. That recognition marked the close of the second stage of development.

## REVISION AND REVOLT (1928–1939)

When Francis J. McConnell, who was already a Methodist bishop and president of the Methodist Federation for Social service, was elected as president of the Federal Council in 1928, he seemed to personally unify the long-time cooperation among these organizations. But events in the next eleven years shattered that institutional collaboration and marked these years as a third distinct period in the evolution of the Social Creed.

During his four-year leadership, the Council endured the social, economic and political ravages of the Depression but managed to produce a new Social Ideals declaration. The ten person revision committee included three Methodists: chairman Edward Devine, Frank Mason North, and Worth Tippy, who directed the Council's Social Service Commission. All three were members of the Methodist Federation from its inception. Professor Devine was the primary author of the new document. The seventeen point platform looked much like its 1912 predecessor and incorporated much of it. But it contained striking innovations that fit the circumstances of the Depression Era. Its first two articles boldly confronted traditional laissez-faire economic theory by asserting the subordination of the profit motive to the cooperative spirit and advocated "social planning and control of the credit and monetary system . . . for the common good." Other affirmations dealt with urgent problems in agriculture, race relations, international affairs, prison reform, and rights of free speech, assembly, and press. In the opinion of Methodist F. Ernest Johnson of the Federal Council staff in 1932 Social Ideals "showed a definite movement toward the 'left'" when compared to the 1912 predecessor. But the justification for the declaration had cautious expectations: "This statement is not intended to provide a creed. It is rather intended as a contribution to the process of meeting problems by creating programs."[22] Dr. North presented the report, as he had twenty years earlier, and the delegates sang his hymn "Where Cross the Crowded Ways of Life," before approving it without dissent.[23]

Despite the obvious leadership of Methodists in this revision, and contrary to the prevailing interpretation of Methodist historians, the Methodist Episcopal Church did not adopt the revised Federal Council Social Ideals or any other new Social Creed at its General Conference in 1932. Walter G. Muelder in *Methodism and Society in the Twentieth Century* has argued that the General Conference took action that had "historic character" and deserved special attention. But comparison of the Social Creed in the 1932 Discipline of the Methodist Episcopal Church, on which he based his analysis, was identical in wording to that in the 1928 *Discipline*. As noted above that was borrowed from the amplified Social Creed adopted by the Congregational Church in 1925 rather than based on Methodist initiative or depression conditions. In fact, northern Methodism took no action concerning the Social Creed in 1932, and the 1932 revised Social Ideals became part of the denominational tradition through the Methodist Episcopal Church, South, which embraced it with minor changes in 1934.[24]

One reason for that result in the Methodist Episcopal Church was Harry Ward's refusal to work for changed words rather than actions. His growing radical convictions that had been suppressed in the twenties were freely expressed in the thirties. By 1931 he was convinced that the official social program of the churches depended on "the capacity of capitalistic industrialism to transform itself" by evolutionary development and he now doubted that necessary changes could be achieved without revolutionary methods. He agreed with the evaluation of the *Christian Century* that the 1932 Methodist General Conference had "flickered out in futility" and concluded that it was necessary for the Methodist Federation to become more revolutionary in order to remedy the situation. By November 1933 he urged his organization to work for the abolition of "a dying capitalism."[25]

This steady movement to the left appealed to a few, but it alienated many other Methodists. By 1935 the revolt of the left produced a pendular revolt of the right. A conference of conservative Methodist laymen was organized in Chicago to prepare for the 1936 General Conference at Columbus, Ohio and similar groups were formed in Los Angeles and New Jersey. As their attacks increased, the Methodist Federation for Social Service held meetings across the country to strengthen their cause. By careful planning and maneuvering, denominational leaders guided the moderate majority and avoided an open floor confrontation by enabling the extremists of the contending groups to be heard at length in committee sessions. But in light of that freedom, the chairperson asked the General Conference delegates not to edit or amend their report, which was approved as submitted. Consequently, the anticipated "Battle of Columbus" resulted in the "Peace Pact of Methodism."[26]

However, the peace was purchased at a price—the loss of the Social Creed in the Methodist Episcopal Church. Although there was no report of legislation disavowing Methodist endorsement of the Social Creed in the records of the 1936 General Conference, the *Discipline* that year no longer included that pronouncement. In the place formerly occupied by the Social Creed in the 1932 *Discipline* were statements on The Spiritual Life of the Church and on Social and Economic Questions in the 1936 *Discipline*. Evidently the divided condition of the denomination described in the latter document was intended to explain the absence of the social platform in the *Discipline* for the first time since 1908.[27] However it occurred, that result was an obvious victory for the laymen's groups, which had wanted the General Conference to disavow its earlier social statements. While the laity were unable to get Methodism to repudiate the Federation they succeeded in getting rid of the Social Creed. As a consequence, when the Methodist Episcopal Church entered into the Methodist Reunion of 1939 with the Methodist Episcopal Church, South and the Methodist Protestant Church it did not carry with it the Social Creed it had created and supported for twenty-eight years. Moreover, by 1939 the close institutional unity on the Social Creed previously enjoyed by the Methodist Episcopal Church, the Methodist Federation for Social Service, and the Federal Council of Churches was dissolving.

## A NEW METHODIST SOCIAL CREED (1939–1952)

As three branches of Methodism united at Kansas City in April 1939, the formation of the new institution known as The Methodist Church stimulated a new sense of denominational pride. One product of that pride was a new Social Creed that was distinctly denominational in form and commitment, although it was rooted in earlier versions. Adoption of a new Methodist Social Creed identifies a fourth stage of development, which extended from 1939 to 1952.

While this history of the Social Creed has been traced primarily in the Federal Council of Churches and the Methodist Episcopal Church, which were instrumental in its creation, the other two Methodist bodies also had endorsed the platform to some degree. The Methodist Protestant Church adopted a Social Creed in 1916, although its version was the original Methodist Social Creed of may 1908, not the later Social Creed of the Churches. By the 1920's, however, the declaration no longer was included in its *Discipline*. Southern Methodism embraced the 1912 Federal Council version in 1914 and consistently printed it in its *Disciplines* until they endorsed a slightly modified recension of the Council's 1932 revised Social Creed.[28] Since the 1936 *Disciplines* of both northern Methodism and the Methodist Protestants did not include a Social

Creed statement, the single thread of its continuity into the Methodist Church was provided by the 1938 *Discipline* of the southern branch.

Thus, it was not surprising that the initiative to adopt a Social Creed in the united church came from William P. King, editor of the *Christian Advocate* at Nashville, Tennessee. He called for a committee to harmonize the Social Creed statements in earlier *Disciplines* of each predecessor church since the plan of union failed to include such a platform. On May 9, 1939 that committee reported on "A Social Creed" that simply harmonized prior pronouncements by piecing them together into a single declaration. A 1932 provision advocating social planning and economic control was deleted by a close vote but every other alteration was delayed to future General Conferences. At the first General Conference in 1940 several changes of an editorial nature were approved but they only perfected the earlier hasty work. The basis for the harmonization was the 1912 Social Creed rather than the more recent 1932 revision.[29]

The distinctive feature of the new Methodist social platform was its obvious denominational character. In 1940 it was titled "Our Social Creed" and four years later it was designated "The Methodist Social Creed," a title it carried until 1968. Its affirmations were rooted in the social concerns of John Wesley and expressed Methodism's sense of responsibility in the social order. And the document henceforth contained a provision that every *Discipline* hereafter should include the Social Creed as revised unless otherwise instructed by future General Conferences.[30] From 1940 to 1952 the Methodist Social Creed consistently contained twenty articles but the wording did not remain constant as every General Conference revised one or more articles. The principle that the Social Creed remained a regular part of the *Discipline* while its ingredient statements were subject to change became a fundamental policy of the Methodist Church.

In the mid-forties the relationship of the Methodist Federation to the denomination again became an issue. The retirement of Harry Ward and Bishop McConnell in 1944 triggered both internal dissension and external criticism for the Federation. New leader Jack McMichael, who was even more radical in ideas and methods than Ward, alienated many members and attracted critical attack. Requests that the Methodist Church create its own official social action agency and sever its relations with the organization increased as Federation leaders and programs became targets of the *Reader's Digest* and congressional investigations during the McCarthy era.[31] Finally in 1952 the General Conference voted to break its ties to the Federation and to create a Board of Social and Economic Relations within the denomination. Among the official board's assigned functions was responsibility to revise and clarify the Social Creed and make it effective.[32] When The Methodist Church authorized its own board for social action it entered a new stage and social responsibility with regard to the Social Creed.

As Methodist commitment to the Social Creed became stabilized, ecumenical Protestantism gradually abandoned use of that type of social platform. A thirtieth anniversary review of progress by the Federal Council in 1938 made no reference to the Social Creed or Social Ideals by name, in contrast to the acclaim they received in 1928. And there was no mention of them in its 1948 evaluation.[33] In an appraisal of the Social Ideals in 1942 F. Ernest Johnson compared them to a similar study in 1930 and saw much progress in implementation, but he concluded that it was due to New Deal legislation rather than the churches.[34] He did not suggest that the Federal Council had lost its Christian concern for the social order, but rather had altered its methods in light of a major theological shift that had affected Protestantism. Reinhold Niebuhr's *Moral Man and Immoral Society*, published in 1932, was a sharp critique of Social Gospel optimism and methods and advocated social action based on realism and power. His book transformed social ministry by leading most denominations to abandon paper social pronouncements in favor of specific programs of action. When the Federal Council was absorbed into the larger National Council of Churches in 1950 the concerns once expressed in the Social Creed were cared for in four of the six departments of the new organization's Department of Christian Life and Work, and there was no provision for such a pronouncement.[35] The Social Creed was no longer a part of ecumenical Protestantism; henceforth it existed only in The Methodist Church.

## OFFICIAL CREED—OFFICIAL BOARD (1952–1968)

Entrusting the Social Creed to a new Board of Social and Economic Relations ushered in a new stage of development for the document within The Methodist Church, a stage that lasted from 1952 to 1968. In 1953 A. Dudley Ward, who was no relation to Harry Ward, became the Executive Secretary of the new board. Previously he had served on the staff of the National Council of Church's Department of Church and Economic Life for three years and carried some of the theology and strategy of that agency with him. His vigorous leadership was devoted to implementing the responsibilities assigned by the General Conference, which by 1956 was evident in a new format for the Methodist Social Creed.

Since the Board of Social and Economic Relations was empowered "to implement and make effective the provisions of this Social Creed," it requested authority to rearrange the order of items more logically, to rewrite an out of date section, and to add new subjects. Rearranging the paragraphs involved the insertion of topical headings that became the organizing principle for listing affirmations. To do this smoothly required rewriting, which made possible the insertion and deletion of ideas. In addition, the board created four major sections in the Social Creed: I. Our Heritage; II. Our Theological Basis; III. Our Declaration of Social Concern (under which all the topical headings were listed); IV. Our Mandate—Read, Study, Apply. Emphasizing the Wesleyan heritage and theological component strengthened the denominational basis of the Creed, the social declarations broadened its areas of concerns, and the mandate enhanced its usefulness at all levels of the church.[36]

Four years later the Board of Social and Economic Relations was combined with the boards for Temperance and World Peace to form a new Board of Christian Social Concerns, in which each became a separate division. The unification created a strong official Board to implement the denomination's official Creed, reduced duplication of work, and provided a strategic and symbolic headquarters in Washington, DC, across from the Capitol.[37] Eventually Dudley Ward became Executive Secretary of the enlarged Boards which had responsibility for the Methodist Social Creed when The Methodist Church united with the Evangelical United Brethren Church in 1968.

Neither the United Brethren nor the Evangelicals had developed the commitment to social responsibility or the machinery to implement it that characterized the Methodist tradition. When the two merged in 1946 to form the Evangelical United Brethren Church their social pronouncements were more paper affirmations than actions because the denomination never had the social leadership of more than a part-time executive. Since Methodist and Evangelical United Brethren social platforms were not in conflict, it was agreed that in the first *Discipline* of the United Methodist Church the existing social declarations of both former bodies be printed as the new denomination's Social Principles.[38] Thus, church union provided an opportunity to rethink the Social Creed and another period of development opened up because the Social Principles Study Commission appointed by the 1968 General Conference took a totally new approach to the task.

## A NEW BIRTH: PRINCIPLES AND WORSHIP (1968–1988)

Guided by Bishop James S. Thomas, the Commission on Social Principles worked to restate the denomination's Social Creed in one of the most dynamic periods in the nation's history. The Uniting Conference of The United Methodist Church in April 1968 met only blocks from the site where President John F. Kennedy was fatally shot and just two weeks after the assassination of Martin Luther King, Jr. There were also the violence of burning cities, hateful race relations, protests against the Vietnam War, and demands for social justice from countless groups during the four years the Commission met.

Amid such conditions it was determined that it would not be enough simply to select one of the existing statements or to merge the two, even if they were updated. Rather the Commission determined thoroughly to study the history, content, and implications of the existing platforms, and then in light of that and the social problems that were "literally exploding all around us" to develop the best current social principles to submit to the 1972 General Conference. Their priorities were formed on the basis of regional hearings, ideas solicited from individuals and congregations, and study papers by specialists. Moreover, they set out to prepare Social Principles that could be used in congregational worship as well as in planned social action. The Commission believed that "the General Conference expected us to begin a new era in the writing of Social Principles."[39]

In form the resulting document differed from all previous Social Creeds. It had a new title: Social Principles of The United Methodist Church. It began with a theological preamble and ended with "Our Social Creed," which was a creedal affirmation more akin to the classical creeds of early Christianity and appropriate for congregational worship. Between these two components were the Social Principles themselves divided into six major sections: I. The Natural World, II. The Nurturing Community, III. The Social Community, IV. The Economic Community, V. The Political Community, and VI. The World Community. More inclusive and extensive than all previous pronouncements, the subjects were expressed as a series of principles that were not specific resolutions because the Commission was convinced "that social principles should be specific enough to be meaningful but general enough to allow for the framing of specific resolutions within their broad limits." [40]

Despite these careful preparations the Commission's report was subjected to major revisions by a legislative committee of the 1972 General Conference. From beginning to end it was extensively altered in ideas as well as wording. When the revised form was presented to the assembled delegates for consideration numerous changes were proposed but only a dozen were enacted. The two that attracted the most attention concerned abortion and homosexuality. After this lengthy process, the Social Principles were adopted by the General Conference and Bishop Thomas led the delegates as they affirmed the new Social Creed for the first time.[41] The Social Creed had attained the status of an authorized creed appropriate for use in public worship, which was several stages removed from the original promulgation of a platform concerning only economic problems in 1908.

The significance of this worship dimension of the Social Creed must be read in proper perspective, for the document differs in content, tone, and intention from all previous versions. As an affirmation of integrated statements of theology and social, communal, economic, political and natural commitments it is a unique development. However, it must be recognized that the entire Social Principles pronouncement, not just the final portion designated Our

Social Creed, is the legitimate successor to previous Social Creeds. The worship was added to the forms that had developed earlier; it did not supercede them.

Succeeding General Conferences of The United Methodist Church have modified the originally adopted statement every four years in order to implement growing concerns about gender, ethnicity, age groups, inclusive language, and other contemporary issues. But the basic design of the Social Principles as a modern expression of the Social Creed tradition has proved workable. Until the General Conference changes the format again, the Social Creed continues in its sixth stage of development.

In its present form in Methodism the Social Creed has resolved several issues that arose during its development. It is an official pronouncement that symbolizes the commitment of The United Methodist Church to a role of social responsibility in the world. While it states ideals and provides the basis for platforms it is a statement of principles grounded in Christian theology and political realism. At the same time it enables United Methodists not only to declare their position on issues but also to unite in a creedal affirmation of its content in the context of public worship.

The document has ended where it began, in a denominational rather than an ecumenical heritage. Other churches embraced it but then concluded it was only an expression of words. But as the Methodist Church retained the declaration, severed its relationship to the Methodist Federation for Social Service, and formed its own official Board of Church and Social Service, the social platform came to have continuing support and influence in the denomination. Over the years, and through church mergers, the document has changed in basis, content, format, and purpose, but its essential functions of stating and symbolizing the church's concern for the social order have remained constant. As a unique literary genre it has been useful and pliable in its relationship to Methodism through eighty years.

# The Revival of Stewardship and the Creation of the World Service Commission in the Methodist Episcopal Church, 1912–1924

Stephen Perry

Bishop Edwin Holt Hughes, who served as first president of the World Service Commission of the Methodist Episcopal Church, resided in the Chicago episcopal area when the Chicago Temple was dedicated. Years later, he remembered the day of the dedication and recalled, as he had entered the building, "a querulous voice, issuing from a man who gazed at the tallest church steeple in the world and said, 'Where [in a certain location] do these [adjectival] Methodists get all their money?'" [1]

That, in a more analytical form, is the question of this essay, and the answer lies in the creation of Bishop Hughes' own World Service Commission during the early twentieth century.

The World Service Commission of the Methodist Episcopal Church constituted that church's budgetary authority and treasury from 1924 to 1939. It was also the direct ancestor of the General Council on Finance and Administration of The United Methodist Church, and so its establishment in 1924 marked a major beginning of central financial administration in American Methodism.

Like the present-day General Council on Finance and Administration, the World Service Commission formulated a budget for General Conference-level agencies in order to unify their fund-raising appeals to local churches. It calculated the apportionment of this budget among the annual conferences, treasured the funds raised on apportionment, and distributed them according to a budgetary formula to the church's national agencies.

The beginning of such unexceptional activities merit the attention of historians for several reasons. How a major Protestant denomination reorganized itself to deal with the unprecedented wealth of twentieth-century America involved nothing less than a redefinition of the church in its relation to society. The incapacity of a nineteenth-century denominational apparatus to manage millions of dollars consistently with its spiritual purpose raised questions no less serious than those presented by the motives and the means which church members had used to acquire this wealth.

Furthermore, the creation of the World Service Commission attempted, by giving the church central control over its vastly increased financial resources, to make its national agencies accountable for their actions. Because of this attempt to use money to achieve central control over decentralized decision-making what happened to the Methodist Episcopal Church in the early twentieth century paralleled much of what was happening to American society at large. Scholars have used the concept of "organizational revolution" to describe the transformation of the United States from a nation of farmers, small towns, and general stores to the industrialized, urbanized national marketplace familiar today.[2]

The World Service Commission constitutes a chapter in the larger story of this organizational revolution, but it also raises questions about the way the story has often been told. Employing the metaphor invented by Max Weber and others of transformation from "community" to "society," scholars have seen the centralization of finance and the rise of bureaucracy and professions as typical of the modern world. They have also discovered, concurrent with these phenomena, a shift to more "secular" and rational values.

The creation of the World Service Commission suggests instead a story of the persistence of traditional religious values. Management of debt on an unprecedented scale certainly precipitated organizational change in the Methodist Episcopal Church, but the Methodists who changed their organization and redefined the relation of their church to their society drew on a long heritage of approaching church structure as social strategy and of treating the church instrumentally as a means to an end. This heritage went back at least to John Wesley[3] and belied any recent origin for the values implied by twentieth-century organizational rigor.

This essay attempts to explain why the Methodist Episcopal Church created the World Service Commission. The explanation comes in two parts: (1) the political sources of the World Service Commission and (2) the theology and the piety of the people most actively involved in its creaton.

# I

Pressure for central financial administration in the Methodist Episcopal Church mounted in the late nineteenth century as General Conferences from 1884 to 1908 tried, on the whole unsuccessfully, to consolidate their national boards.[4] These boards, to which each quadrennium a General Conference would delegate the work of publishing, ministerial pensions, missions in the United States and abroad, and education, constituted the denomination's church-wide organization. Each board conducted its work independently of the others, and this included financial campaigns directed to local congregations across the country.

As the work of the national boards expanded, their constant and conflicting appeals for money became increasingly unacceptable, especially since they failed to raise enough to realize growing expectations for the church's role in the world. This failure particularly distressed supporters of missionary expansion who were rapidly emerging as a vocal and nationally organized constituency. They pointed to Methodist students who yearned to cross the sea and spread the gospel but whose hopes were severely constrained by lack of funds. Created by the Student Volunteer Movement, the Laymen's Missionary Movement sought to mobilize lay support for missions.

The Laymen's Missionary Movement was largely responsible for the General Conference action in 1912 that established the Commission on Finance of the Methodist Episcopal Church.[5] The Commission on Finance constituted the church's first attempt at central financial administration. For reasons associated with its origins in the missionary movement, the Commission remained during the eight years of its existence only an attempt. It was instructed to unify the budgets of the national boards, with authority to revise those budgets, and to apportion budget askings among the annual conferences. The membership of the Commission included, however, the secretaries of the very boards whose budgets it was supposed to coordinate. Inevitably, the board chiefs, especially S. Earl Taylor of the Board of Foreign Missions, and, after 1916, David D. Forsyth of the Board of Home Missions and Church Extension, dominated the episcopal, ministerial, and lay representatives whose primary church responsibilities lay elsewhere.

The Commission on Finance never became more than an officially sanctioned version of the informal consultations among board secretaries that had preceded it, and so the national organization of the church remained bound to its nineteenth-century roots. During the Commission's first quadrennium, 1912–16, accounts separate from its own treasury in Chicago were maintained in New York and Philadelphia, the respective headquarters cities of the foreign missions and home missions boards.[6] General Conference provision for the

Commission's administrative budget to be financed by the boards further guaranteed their control of its affairs.[7]

In spite of this dependence on the national boards, which prevented it from becoming an effective budgetary authority and treasury for the church, the Commission on Finance demonstrated the promise that central financial administration held out. Under John Lowe Fort of New York, its field department made a determined effort to reform local church financial organization by meeting frequently from 1916 to 1920 with district superintendents across the country and helping them to spread the "every-member canvass" and a revised form of Methodist classes, the "unit system," that emphasized fund-raising in small groups.[8] The department of apportionments and surveys, headed by C. M. Barton, gathered local church statistics never before available to the national boards, and it used this new information to attempt a more equitable apportionment of support for board budgets. The department also found that price inflation during World War I had eaten into the salaries of Methodist ministers. The Commission then began a campaign through the district superintendents to increase local church support for pastors.[9]

In the midst of the Commission's second quadrennium occurred the organization of the great Centenary fund-raising campaign that dwarfed the Commission's work and, eventually, subsumed it. With General Conference authorization, an *ad hoc* committee of one hundred church leaders met at Niagara Falls in September 1917 to plan a celebration for the one hundredth anniversary of the Missionary Society of the Methodist Episcopal Church. Two successors of the Missionary Society, the Board of Foreign Missions and the Board of Home Missions, provided much of the leadership and staff support for this conference. The Niagara Conference concluded that the most appropriate celebration would consist in a fund-raising campaign to bring millions of dollars under the control of the national boards. By early 1918 a new organization, the Joint Centenary Commission ("Joint" because of participation by the Methodist Episcopal Church, South), was in place with an impressive list of names on its letterhead.[10]

Actually, the official organization of the Centenary campaign in the Northern church reflected a complicated series of formal and informal arrangements negotiated principally by S. Earl Taylor and David D. Forsyth with the Commission on Finance and the national boards.[11] No one seemed worried that by the time these arrangements were complete the Centenary organization had completely usurped the budgetary authority of the Commission on Finance. During 1918 and 1919 individuals, offices, and organizations worked enthusiastically for the campaign on promises that some of the funds raised would go to their particular church concerns.

An incident at Garrett Biblical Institute in Evanston, Illinois, illustrated the tendency of the entire denomination to get caught up in the prospect of millions of dollars flowing into church coffers. During the summer of 1919, as a new financial organization, the Centenary Conservation Committee, was formed to collect on pledges made in the original campaign, President Charles M. Stuart of Garrett met with Taylor and Frank Mason North from Foreign Missions and Forsyth from Home Missions to discuss funding of a program of religious education for missionary workers. This program would have involved Northwestern University as well, and the secretaries also talked with Dean James Alton James of the university's graduate school. Stuart understood, however, that Garrett was to receive funding for faculty positions independent of the Northwestern program, and he hoped that this would release other sources of income at Garrett to finance building projects.

Stuart thought that Garrett would receive a proportion up to a certain specified amount of all money raised beyond the initial Centenary campaign goal of $105,000,000. The money would come through the missionary boards for the purpose of religious education. By the fall, however, board receipts on Centenary pledges began a decline from which they never recovered, the nation as a whole taking a business downturn in 1920. But the lessening amount involved was not the only issue between Garrett and the boards. Forsyth of Home Missions maintained that Garrett had never been promised any money apart from the program at Northwestern; Taylor of Foreign Missions assured Stuart that Garrett was perfectly correct in its claim on the boards, but he would not raise the matter with Forsyth. When Taylor began avoiding any personal contact with Stuart, Garrett's Board of Trustees had no alternative but to request Forsyth to present its case to the Board of Home Missions and Church Extension in the rather futile hope that the full board would overrule its own secretary.[12]

The national career of S. Earl Taylor, which was bound up from the beginning with the fortunes of the missionary movement and early attempts at central financial administration, ended abruptly soon after this. Taylor had risen from the Student Volunteer Movement in the first years of the century to denominational prominence in the Board of Foreign Missions as a paperwork saint whose negotiating skill and single-minded devotion to the missionary cause were largely responsible, in contemporary opinion, for the initial success of the Centenary fund-raising campaign. Men around him admired his ability to bring church leaders together and considered him a self-effacing diplomat who, by means of discussion, got his point of view and his vision across to subordinates as well as peers. He won not only the verbal assent but also the hearts and minds of people who at first disagreed with him.[13]

The incident at Garrett Biblical Institute suggested, however, a display of characteristic but naive generosity—an innocence of the financial dangers inherent in a pledge campaign and an ignorance of the mind of his colleague, Forsyth. At this point, however, Taylor could hardly have been expected to confront Forsyth over Garrett because it had become clear that the missionary boards would have to institute a program of austerity. Furthermore, in the meantime, the Board of Foreign Missions and a reluctant Board of Home Missions and Church Extension had ventured into the Interchurch World Movement, an interdenominational fund-raising project, and come out after the failure of this effort with a considerable debt to the banks that had financed administrative expenses. Taylor may well have felt disgraced. At any rate, his long hours and years of work for the church made him a very sick man. In the spring of 1921, he retired to the desert of New Mexico to recover his health, but he would never again serve the Board of Foreign Missions.

The Methodist Episcopal Church had, nevertheless, to deal with the debt at the Board of Foreign Missions, a figure that eventually ran into the millions of dollars.[14] The severity of the crisis did not fully appear at the General Conference of 1920, but the delegates certainly perceived the problem of collecting on Centenary pledges. They combined the Centenary Conservation Committee and the old Commission on Finance to form a new financial organization for 1920–24, the Council of Boards of Benevolence, a very large group of church leaders charged with collecting on the Centenary and performing the duties of the old Commission.

The General Conference of 1920 also directed the new Council of Boards of Benevolence to formulate a reorganization plan for the 1924–28 quadrennium and submit it to the 1924 General Conference. The Council of Boards proceeded to appoint a committee of twenty-one to accomplish this task. This committee worked for almost two years interviewing the personnel of the various boards and meeting in an atmosphere of increasing urgency as the debt at the Board of Foreign Missions mounted. The Committee of Twenty-One reported to the Council of Boards a plan to preserve the autonomy of most of the boards but subject to the budgetary authority of a commission made up of independent representatives of the church as well as board representatives. The Council of Boards made major changes in this plan but succeeded only in throwing the question back to the General Conference of 1924.[15]

What had really happened became apparent when the General Conference of 1924 took up the question of reorganization. A controversy had emerged within and around the Board of Foreign Missions. When a majority of the General Conference's Committee on Temporal Economy, chaired by William B. Farmer of Indiana, reported a reorganization plan similar to the Committee of Twenty-One's proposal, an extended floor debate occurred. The principals in the debate consisted largely of members of the Board of Foreign Missions. David G. Downey, a board member from the New York East Annual Conference and secretary of the Committee of Twenty-One, seems to have served as floor manager for the majority report. Frank A. Horne, another board member and a lay delegate from the same annual conference, delivered a major speech in favor of this report. George Fowles, Foreign Missions treasurer, drafted an alternative proposal to merge all the boards into one "straight commission," and a considerable number of the Committee on Temporal Economy supported this proposal for radical centralization as the minority report.

The General Conference of 1924 eventually adopted the majority report (with minor amendments) by a considerable margin.[16] Coming after three days of debate, this action created the World Service Commission of the Methodist Episcopal Church whose direct descendant is the General Council on Finance and Administration of The United Methodist Church. The World Service Commission constituted a central treasury and truly independent budgetary authority for the autonomous, individually incorporated boards that developed and administered the denomination's programs. Except for bishops, no member of this commission was to have any connection with any other national board or agency.

Such a momentous development in the means by which a major Protestant denomination carried out its work calls for explanation. Tactically, supporters of the majority report had fended off an attempt to amend their proposal from supporters of an independent Board of Negro Education, co-opted the Epworth League (youth work) constituency, made the majority report look more attractive as a prospective means of reunification with the Methodist Episcopal Church, South, and, most significantly, pinned the blame for the debt at the Board of Foreign Missions on its treasurer, George Fowles, and the supporters of his minority report. Fowles' opponents within his board won on the floor of the General Conference.[17]

The delegates understood this fight, however, as a constitutional debate rather than a personal feud. Some sort of central control had to be imposed on the chaos of independent boards, but the total consolidation proposed in Fowles' minority report seemed to run against the grain of Methodist connectional polity. William Farmer, the Indiana pastor who chaired the Committee on Temporal Economy that submitted the majority report, interpreted the General Conference's desire for change in terms of three criteria: (1) efficiency, (2) accountability or "no dodging of responsibility," and (3) economy.[18] Supporters of Fowles' minority report as well as supporters of the majority report claimed the business virtues of economy and efficiency for their respective proposals. Fowles stated that his plan had the approval of leading businessmen: " . . . for almost three years I have been checking it up with outstanding business men throughout the United States, and it has been considered by them, with some few additions which have been made, as the best plan ever presented to an ecclesiastical organization."[19] Against Fowles, Frank Horne maintained, " . . . The minority report violates modern business principles of management and administration. The committee or commission form of management has been tried by big business, and has been abandoned."[20]

Both sides, throughout the debate, appealed to the "business principles" of using resources efficiently and spending money economically. The universality of this appeal leads one to question its power of historical explanation and to regard the appeal to business as a rhetorical convention designed to win the votes of those lay delegates who earned their living as business people. Farmer's second criterion, accountability, proved more critical. Although this, too, constituted a principle of some American business and many reform movements, the source of its value to Methodists lay in traditional ideas of church polity. Raymond J. Wade of Indiana, then running for bishop, insisted,

> . . . the church is not analogous [sic] to big business. Practically every dollar that can be saved by the commission plan [the minority report] is saved by the board plan [the majority report]. [The minority report] is a centralization of power to the extreme. It is a dangerous experiment. It centers everything in the hands of a few.[21]

The criticism of concentration of power and consequent absence of accountability proved to be the most telling argument against Fowles' minority report. The measure of its significance lay in Fowles' own acceptance of an amendment to make his "straight commission" more representative of the whole denomination rather than just the bishops. Furthermore, before Fowles accepted this amendment, one of his opponents on the Board of Foreign Missions and the apparent floor manager for the majority report, David G. Downey, tried to get the amendment tabled. In other words, Downey saw any attempt to decentralize power in the minority report as making that report more attractive to the General Conference while Fowles accepted the amendment for precisely this reason. Downey had concluded his major speech in favor of the majority report with these words: "If you are looking for Boards that will be responsive to your action and amenable to your authority, you will take hold of this idea that has been presented to us in the majority report."[22]

The majority report proved to be defensible on traditional grounds of connectional polity as well as modern grounds of business principles, and, as we will see more clearly in the final section of this essay, religious values provide the more likely explanation for the creation of the World Service Commission. The Methodist Episcopal Church determined that it could achieve central financial control by continuing to decentralize decision-making—that is, by making specific persons and agencies accountable to a central budgetary authority.[23] It made this determination because independent boards subject to the budgetary authority of the World Service Commission constituted a structure that promised to preserve a cherished principle of church polity in a world dominated by industrial wealth. Forced into this world by missionary zeal and the indebtedness of their foreign missions board, the Methodists sought to deal with their constitutional crisis on their own terms.

The conclusion of this story of the political origins of the World Service Commission occurred immediately after the General Conference of 1924 with the first meetings of the new body. One of the most significant decisions taken at these meetings consisted in the election of a treasurer. This office did not, perhaps, appear so important at first, but, under Orrin W. Auman, the treasury became the center of staff responsibility and power, especially as the educational and promotional activities originally contemplated for the national board secretaries were phased out during subsequent General Conferences. The new treasurer of 1924 did not retire until 1944, five years after the denominational union of 1939 that created The Methodist Church.

Auman may strike us as a new figure on the national Methodist scene, and, of course, the members of the World Service Commission may have chosen him for this reason. A little exploration sheds another light, however. Elected episcopal area representative for Denver to the World Service Commission, Auman had served on the World Program Committee for the Centenary, the Council for Boards of Benevolence, and the latter's Committee of Twenty-One. His most conspicuous work had occurred as district superintendent for the Denver district of the Colorado Annual Conference. Before coming to this position, Auman pastored a large church in Denver.

Back in 1912 Auman had joined, as an original member, the Colorado Annual Conference Social Service Commission, a local ancestor of today's Methodist Federation for Social Action. His associations here have great relevance for understanding his election as treasurer of the World Service Commission twelve years later. The other members of the Social Service Commission in Colorado were Bishop Francis J. McConnell, resident bishop of the Denver episcopal area from 1912 to 1916; Harris Franklin Rall, President of Iliff School of Theology from 1911 to 1916; and David D. Forsyth, district superintendent of the Denver district from 1909 to 1915.

Together, these men commended various social causes to the annual conference, most notably favoring collective bargaining during the Colorado Coal Strike of 1914. Of the original members, Forsyth moved on to the Board of Education and later, as we have seen, to the Board of Home Missions and Church Extension, and McConnell appointed Auman as district superintendent in his place. Auman and Forsyth served together again on the Committee of Twenty-One that originally proposed establishing a World Service Commission. Rall became a professor at Garrett Biblical Institute. McConnell himself continued to live a life of controversy in the Pittsburgh episcopal area, heading a nationally publicized investigation into the Steel Strike of 1919. In 1924 the Board of Bishops appointed him to the new World Service Commission, and here, one suspects, he played a role in the election of his former district superintendent, Orrin Auman, as treasurer.[24]

Auman's career reveals, therefore, another force in the church, in addition to the missionary boards and the Laymen's Missionary Movement, working for some kind of central financial administration. Except for the membership of Auman and Forsyth on the Committee of Twenty-One, it is not clear whether McConnell or his associates influenced the General Conference of 1924 in its decision to establish the World Service Commission. They did, however, have a great deal to do with the shape that body took over the rest of its corporate life to 1939.[25] This knowledge will assist us as we try now to understand the theology and the piety of the Methodists who created the World Service Commission.

## II

Although we have been looking at church politics on the national level and have, because of the nature of the readily available documents, dealt primarily with the activities of a few church leaders, the World Service Commission grew out of the lives of many thousands of Methodists across the country. For example, 60,000 laymen participated in the Centenary campaign as "Methodist Minute Men" and accomplished the door-to-door and local church meeting work that actually raised money.[26] In fact, the events of 1912 to 1924 constituted nothing less than a revival of Methodist understanding of and conviction about "stewardship."

Since the term "stewardship" has become part of the vocabulary of American Christianity generally, its meaning for early twentieth-century Methodists should be recalled. The "stewards" of a local congregation constituted the lay officers of the church and were charged with taking care of the temporal resources of their congregation. They raised funds, for example, to pay the pastor's salary.[27]

This semantic background suggests an important point; that the theology and the piety emerging in the early twentieth century around the word "stewardship" constituted an essentially *lay* theology and piety. Although articulated principally by ministers, the notion of stewardship at its roots concerned the life of the laity in Methodism. So, we need to gain at least an impressionistic sense of what stewardship came to mean for Methodist laypeople in the years immediately preceding the creation of the World Service Commission.

The periodical literature of the Centenary campaign—*Missiles for Methodist Minute Men*, for example, with model five-minute speeches on the mission of the church and individual responsibility to donate money—gives a flavor of lay participation in fund-raising. Harvey Reeves Calkins' little magazine, *Men and Money*, allowed for thoughtful expression by laypeople as well as ministers. A serial novel, "The Centenary at Old First," by Calkins himself, appeared throughout the two-year life of this magazine and portrayed various laypeople in a local urban congregation—the pastor's best friend, a banker; the banker's wife whose quest for a spiritual high led her to abandon Methodism for the "Church of the Reality"; and a missionary, returned from India, with whom the pastor fell in love. The reader saw these characters from the perspective of their warm-hearted pastor who did youth work in a poor Italian neighborhood and was trying his best to raise money and persuade his ailing downtown congregation that they were stewards of the church, not owners of it.

Two plays by women authors appeared in *Men and Money*. "Thanksgiving Ann" by Kate W. Hamilton opened at the Columbus, Ohio, Centenary celebration in 1919. The plot concerned a prosperous young white couple whose fondness for worldly pleasures made them scoff at the idea of tithing their income to the church. They rejected the calculation and lack of spontaneity involved in tithing as unspiritual and legalistic. The direct but apolitical sarcasm of a poor black woman, "Thanksgiving Ann" (played by a white woman in blackface), made them see their hypocrisy.[28] Ada Luella Woodruff's "The Transformation of Mabel Morris" told a similar story of a rich young woman mainly worried about where her next fancy dress was coming from. The song of a little child about missionaries changed her heart, and she decided immediately to lay aside a tenth of her income for the church. The curtain fell as the characters began the Doxology.[29]

Reading these plays today, one senses the ethos of a white middle class struggling to establish wealth as a virtue and projecting its own conscience onto two of the most exploited groups in early twentieth-century American society, blacks and children. It is interesting, too, that, on the eve of ratification of the Nineteenth Amendment granting women the right to vote, the Calkins novel as well as the two plays portrayed a materially wealthy but spiritually empty white female who eventually, through religious conversion, achieved maturity and self-understanding. On one occasion the editorial section of *Men and Money* addressed the role of women directly. "Can a Woman Tithe?" insisted that a wife ought to participate equally with her husband in the disposal of his income. "He may earn it; but he earns it because she keeps house; . . . "[30] The spiritual struggle of Methodist women at this time, seen as the struggle of the Christian, received articulate expression in "The Steward's Strength," a poem by Mabel C. Falley and a theologically perceptive statement about prevenient grace.[31]

All of this literary evidence suggests the conclusion that the wealth acquired by many Methodist businessmen during the early years of this century precipitated an inner crisis for these laymen and their families. They resolved the crisis with the piety of stewardship. Of the two alternatives generally proposed in the early twentieth century for America's future, capitalism or socialism, Methodist advocates of stewardship tended to reject both. They refused to say that their newly acquired wealth constituted a sign of divine favor, and yet neither did it convict them of sinful profiteering. Rather, whatever one's financial resources, God had given them in trust to be used for good, and the test of a Christian lay in the end achieved by the means of wealth.

No better demonstration of the resulting attempt to sanctify the social and economic life of the world may be found than in the early twentieth-century ritualization of the collection of money during Methodist worship. The *Discipline* of 1920 encouraged pastors to highlight the role of the offering plate in the Sunday morning service, and a column in one of the first issues of *Men and Money* compared the offering to the elevation of the host during Mass, calling for a sacramental silence throughout the congregation as the minister spoke the offertory prayer.[32]

The religious sources of the revival of stewardship were also reflected in the development of Methodist doctrinal understanding. Sometimes, the wind of doctrine blows out in the distance before it ever disturbs the realms of theological glory. Just so, the vitality of the concept of stewardship for early twentieth-century Methodist understanding of Christian doctrine may be observed in the velocity with which that understanding moved from the problem of collecting membership dues to the problem of defining the Church in the twentieth century. A comparison of the emphasis placed on tithing in the stewardship section of the 1912 *Discipline* with the adumbration of a doctrine of creation in the similar section of the 1920 *Discipline* shows how quickly this movement occurred.[33]

Who were the official theologians of stewardship? The circle of associations around Bishop Francis J. McConnell bore responsibility for much of the intellectual content of Methodist fund-raising propaganda. Harris Franklin Rall produced a pamphlet, *A Christian's Financial Creed*, in 1914 for the Colorado Annual Conference which he revised that same year for the Commission on Finance. A reading of this document alongside Rall's "A Stewardship Creed" of 1920 reveals a movement of thought similar to that of the *Disciplines* of 1912 and 1920; from a focus on money to a broader conception of stewardship that included but was not limited to the Sunday-morning collection plate.[34] Another significant work, Harvey Reeves Calkins' *A Man and His Money* (1914), cannot be associated easily with McConnell; as a missionary and official propagandist for the Commission on Finance, Calkins drew on many sources for his biblical scholarship and economic thought. By the time of the Centenary in 1918, however, his theological statements were showing the influence of McConnell and McConnell's teacher at Boston University, Borden Parker Bowne (1847–1910).[35] McConnell himself, apostle of Bowne's "personalism," expressed his views in *Church Finance and Social Ethics* (1920), a small book whose acceptance of large amounts of money in the organized church and simultaneous sensitivity to the resulting problems almost let us see his hand in the founding of the World Service Commission four years later.

The books by Calkins and McConnell reveal in detail the development of Methodist doctrinal understanding of stewardship. Calkins began in 1914 with the problem of defending tithing against the charge that concern with money was essentially unspiritual. In the course of his argument, he expounded a theory of value that located the economic worth of things in the collective estimation of human minds rather than in the things themselves. Since human evaluation of things consisted in estimating their utility as means to an end rather than concern with the things themselves, spiritual life could include money and the material world it represented. "That men themselves demand *value*, and are not content with *things*, shows, indeed, that they are made in the very image of God." [36]

Writing six years later in light of the accumulation of wealth within the church, McConnell moved boldly into the theological territory that Calkins had just managed to penetrate. McConnell believed that creation was potentially good because the incarnation—God taking on a material body in Christ—had made its goodness actual. Given such a presupposition, money could not, at its root, constitute evil, and yet, as the present distribution of wealth in American society and recent Methodist experience demonstrated, money lay at the root of a great many real and possible evils.

McConnell's major contribution lay in defining the church's relation to money and the material world it represented. The church's task consisted in sanctification, in "teaching truth by incarnation." [37] The church in the twentieth-century United States possessed a high calling to use money properly in order that the world might learn how to employ wealth. The church's stewardship of wealth would bring ecclesiastical organization to perfection as the church brought the world to perfection. The ethical handling of money by the church provided a practical means to the ultimate spiritual goal.

A hymn by Ralph Cushman, "My Temple" (1919), also attempted to embody theological insight in language but in a form more characteristic of the Methodist heritage. Just as Methodists followed their political tradition of fighting about organizational strategy when they created the World Service Commission, so Cushman drew on his heritage of praying, preaching, and singing to write a poem about stewardship for Calkins' magazine, *Men and Money*.

Cushman, one of the original members of the World Service Commission in 1924, directed the stewardship education programs of the Joint Centenary Commission and the Interchurch World Movement and helped to found the United Stewardship Council of the Churches of Christ in America in 1920. Until 1932 when the General Conference elected him bishop, he served churches in western New York, assisting his congregation in Geneva to pay a large debt with a very successful tithing campaign.

Both this active interest in the details of church finance and appreciation for the beauty of the land the Iroquois once controlled found expression in Cushman's hymn, the incongruity of the two concerns held together by his belief in stewardship. It seems fitting to conclude this essay with an example of the piety as well as the ideas of the stewardship revival because, perhaps incongruously to the eyes of later observers, the World Service Commission itself would begin its discussions of finance by singing Methodist hymns.

> There's a Temple I know in the heart of the woods,
>> Where the wood bird sings its sweet song,
> And a silence, aware with the fragrance of prayer,
>> Is lingering all the day long.
>
> There wood flowers worship in reverence profound,
>> In this living cathedral of pine,
> And the winds wafting by lift their prayer to the sky,
>> To the God of the Temple divine.
>
> A brook tumbles down through this temple I know,
>> O'er its altars of moss and of stone,
> And it chants all the day in its soft solemn way,
>> To the God who is Lord there alone.
>
> Sweet music is here in the heart of the woods;
>> And he who is listening hears
> A breathing of peace, a soul's sweet release,
>> And the thoughts that lie deeper than tears.
>
> O hie me away to the heart of the woods,
>> Where the temples are made without hands,
> Midst the birds and the breeze and the tall tow'ring trees,
>> Let me worship—my heart understands.[38]

A dialogue took place here between the inner and the outer, which became symbols for the spiritual and the material, respectively. Ostensibly, "My Temple" described an imaginary scene "in the heart of the woods" where, with full poetic license, "the birds and the breeze and the tall tow'ring trees" became sanctuary and congregation combined. A closer look at the geography of the poem reveals, however, something besides charming anthropomorphism. "Heart of the woods" carried a double meaning: the midst of an actual forest *and* the inner being and life of that forest. Cushman's temple looked like an actual forest complete with birds, flowers, trees, and brooks, but the essential activity of these woods consisted in the worship of God. Knowing what we do about the notion of stewardship, we have to conclude that Cushman intended

413

to describe a real forest and also to assert the glory of God as the ultimate purpose of that natural and material world.

Cushman saw the physical world of his woods and tried to penetrate to its spiritual heart, its value as Harvey Reeves Calkins would have said. The resulting vision of all creation as a temple included, of course, human beings themselves who, at *their* hearts, could understand the purpose of creation and deliberately participate in its fulfillment. In this participation Cushman found a resolution of the spiritual and the material, symbolized respectively by the spatial categories, inner and outer. In other words, the thought of the poem involved an introjection of landscape—the conceptualization of spiritual life in terms of geography—and a projection of values onto the material world. Furthermore, this concurrent introjection and projection constituted the role of humanity in the universe, the simultaneous impinging of a material world that did not belong to the human being and acceptance of responsibility for it which together defined "stewardship." From such a perspective, money itself functioned as a means of projecting and sharing Christian values.

The conclusion of a historical essay is not the place to engage one's own thoughts and those of his readers in a final judgment on the piety or the aesthetic sensibility of a previous generation. Nor is it the place to refine the theology of stewardship and church administration. Nevertheless, we might imagine a man and a woman standing under a tree in the heart of the forbidding vastness of America. They reach out to pick some of its luscious, untouched fruit. We would be justified in concluding that the Methodist Episcopal Church did not have much to say about the impulse that led this couple to want the fruit. But the Methodists surely said a lot about what these people should do after they have the fruit and, in 1924, created the World Service Commission to help them do it.

## CHAPTER 28

# The United Methodist System of Itinerant Ministry

## E. Dale Dunlap

Methodism began as a missionary movement. The strategies and structures of the movement developed, largely pragmatically, as a means of fulfilling that missionary vocation.

Methodism has always been, and The United Methodist Church continues to be, connectional rather than congregational in polity. The essence of a connectional system is that every church is a part of every other church, and that no one church can live to itself alone. Within such a system common consideration is given to the needs of all the churches, the good of all the churches is promoted, and decisions take account of all the churches. Connectionalism is a corporate covenant as one means of fulfilling the church's reason for being—God's call to embody and carry forth Christ's ministry in and for the world.

The promise of connectionalism is best fulfilled by an itinerant system of ministerial supply. A writer in *The Methodist Magazine* in 1843 identified an itinerating ministry as the distinguishing feature of Methodism, "that feature which constitutes the main difference between ourselves and other evangelical denominations. . . ."[1] In one way and another Abel Stevens' judgment that "the grand peculiarity of the Methodist *ecclesiastical system* is the *itineracy of its ministry* . . . the cornerstone of the whole structure"[2] has been a recurring theme throughout the years. Even those who have been critical of some aspects, or even most of the system, form a consensus that it still is the best system: Distinctive of United Methodism, the itinerant system accounts in very large measure for the phenomenal effectiveness of the movement in the United States.

Itinerant ministry is a kind of team ministry created by and for the connection as a whole. It is designed to provide careful and strategic deployment of the totality of the ministers for the fulfilling of their corporate goal and reason for being—namely, the effectiveness of the church in mission. It aims to balance the needs of the connection (the totality of the churches) with the opportunity for the minister to make her or his best contribution toward that common goal.

The "bed-rock" essence of the system of itineracy is a disciplined and directed mobility of preachers. This involves three components:

1) The context of mission, and a necessary overall strategy for the deployment of ministerial resources.

2) A covenanted commitment on the part of congregations, clergy, and connection (personified by some kind of third-party appointing power, which historically has been the bishop), which involves the surrender of certain individual rights in order to benefit from the values of convenantal rights and principles, and in the interest of the common cause.

3) The principle of mobility of clergy who are committed to the mission of the Church and the United Methodist system, though requiring no particular length of tenure.

The covenant relationship that characterizes itineracy is double in nature: clergy members of an annual conference covenanting with each other to form an interdependent and complementary "group" ministry, and the clergy covenanting with the connection and the churches to provide their ministerial needs—all within the context of commitment to the mission of the church. The system promises that each church will be provided ministerial leadership, and that each clergyperson will be provided a charge. It requires that each charge must receive and support the minister appointed, and that each clergyperson must go to and serve faithfully the appointed charge. Being a covenant, it is voluntarily entered into and mutually binding. No one called to preach has a "natural," religious right to fulfill that calling as an itinerating United Methodist minister. They become so by voluntarily entering a covenant relationship, the conditions of which are known in advance and accepted, and the fulfillment of which is characterized by obedience—joyful obedience, hopefully. Such a system can operate successfully only when there is a mutual concession on the part of churches and preachers, both giving up the right and power of absolute choice, and in the final analysis accepting the decision of a duly constituted third party—the appointing power, which in United Methodism is the bishop.

Loyalty to the system, albeit sometimes critical—and properly so—is necessary to the effective functioning of itineracy. Historically United Methodism has taken the position that the preacher has voluntarily entered into the covenant relationship for evangelical religious purposes, and that if one becomes convinced that the system is wrong, or finds it unacceptable, or becomes unable to fulfill the covenant, after all constitutional efforts to improve or change the system have failed, the appropriate alternative is to withdraw from the traveling ministry of The United Methodist Church.

The origin of the itinerant ministry in Methodism was incidental and providential. It certainly was not a premeditated and carefully projected design in the mind of John Wesley. His passion was the saving of souls, and his sole aim, as he wrote to Samuel Walker, a clergyman of Truro, in 1736, was and still remained "to promote . . . vital, practical, religion; and order, then, is so far valuable as it answers these ends." [3] Itineracy was a strategy for meeting the spiritual and religious needs of those who responded to Wesley's evangelism—the people called Methodists. Of necessity Wesley was forced to use lay persons to assist him in the various bands, classes and societies. The next step was the use of some of the more promising laity as "sub-pastors." Then came the use of "lay preachers," local and itinerant.

In his description in the *Minutes* of 1766 Wesley says that "after a time a young man named Thomas Maxfield, came and desired to help me as a son in the gospel. Soon after came a second, Thomas Richards; and then a third, Thomas Westell. These severally desired to serve me as sons, and to labour when and where I should direct." [4]

As a matter of fact Wesley had no alternative but to use lay preachers if he was to accomplish anything at all. The clergy would not help. In his *Farther Appeal to Men of Reason and Religion* Wesley defends his use of lay preachers by showing that circumstances forced him to accept "this surprising apparatus of Providence," which certainly ran counter to his own prejudices. [5] As far as he was concerned the fruit of their labors was vindication of their use. The spread of Methodism would have been impossible without the itinerant lay preacher.

John Wesley laid down certain unalterable conditions for itinerant ministers who asked to join him in his work. "None needs to submit to it (his direction)," he says, "unless he will . . . Every Preacher and every member may leave me when he pleases. But while he chooses to stay, it is on the same terms that he joined me at first," [6]—namely, that it was needful that they should do that part of the work which Wesley advised, at those times and places which he judged most for God's glory. [7]

The strategy of being able to send his helpers when, where, and how they were needed for the good of the connection and its mission was only a part of the value of a system of itinerant ministry for John Wesley. He found great value in itineration *per se*. Again replying to Samuel Walker, Wesley insisted that to restrict the preachers to individual societies would ruin the work as well as the preachers themselves—whether ordained or unordained. . . .

417

I know, were I myself to preach one whole year in one place, I should preach both myself and most of my congregation asleep. Nor can I believe it was ever the will of our Lord that any congregation should have one teacher only. We have found by long and constant experience that a frequent change of teachers is best. This preacher has one talent, that another. No one whom I ever yet knew has all the talents which are needful for beginning, continuing, and perfecting the work of grace in an whole congregation.[8]

Wesley was convinced that the societies would become as dead as stones if preachers remained in the same place too long.[9]

Whatever gave promise of usefulness in the promotion of evangelism and meeting the needs of the societies was used by Wesley, and if fruits were forthcoming, that was sufficient validation of divine approval. Nearly everything Wesley did was basically pragmatic and prudential—or, as he would prefer, providential. This is not to say, however, that there was no theological rationale, but only that his mode and means of promotion and administration derived from practicality rather than theory.

It was this system of itinerant ministry that was instrumental in the mission of Methodism to America. And it was this system of itinerant ministry, adapted to a new and radically different environment, that was to be the distinguishing mark and instrumentality of the Methodist Episcopal Church.

There were similarities between the system of itineracy in England and in America. There was the same directed and disciplined mobility, with the same "double" itineracy—movement from circuit to circuit with limited tenure, and movement from charge to charge within the circuit. There were distinct and significant differences also. With the end of the Revolutionary War Methodism became a church, not a connection of societies—an *ecclesia* rather than *ecclesiolae in ecclesia*. It had to operate in a geographic expanse and contour unlike and more expansive than anything in England. It found itself in the context of an unsettled and dynamic cultural climate that was "in process" of becoming in a way unfamiliar to England, even on the eve of social revolution. American Methodism began its independent existence with a notion of ministry markedly different from that in English Methodism of the time. American traveling preachers, for the most part, were ordained, which involved them in a priestly function. In a way and to an extent not to be characteristic in England until sometime after Wesley's death, Methodist ministry in America combined the pastoral office with the prophetic. Dr. J. D. Lynn suggests that an additional factor added by the Americans to the Wesleyan notion of ministry is that of identifying willingness to travel with an authentic call to preach. A call to preach is a call to travel. Itineracy became the norm of ministry.[10]

The system of itinerant ministry was peculiarly suited to the Methodist missionary enterprise in frontier America. Whether positive or negative, the dairies, journals and letters of the preachers attest, as Professor Frederick

Norwood observes, to the "universal domination" of the itinerant system in American Methodism[11] and it is apparent that "until about the end of the Civil War, frontier conditions favored the itinerant system, in spite of the natural difficulties." [12]

Reading the literature of Methodism in general and American Methodism in particular, one is struck by the paucity of direct spiritual and theological apology for the system of itinerant ministry. Claims of a scriptural mandate or warrant for the system are not made by the Methodists, but beginning with Coke and Asbury in their *Notes to the Discipline*, and continuing throughout most of the nineteenth century, Methodists extolled the system as "the primitive and apostolic plan"—". . . *that plan* which God has so wonderfully owned, and which is so perfectly consistent with the apostolic and primitive practice." [13] The theological rationale for the system has to be discovered more by extrapolation from general descriptions and discussion of pragmatic values than from intentional theological analyses. Bishop McKendree's phrase, "the universal spread of the Gospel," provides the clue to the fundamental theological rationale of Methodism's system of itinerant ministry. Itineracy is tied intimately to the mission of the church, an outgrowth of the New Testament message. Pragmatic justifications are voluminous. Methodists have never supposed that there was any particular form of church polity of divine prescription. The mode of governing the church is left, as Abel Stevens wrote, "to its own discretion and the exigencies of time and place." [14]

It has been well observed that "if the itinerant ministry had its beginning under the leadership of Wesley, it had its greatest development under the direction of Francis Asbury." [15] Asbury believed in the plan of itineracy, heart and soul—and he modeled it with uncommon intensity. It was clear to him that it was absolutely essential to the fulfillment of the Methodist mission in the new nation. Very quickly after his arrival he saw that while the work was to be found chiefly in the towns, it could have much greater extension if taken into the villages and crossroads. Within weeks of his arrival in America in 1771 he wrote in his *Journal*:

> I remain in New York, though unsatisfied with our being both (himself and Boardman) in town together. I have not yet the thing I seek—a circulation of preachers, to avoid partiality and popularity. However, I am fixed to the Methodist plan, and do what I do faithfully, as to God. I expect trouble is at hand. This I expected when I left England.[16]

Two days later he wrote:

> I judge we are to be shut up in the cities this winter. My brethren seem unwilling to leave the cities, but I think I shall show them the way.[17]

419

And "show them the way" he did, traveling an estimated 270,000 miles, much of the time suffering illness that normally ought to have caused his death in short order. But he kept it up to the end.

Professor Frank Baker identifies Asbury as "an ecclesiastical Darwinist"(*i.e.*, a religious pragmatist) who honored the past, but for whom no practices were sacrosanct (except the system of itinerancy?). "Even his doctrine of the ministry was functional: you were a minister because you were used of God, and only as long as you were used by God."[18] Asbury was certain that to have

> an efficient itineracy it was essential that the preachers should be tightly ordered and firmly disciplined—though the specific rules and administrative practices to which they must respond and which they in turn would enforce should be flexible enough for variation in face of constantly changing circumstances. To ensure a disciplined people, an adequate ministry, and a smoothly running itinerant organization, it was essential in Asbury's view to have an acknowledged leader or leaders—an apostolate, and episcopacy.[19]

In his "valedictory," his advice offered to Bishop William McKendree in 1813, Asbury was still reinforcing his conviction about an itinerant ministry. "I wish to warn you," he said, "against the growing evil of locality in bishops, elders, preachers, or Conferences."[20] And at the end of the address he commends the itinerancy as distributing talents more broadly and diversifying services more widely than any other system.

The system was a demanding one and the itinerants were subject to rigorous discipline. Once Asbury had been made General Superintendent in 1784 he had the power to send preachers to circuits "with the comprehensive view of a statesman whose eye is on the far horizon, and with the disciplined strategy of an army commander who deploys men as seems best to serve the cause."[21] And he used that power. The "cause" was everything with Asbury, and the preachers (including himself) were servants to that end. It must be remembered, however, that they had voluntarily entered into this covenant of service and sacrifice. While Methodist bishops theoretically had absolute power and discretion in appointing preachers, by 1844 most of them practically received the counsel of their presiding elders and communications from both preacher and people—in greater or lesser degree.

In Coke's and Asbury's view the episcopacy was as itinerant as the traveling preachers—an itinerant general superintendence. In their "Notes" in the *Discipline* of 1798 they wrote:

> It would be a disgrace to our episcopacy to have bishops settled on their plantation here and there, evidencing to the world, that instead of breathing the spirit of their office, they could, without remorse, lay down their crown, and bury the most important talents God had given to men.[22]

In the system bishops are regulated by the same itinerant principle as the other preachers. They go on to say that if through improper conduct the episcopacy loses the confidence of the preachers and conference, the appointing power can be taken from it and invested in other hands.[23]

The cost of the system in human effort and sacrifice was fantastic. The preachers were constantly on the go, exposed to all kinds of weather, especially vulnerable to epidemics and disease, for which, in addition to the expectancy of an eternal reward, they received less than $100 cash per year. Most of the men were young when they died. "Promised nothing either as they entered the traveling ministry or as they retired from it, they were nevertheless expected to give all of themselves to their calling. And they did, by the hundreds worn out before they were forty."[24]

Professor Norwood is right in identifying the early itinerant Methodist preachers as being "as close as one could come in Protestantism to the absolute vows imposed on members of monastic orders."[25]

Demanding as the system was, it was not inflexible. From the beginning it was capable of responding to the ever-changing circumstances of the geographical frontier, and during the two centuries of its development it has adapted itself to the new conditions created by social, economic and cultural changes. There would have been, all along, general agreement with "Nathan Plainspeak" in his view that "the itinerancy is a human invention. As such it is from its very nature constantly in need of repair and renovation, as such is capable of unlimited improvement, as such must be adapted to new conditions as fast as they arise."[26]

Thomas Coke and Francis Asbury were unwilling to consider any change that might run the least chance of "wounding" the itinerant system. To an astonishing extent the dedicated preachers responded to the bishop with an "I'll go where you want me to go." They knew the system was a hard one, but they saw its superiority in the field and "dreaded experimentation" that might disturb the foundations. They viewed "the gospel *and the itinerancy* (as) a fine illustration of power geared to adequate machinery."[27] William Watters wrote in 1806, "I never moved from one Circuit to another, but what it reminded me that I was a Pilgrim—that here I had no continuing city—that I was a tenant at will, and ought to be always ready." Alfred Brunson shared this positive view, opposing the change to the two-year time limit—because it was too long.[28]

Everyone, however, did not view the system as an unmixed blessing or the pinnacle of perfection. Thomas Ware, certainly a committed itinerant, felt that the system was "too severe." Nicholas Snethen and Benjamin Lakin expressed similar reservations.[29] Professor Norwood makes the following cogent observation:

That the system of itinerant ministry was not universally popular is indicated by the number of locations of men who for one reason or another simply couldn't take it any longer. A substantial report of the Committee on Ways and Means of the General Conference of 1816 dealt with the problem and recommended a series of improvements to render the plan more tolerable. Salaries (allowances) should be higher (though still very low); parsonages should be provided, along with fuel and food; provision should be made for support of retired preachers; a plan for a course of study should be set up.[30]

In addition to the severity of the system itself, there was early resistance to the way in which the appointing power was being exercised. Men dropped out rather than continue under it. Others balked and were disciplined. There were frequent trials and expulsions. All of this surfaced under the leadership of Thomas O'Kelly, who enlisted Coke's aid in calling a conference on October 31, 1792, to consider abolishing arbitrary aristocracy (Asbury's), giving the conference of the district the right to nominate presiding elders, limiting of districts in the general conference, allowing each preacher to appeal his appointment to the conference, and establishing a conference of at least two-thirds of the preachers to check up on everything. The crux of the matter is found in the following motion offered by O'Kelly on the second day of the conference: "After the bishop appoints the preachers at conference to their several circuits, if any one thinks himself injured by the appointment, he shall have liberty to appeal to the conference and state his objections; and if the conference approve his objections, the bishop shall appoint him to another circuit."[31] After lengthy debate the motion was overwhelmingly defeated. O'Kelly and others, including young William McKendree, later to return and become Asbury's "successor," walked out and left the Methodists.

"The itinerary," President Horace G. Smith wrote some time ago, "proved to be a system tailor-made to reach the people and to create a church under conditions that prevailed for half a century after the organization of Methodism." Adapted to reach the multitudes moving westward, it was marked by discipline and flexibility. "Only the other system," he says, "—the lay ministry of the Baptist Church—was able to cope with this pioneering situation."[32] The success of the system needs no proof beyond the telling of the story itself. Professor Norwood quotes Abel Stevens to the effect that the operation of the Methodist itinerant system was analogous, not to American democracy, but to military discipline, and then observes:

> The frontier produced a curious combination of rigid authoritarian discipline associated with a high degree of independent responsibility—authoritarianism tempered with individualism, obedience invested with freedom. Sent out under the sole authority of the bishop from the annual conference, his was not to reason why but only to accept obediently whatever appointment was his, always under the necessity of giving up that appointment in return for another at regular

intervals—this same preacher enjoyed a degree of freedom in the accomplishment of his task almost unparalleled in the annals of the ministry. . . . This curious combination of discipline in the annual conference with freedom on the circuit has entered into the permanent fabric of the American Methodist ministry.[33]

Bishop F. Gerald Ensley observed that "while the Methodist system may have been Hamiltonian in its ideals of authority and efficiency, the personnel who made it go were Jeffersonian in their sympathies and willingness to sacrifice for the people." [34]

The values of the system were simple and clear. It was intensely motivated by the missionary objective to "go into all the world" that all might be saved. It was mobile, following people wherever they went on the frontier. It was strategic, putting preachers where and when they were needed for purposes that meshed into an overall pattern of missionary and evangelistic endeavor. It provided a freedom from congregational control that encouraged and made possible prophetic preaching and pragmatically creative pastoral functioning.

There were problems also. To begin with there was the difficulty of finding men who would submit to the rigors of the system. "I am shocked," wrote Asbury in 1801, "to see how lightly the preachers esteem, and how readily they leave, the traveling plan. O Lord, by whom shall Jacob arise?" [35] Apparently some of the itinerants could not discipline themselves in their freedom, and there were complaints that some developed the habit of appearing for the first time on their appointed circuits immediately prior to the first quarterly conference and departing immediately after the fourth, and while preaching and classes were promoted, pastoral duties and instruction of children were neglected.[36] For the total sacrifice required of the itinerants, there was no security for families, which had to be neglected during their almost continuous absence; no provision in the case of disability, which was almost the rule; and no support in old age. Even at the earliest stages there were pressures from the laity to obtain and retain "the most able and lively preachers for their respective circuits," thereby subverting the itinerant plan.[37]

The most serious and prevailing problem had to do with marriage. Anyone involved in the discipline of the itineracy could never expect to have a normal home and family life. It was almost impossible to stay with the traveling ministry for any length of time unless one remained celibate. Most of the men who continued in the itineracy did not marry. Asbury preferred it this way. When it was called to his attention that the low and precarious financial support resulted in an "involuntary celibacy," he responded, "All the better!" [38] That this was not widely accepted by the preachers is attested by Asbury's response to the news that a favored preacher was to be married: "I believe the devil and women will get all my preachers." [39] Not only did marriage make for problems of appointment, it also was resisted by the circuits who were in no mood to support a minister's wife. If a preacher did marry, it often meant that he would locate. The early *Disciplines* admonish: "Take no step toward marriage without first consulting with your Brethren." [40] The whole matter of marriage and location constituted a serious problem, summarized by Dr. W. W. Sweet:

> The great loss of traveling ministers through their 'location' is showed by the fact that, of the 1,616 preachers received into the conferences from the beginning of American Methodism to 1814, 821 had located, most of them within a relatively few years after their admission; 131 had died in the service; 34 had been expelled; and 25 had withdrawn. As late as 1809, of the 84 preachers in the Virginia Conference, only 3 had wives.[41]

Bishop Coke did not agree with Asbury on the desirability of a celibate traveling ministry, believing that preachers could do better work and serve longer in effective ministry if consideration was given to basic needs, normal family life, and provision of old age.[42] But Coke did not stay around long enough to have any moderating influence. Actually, however, the celibate ministry of Asburian Methodism appears to have been on the way out by the time Asbury died in 1816.[43] With the change in the time limit set on tenure in a circuit, Methodist ministers began to marry and establish homes. Even so, the episcopal address to the 1844 General Conference addresses a continuing concern:

> The admission of married men into the itinerancy (has) had a debilitating influence upon the energies of the itinerant system. . . . A large proportion of the young preachers marry before they graduate to the Eldership, and no small number while they are on trial. And this has almost ceased to be an objection to their trial. In general it is quite sufficient that they have '*married prudently*.'
> It is not easy to calculate the extent of the influence of this practice to enervate the operations of the itinerant ministry. . . . The circuits which would have received and sustained them with cordiality as single men, in consideration of their youth and want of experience, have very different views and feelings when they are sent to them with the encumbrance of a family . . .
> It is to be feared that these men have either mistaken their calling in the beginning, or by early temptation lost the spirit and power of it.[44]

Given the very nature of the system of itinerant ministry, the length of time an itinerant is permitted to stay in the same place is a crucial issue. It appears to be the perennial concern that has engaged the traveling preachers more existentially than any other.

The first *Discipline* of the Methodist Episcopal Church, printed in 1785, but containing the actions of the organizing Conference of 1784, identifies the duty of the superintendent (bishop) among others, "to fix the Appointments of the Preachers for the several Circuits: and in the Intervals of the Conference, to change, receive, or suspend Preachers, as Necessity may require; . . . " [45] In the beginning, at Asbury's discretion, the appointments were changed every three months, with a tenure rarely exceeding six months. The first formalization of a time limit seems to be the following note in the *Minutes* of 1794: "The bishop and Conferences desire that the preachers would generally change every six months, by the order of the presiding elder, whenever it can be made convenient."[46] In fact, "between 1794 and 1804 the terms greatly lengthened. Many remained *two* years, and several stayed *three* years, and Francis Asbury *could not* prevent it."[47]

In 1800 a pastor named Stebbins was appointed to Albany, New York. He was very popular and the people wanted continued reappointments. Asbury thought it a mistake, but the pressure was so great that he did so against his better judgment. Some of the preachers proposed that to avoid this kind of thing, the conference set a maximum limit. Asbury had some reservations about this restricting of the appointive power, but made no real objection. As a result the conference of 1804 directed that no preacher was to remain in the same station more that two years successively (excepting the presiding elders, the editor and general book steward, the assistant editor and general book steward, the super-numerary, superannuated, and worn-out preachers).[48]

Bishop Asbury made the appointments without consultation. This changed with William McKendree who was elected bishop in 1808 and took the leadership after Asbury. He introduced the practice of consulting with the cabinet on ministerial appointments, "getting around Asbury's objections to this innovation adroitly by explaining that, unlike his old father in the faith, he needed the help of the presiding elders."[49]

From 1836 onward efforts were made to lengthen the time limit, but without immediate success. The conference that year held that "it is inconsistent with the genius of Methodism to continue a preacher for many years in succession in the same part of the work, and, therefore, the bishops are advised not to continue any preacher for many years in succession in the same city, town, or district."[50] "The *Journal* of the General Conference of 1840 recorded the opinion of the Committee on Revisals that 'the time has not yet arrived for such alteration of the *Discipline.*'"[51]

The General Conference of 1844 provided "that, with the exceptions above mentioned, he (the bishop) shall not continue a preacher in the same appointment more than two years in six, nor in the same city more than four years in succession, nor return him to it after such term of service till he shall have been absent four years."[52] This was repealed in 1856. The Methodist Episcopal Church, South, carried the two-year limit into its structure in 1844. (Eventually an exception was made for New Orleans, where a man might serve longer because it was felt it took at least two years to build up immunity to yellow fever.)[53]

The pressures of changed circumstances, however, could not be resisted forever. As Bishop Harmon observes, "with the development of more and more station churches, and the establishment of parsonage homes in connection with these, and also with the growth in membership and the ongoing of time, there was increased pressure to obtain relief from the ironclad time limit of earlier years. In every Annual Conference there proved to be situations where it was clearly in the interest of the work for a man to be continued longer in a special situation than the law allowed." [54] Evidence suggests that the real breakthrough on the time limit began with the appointment of special editors, secretaries, missionary personnel, and other ministries, whose work could not be adequately consummated under the strict time limits applied to the regular traveling preachers.

The Methodist Episcopal Church was the first to respond to these pressures. In 1864 the limit was extended to allow an appointment of not more than "three years in six." [55] As an experiment, it was further extended to five years for regular preachers-in-charge in 1888. [56] By 1900 that experimental rule was dropped, and there was no further time limit established. In the Methodist Episcopal Church, South, there was growing feeling that a more settled pastorate would greatly enhance the interests of the church, and at the conference of 1866 a committee recommended the removal of all time limits. The recommendation was overwhelmingly accepted. Under the pressure of conservative "elders," led by Bishop Pierce, who threatened to resign, the action was reconsidered the following day and the conference settled for a maximum limit of four consecutive years. [57] Provision was made later for exceptions if the bishop had the approval of a majority of district superintendents given by ballot. This legislation continued until the time of union in 1939.

The Methodist Church, in its initial *Discipline* in 1939, placed no time limits upon the tenure of a traveling preacher in a given charge. At this point, however, changes begin to appear in the conditions under which appointments are to be made. In that first *Discipline* it is stated that the bishop "shall appoint Preachers to Pastoral Charges annually after consultation with the District Superintendents; *provided* that, before the official declaration of the assignments of the Preachers, he shall announce openly to the cabinet his appointments." [58] The 1940 *Discipline* stipulates that *"provided,* further, that before the final announcement of appointments is made the District Superintendents shall consult with the Pastors when such consultation is possible." [59] A move to force the Superintendent to consult also with the Pastoral Relations Committee involved was voted down. [60] This seemingly modest provision was a significant restriction upon the unlimited authority of a bishop to make appointments that was to lead to even further modifications. This restriction was made explicit in 1953 when an Annual Conference appealed to the Judicial Council for an interpretation of the meaning of "consult." The decision makes clear that while the final authority in appointing preachers to their charges rests upon the presiding bishop, "it does not relieve the District Superintendent of the responsibility of consulting with the preacher in order to ascertain whether there are

426

any reasons why the appointment should not be made. Therefore, the final reading of the appointment of preachers to their charges must be preceded by consultation of the District Superintendent with the preacher." [61] Clearly, the District Superintendent is now mandated to participate in the appointing process which up to this point legally had been the exclusive prerogative of the Bishop. A minor revision in 1948 provided that the District Superintendent did not have to consult the pastor when that person had left the seat of the Annual Conference without permission. [62] In 1964 a further provision was made: "Bearing in mind the stated goals of an inclusive church, he shall seek the co-operation of the Cabinet and congregations in the appointment of pastors without regard to race or color." [63]

The Evangelical United Brethren Church and The Methodist Church came into the union of 1968 with no time limits upon the tenure of a traveling preacher in a given charge. The first *Book of Discipline* of The United Methodist Church contains Paragraph 432.1 (now 391.1) of the 1964 *Discipline* of The Methodist Church without a change of any kind. [64]

The movement to require consultation with the Pastoral Relations Committee in the appointment-making process that failed in The Methodist Church in 1940 came to fruition in The United Methodist Church in 1972. That legislation provided that "the bishop shall provide for consultation with the Pastor-Parish Relations committee or its representative," and that "before any announcement of appointments is made, the district superintendents shall consult with the pastors and the local Pastor-Parish Relations committees or their chairpersons concerning their specific appointments. . . . " [65]

Dramatic evidence of the movement to restrict the power, if not the authority, of both bishop and cabinet and to broaden the participation of both pastors and local churches in the decision-making process of appointment-making is provided in the 1976 *Book of Discipline*. In it there is an entire section on appointment-making that requires consultation with the parties affected by the process of appointment-making and announcement of the appointment to these parties before public announcement is made. It spells out the consultative process in detail and identifies the criteria to be used in making appointments. [66]

Both the fact and the far-reaching implications of this action constitute the most revolutionary adjustment of the system of itineracy to the challenge of changing circumstances in the two centuries since it was laid down as the foundation of American Methodism. One can almost feel the vibrations of Bishop Asbury turning over in his grave. The extent to which it is responsive to the concerns the traveling preachers have with the system is astonishing. The test, of course, lies in the extent and spirit of its implementation.

The simplest description of what has happened to the system of itineracy in American Methodism is that it has undergone a slow but steady change from radical itineracy to localism. In different ways Dr. Lynn and Professor Norwood provide impressive illustration of this thesis.[67] Dr. Lynn holds that between 1784 and 1844 the role of minister in Methodism shifted from simple evangelical proclamation to denominational promoter and administrator, with the concomitant change that called for a more settled ministry.[68] Professor Norwood says that during the nineteenth century the traveling ministry became localized, both in the sense of the increase of stations as against circuits and the lengthening of pastorates. In this process he sees two sociological factors at work, the western movement of the frontier which tended to foster the itineracy, and the urbanization of society which tended to destroy it. He makes an interesting value judgment:

> The change was probably necessary, to fit the changing times, for, after all, the itineracy was a human invention. But something of the light of the Wesleyan tradition was extinguished, for out with the itineracy went the fundamental concept of a world parish, an unlimited ministry called to publish the glad tidings in the great unknown. Location could too easily mean stagnation. That is why I suggest that the missionary has inherited one of the central features of the Methodist ministry.[69]

As early as 1774 Asbury was having to deal with the pressures toward localization when friends of Thomas Rankin requested that he be left in New York for a longer time. His *Journal* recounts other similar requests.[70] While the system was being regularly extolled in the literature, the frequent expression of concerns about this aspect of the itineracy in the bishops' addresses to conference—as early as 1828—underscore the reality of the problem. By 1844 there were few circuits left in the north and east. That year in their Address to conference the bishops deplored the fact that "in some Conferences little or nothing remains of the itinerant system, but the removal of the preachers once in two years from one station to another." At the same time they were insisting that "the itinerant plan of preaching the Gospel is an essential element of this system. It was laid as the chief stone in the foundation of the whole building."

A major problem arose with the appearance of the large churches. Increasingly the prestigious city churches tended to disregard the obligations of the itinerant system and to subvert the appointive system by operating on what was practically a "call" system—initiating and making prearrangements with a pastor, and then "seeking" the consent of the bishop to make the appointment. Some even thought their decision should be final. The Methodist Episcopal Conference of 1884 took the position that "direct negotiations between pastor and churches in advance of the making of the appointments by the bishops are contrary to the spirit of our itinerant ministry and subversive of our ecclesiastical polity, and as such should be discouraged by our Bishops, Pastors, and people." [71] Apparently this did not have the desired effect, for in 1912 conference enacted the same resolution again. The episcopal address that year dealt with the problem at length. Bishop Thomas B. Neely felt strongly that if the practice was allowed to continue it would weaken or even destroy the appointing power, work injury to everyone, and work disaster in the church. He observed that the problem was not with the system, but with too many interfering with it—a few laymen of prominent churches, some preachers, and some presiding elders.[72] More than half a century later this problem is still not unknown.

Further pressure was put on the system and the goodwill of the regular traveling preachers by the steady increase of special appointments, which by 1880 involved over three hundred ministers in the Methodist Episcopal Church. While still remaining officially traveling preachers, they were virtually located. This phenomenon, too, has increased steadily to the present.

The very success of the itinerant system was a significant factor in its modification. As membership in local congregations grew and more churches developed on a circuit, it became necessary for the traveling preacher to travel less extensively and devote his time to fewer churches. The inevitable outcome was that the station (a one-point charge) became common. And, as Dr. Gerald F. Moede has observed, in this development the pastoral office assumed a new importance, occasioning a new relationship between Methodist preachers and their people.[73] When this relationship grew into mutual satisfaction and appreciation, the natural tendency was to resist change and to seek a continuation of it.

By the turn of the century it was clear that the Methodist system of itinerant ministry was experiencing an irresistible and irreversible metamorphosis. During the early period of American Methodism itineration meant that a preacher literally was constantly traveling—on the move from place to place within a circuit and from circuit to circuit, at the direction of an appointing power with absolute authority. For a long while now itineracy basically has meant that the preacher is amenable to periodic (at increasingly lengthening intervals) change of appointment, with increasing participation in the decision-making related to it. There is almost no comparability between the present condition of relative stability of time, opportunity for settled family life, adequate to luxurious parsonages, minimum salaries, and health and retirement provisions, and the earlier one of constant mobility, no chance for a settled family life, few amenities for living, meager financial support, and no security in infirmity or old age. How the change has affected the traveling preachers' ministry, particularly its missionary thrust and sacrificial mode, is a moot matter.

The social and cultural context in which connectionalism and itineracy have to do mission and ministry today, if it is to be done at all, has changed—as it always has. The rigors of a radical itineracy were relatively subject to acceptance and fulfillment by a celibate itineracy to a degree not realistic by a largely married one. Legitimate family responsibilities mean that some kind of accommodation is required between the claims of itineracy and family.

Spouses' right to self-identity and fulfillment in their own vocations has to be acknowledged. The insistence upon a greater measure of participation in self-determination, by both clergy and congregation, cannot be ignored.

The system of connectionalism and its strategy of itinerant ministry has worked well throughout Methodist history, and in the light of past crises calling for change and adaptive responsiveness of the systems, there is hardly warrant for anticipating or predicting its demise at this time. It has always been a pragmatic and flexible system in its functioning—and still is. The working of the system obviously requires a very high level of commitment and willing cooperation of churches and preachers. In the last analysis, however, the effectiveness of the system is going to lie in great measure with bishops and cabinet—prepared to work the system with equity, sensitivity, and as much skilled consultative collegiality as possible, but ultimately clearly on the basis of missional strategy and thrust.

Without doubt United Methodism finds itself in this kind of a situation. It is a moot question whether the new social order is either in principle or in fact any more fluid than the frontier society of Methodism's first century in America. There is a remarkable similarity between them. Once again the flexibility and adaptability of the system is being put to the test. Historically the system has always been able to adapt, but always in such a way as to preserve the integrity and essence of connectionalism and itineracy. The question is, Can and will we adapt the present-day version of United Methodism's system of connectionalism and itinerant ministry to meet the challenge?

## CHAPTER 29

# A Critical Analysis of the Ministry Studies Since 1948

Richard P. Heitzenrater

Let me first say a word or two about my approach to this analysis of the ministry study. I can illustrate my approach in my reaction to the invitation. When Don Treese initially asked me to analyze the ministry studies since 1948, my first response was, "Why me? I am not a theologian. I am a historian." He said, "That's no problem." I replied, "I have not been involved in the ministry studies at all—I have not read most of them, quite honestly." He said, "That's no problem. That's an advantage." So I come then as a Wesley historian to analyze work on which some of you have worked very hard yourselves and towards which you already have definite attitudes. I have done my best to analyze these reports from my perspective as a Wesley historian. I will give my apologies ahead of time to anyone whom I might offend. But that apology will not keep me from offending some.

My contact with the church in most recent years has been primarily at the local church level, more or less as a layperson, although I am an ordained United Methodist minister in the Western Pennsylvania Conference. My work in the seminary is, as I have said, mostly in historical studies. My work in the general church has been primarily with the General Commission on Archives and History, and I have never been to General Conference. I say that with some self-assured pride that will perhaps help explain my innocence if not naiveté towards the operation of General Conference.

As one might expect, the material that I accumulated in my analysis was a stack of papers about four or five inches deep, which included the ministry

N.B. This paper was originally given at the United Methodist European Theological Conference, July 15–22, 1987, in Hasliberg Reuti, Switzerland.

studies and the discussions at General Conference as recorded in the *Daily Christian Advocate* and/or the *Journal of the General Conference*. I have tried to digest all of those, though I do not think all of the studies of ministry are of equal importance to the task at hand. Six of the eleven quadrennial studies will be the focus of my survey: the reports of 1952, 1964, 1968, 1976, 1980, and 1984. Although my assignment ends with 1986, I will also make a few observations on the current draft of the statement that is being proposed for 1988.

Actually, the first ministry study in the Methodist Church was in 1944. It was very similar to one that was done in 1948, the date at which my study is supposed to start. This first study was done by Murray Leiffer at Garrett.[1] It was a sociological and demographic study of ministry in the Methodist Church. It attempted to analyze the state of Methodist ministry at that time in order to improve the church's role in recruitment, training, deployment and retirement. The 1952 study is the first major attempt by The Methodist Church to deal with definitions and, to some extent, theological understanding of ministry.[2] In the 1952 study, the commission was asked to examine the ministry of the church in all of its orders and offices. To that commission were referred all matters concerning the ministry of the church, including the non-concurrent matters from the Committee on Ministry of the General Conference of 1948. Here we see one of the problems that faces any committee charged with studying the ministry. Part of their charge is to gather up the loose ends left over from the previous General Conference. The report of 1952 tried to explain that a Methodist concept of ministry represented a middle ground between sacerdotal and evangelical concepts of orders. It explained the concept in this way: an *order* has carried historically the idea of a supernatural *endowment* bestowed on the candidate by one who performs the ordination ceremony. An *office*, on the other hand, suggests an ecclesiastical status, granted to one who has demonstrated he has the spiritual gifts to perform a certain *function* in the church. Two distinctions emerge here: first, between divine origin and human origin; second, between performing duties correlative to ordination and performing other functions in the church. The point of the report (and of those definitions) was summarized by the statement, "We must not in any way despise or discount the divine meaning of ordination" (p. 4). At the same time, the report recognized that American Methodism tended to make admission on trial and acceptance into full membership in conference more important than ordination (p. 5). It also had addressed the question of the relationship between ordination and sacraments. This issue had first arisen in the act of the Methodist Episcopal Church, South, in 1926, which adopted legislation permitting unordained supply pastors to administer the sacraments within the bounds of their own parish. The uniting conference of 1939 adopted this practice. In an attempt to deal with the seeming incongruity of the situation, however, the 1948 conference had "reaffirmed the historic position of Methodism" and made it unlawful for unordained ministers to administer the sacrament of holy communion. But the 1948 conference went on to state that a bishop *may* give unordained pastors permission to do baptism and marriage in the parish where the law of the state permits.

The Conference in 1952 was very concerned (as was the report of the Study Committee) about the relationship between ordination and administration of the sacraments. It tried to hold a hard line on the matter and presumed that any practical problem of short supply of ordained ministers would be solved in the coming years through recruiting and training an increased number of ordained ministers (pp. 8–13).

The 1956 report of the Study Commission on Theological Education was primarily concerned with the support of theological schools;[3] it tried to continue the increase of ministry and proper training of ministry through an emphasis on numbers and deployment of seminaries in the United States. Following the recommendations in this report, the General Conference established two new seminaries (one in Ohio and one in Kansas City), relocated one to Washington (Wesley), and relocated Claremont in California. The tone of the conference relative to the matter of education and training is perhaps best summarized by a statement by Bishop Cannon who said, "As we promote our theological education, we promote the church and we bring the Kingdom of God a little nearer to realization on earth." Further, he said, "If we support this program and then go on to bigger programs, generations yet unborn will rise up and call this General Conference blessed."[4]

The 1960 Study of Ministry, as well as its report to General Conference, is not really as significant as the publication in 1960 of a series of papers from a consultation the previous year of Methodist theological faculties, published as *The Ministry in the Methodist Heritage* and edited by Gerald McCulloh.[5] Several concerns, indicative of the issues of the times, are evident in that publication. Here we begin seeing reflections upon the phrase, "the priesthood of the laity" (p. 54), and that phraseology raises the question of terminology. When we talk about the ministry of the laity, are we talking about the laity as ministers? I am not sure if anyone at that point could have possibly anticipated the following twenty-five years of development, but the question certainly indicates that the problem had surfaced at that time. One chapter of this publication also deals with the question of ordination and its relationship to the sacraments. The author takes a very firm stand: ordination is historically and theologically and necessarily tied to the administration of the sacraments. The question of the priesthood of all believers is also raised: does the priesthood of all believers, as being mentioned and discussed in our denomination, mean in fact the profanation of all ministries? (p. 78)

These questions and others were presented to a Committee to Study the Ministry, which was to report in 1964. Their mandate was the following: "Study the ministry of the Methodist Church in the light of historic Christianity for the purpose of clarifying the doctrine of the church in relation to its ministry and as bearing on the proper use of terms, such as 'minister,' 'pastor,' 'ordination' (including the ordination of local preachers, the status of local preachers), administration of the sacraments, the relation of supply pastors to the annual conference (that is to say, the question of full membership in conference), the responsibilities of ministry, careers properly included in the ministerial office and offices to which episcopal appointments may be made (those are code words that deal with the question of special appointments), problems of recruitment and the most effective use of our ministerial manpower."[6]

This study committee explained in its report that the concept of an ordained laity is indefensible, while at the same time it recognized that the Methodist Church in fact had an ordained laity (p. 28). It went on to say that within our tradition, ordination is not definition; ordination does not define the essence of ministry (p. 31). This tension that had been in evidence within the church at that time for nearly fifty years was somewhat resolved by the 1964 report and its reaction to those issues in the assertion that the term minister should be reserved for those who are ordained and in full connection (pp. 33–34). The question of *when* one becomes a minister (when one is ordained? or when one is brought into full connection? or some time in between?) was resolved by the assertion that being ordained and being brought into full connection are in fact simultaneous ecclesial acts (p. 52). The problem then of having to be ordained before being brought into full connection and having to be in full connection before being ordained was therefore, by definition, resolved. Full connection and ordination, no matter what the chronological sequence, are seen as "simultaneous ecclesial acts."

The commission went on to propose, on the basis of its study, that the Methodist Church should have *one* ordained *order*, that of elder. Further, it should have *one* office—unordained *office*, that is—of deacon. Additionally, those persons previously known as "supply pastors" should be more explicitly defined as "lay pastors." After having carefully distinguished between the *order* of elder and the *office* of deacon, the report to the floor confused the issue by noting that "in the end, all ministerial *orders* are *offices*."[7] This strange incongruity between the study and its presentation is only one of a number of problems evident in 1964.

The report of 1964 was not accepted by the General Conference, which by that time was anticipating union with the Evangelical United Brethren and felt that any major steps in the matter of ministry should be held over until discussions with the Evangelical United Brethren could be brought to fruition at the uniting conference. Therefore, the General Conference voted non-concurrence with the report. In fact, Bishop Cannon, who was on the Committee to Study the Ministry, was the chair of the legislative committee. Therefore, his strong words at the outset asking the General Conference to support the report are in odd contrast to his report from the legislative committee of their non-concurrence as a result of a close vote (43–41 for a substitute recommendation).[8] The General Conference followed the legislative committee's recommendation to establish a new study commission for the following quadrennium to consider both the majority report as it came to the 1964 conference *and* the minority opinion. The new study was to consider primarily the theological issues relating to ministry and the matter of merger with the Evangelical United Brethren.[9]

In 1966 at the special conference in Chicago, the study committee made a preliminary report which by and large said that we are working together to develop a unified view of ministry. The only actual significant legislation relative to that process was a proposal to change the constitution to allow the committee more flexibility in its discussion. The proposal was to change the phrase "traveling preacher in full connection" to "effective full-time ministerial member" because this change would allow the committee more flexibility.[10] It is interesting that what is lost in such a change are two of the key historic terms, "traveling preacher" and "full connection"—what is lost in that change are the basic concepts of *itinerancy* and *connectionalism*! Nevertheless, that tentative change was felt to be necessary at that time.

The report in 1968 that was brought to the Uniting General Conference was a careful and comprehensive study, and took into consideration a wide variety of views. With regard to the question of orders and sacraments, the report tied together the concepts of ministry (I should say ministers), the sacraments, and ordination: only a minister may administer the sacrament; the minister must, therefore be ordained. Walter Muelder emphasized in the discussion on the floor of the conference that there is a fundamental distinction between laity and ordained clergy, that this distinction is related precisely to the question of the administration of the sacraments, and that this distinction is "absolutely fundamental."[11] No one should administer the sacraments without ordination. Lay pastors (new terminology for "approved supply pastors") were, therefore, not authorized to administer the sacraments. Ordination signifies the *authorization* from the ordained ministry of the annual conference. The study committee was convinced that this approach was altogether consistent with the understanding of what ordination is, and they saw it as putting the Methodist Church and the Evangelical United Brethren (as they were joining together in the United Methodist Church) in an ecumenical stance that made it possible to discuss intelligently the question of ordination with other churches.[12] With the adoption of this report, the church (at least for the following quadrennium) prevented unordained local pastors from administering the sacraments—the first time such a situation existed (to my knowledge) since 1926 in the South and 1939 in the unified church.

Another interesting comment that comes from the report of 1968 has to do with the status of Evangelical United Brethren pastors who were not ordained elders but who would qualify in the new church as "associate members" (another new term) with deacon's orders. The terminology used here is informative: a deacon's ordination was seen as *terminal* ordination.[13] Although it sounds strangely like a terminal disease, terminal here is meant to indicate permanent orders at that level.

The 1968 report was basically adopted by the legislative committee and passed on to the Conference. In the midst of a lively debate on an amendment touching on the theology of ordination, Walter Muelder, speaking from the floor of the session, objected that the job of the General Conference was to write *legislation*, not *theology*, and that the Conference should not spend its time with twelve hundred people trying to "write a theology of ordination and correct it from the floor." [14] His point was well made, from a practical point of view: a General Conference cannot write a consistent theology of ministry or ordination in a floor debate.

The 1968 conference accepted the report; as you know, The United Methodist Church retained two orders. In retrospect, one might note that Methodism passed up a prime opportunity to adopt a single order of ministry, a move that many had anticipated would be proposed at the Uniting Conference since it was the structure of ministry in the Evangelical United Brethren Church. The report as it went to the Conference, however, proposed two orders and also tried to distinguish very carefully between ordained and lay positions in the church. In receiving and accepting the report, the General Conference also established the Ministerial Education Fund, an important step ahead in the support of seminary education.

The report to the 1972 General Conference focused primarily upon theological education, the recruitment, nurture, and continuing education of the ministry; the best utilization and deployment of theological schools; and the appropriate promotional and administrative structure for the advancement of the church's ministry.[15] It developed the basic administrative structure that led to what is familiar to us today: the Board of Higher Education and Ministry with three divisions; at that point, Ordained Ministry, Lay Ministry, Chaplains and Related Ministries. The report did ask for a continuing study of ministry that would evaluate the geographic distribution and use of the seminaries, look at the question of continuing education, special appointments, enlistment of women in ministry, and examine the meaning of ordination and the covenant relationship (conference membership).[16]

The report of the 1976 commission marks a radical shift in the church's view of ministry. Two new elements are highlighted for the first time: the concepts of "general ministry" and "representative ministry." [17] The report "attempts a theological definition both of the general ministry and of the ordained ministry, showing thereby their inherent relationship and interdependence, yet at the same time delineating their distinctiveness." [18] In a remarkable turnaround from the sentiment of the previous decade, the commission proposed that the use of the word "ministry" as being particularly or even predominantly identified with those who are ordained was indefensible from the standpoint of our accepted theological standards (which had been defined four years earlier as scripture, tradition, reason, and experience). [19] Ministry was said to be in the name of Jesus Christ, whether carried out by clergy or laity. This broader conceptualization of ministry was grounded in baptism and confirmation, as rites of entry into ministry (supposedly in keeping with the idea of the priesthood of all believers). [20] Thus, in a brief span of eight years, the loudest voices in the commission and at General Conference shifted from talking about ministry as being valid only in the light of ordination to talking about ministry as being open to all in the light of their baptism.

The basic concern at that point was to include somehow within the conception of ministry all those who serve the church in professional ministries, both lay and ordained. The phrase "representative ministry" was coined to designate two categories of ministry within the general ministry of all Christians: diaconal ministers, called to ministries of service, and ordained ministers, called to specialized ministries of Word, Sacrament, and Order. Ordained ministers are representative *of* the entire ministry of Christ and *of* the ministry required of the entire church to the world. [21] In this report, the longtime tension between authoritarian and democratic tendencies in Methodism surfaces and is generally resolved in favor of the latter at nearly every turn.

The 1976 report notes that the ordained ministry is defined by its intentionally representative character (cf. earlier statement). Ordination is seen as "that act by which the Church symbolizes a *shared relationship* between those ordained for sacramental and functional leadership and the Church community from which the person being ordained has come." Now it is "this *relationship*" that is "a gift which comes through the grace of God." [22] At every opportunity, the point is repeated that there is no rivalry between the general and representative orders of ministry and that neither is subservient to the other: "The validity [!] of the mission of the Church is dependent on the viable interaction of the general ministry and the ordained ministry of the Church." [23]

Besides this concern for defining and positioning general ministry, the commission reflected a growing concern for recognition of unordained persons who serve the church on a full-time professional basis as part of the ministry of the church. Many of these persons were seen as powerless, having no participation in annual conference, and beset with such practical problems as benefits and pensions. [24] This need for empowerment was met in the short run by the designation of an office of diaconal minister, into which persons were consecrated for ministries of love, justice, and service. It was thought that these persons would be those in the professions (counseling, law, social service) whose ministries would benefit from some authorization from the church. The result was to have both an order of deacon and an office of diaconal minister, a confusing situation that was not directly addressed by the Conference.

On the other matters designated to its agenda, the commission suggested that special appointments be clarified in terms of categories of service (there has always been a certain amount of suspicion on the part of clergy in the annual conferences that people with special appointments are somehow getting away with something). As for women in ministry, the report suggested that recruitment be emphasized and that fairness be exhibited in such matters as examining women for ordination. It also recommended that ordained women be included in all the structures of the church.[25]

On the surface, the most startling recommendation made by this commission was that no commission be appointed by General Conference to study the ministry. It was, as a matter of fact, one of the most crucial political maneuvers in the long history of ministry studies, for this commission did actually call for a study of the diaconate to be made by a joint committee of the BHEM and BGM (DLM).[26] This "in-house" study was weighted from the beginning toward the diaconal interests: the committee was heavily representative of lay interests in the church, half of its membership from the lay division of the BGM and another quarter from the diaconal ministries division of the BHEM. The mandate given the committee was to build upon the approved Guidelines for Recognition of Diaconal Ministry; to do further study to enable the church to move forward in establishing appropriate new structures for the enrichment of its ministry; to monitor progress being made in implementation of the 1976 legislation concerning diaconal ministry; and to report to the 1980 General Conference.

The language of the 1980 report heightens the tendencies begun in 1976 to shift away from traditional conceptualizations of ministry, ordination, and even sacraments. New ideas flow almost too easily with a rhetorical flourish.

There is, for instance, the "primacy of general ministry": "The United Methodist heritage in all of its forms has recognized consistently in its practical life and theology the primacy of the ministry of all believers"—a statement that should make historians blink twice.[27] But there is also, as seen in the report, the "primacy of service": "Serving the needs of all of God's creatures, in Christ's name, constitutes the primary outward and visible sign (sacrament) of God's redemptive presence in the world." [28] Not only does this statement represent an innovative and questionable designation of "sacrament" (seen also in the context of "the sacramental character of all ministry") but the linkage of "primacy of service" (within the general ministry) with the Greek term for service (*diakonia*, sometimes translated as "servanthood") must be seen as an important tactical step in the politicization of scripture to support specific empowerment issues within the structure of the church for a particular group that has already been designated as diaconal ministers. The political tensions that lay behind the "empowerment" issues, as well as the bias of a majority of the committee, are quite evident in the repetitive "non-hierarchical" "non-authoritatarian" emphases in this document.

The most radical proposal in the report was for a new *order* of diaconal minister. Whereas the previous Conference had provided for consecrated diaconal ministers in ministries of service and ordained ministers in specialized ministries of Word, Sacrament, and Order, this report tried to define both ministries in the same terminology: two specialized ministries within the representative ministry, both ordained to particular functions. The elder (ordained to responsibilities primarily for Word, Sacrament, and Order) would have a ministry of leadership within the congregation; the diaconal minister (ordained to responsibilities primarily for Service, Justice, and Love) would have a ministry of service in the world. The report inaccurately describes the historic order of ordained "deacon" as a "temporary" order and suggests that it could be abandoned.[29]

The rhetoric in this report rambles on with little regard for meaning or history, and borders on glibness at points. The way in which strained cleverness with words often results in confusion of thoughts can be seen in the variety of ways the term "representative ministry" is explained: "the calling and intention to present again (re-present) the calling of God to the whole people"; "intending to represent the whole gospel *and* the whole people of God." Leadership is described almost entirely in terms of facilitating; the terms used are revealing: ministry is to enable, embody, exemplify, intensify, and make more effective. Ordination is watered down to consist of "symbolic acts which confer special roles of responsibility." The loss of the divine element in the process is indicated by an interesting shift in language, which may or may not have been intentional but illustrates the mindset in either case: the Wesleyan question, "Have they gifts, as well as grace, for the work . . . ," is changed to "Have they gifts, as well as *graces*, for the work . . . "; the single letter *s* in this case makes all the difference in the world.[30] A divine gift has thereby become cultivated manners! Wesleyan language about "setting apart" is used in the report as a subtle part of the rationale for ordination of diaconal ministers; Wesley himself, though, had no problem "setting apart" his lay preachers without ordination.

The report was so laden with problems that the legislative committee that received the report at General Conference in 1980 unanimously recommended non-concurrence. Accepting instead a BHEM document, the legislative committee recommended that diaconal ministers continue to be consecrated and be allowed lay membership in annual conference (using, if necessary, the lay equalization plan). The language of the study report regarding representative ministry and specialized ministries was shifted slightly in the recommended proposals, and the rationale for diaconal ministry, problematic as it may have been, was incorporated into the legislation that was finally accepted by the Conference.

The Conference also voted to continue the study of ministry during the following quadrennium and asked that the three ministry divisions work together (as well as consult with appropriate general agencies) to develop recommendations that would reflect a "holistic understanding and ordering of ministry" with specific response to a permanent diaconate in the UMC.[31]

The study committee for the 1980–84 quadrennium was again made up of a minority of representatives from the Division of Ordained Ministry. Over two thirds of the committee were representatives from the Division of Diaconal Ministry, the Division of Chaplains and Related Ministries, and at-large members.[32] Following the suggestion of the mandate, the committee developed a set of recommendations that were sent to the Divisions for study in October 1982. Over the next few months, the committee prepared revised recommendations, which were passed by a minority of 9 votes (out of 19, 4 absent, 3 abstaining, 3 against), and sent to the BHEM in October 1983. The following statements reflect the nature of the final report: there should be one order of elder (for Word, Sacrament, and Order); there should be one order of deacon (for Word and Service); the "transitional" deacon should be eliminated. Descriptive terms for diaconal ordination were changed in the last report from "Word and Service" to "Liturgy, Service, and Justice."[33]

The wording and tone of the 1984 report echo its predecessor in 1980. The general ministry is again emphasized as the *basic* ministry of the church; the representative ministry is in and for the basic ministry, embodies the church in the world, and has two non-hierarchical forms differentiated by representative roles, functions, and means of accountability (the distinctions of function not intending to indicate distinctions of dignity, status, or worth). The representative ministry is a special ministry, identified by special gifts, graces (!), fruits, and promise of usefulness.[34]

There is some problem in knowing just what representative means; it seems to mean everything and therefore nothing. The special ministry is representative of Christ (!), of the whole church, of the entire community of Christ, of the Gospel; special ministry represents to the church its identity with Christ and the Gospel itself.[35] Ordination is no longer associated with the sacraments or preaching, but rather is an ordination "for mission": the act "has different intentions according to the tasks and functions of the representative ministers."[36] Presumably, if a church administrator is ordained as a diaconal minister, he or she is ordained to administering. The increase of concern for promoting "mission" in unconventional ways seems in some ways to run the risk of losing sight of the conventional ways (again the language is of equipping, ena-bling . . . ).

The problems in this report were essentially the same as those in the report rejected by the General Conference in 1980, and this report met a similar fate, being turned down in the legislative committee by an overwhelming vote of 84 to 24.[37] A minority report by four members of the committee then became the majority report of the legislative committee (by about the same margin of vote). It stipulated that the diaconal ministry be retained in its current form (as set up in 1976); that the church consider broadening the deaconate to include three types of deacons (those intending to seek elder's orders, those intending to remain as deacons in pastoral ministry; those intending to serve in ministries of love, service, and justice); and that an instrument for ongoing reflection on the theology of the church and ministry be established and report to each session of the General Conference.[38] Our present meeting (United Methodist European Theological Conference), though not directly a result of that last suggestion, is certainly in keeping with that spirit.

A new study committee was established through the Council of Bishops to report to the 1988 General Conference. The mandate stipulated that it study specifically the meaning of ordination, the relationship of ordination to the sacraments, the meaning of itinerancy and the nature of conference member-ship; that it deal with current orders of ministry and the possibility of a permanent diaconate; that it consider all studies of ministry made since 1968.[39] The make-up of the committee is typically representative in the recent mode of quota-recognition (which seems to be more important than expertise in these days of caucus-Christianity). The committee is chaired by a laywoman, the vice-chair is known for her advocacy of what has come to be known as "a permanent diaconate", and the secretary is the general executive of COCU. This membership does not necessarily indicate problems; but the problems in the current draft of the report seem to reflect some confusion that could naturally result within that constellation of influences.

One should acknowledge that the current plan of the committee is to present only a tentative report and ask for continued study for another quadrennium. I would say that this maneuver is the result of the negative reaction from around the church to yet another report that essentially starts and ends at the same places as the last two reports that have both been rejected by the General Conference. Some of the problems in the report can be seen in the wording of specific sentences as published in the Circuit Rider:[40] "Everything the church is and does is 'ministry'—service to God and the world." Ordained ministers "represent Christ to the community and the ministry of all the People of God to the world . . . to them is given the task of publicly presenting and representing those events, authorities and powers which are essential to the ongoing life of the Church." Ordained ministers "represent the Gospel of Christ" "to remind the entire People of their commission." "The ordained ministry is sacramental to the Church as the Church itself is sacramental to the world." "There is also the matter of harmony rather than hierarchy." "Lay persons who are further called to particular, representative service in the church and are ordained, also continue their responsibility for the ministry common to all Christians to which they were called at baptism." "Ordained ministry may be called representative in at least two ways:—the intention to present again (re-present) the calling and acts of God in Christ to the whole people, re-presenting to the Church its own identity and mission in Jesus Christ;—the visible and intentional representation of the general ministry of all baptized Christians, focusing the ministry of all the people of God to the world, and intensifying and effectuating the calling and self-understanding of all God's people as servants (ministers) in Christ's name." "To speak of embodying is to state that the church sets aside those who will intentionally 're-present' to the community that distinct part of its identity and purpose." "Deacons shall be lay members of the annual conference upon their ordination." "Deacons may be licensed as Local Pastors to administer the sacraments in the charges to which they are assigned."

Many of the concepts are less than clear and in fact point toward real problems of understanding: ordination is a sacramental act; Baptism is a mandate for servanthood; the Eucharist in a mandate for ministry; the church must continually reform the ordering of ministry; horizontal relationships are more important than vertical relationships.

Many of the problems of the last three reports can be summarized in several questions raised on the floor of General Conference in 1984 by James Logan and John F. Walker.[41] The essence of these was as follows: In the attempt to relate the sacrament of Baptism and the act of ordination within the concept of ministry, does the proposal *inflate* the category of permanent diaconate to the point of *conflating* it with the baptism of all Christians in the general ministry? What ever happened to lay leadership within a meaningful theology of the laity? Does not a diaconal order based on service undermine the ministry of all Christians? What is representative ministry actually representative *of* or *to*? If ordination and itineration are both intended to facilitate mission, why does the proposal have only one order itinerate? Does not a non-itinerating conference relation change the nature of annual conference relations and episcopal responsibility (just ask Joshua Soule)? Is it fair or even correct to refer to the traditional order of deacon as "temporary" or "transitional" (much less the proposed diaconal order as "permanent")? Two or three other observations made in that discussion also seem pertinent: The report, lacking a global dimension, seems to be insensitive to the UMC outside of the United States. Adoption of the report would seem to short-circuit ecumenical discussions that are still underway. Ordination is not the proper way to recognize lay persons who serve the church, nor is it what many diaconal ministers themselves want—"We asked for rights, and we got orders as an answer."

In conclusion, I would like to present my own analysis and summary of the nature and cause of what seems to me to be a very confusing state of affairs in some very crucial areas of concern in our church. On the matter of *number of orders*, for the first decade after 1944, the studies maintained and defended the traditional scheme of two orders, as well as holding the line on the necessary connection between ministry, sacraments, and ordination; the studies focussed on maintaining high standards (educational and personal) and promoting recruitment and support of ministry. The next decade saw a shift toward restructuring ministry on the basis of proposing one order (elder), partly in anticipation of union between the Methodists and the Evangelical United Brethren. The third decade, after 1964, abandoned the idea of one order and moved rapidly toward a democratization of ministry and a reconceptualization of orders within the prevailing temper of non-authoritative and non-hierarchical tendencies of the 1970s. In the 1980s, the reports have continued the attempt to unravel the relationship between ordination and sacraments and to suggest that the lay diaconate become an order. The most recent study commission, as I understand it, has moved beyond these two orders and is thinking of promoting three orders (including an ordained episcopate). In a period of twenty years, we have moved from advocating one order to contemplating three. In spite of much of the rhetoric to the contrary, some of the emerging views of ministry are often tied more to function and facility than to vision, commitment, or vocation.

At the beginning of these reports, the need to establish positive ecumenical relationships was seen as the rationale for maintaining two traditional orders of ministry. By the 1960s, however, these broader relationships (including our European connection and our talks with the Evangelical United Brethren) were seen as reasons we should be thinking in terms of one order. As we approach 1988, the same rationale (ecumenical viability) is being touted as a reason we should perhaps be thinking of three orders!

There has been a great deal of waffling back and forth on the matter of the *nature and purpose of ordination*. The matter of orders as distinguished from offices has never been made clear in any official statement. The clarity in the earlier reports in distinguishing between clergy and laity on the basis of ordination has now been significantly clouded by the emphasis on general ministry into which one is "ordained" by baptism. And the connection between ordination and the sacraments, already a problem at the outset of these studies, has been alternately clarified, confused, clarified, disregarded, and has generally fallen victim to practical and political pressures quadrennium by quadrennium. A return to the traditional requirement of ordination for anyone who would administer the sacrament was not only short-lived, but was reversed to the extent that lay administration (under certain minimal restrictions) has become commonplace. Whether ordination is essentially a gift of God or a rite of the Church has been voted back and forth by more than one General Conference. Ordination as the mark of a clear distinction between laity and clergy was certain for the first two decades of this period, but that clarity disappeared into the fogginess of representative ministry.

The confusion of starting points between what a minister *is* and what a minister *does* is paralleled in a confusing *doctrine of the church*. This attempt to elucidate a doctrine falls short of the wisdom of what the church *is* (which helps define what it does) or with what the church *does* (which then defines what the church *is*). One point of confusion is in a shift away from the concept of Church as fellowship of believers in which the Word is preached and the Sacraments duly administered (a community of grace in and through which appropriate actions consequential to its nature take place) toward a concept of the Church *as* mission (a community shaped by the actions it takes necessary to meet the needs of the time and place, those actions then defining the nature of the gathered community). Additionally confusing is recent talk about the church as *being* "sacrament" to the world, in terms of it being an "outward and visible sign" (of the fruits and *graces* of ministry?) presumably of God's grace (the similarity in wording to the traditional definition of sacrament overshadowing the omission of the last half of that definition: "of an inward and spiritual grace" [*grace*, after all, has become so meaningless as to be shifted to "graces" without the batting of an editorial eyelash]).

Finally, we seem to have become more interested in rhetoric and image than substance and meaning. Many key *words* that are basic to a clear understanding of the church have become nearly meaningless in the process. In the process of draining many words of any distinctive significance, other words take on special alternative significance because they have become symbols of party issues, and therefore have in essence become tools of power struggles, and are thus unable to convey any intrinsic meaning. Some words such as "ministry" have been used in so many specific contexts (sliding back and forth between a specific and a general meaning and sometimes used interchangeably in both ways) that the term has become nearly meaningless in terms of its derivative, "minister." The term "representative" ("representative ministry") might seem to be clear in many of its separate and specific applications, but looking at the whole picture, one wonders how ministry can in the end be representative *of* everything and *to* everything. The term "sacrament" ("the church is sacrament") is now falling into that familiar bin of favorite words that can be weighted with different and special new meanings so as to broaden their usability. But the terms become then less useful in designating traditional meanings within an understandable context. Some terms, such as "confessional" ("we are not a confessional church"), are at times given particularly narrow uses, so that one has to know the specific hermeneutical usage in the mind of the user to understand the meaning. And some quite central words in the tradition, such as "Lord", have become the focal point of party contentions. Terms become heavy with latter-day connotations that can be used to obscure their primary meanings in a cloud of contention. One difficulty in elucidating a clear doctrine of the church and its ministry becomes apparent in the history of a process that has begun to rely on the parochialized special uses of words and terms that are packed, stretched, and finally squeezed out of the arena of consensual usefulness.

We could also point out that an increasingly significant part of the ecclesiastical ambiance within which many of these developments have taken place has been the burgeoning influence of pastoral care approaches to many areas in the church from educational methods to leadership training. We are so desirous of harmony, so afraid of hierarchical tendencies, so inclined to be non-directive, and wanting so much to facilitate, to embody, to heal, to enable, to lead from behind, and to see it all from the underside, that no one wants to provide any real leadership or is willing to make firm, responsible decisions. We are in dire need of good leadership, but in many of our official actions and statements, we exhibit an implicit understanding of organization and administration in which strong leadership is by nature seen as oppressive, hierarchical, fascist, discriminatory, or capricious, and therefore to be avoided at all costs. And many times the resulting cost of avoiding strong leadership is very high. We do have capable laity and clergy in the church. We simply do not trust them to do anything, say anything, or even make a decision without asking us first. And it is rather ironic that from the same quarter that complain about a clergy-dominated institution comes the cry to recognize outstanding lay workers by creating a new class of clergy or paraclergy.

When this penchant for democracy is combined with a tendency for American experimental pragamatism to prevail in any discussion of how to proceed ("I like it, let's try it; if it works, it must be right!"), one can see how doctrine takes on the appearance of an occasional and ancillary enterprise. Theology and history become relegated to the role of being used as handy tools for retrospective rationalization rather than basic methodological resources that stand behind the development of policies and programs. In many ways, these developments seem to demonstrate the increasing influence of those theologies that start with issues of power and politics and try to derive a theological (if not biblical) rationale to support partisan issues and pressures. At times, it seems as though administrative problems of staff relationships are being confused with theologies of ministry and mission; there is room yet for a good theology of polity, but there is also a need for good administrative structure and know-how.

It is easy in this context to blame the process by which our church proceeds in its attempts at official self-understanding and operation. Nearly everything is up for grabs every four years at General Conference. And given the increasingly large and diverse nature of our church, the possibility of focussed concerns and real unity seems to fade farther into the background behind the activities of pressure groups and specific interest groups. The crucial battles are now fought over who gets named to important committees because in spite of (or in some cases because of) the implicit or explicit quota systems, the outcome of committee deliberations can nearly always be predicted by the makeup of the committee.

In the whole constitutional and legislative process of governing our church, where is theology done? I can sense that it really does not happen in the quadrennial study committees. The activities in those groups are most often characterized by careful jockeying for position, in which theology is sometimes used as the handmaid of politics. As Walter Muelder pointed out in 1968, the theological work cannot be expected to take place on the floor of the General Conference itself. The boards and agencies are perhaps more rightfully concerned with implementing than theologizing. The local church and annual conferences certainly don't exhibit a continuing interest in pursuing serious theological reflection. Where, in the structure of the church then, is theology done? Many of the calls for reports ask that a theological rationale be provided in the final report. Sometimes the mandate even includes a request that decisions be tested by the Wesleyan guidelines of scripture, tradition, reason, and experience, a particularly intriguing dilemma since there seems to be little common agreement as to how these are supposed to function authoritatively within our theological methodology. In the midst of this somewhat troubling picture of our theological dilemma (if not to say doctrinal wasteland), I would suggest that this particular gathering (United Methodist European Theological Conference) represents in my experience one of the few bright lights of hope for serious reflection on basic issues that must be of concern to the church. We must give thought to ways in which this kind of endeavor can be expanded without being trivialized or politicized.

I would also suggest that the legislative processes of the General Conference itself could be adjusted to accommodate two basic concerns that have become evident to me in this study—the need for meaningful levels of *continuity* and *consensus* in our basic self-understanding and the structures that reflect our identity. A church that attempts to change its structures every four years, especially in such basic areas as ministry, seems to lack the basic concern for continuity that might provide some of the strength that it seems so wistfully to desire. And although a diverse group such as ours can never hope for total unity on any given issue, an intentional concern for converging toward consensus might go a long way toward that "unity in diversity" that we would all like to celebrate. We need a way to keep major proposals from being decimated and treated piecemeal if we are to prevent the essential nature of our church from disappearing under continual layers of quadrennially-applied bandaids. The

Book of Discipline in this sense simply reflects the confusion that is promoted by the present process. Without claiming a definitive answer to the problem, I would venture to propose several guidelines that might be helpful in this regard:

1. Require that major proposals (on ministry, doctrinal guidelines, etc.) must be dealt with as a whole, as reported by the committee; the report could not be voted on piecemeal, but must be voted up or down as a whole.

2. Require that a final vote on any such report could come only at the following General Conference, after a four-year study within the church; such a "second reading" policy is not unusual within many polities for important issues.

3. Require that the approval of such proposals finally requires a two-thirds majority; even if not a constitutional issue, such significant issues should represent more of a consensus that 50% plus one.

I make these suggestions with the simple intention of trying to stimulate thinking on ways by which we as a denomination could be more intentional in our concern for continuity and consensus in our dealing with basic issues, be they structural, theological, or missional. I would be encouraged, even re-freshed, by discussions within our denomination that struggled with basic theological issues, for I am convinced that we must know what ministry is (and what the church is) before we can know what the church must do. Further we must understand the nature of the church and its ministry before we can have an effective and meaningful mission.

# United Methodism's Basic Ecumenical Policy

## John Deschner

"We are becoming the Sancho Panza of the ecumenical movement," a United Methodist of my acquaintance remarked to me recently. I laughed until it began to sink in. Sancho Panza was the great realist who wept over Don Quixote's windmills; the eternal survivor who made sure there was a next meal, if not a believable future; the faithful follower, seldom the initiator; the man with an absolutely impenetrable tin ear, who lacked even a trace of his master's soaring imagination.

That ecumenical Sancho needs a vision of his own. Not a triumphal Quixote-like vision, but a realistic vision that suits him—a basic ecumenical policy that does for The United Methodist Church what sound basic foreign policy can do for the nation. This paper aims to provoke something like that by clarifying the importance of United Methodism's ecumenical commitment for its health as a church.

Its main affirmations are these:

First: Our ecumenical commitment is not an extra but is essential and constitutive for United Methodism as church.

Second: An adequate basic ecumenical policy for United Methodism will focus upon four points:

1. The central ecumenical goal is an *inclusive church unity as a witness* to God's way of healing and renewing the broken human community.

2. The attainable sign of integrity in that witness is an inclusive *visible fellowship* around the table in Holy Communion—a fellowship presently not expressed by the divided churches.

3. The unavoidable immediate step toward that witness is the work toward a full inclusive and *mutual recognition* of members and ministers among the divided churches.

4. The historical embodiment of this attainable goal is best viewed as a future, truly ecumenical, *conciliar event of witness.*

## UNITED METHODISM'S ECUMENICAL COMMITMENT AND PRINCIPLES

Let's begin constitutionally. How much do United Methodists care about ecumenism? If ecumenism means church unity and its witness concerning the healing and wholeness of human community, then constitutionally United Methodists put that concern at the top of their self-understanding as a church.

Our constitution begins with church unity as a witness about human community. The preamble mentions the United Methodist denomination only after two substantial paragraphs in which it has already defined the church in ecumenical terms and put its finger on "dividedness" as a fundamental hindrance to that church's mission in the world (*Discipline*, p. 19). Turning to the Constitution proper, Division One, along with our three general articles about Name, Articles of Religion, and Title to Properties (Articles 2, 3, and 6), contains three more articles—all on ecumenism! (Articles 1, 4, and 5 on Church Union, Inclusiveness, and Ecumenical Relations)!

When you consult our Articles of Religion and Confession of Faith to find how United Methodists understand this church, they answer with deep ecumenical insight: as "the one, holy, apostolic and catholic . . . community of all true believers under the Lordship of Christ," gathered around the Word of God purely preached and the sacraments duly administered (Article XIII, of Confession V). And lest there remain any doubt about what "pure" preaching and "due administration" of sacraments imply, we can be reminded by that basic constitutional article about "Inclusiveness of the Church" that all persons without regard to race, color, national origin, or economic condition are eligible to attend, participate, and share membership in the life and koinonia of this worshiping and witnessing "congregation."

We need to repeat and nail down from the beginning this fundamental, thoroughly characteristic United Methodist emphasis about ecumenism. "Church unity," has to do not simply with lessening denominational divisions, but with overcoming whatever divides and alienates *either* Christian fellowship or human community—dogmatism and institutionalism, to be sure, but racism, classism, and sexism no less. The emphasis is on "inclusive" church unity. Indeed, the deeper emphasis is upon a church unity whose *mission* is to bear witness to and visibly demonstrate God's way of healing the broken human community. The first and basic division of our Constitution is utterly preoccupied with laying down this foundational United Methodist concept. Do not misread what follows, then, as pleading merely for a narrow interdenominational view of ecumenism; its aim is to make clear the United Methodist understanding that ecumenism is missionary through and through. It has to do with the integrity of our witness.

What is the basis of this emphasis on ecumenism as wholeness in church and community? First, it lies deep in the Wesleyan vision of *sanctification as the wholeness of salvation*, a personal wholeness which is inseparable from a vision of wholeness in church and society. God's gift is the vision and the power for a renewal of this wholeness, a renewal which God freely offers in all and to all without exception. We are committed to receiving this gift as God gives it, in its wholeness both personally and corporately, and to bearing witness to all, whatever their condition, concerning that gift's "pure, unbounded" powers of reconciliation, liberation, and healing. There is a personal being made "perfect in love"; there is also a corporate perfection as God, in the inspired phrase of Charles Wesley, "perfects us in one" (*The United Methodist Hymnal*, no. 627).

Church unity and church inclusiveness are not mere extras any more than sanctification is a mere extra in personal salvation. They are basic and essential, both as unity and inclusiveness. Wesley, as Albert Outler loved to say, was an "evangelical catholic." One of the most basic meanings of the ancient term *catholicity* is precisely that inclusiveness of the church about which our Constitution speaks. "Catholic Spirit" is Wesley's translation into corporate terms of our characteristic emphasis upon wholeness in personal salvation. There, at the very core of our Wesleyan conviction, lies the reason for our United Methodist ecumenical commitment. We are concerned about church unity because we believe the sanctification of the church belongs to and prepares it for its mission.

That invocation of the traditional Wesley can turn our attention to a crucial feature of our new disciplinary doctrinal statement (*Discipline*, Pars. 66–69). That statement leaves no doubt that our United Methodist doctrinal heritage consists of *two* parts: "Our common heritage as Christians" and "our distinctive heritage as United Methodists" (pp. 41, 44). "Our common heritage" as United Methodists is the faith of the apostles and therefore of the scriptural canon, as it has been generally summarized in the ecumenical creeds (the Apostles, the Nicaean, the Chalcedonian Definition) and interpreted in the developing tradition of the great Eastern and Western teachers (Athanasius and the Cappadocians, Augustine and Aquinas, the Continental and the English reformers)—all as passed on to us via that unresting editorial pencil of John Wesley in our Articles of Religion.

450

"Our distinctive heritage as United Methodists" consists of the distinctive Wesleyan sermon themes capable of being preached to coal miners at five in the morning: prevenient grace and repentance, justification and assurance, sanctification and perfection, faith and good works, mission and service, and the nature and mission of the church.

What interests us here is how our church understands the relation of the "common" and the "distinctive." About that the *Discipline* is quite explicit and emphatic; "The core of Wesleyan doctrine that informed our past rightly belongs to our common heritage as Christians" (*Discipline* p. 50). "The heart of our task is to reclaim and renew the distinctive United Methodist doctrinal heritage, which rightly belongs to our common heritage as Christians, for the life and mission of the church today" (p. 56).

Something momentous is being said here about how to relate the common and the distinctive, something that few other churches have said so explicitly as yet. We are stewards of a distinctive tradition on behalf of the whole church, charged to renew and cherish it and to give it to the other churches as something which belongs to their and our common heritage. Our "distinctive" Wesleyan themes are truly ours only within that ecumenical commitment and stewardship. No "distinctives," no United Methodists—that's a truism. But no ecumenical commitment, no United Methodists either, and that's the point. We can truly have Wesley only by giving him to others in terms which they as well as we can understand. We can truly observe United Methodist services of Holy Communion only as celebrations of the whole church. We can truly have United Methodist ministers and bishops only as recognizable ministers and bishops of the whole church. We can be truly distinctive only as we are one.

Let me try to formulate that commitment into three ecumenical principles:

First, the basic United Methodist commitment to the wholeness of God's grace and our salvation is at once personal, ecclesial, and social. The three unities personal, churchly, and social are inseparable.

Second, inclusive church unity is thus constitutive for United Methodism, as constitutive as personal sanctification is for Wesleyan salvation. United Methodism has its being, its integrity, only in relation to the whole church of Christ. We cannot be ourselves without being ecumenical. That is what Wesley saw in his construal of the relation of the Methodists to the Church of England. It remains utterly clear in principle in the Constitution and *Discipline* of our denomination.

Third: United Methodism's distinctive heritage is constitutive of and—inasmuch as it expresses the apostolic faith—belongs by prior right to the whole church. Our "distinctives" are truly ours only in trust, insofar as we hold them as stewards actively engaged in making them understandable and sharing them with others. This does not deny our mission to the unchurched. But it does take seriously what Wesley knew very well and presupposed in his mission to them:

451

that it is a mission to spread the faith of the one, holy, catholic, and apostolic church, or it is nothing. That requires dialogue with other churches as well as mission to the unchurched.

In a word, ecumenism is of the essence of United Methodism. There can be no more searching question to put to our church than, what is the health of your ecumenical commitment?

# UNITED METHODISM'S BASIC ECUMENICAL POLICY

We turn now to policy, those middle points of strategy that link basic principles and quadrennial programs.

I do not have space here for a methodologically explicit derivation of policy from principle. I frankly ask you to follow my attempt simply to focus upon four basic points which belong to any adequate United Methodist ecumenical strategy today.

1. First, deceptively self-evident, yet most basic, is that *the central goal of United Methodism's ecumenical policy is the quest for an inclusive church unity.* The reason, as the previous section sought to make clear, is that church unity is central for our denominational identity and ecclesiology as such.

This church unity focus in our ecumenism is contested by some. Church unity is a North Atlantic concern, it is said; it belongs to the past. The contemporary challenge lies in the broken human community itself, and our concern is not unity but purposeful conflict and surgical use of power to bring about justice. The commanding theme today is not unity among the churches but justice in the human community. Some therefore call for a quite explicit new "secular ecumenism."

If this is posed as an alternative center, I believe that it is a mistake. Gustavo Gutierrez himself insists that the root problem in oppression is not simply unjust social structures but sin and that any truly radical liberation will begin by generating a new human being. John Wesley agrees: first God's grace and our new birth, then human response in good works. Thus, there is no real sanctification without regeneration and no real regeneration without justification by faith and no true faith without prevenient grace.

We can translate that into ecclesiological and ecumenical terms. Before the renewal of mission there must be a new koinonia, and before the new koinonia there must be grace and receptive participation in the means by which that grace is "normally given," as Wesley puts it—through the apostolic witness in the Scriptures, through faithful contemporary proclamation of that witness today, and through initiation into the apostolic community of faith and participation in its communion and mission. The central theme in a United Methodist ecumenical policy, then, must be the quest for church unity as an ecclesial

452

sanctification in which formerly separated churches are ready to receive together the fullness of the "ordinary" means of grace and are thus visibly capable of bearing witness, as the divided churches cannot be, about inclusiveness and justice in the human community as well. To make the quest for social justice alone the center of our ecumenical policy is to practice an ecumenism without foundations or credible visible signs and to offer a witness without "good news."

This focus on church unity does not imply a retreat into interdenominationalism. It asks, rather, that we discern the Body of Christ, as Paul asks, in our so-called ethical issues. Racism, sexism, classism are for United Methodists ecclesiological and ecumenical issues before they are ethical issues. They have to do with how we *are* the Christian koinonia. That is what our constitutional linkage of church unity and inclusiveness is trying to tell us.

Only a quest for *church* unity, so understood, will have a message of hope for our post-Christendom contemporaries and a real future in the 21st century.

And so our first policy point is this: The central principle of our ecumenical policy is the quest for a credible, visible, and inclusive church unity.

2. What kind of attainable and visible sign of this church unity should our policy seek? The question is important, for if church unity is in any sense our task and not purely and simply a divine gift, then it must be attainable, and if attainable then it must be visibly embodied in signs that communicate it. My conviction is that the attainable sign of an adequate United Methodist ecumenical policy is a *visible fellowship in Holy Communion*. This fellowship must include not only United Methodists but of all persons, especially those whose liberation is at issue and those who are members and ministers of other divided churches.

Other concrete signs could of course be mentioned: various arrangements for common witness, schemes for organizational merger, specific declarations of mutual recognition of other churches' baptisms or ordinations, covenanting together with other churches to "live our way toward unity," or conciliar arrangements of various kinds. Section II of our *Discipline* makes it clear, however, that "sharing in Holy Communion with all God's people" is what these many ways point to (p. 88). It is their acid test. The ultimate ecumenical goal, of course, is God's kingdom. But the kingdom, too, generates "signs" of its presence, according to the Gospels, and visible, common Holy Communion belongs to these signs. Jesus himself asks us to do this "in remembrance" of him.

Eucharistic fellowship is attainable. As it has been threatened and mutilated in history, so it can also be recovered in history.

Is divided Holy Communion that important? Failing to discern the Body of Christ as we eat is that important according to Paul (1 Cor. 11:29), and he regards that failure as a dangerous symptom in the church. I communicate sometimes in a joint "ecumenical" Catholic-Protestant service. We prepare together, repent together, pray together, hear the Word together—and then at the climax of the service turn our backs on each other as we go to our respective Catholic and Protestant ends of the sanctuary to have communion with our God (with our "gods"?) This is behavior I would not tolerate in a restaurant, yet it is the actual situation every day in every service of Holy Communion, including that of The United Methodist Church. It is wrong for churches to tolerate that symbol. It points to a sickness in the church. It is right for our Constitution to name that "dividedness . . . a hindrance to (our) mission".

We should acknowledge that United Methodist willingness to accept all others doesn't solve the problem. The solution is not that all become United Methodists, or that all become Roman Catholics. The solution has to be sought together, because we must also listen to the reasons others give for their refusal to accept our invitation. There is plenty of room for all to repent.

And so our second policy point is this: Our policy is committed to an inclusive visible fellowship in Holy Communion as a credible witness that the Christian gospel can indeed heal broken human community.

3. That point leads to another element in policy: *the immediate step towards that goal is to work toward a full inclusive mutual recognition of members and ministers of the divided churches.* We do not need total doctrinal consensus. We do not need massive new structures. Concretely, what we need is mutual recognition of baptisms and ordinations. In other words, we need that mutual understanding of each other which enables an authentic hospitality at the table of Holy Communion. The way to that unity is not uniformity but genuine mutual recognition in each other of the apostolic faith and fellowship—in that good diversity and plurality which belong to its essence.

I have three short remarks about this. First, United Methodists have been generous when asked officially to recognize the *baptisms and ordinations* of other churches and to seek visible eucharistic fellowship with them, as, for example, in the Consultation on Church Union (COCU). The question is, if that generosity is justified, are we actively pursuing and broadening it, or are we simply going along when others take the initiative? Where do we stand, for example, with our bilateral recommendation of 1984 "to take steps to declare and establish full fellowship of Word and sacrament" with the Lutherans? Is our ecumenical policy strong enough to generate not simply cooperation and compliance but initiative?

A second remark about mutual recognition: It is realized on all sides that the truly tough sticking point in mutual recognition is *bishops.* Here United Methodists have a problem. It's not simply that John Wesley couldn't recognize our General Superintendents as bishops. Neither can the majority of Christians (e.g., the two-thirds who are Orthodox or Roman Catholics, among others). The answer does not lie in some unilateral Methodist commission attempting to theologize about our episcopacy. Rather, it has to do with, as our UMC response to the World Council's *Baptism, Eucharist and Ministry* (BEM) text puts it, our participation with other churches in a succession of multilateral projects of reconciliation of ministries, in COCU for example. I can foresee no widespread mutual recognition of ministers, hence no widespread visible fellowship in Holy Communion, which does not involve, as BEM and COCU recommend, some version of the historic episcopate as "sign though not a guarantee" (as *Baptism, Eucharist, and Ministry* puts it) of the apostolic (i.e., biblical) tradition as the basis of all ministry, lay and ordained. That is the transcending issue represented by the ecumenical discussion about our UMC bishops, namely, the question about the "apostolicity," or in our language, the biblical integrity, of witness in ministry of each church.

This recognizability of our bishops is very nearly the nub of our ecumenical problem concerning an inclusive and visible church unity. The strategic point is certainly the question now being asked of the United Methodist Church by the Consultation on Church Union. Are we preparing our 1992—or our 1996?— decision about COCU with sufficient prudence, care, energy, and initiative? Our response should be influential to many besides ourselves. We are not being asked merely for our consent. We have a responsibility for leadership.

A third remark about mutual recognition: It must include recognition of ordained women.

The United Methodist insistence on an inclusive church unity has vaulted the United Methodist Church way out front in its insistence upon the *ordination of women*. Mutual recognition of ministers as necessary for visible fellowship in Holy Communion will have to come to terms with this insistence upon inclusiveness.

Finally, some words of admonition here from one who profoundly believes that this United Methodist "distinctive" belongs to the whole church: (1) This question will not be quickly solved. Not in a quadrennium. Not in a decade. Not, possibly, in a century. Real love is patient, and it was John Wesley who defined ecumenical or "catholic" spirit as real love. (2) It won't help to assume that the right position is clearly known, and that it is our own position, and that the appropriate action for Orthodox and Catholics is repentance. However right we may be in seeing "non-theological factors" at work here, the discussion is theological, and our case needs to be put in theological terms that speak the language of the whole church. (3) To prevail, or even to be taken seriously, those theological arguments will have to show that ordination of women is an expression of the apostolic faith. It is hopeless to concede the apostolic tradition to those who oppose. (4) Likewise, it is insufficient to think that we are talking merely about securing recognition of women as ordained ministers of the United Methodist Church. Our basic ecumenical principles commit us to more. Just as there is no true denominational doctrine except as expression of the apostolic faith; just as there is no denominational bishop except as bishop of the whole church; so there is no such thing as an ordained denominational minister except as a minister of the one, holy, catholic and apostolic church— the church which our own Constitution puts first. It might be asked whether mutual recognition of ministers requires that other churches ordain women, although we might well work for that. What is clear is that for the United Methodist Church inclusive church unity must include seeking and asking for recognition of United Methodist Church ordained women as ministers of the only church there is—hence as valid con-celebrants in the practice of visible eucharistic hospitality and fellowship.

And so our third policy point is that the unavoidable immediate step towards the visible ecumenical sign is to work toward a full, inclusive, mutual recognition of members and ministers of the divided churches.

4. That brings us to a fourth element of policy. Granted that our ecumenical councils (WCC, NCCC) do not require full mutual recognition of ministers and members or, indeed, of churches as a requirement for membership, and are thus "pre-conciliar" in character in the technical sense of the term. What would be the basic policy of the United Methodist Church with respect to genuine conciliarity—the most likely form of ecumenical life in the century to come? The historical embodiment of our attainable goal is best viewed as a future truly ecumenical conciliar event, an event that could mean for all the churches what Vatican II meant for Roman Catholics.

We can remind ourselves of the function of an ecumenical council in the classical sense (e.g., the Jerusalem "council" of Acts 15, or the Council of Nicaea), namely, as an event called to confess the apostolic faith to the church's religious and non-religious contemporaries. A truly ecumenical council means an event in which authorized representatives of all churches come together, when necessary, to exercise the church's universal or ecumenical magisterium (authoritative teaching office). There is no lack of church attempts to confess the faith today. The tragedy is that the church has lost its capacity to speak authoritatively with one teaching voice. There is no ecumenical magisterium today, a major change from the days in which both Orthodox and Catholic developed rationales for a universal magisterium. There is no instrumentality for addressing the common Word of Christian faith and hope to our contempo- raries in the name of the whole Christian community on issues of enormous import—abortion, birth control, racism, poverty, euthanasia, nuclear energy and weapons, not to mention such issues as baptism and mixed marriages. Although authoritative church teaching today must be rightly and creatively diversified, diversity cannot and should not rationalize the sheer contradiction in much church teaching. Those contradictory teachings are no small reason for what we call the authority crisis today. They cripple witness. Our resolutions end up in archives and footnotes. No particular church can speak for all, not even if its Pope addresses the United Nations. And no present group of churches can either. The WCC constitution, for its part, makes it utterly clear that the WCC has no authority to speak for its member churches any farther than they may ask it to do so. Who speaks for the church?

And yet the impression grows that the churches are increasingly wanting ecumenical organizations to speak and act on their behalf, especially on issues of high technical complexity, such as bio-medical research, for example. Is there a growing conciliar magisterium in our time, and what should United Methodist policy be toward that?

*Baptism, Eucharist and Ministry* provides a highly interesting example of this problem, and perhaps a hint of the way ahead. Strictly speaking, the WCC is a house in which the churches can carry on an ecumenical conversation *with each other*. But in this case the churches asked the WCC to do more—to summarize their sixty-year-long conversation on baptism, eucharist, and ministry, and to submit the result to the churches.

You know the outcome: unprecedented interest. The Lima text on *Baptism, Eucharist and Ministry* is the most widely translated, published, and used text in modern ecumenical history; six volumes of official responses from the churches published already with a seventh in preparation; a hundred-page WCC analysis of the responses now in the hands of the churches; plans for a Fifth World Conference on Faith and Order in 1993 to help the churches assess the import of all this for their future relations with one another.

But the most interesting aspect is that the WCC, rather naturally and without much premeditation, did not simply summarize the discussion. It went on to *ask* the churches four basic questions about the BEM text and its possible role in the churches' lives and ecumenical policies. One church refused to respond, and their letter showed that they understood the point I am trying to make: the WCC has no constitutional authority, they said, to ask such questions of a member church. But the astonishing thing is that 189 churches (so far) did not raise that question but did respond, and moreover wished the project well—including the whole spectrum: the Vatican and the Ecumenical Patriarchate, the Salvation Army and the Quakers, the Pentecostals, the Anglicans, the Protestants, the free churches, and all the major member churches in the WCC. Moreover, they took seriously the invitation to respond to BEM from "the highest appropriate levels of authority," officially.

The WCC's constitution insists that the WCC is not an ecumenical magisterium. But as any teacher knows, questions teach. In these official responses the WCC has been accorded something like a *de facto* authority as a *questioner* in the ecumenical conversation among the churches. It is not a mere host or enabler in the ecumenical conversation house. Moreover, that *de facto* authority is further attested by the remarkable fact that a number of churches have found it advisable or even necessary to create their own more adequate magisterial instrument in order to produce a response on a level this fundamental.

Our own church is an example. As we all know, the General Conference is our highest doctrinal authority under our standards of doctrine. Our General Conference nevertheless saw fit to devise a special magisterial process in order to produce our official response to BEM. Our own ecumenical commission was given authority (and it carried out the task extremely well!) to create a many-sided process of consultation, of local study, of special commissions, of drafting and redrafting. It was then asked to submit the provisional draft to our Council of Bishops who, upon realizing the magnitude of the assignment, docketed it in two of their semiannual meetings before they were ready to approve it—unanimously, if I remember correctly—as the official United Methodist response to BEM from our "highest appropriate level of authority."

Curious! The General Conference itself asked the bishops, who have by Constitution no voice or vote in the General Conference where our denominational magisterium is located, to participate in, indeed to consummate, the process of formulating our church's most authoritative response on questions of basic authoritative church teaching. I submit that something more than an episcopacy of general superintendency was stirring in the instincts which created that process.

But our concern here is what occasioned this remarkable constitutional improvisation on our part, if not the presence of an ecumenical questioner whom we felt in our bones asked questions of us with real authority to do so, and required authoritative answers from us of corresponding weight.

What is happening here exceeds our vision, as yet, but it is going to require a United Methodist policy on conciliarity—or, in our own lingo, an *ecumenical* policy about "connection" and "conferencing." Somewhere between 1990 and a future truly ecumenical conciliar event (say around 2050) will lie hard ecumenical work on developing the presuppositions which can surmount the difficulties preventing such an event today.

Our preparatory work will have to focus the task of such a conciliar event upon an act of common witness, for example, on expressing to our contemporaries the common apostolic faith and our hope about survival on this planet, and it must do so in convergent terms not yet within our grasp. Moreover, such an event would require that we be able to lay our concern before God in a common act of eucharistic worship, a fellowship in Holy Communion still beyond us.

Again, such an event would require mutual recognition of all bishops as ministers of the churches' unity in the apostolic faith, and at the same time bring into the event the inclusive representation of both laity and clergy, both male and female, old and young, which our UMC Constitution is so concerned about—an understanding of representation which neither we nor the Christian tradition yet possesses.

I think you see my point. A future truly ecumenical event will have to presuppose some solution to many of our present day dilemmas. The power to focus is one thing that makes this vision so interesting. And the sharp point of such a vision's demand for United Methodists will be our need for a policy about conciliarity and the ecumenical magisterium.

That truly ecumenical conciliar event will happen only if the churches really want it. Does The United Methodist Church want such an event of ecumenical witness?

I believe that as a visible embodiment of a basic ecumenical policy rooted in our understanding of the gospel itself we should be leaders in asking for it. Like John Wesley, our church understands its own life to require participation in the wider ecumenical church. It believes in the sanctification of the church as well as in the sanctification of persons. It has a missional passion therefore to press for the growth of the ecumenical movement and the common, undivided, unhindered mission of the whole church. It believes that the sign of an inclusive visible fellowship in Holy Communion is not only realistic but attainable in the history of our time (cf. the UMC response to BEM in *Churches Respond to BEM*, Vol. II [Geneva: WCC, 1986] 177). And it believes that this process of church renewal is of decisive importance for the healing and renewal of our broken human community today.

And so our fourth policy point is this: The historical embodiment of our attainable policy goal is best viewed as a future truly ecumenical conciliar event.

## CONCLUSION

I have tried to show that this ecumenical commitment, these ecumenical principles, and much if not most of these ecumenical policies are already implicit in United Methodism's understanding of its own essential constitution. My hope is for a basic ecumenical policy in our church which lets the implicit become very explicit—as explicit as the works of love which evidence real faith—as God "perfects us in one."

# Methodist Worship

## James F. White

The Methodist tradition of worship began in the eighteenth century [ . . . ]. Not only had the controversies of the Reformation era long disappeared but the battle over control of the Church of England that had marked most of the previous century had finally been put to rest. Indeed, too much peace was probably the greatest problem in English religion at the time, manifesting itself in general indifference. But such peace also brought about the possibility of a less partisan and more universal approach to worship.

By Methodist worship, we mean that of the disciples and descendants of John Wesley (1703–91), his brother, Charles (1707–88), and numerous other co-workers, most of them, in the initial stages, Anglican clergymen. This tradition of worship is located most obviously in those churches called "Methodist" or "Wesleyan" in the United Kingdom and the United States. It also continues, in varying degrees, in more than fifty other churches that have separated from Methodists at one time or another: the Salvation Army, the Church of the Nazarene, and various Holiness churches of the non-Pentecostal variety. Some, such as the Salvation Army, have modified the Methodist worship tradition drastically; others have been less innovative. At the same time, Methodists have assimilated others, such as the Evangelical United Brethren Church in 1968. Thus the Methodist tradition has often become anonymous as the result of divisions and mergers. It is easier to define the tradition's central core than its outer boundaries.

The place of the Methodist tradition in the scheme of Protestant worship is not immediately apparent. Because of the time distance from Reformation controversies, John Wesley was able to reintroduce some features of late-medieval piety and practice: the eucharist as it implies a sacrifice, frequent celebrations of the eucharist, vigils, and fasting. These practices alone could place Methodism to the far right of Protestant worship traditions. On the other hand, Methodism is a secondary or even tertiary tradition, reflecting later developments within both Anglican and Puritan traditions. Pietism is certainly present too, especially from the Moravian phase of the Lutheran tradition. Significantly, Wesley made a pilgrimage in 1738 to the Moravian center at Herrnhut just after the heartwarming experience at Aldersgate that began his most significant work.

The Puritan tradition is strongly represented; both of Wesley's grandfathers were nonconformist ministers, and his mother's family included influential Puritans from Dorchester, the Whites. Wesley's alterations to the *BCP* reflect much of the Puritan agenda for worship as expressed in the 1603 "Millenary Petition" and the 1661 "Exceptions of the Ministers." Yet Wesley repudiated the emphasis that Puritans (and many Anglicans) placed on predestination. At the same time, Wesley's eucharistic doctrine is probably closest to that of John Calvin.

But the matrix of Wesley's work was always his beloved Anglican tradition. Whenever possible, he extolled the virtues "of a solid, scriptural, rational Piety" and departed from Anglican practice only when souls were at stake. Thus Wesley would break canon law by invading others' parishes if it were necessary to save souls.

Methodist worship was also greatly transformed by the nineteenth-century experience of the American frontier and both shaped and assimilated the Frontier tradition of worship. In turn, Methodist worship provided the background for yet another worship tradition, the Pentecostal.

Where do we locate Methodist worship on the scheme? It seems most appropriate to consider it a central tradition, not unlike the Reformed tradition. In the general context of American Protestant worship, Methodist worship is probably as central as any.

We shall deal first with Methodism's eighteenth-century origins in Great Britain, then look at worship on the American frontier with its subsequent nineteenth-century developments, and finally turn to the characteristics of twentieth-century Methodist worship.

## EIGHTEENTH-CENTURY ORIGINS

The original reasons for the formation of the Methodist tradition in worship were missional. John Wesley faced the problem of reaching unchurched masses in the new industrial and mining centers of England. We shall call his method "pragmatic traditionalism": that is, use the methods of current practice where they work; otherwise, search the universal tradition for practices that have worked in similar situations. Thus Wesley could accept field preaching (although reluctantly, at first) because it was both apostolic and effective; the love feast he defended because it was the ancient agape; and the watch night was simply a new form of vigils. Hymn singing could be justified on the grounds of biblical precedent, the ancient fathers, and Lutheran practice. In his pragmatic traditionalism, Wesley is not so much an innovator as a restorer. He is a good Anglican in his love of tradition, but it is a tradition that can liberate, that can reform the present. Wesley was a patristics scholar, and no one ever has shown better how relevant the early church can be to practice.

Methodist worship was a countercultural movement in the midst of the English Enlightenment. As we have seen, sacramental worship had been pushed to the margin of church life among both Anglicans and Nonconformists. Sacraments were reduced to social propriety (in the case of baptism) or ethical motivation (in the case of eucharist), with little thought that either sacrament might be divine intrusion into this well-ordered universe. It was not intellectually respectable to make the sacraments central in an atmosphere that so completely dissociated the physical and visible from the inward and spiritual.

If anything was unfashionable in Georgian England, it was enthusiasm. The Wesleyan movement was constantly denounced for producing Spirit-filled Christians or "enthusiasts" rather than staid pewholders. Enthusiasm was especially distrusted because it made religion primarily a matter of the heart rather than the head. Rationalism simply could not tolerate such enthusiasm. Yet Wesley did reflect some of the liberal currents of the time, especially his dislike for the stern denunciations of the Athanasian Creed.

Another reason Methodism was considered not socially respectable was that it reached out primarily to the poor.[1] In an era that placed so much emphasis on power and prestige, a few Anglican priests had no concern with advancement but identified with "the meaner sort," who were powerless politically and economically. To reach the poor urban masses, one had to go beyond the parish system and develop a whole new form of mission. This outreach shaped Methodist worship in definite ways.

Methodism, then, began as a countercultural movement in the midst of an era of rational religion. The members of the Holy Club of students and dons at Oxford were ridiculed for the methodical emphasis on sacraments and daily prayer, hence they were called "Methodists" or "sacramentarians." John Wesley's mission to America in 1735–38 was far less successful than he had hoped, but it brought important contacts with the Moravians and in 1737 Wesley published in Charleston the first Anglican hymnal, *Collection of Psalms and Hymns*. Wesley's return to England led to his Aldersgate experience of inward assurance of salvation in 1738 and the radical step of preaching in the fields. From then on, Wesley's life for over half a century was incessant riding across the British Isles to preach, organize, and guide the people called Methodists.

Charles Wesley poured forth the greatest treasury of hymns in the English language, over six thousand of them. In 1784, John Wesley put his hand to revising the *BCP* for America. His *Sunday Service for the Methodists in North America*[2] was the rather conservative work of one who loved the 1662 *BCP* but saw the need to adapt it to the times. He accepted most of the 1661 Puritan "Exceptions" to the *BCP* and made a number of changes of his own. In particular, he tried to encourage a weekly eucharist by making the combined Sunday services less burdensome. This book provided the background for Methodist rites for over two hundred years. Contrary to his wishes, Methodists in England separated from the Church of England shortly after Wesley's death, while American Methodists had been organized as an independent church since 1784. Nevertheless, English Methodists kept a strong affinity for the worship forms of the established church.

One cannot describe the origins of Methodist worship without attention to the early Methodist people. Wesley faced the problem of ministering to the new urban poor in such places as London, Bristol, and Newcastle. The parliamentary system for creating new parishes had failed to provide a satisfactory means for reaching the vast population jamming the cities. The mines and "dark satanic mills" employed many of the countryfolk who had been forced off the land as "the deserted village" became a widespread phenomenon. Here was a new social system that the established church, largely staffed by younger sons of squires, was poorly equipped to serve.

New forms of mission had to be found in worship as well as new systems for health, education, and public welfare to minister to a largely unchurched population. The inhibitions that restrained educated and affluent people could be ignored. People could sing and shout with uninhibited joy. The level of active participation could be raised by encouraging people to sing with fervor, give personal testimonies, and pray spontaneously in class meetings. Although Wesley was careful not to confuse genuine religious affections with mere boisterous behavior, Methodist worship invited vigorous and loud participation. Scant wonder, then, that it was labeled "enthusiasm," for there was an abundance of outward signs of the Spirit's inward working.

With the fields ripe for harvest, the number of Anglican clergy willing to help was far from sufficient and Wesley early began to use lay preachers, eventually even some women. A constant problem was the lack of clergy willing to celebrate the eucharist frequently. Wesley took the conservative position, that ordained clergy were necessary for the celebration of the eucharist. Late in life, he felt forced to ordain elders (presbyters) for "those poor sheep in the wilderness" in America and finally for the British Isles. He did not take the liberal position of allowing lay leadership of the eucharist but found new roles for laity in preaching and pastoral functions in the societies and classes. Thus although there was a great increase in lay leadership of worship, it did not include the sacraments. Laity were enlisted "to feed and guide, to teach and govern the flock" of societies, penitents, and classes.[3]

Shifts in piety shaped the new Methodist tradition, especially in Wesley's insistence on the instituted means of grace. In his sermon on "The Means of Grace,"[4] Wesley makes it clear that these consist of searching the scriptures, receiving the Lord's Supper, and prayer. Elsewhere he adds to these, as "ordinances of God," "fasting, or abstinence."[5] Christians were to be immersed in scripture through frequent attendance at preaching services and in personal and group Bible study.

The Lord's Supper was of great importance. At a time when frequent celebration of the eucharist was rare in most parish churches, Wesley preached on "The Duty of Constant Communion," insisting that "do this" meant it should be done as frequently as possible.[6] Wesley himself received communion on "an average of once every four or five days" throughout his lifetime.[7] Such frequency had been rare in Protestantism since the sixteenth century, and it required great ingenuity for Wesley to try to provide sufficient Anglican clergy to meet the needs of Methodist people for the sacrament. Wesley observed that for many lukewarm Christians the eucharist could be both a confirming and converting ordinance.

Prayer was the third means of grace and was encouraged in the parish church services (Methodist services being scheduled at other than "church" hours), in the Methodist societies and classes, and in the family.

The "General Rules," which gave Methodism much of the character of a religious third order, encouraged fasting at regular intervals as an important religious discipline. This was about as countercultural as one could be in a self-indulgent century!

Another factor shaping Methodist piety was "Christian conference." Part of Wesley's genius as organizer was to provide support groups for converts, whom he organized in societies, bands, and classes. The Methodist society in a community would meet regularly for lay preaching services and for the eucharist whenever a clergyman was available. But small class meetings provided the place for examination of conscience, spiritual direction, testimony to one's religious growth, and prayer together. Thus worship and discipline were intimately related. Indeed, a ticket from class meeting was necessary for receiving the eucharist with the society. The small class meeting never existed in isolation but was always feeding people back into the larger society or the church. The early Methodist people prayed with their peers in class meeting, with the society in the local community, and frequently in the parish church. At its best, it brought a combination of public prayer, preaching and the eucharist. Such a balance has been hard to achieve at any time in Christian history, but Methodists accomplished it during the eighteenth century in England despite formidable obstacles.

The structuring of time showed important changes for the Methodist people. Wesley hoped everyone would receive the eucharist weekly when possible. Lay preachers could provide weekly preaching services, and the class meetings met on a weekly basis under a lay leader.[8] The preaching services were regarded as supplemental to worship in the parish church: the Anglican Sunday morning prayer, litany, and ante-communion with sermon.

On a monthly basis, there were special services, such as watch night, Wesley's version of vigils.[9] Usually held on a moonlit night (for reasons of safety), these were times for preaching, prayer, testimony, and hymn singing. Occasionally, the love feast[10] would be held when eucharists were not possible. Administered with bread and water, this derived from the ancient church via the Moravians and was an occasion for sharing of prayer, testimony, and hymn singing. Testimony was a spontaneous sharing by any individual present with a story of God's grace in that person's life. In effect, it gave everyone a chance to proclaim God's work.

Unlike many of their contemporaries, the Wesleys regarded the Christian year with enormous seriousness. John Wesley's *Journals* show careful observance of prayer-book feasts such as All Saints' Day.[11] Many of the hymns of Charles Wesley were written to celebrate these events, "Hark! the Herald Angels Sing" and "Christ the Lord Is Risen Today" being the best known. In his *Sunday Service*, John Wesley could not refrain from tidying up the calendar, with Sundays numbered after Christmas until "the Sunday next before Easter" and after Trinity. Nevertheless, he could excise much: "Most of the holy-days (so called) are omitted, as at present answering no valuable end," a thoroughly pragmatic decision. Propers remain only for Christmas, Good Friday, and Ascension in addition to the Sundays.

Wesley added one annual event, the Covenant Renewal service, held New Year's Day.[12] Ultimately deriving from biblical precedents such as Joshua 24, the immediate source was a service developed by Presbyterians Richard (1611–81) and Joseph Alleine (1634–88) in the previous century. In recent times, it has been somewhat duplicated by the annual reaffirmation of baptismal vows at the Baptism of the Lord as introduced since 1976 in many Methodist churches.

The lifetime cycle brought other changes. Wesley kept and defended infant baptism. But, like the Puritans, he saw no purpose in confirmation and omitted the rite from his prayer book. The conscious experience of conversion was the crucial event, but it had no liturgical reflection. This experience of new birth had far more practical consequences than infant baptism, for it brought full assurance that one's sin was forgiven and that one was justified with God. Conversion was an exhilarating experience of justifying grace. Recollection of this event could fill a lifetime with rejoicing. Converts were shepherded in classes and societies where the white flame of conversion could be kept burning brightly.

Wesley made some significant changes in the rites of passage.[13] With no apparent precedent he eliminated the giving away of the bride in the wedding service. He also removed the giving of rings (as the Puritans had advocated). The burial rite was changed to make the ultimate destination of the deceased seem less certain, Wesley finding the *BCP* service too presumptuous. Changes were made in the ordination rites, with forms for ordaining deacons, elders, and "superintendants."[14] All mention of the power to forgive sin was eliminated from the rite for elders. In general, Wesley had problems with any forms that presumed to know the spiritual state of the recipient, whether alive or dead.

There were significant developments in the place for worship. In 1739, Wesley persuaded himself "to be more vile" and began preaching in the fields and anywhere he could reach a crowd. He leap-frogged over five centuries of indoor worship to the days of the early mendicant friars and their preaching at market crosses. When possible, "preaching houses" were built to enable indoor preaching services. Wesley resisted the legal definition of these as dissenting chapels.[15] For many years, his model was the Octagon Chapel in Norwich (1756). Wesley's premise was that such octagonal buildings (with balconies) brought the largest number of people close to the preacher at minimum expense. Late in life, he built City Road Chapel in London (1778). A font appeared, and City Road Chapel functioned almost as a parish church. Eventually, Methodist chapels were built all over England and Wales, unpretentious brick buildings on back lanes without steeple or portico but usually with balconies, an elevated pulpit, and a communion table ringed with rails.

If the times and places of worship changed, so did the style of preaching.[16] Although emotions were not sought for their own sake, they were not avoided either. Methodist preaching was directed to the heart as well as to the head. It was a constant offering of a crucified Savior calling for conversion of life, a far cry from the tepid moral rationalism heard from most Anglican and Nonconformist pulpits of the time. More often than not, the preacher might be a neighbor or local man or woman who had received a call to preach and had been examined and licensed under careful supervision. The link between preaching and pastoral care was always clear. Wesley felt that simply making converts without careful spiritual direction afterward was breeding souls for damnation.

Wesley balanced both sides of the controversy over free and fixed forms of prayer by advocating both at every level of worship. His eucharistic rite concludes (after all the fixed forms) with the rubric, "Then the Elder, if he see it expedient, may put up an Extempore Prayer."[17] Such prayer was to be prepared for the time, not left to chance. Wesley always defended the *BCP* with its fixed prayers and used it faithfully each day. But he was equally firm on the need to supplement the official forms with prayer conceived for the occasion.

Furthermore, he expanded the numbers of those who were to pray in public so that class meetings involved spontaneous prayer offered by anyone present. And what was done in the public session of the class was replicated daily at home in family prayers. Being able to address the Almighty publicly and extemporaneously in prayer was an ability expected of any Methodist, even though read prayers were also encouraged. Wesley advised ministers in America to use the full liturgy "on the Lord's Day, in all their congregations, reading the litany only on Wednesday and Fridays, and praying extempore on all other days."[18]

Methodism's greatest contribution to ecumenical Christianity has been in the form of hymnody. The result of introducing hymnody to wide use in England was to allow a far greater degree of active participation so that all could express their worship with the best of their musical talent. Many of the over six thousand hymns by Charles Wesley consist of doctrine written as poetry, in some instances literally theological treatises versified.[19] But Charles Wesley was able to use the poetic forms of the time to achieve this without being tedious or didactic. "Come, O Thou Traveler Unknown," sometimes called the best of his hymns, is a poetic version of Genesis 32, Jacob at Penuel. What people sang became the theology they learned, and what they learned shaped their lives.

Frequently, the hymns are the best source of Wesleyan theology. The 166 *Hymns on the Lord's Supper*, published in 1745, are one of the greatest treasures in English of eucharistic piety.[20] They also are the chief document for Wesleyan eucharistic theology. With their emphasis on the eucharist as sacrifice, the work of the Holy Spirit, and strong eschatological flavor, they seem to belong much more to the early church or the present than to the eighteenth century.

The hymns gave the people much active participation in worship and punctuated every service. Familiar tunes were used to make them as singable as possible. On the other hand, Wesley's prayer book makes no provision for service music, and organs were too expensive. Nor did he approve of choir anthems, "because they cannot be properly called joint worship." Music was a form for active participation by everyone rather than passive listening.

## NINETEENTH-CENTURY DEVELOPMENTS

The journey across the Atlantic brought a real sea change in Methodist worship. Although many of the themes of Wesley's movement endured, they were transmuted by personalities and circumstances he could not have envisioned. The real founder of American Methodism was Bishop Francis Asbury (1745–1816), whose role it was to preside over the expansion of Methodism from the strip of states along the seacoast to the vast heartland beyond the

Appalachian mountains. Asbury, although English born, was attuned to the new American situation. Wesley's pragmatism had great appeal to him, Wesley's traditionalism very little. The result was a mostly pragmatic reformation of worship for American circumstances.

Wesley's love for the *BCP*, his emphasis on frequent eucharists, his affection for the church year—none of these survived passage across the Atlantic. William Wade has shown that, unlike Wesley, Asbury scarcely noted Christmas Day in his journals, let alone the lesser feasts of the Christian year.[21] Although Asbury successfully stopped an attempt to allow unordained men to administer the eucharist, it seems to have been more a matter of church discipline than to defend a traditional approach to the sacrament. Asbury's piety focused on preaching and disciplined life, not on sacraments and fixed forms for prayer.

The key event came in 1792, a year after Wesley's death. The 314 pages of his prayer book were quietly laid aside in favor of 37 pages of "Sacramental Services, &c." in the *Discipline* of that year. Jesse Lee (1758–1816) tells us that the ministers were convinced that "they could pray better, and with more devotion while their eyes were shut, than they could with their eyes open."[22] All that survived this discarding were services for the baptism of infants and adults, the second half of the Lord's Supper, weddings, burials, and the three ordination rites. These became standard items in the *Discipline;* the rest of the *Sunday Service* seems to have been little missed. After 1808, the *Discipline* was revised every four years, and minor changes frequently appear. The rites in the *Discipline* were named the "Ritual" in 1848 and 1870.

The *Discipline* continued to carry a brief notice as to what should be included in the normal Sunday morning and evening services, especially insisting on the reading of scripture "chapters" or, later, "lessons." The 1828 *Discipline* was concerned to promote "establishment of uniformity in public worship," and frequent appeals were made that the "Ritual invariably be used," probably good evidence that it was not. New services were added in 1864 for the laying of a cornerstone and the dedication of a church building and for the reception into church membership of probationary members. The year 1876 brought the first recommendation of the use of "pure unfermented juice of the grape" for the Lord's Supper. This eventually became mandatory until 1988. Such a move resulted from the work of a pious dentist, Dr. Thomas B. Welch (1825–1903), who discovered in 1869 a means of pasteurizing grape juice that prevented fermentation. As a former Methodist preacher, Welch sought a nonalcoholic sacramental wine. He adapted technology recently developed by Louis Pasteur to make grape juice a possibility.[23]

As the century continued, others became concerned for the recovery of set forms, especially Thomas O. Summers (1812–82), Dean of Vanderbilt Divinity School and general book editor for the Methodist Episcopal Church, South. He oversaw a reprint of Wesley's *Sunday Service*, edited a collection of prayers, *The Golden Censer*,[24] and developed a standard order of worship.

Summers's background was English and he reflects different developments in England, where Wesley's prayer book or even the *BCP* were used by some Methodists through much of the nineteenth century. The Catholic Revival in the Church of England brought a negative reaction from many British Methodists, who moved further from the forms of prayer-book worship and, as a result, from Wesley. In time, however, Methodists began to accept the Gothic revival[25] and some of the practices of the Catholic Revival.

These are the bare bones of nineteenth-century developments. The reality needs flesh and blood, and we must begin with the actual people involved. There seems to have been a split in worship between the settled East Coast and the frontier west of the Appalachians. Ralph Waldo Emerson remarked that England stopped at the Appalachians, America began beyond them. Churches on the seaboard tended to be in settled towns where conventional forms of ministry could function. Worship there tended to be relatively sober and sedate. By contrast, the frontier had few settlements but a widely scattered population of largely unchurched people who ventured up rivers and creeks wherever fertile land could be found to farm.[26] People so isolated could not come to church, so Methodist circuit riders went to them. Incessantly on the move, these itinerant preachers were the friars of the time, mostly celibate, always poor, and obedient to the presiding elder (district superintendent). They visited families, preached to whatever groups they could assemble, and soon adopted the practice of bringing large crowds together for annual camp meetings [ . . . ].

In the process, Methodism learned to adapt worship to the unchurched people on the frontier, who, first of all, had to be brought to Christian faith itself. Certainly no prayer book could appeal to largely illiterate people, but simple songs could. Sedate and fixed forms did not recommend themselves in such situations, but spontaneity and excitement did. For frontier people, freedom was important and structures not. So the frontier developed forms of worship that were demonstrative and uninhibited, abounding with shouts and exclamations and fervent singing. People who had sought freedom on the frontier were not about to sacrifice it in worship. They responded to worship that allowed them to shout their feelings about what the preacher was saying or engage in physical movements such as the altar call, at which converts were summoned to come forward to be welcomed at the communion rail.

A good representative of this period was Peter Cartwright (1785–1872), who preached all over Kentucky, Ohio, and Illinois as circuit rider and presiding elder.[27] As rough-and-ready as the people to whom he ministered, Cartwright was the epitome of pragmatism in introducing whatever new forms seemed effective in worship. He had little regard for tradition, much concern for whatever methods would win souls. His preaching and pastoral care brought

many of the unchurched to Christian conversion. Their worship reflected the
unpolished life-styles of these new Christians.

An important development in this period was the emergence of Christian
worship among blacks, especially in the South and West.[28] Worship had a
particular function for these oppressed people, playing a bonding role for the
community in both suffering and hope. In many ways, blacks adapted the
worship forms of whites, but it also was a reciprocal development as both
cultures affected each other.[29] For example, white spirituals were fused with
African culture to produce black spirituals that became a common treasure of
church music.

Richard Allen (1760–1831) became the first black American bishop in 1816
and led in the formation of the African Methodist Episcopal Church. Like the
church's name, the worship was of the Methodist tradition but in a different
cultural style. Freedom was observed in the usual Sunday service, but a "Ritual"
closely similar to that of the predominantly white Methodist churches appears
in the Disciplines of most of the major black Methodist churches.

As might be expected, the piety of people on the frontier developed along
different lines from that in England or even on the East Coast. The culture was
highly individualistic and this tended to be the case with piety, best expressed
in the camp-meeting songs that focused on first person singular. Charles
Wesley's "Jesus, Lover of My Soul" would more likely have been, on the
frontier, "My Soul, Lover of Jesus." The personal relation of the individual to
God was paramount, and songs expressed contrition for sin, joy in salvation,
and hope of sanctification. Simple lyrics could easily be memorized: "Come to
Jesus just now / Just now come to Jesus." Much of the piety was otherworldly,
as in hymns such as "This World Is All a Fleeting Show" or "There Is a Land
of Pleasure." [30]

In all this, the institutional church played a relatively minor role. Those
converted were put to work in helping to continue revivals or advance some
good cause: distribution of tracts, Bible circulation, Sunday schools, missions,
abolition, women's rights, and temperance. By the end of the century, the
temperance cause had helped women discover political power in America and
led to elimination of fermented wine at the Lord's Supper. All these movements
were celebrated in songs used in worship. A very activist hymnody developed
in addition to the personal "Jesus-and-me" type. Usually the demonic character
of a particular evil (such as rum) was excoriated and then the triumph of virtue
hailed.

Because Methodism expanded so rapidly, the discipline of the class meeting tended to disappear, although the worship function of these sessions was
transferred to the midweek prayer service. Often led by laity, individuals
continued to share their joys and sorrows as they prayed with and for one

another. Such prayer was almost entirely spontaneous and interspersed with hymns.

The Wesleys' sacramental piety did not transplant in American soil. The only available alternative was the prevalent enlightenment attitude to the sacraments, which saw them as divine commands but not as essential means of grace. The Disciplines often mandated that people have access to the sacrament quarterly and made provisions for securing an ordained elder for such occasions. For a number of churches, this remained the norm although the Methodist Episcopal Church, South (1844–1939), always more conservative and Wesleyan, mandated monthly communion in some Disciplines and this survives in parts of the South. Wesley's eucharistic hymns disappeared entirely from the hymnal in 1905 and 1935, only to begin a slow return in the late twentieth century. Defense of infant baptism was the subject of many tracts and the chief point of conflict with Baptists. Fasting was an early casualty, although temperance became an important crusade after the Civil War.

On the frontier, time took on a new sense of meaning. Much depended on the circuit rider's making his way around a vast area. The year was also punctuated by camp meetings. Peter Cartwright went to camp meeting in May 1801 and was converted. Gradually, local preachers were appointed and began to hold weekly preaching services, leaving it to the circuit rider to administer the sacraments on his next visit.

The weekly pattern included both Sunday and midweek services. Sunday morning services were somewhat more formal than the evening service, which was likely to place emphasis on altar prayers in which worshipers knelt at the communion rail (usually called the "altar"). The Disciplines suggest more scripture reading in the morning, probably to allow more time for altar prayers and singing in the evening. The midweek prayer services attracted the inner circle of church members. These included prayer, a lesson, testimony, singing, and a benediction.[31] As the century wore on, Sunday school also came to be an important part in church life, beginning with "opening exercises" of informal worship consisting of prayers and songs, before dividing into classes by age groups for study.

The traditional church year meant little but a new pragmatic calendar developed around local festivals. The quarterly visits of an ordained elder for the sacraments were red-letter days. In addition, periodic revivals were held, frequently lasting the better part of a week. There might be pilgrimages to nearby campgrounds for camp meetings; this gave way after 1874 to the much more refined Chautauqua meetings, a significant transition.[32] As the exodus of youth from farming communities accelerated, homecoming services became an annual feature, with dinner on the grounds. Methodists usually kept an annual watch night at New Year's Eve when others were less piously occupied. It was not the church year Wesley envisioned but one that functioned well in a period of Christianizing a continent.

In the life cycle, the chief change came about mid-century with the realization that Methodism was not just a religious society that could be attached to other churches but a church in its own right. The chief sign of this was the new "Form for Receiving Persons into the Church after Probation" of 1864. Probationary members were adults who had been baptized but for whom a six-month period of scrutiny was required after their baptism rather than before it. Eventually, as discipline slackened, the term was changed to "preparatory members" and finally applied only to those baptized as infants. The attempt to keep a disciplined church had finally been turned over to the Sunday school. In 1964, the term for the service introduced in 1864 was changed to "The Order for Confirmation and Reception into the Church," unleashing even greater theological confusion. But, with the stubbornness of a recent tradition, the term "Confirmation" proved impossible to dislodge even when attempts to remove it were made in the post-Vatican II reforms.

A significant change in the wedding rite was dropping the term "obey" from the betrothal vows as early as 1864 in the Methodist Episcopal Church and in 1910 in the Methodist Episcopal Church, South. This progressive act was balanced by restoring the giving away of the bride in 1916, recovering the ring ceremony in the 1860s, and making the service more like that of the 1662 *BCP*. Burial and ordination rites underwent minor revisions during this century.

If the times of worship changed throughout the century, places did likewise. The period began with much worship being held outdoors, in temporary brush arbors in wooded regions. Eventually, more-or-less permanent camp-meeting grounds were established, with tents for people to camp on the grounds for a week or so, and these finally gave way to cottages.[33] Eventually, Methodists built churches in virtually every town and village in America, some 39,000 of them. A reminder of the primitive brush arbors remains in many country churches in the form of outdoor tables for gathering "on the grounds" at homecomings.

As civilization intruded on the frontier, church buildings evolved through all the fashionable styles of the nineteenth century. Methodist churches were identifiable on the interior by always having a communion rail, which frequently encircled the altar-table and pulpit platform. The pulpit evolved from a wineglass form or tub pulpit to a desk on a platform behind which invariably stood three chairs: one each for minister, visiting preacher, and song leader. A pedestal font or portable basin completed the liturgical centers.

A major change in church architecture in the nineteenth century was brought about by the advent of the Sunday school movement. Many wooden churches were jacked up and a lower floor built beneath or else they were floored over at the balcony level. The climax was the advent of the Akron plan, invented by industrialist Lewis Miller (1829–99) in Akron, Ohio, in 1868. Organ pipes, choir, pulpit platform, altar-table, and communion rail were tucked in descending order in a corner, surrounded by semicircular pews on a sloping floor. Adjacent Sunday school space could be opened by sliding doors on festive occasions, revealing the school's central space for opening exercises and classrooms on floor and balcony levels. It was a highly functional arrangement of space that occurred at a time of eclecticism in architectural style. Because of the eclectic styles, most leave much to be desired aesthetically but they do document the worship form.

These churches were especially designed for preaching, which was to be the principal focus and climax of the usual service. The type of evangelistic preaching for conversion that thrived on the unchurched frontier gradually became institutionalized, even for East Coast churches. The function of preaching seemed to be largely to call people to conversion or to rekindle the white heat of that moment of one's personal experience. Special seasons of the year might feature revival preaching, with emphasis on repentance and conversion.

A distinctive feature of nineteenth-century Methodist worship was that people knelt for prayer, usually facing the pew. Indeed, some editions of the 1905 *Hymnal* carried a rubric advising worshipers to face the preacher when they knelt. Prayer was important in worship but it became almost exclusively clericalized in the Sunday morning service in what came to be known as the "pastoral" or "long" prayer. In this, the preacher covered the whole gamut of prayer from confession to oblation, from praise to intercession, using Elizabethan rhetoric. In Sunday evening services, those who wished to were invited to kneel in prayer at the communion rail. In the midweek prayer service, all could express their concerns aloud in prayer. Some felt the need for more guidance, and collections such as Thomas O. Summer's *The Golden Censer* must have been used in some churches. But protests over increasing "formalism" occurred over such moderate innovations as a full order of worship for the first time in a Methodist hymnal in the 1880 *New Hymnbook*. An order had appeared in the 1870 southern church's *Discipline* and another followed in the northern *Discipline* of 1888. Family prayers flourished, and there was no lack of small books designed to guide families in praying together.

Music thrived in Methodist worship. The frontier had known black and white spirituals. A specific type of revival music developed, simplistic in wording, theology, and music but capable of expressing the heartfelt yearnings of new converts.

A peculiarly Methodist contribution was the work of Fanny Crosby (1820–1915), who, though blind, wrote over two thousand hymns. They represent the individualism of the day with concern for the state of one's own soul, such as "Safe in the Arms of Jesus," "Pass Me Not, O Gentle Savior," and "Blessed Assurance, Jesus Is Mine!" Few if any other women have had such an impact on Protestant worship in America as this devout poet. Hers was a hymnody of personal experience, and that was just what the times wanted.[34]

The more flamboyant music of Ira D. Sankey (1840–1908) accompanied the preaching of Dwight L. Moody (1837–99) and was supported by Rodeheaver Publishers of Sacred Music, which flooded the market with books of gospel music. Charles A. Tindley (1856–1933), black pastor of a Philadelphia church, helped develop the black gospel hymn, and Thomas A. Dorsey (1899–1965) continued the tradition.[35]

Choral music was an innovation for nineteenth-century Methodists. It was found in revival services that music could melt the hardened hearts of sinners. Soloists, duets, quartets, and octets became increasingly frequent, first at revivals and then at normal services. Eventually, full-fledged choirs made their advent. Much of their original function was to manipulate emotions, creating an atmosphere for preaching for conversion. Gradually, choirs came to have other functions in worship. At the same time, instrumental music made its appearance, especially in the form of parlor organs and pipe organs. Wesley's belief that organs were better "not seen or heard" in Methodist chapels was long forgotten. Service music was late in arriving, not very apparent until the 1935 hymnal, although chants and some service music had appeared in the 1905 hymnal.

## TWENTIETH-CENTURY METHODISM

If the nineteenth century brought major developments to Methodist worship, the twentieth century saw equally as much change. We can only sort out the essentials here, but they reflect similar experiences among several other traditions in twentieth-century Great Britain and North America.

Nineteenth-century revivalism had filled the churches, but as the days of the frontier ended the price became apparent. Worship tended to be treated as a means to an end—making converts—rather than an end in itself. Making converts certainly worked, especially on the frontier and in unchurched areas, but with the closing of the frontier and with a Methodist church in every village, worship with this orientation had drawbacks. As Methodist people became more affluent and educated, they became more middle class and more self-conscious. Emotional displays were discouraged and spontaneity was relegated to the prayer meeting. Typical was a Vermont congregation which built a new Gothic church in the 1920s and resolved to discourage shouts of "amen" during the sermon.

The substitutes for emotionalism and spontaneity came to be aestheticism and new types of social activism. The combination did much to move Methodist worship toward greater social respectability. Aestheticism was manifested in efforts at "enriching worship," a phrase that did not seem redundant at the time. Such enrichment took the form of sophisticated architect-designed buildings in whatever style was fashionable. Methodists made the most of the second Gothic revival, popular at such places as Yale, Duke, Princeton, and West Point in the first four decades of this century. Indeed, Duke University Chapel remains the greatest Methodist monument of this period. Such buildings on a much reduced scale were the goal of Elbert Conover (1885–1952), who directed the Methodist architectural bureau and for decades advocated Gothic or Georgian revival churches with divided chancels (i.e., altar-table at far end between choir stalls) and a cross on the steeple.[36]

Aestheticism revealed itself musically in improving the "quality" of music sung with more and more professionally trained musicians employed in the larger churches. Choral responses replaced the people's parts as choirs became standard in all but the smallest congregations. The 1935 *Hymnal* reflected growing musical sophication. Lowell Mason (1792–1872) and John B. Dykes (1823–76) were still the favorite composers, but the number of their hymns had dropped since the 1905 hymnal. Choral anthems were becoming important parts of worship despite Wesley's reservations. An abundance of service music was provided in the 1935 hymnal for "the Holy Communion" plus a collection of "Ancient Hymns and Canticles."

Methodists were in the forefront of uniting worship and social action. The social gospel was captured in such hymns as "Where Cross the Crowded Ways of Life" by Philadelphia pastor Frank Mason North (1850–1935). A Methodist minister from Springfield, Massachusetts, Fred Winslow Adams, led the effort to set up a new Christian calendar through the Federal Council of Churches. In 1937, the Council published *The Christian Year*[37] with a new season, King-domtide, reflecting the social gospel optimism of the time. Other denominations were reluctant to accept this innovation, although Congregationalists did so briefly. Only Methodists have retained this reminder of the social gospel era.

A tendency to use worship as a means of promoting peace and social justice flourished during this period. The prophets of the Old Testament provided favorite lections and many sermon texts. There was concerted effort to make worship relevant to daily life and the topical sermon flourished. Typical was William L. Stidger's admonition to preach "to real-life situations." Solving problems in daily life or resolving moral dilemmas tended to characterize Methodist preaching during much of this period. Advocacy of social reforms often replaced calls for conversion in the preaching of this period of liberal theology.

Aestheticism and worship as social crusade may have held people's interest in the first half of the century, but in the quarter century after World War II it became increasingly obvious that this was insufficient. Twentieth-century Methodist liturgical scholarship had been born with Nolan B. Harmon's *The*

*Rites and Ritual of Episcopal Methodism*, published in 1926.[38] After fifteen hundred copies had been run off the publisher broke up the plates, foreseeing neither further sales for such an esoteric subject nor a future bishopric for the young author! But there were people who were interested. Bishop Wilbur P. Thirkield and Oliver Huckel published a *Book of Common Worship* in 1932,[39] compiling a large collection of prayers. Books such as Johnston Ross's *Christian Worship and Its Future*[40] and Fitzgerald Parker's *The Practice and Experience of Christian Worship*[41] began to appear. And pastors such as Oscar T. Olson of Epworth-Euclid Church, Cleveland, Ohio; Fred Winslow Adams, Wesley Church, Springfield, Massachusetts; J.N.R. Score, St. Paul's, Houston, Texas; and George Hedley, chaplain of Mills College, Oakland, California, were pointing Methodism to a new era.

In general, these men were neo-Wesleyan in their worship concepts. Their preference was for the fixed forms that Wesley had provided in his *Sunday Service*, now for a century and a half left in oblivion. Scholarly support came from the English Methodists, especially John Bowmer, *The Sacrament of the Lord's Supper in Early Methodism* (1957), John Bishop, *Methodist Worship* (1950), and J. Ernest Rattenbury, *The Eucharistic Hymns of John and Charles Wesley* (1948), to cite a few. Their work gave an important foundation for Methodist restorationism. Another impetus was given by the founding of the Order of St. Luke in 1946 under the guidance of Romey Marshall and William Slocum.[42] In its early years, this organization of Methodist clergy worked to restore the Wesleyan side of Methodist worship but moved to a new agenda in the 1970s.

The result of many efforts was the publication in 1945 of the first *Book of Worship*, approved by the General Conference in 1944. If we remember that a single order of worship had caused protests of "formalism" in 1870, the publication of an entire volume of services and prayers seventy-five years later was a significant event indeed. Two decades later, a second *Book of Worship* was authorized and published in 1965. By this time, the agenda had become much clearer. Methodists and others had found the liberal sentiments of the early twentieth century too glib after a decade and more of depression and war. Neo-orthodoxy now had a profound appeal reflected throughout the 1965 book. Many of the affirmations of the Reformation era now rang true, especially the dependence on God's grace in the face of human rebellion and sin. For Methodists, the liturgies of Wesley (which were largely those of the *BCP*s of 1662 and 1552) said it all very well. The only part provided in full in the normal Sunday order of worship was the confessional portion introduced into morning prayer by Cranmer in 1552. Penitential piety was back in fashion; Methodists had discovered sin again after fleeing from generations of hellfire preaching. In effect, a selective image of Wesleyan worship was being recovered: the emphases on confession and the creeds.

The 1965 *Book of Worship* and 1966 *Hymnal* signaled the fusion of the eucharistic rites of the northern and southern churches, printed next to each other in the 1935 hymnal. Now it was the same service but printed in versions for a full service of word and table and a shorter version for the table service, to be appended to the usual Sunday service. It is still quite clear that the eucharist was regarded as an occasional service, although by 1966 it was being celebrated weekly in some of the Methodist seminaries. Restoration of the sacramental half of Wesleyan worship still had a long way to go.

Scarcely were the new *Book of Worship* and *Hymnal* published before the post-Vatican II era of liturgy erupted. Much of the euphoria among Roman Catholic clergy reached Methodists too. Those were the 1960s when defiance of authority was almost mandatory, when the best-publicized Roman Catholic services were so-called "underground masses," which frequently ended up in print.[43] In 1965, Methodists had just published the last service book in Elizabethan English. But instead of being able to sit back and absorb the products of a process of liturgical revision that had lasted a decade, suddenly they had to begin the same work all over again.

The revolution of the 1960s was a time when all worship conventions and traditions were questioned. Even matters as seemingly sacrosanct as the 11 A.M. Sunday hour for worship were found to be entirely arbitrary. Some regarded this period as a temporary storm they could ride out by never venturing from harbor. More venturesome congregations entered with gusto into what was called "experimentation." For the timid, an early service could try balloons and banners and leave the eleven o'clock service undisturbed. The balloons are gone, now, and the banners fading, but one thing that has lasted is the realization that a large part of worship is visual experience. The visual participation that the medieval Christian knew is slowly becoming available to modern Christians. For Methodists, the change is seen most graphically by comparing the colors and objects offered in the Cokesbury church-supply catalogs of the 1980s with those of the 1950s.

In 1970, the Commission on Worship started the process of Methodist liturgical revision once again. By that time, the reformed Roman Catholic rites were becoming available and other churches were retooling to produce their own revisions (except the Presbyterians, who had just finished, it turned out, too soon). Four goals motivated the development of the new United Methodist rites: use of contemporary English, a classical and ecumenical shape to the rites, expressing contemporary theology, and the maximum of pastoral flexibility. The first new rite, *The Sacrament of the Lord's Supper*, published in 1972, was received with enthusiasm and inaugurated the *Supplemental Worship Resources* series, which eventually reached seventeen volumes.[44] Second-generation revisions of the five basic services (word, table, baptism, marriage, funeral) appeared in *We Gather Together* (1980); third-generation revisions in

*The Book of Services* (1985), and final versions in *The United Methodist Hymnal* (1989).[45]

In the process of liturgical revision, it became apparent that when choices had to be made they were generally between late-medieval practices mediated through Cranmer or early Christian services documented by Hippolytus. In almost every case, the preference was for early Christian over late medieval. A good instance is in *An Ordinal* (1980)[46] where the laying on of hands is accompanied by a prayer of invocation rather than by the medieval imperative formula.

The most conspicuous change in American Methodist worship in recent decades has resulted from widespread use of a lectionary. The *Common Lectionary*[47] version of the Roman Catholic Sunday lectionary of 1969 has been adopted in slightly more than half of United Methodist congregations. It has brought a major shift to more exegetical preaching, aided by the availability of a variety of lectionary-based commentaries. An unexpected concomitant result has been the use of a much fuller calendar, with new feasts (Baptism of the Lord, Transfiguration, Christ the King) previously not observed by Methodists.

In most of the new rites there are clear parallels between the new rites of Roman Catholic and other Protestant churches. In two areas, the United Methodist rites are distinctive. The first is in the large number of eucharistic prayers, twenty-two in *At the Lord's Table* (1981) and twenty-four in *Holy Communion* (1987). Many are seasonal (Lent I) or for pastoral occasions (Christian Marriage), but in each case the entire prayer changes as in the Gallican liturgies of early medieval Western Europe. The other major change is in the process of Christian initiation, where an effort has been made to make the process complete at whatever age performed (with baptism, laying on of hands, and first communion), yet with possibilities for subsequent renewals through reaffirmation of baptism by individuals when they reach maturity (confirmation) or upon return to faith or by the entire congregation on an annual basis.

A major feature of recent years has been the concern to make worship fully inclusive. This has led many congregations to eliminate exclusively masculine language when referring to human beings ("man," "mankind") and to move in some quarters to change God language by eliminating pronouns and using more feminine images of God. "Father," "Son," "Lord," "King," and "kingdom" still remain in place generally despite protests. Compromises on God language mark the 1989 *Hymnal*.

*The United Methodist Hymnal* also recognized a high level of awareness of the need for ethnic and cultural pluralism. Songbooks for blacks, Asian Americans, and Hispanics were published in the early 1980s. A conscious effort was made to make the *Hymnal* as inclusive as possible for a denomination that includes more different constituencies than most American Protestant churches. The compilation of a hymnal is a highly political task, and the 1989 *Hymnal* certainly reflects that. It will be anathema to elitists of any kind, yet it will be the most representative hymnal ever compiled in America. Of course, pluralism leaves many wondering just what consensus is still possible today. Whether the revised services, the recovery of the psalter (noted and with antiphons), higher standards of visual design, and the wide variety of hymn texts and music will lead to a new consensus or promote further fragmentation remains to be seen. English Methodists have been through a similar process in recent years, resulting in *The Methodist Service Book*[48] (1975) and *Hymns and Psalms* (1983).[49] The next few years would seem to require time to assimilate so much recent change.

## CHAPTER 32

# History as a Bearer
# of Denominational Identity:
# Methodism as a Case Study

Russell E. Richey

> So it was that Methodism, with a system more mobile than that of any other
> church, with a message more democratic and inclusive, and with a ministry
> which was part and parcel of the life of the frontier, came over the mountains
> with the great rush of emigration, and took over the spiritual command of the
> commonwealths which men were hewing from the wilderness—a command
> which it maintains to this day (Luccock and Hutchinson, 1926: 270).

Well into the 20th century, Methodists held several propositions about
themselves and their role in society.[1] The propositions, still implicit in the
above, are (1) Methodism was/is a child of providence.[2] (2) Providence especially fitted Methodism and the Methodist connection for American society.[3]
(3) Methodist response to and stewardship of that providential calling had
benefitted both church and nation, blessing the church with great numbers and
the nation with troops of true believers in the American system.[4] (4) The
purposes and ultimately the health—spiritual and physical—of Methodism are
bound up in this linked mission of nation and church.[5]

Had Methodists conflated the kingdom of God with the nation, construed
denominational purposes in terms of those of a Christian America, and in
making the church subservient to Christian nationalism, intimately tied the
former's health to the latter's? As the above propositions suggest, this paper
answers those questions affirmatively, at least insofar as propositional or
ideational evidence will allow.[6] It goes on to draw the implications of those
questions—that the demise of Christian America, the event that Robert Handy

called "the second disestablishment," (1984: 159–84) shattered this mission that the church had taken as its own, that no comparable purpose of such energizing dimensions has arisen to take its place, and that the present malaise of mainline denominations in general and Methodism in particular roots in this loss of purpose. This analysis locates mainline Protestantism's problem, if problem is the right word, not only, perhaps not primarily, in present agendas so much as in a faulty earlier purpose. The wedding of denomination to nation, however stimulating it proved to denominational growth, built a fundamental flaw into the church's foundations. When the promises of the First Amendment and the realities of pluralism exposed the fault line in Christian America, Methodists and perhaps also other mainline denominations suffered structural damage.[7]

This paper works on the propositional level, that is, with what Methodists affirmed about themselves. Those affirmations are derived from Methodist histories. The paper will endeavor to show how historians initially conceived Methodism's propositions, how they altered those propositions into the above form as nation and church changed, and how they struggled to make sense of the Methodist saga when the propositions no longer made sense.

The propositions about denominational identity were widely shared among what are sometimes termed mainline denominations. The Methodist pattern then is but an instance of a common story. So also the ideological use of history was widely shared. The premium Methodists put on a historical fabrication of identity allows us to use them as a case study, an illustration of how in the quest for a Christian America, Methodists (and other Protestants) wrought fundamental changes in their purpose and perhaps in their character.

## WHY HISTORY?

At the 1988 General Conference of The United Methodist Church, individuals and groups concerned to redirect the denomination and to return it to full health chose a curious vehicle for renewal. They recast the history of Methodism. They rewrote the "doctrinal history" in the *Discipline* (1988: 40–60) so as to accent those aspects of Methodism which, if reemphasized, would rejuvenate the church. The strategy, perhaps a strange one for some communions, was an obvious and well-tried maneuver for Methodists.

From the earliest *Disciplines* down to the most recent, Methodists have begun these formal, official self-presentations with a history of the movement. The first word that Methodists have wanted to say about themselves was an historical one. For the most part, these historical statements functioned to state and hence transmit the received Methodist identity. For long periods they would be carried over intact from one *Discipline* to another. But at points of significant change, Methodists struggled to reshape the history to warrant the change (Richey, 1989).

That orientation to historical self-understanding—a preoccupation derived from Wesley's practice and precept—reflected itself at a variety of points in the life of Methodism. It both stimulated and derived sustenance from the common Pietist passion for recounting individual and corporate religious experience; it 'authorized' the production of endless histories of the movement, from competent surveys of the whole denomination to quite amateurish local and conference narratives; it expressed itself in myriad studies of Methodist 'worthies', the bearers of the Methodist standard; it found expression in the papers and magazines, particularly the *Christian Advocates*, which reserved disproportionate space for the stories of Methodism; and it led them to require and feature history, particularly the history of the movement, in the preparation of Methodist ministers.[8] History served to express and even to shape Methodist identity and to transmit denominational culture. Like Lee, Bangs was an actor in that which he interpreted. He also made his mark on New England Methodism, particularly as Methodism's foremost spokesperson for Arminianism and against Calvinism. *Nathan Bangs: Apologist for American Methodism* one interpreter called him (Hermann, 1973). That he was and more. Bangs labored effectively not only to speak on Methodism's behalf to "its cultured critics" and the religious establishment, but also to remake Methodism so that it might claim its place in the American religious establishment. Bangs played that reshaping role from his office as book agent, effectively the executive secretary and the teaching office of the church. What he wrought might be termed the revolution of the 1820s, the wholesale restructuring of Methodism—creating missionary, Sunday school and tract societies; launching and editing a major weekly, *The Christian Advocate*, and a journal of theological opinion, *The Methodist Magazine*; establishing educational institutions; and founding the course of study, Methodism's four year national reading course in preparation for ministry (Pilkington, 1968: 169–219). Bangs sought to make the church an effective force in national life.

This chapter will explore shifts in Methodist identity and/or culture as they are reflected in Methodist histories and proceed then to reflect about history as bearer and transmitter of denominational identity. The historians treated are Jesse Lee, Nathan Bangs, Abel Stevens, Matthew Simpson, James M. Buckley, the team of Halford E. Luccock and Paul Hutchinson, William Warren Sweet and Frederick Norwood, each of whom, in some sense, spoke authoritatively for and about the movement.[9]

# PROVIDENCE

In 1784, the newly organized Methodist Episcopal Church provided itself a constitution or quasi-constitution, adapting one elaborated by the British Methodists under John Wesley, a document known as *The Large Minutes*. The first American *Discipline*, that of 1785, followed the question and answer format of the British *Minutes* and its sequence of questions (Tigert, 1908: 532–602). The 1787 revision of the first *Discipline* put a new order to the questions and a historical frame on the constitution. The first asked, "What was the Rise of Methodism, so called in Europe?" the second, "What was the Rise of Methodism, so called in America?" the third "What may we reasonably believe to be God's design in raising up the Preachers called Methodists?" The answers briefly sketched the founding acts and founding impulses of the movement. The third answer deserves citation; it has been recited down to the present as a statement of Methodist purpose; it retained the substance of Wesley's answer but now nuanced to fit the new land. God's design was

> To reform the Continent, and spread scriptural Holiness over these Lands. As a Proof hereof, we have seen in the Course of fifteen Years a great and glorious Work of God, from New York through the Jersies, Pennsylvania, Delaware, Maryland, Virginia, North and South Carolina, even to Georgia (1787: 3–4).

These early Methodists had a vivid sense of America. Even as a small band of itinerants, they had travelled its roads, forded its waters, crossed its mountains and penetrated its wilderness. This litany of states evoked their direct experience with the outpouring of God's spirit upon the American landscape. The first proposition—that Methodism was providentially given and directed—expressed their very being. They found it axiomatic. Methodism was providential. The other propositions they would have found strange and discordant.

Jesse Lee shared the Christmas Conference's vision of Methodism as an impulse of providence. Indeed, we may fittingly view his *Short History* as a fleshed out version of this initial providential reading of the Methodist saga. Jesse Lee missed the 1784 constitutional gathering known as the Christmas Conference, missed it because he was some five hundred miles distant when he received the summoning word and nursed some grudges for being so belatedly informed (Thrift, 1823: 67 ff.). He began travelling with Bishop Francis Asbury immediately thereafter, came to exercise considerable influence in the Methodist leadership, blazed the way for Methodism into New England, and served as chaplain to Congress. Lee missed election to the episcopacy by a narrow margin. And, of course, he could serve Methodism in only one place at a time. However with due allowance for his frailty and finitude, we can say that otherwise Lee left his imprint on early Methodism. Sweet termed him "the most popular of all the early Methodist preachers" (Sweet, 1953: 176). He both made and wrote Methodist history, as would be the case for Methodist historians throughout the 19th century. His *A Short History of the Methodists* (1810) was the first serious effort to sketch the contours of the movement. Lee's construction of the movement did not, however, please all. The General Conference actually rejected the volume; Asbury thought it inadequate on his own role (Bangs, 1860, II: 322–23; Asbury, II: 640–41; Lee, 1848: 466). Certainly part of the reason for controversy derived from the very personal vision that Lee provided.

Lee told the Methodist story as he saw it. He had seen enough of the whole that we get from him a remarkably well rounded account. Subsequent historians have consistently drawn upon him for the documents that he reproduced, the events for which he provides the most complete eyewitness account, the very vividness of his portrayal. The revivals that he experienced and led; the conferences he attended and whose legislation he could then report first hand; the penetration of 'enemy' Puritan territory that he led; the general explosion of the movement over the new nation, that his extensive travels documented; the advent of the camp meetings which he witnessed—these personal involvements in the development of Methodism give shape and vigor to his narrative. Doubtless that very personal, idiosyncratic perspective offended his colleagues who could not help but feel that Lee had implicitly claimed for his own what belonged to them all. And yet in another sense, this very personal vision did stand for them, in the way that the historical preface to the *Discipline* stood for them, for their conception of their history, history as immediate and perceivable instances of God at work. For that is how providence functioned for Lee. He offered no grand theory of providence at work. Nor did he explicitly claim the Methodist connectional system to be providential. Rather, he pointed concretely and specifically to the presence of God among the Methodists. For instance, of a 1788 Baltimore conference Lee reported:

> During the time of the conference, we were highly favoured of the Lord, and souls were awakened and converted. On Sunday, the 14th of September at 3 o'clock in the afternoon, Mr. Asbury preached in Mr. Otterbein's church; and the people were generally solemn and much affected; he then asked another preacher to pray and conclude: and whilst he was praying, an awful power was felt among the people. Some of them cried out aloud . . . and in a little time there was such a noise among them, that many of the christian people were measurably frightened, and as there was no opportunity for them to escape at the door, many of them went out at the windows, hastening to their homes. The noise had alarmed hundreds of people who were not at the meeting, and they came running to see what was the matter, till the house was crowded, and surrounded with a wondering multitude. In a short time some of the mourners lost the use of their limbs, and lay helpless on the floor, or in the arms of their friends. It was not long before some of them were converted. . . . This day of the Lord's power will never be forgotten by many who were present (Lee, 1810: 139–40).

Lee claimed Methodism to be providential by showing providence at work.

In similar fashion, he showed Methodism's attachment to the United States. He did not, most certainly did not, wrap the nation around the church. Indeed, with most early Methodists, Lee evidenced the pattern of affection-but-alienation that R. Laurence Moore (Moore, 1986) shows to be so prototypically American—a kind of sectarian distancing of self and movement from nation and society at the same time that full loyalty is proclaimed and efforts are even made to convert and transform the society. Lee did make unmistakable his own and American Methodism's patriotism. He criticized, for instance, the "head preachers all from Europe," some of whom "were imprudent too freely against the proceedings of the Americans" during the Revolution (Lee, 1810: 60). And he presented the Methodists' own march to independence from Wesley and the British connection as an appropriate development.[10] But Lee did not providentially connect church and nation. Lee thought providence to be rather specifically focussed on the work of salvation. Connections of general providence and the fate of nations therein did not interest him.

## PROVIDENTIAL DESIGN

As he drew his first volume to a close and took the measure of the Methodism of 1792, Nathan Bangs calculated that its 66,246 actual members represented about 198,000 family members and dependents who attended. Using four million as the total U.S. population, Bangs gauged that "about one-twentieth part of the entire population were brought under Methodist influence in the short space of thirty-six years." This growth, he noted, came from a dead start and despite the presence of and advantages enjoyed by other denominations. Dismissing other explanations of Methodist growth, Bangs found himself forced "to the conclusion that their prosperity must be attributed to the blessing of God upon their labors." He continued,

> We therefore say again, that its forward course can be accounted for only by supposing the sanction of the most high God upon their labors (1860, I: 356–59).

At the end of the fourth volume, having brought the church down to 1840, Bangs rendered the same judgment—that the "success and influence of Methodism" had "one true original cause, namely, the divine agency" (IV: 436). Concern with Methodist numerical success led Bangs from the providential character of Methodism towards a second proposition—the providential connection of church and nation.

Like Lee, Bangs was an actor in that which he interpreted. He also made his mark on New England Methodism, particularly as Methodism's foremost spokesperson for Arminianism and against Calvinism. *Nathan Bangs: Apolo-*

*gist for American Methodism* one interpreter called him (Hermann, 1973). That he was and more. Bangs labored effectively not only to speak on Methodism's behalf to "its cultured critics" and the religious establishment, but also to remake Methodism so that it might claim its place in the American religious establishment. Bangs played that reshaping role from his office as book agent, effectively the executive secretary and the teaching office of the church. What he wrought might be termed the revolution of the 1820s, the wholesale restructuring of Methodism—creating missionary, Sunday school and tract societies; launching and editing a major weekly, *The Christian Advocate*, and a journal of theological opinion, *The Methodist Magazine*; establishing educational institutions; and founding the course of study, Methodism's four year national reading course in preparation for ministry (Pilkington, 1968: 169–219). Bangs sought to make the church an effective force in national life.

When sketching the hand of providence in this Methodism on which he also had laid a hand, Bangs could not be content with simple and discrete providential instances, though he like Lee eagerly pronounced events both large and small to be of divine agency. No, Bangs saw that the divine agency extended also to Methodism as a system and its operation. And Bangs also recognized a providential connection between church and nation. To that end, he chose to begin the saga of American Methodism not with Wesley but with Columbus and proceeded to an examination of "the civil and religious state of the people at the time Methodism was introduced (I:11)." This was a self-consciously interpretive gesture on the part of a man with quite keen historical skills.[11] Bangs saw "benignant Providence" in the peopling of the land, the development of civil and religious liberties, the respect accorded scripture and the sabbath, the widespread profession of Christianity, the influence of revivals, the atmosphere of toleration—in short, the creation of a situation "highly favorable" to Methodist "evangelical labors" (I: 22, 26, 30). Methodism's introduction into the land also showed providential design (I: 46).

At various points, his providential treatment of America was evocative of the Christian republicanism now recognized to be so significant in both national and mainstream Protestant life (Noll, 1988: 35–43; Shalhope, 1982). And yet Bangs did not really offer a providential reading of the nation as such; he did not provide a public theology. Bangs took interest in providence and Methodism, not providence and America. Or perhaps we should say, he was interested in the public roles that providence exercised through Methodism. For instance, in measuring the impact of camp meetings and the revivals at the turn of the 19th century, Bangs spent some five pages on the "most happy and conservative influence upon our national character," "the conservative influence which vital, experimental, and practical Christianity exerts upon individual character, upon social and civil communities, and of course upon states and empires" (II: 146–48). Though Methodism exercised a politically and socially constructive influence, Bangs insisted that it was purely religious in its intent and operation:

> The influence therefore, which she has exerted upon the civil destinies of the republic, has been altogether of an indirect and collateral character, growing out of that moral and religious stamp with which she strives to mark and distinguish all her children. (II: 150)

Bangs could be quite effusive about the political consequences of such indirection. For instance, he thought the national operation of Methodism functioned to cement the union together and to counter the politically divisive force of state governments.[12] But such notes were quite occasional. Bangs focused upon Methodism. It was the providential character of Methodism, not the providential character of the nation, that interested him. Incidentally, providence worked through Methodism and Methodists for the good of the nation. However, church not state remained providence's aim.

## PROVIDENTIAL CONNECTION

Bangs had tentatively connected church and nation. Abel Stevens drew the providential connection of church and nation firmly. Firmness was characteristic of Stevens, who held a series of important editorships in the tumultuous middle decades of the 19th century, *Zion's Herald*, the New England Methodist paper, then *The National Magazine* and finally *The Christian Advocate*. Through those immensely influential posts, he spoke a moderating, even conservative word to the church, prizing its unity at the cost, some thought, of its witness.

Stevens entitled the first chapter in his *Compendious History*, "Methodism—Its Special Adaptations to the New World" (1868: 17).[13] The chapter and the volume begins with a striking, but imaginary event of 1757.[14] That year, John Wesley, 'inventer' of Methodism, and James Watt, inventor of the steam engine, found themselves at Glasgow University. Stevens imagined a chance meeting of these two in the university quadrangle, the inventors of the two machines for the conquest of the new world. "Watts and Wesley might well then have struck hands and bid each other godspeed at Glasgow in 1757: they were co-workers for the destinies of the new world (19)." Watts had produced the engine for the conquest of the new world physically, Wesley that for the conquest of the new world morally.

> Methodism, with its 'lay ministry,' and 'itinerancy,' could alone afford the ministrations of religion to the overflowing populations; it was to lay the moral foundations of many of the great states of the West (18).

487

A religious system, energetic, migratory, 'itinerant,' extempore, like the population itself, must arise; or demoralization, if not barbarism, must overflow the continent.

Methodism entered the great arena at the emergent moment. . . . It was to become at last the dominant popular faith of the country, with its standard planted in every city, town, and almost every village of the land (22–23).

Methodism thus seems to have been providentially designed more for the new world than for the old. The coincidence of its history with that of the United States does indeed seem providential . . . (24).

Between and among these affirmations, Stevens sketched the contours of the Methodism system, a machine the elements of which seemed providentially suited to this American mission. Providence had indeed blessed America with Methodism and Methodism with America. Stevens saw in this new order that vision that Augustine had sought, "the city of God" (176).

Though enunciating the third of the Methodist axioms, Stevens like his predecessors stopped short of a full-fledged public theology. Indeed, his affirmations about America touched land as much as state, the new world as much as the new republic. Watt and the steam engine, Wesley and the Methodist engine imaged a providential ordering of America as a whole—land, culture, peoples, society, economy. Providence extended its rule over America preeminently through Methodism.

## A CONJOINT MISSION

Matthew Simpson focused Methodist attention more sharply on the American state and so articulated the fourth Methodist axiom. This was a fitting service for a man whose life was dedicated to politics, in church and in state.[15] College professor and president, like Bangs and Stevens an editor (*Western Christian Advocate*), delegate to General Conferences, then in 1852 a bishop, Simpson employed pen, platform, and power on behalf of anti-slavery and union. Confidant to Lincoln, Simpson used his access to Washington inner circles to gain appointments for Methodists and control over Methodist Episcopal Church, South buildings in territory that fell to Union troops. When Lincoln fell, Simpson preached funeral sermons in Washington and at graveside (Crooks, 1891: 397–403). Simpson's history, unlike that of Stevens (1868), reflected Methodism's Civil War experience, an involvement which had wedded the Methodist Episcopal Church to the nation.[16]

Simpson's *A Hundred Years of Methodism* appeared in observance of the American centennial. Appropriately, he began with a survey of national accomplishments, the contributions of America to the world. Then he flashed back to

Wesley and British Methodism. It was American origins, however, not these 'foreign' ones that stamped American Methodism. "The rise of Methodism," he insisted, "was coeval with the Revolutionary spirit" (41). Both during the Revolution and thereafter Methodism suffered because of its British connection.

> It is somewhat singular that nearly all the troubles and secessions in Methodism have arisen from trying to introduce English ideas and plans into our American Church, or, in other words, from trying to condense our immense continent into the area of a little island. Every agitation has begun by extolling British usages and depreciating American.
>
> In every instance, however, the Church has adhered to American ideas, and has resolutely refused to change her policy at such dictation (68).

An 'American' Methodist church, that was Simpson's topic. It was this dynamic and rapidly growing church, the success story of American Methodism, that Simpson sought to explain. Like his predecessors, Simpson gloried in statistics, in growth.[17] He found "reasons of the remarkable increase of the Methodist Church" in three superior features of its life, "the superiority of its doctrines, the efficiency of its organization, . . . the piety, earnestness, and activity of its ministers and members" (345). Such claims had led his predecessors almost inevitably and immediately to invocation of providence. Simpson made much less of providence than they. When he did speak of it, the nation rather than the church came into focus. Of the war and emancipation, for instance, he said:

> We can now . . . see the guidance of an all-wise Providence, which overruled the counsels of men in the midst of all these commotions. It was the Divine will that slavery should be destroyed. With determined purpose, step by step, the South moved forward in the separation, first, of the Christian Churches, and then in the attempted division of the States, to that fearful war which resulted in the emancipation of the slaves. No instance in history more clearly shows how God has made 'the wrath of men to praise him, and the remainder of wrath' he has restrained (156–57).

Here was Mead's "nation with the soul of a church," (Mead, 1975) or perhaps even a church whose soul was the nation. Simpson doubtless held all four Methodist propositions. However, the accent fell on the last, the providential linked mission of church and state. In the spirit of the centennial, Simpson spoke with confidence of this conjoint mission, mindful to be sure of the great cost with which it had been vindicated, but even so, especially so, with a providential, even millennial confidence (209).

# WHITHER PROVIDENCE?

James M. Buckley struck no such ebullient note. Rather he concluded his assessment and essayed twentieth century prospects by pondering the question, "Has Methodism lost to a dangerous degree its original vital impulse?" and by invoking John Wesley's worry that "the people called Methodists" might become "a dead sect, having the form of religion without the power." Buckley obviously shared Wesley's worry:

> The founders of Methodism had no enterprises that were not distinctly subordinate to the conversion of men and their spiritual training. Now its enterprises are many and complex, often pervaded by a distinctly secular element, which contends constantly with the spiritual (1900: 685, 686).

American Jeremiahs have typically prophesied doom to achieve revival and reform (Bercovitch, 1978). Buckley was no exception. He called for the renewal of the Methodist spirit and identified the requisite resources (685–86). And yet his rendering of Methodism's history, if carefully read, suggested grounds for pessimism. In Buckley's account, providence had seemingly loosed her grasp on church and on nation.

This judgment about Buckley and providence is extremely ironical, for in some ways Buckley was more self-conscious about providence than his predecessors. That concern he shared with the general editor of the important series in which his volume figured, the American Church History series.[18] Philip Schaff designed the series to display the professional prowess of The American Society of Church History. For the Methodist volume he chose its preeminent spokesperson. Buckley played a major and a conservative role in its national affairs. He was delegate to General Conferences from 1872 to 1912. He edited the official and national paper of the denomination, *The Christian Advocate*, from 1880 to 1912. On several important matters, most notably women's role in the church, he stood steadfast and effectively against change. The past and history seemed, at times, to be his forte.

At two important places, Buckley stopped to consider the relation of the human and the divine. Chapter VIII he devoted to the work of the Spirit in early Methodists, specifically considering Benjamin Abbott, John Dickins, Caleb B. Pedicord, Thomas Ware, and Jesse Lee and the responses they elicited. Noting that Methodists construed the highly demonstrative behavior evident in conversions and revivals "to be direct results of the power of the Holy Spirit, and manifest proofs of His presence and approval of the work" (217), Buckley inventoried other explanations—naturalistic and particularly psychological explanations—of the phenomena. He conceded that "Various factors were involved in producing the effects of Methodist preaching and methods," but that among them "was the might of the Holy Spirit" (220). And the effects when carefully essayed and correlated with Scripture, Buckley affirmed, establish "the divine origin of the movement as conclusive as that furnished when holy men of old spake not of themselves, but as they were moved by the Holy Ghost" (220–21). So Buckley wrenched a providential meaning out of Methodism.

Buckley returned to the theme of providence at the end of his narrative, to the worries over Methodism's current prospects initially mentioned. For the most part, however, Buckley remained uninterested in the providences underlying Methodist development and content to explain Methodism in naturalistic fashion. Quite a few of the stray exceptions—statements that God's hand can be found in Methodist affairs—occur in passages that he cited (170–71, 173, 176–77, 179, 203, 205, 248). Buckley offered us, then, a curious irony. He insisted vehemently on the importance of providence but proved curiously unwilling or unable to point to its presence and activity. Providence had assumed doctrinal rather than historiographical force for him.

One could hardly assert that his reluctance to advance providential claims for Methodism typified the turn-of-the-century movement. Methodists generally continued the triumphalism so clearly evidenced in Scudder and Simpson.[19] Nor was he typical in his neglect of similar triumphal claims for the nation. Historians after him would entertain the four propositions and search for appropriate meaning thereof. Nevertheless, Buckley had taken Methodism around an important turn. He had effectively given up the affirmation that lent plausibility to the four propositions—that providence could be seen at work in Methodism.

This was a fitting posture to be taken in a volume that would stand cover-to-cover with histories of other American denominations. Buckley may well have felt constrained by the series. He certainly forewarned the reader that he could not, in good conscience, advance providential claims:

> It is not within the province of the historian of his own communion, and in part of his own time, to pronounce judgment upon the motives of those professing 'like precious faith' (xviii).

At most, he should aspire to present the developments so fairly that the reader would draw that conclusion.[20]

The reader intent on drawing the four propositional conclusions would have received help from Buckley only on the first. He did present Methodism as "the lengthened shadow" of Wesley and construe Wesley as "The Man of Providence" (1–2, 40–72). As we have seen, a limited providential meaning for Methodism can be detected. The other claims apparently did not interest him. He chose, in fact, an interesting place to begin the Methodist story, one wholly out of keeping with the other three propositions. He started with Henry VIII and the English Reformation. From such national and denominational humility interesting consequences flowed. They flowed gradually.

## HUMPTY DUMPTY

In spirit and assertions, Luccock and Hutchinson's *The Story of Methodism* resembled Simpson, not Buckley.[21] They chatted with the reader about Methodism; provided upbeat, celebrative and personal estimates of its power and significance; claimed providential guidance for the movement with a frequency that recalls Lee or Bangs. Yet, their very easiness with the providential claims is striking, perhaps worrisome. Do Buckley's critical premises haunt their breezy confidence? Do their assertions betray superficiality or conviction?[22]

Halford E. Luccock held pastorates, served as editorial secretary of the Board of Foreign Missions (1918–24), taught in several theological schools, including a long stint as professor of preaching at Yale (1928–53). A prolific writer, from 1924 till his death he contributed to *The Christian Century*. The *Century's* managing editor from 1924 to 1947 and its editor from 1947 to 1956 was Paul Hutchinson. Hutchinson shared Luccock's literary and missionary activities and concerns. He, too, was prolific. Their common journalistic bent is evident in this popular account of Methodism.[23]

Evident also is the premise they shared that the 20th would be *The Christian Century*. They confidently traced the parallel development of nation and church. One early chapter, entitled "A Tale of Two Villages," examined two English towns "which gave to the English speaking world the most transforming spiritual forces of the seventeenth and eighteenth centuries" (28). Scrooby launched the Pilgrims; Epworth was home to Wesley. "From the first, in truth if not in actual chronicle, the Mayflower set sail to plant a new world. From the second, John Wesley went out to save an old one" (34).

Once they had Methodism firmly planted on these shores, they returned to the parallels of church and nation. In "Methodism in the New Republic," for instance, they implicitly compared Asbury and Washington and explicitly compared James O'Kelly and Patrick Henry (213–17). They dwelt on Methodism's popular, even democratic, character and celebrated its pioneer and frontier spirit (217–300). The genius of the movement, in fact, is its spirit of adventure, its willingness to experiment, its pragmatism. They did not invoke Frederick Jackson Turner explicitly but found their own term for the frontier spirit, Methodism's "irregularity" (333–34, 494–95). The camp meeting typified Methodism's irregularity (264). They found that spirit of adventure also in missions, to which they devoted considerable attention, making their volume in some respects a study of world Methodism. But again and again, they returned to Methodism and the nation. In the late 19th century, nation and church were paralleled on seven particulars—the application of polity, spirit and organization to new conditions; elaboration of national organization; extensive building; the closing of the frontier; an increase in democracy; foreign affairs and Negro education (440–42). They also paralleled the international perspectives of nation and church in the period after the First World War (486–87). And of course, they took great interest in the causes that riveted the church's attention on the nation—the civil war, reconstruction, temperance, the social gospel and world war.

Such challenges evoked the Methodist spirit, of adventure, of irregularity. Luccock and Hutchinson end the volume on that positive note, hopeful that Methodism will in the future draw upon that experimental spirit and reach out to the world (494–95). That note concluded a thoughtful discussion of problems—modern developments, post World War I developments—that tested Methodism. They listed ecumenism, peace, technological-industrial matters, race. They also examined the great campaign that sought to address such challenges by transforming wartime religious mobilization into peacetime enterprise. This Centenary financial campaign Methodism initially pegged at one hundred million dollars.[24] Luccock and Hutchinson entered their skepticism about the campaign, deftly but clearly. Their comments bear citation, for they point to the overreaching that Handy analyzes as constitutive of Protestantism's "second disestablishment" (Handy, 1984: 161–64).

> That the Centenary was not all permanent advance will be admitted. There was, it is probable, too much use of war psychology. . . . Moreover, the Centenary did, by certain of its promotional methods, tend to make shoddy thinkers believe that the task of building the kingdom of God is simply a task of perfecting a high-pressure organization of churches and ministers for the raising of certain definitely ascertainable sums of money. In these, and perhaps some other ways, an atmosphere of false excitement and achievement was created, which could not be kept up. Gradually this promotional fever evaporated. With its passing there were left certain problems of adjustment which have perplexed many leaders, and many whom the church had commissioned for work in various difficult fields. The solution of these problems is a matter of time and hard thinking. When the readjustments are completed, the permanent benefit which has grown out of the Centenary will be clear (487–88).

The hard-thinking that followed—Neo-orthodoxy it has been called—saw ironies where liberals had claimed providences, perceived an immoral nation where the Centenary had glimpsed the kingdom, recognized cultural enslavement in visions of a *Christian Century*. In Luccock and Hutchinson we find the now liberal Protestant establishment facing the implausibility of its premises. Methodism's four propositions come to rest on 'irregularity' not providence, a sandy 'human' foundation where Methodists had once found rock.

## PROFESSIONAL NOT PROVIDENTIAL ESTIMATE

Luccock and Hutchinson wrote a historical idiom that Lee and Bangs would have understood. Sweet (1953 [1933]) and Norwood (1974) simply did not.[25] The "second disestablishment" rendered the privileged, providential reading of American history impolitic and implausible. So for Methodists, the four propositions no longer guide historical analysis. Or perhaps it would be more accurate to say, those dogmas have now recast themselves as historical generalizations.

Sweet found difficulty in claiming Methodism providential, but in his second chapter, he treated "The Message of Wesley to His Time." That, once 'providential', fit of movement and age could be diagnosed. "Methodism arose out of two great urges: the first was the religious experience of John Wesley; the second was the vast spiritual destitution of eighteenth-century England (27)." So the first proposition found objective form.

The second proposition, the relation of Methodism to American society consumed Sweet. However, he found the relation to hinge not on providence but on Frederick Jackson Turner's frontier thesis.

> The greatest accomplishment of America has been the conquest of the continent. . . . the most significant single factor in the history of the United States has been the Western movement of population, and the churches which devised the best methods for following the population as it pushed westward were the ones destined to become the great American churches (143).

A series of chapter titles charted that destiny:

Organizes for a Great Task
Invades New England
Crosses the Alleghenies
The Circuit Rider Keeps Pace with the Westward March
Shares in the Missionary Enterprise
Begins her Educational Task.

Conquest defines destiny. Methodism charted its destiny in the 19th century in conquest of the frontier, the conquest really of America, the missionary impulse to take the continent.

Stewardship of its missionary calling constituted the reason for Methodism's success, its rapid growth to become the largest Protestant denomination. Sweet rendered that third proposition also in objective or human rather than providential terms. Why did Methodism succeed? Sweet insisted that the Methodist Episcopal Church "possessed, or developed, the best technique for following and ministering to a moving and restless population" (143). What were factors in that technique? Itinerancy, a centralized appointive power, circuits, short appointments, few repreached sermons, "zealous, energetic ministry," lay leadership, Arminian theology, a populist episcopacy, ample religious literature, and an "emphasis upon singing" (143–53).

Sweet's version of the fourth proposition followed readily. Sweet conceived of Methodism as the prototypical American church. He understood Methodism in terms of American society and American society in terms of Methodism.[26]

> As the title of this book implies, the history of American Methodism is here considered as a phase of American history, and it is assumed that it can best be understood in relation to the history of the American people (8).

So the church found itself caught in society's web, captive to American developments. Wealth was one.

> But such changes as were taking place in American Methodism were inevitable, for the church could not stand apart from the social, educational, and economic changes which were taking place in the nation. In the very nature of the case Methodists were bound to become economically prosperous (336).

And "the most serious problem faced by American Methodism as a whole at this time was its rapidly increasing wealth (336)."

In this and a variety of ways, Sweet transformed Methodist belief about itself into historical axioms. As such they could be tested by his graduate students at the University of Chicago. Sweet's intentions were laudable and widely shared by church historians. Church history would be a historical science, a species of history, a respectable university discipline. Sweet wanted American historians as colleagues. As president of the American Society of Church History and mentor to several generations of church historians, Sweet played a major role in secularizing and professionalizing the discipline. He gave such a reading to Methodist history.

Sweet taught at the University of Chicago from 1927 to 1946. For two years thereafter, from 1946 to 1948, he plied his craft at Garrett Theological Seminary. Soon after his departure, in 1952 to be precise, Frederick Norwood assumed that Garrett position, which he held until his recent retirement. Norwood achieved what Sweet intended, the execution of a Methodist history fully respectful of 'secular' historical canons. From its appearance, his *Story of American Methodism* (1974) enjoyed preeminence as the text of choice in the course required of United Methodist seminarians. Had these theologs known about and gone searching for the Methodist propositions, they would have found them, but in such a subtle and historiographically nuanced form as to be scarcely recognizable. Norwood dealt self-consciously and explicitly with these motifs that have been so important to Methodists. He did so in responsible interpretive fashion. A few citations provide some sense of his handling of Methodism's propositions:

1) Methodism began as a revival, and its history has been marked repeatedly by continuing revivals. From this point of view the denominational story is part of a constant theme in the history of Christianity in all times and places—continuing reformation. Inevitably, it seems, the church must go through such a process, as strong institutions languish and traditions ossify. The history of Methodism consistently demonstrates this theme (15).

2) American Methodists, and to a lesser extent United Brethren and Evangelicals, were caught up in the heady surge of the westward movement. A couple of generations of historical scholars have attempted to disparage the hoary Turner thesis on the westward movement as the determinative factor in American History. But all they have been able to accomplish is to qualify it as one factor playing a part with others. For Methodism this surge west determined at least the size and influence of the growing institution, and to some extent its quality and spirit (16).

3) [The Wesleyan or Methodist working theology] was so successfully peddled that it became a characteristic mark of American Christians of all kinds. The question remains to be discussed, whether this development was peculiarly Methodist or just plain American. Even Calvinism . . . was deeply affected. . . . Methodism became in many ways the most American of the churches. Not only in its inception but throughout its development it was most in tune with the American song (17).

4) Does this mean that America was Methodized or that Methodism was Americanized? Probably some of both. . . . [Methodism's various developments] all point to a close and continuing love affair, for better or worse, between the Methodist Church and the United States. Who was the dominant partner? The process of Americanizing and Methodizing brought on a tension which might be judged as the overriding theme of Methodist history in America (17).

Here Methodism's four propositions found scholarly expression.

## WHY METHODISM?

It would be uncharitable to lay at the feet of Sweet and Norwood a transformation that most church historians, including the present writer, presume and one that the whole denomination effected. The "second disestablishment," in fact, enveloped all mainline denominations. It would be more appropriate to see Sweet and Norwood as mirrors, as their predecessors were mirrors, reflecting the church's self-understanding back to church members. We should underscore, however, the importance of this historical reflection, this historical estimate of Methodist identity. As we noted above, Methodists have consistently turned to history when called upon to say who they were, to state purposes, to define themselves. History looms first in the *Discipline*. And these secular versions of the Methodist propositions now render United Methodism's understanding of itself and its belief. In the 1988 *Discipline's* "Historical Statement" (7–15) Methodism's propositions survive, as in Sweet and Norwood, only as historical axioms. Methodists continue to turn to their history for self-understanding. They find a narrative from which providence has departed. In this sense the making of church history into a historical rather than theological science has interesting consequences for the church. For it means that theological claims that once came readily to Methodist lips now simply are not heard.

"What may we reasonably believe to be God's design in raising up the preachers called Methodists?" Many now do not find that Wesleyan purpose appropriately rendered by the four propositions and a vision of a Christian America. Certainly those propositions and vision no longer shape Methodist histories or the *Discipline*. That particular constellation is not, however, the only appropriate statement of the Wesleyan purpose. Early Methodists and their first historian, Jesse Lee, claimed providence but did not find it expressed in nationalism or a national ideology. It may be time for Methodists once again to recognize that they may be about reforming the continent and spreading scriptural holiness over these lands without domesticating that purpose into a vision of a Christian America.

## Preface

1. Russell E. Richey and Kenneth E. Rowe, eds. (Nashville: Kingswood, 1985).
2. Rosemary Skinner Keller, Hilah Thomas, and Louise Queen, eds., 2 vols. (Nashville: Abingdon, 1981–82).
3. (Nashville: Abingdon, 1992). Inclusion in the United Methodist bibliography served as one criterion for this collection. Items were also suggested by United Methodist scholars whom we wrote explicitly asking for commentary on the essays in *Rethinking Methodist History* and for alternative selections from *Women in New Worlds* and elsewhere.
4. Both of these items are published by The General Commission on Archives and History, Madison, N.J., 1991.
5. Two vols. (Nashville: Board of Higher Education and Ministry, 1989). The five journals are *The Methodist Magazine, The Methodist Quarterly Review, The United Brethren Review, Religion in Life*, and *Quarterly Review.*
6. In addition to monographs, Kingswood features several other collections of essays either from a single hand or devoted to specific themes: Richard P. Heitzenrater, *Mirror and Memory: Reflections on Early Methodism* (1989); Thomas A. Langford, ed., *Doctrine and Theology in the United Methodist Church* (1990); Randy L. Maddox, ed., *Aldersgate Reconsidered* (1990); M. Douglas Meeks, ed., *What Should Methodists Teach?* (1990); S T Kimbrough, Jr., ed., *Charles Wesley: Poet and Theologian* (1991).

## Chapter 1

Mathews, *Evangelical America—The Methodist Ideology*

1. Clifford Geertz, "Ideology as a Cultural System," in David Apter, *Ideology and Discontent* (London: Free Press of Glencoe, 1964), 47–76.
2. Thomas B. Houghton to James Iredell, Jr., 2 February 1807, James Iredell Papers, Duke University.

3. Walter J. Ong, *The Presence of the Word: Some Prolegomena for Cultural and Religious History* (New Haven: Yale University Press, 1967), especially Chapter 3.

4. Frederick Dreyer, "Faith and Experience in the Thought of John Wesley," *American Historical Review,* 88 (February, 1983), 12–30.

5. Donald G. Mathews, *Religion in the Old South* (Chicago: University of Chicago Press, 1977), 194.

6. Raymond Williams, *Marxism and Literature* (Oxford: Oxford University Press, 1977), 110.

7. Victor Turner, *The Ritual Process: Structure and Anti-Structure* (Chicago: Aldine), 94–120; Turner, *Dramas, Fields, and Metaphors: Symbolic Action in Human Society* (Ithaca: Cornell University Press, 1974), 272–99. See also Sally Falk Moore, "Epilogue" in Moore and Barnara G. Myerhoff, eds., *Symbol and Politics in Communal Ideology* (Ithaca: Cornell University Press, 1975), 210–39.

8. Dreyer, "Faith and Experience in the Thought of John Wesley," 27.

9. Diary of William McKendree, September 18, 1790, Vanderbilt University Library.

10. Mathews, *Religion in the Old South,* 66–73.

11. Ibid., 66–80.

12. See Turner, *Ritual Process,* 94–165; Turner, *Dramas, Fields, and Metaphors,* 23–59, 271–99; Donald G. Mathews, "Evangelicalism in the Old South—*Communitas* and *Apocalypse,*" unpublished essay.

13. Quoted in Dickson D. Bruce, Jr., *And They All Sang Hallelujah: Plain-folk Camp Meeting Religion, 1800–1845* (Knoxville: University of Tennessee Press, 1974), 87.

14. Harriet Beecher Stowe, *Uncle Tom's Cabin or Life Among the Lowly,* edited and with an introduction by Ann Douglas (Penguin American Library, 1981) 582–83.

## Chapter 2

### Williams, *The Attraction of Methodism: The Delmarva Peninsula as a Case Study, 1769–1820*

1. William Morgan, Memoir, 20, 21, Hall of Records, Dover, Del.

2. Statistics on blacks compiled from *First Census of the United States, 1790* (Philadelphia, 1791), passim.

3. Figures used in calculating Methodist percentages came from *Minutes of the Annual Conferences of the Methodist Episcopal Church, 1773–1828,* and *Fourth Census of the U.S., 1820* (Washington, 1820). Working on the assumption that very few Methodists were fifteen or under and finding that approximately one-half of the Peninsula's population was sixteen and over in 1820, I used the latter half to compute the percentage of adult Delmarvans who were Methodists. For an estimate of church membership across the U.S. in the first half of the nineteenth century, see Edwin S. Gaustud, *The Rise of Adventism, Religion, and Society in Mid-Nineteenth Century America* (New York, 1974), xiii.

4. Morgan, Memoir, 2, 101, 102; William Duke, *Observations on the Present State of Religion in Maryland* (Baltimore, 1795), 44; John Lednum, *A History of the*

*Rise of Methodism in America* (Philadelphia, 1859), 418; Francis Asbury, *Journal and Letters*, I, 470, 471.

5. Isaac Davis, Autobiography, 1, typed copy in possession of Mrs. James McNeal of Bethany Beach, Del.; Joseph Everett, "An Account of the Most Remarkable Occurrences in the Life of Joseph Everett," *Arminian Magazine* (1790), 505; Adam Wallace, *The Parson of the Islands* (Baltimore, 1906), 69, 88, 89; Thomas Smith, *The Experience and Ministerial Labors of the Rev. Thomas Smith* (New York, 1840), 72–78; Asbury, *Journal and Letters*, I, 387.

6. Lednum, *A History of the Rise of Methodism in America*, 417; Smith, *The Experience and Ministerial Labors of the Rev. Thomas Smith*, 105; James Mitchell, *The Life and Times of Levi Scott* (New York, 1885), 32; Nathan Bangs, *The Life of the Rev. Freeborn Garretson* (New York, 1832), 74, 218; Andrew Manship, *Thirteen Years of Experience in the Itinerancy* (Philadelphia, 1881), 157; Asbury, *Journal and Letters*, I, 303, 496; Thomas Rankin, The Diary of the Rev. Thomas Rankin, 160, typed copy, Drew University, longhand at United Library, Garrett Theological Seminary, Evanston, Ill.

7. *Laws of Delaware*, II, 1218; III, 155; IV, 495; Edmund deS. Brunner and Wilbur C. Hallenbeck, *American Society: Urban and Rural Patterns* (New York, 1955), 216; William Wade, *Sixteen Miles from Anywhere: A History of Georgetown, Delaware* (Georgetown, Del., 1976), 7, 11, 12; William H. Williams, *A History of Wesley United Methodist Church, 1779–1978* (Georgetown, Del., 1978), 7, 8.

8. Rev. Henry Davis to Bishop John Claggett, Annapolis, Md., June 3, 1816, Maryland Diocesan Archives, Maryland Historical Society, Baltimore, Md; Proposals offered to the parishioners of St. Peter's Parish [Easton, Md.] May, 1788, Maryland Diocesan Archives; Smith, *The Experience and Ministerial Labors of the Rev. Thomas Smith*, 74; Asbury, *Journal and Letters*, II, 633; I, 612; St. Stephen's Parish Vestry to Bishop James Kemp, Sassafras Neck, Cecil Co., Md., Nov. 1816, Maryland Diocesan Archives. For specific examples of Methodism pushing Episcopalianism out of most of Maryland's Eastern Shore, see Rev. Henry Davis to Bishop Claggett, May 16, 1808; Rev. William Wicks to Bishop Kemp, Princess Anne, Md., Aug. 23, 1819; and Rev. Purnell Smith to Bishop Kemp, May 27, 1820; in Maryland Diocesan Archives.

9. Ethan Allen, *Clergy in Maryland of the Protestant Episcopal Church Since the Independence of 1783* (Baltimore, 1860), 5, 6; Kirk Mariner, *Revival's Children* (Salisbury, Md.), 83; Charles A. Silliman, *The Episcopal Church in Delaware, 1785–1954* (Wilmington, Del., 1982), 22; *Minutes of the Annual Conferences of the Methodist Episcopal Church 1773–1828*, 285; Asbury, *Journal and Letters*, II, 633; Duke, *Observations on the Present State of Religion in Maryland*, 18–21; Thomas Coke, *Extracts of the Journals of the Rev. Dr. Coke's Five Visits to America* (London, 1793), 18; Morgan, Memoir, 15.

10. James H. Lappen, *Presbyterians on Delmarva, The History of the New Castle Presbytery*, 26; John W. Christie, "Presbyterianism in Delaware," H. Clay Reed, ed., *Delaware, A History of the First State*, II, 652.

11. Mariner, *Revival's Children*, 12–16, 28; Blanche Sydnor White, *History of the Baptists on the Eastern Shore of Virginia 1776–1959* (Baltimore, 1959), passim; Albert Henry Newman, *A History of the Baptist Church in the United States* (New York, 1915), 273; Morgan Edwards, "Materials Towards a History of Baptists in Delaware State," *Pa. Mag. of Hist. and Bio.* IX (1885), 52. For Methodist responses to the Baptist

challenge see Asbury, *Journals and Letters*, I, 305, 306, 344; Asbury to Ezekiel Cooper, Bolingbroke, Talbot Co., Md., Nov. 12, 1790, Ezekiel Cooper Collection, No. 16, United Library, Garrett Theological Seminary, Evanston, Ill.

12. Nicholites were followers of Joseph Nichols (1730–1770) of Kent Co., Del. Believing in approximately the same principles as the Quakers, the Nicholites were numerous in southern Kent Co., and northern Sussex Co., Del., and in Caroline Co., Md. By the end of the eighteenth century, most of the Nicholites on Delmarva had migrated to North Carolina or were absorbed into nearby Quaker Meetings. For an overview of the Nicholites see Kenneth Carroll, *Joseph Nichols and the Nicholites* (Easton, Md., 1962). For examples of Methodist concern for the Deists and Catholics see William Colbert, A Journal of the Travels of William Colbert, II, 88, 89, typed copy, St. George's U.M. Church, Philadelphia; Robert Ayres Journal, Jan. 9, 1786, Hist. Soc. of Western Pa., Pittsburgh, Pa.

13. Wallace, *The Parson of the Islands*, 89.

14. The value system of eighteenth century Delmarva seems to have paralleled the value system found on Virginia's Western Shore by Rhys Isaac, "Evangelical Revolt: The Nature of the Baptist Challenge to the Traditional Order in Virginia, 1765–1775," *William and Mary Quarterly* (July 9, 1974), 345–368. The sources for the generalization concerning Delmarva's value system and the rejection of that value system are far too numerous to list here. These sources will be individually cited in a detailed treatment in my forthcoming book, "The Methodist Revolution, The Delmarva Peninsula as a Case Study, 1769–1820."

15. Landed gentry of Maryland's Eastern Shore who became Methodist included: Benton Harris of Worcester Co.; Henry Airey and Henry Ennalls of Dorchester Co.; General James Benson, Thomas Harrison, William Hindman, and Henry Banning of Talbot Co.; Capt. William Frazier, Phillip Harrington, and Henry Downes, of Caroline Co.; Col. William Hopper, William Bruff, Robert Emory, and James Bradley of Queen Anne's Co. In Delaware, Methodist converts from the gentry included: Thomas White, Philip Barratt, and Allen McLane of Kent Co.; David Nutter, Rhoads Shankland, John Wiltbank, and Lemuel Davis of Sussex Co. Peninsula attorneys and physicians who became Methodists included Richard Bassett of Dover, who also owned considerable land in Cecil Co., Md., Dr. Charles Ridgely of Dover, Dr. James Anderson of Chestertown, and Dr. Sluyter Bouchell of Cecil Co. Even on Virginia's Eastern Shore, the last sector of the Peninsula reached by circuit riders, Methodist converts of the "middling and lower sorts" were proud to note that their ranks had been joined by the likes of Col. Thomas Paramore of Northampton Co. and Capts. Thomas Burton and William Downing of Aecomack Co. All but one of the early membership records (class meeting records) of Methodist societies on the Peninsula have been lost. Nevertheless, the Methodism of the above people has been established by the use of a number of sources including *Biographical Dictionary of Maryland Legislatures, 1635–1789*, I, passim; Trustees' Minutes Bethel Methodist Church, Cecil Co., Md; Barratt's Chapel Archives, Frederica, Del., 1, 3; Asbury's *Journal and Letters*, passim; Emerson Wilson, *Forgotten Heroes of Delaware* (Cambridge, Mass., 1969), 167, 254–62, 416; Colbert, *Journal*, passim; as well as numerous other primary and secondary sources. For a short list of wealthy American Methodists who lived beyond the Peninsula see Lednum, *A History of the Rise of Methodism in America*, 167.

16. John B. Boles, *The Great Revival, 1787–1805* (Lexington, Ky, 1972), 169, 170; and Frank Baker, *An Introduction to the History of New England Methodism, 1789–1839* (Durham, 1941), 16–19 indicate the lower-class nature of early Methodism beyond the Delmarva Peninsula.

17. For a brief introduction to "old Methodism" and Asbury's use of it to fight the schismatics see Asbury, *Journal and Letters*, I, 85, 346; *Minutes of the Methodist Conferences Annually Held in America, 1773–1813* (New York, 1813), 19, 25, 26, 28; James W. May, "From Revival Movement to Denomination: A Re-Examination of the Beginnings of American Methodism" (Ph.D. diss., Columbia University, 1962), 105–12.

18. Asbury and his preachers got along particularly well with Anglican rectors Samuel Magaw of Dover, Del., Sydenham Thorne of Milford, Del., and Hugh Neill of Queen Anne's Co., Md. Once these three Anglican clerics became aware of the nature of "old Methodism," they became very friendly and even participated in Methodist services on the Peninsula. Asbury, *Journal and Letters*, I, 300, 310, 319, 341, 342, 345, 390; III, 28. By 1783, Methodism had spread to such singular Anglican families as Barratt, Bassett, Sipple and White in Kent Co., Del.; Anderson in Kent Co., Md.; Bruff and Benson in Talbot Co.; Downes and Frazier in Caroline Co.; and Airey, Ennalls and Hooper in Dorchester Co. See Lednum, *A History of the Rise of Methodism*, 166, 167, passim; Asbury, *Journal and Letters*, I, passim; Freeborn Garrettson Collection, Drew University, Madison, N.J., passim; "Memoir of Mrs. Anna Matilda Moore," *Methodist Magazine* (New York, 1828), 136–37. For the impact of conversions among the gentry on the lower orders see Smith, *Experience and Ministerial Labors of the Rev. Thomas Smith*, 97; John Wesley Andros Elliott, [Septuagenarian] Unwritten History of Eastern Shore Methodism, #5 (Circa 1885–86), xeroxed copy in the possession of the Rev. Dr. Kirk Mariner, Vienna, Va.

19. Isaac Davis, Autobiography, 3, 6, 8–12; *Smyrna Times*, April 2, 1856.

20. *Discipline of the Methodist Episcopal Church*, fifth ed. (New York, 1789), 49; Ethan Allen, St. Peter's Parish in Talbot Co., III, 36, Hall of Records, Annapolis, Md.

21. Asbury, *Journal and Letters*, I, 651, 335, 497, 612; II, 635; Boles, *The Great Revival*, 166–69.

22. Asbury, *Journal and Letters*, I, 497, 397; Morgan, Memoir, 17–19, passim.

23. William Colbert, Journal, II, III, (typed copy at St. George's U.M. Church, Philadelphia. Original is at United Library, Garrett Theological Seminary, Evanston, Ill.). The use of the prefix "brother" and "sister" is too common in the primary source materials to cite.

24. State laws for the incorporation of individual church congregations limited voting rights to free, white adult males. These state laws reflected restrictions on women already in practice. See, for example, Dudley's Chapel Minutes of Board of Trustees, 1797–1900, 5, Hall of Records, Annapolis, Md. For examples of state mandated voting restrictions in Maryland see Trustee's Minutes, 1809–1847, Zion U.M. Church, 6, 7, Cambridge, Md. See Trustees' Book, 1807, Wesley U.M. Church, Georgetown, Del., for restrictions in Delaware. For a typical example of an all female class meeting led by a male, see Smith, *Experience and Ministerial Labors of Rev. Thomas Smith*, 27; *Discipline of the Methodist Episcopal Church*, fifth ed. (New York, 1789), 31; Charles Johnson, *The Frontier Camp Meeting* (Dallas, 1955), 46; John D. C. Hannah, ed., *The Centennial of Asbury Methodist Episcopal Church* (Wilmington, 1889), 140, 151; Frank

C. Baker, Jr., *An Introduction to the History of Early New England Methodism 1789–1839* (Durham, N.C., 1941), 21; Lednum, *A History of the Rise of Methodism in America*, 270. Since early membership records for individual Methodist societies on the Peninsula—with the exception of Asbury Church, Wilmington—aren't exact, it is impossible to present a statistical breakdown of male vs. female members. However, Colbert, *Journal*, IV, 60; Ayres, *Journal*, 15 and passim; Records of Asbury M.E. Church, Wilmington, V, Hall of Records, Dover, Del.; and a study by Terry David Bilhartz, "Urban Religion and the Second Great Awakening: A Religious History of Baltimore, Maryland, 1790–1830" (Ph.D. diss., George Washington University, 1979), 62, indicates that Methodists, on the Peninsula and on the west side of the Chesapeake, were overwhelmingly female. In the case of Asbury Church, Wilmington, women outnumbered men almost two to one.

25. Jeffrey Savor, "Edward O. Wilson, Father of a New Science," *Science Digest* (May, 1982), 86; John D. C. Hanna, ed., *The Centennial Services of Asbury Methodist Episcopal Church*, 151.

26. Morgan, *Memoir*, 102; "Memoir of Mrs. Anna Matilda Moore," *Methodist Magazine* (New York, 1828), 135; Davis, *Autobiography*, 7.

27. Smith, *The Experience and Ministerial Labors of Rev. Thomas Smith*, 99. For the behavior of Garrettson and other itinerants in the face of persecution see William H. Williams, *The Garden of American Methodism: The Delmarva Peninsula, 1769–1820* (Wilmington, Del., 1984), chap. II. For particularly interesting views on why more women than men joined churches in New England during the eighteenth and early nineteenth century see Nancy F. Cott, *The Bonds of Womanhood: "Woman's Sphere" in New England, 1780–1835* (New Haven, Conn., 1977), 126–59; and Laurel Thatcher Ulrich, *Good Wives: Image and Reality in the Lives of Women in Northern New England, 1650–1750* (New York, 1982), 215–16.

28. Boehm, *Reminiscences*, 59–60; Smith, *The Experience and Ministerial Labors of Rev. Thomas Smith*, 30, 31; Abbott, *The Experience and Gospel Labours of The Rev. Benjamin Abbott*, 109. A real opportunity for female leadership in Methodism opened up with the sectarian development of the Sunday School in the 1830s. See Mariner, *Revival's Children*, 82.

29. Figures on black and white membership are drawn from *Minutes of the Annual Conferences of the Methodist Episcopal Church, 1773–1828*, passim; and the first four U.S. census returns.

30. Frederick E. Maser, ed., "Discovery," *Methodist History* (Jan., 1971), 35; Asbury, *Journal and Letters*, I, 273, 274, 582; Boehm, *Reminiscences, Historical and Biographical of Sixty-four Years in the Ministry* (New York, 1865), 26, 70; Allen, St. Peter's Parish in Talbot Co., III, 35; Colbert, *Journal*, II, 104, 126, 216, IV, 8, 41, 48.

31. For just a few examples of "the better sort" and the emotional side of Methodism see Rachel Bruff in Garrettson Collection, Drew University; Boehm, *Reminiscences*, 151, 152; John A. Munroe, *Louis McLane* (New Brunswick, N.J., 1973), 11, 12; Nathaniel Luff, *Journal of the Life of Nathaniel Luff, M.D.* (New York, 1848), 126, 127; Kirk Mariner, *Revival's Children*, 59. For black religious enthusiasm and white reaction see Colbert, *Journal*, IV, 49, 56, passim, III, 129; Asbury, *Journal and Letters*, I, 274, 655; R. W. Todd, *Methodism of the Peninsula* (Philadelphia, 1886), 183–85; A. Chandler, *A History of the Churches on the Delmar Circuit* (Wilmington, Del., 1886),

10; Minutes of Board of Trustees, Asbury M. E. Church, Wilmington, Del., June 9, 1805, Barratt's Chapel, Frederica, Del.; Barratt's Chapel Record Book, 7–9, Barratt's Chapel.

32. Did African culture and, in particular, African religion survive among American slaves? This has become a subject of considerable controversy among historians. Melville J. Herskovitz in *The Myth of the Negro Past* (Boston, 1958) argued that the African heritage survived among American blacks despite the trauma of slavery. E. Franklin Frazier in *The Negro Church in America* (New York, 1964), and in other works, maintains that the African in America was almost totally stripped of his culture by American slavery. A particularly stimulating treatment of the survival of African religious traits among American slaves can he found in Eugene D. Genovese, *Roll Jordan Roll: The World the Slaves Made* (New York, 1976), 161–284. I have found the most satisfactory study of African religious remnants in White Christianity in Albert J. Raboteau, *Slave Religion: The Invisible Institution in the Antebellum South* (New York, 1978), 43–92.

33. Daniel Blake Smith, *Inside the Great House: Planter Family Life in Eighteenth Century Chesapeake Society* (Ithaca, N.Y., 1980), 265–67; George A. Phoebus, *Beams of Light on Early Methodism* (New York, 1887), 12.

34. William Watters, *A Short Account of the Christian Experience of William Watters* (Alexandria, Va.). 38; Bishop James Kemp to Rev. William Duke, Baltimore, Sept. 19, 1815, Maryland Diocesan Archives (Kemp had observed Peninsula Methodism while Episcopal rector in Dorchester Co., for nineteen years.); Asbury, *Journal and Letters*, II, 388, I, 302; David, Autobiography, 2, 7, 8, 10, 14; Robert Emory, *The Life of the Rev. John Emory, D.D.* (New York, 1841), 12; William Coulter to Ezekiel Cooper, Dorchester Co., Md., March 29, 1800, Ezekiel Cooper Collection, United Library, Evanston, Ill.; Lednum, *A History of the Rise of Methodism in America*, 229.

## Chapter 3

### Baker, *The Doctrines in the* Discipline

First published in The Duke Divinity School Review, XXXI (1966), 39–55.

1. Journal of Thomas Haskins at the Christmas Conference, Jan. 1, 1785, quoted in William Warren Sweet, *Men of Zeal* (New York: Abingdon, 1935), 173.

2. John J. Tigert, *A Constitutional History of American Episcopal Methodism*, 6th ed. (Nashville: Smith and Lamar, 1916), 533–602. See also above, p. 151.

3. John Wesley, *The Sunday Service of the Methodists* (London: n.p. 1784, 1788, 1790, 1792), 322–55. This particular edition is briefly described in Frank Baker, *A Union Catalogue of the Publications of John and Charles Wesley* (Durham: Duke Divinity School, 1966), 174, as No. 376[E]. There were also "British" editions in 1786 ([C], [D]), and other years. These contained variants in the prayers and the Articles, suited to members who still owed allegiance to the British Crown, though otherwise the editions were the same.

4. See the editions of 1787, 1788, 1789, 1790, and 1791; cf. Baker, *Union Catalogue*, No. 425.ii, 216–17.

5. Tigert, op. cit., 535. In 1876 the footnote was brought into the text. In 1892 this section was transferred to a "Historical Statement," where it remained until 1944,

to be replaced at the following General Conference by a statement emphasizing Wesley's experience of May 24, 1738.

6. Tigert, op. cit., 146. Their place and manner of appearance varied greatly, however, so that omission and error can readily be understood. In the 1785 *Minutes* the doctrinal sections appear without any titles, the discussion of antinomianism forming the questions and answers of the two closing sections, 80 and 81, while the statement on perfection forms the lengthy closing paragraph of the answer to question 73 (see Tigert, op. cit., 585–86, 600–602). In 1787 their order was reversed, "Against Antinomianism" forming section 16 and "On Perfection" section 22, as noted above. This remained true until 1790, when each was elevated one step, to slip back once more in 1791 through the insertion of a new section on Band Societies.

7. See Frank Baker, *From Wesley to Asbury* (Durham: Duke University Press, 1976), 158.

8. Tigert, op. cit., 146.

9. M. E. Church, *Journals of Gen. Conf.*, I, 82–83, 89; cf. Tigert, op. cit., 304–14.

10. The United Methodist Church, *The Book of Discipline 1972*, pp. 21 (16, Article 1), 43–44.

11. *Discipline 1972*, 157 (334).

12. The United Methodist Church, *The Book of Discipline 1968*, 455–56 (1419).

13. Ibid., 35–36, which make it clear that although the restrictive rule of 1808 is thus continued through 1968 the Wesleyan standards are to be interpreted as "negative limits of public teaching" rather than "the positive prescription of an inflexible system of doctrine."

14. Harold Spencer and Edwin Finch, *The Constitutional Practice and Discipline of the Methodist Church* 4th ed. (London: The Methodist Publishing House, 1964), 276–77, 285.

15. Even the homespun evangelist Benjamin Abbott introduced an appeal for members by reading the Articles after preaching at a new place in 1792. Benjamin Abbott, *Experience and Gospel Labors*, ed. John Ffirth (New York: Waugh and Mason, 1833; 1st published in 1809), 204.

16. *Discipline 1968*, 43, 47, and *1972*, 60, 63–64.

17. Ibid., *1968*, 36.

18. Ibid., *1972*, 40–43.

19. Tigert, op. cit., 589–91. This Model Deed was earlier used by American Methodists, as in New York for John Street Chapel, and also for Old St. George's, Philadelphia. (See Baker, *From Wesley to Asbury*, 78, 87–88.)

20. *Discipline, 1972*, 41.

21. Ibid., 39n.

22. Ibid., 484–86.

23. *Minutes* (American, 1795), p. 5.

24. Samuel A. Seaman, *Annals of New York Methodism* (New York: Hunt and Eaton, 1892), 421.

25. In the Methodist Publishing House Library, Nashville, Tennessee, inscribed on the flyleaf of each volume: "William Duke/May 10th—1775/Mr. Wesley's Gift." Overleaf is a note by the Reverend J. B. Hagany describing how he received the volumes from Duke, who informed him that "Mr. Wesley sent over a copy of his *Notes* to each

of the preachers who composed the Conference of 1775." It seems quite probable that Wesley also presented them with copies of his *Sermons*.

26. *Minutes* (American, 1795), 41.

27. Ibid., 72–73. Cf. Wesley's 1783 charge to Asbury, quoted in Baker, *From Wesley to Asbury*, 128–29.

28. See Tigert, op. cit., 542.

29. Ibid., 592.

30. Ibid., 562, 570, 576, 585, 600.

31. David Sherman, *History of the Revisions of the Discipline of the Methodist Episcopal Church*, 3rd ed. (New York: Hunt and Eaton, 1890), 200.

32. There was one major and important change in this document—the addition of a provision against slaveholding. See Baker, *From Wesley to Asbury* n. 42 p. 152.

33. Actually it was not Wesley's own composition, but was extracted by him from *The Order of Causes*, originally published in 1654 by Henry Haggar, and first appearing in Wesley's abridgment in 1741. See Baker, *Union Catalogue*, No. 27.

34. Baker, *Union Catalogue*, No. 153; first published in 1751.

35. Ibid., No. 238, first published in 1766. An early edition was apparently used, for from the fourth edition onwards the terminal date was altered to 1777. In the 1789 *Discipline* the added tracts were paginated separately, but the signatures of the gatherings show that the work was printed as a unit: see *Union Catalogue*, No. 425.ii(5), 216.

36. That this was added to the printer's copy at the last minute, and presented some kind of a problem (perhaps its late substitution for other matter) is shown by the signatures of the gatherings. Up to this point they are signed A-P$^6$, and Wesley's *Plain Account* ends on pp. 177–78, sig. Q. The title page to the *Treatise* is apparently Q2—the matching chainlines confirm the conjugacy—but the drop title to the *Treatise* on p. (181) not only varies from the title page but begins a fresh gathering signed R, after which the book proceeds regularly R-Y$^6$, Z$^2$.

37. Altered to "who" in 1798.

38. Asbury, *Journal*, III, 159.

39. Ibid.

40. M. E. Church, *Journals of Gen. Conf.*, I, 40, 43–44.

41. Ezekiel Cooper had just taken over as editor and publisher upon the death of John Dickins, but his manuscript printing records for 1799–1804 reveal no such item. See Lester B. Scherer, *Ezekiel Cooper, 1763–1847* (Lake Junaluska: Commission on Archives and History, 1968), 116–17.

42. M. E. Church, *Journals of Gen. Conf.*, I, 121.

43. Tigert, op. cit., 145–48.

44. I wish to record here my indebtedness to the librarians of the following institutions, who made it possible for me to have access to their treasures, including the rare editions of the *Collection of Interesting Tracts* noted, for which see Baker, *Union Catalogue*, No. 425.ii(16), 217–18: American Antiquarian Society (1814, 1817); Bangor Theological Seminary (1825); Library of Congress (1814, c. 1856–60 [Carlton and Porter], c. 1872–80 [Nelson and Phillips]); Depauw University (1836, 1856, c. 1856–60 [Carlton and Porter]); Drew University (1814, 1817, 1831, 1836); Duke University (1814, 1817, 1825); Emory University (1814, 1817, 1825); Garrett Theological Seminary (1817, 1861); The Methodist Publishing House, Nashville (1817, 1836, 1850, 1856

c. 1892 [Hunt and Eaton, etc.]); Methodist Theological School in Ohio (1847); Southern Methodist University (1814, 1834, 1850, 1854); Syracuse University (1825); Xenia-Pittsburgh Theological Seminary (1847); Vanderbilt University (1814, 1850). Dr. Kenneth E. Rowe kindly informs me of several other institutions who hold some of these editions, full details of which will be published in the forthcoming Methodist Union Catalog which he is preparing.

45. Baker, *Union Catalogue*, Nos. 24, 70–71, 155.

46. Ibid., Nos. 11, 274, 212; the other items were *Serious Considerations concerning the Doctrine of Election and Reprobation* (No. 16), abridged from *The Ruin and Recovery of Mankind*, by Isaac Watts; *Serious Considerations on Absolute Predestination* (No. 22), abridged from Robert Barclay's *Apology*; and *Thoughts on the Imputed Righteousness of Christ* (No. 211), an original work by Wesley. There were also two non-Wesleyan pieces, "A Plain Definition of Saving Faith," and "How the Doctrines of the Gospel come into the Succour of Morality," the latter being dropped after the 1817 edition.

47. Ibid., Nos. 191.vi, 149.

48. *The Doctrines of the Methodist Episcopal Church in America, as contained in the Disciplines of said Church from 1788 to 1808, and so designated on their Title-pages. Compiled and edited with an historical introduction by Jno. J. Tigert, D.D., LL.D.*, 2 vols, Cincinnati: Jennings and Pye, 1902). Tigert does not print the complete contents of the 1814 doctrinal tracts, however, but only the four which had appeared by 1792, together with the two brief sections "On Christian Perfection" and "Against Antinomianism." The four presented comprise not only *The Scripture Doctrine of Predestination, Election, and Reprobation, Serious Thoughts upon the Perseverance of the Saints*, and *A Plain Account of Christian Perfection*, all by Wesley, but also Hemmenway's *Nature and Subjects of Christian Baptism*, even though this was dropped from the 1797 *Discipline*, and never restored, so that it could hardly have been included in the "present existing and established standards of doctrine" referred to by the restrictive rule of 1808, as the others surely were.

49. The United Methodist Church, "The Theological Study Commission on Doctrine and Doctrinal Standards: A Report to the General Conference, April, 1972," 7; cf. *Discipline, 1972*, 44.

50. "The Theological Study Commission . . . ," 13, 27–38; cf. *Discipline, 1972*, 48–49, 75–82.

## *Chapter 4*

## Heitzenrater, *At Full Liberty: Doctrinal Standards in Early American Methodism*

1. Richard P. Heitzenrater's article is published in *Quarterly Review* (Fall 1985) and is republished in *Mirror and Memory* (Nashville: Abingdon, 1989) and is used with permission.

2. *Journals of the General Conference of the Methodist Episcopal Church* (New York: Carlton & Lanahan, n.d.), vol. 1, 1796–1836, 89, hereafter cited as *Journal*. Curiously, only the first volume has a number; others bear only dates. The 1984 Book

of Discipline (¶ 16) contains only slight revisions: "nor" has been changed to "or"; "articles of religion" has been capitalized; most commas have been omitted.

3. The terms *doctrine* and *doctrinal standards* are used in this paper with the specific connotation that their role is distinctly different from the task of *theology* or *theological reflection*. *Doctrinal standards*, established by and for the church, provide criteria for measuring the doctrinal adequacy of the witness of clergy and laity in the church, whereas *theological reflection*, based on norms such as Scripture, tradition, reason, and experience, necessarily is not subject to such standards and in fact is intentionally and appropriately critical in its task of examining such standards. See Schubert M. Ogden's essay, chapter 3 in Thomas A. Langford, *Doctrine and Theology in the United Methodist Church* (Nashville: Kingswood, 1991). Doctrinal *standards* can also be distinguished from other doctrinal writings in that the standards are carefully formulated documents that provide established norms for measuring the adequacy of various other doctrinal writings ("our doctrines" and "our doctrinal *standards*" are not the same thing, a distinction which Professor Oden totally misses in his discussion of the question; see chapter 9 in Langford, *Doctrine and Theology*.

4. Preface to Part II, *The Plan of Union, as Adopted by the General Conferences* (the "Blue Book," copyright 1967 by Donald A. Theuer for the Joint Commissions on Church Union of the Methodist Church and the Evangelical United Brethren Church), p. 22 (subsequently contained in the 1968 Book of Discipline, p. 35).

5. 1984 Book of Discipline, ¶67, p. 49. This section of the Discipline, which is not a part of the constitution, was adopted in 1972 from the report of the Theological Study Commission on Doctrine and Doctrinal Standards. The line of interpretation contained in the statement reflects in large part the opinions of the last generation of Methodist constitutional historians, who were writing at the turn of the twentieth century. See note 37, following. I began this research in order to *support* that claim with historical evidence, not just historical inferences; the task has concluded just the opposite. As of the republication of this article in 1990, no one has yet provided *any* actual reference (1785–1840) or other solid historical evidence to back up the claim of the 1972 Discipline, and even the author of that sentence has admitted that he may have "fudged a bit" in making that claim (see chapter 7, n. 9, in Langford, *Doctrine and Theology*).

6. *Minutes of the Methodist Conferences, Annually Held in America from 1773 to 1794* (Philadelphia: Henry Tuckniss, 1795), 77.

7. Benson's proposal to organize Methodism into a distinct denomination separate from the Church of England was passed on to Wesley by Fletcher with some alterations and additions. Two items are of particular note:

> 4. That a pamphlet be published containing the 39 articles of the Church of England rectified according to the purity of the gospel, together with some needful alterations in the liturgy and homilies. . . .

> 10. That the most spiritual part of the Common Prayer shall be extracted and published with the 39 rectified articles, and the minutes of the conferences (or the Methodist canons) which (together with such regulations as may be made at the time of this establishment) shall be, next to the Bible, the *vade mecum* ["constant companion" or "handbook"] of the Methodist preachers. (*The Journal of the Rev. John Wesley* [London: Epworth, 1960], 8:332–33.)

Frank Baker comments that this proposal "was almost certainly present in Wesley's mind, and possibly before his eyes" in 1784 when he put together his scheme for American Methodism. *John Wesley and the Church of England* (Nashville: Abingdon, 1970), 212.

8. This assumption is clearly alluded to in an account of a private interview held during the Christmas Conference, at which Coke, Asbury, William West, and John Andrews (the latter two Protestant Episcopal priests in Baltimore County) discussed the possibility of merging the two emerging episcopal churches in America. Andrews's account of the conversation, in a letter to William Smith, notes that *The Sunday Service of the Methodists* makes plain that "the people called Methodists were hereafter to use the same Liturgy that we make use of, to adhere to the same Articles, and to keep up the same three orders of the Clergy" (interesting that he notes no basic difference between the Wesleyan version of these documents and their English counterparts). Andrews also points out that, "as to Articles of faith and forms of worship, they already agreed with us." Emora T. Brannan, "Episcopal Overtures to Coke and Asbury during the Christmas Conference, 1784," *Methodist History* 14 (April 1976): 209.

9. In fact, the interview mentioned above failed to produce a working agreement in part because West and Andrews perceived that Coke and Asbury considered it "indispensably necessary that Mr. Wesley be the first link of the Chain upon which their Church is suspended." The "binding minute" makes it clear that the American preachers at the Christmas Conference were willing to acknowledge themselves as Wesley's "Sons in the Gospel, ready in matters belonging to church government, to obey his Commands," a very polite and precise acknowledgement of Wesley's relationship to them in matters of polity. This approbation of Wesley's personal leadership disappeared from the Discipline after 1786, and Wesley's name was omitted from the published minutes of the American annual conferences from 1786 to 1788.

10. James Everett (who was present at Baltimore in 1785), in his autobiographical reflections written to Asbury in 1788, makes a reference to "the Christmas conference, when Dr. Coke came from England, and the Methodist church separated from all connection or dependence on the church of England, *or any other body or society of people*" (italics mine). "An Account of the Most Remarkable Occurrences of the Life of Joseph Everett," *Arminian Magazine* 2 (Philadelphia, 1790): 607.

11. *Minutes of Several Conversations between the Rev. Thomas Coke, the Rev. Francis Asbury, and Others . . . Composing a Form of Discipline* (Philadelphia: Charles Cist, 1785), 3.

12. This point is not taken seriously by Professor Oden, who spends a great deal of time discussing pre-1785 American Methodism (still a part of British Methodism) in his arguments; all of the "evidence" he quotes concerning the *Sermons* and *Notes* is from documents prior to 1785, which he wrongly assumes continued in effect into the new church (see chapter 9 in Langford, *Doctrine and Theology*). The references to "Minutes" in the 1785 Discipline clearly refer to that document itself, as can be seen in the answer to Question 3, cited above. Also in Question 69, "Questions for a New Helper," where the prospective preacher is asked, "Have you read the *Minutes of the Conference?*," the reference is clearly to the American document, and not to the British *Minutes*, because in 1787, when the third edition of the disciplinary *Minutes* changed its title to *A Form of Discipline*, the question was changed to read, "Have you read the Form of Discipline?"

13. *Minutes of Several Conversations between the Rev. Mr. John and Charles Wesley and Others* (London: Paramore, 1780), 43. This edition of the "Large Minutes" was in effect at the time of the Christmas Conference; the "model deed" had been included in the three previous editions of the "Large Minutes": 1763, 1770, 1772.

14. The first conference in 1773 agreed that the doctrine and discipline of the British Methodist *Minutes* should be "the sole rule of our conduct who labour, in the connection with Mr. Wesley, in America." The conference in 1781 noted that the preachers were determined "to preach the old Methodist doctrine, and strictly enforce the discipline, as contained in the notes, sermons, and minutes, as published by Mr. Wesley." At the conference of 1784, held the spring previous to the specially called Christmas Conference, the preachers agreed to accept among them only those European preachers who would, among other things, "preach the doctrine taught in the four volumes of Sermons, and Notes on the New Testament . . . [and] follow the directions of the London and American minutes." *Minutes of the Methodist Conferences* (1795), 5, 41, 72.

15. Question 64 in the "Large Minutes." Part of the answer to Question 65 was retained (as Question 74 in the Discipline): "Let all our Chapels be built plain and decent; but not more expensively than is absolutely avoidable: Otherwise the Necessity of raising Money will make rich men necessary to us. But if so, we must be dependent upon them, yea, and governed by them. And then farewell to the Methodist-Discipline, if not Doctrine too." *Minutes . . . Composing a Form of Discipline* (1785), 32. A parallel comparison of the "Large Minutes" with the first American Discipline is published in Appendix VII of John M. Tigert's *Constitutional History of American Episcopal Methodism*, 4th ed. (Nashville: Publishing House of the Methodist Episcopal Church, South, 1911), 532–602. The fact that the Americans did not include the Model Deed in their constitutive documents does not mean that they "rescinded" or "rejected" the British document—starting anew, they simply never implemented it in their new church structure. No evidence of any use in America after 1785 of the British model deed (containing the reference to Wesley's *Sermons* and *Notes*) has turned up.

16. The wording in the American deed follows very closely the wording of the British document before and after the omitted section, indicating that the doctrinal stipulation ("preach no other doctrine than is contained in . . . ") was consciously dropped from the American form, or more precisely, never implemented in the new American church. Documents previously authoritative in America (before 1785, such as the British *Minutes*) had no constitutional standing in the new church.

17. The "fifth edition" of the Discipline (New York: William Ross, 1789), section XXXIII.

18. This wording is on the title page of the Discipline; the "useful pieces" have separate title pages but are paged continuously in the volume. Some are written by Wesley, whose doctrines and writings still provided the basic shape of American Methodist doctrine (in addition to the "standards" he also had provided in the form of Articles). In 1790, the Articles of Religion became section XXXV of the *Form of Discipline*; in 1791, section XXXVI.

19. The answer stipulates that the preacher of such "erroneous doctrines" shall confront the same process as is observed "in cases of gross immorality," which had just been spelled out.

20. This wording, not only used in 1808 in the Restrictive Rules but also still in effect today in the section on trials, implies a method of measure quite different from the early British rule that allowed preaching of "*no other doctrine* than is contained in Mr. Wesley's Notes upon the New Testament and four volumes of Sermons," which is strictly delimiting in its intention (my italics). The "contrary to" concept and language was adopted by the British Conference in 1832.

21. The explanatory notes of Asbury and Coke, included in the 1796 Discipline, for the section on trial of a minister for erroneous doctrines, point out that "the heretical doctrines are as dangerous, at least to the hearers, as the immoral life of a preacher." The heresies mentioned specifically were "arian, socianian, and universalian." *The Doctrines and Discipline of the Methodist Episcopal Church in America* (Philadelphia: Tuckniss, 1798), 113.

22. E.g., Wesley's *Works, Notes, Christian Library, Primitive Physick*, Fletcher's tracts, Richard Baxter's *Gildus Salvianus*, Kempis, and the *Instructions for Children*. These were all carried over from the British *Minutes*; the American Discipline omitted some, such as the reference to Wesley's fourth volume of *Sermons* in Question 33 (Question 51 in the Discipline). The bishops' notes in the 1798 Discipline say nothing after the two doctrinal sections, simply referring the reader to "Mr. Wesley's excellent treatise" after the section "Of Christian Perfection," and to "that great writer, Mr. Fletcher" after the section "against Antinomianism." A footnote in Bishop Roberts's address to the conference at Baltimore in 1807, in a section headed "take heed unto the doctrine," refers the reader to several guides to understanding the Bible, including works by Stackhouse, Doddridge, Bonnett, Watson, Addison and Beattie, Jenny, Wilberforce, Leland, and Ogden, but no mention is made of Wesley's *Notes*. These references (or the wide availability or scarcity of particular publications), however, do not speak to the question of officially "established standards" of doctrine.

23. In 1790 when the doctrinal treatises were introduced into the body of the Discipline (with section numbers), the title was altered to read, *A Form of Discipline . . . (now comprehending the Principles and Doctrines) of the Methodist Episcopal Church in America*. Two years later, the sacramental services were added and the title became *The Doctrines and Discipline of the Methodist Episcopal Church in America* as we noted above. The doctrinal treatises were by and large "Wesleyan" tracts, though only half of them were by John Wesley: *Scripture Doctrine of Predestination, Election, and Reprobation*, by Henry Haggar, abridged by Wesley (inserted beginning in 1788); *Serious Thoughts on the Infallible, Unconditional Perseverance of All That Have Once Experienced Faith in Christ* (beginning in 1788); *A Plain Account of Christian Perfection* (beginning in 1789); *An Extract on the Nature and Subjects of Christian Baptism*, by Moses Hemmenway (beginning in 1790). The tracts were omitted from the 1798 Discipline (tenth edition) to make room for the bishops' explanatory notes, but (with the exception of the treatise on baptism) were restored in the following (eleventh) edition of 1801.

24. These treatises were removed from the Discipline by action of the General Conference of 1812 to be published separately. The directions of the conference were only slowly and inaccurately heeded. See Frank Baker's article above.

25. One document, by Coke, contained twenty-eight Articles; the other, probably by Clarke and Benson, contained thirty-eight Articles. See *Articles of Religion Prepared*

*by Order of the Conference of 1806*, publication no. 2 of The Wesley Historical Society (London: Kelly, 1897).

26. *Journal*, 1:76, 79.

27. *Journal*, 1:82; compare "A Journal of the Proceedings of the General Conference of the Methodist Episcopal Church, 1800–1828" (MS, Drew University Library), p. 168; referred to hereafter as "manuscript journal" or "MS journal." The last phrase, starting "contrary to," was inadvertently omitted in the printed version. Contrary to Professor Oden's argument, the reference to "Articles of Religion" can surely be seen as plural, referring to the several articles contained therein as standards of doctrine.

28. *Journal*, 1:89.

29. MS journal, 68; this page also contains the Restrictive Rules (see illustration).

30. *Journal*, 1:128–29. The committee that had determined the necessity for such a committee of safety, based on the episcopal address, consisted of one member from each conference and included Philip Bruce and Nelson Reed, two members of the 1808 "committee of fourteen" that had drawn up the Restrictive Rules.

31. Horace M. Du Bose, *Life of Joshua Soule* (Nashville: Publishing House of the Methodist Episcopal Church, South, 1916), 110.

32. *Journal*, 1:155. The Committee of Safety ended its report with eight resolutions which were passed by the conference, including, "1. That the General Conference do earnestly recommend the superintendents to make the most careful inquiry to all the annual conferences, in order to ascertain whether any doctrines are embraced or preached contrary to our established articles of faith, and to use their influence to prevent the existence and circulation of all such doctrines" (*Journal* 1:157). It might also be noted that the following day, the conference adopted the report of the Committee on Ways and Means which included a proposal that the section of the Discipline on "The Method of Receiving Preachers" include the stipulation, "It shall be the duty of the bishops, or of a committee which they may appoint at each annual conference, to point out a course of reading and study proper to be pursued by candidates for the ministry . . . " (*Journal*, 1:160–161).

33. Ibid., 348.

34. Ibid., 350–351.

35. *Guide-Book in the Administration of the Discipline* (New York: Carlton & Phillips, 1855), 152.

36. *A Manual of the Discipline of the Methodist Episcopal Church, South* (Nashville: Publishing House of the Methodist Episcopal Church, South, 1870), 131.

37. Discipline (1880), ¶213; see also *Journal* (1880, no vol. no.), 323.

38. *Constitutional and Parliamentary History of the Methodist Episcopal Church* (New York: Methodist Book Concern, 1912), 157–69. See also John M. Tigert, *A Constitutional History of American Episcopal Methodism* (Nashville: Publishing House of the Methodist Episcopal Church, South, 1894), 113, 139–48, and Thomas B. Neely, *Doctrinal Standards of Methodism* (New York: Revell, 1918), 225–37.

39. At about the same time, the southern church received a report by the College of Bishops to the General Conference of 1914, stating that Wesley's *Notes* and *Sermons* "have never been adopted by organized Episcopal Methodism" and therefore "it is not clear that [they] are standards of doctrine." See the eighteenth edition of Bishop McTyeire's *Manual of the Discipline* (1924; edited by Bishop Collins Denny), 147–48.

## Chapter 5
### Sanders, *The Sacraments in Early American Methodism*

1. P. Tillich, "Nature and Sacrament," in *The Protestant Era* (Chicago, 1948), 94–119.

2. J. Wesley, Minutes of the Conference; quoted in L. Tyerman, *The Life and Times of John* Wesley (6th edition, 3 vols.; London 1890), II, 576.

3. J. Wesley, *Journal* (Standard Edition, ed. N. Curnock, 8 vols.; London 1909–1916), II, 293.

4. Cf. G. C. Cell, *The Rediscovery of John Wesley* (New York, 1935), 145. "Wesley's life-long resistance to the separation of his societies from the Anglican Church was therefore dictated by something far more significant than a blindly tenacious conservatism. It was dictated by an intelligent religious appreciation of the Christian Church as the means of grace. It was rooted and grounded in a profoundly *soteriological* evaluation of the Church" (italics Cell's).

5. J. Whitehead's *Life of the Rev. John Wesley* (London, 1793) was the first official biography. See also T. Coke and H. Moore, *Life of the Rev. Mr. Wesley* (American edition; Philadelphia, 1793); R. Watson, *Life of Rev. John Wesley* (First American edition; New York, 1853). Even Tyerman concludes that if Wesley appears inconsistent, "we must take [him] as we find him" (*op. cit.*, I. 496).

6. E.g., W. H. Holden, *John Wesley in Company with High Churchmen* (London, 1870); F. Hockin, *John Wesley and Modern Methodism* (4th edition; London, 1887); R. D. Urlin, *John Wesley's Place in Church History* (London, 1870); A. S. Little, *The Times and Teaching of John Wesley* (Milwaukee, 1905).

7. E.g., J. H. Rigg, *The Churchmanship of John Wesley* (revised edition; London, 1886); *The Living Wesley* (2nd ed.; London, 1891); G. J. Stevenson, *Memorials of the Wesley Family* (London, 1872).

8. G. Every, *The High Church Party, 1688–1718* (London, 1956).

9. C. J. Abbey and J. H. Overton, *The English Church in the Eighteenth Century* (2 vols.; London, 1878), I, 135f.; II, 67–72. See also G. W. O. Addleshaw, *The High Church Tradition* (London, 1941); P. E. More and F. L. Cross, *Anglicanism* (Milwaukee, 1935), especially P. E. More, "The Spirit of Anglicanism" and F. R. Arnott, "Anglicanism in the Seventeenth Century."

10. Cell, *op. cit.*, 185.

11. J. Wesley, Minutes of the 1745 Conference; quoted in Cell, *op. cit.*, 243.

12. S. Dimond, *The Psychology of the Methodist Revival* (London, 1926), 235.

13. Cf. Cell's comment, "The Wesleyan reconstruction of the Christian ethic of life is an original and unique synthesis of the Protestant ethic of grace with the Catholic ethic of holiness" (*op. cit.*, 347).

14. E. Underhill, *Worship* (New York, 1937), 303–7.

15. See J. E. Rattenbury, *The Eucharistic Hymns of John and Charles Wesley* (London, 1948) for discussion and for a reprint of the hymns and the "extract" of Brevint's tract.

16. The chief sources for ascertaining Wesley's Eucharistic doctrine are, besides the hymns, the following: "The Duty of Constant Communion" (*Sermons on Several Occasions*, ed. by T. Jackson, 2 vols.; New York, 1831, Sermon No. CVI, written 1732,

revised 1788); "The Means of Grace" (Standard Edition of the *Standard Sermons*, ed. by E. H. Sugden, 2 vols.; London, 1921, sermon XII); "Upon our Lord's Sermon on the Mount, Discourse VI" (ibid., sermon XXI); *Explanatory Notes upon the New Testament* (London, 1755; based on Bengel's *Gnomon*, and constituting with the Standard Sermons the doctrinal standard of British Methodism); *A Roman Catechism, with a Reply Thereto* (*Works*, 3rd American edition, ed. by J. Emory; 7 vols.; New York, 1831, Vol. V); *Popery Calmly Considered* (ibid.); besides hundreds of occasional and incidental references in the *Journal* and the *Letters* (Standard Edition, ed. J. Telford, 8 vols.; London, 1931), together with his revision of the Prayer Book offices and the Thirty-Nine Articles of Religion for the Americans in 1784. See also J. C. Bowmer, *The Sacrament of the Lord's Supper in Early Methodism* (Westminster, 1951).

17. Cf. G. Dix, *The Shape of the Liturgy* (Westminster, 1945), 161.

18. Petition presented to the Virginia Assembly; quoted in C. F. James, *Documentary History of the Struggle for Religious Liberty in Virginia* (Lynchburg, 1900), 75.

19. *Letters*, VII, 237ff.

20. *A Pocket Hymn-Book, designed as a Constant Companion for the Pious* (10th edition; Philadelphia, 1790).

21. J. Lee, *Short History of the Methodists in the United States of America 1766–1809* (Baltimore, 1810), 107.

22. A comparison of the text of Wesley's revision of the Thirty-Nine Articles with the original may be found in R. Emory, *History of the Discipline of the Methodist Episcopal Church* (New York, 1844), 95–109.

23. The sources for Wesley's teaching on Baptism are chiefly the following: *A Treatise on Baptism* (Works, Vol. VI); *Notes upon the New Testament*; the following Standard Sermons: XII, "The Means of Grace;" XIV, "The Marks of the New Birth;" XV, "The Great Privilege of Those That Are Born of God;" XXXVIII, "Original Sin," and XXXIX, "New Birth;" together with Wesley's revision of the Articles of Religion and the offices of the Book of Common Prayer.

24. See especially Standard Sermons XIV, XV, and XXXIX. Wesley very nearly overstated his case in the sermon on Original Sin (XXXVIII), so anxious was he to confute the Socinian views of Dr. John Taylor. Proper emphasis must be allowed his insistent stress on prevenient grace.

25. See N. B. Harmon, *The Rites and Ritual of Episcopal Methodism* (Nashville, 1926) for a detailed study of changes in the offices.

26. H. Wheeler, *History and Exposition of the Twenty-five Articles of Religion of the Methodist Episcopal Church* (New York, 1908), 281.

27. Emory, *op. cit.*, 45. This was in 1784; the action was rescinded in 1786. All subsequent references to Disciplinary provisions are taken from Emory.

28. Cf. F. G. Hibbard, *Christian Baptism* (New York, 1842); *The Religion of Childhood* (Cincinnati, 1864).

29. Cf. L. H. Scott, "Methodist Theology in America in the Nineteenth Century," *Religion in Life*, XXV, 1 (Winter, 1955–56), 87–98.

30. Wheeler, *op. cit.*, 314.

31. Emory, *op. cit.*, 323.

32. Cf. S. E. Mead, "American Protestantism During the Revolutionary Epoch," *Church History*, XXII, 4 (December 1953), 279–97.

*Chapter 6*

Mickle, *A Comparison of the Doctrines of Ministry of Francis Asbury and Philip William Otterbein*

1. These observations are made on the basis of the author's personal experience in dealing with local churches, both of E. U. B. background and of Methodist background.

2. Jack M. Tuell, *The Organization of the United Methodist Church* (Nashville: Abingdon, 1977), 12. Other examples of this conclusion are cited in Paul F. Blankenship "Bishop Asbury and the Germans," *Methodist History*, 4, (April, 1966), 5.

3. Frederick A. Norwood, *The Story of American Methodism* (Nashville: Abingdon, 1974), 429. These differences are outlined more fully in pp. 426–30.

4. "Ministry" is here used in the narrow sense of the professional, full-time office of leadership in the broader ministry of all Christians.

5. Due to limitations of space, we shall ignore the contribution of Jacob Albright and the Evangelical Association.

6. See, e.g., John Lawrence, *The History of the Church of the United Brethren in Christ* (Dayton, Ohio: United Brethren Printing Establishment, W. J. Shuey, Publisher, 1868), who traces the history of the U. B. back through the Waldensians to the primitive church; Nathan Bangs. *A History of the Methodist Episcopal Church,* (New York: Mason and Lane, 1839–1841); Arther C. Core, ed., *Philip William Otterbein: Pastor, Ecumenist* (Dayton, Ohio: The Board of Publication of the Evangelical United Brethren Church, 1968). Or, see Blankenship, *op. cit.*, 5–13.

7. Core, *op. cit.*, 17, 43–49.

8. Francis Asbury, *The Journal and Letters,* ed. Elmer T. Clark, J. Manning Potts, and Jacob S. Payton (Nashville: Abingdon, 1958), I, 4, 10, 16.

9. Frank Baker, *From Wesley to Asbury* (Durham: Duke University Press, 1976), 93–94.

10. Asbury, *Journal*, I, p. 105. The entry is from February 3, 1774, before Otterbein had moved to Baltimore and, presumably before he had met Asbury. It should be noted that Lawrence claims an acquaintance between Asbury and Otterbein as early as 1771, *op. cit.*, 218.

11. A. W. Drury, *History of the Church of the United Brethren in Christ* (Dayton Ohio: Otterbein, 1924) 115.

12. Asbury, *Journal*, I, p. 114. Drury says that this meeting took place on the first day of Otterbein's work in Baltimore, *op. cit.*, 144.

13. Core, *op. cit.*, 32–33; cf., Drury, *op. cit.*, 144. The "Minutes of the Association of Reformed Congregations of Maryland, including Canawacke, Pennsylvania," (known as the Pipe Creek United Brotherhood) from May 1774 to June 1776 are printed in Core, *op. cit.*, 115–19, detailing the organization of these "classes."

14. John Dallas Robertson, "Christian Newcomer (1749–1830), Pioneer of Church Discipline and Union Among the United Brethren in Christ, the Evangelical Association, and the Methodist Episcopal Church" (Ph.D. diss., George Washington University, 1973), 92.

15. Asbury, *Journal*, I, 153.

16. Drury, *op. cit.*, 147.

17. Core, *op. cit.*, 65. Asbury was ordained as deacon and elder at the same conference. It should be noted that Wesley intended Asbury to be "superintendent," not "bishop." Asbury took the title of bishop on his own, in spite of Wesley's objections.

18. Norwood, *op. cit.*, 119–27.

19. Ibid., 133–44. An expanded treatment of this topic by Norwood can be found in "The Shaping of Methodist Ministry," *Religion in Life*, 43 (Autumn 1974), 337–51.

20. This insight came from a lecture by Dr. David C. Steinmetz, September 20, 1979, in the course, "Ordination in the Protestant Tradition."

21. Asbury, *Journal*, I, 513.

22. Henry G. Spayth, *History of the Church of the United Brethren in Christ* (Circleville, Ohio: Conference Office of the United Brethren in Christ, 1851), 59. Spayth was the earliest U. B. historian. Also, Lawrence, *op. cit.*, I, 203–77.

23. Robertson, *op. cit.*, 90, 105. These conclusions are deduced from several primary sources including the *Journal* of Christian Newcomer, the *Reminiscences* of Henry Boehm, and the Minutes of the United Brethren in Christ after 1800.

24. Robertson, *op. cit.*, 101–3. These conclusions are drawn from the *Journal* of Christian Newcomer. It should be noted that when regulations were drawn up, the big meeting (not the annual conference) was the site of examinations and licensing of lay preachers; see the Minutes of the United Brethren in Christ from 1808.

25. Minutes of United Brethren in Christ, September 25, 1800, printed, in Core, *op. cit.*, 120-21, 123, 125-26. The special approval can only be documented in 1800 and afterwards.

26. Spayth, *op. cit.*, 147; Robertson, *op. cit.*, 97–98. Christian Newcomer was an exception in the early years to the general "anti-ecclesiastical order" attitude. He favored a Methodist-like plan among the United Brethren early on, but was constantly opposed until after 1805. Robertson, *op. cit.*, 113–16.

27. Minutes, Core, *op. cit.*, 121.

28. Spayth, *op. cit.*, 83. These details are not recorded in the Minutes.

29. Ibid. Emphasis is mine. Cf., Asbury's claim for episcopal authority which includes the reason, "Because the signs of an apostle have been seen in me." *Journal*, II, 470. Such a self-description is not identical with the description of Otterbein given by Spayth: "he would not be called Chief," *op. cit.*, 133. These two excerpts give some insight into the difference between the two men and their understanding of their office.

30. Spayth, *op. cit.*, 90, 105, 132, 153–54 Minutes, Core, *op. cit.*, 121, 125. Newcomer's *Journal*, even when Otterbein ordained Newcomer, the reference is to "Father Otterbein," quoted in Robertson, *op. cit.*, 172; Asbury, too, called Otterbein "Father," *Journal*, III, 333. It seems significant that, in the official records of the United Brethren in Christ, Otterbein's title does not distinguish him from any of the other brethren. All are "brothers." Asbury, of course is referred to as "Bishop" from the start. The distinction probably rests on the difference between Anglican and Reformed background, which we shall consider in more detail later.

31. We have few extant writings of Otterbein; therefore, we have to extrapolate from a variety of sources to arrive at his understanding of ministry. It seems fair to assume that his unquestioned influence in these first conferences shaped the decisions concerning ministry which are made therein. Thus, we feel justified to use the data from

the 1800–1805 Minutes (the Conferences which Otterbein attended) as sources for his doctrine of ministry.

32. Minutes, Core, *op. cit.*, 122, 123. Emphasis is mine. Virginia followed a kind of *via media*: "Resolved that Daniel Strickler and Christian Krum shall call the preachers in Virginia together and with one another determine how they should preach and rightly arrange their plan."

33. Asbury, *Journal*, II, 400. The one reservation about that statement is that Otterbein may not have considered his connection of "unsectarian preachers" as a "Church."

34. Spayth, *op. cit.*, 143–44. Some exceptions for disciplinary reasons prove the rule. Minutes, Core, *op. cit.*, 121–27, Authorization to preach could also be issued at big meetings by other preachers. See above, n. 24.

35. Drury, *op. cit.*, 237, based on Newcomer's *Journal*.

36. These negotiations have been thoroughly treated in two recent sources: Robertson, *op. cit.*, 117, 155, and Paul F. Blankenship, "History of Negotiations for Union Between Methodists and Non-Methodists in the United States" (Ph.D. diss., Northwestern University, 1965), 177–95. My conclusions are drawn from these two sources.

37. Correspondence on May 10, 1809, quoted in Lawrence, *op. cit.*, I, 350.

38. Correspondence quoted in Robertson, *op. cit.*, 142. Emphasis is mine.

39. Blankenship, "History of Negotiations," *op. cit.*, 193.

40. Drury, *op. cit.*, 258.

41. Quoted in Francis Hollingsworth, "Notices of the Life and Labours of Martin Boehm and William Otterbein; and Other Ministers of the Gospel among the United German Brethren," *The Methodist Magazine*, 6 (July 1823):253.

42. Robertson, *op. cit.*, 153.

43. Asbury, *Journal*, III, 475–92.

44. Core, *op. cit.*, 91.

45. Drury, *op. cit.*, 188, quoting from Newcomer's *Journal*.

46. Core, *op. cit.*, 109–14.

47. Asbury, *Journal*, III, 480.

48. Ibid., 483–84.

49. Ibid., 483.

50. Ibid., 480, 484, quoting Haweis.

51. Ibid., II, 290.

52. Robert Emory, *History of the Discipline of the Methodist Episcopal Church* (New York: Carlton and Porter, 1843), 134–35, 345. It is reasonable to assume that Asbury's doctrine of ministry was congruent with the early *Discipline*.

53. Ibid., 124, 134, 135, 183, 184, 345.

54. David C. Steinmetz, "Asbury's Doctrine of Ministry," *Duke Divinity School Review*, 40 (Winter 1975), 11–12, 17.

55. Ibid., 16; Emory, *op. cit.*, 115.

56. Core, *op. cit.*, 112–14.

57. Spayth, *op. cit.*, 145, 148.

58. "The Constitution," Core, *op. cit.*, 112.

59. See the "Minutes of the Association of Reformed Congregations," Core, *op. cit.*, 115–19.

60. Spayth, *op. cit.*, 105.

61. In what follows, the term "elder" refers to the single order of ordained ministry, not the lay office mentioned above. Spayth, *op. cit.*, 56. Remember also that Otterbein takes part in Asbury's ordination.

62. The office is "not thought to carry any sacerdotal or spiritual authority above that of an ordinary preacher," Robertson, *op. cit.*, 173.

63. Lawrence, *op. cit.*, II, 57, quoted from Minutes of Miami Conference Journal of 1813.

64. Robertson, *op. cit.*, 172–73, relying on Newcomer's *Journal*.

65. We can assume that the ministry of Word and Sacrament is given at the time of ordination, if it has not been previously received.

66. It is noteworthy that Otterbein's will, written in 1805, begins with the words, "In the name of God Amen: I, William Otterbein, Pastor of the Evangelical Reformed Church, do make . . . " It does not mention the United Brethren, let alone the episcopacy. Core, *op. cit.*, 74.

67. Asbury, *Journal*, II, 474; III, 490–492.

68. Emory, *op. cit.*, 130–156; Norwood, *op. cit.*, 138–39; Asbury, *Journal*, III, 487–88.

69. Core, *op. cit.*, 111.

70. Ibid., 113, 110. The preacher was to be chosen by "the male members of the church." Undoubtedly, female preachers were not acceptable, p. 112.

71. Core, *op. cit.*, 102; from one of Otterbein's letters. Cf., Spayth, *op. cit.*, 145–47.

72. Minutes, Core, *op. cit.*, 125; Spayth, *op. cit.*, 165. This late verification (1825) was probably grounded in an earlier practice respecting the customs of the Mennonites.

73. Tuell, *op. cit.*, 92–93.

74. These last three differences are cited in Norwood, *op. cit.*, 427.

## Chapter 7

Gravely, *African Methodisms and the Rise of Black Denominationalism*

1. Woodson, *History of the Negro Church* (Washington: Associated Publishers, 1921). Recent examples of the concept occur in Carol V. R. George, *Segregated Sabbaths: Richard Allen and the Rise of Independent Black Churches, 1760–1840* (New York: Oxford University Press, 1973) and Gayraud S. Wilmore, *Black Religion and Black Radicalism* (New York: Anchor, 1973).

2. *Sketch of the Early History of the African Methodist Episcopal Zion Church with Jubilee Souvenir and an Appendix* (n.p., n.d.), 61–62; *One Hundred Years of the African Methodist Episcopal Zion Church* (New York: A. M. E. Zion Book Concern, 1895), 5–7.

3. John H. Bracey, Jr., August Meier, Elliott Hudwick, eds., *Black Nationalism in America* (Indianapolis: Bobbs-Merrill, 1970), xxvi-xxvii, 3ff; Alain Rogers, "The African Methodist Episcopal Church: A Study in Black Nationalism," *The Black Church*, I (1972), 17–43.

4. For examples of this interpretive perspective, see Theodore Hershberg, "Free Blacks in Antebellum Philadelphia," *Journal of Social History*, 5 (1971–72), 183–209; Ira Berlin, "The Structure of the Free Negro Caste in the Antebellum United States,"

*Journal of Social History*, 9 (1975–76), 297–318 and "Time, Space, and the Evolution of Afro-American Society on British Mainland North America," *American Historical Review*, 85 (February, 1980), 44–78. More directly applicable to the black church are two exceptional essays, George A. Levesque, "Inherent Reformers—Inherited Orthodoxy: Black Baptists in Boston, 1800–1873," *Journal of Negro History*, 60 (October, 1975), 491–525 and Emma Jones Lapansky, "'Since They Got Those Separate Churches': Afro-Americans and Racism in Jacksonian Philadelphia," *American Quarterly*, 32 (Spring, 1980), 54–78. See also Gayraud S. Wilmore, "Reinterpretation in Black Church History," *The Chicago Theological Seminary Register*, 73 (Winter, 1983), 25–37, with the phrase "nationalist aspirations" quoted on p. 30.

5. E. Franklin Frazier, *The Negro Church in America* (New York: Schocken, 1974 ed.), ch. 3 and W. E. B. DuBois, "The Souls of Black Folk" in *Three Negro Classics*, intro. by John Hope Franklin (New York: Avon, 1965), 215.

6. Floyd J. Miller, *The Search for a Black Nationality: Black Colonization and Emigration* (Urbana: University of Illinois Press, 1975), 6–15; Dorothy Sterling, ed., *Speak Out in Thunder Tones: Letters and Other Writings by Black Northerners, 1787–1865* (Garden City: Doubleday, n.d.), 3–12. The manuscript records of the Free African Society of Newport show an entry for June 20, 1793 which notes a contribution by the Rhode Island organization to the African Church building project in Philadelphia, in the Newport Historical Society.

7. *A Dialogue Between a Virginian and an African Minister* (Baltimore: Benjamin Edes for Joseph James, 1810), 37–42. This paper omits consideration of black Methodist churches on Long Island, in Salem, New Jersey, Annapolis, Maryland and West Chester, Pennsylvania which are on Coker's list. There was also an African Presbyterian church in Philadelphia which he did not include, and an African church in Wilmington, North Carolina in 1807, mentioned in *The Journal and Letters of Francis Asbury*, ed. Elmer T. Clark (Nashville: Abingdon, 1958), II, 556, n. 117.

8. The historiographical context of blacks within Methodism is ably demonstrated in Harry V. Richardson, Dark Salvation (Garden City: Doubleday, 1976).

9. Russell E. Richey begins to raise the kind of questions of black denominationalism that American church historians have neglected. See his edited volume, *Denominationalism* (Nashville: Abingdon, 1977), 207–9.

10. *The Letters of Francis Asbury*, 366–67.

11. Allen dates the opening in July, 1794, in *The Life Experience and Gospel Labors of the Rt. Rev. Richard Allen* (New York: Abingdon, 1960), 31. *The Journal of Francis Asbury*, II, 18.

12. Allen, *The Life Experience*, 24, and *Minutes of the Methodist Conferences, Held Annually in America; From 1773 to 1813* (New York: Daniel Hitt and Thomas Ware, 1813), 60.

13. The first published reference to the incident is in the preface to *The Doctrines and Discipline of the African Methodist Episcopal Church* (Philadelphia: John H. Cunningham, 1817), 4. Milton Sernett has refuted the traditional date of 1787 on the basis of records showing that the first gallery at St. George's was constructed in 1792–93. Without denying that the event happened, he proposes a closer chronological connection to the dedication of the first building and the public statement of 1794. See his *Black Religion and American Evangelicalism* (Metuchen: Scarecrow, 1975), 116ff.,

218ff. and Benjamin Tucker Tanner, *An Outline of Our History and Government for African Methodist Churchmen, Ministerial and Lay* (Philadelphia: A. M. E. Book Concern, 1884), 142–48. Allen's account in *The Life Experience* is undated, 25–26, but he attested to the veracity of the incident to answer a disaffected church member, Jonathan Tudas. See Trustees of Bethel and Wesley Churches, *The Sword of Truth* (Philadelphia: J. H. Cunningham, 1823), 13.

14. Allen, *The Life Experience*, 24, and *Minutes of the Methodist Conferences, 1773–1813*, 74, 93, 104.

15. William Douglass, *Annals of the First African Church in the United States of America* (Philadelphia: King and Baird, 1862) 10–11, 15–22, 33–40,45–46; L. H. Butterfield, *Letters of Benjamin Rush* (Princeton: Princeton University Press, 1951), I, 599–600, 602–3, 608–9, 716–17; II, 1071; George W. Corner, ed., *The Autobiography of Benjamin Rush* (Princeton: Princeton University Press, 1948), 202–3, 221; Allen, *The Life Experience*, 29–30.

16. Tanner, *An Outline*, 142–48, contains this important document.

17. Allen, *The Life Experience*, 26–27, and *Minutes of the Methodist Conferences, 1773–1813*, 116, 161. See also George A. Phoebus, ed., *Beams of Light on Early Methodism in America* (New York: Phillips and Hunt, 1887), 217, 222–23.

18. *Articles of Association of the African Methodist Episcopal Church, of the City of Philadelphia, in the Commonwealth of Pennsylvania* (Philadelphia: John Ormred, 1779; reprinted Philadelphia: Historic Publications, n.d.), 3–4, 8, 10; Douglass, *Annals*, 104–6.

19. Jesse Lee, *A Short History of the Methodists* (Baltimore: Magill and Clime, 1810), 271–72; Reginald Hildebrand, "Methodist Episcopal Policy on the Ordination of Black Ministers, 1784–1864," *Methodist History*, 20 (April, 1982), 125–26.

20. Hildebrand, 126–27.

21. *Minutes of the Methodist Conferences, for 1799*, 223–26; for 1805, 343–47. J. R. Flanigen, *Methodism: Old and New* (Philadelphia: J. B. Lippincott, 1880), 51–52, 61–62. The building at Bethel was expanded in 1800. On Allen's secular employment, see George, *Segregated Sabbaths*, 75, 90; Charles H. Wesley, *Richard Allen: Apostle of Freedom* (Washington: Associated, 1935), 99–123; *The Philadelphia Directory for 1798* (n.p., n.d.), 15.

22. *A Collection of Spiritual Songs and Hymns Selected From Various Authors by Richard Allen, African Minister* (Philadelphia: John Ormred, 1801), with a second edition issued later the same year which added ten additional hymns. See Eileen Southern, *The Music of Black Americans: A History* (New York: W. W. Norton, 1971), 86ff., 517.

23. Phoebus, ed., *Beams of Light*, 252–54; *The Journal of Francis Asbury*, 235, 432; Francis H. Tees, *The Ancient Landmark of American Methodism or Historic Old St. George's* (Philadelphia: Message, 1951), 94.

24. George, *Segregated Sabbaths*, 66–69; Allen, *The Life Experience*, 32, 37–41 (for a text of the African Supplement).

25. Allen, *The Life Experience*, 37–41.

26. *The Letters of Francis Asbury*, 366–67.

27. *Minutes of the Methodist Conferences* for 1812, 562. The reconstruction of these events comes from notes taken in the 1816 legal suit (see below, 15), in the Edward

Carey Gardiner Collection, Pennsylvania Historical Society. Though there is no record in his *Letters* or *Journal*, at least one conference was held with Asbury according to these notes and the *A. M. E. Doctrines and Discipline*, 6.

28. J. Emory to "Sir," 6 April, 1815 in the Gardiner Collection articulated the logic of the white elders.

29. Allen, *The Life Experience*, 33–34; *A. M. E. Doctrines and Discipline*, 5–6.

30. See my essay, "Early Methodism and Slavery: The Roots of a Tradition," *The Drew Gateway*, 30 (Spring, 1964), 150–65. A copy of one of the expurgated versions of the Methodist Episcopal *Discipline* is in the Perkins Library Rare Book Room, Duke University. See also George, *Segregated Sabbaths*, 77–80.

31. See the entry for 5 February 1809 in *The Journal of Francis Asbury*, 591. Lorenzo Dow accused Asbury of being jealous of the rising power of Richard Allen, first in print in 1816. See *History of Cosmopolite* (Cincinnati: H. M. Rulison, 1856), 545–48.

32. See notes of the legal suit of 1816 in the Gardiner Collection for confirmation of the public letter by Emory, also mentioned in Allen, *The Experience*, 33–34. For the case of Green v. African Church Called Bethel, see miscellaneous legal notes in the Yeates Papers, Pennsylvania Historical Society and Wesley, *Richard Allen*, 147–48.

33. Allen, *The Life Experience*, 34, and Robert Burch, 16 December 1815, in notes for the legal suit of 1816 in the Gardiner Collection.

34. *Minutes Taken at the Several Annual Conferences of the Methodist Episcopal Church in the United States of America for the Year 1815* (New York: J. C. Totten, 1814), 36.

35. See notice of "Sheriff's sale," dated June 12, 1815 and a copy of the certificate of sale, stating that Allen had purchased the "brick meeting house and Lot of ground" for $9,600, plus two year rent charges amounting to $525. Wesley links the sale to the legal case of 1816, but it clearly belongs to the settlement involving Robert Green, for which see *Richard Allen*, 146.

36. Allen, *The Life Experience*, 34–35, and Richard Allen to Daniel Coker, 18 February 1816, as reprinted in Tanner, *An Outline*, 152–55. See also legal notes for the case of 1816 and Burch's letter of 16 December 1815, in the Gardiner Collection and Wesley, *Richard Allen*, 140–141.

37. *A. M. E. Doctrines and Discipline*, 8–9; Daniel A. Payne, *History of the African Methodist Episcopal Church* (Nashville: A. M. E. Sunday School Union, 1891, reprinted by Arno Press, 1969), 13–14. Blacks in Philadelphia Methodism left to join the Bethel movement, dropping their number from 1371 in 1815 to seventy-five in 1816. See *Minutes* for 1815, 21–29, and for 1816 (New York: J. C. Totten, 1816), 27–35.

38. James A. Handy, *Scraps of African Methodist Episcopal History* (Philadelphia: A. M. E. Book Concern, n.d.), 13–14.

39. *Minutes of the Methodist Conferences, 1773–1813*, 60–61, 75, 154–56.

40. *The Journal of Francis Asbury*, II, 51, 65.

41. Ibid., 129 and *The Letters of Francis Asbury*, 160.

42. Handy, *Scraps*, 14, 24, and James M. Wright, *The Free Negro in Maryland* (New York: Columbia University, 1921), 216.

43. Bettye C. Thomas, "History of the Sharp Street Memorial Methodist Episcopal Church, 1787–1920," pamphlet (n.p., n.d.), unnumbered page 2; Cornelius William

Stafford, *The Baltimore Directory, for 1802* (Baltimore: John W. Butler, n.d.), 64 and A. Hoen, "Baltimore in 1804," Peale Museum, Baltimore; "Improved Plan of the City of Baltimore" in the Lovely Lane Museum and Methodist Historical Society, Baltimore; Wright, 213.

44. Thomas, unnumbered page 3; Wright, 213, 217–18, 222–23; Baltimore City Station Class Records, Lovely Lane Museum; *Biography of Rev. David Smith, of the A. M. E. Church* (Lenia: Xenia Gazette Office, 1881), 28–29. Even after the separation of 1815, the loyalists continued to use the name "African Methodist Episcopal."

45. Coker, *Dialogue*, 41; *Minutes of the Methodist Conferences, 1773–1813*, 420–25, 592–99.

46. Baltimore City Station Class Records.

47. Ibid.

48. Glen A. McAninch, "We'll Pray For You: Methodist Ethnocentrism in the Origins of the African Methodist Episcopal Church in Baltimore," M. A. thesis, University of North Carolina at Chapel Hill, 1973, 41, 50.

49. *Biography of Rev. David Smith*, 26–30. The Baltimore City Station Class Records show forty black classes with 1274 members after Coker's secession. I counted 217 names stricken from the lists.

50. McAninch, 73; Wright, 217–18, 222–23; *Minutes of Two Conferences of the African Methodist Preachers Held At Baltimore and Philadelphia in April and May, 1818* (Philadelphia: Richard Allen, 1818), 9, 14. There were 1322 black Methodists remaining with the Methodist Episcopal societies in 1818, see *Minutes of the Methodist Conferences* for 1818, 22–31.

51. The only extant copy, apparently, of Coker's sermon in the New York Public Library's main branch was torn out of a bound volume of collected pamphlets. A summary of the sermon is in Wesley, *Richard Allen*, 141–42, 150, and an extract is in Herbert Aptheker, ed., *A Documentary History of the Negro People of the United States* (New York: Citadel, 1969, original ed., 1951), 67–69.

52. *A. M. E. Doctrines and Discipline*, 1817, 190. The complete title of Coker's sermon is *Sermon Delivered Extempore in The African Bethel Church in The City of Baltimore, on the 21st of January, 1816, to a Numerous Concourse of People, on Account of the Coloured People Gaining Their Church (Bethel) in The Supreme Court of the State of Pennsylvania, by the Rev. D. Coker, Minister of the Said Church, to Which Is Annexed a List of the African Preachers in Philadelphia, Baltimore &c Who Have Withdrawn from Under the Charge of the Methodist Bishops and Conference, (BUT ARE STILL METHODISTS)*, n.p., n.d.

53. *The Discipline of the African Union Church of the United States of America*, 3rd. ed. enlarged (Wilmington: Porter & Eckel, 1852), iv.

54. John D. C. Hanna, *The Centennial Services of Asbury Methodist Episcopal Church, Wilmington, Delaware. October 13–20, 1889* (Wilmington: Delaware, 1889), 146, 160.

55. See notice in *Mirror of the Times and General Advertiser* (Wilmington), 6 February 1805.

56. Asbury preached in "the African chapel in Wilmington" on May 2, 1810. *The Journal of Francis Asbury*, 636.

57. Hanna, *Centennial Services*, 160, and *The Discipline of the African Union Church*, iii-v.

58. The "Articles of Association" are recorded in the Division of Historical and Cultural Affairs, Department of State, Hall of Records, Dover, Del. Typed versions are in the Historical Society of Delaware, Wilmington. *A Directory and Register for the Year 1814 . . . of the Borough of Wilmington and Brandywine* (n.p.: R. Porter, 1814), as a typed copy in the Historical Society of Delaware, 45–52 shows home addresses and vocations for three-fourths of the charter members of the African Union church.

59. Union Church of Africans v. Ellis Sanders, Court of Errors and Appeals, June term, 1855, typed copy in Historical Society of Delaware, unnumbered page 4; Lewis V. Baldwin, "Invisible Strands of African Methodism," (Ph.D. diss., Northwestern University, 1980), 103–5, 118–22. There were 1263 members in four states in 1837.

60. Baldwin, 105–8.

61. Ibid., 87, and *A Directory and Register for The Year 1814*, 45–52.

62. William J. Walls, *The African Methodist Episcopal Zion Church: Reality of the Black Church* (Charlotte: A. M. E. Zion Publishing House, 1974), 49, quoting the first *Discipline*.

63. Samuel A. Seaman, *Annals of New York Methodism* (New York: Hunt & Eaton, 1892), 465.

64. Walls, *The A. M. E. Zion Church*, 47–48; *The Journal of Francis Asbury*, 55, 95–96.

65. *American Citizen and General Advertizer* (New York), 21 March 1800 as quoted in Walls, *The A. M. E. Zion Church*, 53; also 56–57 where the General Conference report instructed the Zion Society to model itself after the Bethel "Articles of Agreement" or to obtain a charter like white congregations within the New York Conference. *Minutes of the Methodist Conferences 1773–1813*, 247 (for 1800).

66. *Articles of Agreement Between the General Conference of the Methodist Episcopal Church, and the Trustees of the African Methodist Episcopal Church, in the City of New York* (Brooklyn: Thomas Kirk, 1801), 6–7; Walls, *The A. M. E. Zion Church*, 56–57.

67. *The Journal of Francis Asbury*, 506, 568; Walls, *The A. M. E. Zion Church*, 65–69.

68. Dorothy Porter, ed., *Early Negro Writing 1760–1837* (Boston: Beacon, 1971), 343ff., 365ff., 374ff. for three orations. See also Adam Carman, *Oration Delivered at the Fourth Anniversary of the Abolition of the Slave Trade, in the Methodist Episcopal Church, in Second-Street, New York, January 1, 1811* (New York: John C. Totten, 1811) and William Miller, *A Sermon on The Abolition of the Slave Trade: Delivered in the African Church, New York, on The First of January, 1810* (New York: John C. Totten, 1810).

69. David Henry Bradley, Sr., *A History of the A. M. E. Zion Church* (Nashville: Parthenon, 1956), 65–66.

70. There were 963 members of Zion and Asbury churches in 1818. *Minutes Taken at the Several Annual Conferences of the Methodist Episcopal Church in the United States of America. For The Year 1818* (New York: John C. Totten, 1818), 28–37; Christopher Rush, *A Short Account of the Rise and Progress of the African M. E. Church in America* (New York: Christopher Rush, et al., 1866), 32ff.

71. John Jamison Moore, *History of the A. M. E. Zion Church in America* (York: Teachers' Journal Office, 1884), 59.

72. Walls, *The A. M. E. Zion Church*, 76–82.

73. Ibid., 83.

74. *Journal of the General Conference of the Methodist Episcopal Church, 1824*, 244, 246, 254 and Peter Cartwright et al., "Report of the committee to whom was referred the affairs of the people of colour," May 27, 1824, General Conference Papers, Drew University, Madison, N.J.

75. I have examined the beginnings of the fourth black Methodist denomination, "The Social, Political and Religious Significance of the Formation of the Colored Methodist Episcopal Church (1870)," *Methodist History*, 18 (October, 1979), 3–25.

76. Cartwright, "Report of the committee," General Conference Papers.

77. These comparative conclusions come from my current research, a version of which in unpublished form was presented to the Society for Historians of the Early American Republic, July, 1982 in Memphis under the title, "The Exodus: The Emergence of Independent Black Churches in the New Nation, 1787–1821."

78. Mathews, "The Second Great Awakening as an Organizing Process," *American Quarterly*, 21 (1969), 23–43.

## Chapter 8

Lobody, *"That Language Might Be Given Me": Women's Experience in Early Methodism*

1. Margaret Atwood, "Spelling," in Sandra M. Gilbert and Susan Gubar, eds., *The Norton Anthology of Literature by Women: The Tradition in English* (New York: W. W. Norton, 1985), 2299.

2. Ibid., 2298.

3. Russell E. Richey, *Early American Methodism* (Bloomington: Indiana University Press, 1991); Nathan O. Hatch, *The Democratization of American Christianity* (New Haven: Yale University Press, 1989); Donald G. Mathews, "Evangelical America - The Methodist Ideology" in this volume.

4. Maria Harris, *Women and Teaching* (Mahwah: Paulist, 1988), 17.

5. Carol Gilligan, *In A Different Voice: Psychological Theory and Women's Development* (Cambridge: Harvard University Press, 1983); Nancy Seifer, *Nobody Speaks for Me: Self-Portraits of American Working Women* (New York: Simon and Schuster, 1976); Tillie Olsen, *Silences* (New York: Delacorte, 1978); Theodora Penny Martin, *The Sound of Our Own Voices: Women's Study Clubs 1860–1910* (Boston: Beacon, 1987); bell hooks, *Talking Back: Thinking Feminist, Thinking Black* (Boston: South End, 1989).

6. Mathews, op.cit.; see also his *Religion in the Old South* (Chicago: University of Chicago Press, 1977), 101–24; William H. Williams, *The Garden of American Methodism: The Delmarva Peninsula 1769–1820* (Wilmington: Scholarly Resources, 1984); Doris Andrews, "Popular Religion and The Revolution in The Middle Atlantic Ports: The Rise of the Methodists 1770–1800" (Ph.D. diss., University of Pennsylvania, 1986).

7. Nelle Morton, *The Journey Is Home* (Boston: Beacon, 1985), 127–29.

8. Garrettson's manuscripts are held in the Archives of the United Methodist Church at Drew University, Madison, N.J. Her early diaries have been edited by Diane Lobody in "Lost In The Ocean of Love: The Mystical Writings of Catherine Livingston Garrettson" (Ph.D. diss., Drew University, 1990). Preachers' journals cited in this article include "The Journal of Benjamin Lakin, 1794–1820" and "The Journal of Bishop Richard Whatcoat, August 1, 1789 - December 31, 1790" in William Warren Sweet, *Religion on the American Frontier 1783–1840*, vol. 4, *The Methodists* (New York: Cooper Square, 1964), 202–260 and 73–122; Robert Drew Simpson, ed., *American Methodist Pioneer: The Life and Journals of the Rev. Freeborn Garrettson 1752–1827* (Rutland: Academy, 1984); William Watters, *A Short Account of The Christian Experience and Ministerial Labours of William Watters* (Alexandria: S. Snowden, 1806); Thomas Ware, *Sketches of the Life and Travels of Rev. Thomas Ware* (New York: T. Mason and G. Lane, 1839).

9. CLG in Lobody, p. 139. Diaries themselves were a significant place where women found their voices, but that is a whole different line of research. See Harriet Blodgett, *Centuries of Female Days: English Women's Private Diaries* (New Brunswick: Rutgers University Press, 1988).

10. G. B. Trudeau, *You're Never Too Old for Nuts and Berries* (New York: Holt, Rinehart and Winston, 1975, 1976).

11. See Linda Kerber, *Women of the Republic: Intellect and Ideology in Revolutionary America* (New York: W. W. Norton, 1980); and Mary Beth Norton, *Liberty's Daughters: The Revolutionary Experience of American Women 1750–1800* (Boston: Little, Brown, 1980).

12. CLG to Mercy Otis Warren, August 18, 1781.

13. Margaret Livingston to Catharine Livingston (not CLG), October 20, 1776, quoted in Kerber, p. 35.

14. Nathan Hatch, *The Sacred Cause of Liberty: Republican Thought and the Millennium in Revolutionary New England* (New Haven: Yale University Press, 1977), 67.

15. Linda Kerber, "'History Can Do It No Justice': Women and the Reinterpretation of the American Revolution" in Ronald Hoffman and Peter J. Albert, *Women in the Age of the American Revolution* (Charlottesville: University Press of Virginia, 1989), 35.

16. CLG to Mercy Otis Warren, n.d. and CLG to Edward Livingston, October 30, 1785.

17. CLG to Mr. Otis, n.d.

18. Denise Levertov, "Cancion", in Gilbert and Gubar, 1954.

19. Quoted in Hatch, *Sacred Cause*, 64.

20. Benjamin Lakin in Sweet, 226.

21. Marge Piercy, "Unlearning to Not Speak", in *Circles on the Water: Selected Poems* (New York: Alfred A. Knopf, 1985), 97.

22. Thomas Ware, 90.

23. CLG in Lobody, 257–58.

24. William Watters, 76.

25. Ibid., 65–66.

26. CLG to Freeborn Garrettson, March 19, 1792.

27. bell hooks, p. 2.

28. Carolyn Kizer, "Pro Femina," in Gilbert and Gubar, p. 1974.

29. *The Doctrines and Discipline of the Methodist Episcopal Church, in America. With Explanatory Notes, by Thomas Coke and Francis Asbury* (Philadelphia: Henry Tuckniss, 1798), 134.

30. CLG in Lobody, 180, 153, 167.

31. Ibid., 205.

32. Ibid., 204.

33. Ibid., 275.

34. CLG to Kitty Rutsen, March 11, 1793.

35. CLG to Kitty Rutsen, March 17, 1791.

36. CLG in Lobody, 255–56.

37. Ibid., 293.

38. Ibid., 279.

39. CLG to Janet Montgomery, April 1, 1790.

40. Ursula K. LeGuin, *Dancing At the Edge of The World* (New York: Harper and Row, 1989), 160.

41. Richey, 5–11.

42. Ibid., 82.

43. This language riddles the journals and memoirs of the Methodist preachers. See Lakin, Whatcoat, Garrettson, Watters, and Ware, passim.

44. CLG in Lobody, 241.

45. Williams, 110.

46. The Earl of Chesterfield, *Letters to His Son on the Fine Art of Becoming a Man of the World and a Gentleman* (New York: Dingwall-Rock, 1901 reprint edition), vol. 1, 107–8, 267–8.

47. Watters, 46–7.

48. CLG to Kitty Rutsen, December 3, 1791.

49. Richey, 1–20.

50. Jon Butler cites the frequent use of "Father" as a title used by Methodists in referring to the preachers, but Catherine Garrettson uses the term "Brother" exclusively, and the phrase "our brothers in the ministry" regularly. See Butler, *Awash in A Sea of Faith: Christianizing The American People* (Cambridge: Harvard University Press, 1989), 237–38.

51. CLG to Kitty Rutsen, April 4, 1791.

52. A poignant instance of a preacher's attention to women may be found in Freeborn Garrettson, 184–85.

53. Watters, 65–66; Lakin, 240; Garrettson, 177–78; Watters, 27; Ware, 73, 165–67. A similar tradition of gender exchange occurs in the martyrdom accounts of the early Christian churches in the Roman empire.

54. CLG in Lobody, 289, 300–301, 308–9, and passim.

55. Linda Mercadante, *Gender, Doctrine, and God* (Nashville: Abingdon, 1990).

56. CLG in Lobody, 300–301.

*Chapter 9*

Andrews, *The African Methodists of Philadelphia, 1794–1802*

1. Richard Allen, *The Life Experience and Gospel Labours of the Rt. Rev. Richard Allen* (Reprint edition, Nashville, 1960). My description of the black community in late eighteenth-century Philadelphia is based on Gary B. Nash, "Forging Freedom: The Emancipation Experience in the Northern Seaport Cities, 1775–1820" in Ira Berlin and Ronald Hoffman, eds., *Slavery and Freedom in the Age of the American Revolution*, Perspectives on the American Revolution (Charlottesville, Va., 1983), 3–48.

2. Benjamin T. Tanner, *An Apology for African Methodism* (Baltimore, 1867); Daniel A. Payne, *History of the African Methodist Episcopal Church*, 2 pts. (Nashville, 1891); Charles H. Wesley, *Richard Allen: Apostle of Freedom* (Reprint edition, Washington, D.C., 1969); George A. Singleton, *The Romance of African Methodism: A Study of the African Methodist Episcopal Church* (New York, 1952); Carol V. R. George, *Segregated Sabbaths: Richard Allen and the Emergence of the Independent Black Churches, 1760–1840* (New York, 1973); Milton C. Sernett, *Black Religion and American Evangelicalism: White Protestants, Plantation Missions, and the Flowering of Negro Christianity, 1787–1865*, American Theological Library Association Monograph Series, No. 7 (Metuchen, N.J., 1975); Harry V. Richardson, *Dark Salvation: The Story of Methodism as It Developed Among Blacks in America*, C. Eric Lincoln Series on Black Religion (Garden City, N.Y., 1976); Clarence E. Walker, *A Rock in a Weary Land: The African Methodist Episcopal Church During the Civil War and Reconstruction* (Baton Rouge, La. and London, 1982); Julie Winch, "The Leaders of Philadelphia's Black Community, 1787–1848" (Ph.D. diss., Bryn Mawr College, 1982).

George Singleton refers to the list of Bethel's members in his preface to the reprint of Allen's memoir, but does not reproduce or analyze it. Allen, 6.

3. The register covers the years 1793 to 1814, including both classes and admissions, and is recorded in the middle of a volume with "Births & Baptisms 1785 to 1816 St. George's M.E. Church Philada" at one end, and "Marriages 1789–1817 St. George's M.E. Church Philada" at the other, located at the Historical Society of the Eastern Pennsylvania Conference of the United Methodist Church, St. George's United Methodist Church, 4th and New Streets, Philadelphia [hereafter cited as HSEPC]. A microfilm copy is at the Historical Society of Pennsylvania.

4. Thomas Morrell, "Journal," 1789–1809, typescript, Drew University Library, Madison, N.J. For Morrell's stationing in Philadelphia, see Methodist Episcopal Church, *The Minutes of the Methodist Conferences, Annually Held in America from 1773 to 1813, inclusive* (New York, 1813).

5. The register for members received on trial begins with December 10, 1793. Thomas Morrell's admissions begin on May 11, 1794 following the note "The above admitted by Freeborn Garritson. The following by Thos. Morrell." Black members whose names appear from January through September 1794 are: Mary Holmes, Jane Vandergraff, Lydia Posey, Thomas Jonson, Benjamin Ellis, John Burkib, Jenny Gibbs, James Gibbs, Dinah Richardson, Betty Sampson, Henry Norton, and Peter Sampson.

6. Smith was a house carpenter and Blair, a shoemaker. *The Philadelphia Directory*, ed., Clement Biddle (Philadelphia, 1791); *The Philadelphia Directory and Register*, ed., James Hardie (Philadelphia, 1793).

7. Jonathan York's occupation and residence are listed in *The Philadelphia Directory and Register* and U.S. Bureau of the Census, Department of Commerce and Labor, *Heads of Families at the First Census of the United States Taken in the Year 1790: Pennsylvania* (Reprint edition, Washington, D.C., 1908). He is identified as a "Negroe" in the Philadelphia County Tax Assessment Ledger, Southwark (West) Ward, 1799, Philadelphia City Archives.

A full discussion of African Methodists forms part of my longer study, "Methodists and Early American Society: The Shaping of Popular Religion in the Middle Atlantic, 1770–1800," to be submitted as a dissertation at the University of Pennsylvania.

8. Allen, 15–24; [Free African Society], "Minutes" in William Douglass, comp., *Annals of the First African Church* (Philadelphia, 1862), 15ff. The context for the founding of the Free African Society is discussed in Gary B. Nash, "'To Arise Out of the Dust': Absalom Jones and the African Church of Philadelphia, 1785–1795," Paper delivered at Philadelphia Center for Early American Studies seminar, 24 September 1982. Nash comments on the compatibility of American Anglicanism with many of Philadelphia's blacks. ibid., 13, 19.

9. Allen, 25.

10. "Acct of the Carpenter Work done by Moseley & Smith at the Methodis [sic] Church 4th Street," 28 May 1792–25 October 1792, HSEPC. Milton Sernett corrects the date of the episode in *Black Religion and American Evangelicalism*, 117–18. Asbury writes in a journal entry dated 8 July 1792: "After twenty years' standing of the house in our hands, the galleries are put up in our old *new* church." *The Journal and Letters of Francis Asbury*, ed., Elmer T. Clark, J. Manning Potts, and Jacob S. Payton, (Nashville, 1958), I, 719.

11. Nash, "Absalom Jones," 18–24; on White and the Quakers, see Benjamin Rush, *The Autobiography of Benjamin Rush: His 'Travels Through Life' Together with his Commonplace Book for 1789–1813*, ed., George W. Corner (Princeton, 1948), 202–3; on the Methodist elder, see Allen, 28–29. The preacher was probably Henry Willis, stationed in Philadelphia in 1792. Methodist Episcopal Church, *Minutes.*

12. Jones, Jennings and White appear in St. Thomas's first membership register in 1794. Douglass, 107–9.

13. Allen, 29; Wesley, 77–81. The first trustees for Bethel, appearing on the chapel's deed of October 13, 1794, are John Allen, Robert Green, William Hoggins, Jacob Johnson, John Morris, and Jonathan Trusty. Cited in Wesley, 79.

14. Allen, 31. Allen dates the opening of Bethel to July, but Asbury first preached there on June 29, 1794. Asbury, II, 18. For a discussion of the neighborhood in which Bethel was located, see Emma Jones Lapsansky, "South Street Philadelphia, 1762–1854: 'A Haven for Those Low in the World'" (Ph.D. diss., University of Pennsylvania, 1975).

15. James Gibbs may have left Bethel for St. George's, but this seems less likely than *vice versa*. [St. George's Methodist Episcopal Church], "The Names of the Officers"; Benjamin T. Tanner, *An Outline of Our History and Government for African Methodist Churchmen, Ministerial and Lay, in Catechetical Form* (n.p., 1884), 19, cited in Nash, "Absalom Jones," note 90.

16. [St. George's Methodist Episcopal Church], "The Names of the Officers."

17. *Articles of Association of the African Methodist Episcopal Church, of the City of Philadelphia, in the Commonwealth of Pennsylvania* (1799, reprinted, Philadelphia,

1969), articles 3, 4, 11, and also 9, 10, 13. Bethel's ecclesiastical battles with St. George's continued until the founding of the separate African Methodist Episcopal Church in Baltimore in 1816. See Wesley, chap. 7, and George, chaps. 2–3.

18. *Articles*, articles 6–8, 10, 11.

19. The dates of admission are omitted here. Asbury, II, 93; on Campington, see Emma Jones Lapsansky, *Before the Model City: An Historical Exploration of North Philadelphia* (Philadelphia, [1968]), 10.

20. McCombs's, Coate's, Higby's and Chandler's appointments are cited in Methodist Episcopal Church, *Minutes*, 246, 262, 278. On the circumstances of Sneath's appointment, see Andrews, chap. 6.

21. The leaders' names have been omitted here. They are: John Walker, William Sturges, John Sullavan, William Fisher, Daniel McCurdy, Hugh McCurdy, and Davis [first name not identifiable].

22. Methodist Episcopal Church, *Minutes*, 243, 259. The opportunity for advancement at Bethel is apparent in the greater power wielded there by members of St. George's and Bethel's first classes once the church was incorporated. Robert Green and Peter Lux from York's class, John Morris from Smith's class, and Allen, William Hogan and Jonathan Trusty from Wildgoose's class were all trustees when the Articles were enacted in 1796. The other trustees are Jupiter Gibson, William Jones and Prince Pruine. *Articles*, 3. See also footnote 13 above.

Bethel's members were also able to achieve rank in the Methodist Episcopal Church: Allen was ordained a deacon in 1799. Wesley, 90.

23. [Philadelphia Yearly Conference], "Deficiencies of the Preachers at the Duck Creek Conference," 2 May 1803, HSEPC.

24. Rush to Sharp [August 1791] in *Letters of Benjamin Rush*, ed., L. H. Butterfield, 2 vols. (Princeton, 1951), I, 608; Nash, "Forging Freedom," 11–15. When two female members with the same last name appear, I have matched just one with a male of the same last name. Hester Thompson was counted once.

25. *The Prospect of Philadelphia, and Check on the Next Directory*, ed., Edmund Hogan (Philadelphia, 1795). Hester Vanderill appears as "Hester Vandergrief." Hester and Jane Vandergrief's last name is variously spelled Vanderill, Vanderiff, Vandergraff and Vandergrief in St. George's records. "Hester Vandergrief" married Lunar Brown in 1796. [St. George's Methodist Episcopal Church], "Marriages 1789–1817," HSEPC.

26. [Port of Philadelphia], Maritime Records, Section V: Alphabetical Masters and Crews, 1709–1880, Historical Society of Pennsylvania, I–V (1798–1805). I consulted these records on the recommendation of Gary Nash.

On Zoar, see *Oxford English Dictionary*, I, 829. Bethel, Zoar, Zion and Bethesda were all names used regularly by Methodists to designate chapels. Ibid.

27. Jane Gray and Favorite Bush left for St. Thomas's. Douglass, 107–9.

28. Winch, 85–87; Philadelphia County Tax Assessment Ledger, New Market Ward, 1791–1794.

29. Philadelphia County Tax Assessment Ledger, South Mulberry Ward, 1794, 1795.

30. Philadelphia County Tax Assessment Ledger, New Market Ward, 1796. Robert Green was a trustee at Bethel by this date: *Articles*, 3; John Burkib appears as "John Burkett" in the Ledger.

31. Philadelphia County Tax Assessment Ledger, Southwark (West), 1799.

32. [Port of Philadelphia], Maritime Records, I, 22, 71, II, 163; Philadelphia County Tax Assessment Ledger, Northern Liberties (East), 1798; [St. George's Methodist Episcopal Church], "Marriages 1789–1817"; *The Philadelphia Directory for 1800*, ed., Cornelius William Stafford (Philadelphia, 1800).

33. A[bsalom] J[ones] and R[ichard] A[llen], *A Narrative of the Proceedings of the Black People During the Late Awful Calamity in Philadelphia* (Philadelphia, 1794), 11; [St. George's United Methodist Church], "Marriages 1789–1817."

34. This important document is reproduced in Sidney Kaplan, *The Black Presence in the Era of the American Revolution*, National Portrait Gallery (Greenwich, Conn., 1973), 238. Pruine appears as "Prince Sprunce." Since he signed with a mark, this was apparently a mishearing of his name. He is listed as a trustee at Bethel in *Articles*, 3.

## Chapter 10

Carwardine, *Methodist Ministers and the Second Party System*

1. See, in particular, M. J. Heale, *The Making of American Politics 1750–1850* (London, 1977), pp. 140–202; Lee Benson, *The Concept of Jacksonian Democracy: New York as a Test Case* (Princeton, 1961); Richard P. McCormick, *The Second American Party System: Party Formation in the Jacksonian Era* (Chapel Hill, 1966); Ronald P. Formisano, *The Birth of Mass Political Parties: Michigan, 1827–1861* (Princeton, 1971); Michael F. Holt, *The Political Crisis of 1850s* (New York, 1978).

2. Charles C. Goss, *Statistical History of the First Century of American Methodism* (New York, 1866), p. 110.

3. Thomas B. Alexander, 'Presidential Election of 1840 in Tennessee', *Tennessee Historical Quarterly*, 1 (1942), 26–27, 34–36; Hugh McCulloch, *Men and Measures of Half a Century* (New York, 1888), pp. 54–56; *Western Christian Advocate* [Cincinnati], 7 Aug. 1840. For cross-fertilization from the world of politics to the churches, see the New York *Christian Advocate and Journal*, 29 Sept. 1841, which advocated the use of 'reclaiming committees' in pursuing backsliders.

4. Formisano, *Mass Political Parties*, pp. 153–55, 312–15. Seymour M. Lipset, 'Religion and Politics in the American Past and Present' in Robert Lee and Martin E. Marty, eds. *Religion and Social Conflict* (New York, 1964), 69–126, is a suggestive essay.

5. Heman Bangs, *The Autobiography and Journal of Rev. Heman Bangs...* (New York, 1872), 316; T. M. Eddy to A. White, 9 Nov. 1844, 1 Mar. 1845, Thomas M. Eddy Papers, Garrett-Evangelical Theological Seminary Library; Walter C. Palmer, *Life and Letters of Leonidas L. Hamline* (New York, 1866), 88; *Pittsburgh Christian Advocate*, 11 Nov. 1840; Daniel Dorchester, 'Rev. Daniel De Vinne', New England Conference Collection, Boston University; Thomas B. Miller, *Original and Selected Thoughts on the Life and Times of Rev. Thomas Miller and Rev. Thomas Warburton* (Bethlehem, Pa., 1860), 17; *Christian Advocate and Journal*, 28 Oct. 1840; *Western Christian Advocate*, 12 Feb. 1841.

6. George R. Crooks, *The Life of Bishop Matthew Simpson* (London, 1890), p. 168; *Pittsburgh Conference Journal*, 26 Mar. 1840; *Western Christian Advocate*, 30 Nov. 1840, 11 June 1841; *Christian Advocate and Journal*, 25 Sept. 1856, 20 Dec. 1860.

Cf. *Southern Christian Advocate* [Charleston, S.C.], 23 Oct. 1856; David Lewis, *Recollections of a Superannuate; or, Sketches of Life, Labor and Experience in the Methodist Itinerancy* (Cincinnati, 1857), 293–96; Bangs, *Journal and Autobiography*, 257.

7. R. Emory to J. McClintoch, 14 Sept. 1840, and J. P. Fort, 'Reminiscences', 238, manuscript collection, Drew University; *Pittsburgh Christian Advocate*, 11 Nov. 1840. The impact of electoral campaigns on Methodist patterns of revival—as compared to the *supposed* impact, which is all that matters in the present context—deserves attention in its own right.

8. *Western Christian Advocate*, 10 July, 18 Dec. 1840, 30 July 1841; *Christian Advocate and Journal*, 2 Sept., 4 Nov. 1840; Chauncey Hobart, *Recollections of My Life: Fifty Years of Itinerancy in the Northwest* (Redwing, Minn., 1885), 202–3; Benjamin F. Tefft, *The Republican Influences of Christianity: a discourse delivered on occasion of the death of William Henry Harrison . . .* (Bangor, Maine, 1841), especially pp. 13–15; Alfred Brunson, *A Western Pioneer: or, Incidents of the Life and Times of Rev. Alfred Brunson, A.M., D.D., embracing a period of over seventy years*, 2 vols. (Cincinnati, 1880), 2: 136–37; La Roy Sunderland to E. Kibby, 9 Sept. 1835, and R. M. Burt to 'Mr. Cox', 20 June 1848, New England Conference Collection.

9. *Western Christian Advocate*, 30 Oct., 25 Dec. 1840, 17 Dec. 1841, 19 Aug., 16 Sept., 11 Nov. 1842; George Peck, *National Evils and Their Remedy: a discourse delivered on the occasion of the National Fast, May 14, 1841 . . .* (New York, 1841), 12–13; Matthew Simpson, 'Reasons for Building a Metropolitan Church in Washington', 3–4, manuscript collection, Drew University; *Christian Advocate and Journal*, 23 June 1841; Tefft, *Republican Influences of Christianity*, 15–17.

10. *Western Christian Advocate*, 1 Jan., 21 May, 30 July, 17 Dec. 1841, 19 Aug., 14 Oct. 1842; George Peck, *The Life and Times of George Peck, D.D.* (New York, 1874), 217–19; R. Emory to C. W. Emory, 9 Nov., 13 Nov. 1844, manuscript collection, Drew University; *Christian Advocate and Journal*, 23 Oct. 1856; Brunson, *Western Pioneer*, 1: 334–45; Dan Young, *Autobiography of Dan Young*, ed. W. P. Strickland (New York, 1860), 273–75.

11. William Warren Sweet, *Religion on the American Frontier*, vol. IV: *The Methodists, 1783–1840* (Chicago, 1946), 455; E. Mudge to B. Pitman, 22 Oct. 1844, and J. Bontecou to S. L. Pease, 17 Aug. 1840, New England Conference Collection; *Western Christian Advocate*, 17 July 1844. For Garrisonian anarchism, see especially, Lewis Perry, *Radical Abolitionism: Anarchy and the Government of God in Anti-slavery Thought* (Ithaca, 1973).

12. H. H. Green, *The Simple Life of a Commoner: An Autobiography* (Decorah, Iowa, 1911), 51–52; *Christian Advocate and Journal*, 3 Aug. 1842. Cf. William E. Gienapp, '"Politics Seem to Enter into Everything': Political Culture in the North, 1840–1860", in Stephen E. Maizlish and John J. Kushma, eds. *Essays on American Antebellum Politics, 1840–1860* (Arlington, Tex., 1983).

13. *Western Christian Advocate*, 19, 26 Feb., 9 Apr. 1841; Tefft, *Republican Influences of Christianity*, 6 and passim.

14. See, for example, Leonidas Hamline's editorials on 'Christian Patriotism' in *Western Christian Advocate*, 31 July, 7 Aug. 1840.

15. Ibid., 17 Dec. 1841, 22 Jan. 1842.

16. Ibid., 7 Aug., 25 Sept. 1840, 24 Sept. 1841; Thomas O. Summers, *Christian Patriotism: a sermon preached in Cumberland-St. M. E. Church, Charleston, S.C., on Friday, Dec. 6, 1850...* (Charleston, S.C., 1850), passim.

17. *Christian Advocate and Journal,* 28 Oct. 1840, 30 Oct. 1856; *Western Christian Advocate,* 30 Oct. 1840, 26 Mar. 1841; William G. W. Lewis, *Biography of Samuel Lewis, first superintendent for common schools for the state of Ohio* (Cincinnati, 1857), 369; Lewis, *Recollections of a Superannuate,* 294; A. Wood to L. Smith *et al.,* Aug. 1860, Matthew Simpson Papers, Library of Congress.

18. George Coles, 'Journal', 5 Nov. 1844, manuscript collection, Drew University; cf. 5 Nov. 1854, where he condoned a 'harsh and vulgar' translation of a Pauline epistle since it was designed to drive home the Methodist's duty to vote.

19. Sweet, *The Methodists,* 428, 436; newspaper cutting from the *Madison Courier,* n.d., Eddy Papers, Garrett-Evangelical Theological Seminary Library; T. M. Eddy, 'Sermon on the Death of General Z. Taylor ... July 1850' in ibid.; *Christian Advocate and Journal,* 28 Oct. 1840; *Western Christian Advocate,* 7 Aug., 30 Oct. 1840, 21 May, 4 June 1841, 9 Dec. 1842; *Pittsburgh Conference Journal,* 5 Sept. 1839, 17 Sept. 1840; Calvin Fairbank, *Rev. Calvin Fairbank during Slavery Times: How He "Fought the Good Fight" to Prepare "The Way"* (Chicago, 1890), 168; Lewis, *Samuel Lewis,* 325, 343.

20. John F. Wright, *Sketches of the Life and Labors of James Quinn* (Cincinnati, 1851), 188–89; W. J. Rorabaugh, *The Alcoholic Republic: An American Tradition* (New York, 1979), 220; *Christian Advocate and Journal,* 2 Sept. 1840, 3 Aug. 1842, 25 Sept., 30 Oct. 1856; *Western Christian Advocate,* 10 July, 4 Sept. 1840, 26 Mar. 1841; Sweet, *The Methodists,* 643; *Pittsburgh Conference Journal,* 21 Mar. 1840; Jacob B. Moore, *The Contrast: or, plain reasons why William Henry Harrison should be elected President of the United States...* (New York, 1840), 5; L. W. Berry to M. Simpson, 30 July, Simpson Papers, Library of Congress.

21. T. A. Morris to M. Simpson, 16 Aug. 1848, Simpson Papers, Library of Congress.

22. *Christian Advocate and Journal,* 19 Aug. 1840, 23, 30 June 1841, 13 July 1842, 21 Jan. 1846, 17 Jan. 1856; *Pittsburgh Christian Advocate,* 2 Apr. 1841; Enoch M. Marvin, *The Life of Rev. William Goff Caples of the Missouri Conference of the Methodist Episcopal Church, South* (St. Louis, 1871), 258–59.

23. Frances M. B. Hilliard, *Stepping Stones to Glory: From Circuit Rider to Editor and the Years in Between: Life of David Rice McAnally, D.D. 1810–95* (Baltimore, 1975), 55–61; *Ohio State Journal,* 14 Dec. 1839, 16 Sept. 1840; Brunson, *Western Pioneer,* 2: 212–13; Helen H. Grant, *Peter Cartwright: Pioneer* (New York, 1931), 148–55; *Western Christian Advocate,* 10 July 1840; *Christian Advocate and Journal,* 2 Sept. 1840; William McDonald and John E. Searles, *The Life of Rev. John S. Inskip, President of the National Association for the Promotion of Holiness* (Chicago, 1885), 49. Joseph Creighton believed that it was his own Democratic political allegiance that spurred his Whig presiding elder to obstruct his entry into the travelling ministry. Joseph H. Creighton, *Life and Times of Joseph H. Creighton, A.M., of the Ohio Conference* (Cincinnati, 1899), 24, 67.

24. George C. Baker, *An Introduction to the History of Early New England Methodism 1789–1839* (Durham, N.C., 1941); Brunson, *Western Pioneer,* 1: 27–30,

35–43, 171–73; A. Hunt, 'Reminiscences'; 22 Mar. 1847: J. B. Thomas to A. Stevens, 8 Oct. 1860: D. D. Kilburn, ms. recollections: G. Bickering to E. Kibby, 19 Dec. 1798: manuscript collection, Drew University; Daniel De Vinne, *Recollections of Fifty Years in the Ministry . . .* (New York, 1869), 14–15, 31–32; *Christian Advocate and Journal*, 23 Oct. 1856. In Connecticut in the first decade of the century, '[t]he great mass, if not the entire, of the Methodist Church and her adherents were Republicans, and so were the entire infidel portion of the community . . . [E]very convert to Methodism . . . became a Republican, if he was not one before.' Brunson, *Western Pioneer*, 1:43.

25. Ray Holder, *William Winans: Methodist Leader in Antebellum Mississippi* (Jackson, Miss., 1977), 36; Selah Stocking, 'A Brief Sketch of the History of the Rev. Jeremiah Stocking, New England Conference Collection; Young, *Autobiography*, 4, 101–3, 278–90.

26. Arthur M. Schlesinger, Jr., *The Age of Jackson* (Boston, 1945), 350–60; Benson, *Concept of Jacksonian Democracy*, 86–109.

27. Septimus Stocking, 'A Brief Historical Sketch of the life of the Rev. Solon Stocking', New England Conference Collection; William Gordon, 'Autobiography', ibid.; McCulloch, *Men and Measures*, 75; Benson, *Concept of Jacksonian Democracy*, 191–92; Formisano, *Birth of Mass Political Parties*, 153–55; Donald B. Cole, 'The Presidential Election of 1832 in New Hampshire', *Historical New Hampshire* 21 (1966), 40–42, 49; E. R. Ames to M. Simpson, 21 Jan. 1845, 5 Jan. 1849, Simpson Papers, Library of Congress; Thomas H. Pearne, *Sixty-One Years of Itinerant Christian Life in Church and State* (Cincinnati, 1898), 49.

28. S. D. Lewis to G. Peck, 3 Nov. 1828, George Peck Papers, Syracuse University Library; Holder, *William Winans*, 76, 94, 99; William Winans, *A Funeral Discourse on Occasion of the Death of Hon. Henry Clay . . .* (Woodville, Miss., 1852), 9; R. Emory to J. Nicols, 11 Apr. 1831, G. R. Crooks to J. McClintock, 21 Oct. 1848, J. McClintock to R. Emory, 23 Jan. 1848, G. Coles to G. Cubitt, 21 Feb. 1845, manuscript collection, Drew University; Moses M. Henkle, *The Life of Henry Biddleman Bascom* (Nashville, 1856), 105–7, 281–85; George G. Smith, *The Life and Letters of James Osgood Andrew, Bishop of the Methodist Episcopal Church South* (Nashville, 1883), 436; *Western Christian Advocate*, 5, 26 Mar. 1851; Hobart, *Recollections,* 200–202; W. W. Hibben, *Rev. James Havens* (Indianapolis, 1872), p. 182; McDonald and Searles, *Life of Inskip*, 66–67, 75–76; James Dixon, *Personal Narrative of a Tour through a part of the United States and Canada: with notices of the History and Institutions of Methodism in America* (New York, 1849), 63.

29. George Brown, *Recollections of Itinerant Life: including early reminiscences*, 3rd edition (Cincinnati, 1866), 269–70; Brunson, *Western Pioneer*, 1:138.

30. Leonard W. Levy, 'Satan's Last Apostle in Massachusetts', *American Quarterly* 5 (1953), 16–30; Benson, *Concept of Jacksonian Democracy*, 193–97.

31. Benson, *Concept of Jacksonian Democracy*, 171; William G. Brownlow, *A Political Register, Setting forth the Principles of the Whig and Locofoco Parties in the United States, with the Life and Public Services of Henry Clay* (Jonesboro, Tenn., 1844), 77, 109–11, 113–16; *Christian Advocate and Journal*, 27 Apr., 18 Nov. 1842; *Western Christian Advocate*, 12 Nov. 1841, 8 July 1842.

32. Glyndon G. Van Deusen, 'Seward and the School Question Reconsidered', *Journal of American History* 52 (1965), 313–19; Louis D. Scisco, *Political Nativism in*

*New York State* (New York, 1901), 29–38. For an examination of the Whigs as the 'Christian Party' in 1840, see Richard Carwardine, 'Evangelicals, Whigs and the Election of William Henry Harrison', *Journal of American Studies* 17(1983).

33. J. Cutler Andrews, 'The Antimasonic Movement in Western Pennsylvania', *Western Pennsylvania Historical Magazine* 18 (1935), 255–66; Sweet, *The Methodists*, p. 284; T. J. Brown to M. Simpson, 13 Apr. 1850, Simpson Papers, Library of Congress; James Erwin, *Reminiscences of Early Circuit Life* (Toledo, Ohio, 1884), pp. 61–62; John Burgess, *Pleasant Recollections of Characters and Works of Noble Men* (Cincinnati, 1887), pp. 211–13; Holder, *William Winans*, pp. 104, 108; Ronald Formisano, 'Political Character, Antipartyism and the Second Party System', *American Quarterly* 21 (1969), 683–709; *Western Christian Advocate*, 30 Apr. 1841.

34. Branson, *Western Pioneer*, I: 43, 285–86; J. Copeland to D. P. Kidder, 20 Feb. 1839, Daniel P. Kidder Papers, Garrett-Evangelical Theological Seminary Library; *Pittsburgh Conference Journal*, 20 Feb. 1840; *Western Christian Advocate*, 3, 17, Jan., 27 Mar., 13 Nov. 1840, 29 Jan., 19, 26 Mar., 2, 30 Apr., 13 Aug., 15, 22 Oct., 24 Dec. 1841; Luther Lee, *Autobiography of the Rev. Luther Lee, D.D.* (New York, 1882), 233; *Ohio State Journal*, 5 Aug. 1840, 20 Feb., 3 Mar. 1841; *Christian Advocate and Journal*, 25 May 1842; Tefft, *Republican Influences of Christianity*, 10–11.

35. William G. McLoughlin, Jr., *Modern Revivalism: Charles Grandison Finney to Billy Graham* (New York, 1959), 4–165; Richard Carwardine, *Transatlantic Revivalism: Popular Evangelicalism in Britain and America, 1790–1865* (Westport, Conn., 1978), 3–18.

36. *Western Christian Advocate*, 21 Feb., 6 Mar., 4 Sept. 1840, 27 Mar., 4 June, 9 July 1841; *Christian Advocate and Journal*, 14 Dec. 1842, 17, 31 Dec. 1845, 4 Nov. 1846, 24 Feb. 1847; Timothy L. Smith, *Revivalism and Social Reform in Mid-Nineteenth-Century America* (New York, 1957), 103–47. Cf. Daniel Wise, *Popular Objections to Methodism Considered and Answered . . .* (Boston, 1856), 121 and passim.

37. William McDonald, *History of Methodism in Providence, Rhode Island from its Introduction in 1787 to 1867* (Boston, 1868), 47–48, 53–54; Bertram Wyatt-Brown, 'Prelude to Abolitionism: Sabbatarian Politics and the Rise of the Second Party System', *Journal of American History* 58 (1971), 334; Stephen Parks, *Troy Conference Miscellany, containing a Historical Sketch of Methodism within the Bounds of the Troy Conference of the Methodist Episcopal Church* (Albany, 1854), 67. John Durbin, Henry Bascom, John Newland Maffit, George Cookman and William Daily, amongst others, kept the Methodist flag flying in Congress.

38. Stocking, 'Sketch of Selah Stocking', New England Conference Collection; Gordon, 'Autobiography', ibid.; *Christian Advocate and Journal*, 20 Oct. 1847; R. Emory to J. Nicols, 8 July 1813, manuscript collection, Drew University; George Peck, *The Past and the Present: a semi-centennial sermon . . .* (New York, 1866), 10–22; A. G. Porter to M. Simpson, 26 Oct. 1844, Simpson Papers, Library of Congress.

39. J. Drummond to M. Simpson, 20 Apr. 1850, Simpson Papers, Library of Congress; Milton Haney, *The Story of My Life* (Normal, Ill., 1904), 115–16; George Coles, *My First Seven Years in America* (New York, 1852); Talbot W. Chambers, *The Noon Prayer Meeting of the North Dutch Church, Fulton St., New York: Its Origin, Character and Progress* (New York, 1858), 247; *Christian Watchman and Reflector* [Boston], 24 Apr. 1856.

40. Lewis, *Samuel Lewis*, pp. 286–302, 318, and passim; *Western Christian Advocate*, 13 Aug. 1841.

41. Freeborn G. Hibbard, *Biography of Rev. Leonidas L. Hamline, D.D., late one of the Bishops of the Methodist Episcopal Church* (Cincinnati, 1880), pp. 190–222, 239–40; *Christian Advocate and Journal*, 5, 12 Oct., 11, 18, 25 Nov. 1846, 20, 27 Jan., 3, 10, 24 Feb., 6, 27 Oct., 3 Nov. 1847; McDonald and Searles, *Life of Inskip*, 66–67, 75–76; J. McClintock to S. Olin, 31 Oct. 1844, manuscript collection, Drew University.

42. F. D. Hemenway, 'Oration for July 4, 1851', Francis D. Hemenway Papers, Garrett-Evangelical Theological Seminary Library; William T. Worth, 'A sketch of the Life and Labors of the Rev. Asa Kent, 1780–1860', 28–29, New England Conference Collection; J. C. Clambers to M. Simpson, 2 May 1850, J. Drummond to M. Simpson, 8 May 1850, W. Ternell to M. Simpson, 20 Aug. 1851, Simpson Papers, Library of Congress; S. P. Chase to M. Simpson, 26 Apr. 1850, manuscript collection, Drew University.

43. E. Merton Coulter, *William G. Brownlow: Fighting Parson of the Southern Highlands* (Chapel Hill, N.C., 1937), 119; *Christian Advocate and Journal*, 22 Dec. 1847; David M. Potter, *The Impending Crisis 1848–1861* (New York, 1976), 225–65.

44. *Western Christian Advocate*, 11 Aug., 29 Dec. 1852, 2 Feb., 30 Mar. 1853; Hemenway, 'Diary', 8 Feb. 1853, Garrett-Evangelical Theological Seminary; Coles, 'Journal', 8 Nov. 1853 [cf. entries for 27 June, 9 Sept., 5 and 7 Nov. 1854], manuscript collection, Drew University.

45. William H. Daniels, *Memorials of Gilbert Haven, Bishop of the Methodist Episcopal Church* (Boston, 1882), p. 55; *Western Christian Advocate*, 14 Feb. 1855; J. A. Wright to M. Simpson, 23 Oct. 1854, Simpson Papers, Library of Congress. For Methodist and other evangelical opposition to Know-Nothingism, see Lewis, *Samuel Lewis*, 373; Augustus B. Longstreet, *Know Nothingism Unveiled* (Washington, 1855); Richard Carwardine, 'The Know Nothing Party, The Protestant Evangelical Community and American National Identity', in Stuart Mews, ed., *Studies in Church History*, vol. 18: *Religion and National Identity* (Oxford, England, 1982), 449–63.

46. McDonald and Searles, *Life of Inskip*, pp. 75–76; *Western Christian Advocate*, I, 15 May 1850; J. L. Smith to M. Simpson, 23 May 1850, B. F. Crary to M. Simpson, 31 May 1851, Simpson Papers, Library of Congress; *Correspondence of Andrew Jackson*, ed. John Spencer Bassett, 7 vols. (Washington, D.C., 1926–35), 6:84; *Christian Advocate and Journal*, 12 June 1856. Cf. Wesley Norton, *Religious Newspapers in the Old Northwest to 1861: A History, Bibliography, and Record of Opinion* (Athens, Ohio, 1977), 122.

47. *Western Christian Advocate*, 26 Mar. 1841; *Pittsburgh Christian Advocate*, 30 Apr. 1840; *Christian Advocate and Journal*, 2 Sept. 1840, 17 Nov. 1841; Lewis, *Samuel Lewis*, p. 318; L. W. Berry to M. Simpson, 9 Aug. 1849, Simpson Papers, Library of Congress.

48. *Christian Advocate and Journal*, 2 Sept. 1846.

## Chapter 11

### McKay, *Nineteenth-century Black Women's Spiritual Autobiographies: Religious Faith and Self-Empowerment*

1. See William L. Andrews, *To Tell a Free Story: The first One Hundred Years of Afro-American Autobiography*—a groundbreaking book on early Afro-American autobiography. This text includes the exploration of male and female slave and spiritual autobiographies. Andrews also deserves special credit for his work in *Sisters of the Spirit: Three Black Women's Autobiographies in the Nineteenth Century*, the first anthology to focus specifically on black women's spiritual experiences.

2. In addition to the slave and spiritual narratives, there were the male "criminal" confession narratives in the eighteenth and nineteenth centuries. These were stories recorded from testimony given before the subject's execution. Perhaps the most famous is *The Confessions of Nat Turner*, but others such as *The life and confession of Johnson Green, who is to be executed this day, August 17, 1786, for the atrocious crime of burglary; together with his last dying words*, a broadside published in Worcester, Massachusetts, were not unusual.

3. See Pamela S. Bromberg, "The Development of Narrative Technique in Margaret Drabble's Novels," 179.

4. Albert Stone, *Autobiographical Occasions and Original Acts: Versions of American Identity from Henry Adams to Nate Shaw*, 5.

5. Andrews, *To Tell a Free Story*, 2–3.

6. Stone, 10.

7. Robert Stepto, *From behind the Veil: A Study of Afro-American Narrative*, 3.

8. Andrews, *To Tell a Free Story*, 64.

9. See ibid., pp. 32–60, for an extended discussion on this subject.

10. George White, *A brief account of the life, experiences, travels, and gospel labours of George White, an African, written by himself and revised by a friend* (New York: John C. Totten, 1810).

11. As a large number (reprints and new works) of black autobiographical texts have become available for classroom use (in contrast to their paucity even five years ago), critical essays and longer studies of the genre keep pace with other scholarship in Afro-American literature and history. Among longer works in progress are at least two books on black women's narratives.

12. See Cheryl Gilkes, "'Together in Harness': Women's Traditions in the Sanctified Church," 678–99. Although the essay refers specifically to the Sanctified Church, these qualities have been hallmarks of women's groups among all sects within the black church.

13. See Jean McMahon Humez, *Gifts of Power: The Writings of Rebecca Cox Jackson, Black Visionary, Shaker Eldress*, 262. All other references to Jackson's journal come from this text. Humez's fine editing of the journals deserves special commendation. In addition, her excellent introduction to the work provides a good deal of information on Jackson and others in the context of black women's spiritual lives in the nineteenth century.

14. Jarena Lee, *The Life And Religious Experience of Jarena Lee, a Coloured Lady, Giving an Account of Her Call to Preach the Gospel: Revised and Corrected from the*

*Original Manuscript by Herself,* in *Sisters of the Spirit: Three Black Women's Autobi-ographies in the Nineteenth Century,* ed. William Andrews. Further references to this narrative are taken from this text.

15. According to Humez, her research revealed that black and white groups of women assembled in small prayer groups seeking the "blessing of perfect love" as early as 1819 in New York. Rebecca Cox Jackson refers to her mother as belonging to such a group when she (Rebecca) was a girl. Amanda Smith, another black female spiritual autobiographer, reports that in the 1890s she saw modestly dressed (somewhat like Quakers) Methodist women in Philadelphia, New York, and Baltimore who were known as "Band Sisters." See Humez, 315.

16. Often in Jackson's text after she relates an event, she will write—as though aware of a lack of clarity for the reader—"I should have said first . . . ," and then will relate a previously omitted incident that bears on the point she wants to make.

17. Marilyn Richardson pointed out to me that we know very little about the intellectual thought of black women in the nineteenth century: of what they read and with whom they discussed important issues of the time. In some cases, we are unaware of the accurate pronunciations of their names.

18. See Barbara Leslie Epstein, *The Politics of Domesticity: Women, Evangelism, and Temperance in Nineteenth-Century America,* 45–65, for a discussion of white women in the religious movement of the late eighteenth and early nineteenth centuries.

19. Only recently have we begun to address issues of differences among the lives of nineteenth-century black women. Economic and educational status varied widely between them, and were factors that influenced individual vision and individual percep-tions of options.

20. Maria Stewart, born in Boston, was an articulate black feminist abolitionist who is credited as the first American woman to speak from a platform to a "promiscuous" (men and women together) audience. See Marilyn Richardson, ed., *Maria W. Stewart: America's First Black Woman Political Writer, Essays and Speeches* (Bloomington: Indiana University Press, 1987). Frances Harper was a feminist abolitionist writer (poetry, fiction, and nonfiction prose), public speaker, and educator. Her novel *Iola Leroy,* which focuses on black life during Reconstruction, was first published in 1892.

21. Amanda Berry Smith was born of slave parents in Maryland in 1837, but was freed after the death of her mistress, who shortly before had experienced religious conversion. The Berry family moved to Pennsylvania, where at age eight Amanda went to school. Her evangelistic career began in the late 1870s with a trip to England. Later she went to India and then to Africa for eight years. Smith's narrative, *An Autobiogra-phy: The Story of the Lord's Dealings with Mrs. Amanda Smith, the Colored Evangelist,* was published in 1893.

22. Alice Walker, *In Search of Our Mothers' Gardens,* 79.

23. Andrews, *To Tell a Free Story,* 54.

## Works Cited in Chapter 11:

Andrews, William L. *To Tell a Free Story: The First Century of Afro-American Autobi-ography, 1760–1865.* Urbana: University of Illinois Press, 1986.

————, ed. *Sisters of the Spirit: Three Black Women's Autobiographies of the Nine-teenth Century*. Bloomington: Indiana University Press, 1986.

Bromberg, Pamela S. "The Development of Narrative Technique in Margaret Drabble's Novels." *Journal of Narrative Technique* 16, no. 3 (Fall 1986): 179–91.

Epstein, Barbara Leslie. *The Politics of Domesticity: Women, Evangelism, and Temperance in Nineteenth-Century America*. Middletown: Wesleyan University Press, 1981.

Gilkes, Cheryl. "'Together in Harness': Women's Traditions in the Sanctified Church." *Signs: Journal of Women in Culture and Society* 10, no. 4 (Summer 1985): 678–99.

Humez, Jean McMahon, ed. *Gifts of Power: The Writings of Rebecca Jackson, Black Visionary, Shaker Eldress*. Amherst: University of Massachusetts Press, 1981.

Stepto, Robert. *From behind the Veil: A Study of Afro-American Narrative*. Urbana: University of Illinois Press, 1979.

Stone, Albert. *Autobiographical Occasions and Original Acts: Versions of American Identity from Henry Adams to Nate Shaw*. Philadelphia: University of Pennsylvania Press, 1982.

Walker, Alice. *In Search of Our Mothers' Gardens*. New York: Harcourt Brace Jovanovich, 1983.

## Chapter 12

Schneider, *Social Religion, the Christian Home, and Republican Spirituality in Antebellum Methodism*

1. James B. Finley, *Autobiography of Rev. James B. Finley, or Pioneer Life in the West*, ed. W. P. Strickland (Cincinnati, 1854), 240, 241.

2. The methodological focus on ritual here reflects not only the practice of some of the ethnocultural historians cited below, but especially the perspectives of literary critic Kenneth Burke and of his celebrated intellectual borrower, anthropologist Clifford Geertz. See Kenneth Burke, *The Philosophy of Literary Form: Studies in Symbolic Action* (3rd ed., Berkeley 1973), 103ff.; Clifford Geertz, *The Interpretation of Cultures* (New York 1973), 3–30, 112–18; and Geertz, *Local Knowledge: Further Essays in Interpretive Anthropology* (New York, 1983), 55–70.

3. The denominational and regional limits of this paper ought to be avowed and justified. Methodism deserves distinct attention for two reasons. First, Methodist numerical superiority and the dominance of Methodist-style revivalism and social religion in the most widely noted American revivals, such as Charles G. Finney's "New Measures" or the lay-led revivals of 1857–1858, helped give the nineteenth century the title of the "Methodist Age" in American church history. See Sandra S. Sizer, *Gospel Hymns and Social Religion: The Rhetoric of Nineteenth-Century Revivalism* (Philadelphia, 1976), chaps. 3–5; Richard Carwardine, "The Second Great Awakening in the Urban Centers: An Examination of Methodism and the 'New Measures.'" *Journal of American History*, 59 (Sept. 1972), 327–40; Leonard I. Sweet, *The Minister's Wife: Her Role in Nineteenth-Century American Evangelicalism* (Philadelphia, 1983), 78–89; Winthrop S. Hudson, "The Methodist Age in America," *Methodist History*, 12 (Apr. 1974), 2–15; and Edwin Scott Gaustad, *Historical Atlas of Religion in America* (rev.

ed., New York, 1976), 76–80. Second, rather than lump all evangelicals together under a generic label, one ought first to respect the sense of uniqueness the various communities derived from their distinctive usages. On the Methodist sense of uniqueness, see Donald G. Mathews, *Religion in the Old South* (Chicago, 1977), 54–55. This article also attempts to respect what Russell Richey calls the "Southern Accent of American Methodism," (*Methodist History*, 27 [Oct. 1988], 3–24) by focusing on the upper South and lower Midwest, the region of the greatest early Methodist growth and spread. See also Gaustad, *Historical Atlas*, 77–79.

4. Rhys Isaac, *The Transformation of Virginia, 1740–1790* (Chapel Hill, 1982). For similar findings about the role of evangelicalism in the North, see Paul E. Johnson, *A Shopkeeper's Millennium: Society and Revivals in Rochester, New York, 1815–1837* (New York, 1978); and Mary P. Ryan, *Cradle of the Middle Class: The Family in Oneida County, New York, 1790–1865* (Cambridge, England, 1981).

5. Robert Kelley, *The Cultural Pattern in American Politics: The First Century* (New York, 1979). See also Alfred F. Young, ed., *The American Revolution: Explorations in the History of American Radicalism* (DeKalb, Ill., 1976); and Robert E. Shalhope, "Republicanism and Early American Historiography," *William and Mary Quarterly*, 39 (Apr. 1982), 334–56.

6. Bernard Bailyn, *The Ideological Origins of the American Revolution* (Cambridge, Mass., 1967); Gordon S. Wood, *The Creation of the American Republic, 1776–1787* (Chapel Hill, 1969).

7. For a sense of the continuity and change in the historiography of republicanism, compare Shalhope, "Republicanism and Early American Historiography," with the same author's earlier review article, "Toward a Republican Synthesis: The Emergence of an Understanding of Republicanism in American Historiography," *William and Mary Quarterly*, 29 (Jan. 1972), 49–80.

8. This characterization of the ethos of honor and the meaning of liberty within it draws heavily upon Bertram Wyatt-Brown's massive exploration, *Southern Honor: Ethics and Behavior in the Old South* (New York, 1982), esp. chaps. 2 and 3. See also Isaac, *Transformation of Virginia*, chaps. 4–6. On the patriarchal metaphor and its overthrow, see ibid., 20–21; Edwin G. Burrows and Michael Wallace, "The American Revolution: The Ideology and Psychology of National Liberation," *Perspectives in American History*, 6 (1972), 167–306; Winthrop D. Jordan, "Familial Politics: Thomas Paine and the Killing of the King, 1776," *Journal of American History*, 60 (Sept. 1973), 294–308; and, especially, Jay Fliegelman, *Prodigal and Pilgrims: The American Revolution Against Patriarchal Authority, 1750–1800* (New York, 1982).

9. Charles S. Sydnor, *American Revolutionaries in the Making: Political Practices in Washington's Virginia* (1952; rep. New York 1965), 41–42; J. R. Pole, *Foundations of American Independence, 1763–1815* (Indianapolis, 1972), 163–64; Isaac, *Transformation of Virginia*, 20–21; Kelley, *The Cultural Pattern in American Politics*, 94–106. On the persistence of this dispersed, local patriarchy into the nineteenth century and into the West see Wyatt-Brown, *Southern Honor*, 43–45, 66, 70–74; and John Mack Faragher, *Women and Men on the Overland Trail* (New Haven, 1979), 112–21, 144–60.

10. Wyatt-Brown, *Southern Honor*, 50–55; Bailyn, *Ideological Origins*, 55–93; Isaac, *Transformation of Virginia*, 183. On the constricted role of women and its cultural meanings, see Isaac, *Transformation of Virginia*, 354–55; Wyatt-Brown, *Southern*

*Honor*, 247–53; Daniel Blake Smith, *Inside the Great House: Planter Family Life in Eighteenth Century Chesapeake Society* (Ithaca, 1980), 55–79; and Mary Beth Norton, *Liberty's Daughters: The Revolutionary Experience of American Women, 1750–1800* (Boston, 1980), 4–20, 26–39, 110–17.

11. Wyatt-Brown, *Southern Honor*, 362–401, 435–61; Richard Maxwell Brown, *The South Carolina Regulators* (Cambridge, Mass., 1963); Brown, *Strain of Violence: Historical Studies of American Violence and Vigilantism* (New York, 1975). On the rituals of republican consensus in the revolutionary period, see Wood, *Creation of the American Republic*, 53–70; and Isaac, *Transformation of Virginia*, 243–60.

12. Isaac, *Transformation of Virginia*, 88–114; Wyatt-Brown, *Southern Honor*, 327–61; Faragher, *Women and Men on the Overland Trail*, 112–17.

13. Wood, *Creation of the American Republic*, 65–70; Isaac, *Transformation of Virginia*, 255–60; Wyatt-Brown, *Southern Honor*, 34–45.

14. Wood, *Creation of the American Republic*, 68–69; Wood, "Republicanism as a Revolutionary Ideology," in *The Role of Ideology in the American Revolution*, ed. John R. Howe, Jr. (New York, 1970), 86.

15. Isaac, *Transformation of Virginia*, 194–98. On the fear of effeminacy, see Philip Greven, *The Protestant Temperament: Patterns of Child-Rearing Religious Experience, and the Self in Early America* (New York, 1977), 335–37, 348–54; Linda K. Kerber, *Women Of the Republic: Intellect and Ideology in Revolutionary America* (Chapel Hill, 1980), 31. On taxation and dependency, see Wyatt-Brown, *Southern Honor*, 70–71.

16. In addition to the works of Mathews and Isaac, this characterization of social religion relies on Sizer, *Gospel Hymns and Social Religion*, esp. 50–52; Leland Scott, "The Message of Early American Methodism," in *The History of American Methodism*, ed. Emory S. Bucke (3 vols., New York, 1964), I, 291–317; and A. Gregory Schneider, "Perfecting the Family of God: Religious Community and Family Values in Early American Methodism" (Ph.D. diss., University of Chicago, 1981).

17. Robert Emory, *History of the Discipline of the Methodist Episcopal Church* (New York, 1844), 177–85; Rev. John Miley, *Treatise on Class Meetings* (Cincinnati, 1851). For descriptions of love feasts, see "Love Feast," Cincinnati *Western Christian Advocate*, May 9, 1834; Charles Hardy, "Contributions to the Western Methodist Historical Society," ibid., Apr. 3, 1840; and John L. Smith, *Indiana Methodism: A Series of Sketches and incidents, Grave and Humorous, Concerning Preachers and People of the West* (Valparaiso, Ind., 1892), 25–26.

18. On the theme of liberty in evangelical religious practice, see Fred Hood, "Community and the Rhetoric of Freedom: Early American Methodist Worship," *Methodist History*, 9 (Oct. 1970), 13–25; Mathews, *Religion in the Old South*, 237–50; and Mathews, "Evangelical America—The Methodist Ideology," in this volume. For examples of the expression of these themes in Methodist social religion, see Finley, *Autobiography*, 240–41; Henry Smith, "Contributions to the Western Methodist Historical Society," *Western Christian Advocate*, Dec. 25, 1840; "Annals of Methodism in the West: Journal of Kobler," ibid., Aug. 30, 1839; Thomas A. Morris, "Historical Scraps," ibid., Oct. 4, 1839; Isaac Robbins, "Contributions to the Western Methodist Historical Society," ibid., Mar. 20, 1840.

19. On shame, see Erik Erikson, *Toys and Reasons: Stages in the Ritualization of Experience* (New York, 1977), 92–103, and Wyatt-Brown, *Southern Honor*, 154–56.

20. James Henthorn to Daniel Hitt, Feb. 12, 1802, Daniel Hitt Letters (The Upper Room Devotional Library, General Board of Discipleship, United Methodist Church, Nashville, Tenn.: typescript of originals in the Archives of Ohio United Methodism, Beeghly Library, Ohio Wesleyan University, Delaware, Ohio).

21. James B. Finley, "Experience and Travels of a Western Preacher," *Western Christian Advocate*, May 8, 15, 1835. See also John Scripps, "Early Methodism in the Far West—No. 2," ibid., Jan. 6, 1843; Allen Wiley, "Methodism in Southeastern Indiana," *Indiana Magazine of History*, 23 (June 1927), 175–76; and M. L. Haney, *The Story of My Life: An Autobiography* (Normal, Ill., 1904), 25.

22. William W. Jones, "Class Meetings," *Western Christian Advocate*, Dec. 16, 1842. See also William I. Fee, *Bringing the Sheaves: Gleanings from Harvest Fields in Ohio, Kentucky, and West Virginia* (Cincinnati, 1896), 16–17; J. T., "Class Meetings," *Gospel Herald*, 2 (Oct. 1830), 58; Henry Smith, "Contributions to the Western Methodist Historical Society," *Western Christian Advocate*, Jan. 15, 1841; "Annals of Methodism in the West: Journal of Kobler," ibid., Aug. 9, 1839.

23. Thomas Coke and Francis Asbury, "Extracts from Notes on the Discipline," in Emory, *History of the Discipline*, 304; "Class Meetings and Love Feasts," *Western Christian Advocate*, Aug. 8, 1834; J. T., "Class Meetings," 58. See also "Class Meeting and Love Feast," *Western Christian Advocate*, Apr. 1, 1836.

24. See, for example, "Class Meetings—No. IV," ibid., May 23, 1834; and Miley, *Treatise on Class Meetings*, 166–68.

25. Examples of the application of such titles to lay persons may be found in Smith, *Indiana Methodism*, 74; Finley, *Autobiography*, 281; Finley, "Experience and Travels," *Western Christian Advocate*, May 22, 1835; Wiley, "Methodism in Southeastern Indiana," *Indiana Magazine of History*, 23 (Mar. 1927), 55; and James Quinn, "Memoir of White Brown, A Lay Pioneer and Patriarch of the Scioto Valley," *Western Christian Advocate*, July 22, 1842.

26. Jacob Young, *Autobiography of a Pioneer: Or, The Nativity, Experience, Travels, and Ministerial Labors of Rev. Jacob Young, with Incidents, Observations, and Reflections* (Cincinnati, 1857), 56. See also James B. Finley, *Sketches of Western Methodism: Biographical, Historical, and Miscellaneous, Illustrative of Pioneer Life*, ed. W. P. Strickland (Cincinnati, 1854), 109.

27. Finley, *Autobiography*, 268–69, 416–17; John Scripps, "Early Methodism in the Far West—No. 3," *Western Christian Advocate*, Jan. 13, 1843; Allen Wiley, "Introduction and Progress of Methodism in Southeastern Indiana," *Indiana Magazine of History*, 23 (Sept. 1927), 299; Peter Cartwright, *Autobiography of Peter Cartwright* (1856; rep. New York, 1956), 128–30.

28. Benjamin Webb, "Contributions to the Western Methodist Historical Society," *Western Christian Advocate*, Sept. 18, 1840. See also John Meek's letter in *Extracts of Letters, Containing Some Account of the Work of God Since 1800: Written by the Preachers and Members of the Methodist Church to their Bishops* (New York 1805), 32; Young, *Autobiography*, 36; Finley, *Autobiography*, 203–4; and Charles Hardy, "Contributions to the Western Methodist Historical Society," *Western Christian Advocate*, Apr. 3, 1840.

29. Quoted in Wyatt-Brown, *Southern Honor*, 134. See also Reuben Davis, *Recollections of Mississippi and Mississippians* (Boston 1889), 20.

30. See, for instance, J. C. Smith, *Reminiscences of Early Methodism in Indiana* (Indianapolis, 1879), 189–90; Finley, *Sketches*, 360–1, 519, 527–29; Cartwright, *Autobiography*, 232–33; and Maxwell P. Gaddis, *Brief Recollections of the Late Rev. George W. Walker* (Cincinnati, 1857), 61–68.

31. Emory, *History of the Discipline*, 178.

32. Rev. C. R. Lovell, *Methodist Family Manual . . .* (Cincinnati, 1852), 192. On the rhetorical pattern of qualitative progression of which the conversion seems to have partaken, see Kenneth Burke, *Counter-Statement* (1931; rep. Berkeley 1968), 124–25.

33. James Henthorn to Daniel Hitt, Oct. 3, 1797, Hitt Letters. For examples of the use of the phrase, "way of the cross," see Miss Polly Jennings to Daniel Hitt, Dec. 25, 1801, ibid.

34. James Henthorn to Daniel Hitt, June 19, July 7, 1803, ibid.

35. Examples of the usage of the term, "friends," are found in Benjamin Hitt to Daniel Hitt, Oct. 14, 1792, and A. B. Thompson to Daniel Hitt, Feb. 18, 1796, ibid. See also George Shane Phillips, Diary, Sept. 11, 1841, Jan. 22, 1842; and Sarah Phillips to John H. Phillips, Sept. 12, 1852, both in the George Shane Phillips Papers (Huntington Library, San Marino, Calif.). Examples of the sentimental rhetoric which identified heaven, church, family and friendship are H. Tooley, "Zion Travellers," *The Western Methodist Preacher, or, Original Monthly Sermons, by Ministers of the Methodist Episcopal Church* (2 vols., Nashville, 1835, 1836), I, 189–90; "Re-union in Heaven," *Western Christian Advocate*, Jan. 10, 1840; James Quin, "A Journal, ibid., June 18, 1841; Finley, *Autobiography*, 373–78; James Henthorn to Daniel Hitt, Feb. 12, 1802, Hitt Letters; Mary S. Wall to William McKendree, Mar. 28, 1834, William McKendree Collection (Jean and Alexander Heard Libraries, Vanderbilt University, Nashville, Tenn.); and Abraham Knicely to George Washington Maley, Feb. 5, 1835, Rev. George Washington Maley Papers (Archives of Ohio United Methodism).

36. On the rise and meaning of the doctrine of "woman's sphere" in the Northeast, see Kathryn Kish Sklar, *Catharine Beecher: A Study in American Domesticity* (New Haven, 1973); and Nancy F. Cott, *The Bonds of Womanhood: "Woman's Sphere" in New England, 1780–1835* (New Haven, 1977). Cott suggests that the origins of the doctrine might be found in the thought of British evangelicals like Hannah More, whose writings, incidentally, show up frequently in Methodism's Cincinnati-based *Ladies Repository*. See Cott, *Bonds of Womanhood*, 64–65. On the Christian republican thinking in the Northeast from which Methodists borrowed and to which they contributed, see Perry Miller, *The Life of the Mind in America from the Revolution to the Civil War* (New York, 1965), 66–72; Lois W. Banner, "Religious Benevolence as Social Control: A Critique of an Interpretation," *Journal of American History*, 60 (June 1973), 35–39; and Timothy L. Smith, "Righteousness and Hope: Christian Holiness and the Millennial Vision in America, 1800–1900," *American Quarterly*, 31 (Spring, 1979), 21–45.

37. *Ladies Repository*, 1 (Nov. 1841), 349.

38. "Moral Qualifications of Rulers," *Western Christian Advocate*, Jan. 26, 1839; "Christian Patriotism," ibid., July 31 and Aug. 7, 1840; "What Next?" ibid., July 30, 1841; "Celebration of American Independence," ibid., Aug. 1, 1834.

39. "Duties of American Citizens," ibid., Jan. 29, 1839; "Christian Patriotism," July 31, 1840; Bishop McIlvaine, "Necessity of Religion to the Prosperity of a Nation," ibid., Feb. 2, 1838.

40. "Motives to Union," Pittsburgh *Conference Journal*, Apr. 30, 1840. This article was one of several published by the Pittsburgh Conference in 1840 concerned with the need for unity within and among evangelical churches for the sake of both religious prosperity and civil liberty. See Nathan Bangs, "Necessity of Union," ibid., Feb. 27, Mar. 12, 19, 1840; "Religious Politicians," ibid., Mar. 19, 1840; and "United Action," ibid., Mar. 26, 1840.

41. "Fourth of July," ibid., June 14, 1834; "The Fourth of July," ibid., June 18, 1835; William Hunter, "The Fourth of July," ibid., Nov. 26, 1835; A Parent, "Sabbath Schools—Christmas, New Years, and the Fourth," ibid., Dec. 14, 1837; "Great Sabbath School Jubilee at Pittsburgh," ibid., July 16, 1840; "Fourth of July Sabbath School and Temperance Celebrations," ibid., July 25, 1839; "Celebration of American Independence," *Western Christian Advocate*, Aug. 1, 1834; "Editorial: Fourth of July," ibid., July 16, 1841; "Editorial: Fourth of July Visit," ibid., July 19, 1844.

42. A detailed analysis of the process whereby Methodism helped transform the meaning of the family is the burden of my Indiana University Press book, "The Way of the Cross Leads Home: Religious Community and Domestic Ideology in Early American Methodism." For other studies which shed light on this process see Johnson, *A Shopkeeper's Millennium*; Sizer, *Gospel Hymns*; and Ryan, *Cradle of the Middle Class*.

43. For official rules and commentaries pertaining to family prayer, see Emory, *History of the Discipline*, 179; "Thoughts of the General Rules of the Methodist E. Church—No. XIX. Family and Private Prayer," *Western Christian Advocate*, Mar. 10, 1835; and "Family Prayer," ibid., Feb. 17, 1843. For evidence that the preachers and class leaders followed through on the rules, see Young, *Autobiography*, 316–17; Finley, *Autobiography*, 259, 283; and Joseph Tarkington, *Autobiography of Rev. Joseph Tarkington, One of the Pioneer Methodist Preachers of Indiana* (Cincinnati, 1899), 26. For evidence of the continuity in spirit between family religion and class meeting, see Finley, *Sketches*, 197; John Burgess, *Pleasant Recollections of Characters and Works of Noble Men with Old Scenes and Merry Times of Long, Long Ago* (Cincinnati 1887), 48; Scripps, "Early Methodism in the Far West—No. 2"; Cartwright, *Autobiography*, 289–90; and Gaddis, *Brief Recollections*, 77–78. For evidence of a sense of opposition between praying families and the world, see "Miscellaneous," *Western Christian Advocate*, Jan. 16, 1835; "On Family Worship," ibid., Aug. 4, 1837; Cartwright, *Autobiography*, 335; Burgess, *Pleasant Recollections*, 39; Haney, *Story of My Life*, 26; and T. D. Welker, *Conflicts and Trials of an Itinerant, Rev. John Kiger, D.D.* (Cincinnati, 1891), 24.

44. Lovell, *Family Manual*, 177–78. See also Thomas A. Morris, *Miscellany: Consisting of Essays, Biographical Sketches, and Notes of Travel* (Cincinnati 1852), 38; "Family Religion," *Western Christian Advocate*, May 2, 1834; "Winter Evenings," ibid., May 15, 1840; and "Parents' Department," ibid., July 21, 1837. For related remarks, see "Parents' Department: Domestic Peace," ibid., Apr. 10, 1835; and "Visiting," ibid., Dec. 11, 1835.

45. Lovell, *Family Manual*, 3–4; A Young Lady, "Home," *Western Christian Advocate*, Aug. 12, 1836; "Parents' Department: A Christian Father," ibid., June 30, 1827; "Letter," ibid., Oct. 31, 1834; "Re-union in Heaven," ibid., Jan. 10, 1840;

"Self-denial," ibid., June 27, 1834; "Parents' Department: Kindness at Home," ibid., Jan. 31, 1840.

46. Lovell, *Family Manual*, 173–75; "Rules for Husbands and Wives," *Western Christian Advocate*, May 16, 1834; Bates, "Husband and Wife," ibid., May 8, 1840; "Hints on Family Government," ibid., May 30, 1834; "Parents' Department: Influence of Example," ibid., Nov. 27, 1835; "Parental Government," ibid., July 3, 1835; "Parents' Department: Directions," ibid., Apr. 17, 1835; "Parents' Department: The Family Constitution," ibid., Apr. 28, 1837; "Parents' Department: My Mother Never Tells Lies," ibid., Mar. 6, 1840; Morris, *Miscellany*, 32. For testimonies to the effectiveness of the recommended family discipline, see Burgess, *Pleasant Recollections*, 39–42; Haney, *Story of My Life*, 6–8; and William Fletcher King, *Reminiscenses* (New York, 1915), 49–50.

47. Rev. John H. Power, *Discourse on Domestic Piety and Family Government in Four Parts*, ed. Rev. B. F. Tefft (Cincinnati, 1851), 142. See also "The Family Constitution," *Western Christian Advocate*, Aug. 10, 1838; and "Cultivation of the Infant Mind," ibid., Apr. 28, 1837.

48. On fostering these virtues in Methodist families, see King, *Reminiscences*, 49–50; Morris, *Miscellany*, 33; "Take Care How You Get Up the Ladder," *Western Christian Advocate*, Sept. 23, 1836; "Parents' Department: To Parents—Extract of an Address Delivered in Ohio by D. P. King, Esq.," ibid., Sept. 9, 1836.

49. D. W., "Woman's Sphere," *Ladies Repository*, 1 (Feb. 1841), 38–39. For elaborations of the official view of woman, see J. S. Tomlinson, "Female Influence," ibid., 1 (Jan., Mar., May, July 1841), 28–29, 77–79, 134–35, 194–97; Samuel Galloway, "An Address Delivered Before the Pupils of the Oakland Female Seminary, at Hillsborough, Ohio," ibid., 1 (Mar., Apr. 1841), 65–68, 98–99; J. Adams, "Woman," ibid., (Apr. 1841), 121; and Hannah More, "Woman," ibid., 1 (May 1841), 137.

50. Joanna Bowen Gillespie, "The Emerging Voice of the Methodist Woman: *The Ladies Repository*, 1841–61," in this volume.

51. Examples are Mary, "Woman's Trust," *Ladies Repository*, 2 (Dec. 1842), 378; Mrs. Cross, "What Can I Do?" ibid., 6 (Apr. 1846), 111–12; Imogen Mercein, "Woman," ibid., 7 (Dec. 1847), 354–58, 8 (Jan., Mar., Apr. 1848), 17–20, 60–69; 105–9; Miss Brown, "Aspirations," ibid., 11 (Mar. 1851), 120; and Sarah T. Bolton, "Aspirations," ibid., 11 (Sept. 1851), 329.

52. After the Civil War, the temperance issue, understood as an extension of the evangelical woman's identity as domestic instrument of morality, took women beyond the domestic sphere into politics. See Susan Dey Lee, "Evangelical Domesticity: The Woman's Temperance Crusade of 1873–1874," in *Women in New Worlds: Historical Perspectives on the Wesleyan Tradition*, ed. Hilah F. Thomas and Rosemary Skinner Keller (2 vols., Nashville 1981, 1982), 1, 293–309; and Carolyn DeSwarte Gifford, "For God and Home and Native Land: The W. C. T. U.'s Image of Woman in the Late Nineteenth Century," ibid., 310–27 and in this volume. See also Carl N. Degler, *At Odds: Women and the Family in America from the Revolution to the Present* (New York, 1980), 298–327.

53. Finley, *Autobiography*, 405; "Children's Department: A Hymn—L. M.," *Western Christian Advocate*, June 24, 1836. See also "Independence Hymn," ibid., May 8, 1840.

54. For an overview of a growing body of historiography which interprets nine-teenth-century evangelicalism as an engine of self-control rather than social control, see Leonard I. Sweet's title essay in Sweet, ed., *The Evangelical Tradition in America* (Macon, Ga., 1984), 1–86, esp. 37–41.

## Chapter 13

Forbes, *"And Obey God, Etc.": Methodism and American Indians*

1. Bruce Forbes, editor, "Thomas Fullerton's Sketch of Chippewa Missions, 1841–1844," *Methodist History* 17 (January 1979), 113.

2. John Telford, editor, *The Letters of the Rev. John Wesley, A.M.* (London: Epworth, 1931) I, 188.

3. J. Ralph Randolph, *British Travelers Among the Southern Indians, 1660–1763* (Norman: University of Oklahoma Press, 1973), 97–104. Also found in Randolph, "John Wesley and the American Indian: A Study in Disillusionment," *Methodist History* 10 (April 1972), 3–11.

4. Nehemiah Curnock, ed., *The Journal of the Rev. John Wesley, A.M.* (London: Epworth, 1938) I, 407–9.

5. Telford, *Letters* I, 188.

6. Telford, *Letters* VIII, 24–25.

7. Wade Crawford Barclay, *History of Methodist Missions* (New York: The Board of Missions and Church Extension of the Methodist Church, 1949) I, 201–2. Cf. Thomas Coke, *Extracts of the Journals . . .*, 95.

8. Barclay I, 200.

9. Sources disagree about the precise date; see Barclay I, 203n. Basic primary sources on the Wyandot mission include books by James B. Finley: *Autobiography of Rev. James B. Finley* (Cincinnati: Methodist Book Concern, 1855), *History of the Wyandot Mission . . .* (Cincinnati: J. F. Wright and L. Swormstedt for the Methodist Episcopal Church, 1840), and *Life Among the Indians* (Cincinnati: Methodist Book Concern, 1857). Also see Charles Elliott, *Indian Missionary Reminiscenses Principally of the Wyandot Nation* (New York: Carlton & Porter, 1835). In addition to Barclay, volumes I (203–5) and II (117–26), recent secondary discussions include Frederick A. Norwood, "Strangers in a Strange Land: Removal of the Wyandot Indians," *Methodist History* 13 (April 1975), 45–60; Robert E. Smith, "The Clash of Leadership at the Grand Reserve: The Wyandot Subagency and the Methodist Mission, 1820–1824," *Ohio History* 89 (Spring 1980), 181–205; and two locally published histories: Myrtle E. Felkner, *In the Wigwams of the Wyandots: The Story of Jonathan Pointer* (Cedar Rapids, Iowa: KQ Associates, 1984) and Thelma R. Marsh, *Moccasin Trails to the Cross: A History of the Mission to the Wyandott Indians on the Sandusky Plains* (Upper Sandusky, Ohio: John Stewart United Methodist Church, 1974).

10. Finley, *History of the Wyandot Mission*, 76.

11. Barclay, I, 203.

12. *Eighth Annual Report of the Missionary Society of the Methodist Episcopal Church*, 1826–27, 5. Cited in Barclay II, 125.

13. Finley, *Life Among the Indians*, 447–89.

14. Quoted by Norwood, "Strangers," 51. See *Western Christian Advocate* 8 (June 4, 1841), 26.

15. Article I, Constitution of the Missionary Society of the Methodist Episcopal Church, in *Fifth Annual Report of the Missionary Society* . . . (1824), 42.

16. Barclay I, 280ff.

17. "American Methodist Missions. Missions of the M.E.C.,S. Indian Missions" (Nashville, Tenn.: Board of Missions, M.E. Church, South, June, 1891), 1. This anonymous pamphlet is Number 3 in a series of "Missionary Handbooks" published by the M.E. Church, South. Summaries of southeastern and Oklahoma Indian missions may be found in Walter N. Vernon, "Beginnings of Indian Methodism in Oklahoma," *Methodist History* 17 (April 1979), 127–54, and in Oklahoma conference histories: Sidney Henry Babcock and John Y. Bryce, *History of Methodism in Oklahoma* . . . (Oklahoma City: Times Journal, 1937); Leland Clegg and William B. Oden, *Oklahoma Methodism in the Twentieth Century* (Nashville: Parthenon, 1968), chap. I; Paul D. Mitchell, *From Teepees to Towers: A History of the Methodist Church in Oklahoma* (Verden, Okla.: 1947). *Chronicles of Oklahoma* has published numerous articles pertinent to Methodist missions. Of the pre-Oklahoma efforts, Cherokee missions have been most thoroughly studied. See Mary Thomas Peacock, "Methodist Mission Work Among the Cherokee Indians Before the Removal," *Methodist History* 3 (April 1965), 20–39, and William McLoughlin's book cited below.

18. The membership estimate is from Babcock and Bryce, 23.

19. William G. McLaughlin, *Cherokees and Missionaries, 1789–1839* (New Haven: Yale University Press, 1984), 290. This is a superb comparative study of the efforts of various denominations among the Cherokees.

20. "American Methodist Missions" pamphlet, 20.

21. Ibid. 21.

22. Clegg and Oden, 28.

23. E. B. Dykes Beachy, "Methodist Outpost," *Christian Advocate* (June 8, 1950), 14–15, 49. Martha B. Caldwell, ed., *Annals of Shawnee Methodist Mission and Indian Manual Labor School* (Topeka: Kansas State Historical Society, 1939). Barclay II, 176–80.

24. The major source for information in the following paragraphs is Barclay II, 143–69. For Canadian missions specifically see Mrs. Frederick C. [Annie D.] Stephenson, *One Hundred Years of Canadian Methodist Missions, 1824–24* (Toronto: The Missionary Society of the Methodist Church, 1925). Another secondary discussion of a portion of the Great Lakes region is Frederick A. Norwood, "Conflict of Cultures: Methodist Efforts with the Ojibway, 1830–1880," *Religion in Life* 48 (Autumn 1979), 360–76.

25. Barclay II, p. 152.

26. Ibid., p. 146.

27. Alfred Brunson, *The Western Pioneer; Or, Incidents in the Life and Times of Reverend Alfred Brunson* (Cincinnati: Hitchcock & Walden, 1872–79), two volumes. John H. Pitezel, *Lights and Shades of Missionary Life* . . . (Cincinnati: Western Methodist Book Concern, 1901). Alvin Torry, *Autobiography of Rev. Alvin Torry, First Missionary to the Six Nations and the Northwestern Tribes of British North America*, ed. William Hosmer (Auburn, N.Y.: William J. Moses, 1861). Barnes Hall published a

biography of Clark: *The Life of Reverend John Clark* (New York: Carlton & Porter, 1856).

28. Bruce Forbes, "Evangelization and Acculturation Among the Santee Dakota Indians, 1834–1864" (Ph.D. diss., Princeton Theological Seminary, 1977), 78–91. Barclay II, 148–49, 188.

29. "George Copway, after a few years of most unsatisfactory connection with the missions made himself notorious by various exploits throughout the country and finally drank himself to death." Chauncey Hobart, *History of Methodism in Minnesota* (Red Wing: Red Wing, 1887), 28; George Copway, *The Life, History, and Travels of Kah-ge-ga-gah-bowh . . .* (Albany: Weed and Parsons, 1847).

30. Ronald A. Brunger, "The History of the Taymouth Methodist Indian Mission" (manuscript, 1974; copy held by National United Methodist Archives, Drew University), 26. John H. Pitezel, *The Life of Rev. Peter Marksman, An Ojibwa Missionary . . .* (Cincinnati: Western Methodist Book Concern, 1901).

31. Barclay III, 324. Cf. *Twenty-sixth Annual Report of the Missionary Society of the Methodist Episcopal Church* (1844–45), 85–86, and *Twenty-eighth Annual Report . . .* (1846–47), 96.

32. Ray A. Billington, "Oregon Epic: A Letter That Jarred America," *Pacific Historian* (Summer 1968), 34. Reprinted from *Together*, November 1959.

33. Quoted by Barclay II, 242. Cf. *Christian Advocate and Journal* 18 (Sept. 13, 1843), 408.

34. Barclay II, 200–262.

35. The most recent, significant book on Lee is Robert J. Loewenberg, *Equality on the Oregon Frontier: Jason Lee and the Methodist Mission, 1834–43* (Seattle: University of Washington Press, 1976).

36. Barclay I, 318–57. William R. Cannon, "Education, Publication, Benevolent Work, and Missions," in *The History of American Methodism*, ed. E. S. Bucke (New York, Nashville: Abingdon, 1964), 586–99.

37. Milton A. Clark, "Work Among the Kiowa and Comanche Indians," *Western Methodist* (August 15, 1907), 4.

38. Robert F. Berkhofer, Jr., "The Political Context of a New Indian History," *Pacific Historical Review* 40 (1971), 357–82.

39. Two major books representing this theme are Robert F. Berkhofer, Jr., *Salvation and the Savage: An Analysis of Protestant Missions and American Indian Response, 1787–1862* (Lexington: University of Kentucky Press, 1965) and Henry Warner Bowden, *American Indians and Christian Missions: Studies in Cultural Conflict* (Chicago: University of Chicago Press, 1981).

40. These points are discussed more fully, applied specifically to the Dakota Indians of southern Minnesota, in Bruce David Forbes, "Evangelization and Acculturation Among the Santee Dakota Indians, 1834–1864" (Ph.D. diss., Princeton Theological Seminary, 1977), 128–53.

41. See Berkhofer, *Salvation*, chap. 2, "Nurseries of Morality," 16–43.

42. *Annual Report of the Missionary Society of the Methodist Episcopal Church*, 1851, 71.

43. Joseph Mitchell, *The Missionary Pioneer, or a Brief Memoir of the Life, Labours, and Death of John Stewart (Man of Colour) Founder, Under God, of the*

*Mission Among the Wyandots at Upper Sandusky, Ohio* (New York: J. C. Totten, 1829), 31–32. Hicks eventually joined the Methodist mission, but the fact does not gainsay the depth of the sentiment.

44. Quoted by Robert H. Keller, Jr., *American Protestantism and United States Indian Policy, 1869–82* (Lincoln: University of Nebraska Press, 1983), 5–6. Cf. ABCFM, transcripts of correspondence, 1827–78, in the Newberry Library, Chicago, F. Ayer to D. Greene, October 31, 1838, MS 141.

45. *Our Brother in Red* 7 (September 15, 1888), 7.

46. William T. Hagan, *American Indians* (Chicago: University of Chicago Press, 1961), 66.

47. Quoted by Hagan, 69.

48. McLoughlin, *Cherokees and Missionaries*, 291–92.

49. Finley, *Life Among the Indians*, 452.

50. McLoughlin, 295.

51. Quoted by Frederick A. Norwood, "The Invisible American—Methodism and the Indian," *Methodist History* 8 (January 1970), 11. Cf. *New York Christian Advocate* 9 (1835), 102.

52. Norwood, "Strangers in a Strange Land," 49.

53. Hagan, 70.

54. For a general overview of the period see Francis Paul Prucha, *American Indian Policy in Crisis: Christian Reformers and the Indian, 1865–1900.* (Norman: University of Oklahoma Press, 1976).

55. Grant's annual message to Congress, December 5, 1870, from James D. Richardson, comp., *A Compilation of the Messages and Papers of the Presidents, 1789–1902*, ten volumes (Washington, D.C., 1904?) 7, 109–10.

56. Keller, 36.

57. Robert Lee Whitner, "The Methodist Episcopal Church and Grant's Peace Policy: A Study of the Methodist Agencies, 1870–1882" (Ph.D. thesis, University of Minnesota, 1959), 280. Frederick A. Norwood concurs in "Serpents and Savages." *Religion in Life* 46 (Autumn 1977), 307.

58. Keller, 55.

59. Keller, 24, 36–37.

60. Keller, 213.

61. Whitner, 281. Many would claim that "Father" James Wilbur of the Yakima agency was an exception to this claim of failure by Methodists. Carl Schurz called Wilbur "the most successful agent in the service." For a less positive view, see Keller, 55–56, 158–60. For other views, see Maurice Helland, *There Were Giants: The Life of James H. Wilbur* (Yakima: Shields Bag and Printing, 1980) and Robert Whitner, "Grant's Indian Peace Policy on the Yakima Reservation, 1879–1882," *Pacific Northwest Quarterly* (October 1959), 135–42.

62. *Annual Report of the Missionary Society of the M. E. Church* 1855, 73–74.

63. Hagan, 141.

64. Norwood, "Serpents and Savages," 309.

65. Ibid., 310.

## Chapter 14

Schmidt, *Reexamining the Public/Private Split: Reforming the Continent and Spreading Scriptural Holiness*

1. Several historians have referred to this. See, e.g. Wade Crawford Barclay, *To Reform the Nation*, vol. 2 of *Early American Methodism, 1769–1844* (New York: Board of Missions of The Methodist Church, 1950), 1–2.

2. Martin E. Marty, *Righteous Empire: The Protestant Experience in America* (New York: Dial, 1970). See chap. 17: "The Two-Party System: A Division Within Protestantism," and reference to my dissertation in Acknowledgments, 268, and Chapter Notes, 270.

3. Dean R. Hoge, *Division in the Protestant House* (Philadelphia: Westminster, 1976); Neill Q. Hamilton, *Recovery of the Protestant Adventure* (New York: Seabury, 1981); George M. Marsden, *Fundamentalism and American Culture* (New York: Oxford University Press, 1980); Donald W. Dayton, *Discovering An Evangelical Heritage* (New York: Harper & Row, 1976). Marsden discusses evangelical social concern in chap. 10, "The Great Reversal," 85–93. The term was also the title of a book by David O. Moberg. See *The Great Reversal: Evangelism and Social Concern*, rev. ed. (Philadelphia: J. B. Lippincott, 1977).

4. Hannah Arendt discusses the meaning of "public" in her book *The Human Condition* (Chicago: University of Chicago Press, 1958), especially chap. 2, 22–78. She emphasizes the public realm as common meeting ground and suggests that healthy public life depends upon discourse about the common good that transcends private interest. Also helpful are Parker J. Palmer, *The Company of Strangers: Christians and the Renewal of America's Public Life* (New York: Crossroad, 1981) and the older, but still useful work by John Dewey, *The Public and Its Problems* (New York: Henry Holt, 1927). A good recent illustration of interdisciplinary inquiry into the meaning of "public" is the "Project on Religion and American Public Life" coordinated through the University of Chicago Divinity School.

5. James M. Wall ed., *Theologians in Transition: The Christian Century "How My Mind Has Changed" Series* (New York: Crossroad, 1981). Interestingly, the basic change noted in most of the essays was the shift during the decade of the 1970s from the secular to the religious.

6. This includes the three denominations which became The Methodist Church in 1939 (M.E.; M.E., South; and M.P.), as well as black Methodist denominations (A.M.E.; A.M.E.Z.; C.M.E.) and holiness groups which broke away from Methodism (such as Wesleyan Methodists). I am not, of course, claiming that the Wesleyan traditions *alone* have such resources.

7. See Kenneth E. Rowe, "Counting the Converts: Progress Reports as Church History," *Rethinking Methodist History*, ed. Russell E. Richey and Kenneth E. Rowe (Nashville: Kingswood, 1985), 11–17.

8. Two basic sources are: Donald G. Mathews, *Slavery and Methodism: A Chapter in American Morality 1780–1845* (Princeton: Princeton University Press, 1965) and William B. Gravely, "Methodist Preachers, Slavery and Caste: Types of Social Concern in Antebellum America," *Duke Divinity School Review* 34 (Autumn 1969),

209–29. See also Donald G. Mathews, *Religion in the Old South* (Chicago: University of Chicago Press, 1977).

9. From Asbury's *Journal*, II, 591. Quoted in Gravely, "Methodist Preachers," 214.

10. William B. Gravely makes this point in his article "Methodist Preachers," 215–15. See also Donald G. Mathews, *Slavery and Methodism*, 25–26, 28.

11. Mathews, *Slavery and Methodism*, chaps. 3 and 4, 62–110.

12. Gravely, "Methodist Preachers," 217–18.

13. Ibid., 219; Mathews, *Slavery and Methodism*, 196–211.

14. Mathews, *Slavery and Methodism*, 221–25, 229–31; quote on 231.

15. For the Wesleyan Methodists see Donald W. Dayton, *Discovering An Evangelical Heritage*, chap. 7, 73–84; also Luther Lee, *Five Sermons and a Tract*, ed. Donald W. Dayton (Chicago: Holrad, 1975). Quotes in Dayton, *Discovering*, 74–75, 77.

16. Ibid., 81.

17. Donald G. Mathews, quoted in Dayton, *Discovering*, 84.

18. James W. May, "The War Years," in Emory Stevens Bucke, ed., *The History of American Methodism*, vol. 2 (New York: Abingdon, 1964), 207–8.

19. James E. Kirby, "Matthew Simpson and the Mission of America," *Church History* 36 (1967), 301.

20. Quoted in Donald G. Jones, *The Sectional Crisis and Northern Methodism: A Study in Piety, Political Ethics and Civil Religion* (Metuchen, N.J.: Scarecrow, 1979), 37.

21. Louise Queen, "The Centennial of American Methodism," *Methodist History* 4 (January 1966), 42–46.

22. John O. Gross, "The Romance of American Methodism," *Methodist History* 6 (October 1967), 19.

23. Queen, "Centennial," 48.

24. The major study of Haven is William Gravely, *Gilbert Haven Methodist Abolitionist: A Study in Race, Religion, and Reform, 1850–1880* (New York: Abingdon, 1973).

25. Gilbert Haven, *National Sermons. Sermons, Speeches and Letters on Slavery and Its War: From the Passage of the Fugitive Slave Bill to the Election of President Grant* (Boston: Lee and Shephard, 1869), 88–89.

26. See Gravely, *Gilbert Haven*, 117 (especially footnote 29).

27. Haven, *National Sermons*, 375.

28. Ibid., 405.

29. Gravely, *Gilbert Haven*, 127.

30. Ibid., 150, 140.

31. Ibid., 152.

32. Haven, *National Sermons*, 151.

33. Ibid., 626–30; Gravely, *Gilbert Haven*, 159–60. See also Nancy N. Bahmueller, "My Ordination: Anna Howard Shaw," *Methodist History* 14 (January 1976), 127.

34. Quoted in Gravely, *Gilbert Haven*, 256.

35. Henry F. May, *Protestant Churches and Industrial America* (New York: Harper & Brothers, 1949); Charles Howard Hopkins, *The Rise of the Social Gospel in American Protestantism 1865–1915* (New Haven: Yale University Press, 1940).

36. Philip D. Jordan, "Immigrants, Methodists and a 'Conservative' Social Gospel, 1865–1908," *Methodist History* 17 (October 1978), 19–25.

37. The Episcopal Address of 1888 (M.E. Church) referred to the labor problem as "comparatively new with us" and "not of easy solution." (*Journal of the General Conference*, 1888, 57.) It also raised the issue of the alienation of the workers for the first time. As late as 1891, J. W. Mendenhall, ed. *Methodist Review*, responded to criticism of the church for this inattention by claiming that "such questions are new, and it is a problem to know what more to do than discuss them." Wade Crawford Barclay, *Widening Horizons*, vol. 1 of *The Methodist Episcopal Church, 1845–1939* (New York: Board of Missions of The Methodist Church, 1957), 51.

38. Beverly Wildung Harrison, "Sexism and the Contemporary Church: When Evasion Becomes Complicity," in Alice L. Hageman, ed., *Sexist Religion and Women in the Church* (New York: Association, 1974), 202.

39. *Journal of the General Conference*, 1884, 380–81; Randolph S. Foster, *Centenary Thoughts for the Pew and Pulpit of Methodism in 1884* (New York: Phillips & Hunt, 1884), 166–69.

40. See her own account of the 1888 General Conference: Frances E. Willard, *Glimpses of Fifty Years: The Autobiography of An American Woman* (Chicago: Woman's Temperance Publication Association, 1889), 617–21.

41. Kenneth E. Rowe, "Counting the Converts," on Buckley.

42. Rosemary Skinner Keller, "Lay Women in the Protestant Tradition," in Rosemary Radford Ruether and Rosemary Skinner Keller, eds., *Women and Religion in America*, vol. 1, *The Nineteenth Century* (New York: Harper & Row, 1981), 242–43.

43. Carolyn D. Gifford, "Home Protection: The WCTU's Conversion to Woman Suffrage" (Unpublished paper, December 1980). Gifford describes the women's temperance crusade against the saloons in the 1870s, and the conversion of evangelical Protestant women to the cause of woman suffrage on realizing that laws were necessary to deal adequately with the liquor traffic rather than the persuasive tactics of "praying and pleading."

44. See, e.g. Carolyn DeSwarte Gifford, "For God and Home and Native Land: The W.C.T.U.'s Image of Woman in the Late Nineteenth Century" in this volume. Also Gifford, "Women in Social Reform Movements," in Ruether and Keller, eds., *Women and Religion*, 294–303; and Ida Tetreault Miller, "Frances Elizabeth Willard: Religious Leader and Social Reformer" (Ph.D. diss., Boston University, 1978).

45. Willard, *Glimpses*, 334–41, 576–89.

46. Mary Earhart [Dillon], *Frances Willard: From Prayers to Politics* (Chicago: University of Chicago Press, 1944), especially chap. 9, "National President of the Union." On the subsequent narrowing of W.C.T.U. concerns after Willard's death, see Miller, "Frances Elizabeth Willard," 163.

47. Gifford, "For God and Home," 317.

48. Ibid., 327.

49. On Willard's developing commitment to labor, see Miller, "Frances Elizabeth Willard," 146–52. Also Earhart, *Frances Willard*, chap. 13, "Temperance and Labor," and 16, "Views on Many Subjects," and Mary Earhart Dillon, "Willard, Frances Elizabeth," in *Notable American Women*, vol. 3, 618.

The question has often been raised as to how the issue of temperance/prohibition fits into the public/private scheme. Like prostitution, drugs, and gambling, this is an issue of personal behavior that has clear public consequences. On the one hand, the temperance crusade was part of the evangelical Protestant effort to create (and maintain) a "Christian America." On the other hand, it had deep kinship with the social gospel in its concern for the urban poor and its attack on big business, including the powerful liquor interest. It was primarily *after* the passage of Prohibition that this issue became a surrogate for the social gospel. On temperance/prohibition, see Richard M. Cameron, *Methodism and Society in Historical Perspective*, and Walter G. Muelder, *Methodism and Society in the Twentieth Century*, vols. 1 and 2 of *Methodism and Society* (New York: Abingdon, 1961); also Robert Moats Miller, "Methodism and American Society, 1900-1939," in Bucke, ed., *History of American Methodism*, vol. 3, 329-43.

50. Miller, "Frances Elizabeth Willard," 124. On Willard's religious development, see Willard, *Glimpses*, 622-28.

51. From Willard's Presidential Address to the W.C.T.U., 1897, quoted in Miller, "Frances Elizabeth Willard," 185.

52. Mary Agnes Dougherty, "The Social Gospel According to Phoebe," in this volume and also in Thomas and Keller, eds., *Women in New Worlds*, 1981, 200-16; Keller, "Lay Women," 242-53; Catherine M. Prelinger and Rosemary S. Keller, "The Function of Female Bonding: The Restored Diaconessate of the Nineteenth Century," in Rosemary Skinner Keller, Louise L. Queen, and Hilah G. Thomas, eds., *Women in New Worlds*, vol. 2 (Nashville: Abingdon, 1982), 318-37.

53. Isabelle Horton, *High Adventure: Life of Lucy Rider Meyer* (New York: Methodist Book Concern, 1928); Lucy Jane Rider Meyer, *Deaconesses, Biblical, Early Church, European, American, with the Story of the Chicago Training School for City, Home and Foreign Missions and the Chicago Deaconess Home*, 3rd ed., rev. and enlarged (Chicago: Cranston & Stowe, 1892).

54. Horton, *High Adventure*, 117.

55. Dougherty, "The Social Gospel," 206-10. On holiness social work, see Norris Magnuson, *Salvation in the Slums: Evangelical Social Work, 1865-1920* (Metuchen, N.J.: Scarecrow, 1977); also Timothy L. Smith, *Revivalism and Social Reform* (New York: Abingdon, 1957), 163-77, and Smith, *Called Unto Holiness: The Story of the Nazarenes* (Kansas City: Nazarene, 1962).

56. Dougherty, "Social Gospel," 215-16.

57. John Patrick McDowell, *The Social Gospel in the South: The Woman's Home Mission Movement in the Methodist Episcopal Church, South, 1886-1939* (Baton Rouge: Louisiana State University Press, 1982).

58. Mrs. R.W. [Tochie] MacDonell, *Belle Harris Bennett: Her Life Work* (Nashville: Board of Missions, MECS, 1928). See also Carolyn L. Stapleton, "Belle Harris Bennett: Model of Holistic Christianity," *Methodist History* 21 (April 1983), 131-42. Stapleton stresses Bennett's integration of "traditional Christian piety with a deep commitment to social action." (131)

59. McDowell, *Social Gospel in the South*, chap. 5, 116-43; also Virginia Shadron, "The Laity Rights Movement, 1906-1918: Woman's Suffrage in the Methodist Episcopal Church, South," in Thomas and Keller, eds., *Women in New Worlds*, 1981, 261-75.

60. MacDonell, *Belle Harris Bennett*, 90.

61. Noreen Dunn Tatum, *A Crown of Service: A Story of Woman's Work in the Methodist Episcopal Church, South, from 1878–1940* (Nashville: Parthenon, 1960), 36.

62. David W. Wills, "Introduction," in David W. Wills and Richard Newman, eds., *Black Apostles At Home and Abroad: Afro-Americans and the Christian Mission from the Revolution to Reconstruction* (Boston: G. K. Hall, 1982).

63. Ibid. See also Vincent Harding, *The Other American Revolution* (Los Angeles: Center for Afro-American Studies, UCLA, and Atlanta: Institute of the Black World, 1980), 79: "For a brief time, Reconstruction had provided the nineteenth century's most complete opportunity for the nation to forge a binding chain between the best possibilities of the white American revolution and the deep and pulsing movement of the black struggle for freedom. It was a magnificent chance for the two revolutions to become one in the creation of a new society. . . . Instead, America chose a 'New South.'"

64. David Wood Wills, "Aspects of Social Thought in the African Methodist Episcopal Church 1884–1910" (Ph.D. diss., Harvard University, 1975).

65. Ibid.

66. Robert Moats Miller, "Methodism and American Society," in Bucke, ed., *History of American Methodism*, vol. 3, 400–1.

67. Harding, *Other American Revolution*, 101 (the quote is from W. E. B. DuBois).

68. David Wills, "Reverdy C. Ransom: The Making of an A.M.E. Bishop," in *Black Apostles: Afro-American Clergy Confront the Twentieth Century*, eds. Randall K. Burkett and Richard Newman (Boston: G. K. Hall, 1978), 181–212.

69. William McGuire King, "The Emergence of Social Gospel Radicalism in American Methodism" (Ph.D. diss., Harvard University, 1977).

70. Wills, "Aspects of Social Thought," chap. 6, "The Vision of Reverdy C. Ransom," 243–44; Wills, "Reverdy C. Ransom," 197.

71. Wills, "Aspects of Social Thought," 247–52; Wills, "Reverdy C. Ransom," 195.

72. Reverdy C. Ransom, "The Negro and Socialism," *A.M.E. Church Review* 13 (October 1896), 196–97.

73. Quoted in Wills, "Aspects of Social Thought," 261.

74. Ibid.

75. Wills, "Reverdy C. Ransom," 205.

76. King, "Emergence of Social Gospel Radicalism," 118–21.

77. On the steel strike investigation, see ibid., 292–326; also Muelder, *Methodism and Society*, 96–103.

78. Francis J. McConnell, *By the Way: An Autobiography* (New York: Abingdon-Cokesbury, 1952), 219.

79. Harris Franklin Rall, "Francis John McConnell," in Harris Franklin Rall, ed., *Religion and Public Affairs: In Honor of Bishop Francis John McConnell* (New York: Macmillan, 1937), 9–10.

80. McConnell, *By the Way*, 223.

81. King, "Emergence of Social Gospel Radicalism," 333.

82. King dissertation; also William McGuire King, "The Emergence of Social Gospel Radicalism: The Methodist Case," *Church History* 50 (December 1981), 436–49.

83. Reinhold Niebuhr, *Radical Religion*, quoted in King, "Emergence of Social Gospel Radicalism," 126.

84. Francis John McConnell, *The Essentials of Methodism* (New York: The Methodist Book Concern, 1916).

85. Reverdy C. Ransom, *The Pilgrimage of Harriet Ransom's Son* (Nashville: Sunday School Union, n.d.), 31–33; McConnell, *By the Way*, 36. See the group profile of the charter membership of the M.F.S.S. in King, "Emergence of Social Gospel Radicalism," 126.

86. For example, one of the chapters in the 1910 volume entitled *Social Ministry*, edited for the M.F.S.S. by Harry F. Ward, was on the "social activities" of John Wesley. Close to one-fourth of Bishop McConnell's 1939 biography of John Wesley was devoted to the social consequences of Wesley's evangelical revival. The literature here is considerable and generally well known. For a good recent essay on Wesley's theology in this connection, see Theodore Runyon, "Introduction: Wesley and the Theologies of Liberation," in Theodore Runyon, ed., *Sanctification and Liberation* (Nashville: Abingdon, 1981), 9–48.

87. See Runyon, "Introduction," 30–39.

88. Wellman J. Warner, *The Wesleyan Movement in the Industrial Revolution* (New York: Longmans, Green, 1930), especially chap. 3, "The Basis of Wesleyan Social Ethics," 55–72.

89. Arthur Meier Schlesinger, "A Critical Period in American Religion, 1875–1900," Massachusetts Historical Society, *Proceedings* 64 (1932), 523–47.

90. Robert T. Handy, *A Christian America: Protestant Hopes and Historical Realities* (New York: Oxford University Press, 1971). Handy made the same point in *The Social Gospel in America* (New York: Oxford University Press, 1966), 4.

91. Among the works on modernization that I have found most helpful have been Richard D. Brown, *Modernization: The Transformation of American Life, 1600–1865* (New York: Hill & Wang, 1976) and Brown, "Modernization: A Victorian Climax," in Daniel Walker Howe, ed., *Victorian America* (University of Pennsylvania Press, 1976), 29–44. Robert Bellah, Peter Berger, and Joseph Kitagawa have also written extensively about modernization and religion in modernization.

92. Martin E. Marty, *The Public Church: Mainline-Evangelical-Catholic* (New York: Crossroad, 1981).

93. Dieter T. Hessel, *Social Ministry* (Philadelphia: Westminster, 1982); Jane Cary Peck, "A Model for Ministry," *The Christian Century* 100 (February 2–9, 1983), 94–97.

94. Hessel, *Social Ministry*, chap. 1, "To Reconstruct a Whole Ministry," 13–33.

95. Parker J. Palmer, *The Company of Strangers: Christians and the Renewal of America's Public Life* (New York: Crossroad, 1981), chap. 1, "Life Among Strangers," 17–33.

96. Earl D. C. Brewer, *Continuation or Transformation? The Involvement of United Methodism in Social Movements and Issues* (Nashville: Abingdon, 1982), 118.

97. *Journal of the General Conference*, 1884, 384.

## Chapter 15

Gillespie, *The Emerging Voice of the Methodist Woman:* The Ladies' Repository, *1841–61*

1. *Methodism and Literature, A Series of Articles from Several Writers on the Literary Enterprise and Achievements of the Methodist Episcopal Church*, ed. Frederick A. Archibald (Cincinnati: Walden and Stove, 1883), 267, 264, 82. The magazine was titled *The Ladies' Repository and Gatherings of the West* from 1841–48, after which the latter phrase was dropped.

2. Frank Luther Mott, *The History of American Magazines*, Vol. I, 1741–1850 (Cambridge: Harvard University Press, 1957), 388.

3. Lee Soltow and Edward Stevens, *The Rise of Literacy and the Common School in the United States: A Socioeconomic Analysis to 1870* (Chicago: The University of Chicago Press, 1981), 78; Mott, *History of American Magazines*, 388.

4. James Penn Pilkington, *The Methodist Publishing House: A History*, Vol. I (Nashville: Abingdon, 1968), 276–79.

5. E.g., *Memoirs of Fanny Newell (1793–1824) Written by Herself; and Published at her Particular Request and the Desire of Numerous Friends* (Hallowell, Maine: 1824).

6. As early as Vol. II (1842), one parodistic story, "The Faulty Mistress," was published, with characters such as Paul Censor and Mrs. M. B. Fretful—but it was intended to be above the label "fiction," more a cautionary parable. Vol. V (1845) had one story in it by a bishop's wife. Vol. VI (1846) produced a story, "The Exile," plus an editorial defense of its conclusion on the grounds that it was *history*. Evidently this hardly silenced opponents of fiction because in 1847, Vol VII, No. 4., the editor expostulated: "My readers know I don't write fiction and have often spoken against it." And again in 1849, a feverish editorial denial of any stance favorable to printing fiction (Vol. IX, No. 7, 191): "I never wrote a line of fiction in my life and never knowingly put any in the *Repository*, unless I was deceived by contributors." Nevertheless the antifiction policy was quietly eroded during the 1850s, and much weakened by 1860.

7. In Vol. XVI, No. 1, January 1856, there is a long scholarly article "Phonography and Phonotypy" by the Rev. D. D. Whedon, recommending it as a variety of what we now call shorthand or phonetic symbol writing (pp. 30–32).

8. The Methodist women's magazine *The Heathen Woman's Friend* (1869–1940) was immensely popular and influential, and undoubtedly drew much of the readership away from *LR* in its later years. See Joan Jacobs Brumberg, "Zenanas & Girlless Villages: The Ethology of American Evangelical Women, 1870–1910," in *Journal of American History*, 69, No. 2 (Sept. 1982) 347–71.

9. Mott, *History of American Magazines*, 388.

10. David Tyack, in "The Kingdom of God and the Common School: Protestant Ministers and the Educational Awakening in the West," *Harvard Education Review*, 36, No. 4 (Fall, 1966), 447–69. His phrase "Protestant paideia" describes the institution-building repeated in community after community across the nation—family, church, and school reinforcing one another. In "From Social Movement to Professional Management: An Inquiry into the Changing Character of Leadership in Public Education" (with

Elizabeth Hansot), *American Journal of Education*, 88 (May 1980), 291–310, Tyack points out the contribution of evangelical religion to the spread of common schools.

11. Maggie Newton Van Cott, *The Harvest and the Reaper; Reminiscenses of Revival Work* (New York: N. Tibbals & Son, 1876), Introduction, Bishop Haven, xxxvii.

12. *Ladies' Repository*, XVI, No. 1 (January 1856), 19.

13. "Sunday School Literature" (unsigned), *Methodist Quarterly Review*, 1850, 283.

14. Archibald, *Methodism and Literature*, 51.

15. Abel Stevens, *The Centenary of American Methodism: A Sketch of its History, Theology, Practical System and Success* (New York: Carlton & Porter, 1865), 126.

16. Stevens, *The Century of Methodism*, 107.

17. Ibid., 145, 162. Obviously the central concept for Prof. Stevens was the word "system" which he uses positively throughout.

18. Archibald, *op. cit.*, 54.

19. Nathan Bangs, *A History of the Methodist Episcopal Church,* Vol. IV: 1829–40 (New York: Lane & Sanford for the Methodist Episcopal Church), 452.

20. J. C. Smith, *Early Methodism in Indiana: Biographical Sketches* (Indianapolis: J. M. Olcott, 1879), 75. Jed Dannenbaum, "The Origin of Temperance Activism and Militancy Among American Women," *Journal of Social History*, 15, No. 2 (Winter, 1991), 236–52, connects the perception of women in the temperance movement as "aggressive" with their usurping the public platform, otherwise still culturally proscribed for women.

21. Ann Douglas, *The Feminization of American Culture* (New York: A. A. Knopf, 1977), 254.

22. Ibid.

23. Carl N. Degler, *At Odds*, New York: Oxford University Press, 1980, 191–94. Although he gives religion some credit for helping women discover individualism he is apparently unaware that evangelicalism was the key to it for American women not in elite circumstances or sophisticated circles. The only place he deals with evangelical religion is in the chapter on domestic reform chap. XIII, "The World Is Only a Large Home."

24. "Female Influence," *Ladies' Repository*, I, No. 1 (Jan. 1841), 29.

25. Ibid.

26. Ibid.

27. Ibid.

28. *Ladies' Repository*, II, No. 12 (Dec. 1842).

29. *Ladies' Repository*, IV, No. 6 (June 1844), 286.

30. *Ladies' Repository*, IX, No. 1 (Jan. 1849), 48.

31. *Ladies' Repository*, VI, No. 7 (July 1846), 222.

32. Ibid.

33. *Ladies' Repository*, X, No. 10 (October 1850), 380.

34. *Ladies' Repository*, XVI, No. 1 (Jan. 1856), 63.

35. *Ladies' Repository*, XVI, No. 11 (Nov. 1856), 704.

36. Ibid.

37. *Ladies' Repository*, XVI, No. 8 (August 1856), 511. Two secondary references provide an understanding of the general change in America regarding childrearing,

toward more permissive and less authoritarian parental stance: Bernard Wish, *The Child and the Republic* (Philadelphia: University of Pennsylvania Press, 1968) and Joseph F. Kett, *Rites of Passage* (New York: Basic, 1977). They drew on such mid-nineteenth-century religious and parental advice books as Horace Bushnell's *Views of Christian Nurture* (1847) and Lyman Cobb's *The Evil Tendencies of Corporal Punishment* (1847). "Mother's love replaced father's discipline as the central gesture of the nuclear family." (William G. McLoughlin, *Revivals, Awakenings, and Reforms* (Chicago: University of Chicago Press, 1978), 124).

38. *Ladies' Repository*, XVI, No. 1 (Jan. 1856), 64.
39. *Ladies' Repository*, XVI, No. 3 (March 1856), 192.
40. Ibid.
41. *Ladies' Repository*, VI (1846), 192.
42. Ibid.
43. Ibid.
44. Ibid.
45. Ibid.
46. *Ladies' Repository*, XVI, No. 2, 128.
47. *Ladies' Repository*, XVI, No. 3 (March 1856), 192.
48. *Ladies' Repository*, XVI, No. 2, 128.
49. *Ladies' Repository*, XXl, No. 7 (July 1861), 447.
50. Ibid.
51. *Ladies' Repository*, XVI, No. 11 (Nov. 1856), 647.
52. *Ladies' Repository*, XVI, No. 2 (Feb. 1856), 114.
53. Mary Watters, *The First Hundred Years of MacMurray College* (Springfield, Ill.: Williamson, 1947), 49.
54. Ibid., 66.
55. Ibid., p. 59–60.

## Chapter 16

### Marti, *Rich Methodists: The Rise and Consequences of Lay Philanthropy in the Mid-Nineteenth Century*

1. William Dean Howells, *The Rise of Silas Lapham* (Boston: Houghton Mifflin Co., Riverside Editions, 1957), 21. Howells mentions Lapham's philanthropies in a single sentence. The hazards of wealth are bemoaned in Wade Crawford Barclay, *History of Methodist Missions*, Vol. 3 (New York: The Board of Missions of the Methodist Church, 1957), 49–50, which draws upon William Warren Sweet, *Methodism in American History* (New York: The Methodist Book Concern, 1933). Sweet and Barclay perceive a generalized softening of moral fiber following from the denomination's growing prosperity. This essay intends to be concrete about some of the results of that prosperity. It is obviously a very general sketch of a topic that might be treated in much greater detail. Sydney Ahlstrom has recommended attention to the philanthropies of evangelical laymen, and that might well include detailed study of rich Methodists.

2. Henry F. May, *The Enlightenment in America* (New York: Oxford University Press, 1976), 271–72; *Zion's Herald* 7 January 1869; George Claude Baker, Jr., *An*

*Introduction to the History of Early New England Methodism* (Durham: Duke University Press, 1941), 18.

3. George A. Crawford, *The Centennial of New England Methodism* (Boston: Crawford Bros., 1891), 47–48.

4. Robert D. Clark, *The Life of Matthew Simpson* (New York: Macmillan, 1956), 85–193, 276.

5. Ibid., 192; Matthew Simpson, *A Hundred Years of Methodism* (New York: Phillips and Hunt, 1876), 165; earlier Methodist thinking about church buildings is explained in James Porter, *The Revised Compendium of Methodism* (New York: Nelson and Phillips, 1875), 108.

6. Matthew Simpson, *Cyclopaedia of Methodism* (Philadelphia: Everts and Steward, 1878).

7. Ibid., see especially pp. 504 and 545. Apart from a few farm implement manufacturers, the only people in Simpson's book who were principally identified with agriculture were a black Louisiana farmer, Pierre Laudry, who had participated in politics during Reconstruction (p. 527) and Orange Judd, editor of the *American Agriculturist* and a publisher of agricultural books (p. 504).

8. Ibid., 311–12. The DAB portrays Drew as "sharp-witted, grasping, and unscrupulous," adding that "his trickiness was combined with a sanctimonious devotion to Methodism." Ezra Squier Tipple, *Drew Theological Seminary, 1867–1917* (New York: Methodist Book Concern, 1917), 21 takes a more appreciative view, quoting a contemporary who considered Drew "one of the pleasantest figures in the New York Methodism of that period. . . ."

9. Simpson, *Cyclopaedia*, 48, 768, 357.

10. Ibid., 612, 860–61, 849, 613.

11. Clark, *The Life of Matthew Simpson*, 72–73 reports the bigotry Indiana Methodists of Simpson's time had to confront. A Presbyterian legislator pronounced them too ignorant to conduct a college; Tipple, *Drew Theological Seminary*, 23–24n; Harold F. Williamson and Payson S. Wild, *Northwestern University: A History, 1850–1975* (Evanston: Northwestern University Press, 1976), 2; Frederick A. Norwood, *The Story of Methodism* (Nashville: Abingdon, 1974), 217–20.

12. Williamson and Wild, *Northwestern University*, 2–4; Simpson, *Cyclopaedia*, references throughout the volume.

13. Simpson, *Cyclopaedia*, 220, 754–55, 808; Oscar Handlin, *Boston's Immigrants, A Study in Acculturation* (Cambridge: Harvard University Press, 1959), 219–20 offers some suggestive generalizations about the three.

14. Edward Chase Kirkland, *Dream and Thought in the Business Community, 1860–1900* (Chicago: Quadrangle Paperbacks, 1964), 3; Donald B. Marti, "Laymen, Bring Your Money: Lee Claflin, Methodist Philanthropist, 1791–1871" *Methodist History* XIV (April 1976), 165–85.

15. Marti, "Laymen, Bring Your Money."

16. *Wesleyan Argus*, 31 January 1872; James Mudge, *History of the New England Conference of the Methodist Episcopal Church* (Boston: The Conference, 1910), 263–64; *DAB*; Mary B. Claflin, *Real Happenings* (New York: Thomas Y. Crowell, 1890), 14–22; *Harper's Weekly*, 17 February 1872.

17. *Boston Journal*, 1 April 1869; *DAB*; Mudge, *History of the New England Conference*, p. 265.

18. Handlin, *Boston's Immigrants*, 219–20.

19. Sleeper entry in *DAB; Zion's Herald*, 2 March 1871; Lee Claflin's Sunday Journal, August 12, 18, in Claflin Collection, Rutherford B. Hayes Library; *Wesleyan Argus*, 31 January 1872; Mudge, *History of the New England Conference*, 264.

20. Lee Claflin to William Claflin, n.p., February 2, 1845, Claflin Collection, Hayes Library.

21. Albert C. Outler, ed., *John Wesley* (New York: Oxford University Press, 1964), 238–50.

22. Marti, "Laymen, Bring Your Money," 173–77; Mudge, *History of the New England Conference*, 329.

23. Marti, "Laymen, Bring Your Money," 177–78; William F. Warren, "The Origin of Boston University," *Bostonia* IV (October, 1903), 20.

24. *Wesleyan Argus*, 31 January 1872, p. 118; *Zion's Herald*, 31 August 1871.

25. James A. Woolson, otherwise unidentified letter written in 1892 or soon after, with friendlier letters in Claflin Papers, Hayes Library.

26. Ann Douglas, *The Feminization of American Culture* (New York: Alfred A. Knopf, 1977), especially chapters two and three. Douglas' analysis does not purport to include evangelical clergy, but may have fit Methodists reasonably well by the mid-nineteenth century; *Zion's Herald*, 5 May 1858; 11 February 1852.

27. *Zion's Herald*, 5 May 1858.

28. Ibid., 11 February 1852; 18 April 1855; Mudge, *History of the New England Conference*, 242–43.

29. Mudge, *History of the New England Conference*, 243–44; *Zion's Herald*, 16 March 1859.

30. *Zion's Herald*, 4 February 1852; 10 March 1852.

31. Simpson, *Cyclopaedia*, 766; Simpson, *A Hundred Years of Methodism*, 174.

32. Simpson, *A Hundred Years of Methodism*, 175; Mudge, *History of the New England Conference*, 245; *Zion's Herald*, 3 June 1863; 18 May 1864; 25 May 1864.

33. *Zion's Herald*, supplement to 28 November 1867; Simpson, *A Hundred Years of Methodism*, 187–88.

34. Norwood, *The Story of Methodism*, 257–58.

35. Barclay, *History of Methodist Missions*, Vol. 4, 46n; Simpson, *Cyclopaedia*, especially p. 527.

## Chapter 17

Scott, *The Concern for Systematic Theology, 1840–70*

1. E. P. Humphrey, *Our Theology and Its Development* (Philadelphia: Presbyterian Board, 1857).

2. Tefft, *Methodism Successful* (New York: Derby and Jackson, 1860), 168.

3. See Silas Comfort, *An Exposition of the Articles of Religion of the Methodist Episcopal Church* (New York: Published for the Author at the Conference Office, 1847); and A. A. Jimeson, *Notes on the Twenty-five Articles* (Cincinnati: Applegate and Co., 1853). Jimeson, incidentally, indicates no awareness of Comfort's work.

4. Asbury Lowrey, *Positive Theology* (Cincinnati, 1853); Moses M. Henkle, *Primary Platform of Methodism; or, Exposition of the General Rules* (Louisville: Published by the Author and Company, 1851).

5. Thomas N. Ralston, *Elements of Divinity* (1847); Luther Lee, *Elements of Theology* (1853); Samuel Wakefield, *A Complete System of Christian Theology* (1858). These dates on the first editions of Lee and Wakefield are given in F. A. Archibald, ed., *Methodism and Literature* (New York: Phillips and Hunt, 1883), 172.

6. (New York: Carlton and Porter, 1864).

7. *Systematische Theologie einheitlich behandelt: Einleitung* (Bremen, Verlag des Tractathauses, 1865; Cincinnati: Poe and Hitchcock, 1865). Warren's work was not published in English; some passages are translated in McClintock's review.

8. *The Methodist Quarterly Review*, January, 1866, 106, 104.

9. William F. Warren, "American Infidelity: Its Factors and Phases," in *History, Essays, Orations and Other Documents of the Sixth General Conference of the Evangelical Alliance*, ed. by Philip Schaff and S. I. Prime (New York: Harper & Brothers, 1874), 252. The German philosophies, in various forms, had been penetrating American thought since early nineteenth century—Coleridge and Emerson being among the chief mediators in this earlier period. Cf. *The Life and Letters of Stephen Olin* (New York: Harper, 1853), II, 346 ff.

10. Between 1861 and 1879 a certain nominal support was given by the Methodist Episcopal Church, South, to A. T. Bledsoe's *Southern Review*. Bledsoe's periodical dealt with matters of general literature and history; it included sporadic articles and reviews on religious topics. The *Quarterly Review* of the Methodist Episcopal Church, South, was revived in 1879, and Summers assumed the editorship in 1880.

11. *Quarterly Review*, January, 1859, 143.

12. Ibid., October, 1859, 624.

13. Ibid., January, 1880, 179.

14. See, e.g., W. J. Sasnett, "German Philosophy," July, 1858, 321–47. In his editorial section of the same issue (p. 619) Summers quotes a notice on this article from the Texas *Christian Advocate*: "We are proud to know that the Church has a mind so capable of appreciating the German Philosophy."

15. Whedon, review of *Tracts for Priests and People, The Methodist Quarterly Review*, January, 1863, 163–65. Cf. Whedon's criticism of Bushnell's *Christian Nurture* for its diminution of Christian experience—an appraisal based on the practical imperceptibility therein of any doctrine of radical conversion (MQR, October, 1861, 698–700); also Whedon's summary estimate of Schleiermacher (MQR, January, 1860, 155). See also Summers' comment on Schleiermacher, "whose pantheism utterly precludes all objective Christianity," in Summers' *Systematic Theology* (Nashville: Publishing House of the Methodist Episcopal Church, South, 1888), I, 456.

16. *A Sermon . . . before . . . the legislature of Massachusetts at the annual election* (Boston: White, 1854).

17. See Nathan Bangs, *The Present State, Prospects, and Responsibilities of the Methodist Episcopal Church* (New York: Lane and Scott, 1850) for a specific treatment of this charge. Cf. John Dempster's review of Volume III of Stevens' *History of Methodism*, in *The Methodist Quarterly Review*, April, 1863, 204–26; and Whedon's

remark in the October, 1872, MQR: "The vague depreciation of 'creeds' and 'theologies' is rather new in our Methodism" (p. 667).

18. Whedon, *Statements: Theological and Critical* (New York: Phillips and Hunt, 1887), 183.

19. Ibid., 257 ff.

20. J. A. Reubelt, "Schleiermacher: His Theology and Influence," *Methodist Quarterly Review*, April, 1869, 227.

21. Whedon, *Statements*, 183.

22. "Schleiermacher: His Theology and Influence," 227.

23. A somewhat later exception to this generalization is R. S. Fosters *Philosophy of Christian Experience* (New York: Hunt and Eaton, 1891), which is an apologetic based on the rational significance and theological implications of the concrete facts of Christian experience. The fact remains, however, that American Methodism did not respond creatively to the emergent emphasis on empirical methodologies.

*Chapter 18*

Dayton, *From "Christian Perfection" to the "Baptism of the Holy Ghost"*

1. Cf. his *The Holiness-Pentecostal Movement in the United States* (Grand Rapids, Mich.: Eerdmans, 1971), especially chaps. 1–4.

2. Ibid., 8.

3. Walter J. Hollenweger, *The Pentecostals* (Minneapolis: Augsburg, 1972), 21.

4. "Pneumatological Nomenclature in Early Methodism," *Wesleyan Theological Journal* 8 (Spring 1973), 61–72.

5. Cf. The *Works* (1872 edition or the Grand Rapids, Mich.: Zondervan, 1959 reprint), 7:416.

6. Frederick Dale Bruner, *A Theology of the Holy Spirit* (Grand Rapids, Mich.: Eerdmans, 1970), 40–42, 332–35, etc.

7. (Oberlin: James Steele, 1840).

8. This apparently formed the kernel of *The Enduement with Power* published as an appendix to the British edition of Mahan's *Baptism of the Holy Ghost*.

9. The literature on Mahan is growing. Important for our purposes are the older works by Paul Fleisch, *Zur Geschichte der Heiligungsbewegung. Erstes Heft: Die Heiligungsbewegung von Wesley bis Boardman* (Leipzig: Wallmann, 1910) and Benjamin B. Warfield in articles in the *Princeton Theological Review* (1921), later incorporated into vol. 2 of *Perfectionism* (New York: Oxford University Press, 1931) and the abridged reprint by Presbyterian and Reformed Publishing Co., 1958. Cf. also Barbara Zikmund, "Asa Mahan and Oberlin Perfectionism" (Ph.D. diss., Duke University, 1969) and my essay on Mahan in *Wesleyan Theological Journal* 9 (Spring 1974, 60–69), which amplifies some points of this essay.

10. *Autobiography, Intellectual, Moral and Spiritual (London: Woolmer, 1882).*

11. (London: Wesleyan Conference Office, 1877).

12. *Autobiography*, 321.

13. *Scripture Doctrine of Christian Perfection* (Boston: D. S. King, 1839).

14. *Baptism of the Holy Ghost* (New York: W. C. Palmer, Jr., 1870).

15. This correspondence (two letters from Mahan) is available among the Phoebe Palmer papers held by Drew University Library.

16. Cf. his *Holiness of Christians in the Present Life* (Oberlin: Steele, 1840), first serialized in the *Oberlin Evangelist*.

17. *Oberlin Evangelist* 2 (1840), 93.

18. *Oberlin Quarterly Review* 1 (August 1845), 115.

19. *The Gift of the Holy Spirit*, with an introduction by Finney (Oberlin: E. J. Goodrich, 1875).

20. Bruner, *op. cit.*, 44–45, 340.

21. Cf. the preface to the second edition of his *The Twofold Life* (Chicago: Bible Colportage Association, n.d.). The preface is dated 1884.

22. (New York: Harper, 1856), 354. This work has always been regarded as a holiness classic and remains in print today (published by the Free Methodists).

23. Nelson R. Burr, *A Critical Bibliography of Religion in America, Religion in America*, vol. 4 (Princeton: Princeton University Press, 1961), 165.

24. Cf. the several works on this revival by J. Edwin Orr, and for the place of Phoebe Palmer, Melvin E. Dieter, "Revivalism and Holiness" (Ph.D. diss., Temple University, 1973).

25. These letters (from 1859 and following) were reprinted in *Four Years in the Old World* (New York: W. C. Palmer, Jr., 1870).

26. Ibid., 96. The letter is dated Sept. 16, 1859.

27. Mahan, *Autobiography*, 414.

28. "Baptism of the Spirit," *Guide to Holiness* 20 (February 1874), 1.

29. "Pentecost—What Is It?" *Guide to Holiness* 66 (January 1897), 37.

30. *Christian Perfection*, 158–59.

31. *Baptism of the Holy Ghost*, 21.

32. Ibid., 50.

33. *Christian Perfection*, 7.

34. On this point, see Melvin Dieter, "Revivalism and Holiness," already cited above in note 24.

35. *Baptism of the Holy Ghost*, 150.

36. Ibid., 138–43.

37. *D. L. Moody at Home* (Chicago: Revell, 1886), 168.

38. *Baptism of the Holy Ghost*, 78.

39. Ibid., 47.

40. *Christian Perfection*, 166. Cf. *Baptism of the Holy Ghost*, 113.

41. *Baptism of the Holy Ghost*, 39.

42. Ray Strachey, ed., *Religious Fanaticism: Extracts from the Papers of Hannah Whitall Smith* (London: Faber & Gwyer, 1928).

43. *Anointed to Serve: The Story of the Assemblies of God* (Springfield, Mo.: Gospel Publishing House, 1971), 31.

44. A. M. Kiergan, *Historical Sketches of the Revival of True Holiness and Local Church Polity from 1865–1916* (Fort Scott, Kans.: Board of Publication of the *Church Advocate and Good Way*, 1971), 31.

**Chapter 19**

Rowe, *The Ordination of Women: Round One; Anna Oliver and the General Conference of 1880*

1. Methodist Episcopal Church, General Conference, *Journal*, 1880. Petitions for licensing women to preach: Detroit, p. 107; North Indiana, p. 123; Indiana, p. 189; North West Iowa, pp. 131 and 239; and New York, p. 169. Petitions for the ordination of women: New England, pp. 168 and 262; Pittsburgh, p. 264; Southern Illinois, p. 102; Boston University School of Theology, p. 168.

2. Jeanette E. Newhall. "There Were Giants in Those Days; Pioneer Women and Boston University." *Nexus*, vol. 7, no. 1 (November, 1963) p. 18–19. For essential background, see Elaine Magalis, *Conduct Becoming to a Woman; Bolted Doors and Burgeoning Missions* (New York: Women's Division, Board of Global Ministries, The United Methodist Church, 1973).

3. *One Hundred Years of Methodism in Passaic, New Jersey, 1843–1943* (Passaic N.J.: First Methodist Church, 1943), 1. See also Methodist Episcopal Church, Conferences, Newark, *Minutes*, 1876. [39] for resolution "concerning the Church at Passaic" to "use all proper means to recover the title of this property for the use of said Methodist Episcopal Church."

4. Methodist Episcopal Church, Conferences. Newark, *Minutes*, 1877, [51].

5. Anna Oliver, *Test Case on the Ordination of Women* (New York, Wm. N. Jennings, printer. [1880]), 7.

6. Undated clipping in President William F. Warren papers, Boston University Library, quoted in Newhall, *op. cit.*, 121. Amanda Smith does not seem to mention her evangelistic efforts with Miss Oliver in Passaic in her *Autobiography; The Story of the Lords Dealings with Mrs. Amanda Smith the Colored Evangelist* (Chicago: Meyer & Brother, 1893).

7. Methodist Episcopal Church. Conferences, Newark, *Minutes*, 1877, 56. Although her name does not appear in the Newark Conference minutes, the centennial history of her first church duly lists her on the pastoral roll. *One Hundred Years of Methodism in Passaic, op. cit.*, 4.

8. Newhall, *op. cit.*, 21.

9. "The Methodist Preachers' Meeting," *New York Times*, February 27, 1877, 18, col. 6.

10. Elizabeth Cady Stanton [and others, editors] *History of Woman Suffrage In Two Volumes* (New York: Fowler & Wells, 1881), Vol. I, 784f. "Amativeness" is a Victorian word for being disposed to love or to sexual passion!

11. Willoughby Ave. M.E. Church, Brooklyn, *Methodist Annual*, 1881 (New York, Eagle Job Print [1880]), [3].

12. Oliver, *Test Case, op. cit.*, 7.

13. New England Conference, 81st annual session, report by W. D. Bridge, *Zion's Herald*, vol. 57 no. 16 (April 15, 1880) 122. col. 3–4. See also "The Women's Question Again," *Christian Advocate* (N.Y.), vol. 55 no. 17 (April 22, 1880) 259.

14. Oliver, *Test Case, op. cit.*, 8.

15. "New England Conference, 81st annual session," *Zion's Herald, op. cit.*

16. Ibid.

17. "The Women's Question Again," *op. cit.*

18. "New England Conference, 81st annual session," *Zion's Herald, op. cit.*

19. Anna Howard Shaw, *The Story of a Pioneer* (New York, Harper & Brothers, 1915), p. 123. There was precedent, since the North Indiana Conference of the Methodist Protestant Church ordained a woman, Helanor M. Davidson, as early as 1866, see John C. Coons, *A Brief History of the Methodist Protestant Church in Indiana* ([n.p.] 1939), 27.

20. David H. Wheeler, "Women as Methodist Preachers," *The Methodist* (N.Y.), vol. 21. no. 19 (May 8, 1880), 2, col. 2.

21. Oliver, *Test Case, op. cit.*, 3, 5, and 6. There is no evidence to suggest that the pamphlet was read into the record of the Conference. Only Drew and Garrett have reported copies of this rare pamphlet to the *Methodist Union Catalog.*

22. Methodist Episcopal Church, General Conference, *Journal*, 1880, 262 and 264. See also *Daily Christian Advocate*, May 18, 1880, 1. col. 4.

23. "Exciting Methodist Questions: Women and Temperance before the Conference," *New York Times*, May 18, 1880, 1, vol. 2,

24. Original manuscript in General Conference papers, Drew University Library. Italics in original. Noted, but not published, in General Conference *Journal*, 1880, 262, 264. Printed in an appendix to Anna Oliver's *Test Case*, 8.

25. Printed in General Conference *Journal*, May 27, 1880, 353 and in *Daily Christian Advocate*, May 22, 1880, 79. col. 6. No manuscript appears to have survived. The substance of this judicial decision was printed in the Discipline of the Church until 1920.

26. Original manuscript in General Conference papers, Drew University Library. Noted in General Conference *Journal*, 1880, May 25, 1880, 316; printed in *Daily Christian Advocate*, May 25, 1880, 90, col. 2.

27. Original manuscript in General Conference papers in Drew University Library; italics mine. Noted in General Conference *Journal*, 1880, May 25, 1880, 316; Printed in *Daily Christian Advocate*, May 26, 1880, 90, col. 2.

28. Original manuscript in General Conference papers in Drew University Library; Noted in General Conference *Journal*, May 25, 1880, 316; printed in *Daily Christian Advocate*, May 26, 1880, 90, col. 6.

29. Anna Howard Shaw, quoted in Susan B. Anthony [and others, editors] *History of Woman Suffrage* (New York, Arno & The New York Times, 1969), vol. 4, 207.

30. Willoughby Ave. M.E. Church, *Annual*, 1881, *op. cit.*, 10.

31. Ibid., 3.

32. Ibid., 5 and 9.

33. James M. Buckley, "Two Resignations . . . Miss Oliver," *Christian Advocate*, (N.Y.) vol. 58, no. 12 (March 22, 1883), 1, col. 2.

34. Methodist Episcopal Church. General Conference, 1884, *Journal*, 154. No manuscript papers at Drew for 1884.

35. Ibid., 220 and 314.

36. Although Newhall, *op. cit.*, 21 and Boston University, *General Alumni Catalogue*, 1918, Boston, 111, cite 1893 as the year of death, since Shaw's tribute was delivered in January of 1893, her death date was probably 1892.

37. Anna Howard Shaw, in an address to the National Suffrage Association convention of 1893, Washington, D.C., quoted in Susan B. Anthony [and others, editors] *History of Woman Suffrage* (New York, Arno & The New York Times, 1969) vol. 4., 206–7.

## Chapter 20
## Gifford, *"For God and Home and Native Land"*: The W.C.T.U.'s Image of Woman in the Late Nineteenth Century

1. Quote is from Frances E. Willard, *Home Protection Manual: Containing an Argument for the Temperance Ballot for Woman and How to Obtain It as a Means of Home Protection* (New York: The Independent Office, 1879), 6. The W.C.T.U.'s membership stood at 143,973 in 1890 (Helen E. Tyler, *Where Prayer and Purpose Meet: The W.C.T.U. Story* [Evanston, Ill.: Signal, 1949], 105).

2. See Gerda Lerner, "Placing Women in History: A 1975 Perspective," *Liberating Women's History*, ed. Bernice Carroll (Urbana: University of Illinois Press, 1976); Mary Ritter Beard, *Woman as Force in History: A Study in Traditions and Realities* (New York: Macmillan, 1946).

3. See Annie T. Wittenmyer, *Woman's Work for Jesus* (New York: Nelson & Phillips, 1873); Wittenmyer, *Under the Guns: A Woman's Reminiscences of the Civil War, with an Introduction by Mrs. General U.S. Grant* (Boston, Mass.: E.B. Stillings & Co., 1895). For Wittenmyer's life, see Tom Sillanpa, *Annie Wittenmyer, God's Angel* (Hamilton, Ill.: Hamilton, 1972); Edward T. James et al., eds., *Notable American Women, 1607–1950: A Biographical Dictionary* (Cambridge, Mass.: Harvard University Press, Belknap, 1971), vol. 3, 636–38.

4. Wittenmyer, *Woman's Work*, p. 55. For Methodist home mission work, see Ruth Esther Meeker, *Six Decades of Service, 1880–1940: A History of the Woman's Home Missionary Society of the Methodist Episcopal Church* (Cincinnati: Woman's Home Missionary Society, 1969); Arabel Wilbur Alexander, *The Life and Work of Lucinda B. Helm, Founder of the Woman's Parsonage and Home Missionary Society of the M.E. Church, South* (Nashville: Publishing House of the Methodist Episcopal Church, South, 1898).

5. Jane Marie Bancroft Robinson, *Deaconesses in Europe and Their Lessons for America* (New York: Hunt & Eaton, 1889).

6. Wittenmyer, *Woman's Work*, 5–6.

7. Ibid., 214.

8. Frances E. Willard, "The Dawn of Woman's Day," *Our Day: A Record and Review of Current Reform* 2/11: 345.

9. Ibid., 347.

10. Willard, *Glimpses of Fifty Years: The Autobiography of an American Woman* (Chicago: Woman's Temperance Publishing Association, 1889; reprint ed., New York: Hacker, 1970), 331. Hannah Whitall Smith was a national evangelist for the W.C.T.U. in the early 1880s.

11. Willard, "Organization," *Report of the International Council of Women, Assembled by the National Woman Suffrage Association, Washington, D.C., United States of America* (Washington, D.C.: Rufus H. Darby, 1888), 223.

12. Ibid., 224.

13. Sarepta M. Irish Henry, *The Pledge and the Cross: A History of Our Pledge Roll* (New York: National Temperance Society & Publication House, 1879), 14 (emphasis in original).

14. Margaret Rossiter White, *The Whirlwind of the Lord: The Story of Mrs. S. M. I. Henry* (Washington, D.C.: Review & Herald, 1953); Mary Henry Rossiter, *My Mother's Life: The Evolution of a Recluse* (Chicago: Fleming H. Revell, 1900).

15. Willard, "The New Chivalry," speech given March 3, 1871, typescript. See Mary Earhart Dillon, *Frances Willard: From Prayers to Politics* (Chicago: University of Chicago Press, 1944); James, *Notable American Women*, vol. 3, 613–19.

16. Willard, *A White Life for Two* (Chicago: Woman's Temperance Publishing Association, 1890), 6.

17. Willard, "Woman's Cause Is Man's," *Arena* 5:715.

18. See Susan Dye Lee, "Evangelical Domesticity: The Origins of the Woman's National Christian Temperance Union under Frances E. Willard" (Ph.D. diss., Northwestern University, 1980).

19. Willard, *Occupations for Women* (New York: Success, 1897), 24.

20. Willard, *Woman and Temperance* (Hartford, Conn.: Park, 1883), 310.

21. Willard, "New Chivalry," 1–2.

22. Willard, "Woman's Cause," 715–16.

23. See Julia R. Parish, ed., *The Poems and Written Addresses of Mary T. Lathrap with a Short Sketch of Her Life* (n.p.: Woman's Christian Temperance Union of Michigan, 1895); Aaron Merritt Hills, *Life and Labors of Mrs. Mary A. Woodbridge* (Ravenna, Ohio: F.W. Woodbridge, 1895).

24. Hills, *Life of Mary Woodbridge*, 155.

25. Parish, *Addresses of Mary Lathrap*, 386–87.

26. Rossiter, *My Mother's Life*, 135.

27. Willard, "Temperance," *Report of the International Council of Women* (1888), 114.

28. Willard, *How to Win: A Book for Girls* (New York: Funk & Wagnalls, 1888), 54.

29. Parish, *Addresses of Mary Lathrap*, 322ff.

30. Willard, *Home Protection Manual*, 27.

31. Willard, *Do Everything: A Handbook for the World's White Ribboners* (Chicago: Woman's Temperance Publishing Association, 1895), 45.

32. Willard, *White Life for Two*, 14–15.

33. Willard, *Do Everything*, 181–82.

## Chapter 21

Gorrell, *"A New Impulse": Progress in Lay Leadership and Service by Women of the United Brethren in Christ and the Evangelical Association, 1870–1910*

1. *Woman's Evangel* (Dayton, Ohio), (January 1882):4.

2. *Evangelical Messenger* (Cleveland, Ohio), (October 21, 1884):244.

3. *A History of the Woman's Missionary Association of the United Brethren in Christ* (Dayton, Ohio: United Brethren Publishing House, 1894), 6–7.

4. *Evangelical Messenger* (May 23, 1878):1; (September 14, 1880):1.

5. *Minutes of the Miami Conference of the United Brethren in Christ*, 1872, 9.

6. *Proceedings of the General Conference of the United Brethren in Christ*, 1873, 15, 23, 76 (cited hereafter as *Proceedings of the U.B.*).

7. *Evangelical Messenger* (May 23, 1878):1; (October 17, 1878):4.

8. Ibid., (September 14, 1880):1.

9. Ibid., (October 19, 1880):4.

10. Mrs. S.L. Wiest to Mrs. W.H. Hammer, October 25, 1883, quoted in *The Abiding Past; Or Fifty Years With the Woman's Missionary Society of the Evangelical Church, 1884–1934* (n.p.: The Woman's Missionary Society of the Evangelical Church, 1936), 18–19.

11. *Evangelical Messenger* (June 12, 1883):190.

12. *Proceedings of the General Conference of the Evangelical Association*, 1883, p. 59 (cited hereafter as *Proceedings of the E.A.*).

13. *Religious Telescope* (Dayton, Ohio), (July 28, 1875):345; (August 11, 1875):364.

14. Ibid., (October 27, 1875):36.

15. Ibid., (November 24, 1875):66.

16. *Proceedings of the U.B.*, 1877, 83, 112–18.

17. *Evangelical Messenger* (October 21, 1884):242, 244–47, 250.

18. Ibid., (October 6, 1885):628–29; (October 1, 1889):629, 634; (October 15, 1889):660–61; (October 16, 1894):660; (September 18, 1895):597; (October 19, 1898):660; (September 13, 1899):580; *Proceedings of the E.A.*, 1887, p. 80; 1895, pp. 26, 71, 88; 1899, pp. 88, 101.

19. *Religious Telescope* (May 18, 1881):533, 536; (June 29, 1881):633; *Woman's Evangel* (January 1882):1–2,5–6; (February 1882):20–21.

20. *Proceedings of the U.B.*, 1909, 185, 425–28.

21. Ibid., 429–32.

22. Ibid., 433.

23. *Woman's Evangel* (June 1909):164–65.

24. Ibid., 165–66.

25. Ibid.

26. See J. Bruce Behney and Paul H. Eller, *The History of the Evangelical United Brethren Church*, ed. Kenneth W. Krueger (Nashville: Abingdon, 1979), 181–87, 221–23, 283–85, 296; Raymond W. Albright, *A History of the Evangelical Church* (Harrisburg, Pa.: Evangelical, 1956), 326–33; A.W. Drury, *History of the Church of the United Brethren in Christ* (Dayton, Ohio: Otterbein, 1953), 487–504.

27. *Evangelical Messenger* (November 3, 1891):692, 696, 698.

28. *Missionary Tidings* (Harrisburg, Pa.), (October 1895):1–4.

29. Ibid., (November 1897):1–2; *Proceedings of the General Conference of the United Evangelical Church*, 1898, 19–20.

30. *Proceedings of the General Conference of the United Evangelical Church*, 1910, 45–46, 110.

31. *Evangelical Messenger* (September 20, 1892):602; (October 4, 1892):633.

32. Ibid., (October 16, 1894):660–661.

33. Ibid., (October 16, 1894):660; (September 18, 1895):597; *Proceedings of the E.A.*, 1895, pp. 26, 71, 88.

34. *Evangelical Messenger* (October 19, 1898):660; (September 13, 1899):580; *Proceedings of the E.A.*, 1899, 88, 101.

35. *Evangelical Messenger* (September 2, 1903):552; *Proceedings of the E.A.*, 1903, 106.

36. *Minutes of the Miami Conference of the United Brethren in Christ*, 1883, p. 29; 1884, p. 24; 1885, p. 18; 1886, p. 24; 1889, p. 26; *Minutes of the East Ohio Conference of the United Brethren in Christ*, 1888, unpaginated.

37. *Proceedings of the U.B.*, 1889, 241, 440, 446. See also Donald K. Gorrell, ed., *"Woman's Rightful Place": Women in United Methodist History*, (Dayton, Ohio: United Theological Seminary, 1980), 27–40.

38. *Proceedings of the U.B.*, 1893, 6–7, 16–17.

39. Ibid., 33.

40. Ibid., 1897, pp. 53–55; 1901, pp. 59–62.

41. Ibid., 1905, pp. 45–47.

42. *Religious Telescope* (January 16, 1901):1.

*Chapter 22*

Keller, *Creating a Sphere for Women: The Methodist Episcopal Church, 1869–1906*

1. Lewis Curts, ed., *The General Conferences of the Methodist Episcopal Church from 1792 to 1896* (Cincinnati: Curts & Jennings, 1900), 201.

2. For details of these developments, see Elaine Magalis, *Conduct Becoming to a Woman: Bolted Doors and Burgeoning Missions* (New York: Women's Division, Board of Global Ministries, United Methodist Church, 1973); Patricia R. Hill, "Heathen Women's Friends: The Organization and Development of Women's Foreign Missionary Societies among Methodist Episcopal Women, 1869–1915," *Methodist History* 19/3 (April 1981).

3. Curts, *General Conferences*, 209–11; Magalis, *Bolted Doors*, 119.

4. Curts, *General Conferences*, 214, 219.

5. Ibid., 223.

6. Ibid., 351.

7. For more details, see Edward T. James et al., eds., *Notable American Women, 1607–1950: A Biographical Dictionary*, (Cambridge, Mass.: Harvard University Press, Belknap, 1971), vol. 3, 411–13, 443–44; Clara A. Swain, *A Glimpse of India, Being a Collection of Extracts from the Letters of Dr. Clara A. Swain, First Medical Missionary to India of the Woman's Foreign Missionary Society of the Methodist Episcopal Church in America* (New York: J. Pott, 1909).

8. For more on the Chicago Training School, see Rosemary S. Keller, "The Deaconess Movement: Liberating or Constricting? A Case of the Chicago Training School" (Paper presented at the Missouri Valley History Conference, Omaha, Nebraska, March 11, 1978). On the deaconess movement, see Lucy Jane Rider Meyer, *Deaconesses, Biblical, Early Church, European, American, with the Story of the Chicago*

*Training School for City, Home and Foreign Missions and the Chicago Deaconess Home*, 3rd ed., rev. and enl. (Chicago: Cranston & Stowe, 1892).

9. *The Heathen Woman's Friend* 1/1, (June 1869):1, 2.

10. Frances J. Baker, *The Story of the Woman's Foreign Missionary Society* (Cincinnati: Curts & Jennings, 1898), 9–14; Mary Isham, *Valorous Ventures: A Record of Sixty and Six Years of the Woman's Foreign Missionary Society, Methodist Episcopal Church* (Boston, Mass.: Methodist Episcopal Church, 1936), 7–9.

11. *Heathen Woman's Friend* 1/2, (July 1869):12–13. For Willing, see James, *Notable American Women*, vol. 3, 623–25.

12. *Heathen Woman's Friend* 1/1, (June 1869):1.

13. Ibid., pp. 5–6; 1/2, (July 1869):10–11; 1/4, (September 1869):28; 2/8, (February 1871):86; 2/9, (March 1871) 98; 2/12, (June 1871):134, 139; Isham, *Valorous Ventures*, 11–12.

14. *Heathen Woman's Friend* 1/2, (July 1869):9; 1/3, (August 1869):18; 2/12, (June 1871):135.

15. Ibid., 1/2, (July 1869):10; 1/8, (January 1870):59; 2/9, (March 1871):97; 2/10, (April 1871): 112–14; 2/11, (May 1871):123–25.

16. Ibid., 3/1, (July 1871):146, 151; 2/10, (April 1871):110–13.

17. Ibid., 1/1, (June 1869):3–4; Isham, *Valorous Ventures*, 15–16.

18. *Heathen Woman's Friend* 1/4, (September 1869):29–31.

19. Isham, *Valorous Ventures*, 32–33.

20. *Heathen Woman's Friend* 1/7, (December 1869):52–53.

21. Ibid., 1/1, (June 1869):1.

22. Ibid., 1/3, (August 1869):20; 1/6, (November 1869):46.

23. Ibid., 1/1, (June 1869):7; 1/5, (October 1869):37.

24. Ibid., 1/3, (August 1869):21; Isham, *Valorous Ventures*, 20–25; Baker, *Woman's Foreign Missionary Society*, 27–28.

25. *Heathen Woman's Friend* 1/3, (August 1869):21; 1/2, (July 1869):13.

26. Ibid., 1/1, (June 1869):4–5; Isham, *Valorous Ventures*, 15.

27. Isham, *Valorous Ventures*, 43.

28. *Heathen Woman's Friend* 2/7, (January 1871):77–78.

## Chapter 23

### King, *Denominational Modernization and Religious Identity: The Case of the Methodist Episcopal Church*

1. Russell E. Richey has brought together significant interpretations of the origin and function of the denominational pattern in *Denominationalism* (Nashville: Abingdon, 1977). Useful information on changes in denominational structures after 1865 can be found in Ben Primer, *Protestants and American Business Methods* (UMI Research Press, 1979).

2. Peter R. Rudge, *The Ministry and Management: The Study of Ecclesiastical Administration* (London: Tavistock, 1968), 30.

3. Herbert A. Simon, *Administrative Behavior* (New York: The Free Press, 1952), xvi.

4. *Journal of the General Conference of the Methodist Episcopal Church*, 1872, 217.

5. *Journal of the General Conference of the Methodist Episcopal Church*, 1876, 204.

6. Ibid., 603.

7. According to John Kent, a similar transformation occurred in the British Wesleyan Connection as a result of the acceptance of lay representation in 1878. "This step . . . involved a definite break with the traditional Wesleyan view of the Ministry *[sic]*." *The Age of Disunity* (London: Epworth, 1966), 1.

8. *Journal of the General Conference of the Methodist Episcopal Church*, 1868, 617.

9. Reprinted in Nathan Bangs, *A History of the Methodist Episcopal Church*, vol. 3 (New York: T. Mason and G. Lane, 1840), 418.

10. *Discipline of the Methodist Episcopal Church*, 1832, 40.

11. *Discipline of the Methodist Episcopal Church*, 1852, 194.

12. Bangs, 81f.

13. C. C. Goss, *Statistical History of the First Century of American Methodism* (New York: Carlton and Porter, 1866), chap. 4.

14. John Higham has recently directed scholarly attention "to certain crucial changes in American culture that were already clearly visible in the 1850's—changes that mark the emergence of a pattern of consolidation." *From Boundlessness to Consolidation: The Transformation of American Culture, 1840–1860* (Ann Arbor: William L. Clements Library, 1969), 15.

15. According to the 1892 Aldrich Report, industrial wages rose 64% between 1860 and 1865. U. S. Bureau of the Census, *Historical Statistics of the United States: Colonial Times to 1957* (Washington, D.C.: 1960), 90. In the same period, the purchasing power of the dollar fell 1.43/.65. Frederick Bradford, "Money, Purchasing Power of" in James T. Adams ed., *Dictionary of American History*, vol. 10 (New York: Scribner, 1940), 8.

16. During the Civil War, both the U.S. Sanitary Commission and the U.S. Christian Commission helped to organize national philanthropy. See George M. Fredrickson, *The Inner Civil War* (New York: Harper & Row, 1965), 98–112.

17. Alpha J. Kynett, "Church Extension," *Methodist Quarterly Review* 54 (April, 1972):268–94.

18. Abel Stevens, *The Centenary of American Methodism* (New York: Carlton & Porter, 1866), 247f.

19. Ibid., 225.

20. *Debates and Addresses . . . of the New England Methodist Centenary Convention* (Boston: B.B. Russell, 1866), 137.

21. Ibid., 17.

22. Ibid., 150.

23. Stevens, 267.

24. Quoted in *The Christian Advocate*, 10 May 1972, 171.

25. An explicitly stated reason for turning the benevolent societies into denominational boards was the desire "to close the door against the possibility of danger [of financial mismanagement] in the future." *Journal*, 1872, 297. The delegates were

concerned about this issue at the 1872 General Conference because John Lanahan, assistant agent of the Methodist Book Concern, had charged that the senior agent of the Book Concern was guilty of mismanagement and possible fraud. The 1872 General Conference devoted considerable time to the scandal, but was unable to reach a verdict because crucial evidence had been destroyed. See the various reports and conflicting evidence in the 1872 *Journal*. See also: John Lanahan, *The Era of Frauds in the Methodist Book Concern at New York* (Baltimore: Methodist Book Depository, 1896).

26. Proponents of lay representation argued that "the continuance of the exercise of such [legislative] powers by the ministry alone must in time give to a General Conference of ministers the appearance of exercising lordly authority. A General Conference in which the laity and ministry are both represented can, with the best reason, lay its command upon both." *Journal*, 1868, 612f.

27. Ibid.

28. *Journal*, 1876, 400f.

29. The data are taken from the General Conference journals for these years.

30. "The Annuity Fund," *The Christian Republic* 2 (July, 1908):6.

31. *Journal*, 1876, 621f.

32. Ibid., 401.

33. *Journal of the General Conference of the Methodist Episcopal Church*, 1896, 39.

34. Fayette L. Thompson, "Men and Religion: The Program," *Men and Religion* (New York: Young Men's Christian Association Press, 1911), 6.

35. *Journal of the General Conference of the Methodist Episcopal Church*, 1912, 203.

36. John L. Nuelsen, "Methodism's Achievements and Larger Opportunities," in *Militant Methodism*, edited by David Downey, *et. al.* (New York: The Methodist Book Concern, 1913), 43.

37. "Message to the Church," in ibid., 222.

38. *Journal of the General Conference of the Methodist Episcopal Church*, 1916, 1320.

39. *Journal of the General Conference of the Methodist Episcopal Church*, 1920, 567f.

40. Ralph E. Diffendorfer (ed.), *The World Service of the Methodist Episcopal Church* (Chicago: The Methodist Book Concern, 1923), 698.

41. Ibid.

42. Kynett, 269.

## Chapter 24

Dougherty, *The Social Gospel According to Phoebe: Methodist Deaconesses in the Metropolis, 1885–1918*

1. Charles Howard Hopkins, *The Rise of the Social Gospel in American Protestantism* (New Haven: Yale University Press, 1940), 319

2. Henry F. May, *Protestant Churches in Industrial America* (New York: Harper & Brothers, 1949; reprint ed., New York: Octagon Books, 1963), 91.

3. Hopkins, *Social Gospel*, 318.

4. Aaron Ignatius Abell, *The Urban Impact on American Protestantism, 1865–1900* (Cambridge, Mass.: Harvard University Press; London: Oxford University Press, 1943; reprint ed., Hamden, Conn.: Archon, 1962).

5. John R. Commons, *Social Reform and the Church* (New York/Boston: Thomas Y. Crowell & Company, 1894), 12.

6. *A Dictionary of Religion and Ethics*, ed. Shailer Mathews, (New York: Macmillan, 1921), 416–17.

7. Women's contributions have not been totally ignored. E.g., Abell, *Urban Impact*, and Winthrop S. Hudson, *Religion in America* (New York: Scribner, 1965) note women's work, although they assign it little significance.

8. See Sidney E. Mead, *The Lively Experiment: The Shaping of Christianity in America* (New York: Harper & Row, 1963: paperback ed., 1976), 121. Hopkins called the program the council's "first outstanding pronouncement" and includes the text in *Rise of Social Gospel*, 316–17. Harry F. Ward's *Social Creed of the Churches* (New York: Eaton & Mains; Cincinnati: Jennings & Graham, 1912) is an exposition designed for the instruction of church people. The council's social creed rested on a fourteen-point creed adopted by the Methodist Episcopal Church in 1908. See Donald K. Gorrell, "The Methodist Federation for Social Service and the Social Creed," *Methodist History* 13/2(January 1975):3–32.

9. Men and Religion Forward, *Messages* 2: *Social Service* (New York: 1912), 1-108, quoted in Hopkins, *Rise of Social Gospel*, 296–98. Hopkins argues forcefully that 1912 marks the "official recognition" of the social gospel in the United States, the moment of its maturity.

10. Walter Rauschenbusch, *Christianizing the Social Order* (New York: Macmillan, 1912), 20.

11. Mead, *The Lively Experiment*, 182. Robert T. Handy has described the Men and Religion Forward Movement as the "high tide of the general Protestant interest in the social gospel" (Handy, ed., *The Social Gospel in America* [New York: Oxford University Press, 1966], 11).

12. See Jane Marie Bancroft Robinson, *Deaconesses in Europe and Their Lessons for America* (New York: Hunt & Eaton, 1889); Methodist Episcopal Church, Woman's Home Missionary Society, *The Early History of Deaconess Work and Training Schools for Women in American Methodism, 1883–1885* (Detroit: Speaker-Hines, [1913?]); Mary Agnes Dougherty, "The Methodist Deaconess Movement, 1888–1918" (Ph.D. diss., University of California at Davis, 1979); and Elizabeth M. Lee, *As Among the Methodists: Deaconesses Yesterday, Today and Tomorrow* (New York: Woman's Division of Christian Service, Board of Missions, The Methodist Church, 1963).

13. Quote from Hopkins, *Rise of Social Gospel*, 54.

14. Isabelle Horton, *High Adventure: Life of Lucy Rider Meyer* (New York: Methodist Book Concern, 1928), 78. For Meyer's life, also see Edward T. James et al., eds., *Notable American Women, 1607–1950: A Biographical Dictionary* (Cambridge, Mass.: Harvard University Press, Belknap, 1971), vol. 2, 534–36.

15. For the founding of C.T.S., see Lucy Rider Meyer, *Deaconesses, Biblical, Early Church, European, American* (Chicago: Message, 1889; 3rd ed., rev. and enl., Chicago: Cranston & Stowe, 1892); Dougherty, "Deaconess Movement."

16. E.g., Josiah Strong, *Our Country; Its Possible Future and Its Present Crisis* (New York: American Home Missionary Society, 1885); Washington Gladden, *Applied Christianity; Moral Aspects of Social Questions* (Boston/New York: Houghton Mifflin, 1886); Samuel Lane Loomis, *Modern Cities and Their Religious Problems* (New York: Baker & Taylor, 1887); Richard Theodore Ely, *Social Aspects of Christianity* (Boston: W.L. Greene, 1888).

17. Handy, *Social Gospel in America*, 11–12.

18. May, *Protestant Churches*, 189–90.

19. Handy, *Social Gospel in America*, 11–12.

20. *Daily Christian Advocate* (May 19, 1888):131.

21. Christian Golder, *History of the Deaconess Movement in the Christian Church* (Cincinnati, Ohio: Jennings & Pye; New York: Eaton & Mains, 1903), 307. On Wittenmyer, see Tom Sillanpa, *Annie Wittenmyer, God's Angel* (Hamilton, Ill.: Hamilton, 1972); James, *Notable American Women*, vol. 3, 636–38.

22. The first of the series appeared in *The Ladies Repository* 32(October 1872):242.

23. Edward R. Hardy, "Deacons in History and Practice," *The Diaconate Now*, ed. Richard T. Nolan, (Washington, D.C.: Corpus, 1968), 12.

24. James Dunk, "Phoebe, a Servant of the Church," *Message and Deaconess Advocate* (May 1900):9.

25. I have traced the geographic origins of 164 of the 509 women who served as deaconesses between 1887 and 1914. Of the group researched, 107 (62.5%) came from towns with a population of 2,500 or less. At the zenith of the deaconess movement in 1910, 76.6% of Americans lived in towns designated as rural by the federal census.

26. Dunk, "Phoebe," 9.

27. Brodbeck, "Deaconesses and the City," *Deaconess Advocate* (September 1890):3.

28. W. E. McLellan, "The Open Door of the City," *Deaconess Advocate* (September 1898):4.

29. Brodbeck, "Deaconesses," p. 3; Isabelle Horton, "The Crisis in the Cities," *Deaconess Advocate* (September 1906):9; and "The City Problem," *Deaconess Advocate* (July 1896):15.

30. Editorial, *Deaconess Advocate* (October 1911):8.

31. "Our Bit-of-Heaven House," *Message* (June 1889):1–2. In February 1891, the Chicago deaconesses opened a house of this name located "a stone's throw from one of the worst and neediest localities in the city." Three deaconesses there served a predominantly Italian and Jewish neighborhood.

32. *Message and Deaconess World* (June 1893):11.

33. Some deaconesses entered the ranks of the Progressive movement. A novel vocation as a regularly commissioned policewoman in Ottawa, Ill., was reported for deaconess Viola Miller. She is said to have worn a "*star* along with the deaconess bonnet and worked the night shift, 4–11 p.m., especially among the city's youth" (*Deaconess Advocate* [August 1913]:12).

34. *Message* (October 1890):7.

35. *Message and Deaconess Advocate* (December 1895):9. For Taylor, see Louise Wage, *Graham Taylor: Pioneer for Social Justice, 1851–1938* (Chicago/London: Chicago University Press, 1964).

36. *Deaconess Advocate* (September 1911):1.

37. Isabelle Horton, "The Bad Lands of Chicago," *Christian Cosmopolitan* (n.d.), reprinted in *Deaconess Advocate* (March 1904):4.

38. See, e.g., "Acknowledgments," *Deaconess Advocate* (December 1891).

39. "At the Sign of the Three Gilt Balls," *Deaconess Advocate* (January 1899):1.

40. "What Deaconesses Say to the Churches," *Deaconess Advocate* (March 1896):10.

41. *Deaconess Advocate* (January 1906):9.

42. Ibid. (September 1899):2; for M.F.S.S., see ibid. (October 1908):8.

43. E.g., "Our Sister in the Kitchen," *Message and Deaconess Advocate* (June 1896):5–6.

44. Literature on the Progressives, especially in Chicago, is extensive. For the Christian perspective, see two contemporary writings, Lucy Rider Meyer, "The Italians of Chicago; their religious susceptibility," *Northwestern Christian Advocate* 39/30(July 29, 1891):2; William T. Stead, *If Christ Came to Chicago! A plea for the union of all who love in the service of all who suffer* (Chicago: Laird & Lee, 1894). Also see Ernest P. Bicknell, "Problems of Philanthropy in Chicago," *Annuals of the American Academy of Political and Social Science* 21(May 1903). More recent works include Kenneth Kusmer, "The Functions of Organized Charity in the Progressive Era: Chicago as a Case Study," *Journal of American History* 60/3(December 1973):657–78; Bessie Pierce, *A History of Chicago, 1871–1893; Rise of the Modern City* (New York: Alfred A. Knopf, 1957); Davis Thelen, "Social Tensions and the Origins of Progressivism," *Journal of American History* 56(September 1969):323–41; Robert Wiebe, *The Search for Order, 1877–1920* (New York: Hill & Wang, 1967); and Allen F. Davis, *Spearhead for Reform: The Social Settlements and the Progressive Movement, 1890–1914* (New York: Oxford University Press, 1967).

45. *Deaconess Advocate* (August 1902):5. The article took its position on the basis of studies conducted by Jane Addams' investigators.

46. Ibid. (July 1896):4; (September 1896):13.

47. Ibid. (January 1911):10; (June 1897):5.

48. Deaconesses in this work ran certain risks. Confessed one, "I make mistakes still and sometimes get well laughed at for my trouble. I accosted a little bride once and I'll never forget the air of resentful pride with which she drew herself up and replied, 'He's my husband'" (*Deaconess Advocate* [March 1914]:5).

49. Cited by Hopkins, *Rise of Social Gospel*, 103.

50. John Atkinson, "Methodism in the Cities of the United States," *Methodist Quarterly Review* 59(July 1877):481–505, defended the status of Methodism in America's fourteen largest cities. The Congregationalist *Independent* had run "seven full editorials, besides minor articles" in February and March, 1877, arguing that Methodists were losing ground in the cities.

51. A. F. Pierson, *Message* (November 1889):7.

52. Brodbeck, "Deaconesses," *Deaconess Advocate* (September 1890):3.

53. Chicago Training School Catalogue (1888), p. 12.

54. *Message* (March 1888):2.

55. See Meyer, *Deaconesses* (1889 ed.), p. 86, for the opening of a school on November 28, 1885, at Douglas Park Mission in Chicago.

56. Rauschenbusch, *Christianity and the Social Crisis* (New York, Macmillan, 1920), esp. chap. 7.

57. *Deaconess Advocate* (January 1895):14.

58. "The Coming Billionaire," ibid. (January 1899):6–7.

59. See, for example, *Deaconess Advocate* (May 1900):4; (March 1911):7; (March 1912):4; "Wanted: a Mission for Business Men" (February 1896):7; "Save the Business Man" (January 1907):10.

60. Quoted in Mead, *Lively Experiment*, 178.

61. Quoted in *Deaconess Advocate* (February 1901):10.

62. Rauschenbusch, *Christianizing the Social Order*, 9.

## Chapter 25

McClain, *Pioneering Social Gospel Radicalism: An Overview of the History of the Methodist Federation for Social Action*

1. See William M. King, "The Emergence of Social Gospel Radicalism in American Methodism" (Ph.D. diss., Harvard University, 1978), 70 ff.

2. This title is borrowed from the thesis of William H. King cited above.

3. William H. King, *op. cit.*, 168 ff.

4. This title comes from Milton J. Huber, "A History of the Methodist Federation for Social Action" (Ph.D. diss., Boston University, 1949), 179.

5. Robert Justin Goldstein, *Political Repression in Modern America*, (Cambridge/New York:Schenkman, 1978), 213 ff.

6. Ralph Lord Roy devotes a whole chapter to this controversy in *Communism and the Churches*, (New York: Harcourt, Brace, 1960), 291–324. His perspective, however, is that of Cold War anti-communism and therefore his use of facts and his judgments are not to be trusted.

7. Ralph Lord Roy, *op. cit.*, 301.

8. The Circuit Riders were specifically repudiated by the General Conference of 1960, which stated: "We regret that any Methodists contribute either money or leadership to such organizations as Circuit Riders, Inc., which utilize the 'guilt by association' and 'fellow-traveler' approaches as they stir up unjustified suspicion and develop unfounded fears."

9. Ralph Lord Roy, *op. cit.*, 309–10.

## Chapter 26

Gorrell, *The Social Creed and Methodism Through Eighty Years*

1. Harry F. Ward, *The Social Creed of the Churches* (New York: Eaton & Mains; Cincinnati: Jennings & Graham, 1912), 7.

2. Frederick A. Norwood, *The Story of American Methodism* (Nashville: Abingdon, 1974), 354.

3. Harry F. Ward, "Twenty years of the Social Creed," *Christian Century* (Chicago), 19 Apr. 1928, 502–3.

4. Washington Gladden. "The Church and the Social Crisis," *Minutes of the National Council of the Congregational Churches of the United States*, 1907, 1–21.

5. "Minutes of the Methodist Federation for Social Service, 1907–1930," (Unpublished manuscript, Rose Memorial Library, Drew University, Madison, N.J.), 12–13, 21, 26; Herbert Welch, *As I Recall My Past Century* (Nashville: Abingdon, 1962), 54–55. For more detailed information on this and succeeding events through 1912 see Donald K. Gorrell. "The Methodist Federation for Social Service and the Social Creed," *Methodist History* 13 (Jan. 1975), 3–32.

6. *Journal of the General Conference of the Methodist Episcopal Church*, 1908, 547.

7. *Western Christian Advocate* (Cincinnati), 10 Jun. 1908, 6; *Central Christian Advocate* (Kansas City, Mo.), 10 Jun. 1908, 10; *The Church and Social Problems, Including the Statement of the General Conference of 1908 and the Social Problem in the Episcopal Address*, Federation Pamphlet No. 5 (N.p., n.d.), 8.

8. *Journal of the General Conference of the Methodist Episcopal Church, 1908*, 547–48; *Western Christian Advocate* (Cincinnati), 10 Jun. 1908, 6.

9. *Federal Council of the Churches of Christ in America: Report of the First Meeting of the Federal Council, Philadelphia, 1908*, ed. Elias B. Sanford (New York: Revell, 1909), 226–43, with the revised Social Creed on 238–39; Gorrell, 16–20.

10. *The Outlook* (New York), 19 Dec. 1908, 849–50.

11. In a four volume study of Methodism and Society one volume credits the authorship to Ward while another attributes it to North. Richard M. Cameron, *Methodism and Society in Historical Perspective* (New York, Nashville: Abingdon, 1961), 323; Walter G. Muelder, *Methodism and Society in the Twentieth Century* (New York, Nashville: Abingdon, 1961), 50.

12. Harry F. Ward to Daisy, 17 Feb. 1909, Harry F. Ward Papers, Union Theological Seminary, New York, quoted in Eugene P. Link, *Labor-Religion Prophet: The Times and Life of Harry F. Ward* (Boulder, Colo.: Westview, 1984), 45–46; Creighton Lacy, *Frank Mason North: His Social and Ecumenical Mission* (Nashville: Abingdon, 1967), 129–45; Gorrell, 21–22.

13. Charles S. Macfarland, "The Kingdoms of This World; The Kingdom of Our Lord," *Christian Unity at Work: The Federal Council of the Churches of Christ in America in Quadrennial Session at Chicago, Illinois, 1912*, ed. Charles S. Macfarland (New York: Federal Council of Churches, 1913), 158–60, 165–67; Harry F. Ward, *A Year Book of the Church and Social Service in the United States* (New York: Fleming H. Revell, 1914), 24–28.

14. Macfarland, "The Kingdoms of This World . . . ," 174–77; Gorrell, 24–28.

15. *Discipline of the Methodist Episcopal Church*, 1916, 527–31; *Journal of the General Conference of the Methodist Episcopal Church*, 1916, 602.

16. *The Churches Allied for Common Tasks: Report of the Third Quadrennium of the Federal Council of the Churches of Christ in America. 1916–1920*, ed. Samuel McCrea Cavert (New York: Federal Council of Churches, 1921), 113–14.

17. *Minutes of the General Assembly of the Presbyterian Church in the United States of America*, 1913, 56, 170–171, 186–89, 281, 448; 1914, 52–56, 133–37, 375.

18. *The Churches Allied for Common Tasks*, 312; *Twenty Years of Church Federation: Report of the Federal Council of the Churches of Christ in America, 1924–1928*, ed. Samuel McCrea Cavert (New York: Federal Council of Churches, 1929), 230–31.

19. *Minutes of the National Council of the Congregational Churches of the United States*, 1925, 156–58.

20. "Minutes of the Methodist Federation for Social Service," 22 Nov. 1920, 202–3; 11 Nov. 1927, 235; *Daily Christian Advocate*, 30 May 1928, 706; *Christian Advocate* (New York), 28 Jun. 1928, 815.

21. *Twenty Years of Church Federation*, 62, 229–31.

22. Charles S. Macfarland, *Christian Unity in Practice and Prophecy* (New York: Macmillan, 1933), 298, 312–14; F. Ernest Johnson, *The Church and Society* (New York: Abingdon, 1935), 62, 229–31.

23. *New York Times*, 8 Dec. 1932, 2; 9 Dec. 1932, 44; *Christian Advocate: Western Edition* (Cincinnati), 22 Dec. 1932, 29.

24. Muelder's interpretation is found in "The Social Creed in the Great Depression" chapter of *Methodism and Society in the Twentieth Century*, 126–74, which is restated in A. Dudley Ward, *The Social Creed of the Methodist Church* (New York: Abingdon, 1961), 25 and Norwood, *The Story of American Methodism*, 253–54, 391–94, 400, 401, 402, 419, 422. Cf. *Discipline of the Methodist Episcopal Church*, 1932, par. 561 to ibid., 1928, par. 597, and cf. both to *Discipline of the Methodist Episcopal Church, South*, 1934, par. 593.

25. Harry F. Ward, *Which Way Religion?* (New York: Macmillan, 1931), 6, 180–81; *Christian Century* (Chicago), 8 Jun. 1932, 726; *Social Service Bulletin* (New York), 15 Jun. 1932, Nov. 1933.

26. *Christian Century* (Chicago), 1 Apr. 1936, 486–87; *Daily Christian Advocate*, 18 May 1936, 456–57.

27. Cf. General Conference Reports and Resolutions in *Discipline of the Methodist Episcopal Church*, 1932, 646–66, especially par. 561, with those in ibid., 1936, 651–74, especially pars. 1462 and 1463.

28. *Journal of the General Conference of the Methodist Protestant Church*, 1916, 138–39; *Discipline of the Methodist Episcopal Church, South*, 1914, 373–74; 1934, par. 593.

29. *Journal of the Uniting Conference of The Methodist Church*, 1939, 222, 278, 358–59, 535–38; *Daily Christian Advocate*, 2 May 1939, 113–14; 8 May 1939, 308–9; 11 May 1939. 430–33; *Discipline of The Methodist Church*, 1940, par. 1712.

30. *Journal of the General Conference of The Methodist Church*, 1940, 670–71, 675–76; *Daily Christian Advocate*, 2 May 1940, 257–58; 7 May 1940, 448–49.

31. Muelder, *Methodism and Society in the Twentieth Century*, pp. 205–28; Ralph Lord Roy, *Apostles of Discord* (Boston: Beacon, 1949), 308–36; Stanley High, "Methodism's Pink Fringe," *Reader's Digest*, Feb. 1950, 134–38.

32. *Journal of the General Conference of The Methodist Church*, 1948, 407, 410, 747; 1952, 613–21, 685–90, 1415–21. The Federation continues to the present as the Methodist Federation for Social Action, led now by George McClain.

33. *Twenty Years of Church Federation*, 188–89, 229–31; *Biennial Report of the Federal Council of the Churches of Christ in America*, 1938, 13–15; *Annual Report of the Federal Council of the Churches of Christ in America*, 1948, 9–10.

34. "Social Pronouncements By Religious Bodies," F. Ernest Johnson (ed.) *The Social Work of the Churches: A Handbook of Information* (New York: Dept. of Research and Education of the Federal Council of Churches, 1930), chap. 6; "After Thirty Years: A National Inventory in Terms of the Social Ideals of the Churches," *Information Service* (New York), 20 Jun. 1942, 1–12.

35. *Christian Faith in Action: The Founding of the National Council of the Churches of Christ in the United States of America* (New York: National Council of Churches, 1951), 210, 265–72.

36. *Discipline of The Methodist Church*, 1956, par. 2020, 702–7; *Daily Christian Advocate*, 7 May 1956, 588–91.

37. *Discipline of The Methodist Church*, 1960, 429–38.

38. *Discipline of the Evangelical United Brethren Church*, 1947, 395–402; *Discipline of the United Methodist Church*, 1968, 52–66.

39. *Daily Christian Advocate*, 22 Apr. 1970, 127–28; James S. Thomas, "The Process of Developing Social Principles," *engage* (Washington, D.C.), Mar. 1972, 9.

40. *engage*, Mar. 1972, 9–10, 14–32; *Daily Christian Advocate*, 19 Apr. 1972, 222–25.

41. Cf. *engage*, Mar. 1972, 14–32 with Report 14 of Committee on Christian Social Concerns, *Daily Christian Advocate*, 25 Apr. 1972, 483–87. A summary of major changes was presented by the editor in *Daily Christian Advocate*, 27 Apr. 1972, 593–94. The final document is in *Discipline of the United Methodist Church*, 1972, 83–97.

## Chapter 27

Perry, *The Revival of Stewardship and the Creation of the World Service Commission in the Methodist Episcopal Church, 1912–1924*

1. Edwin Holt Hughes, *I Was Made a Minister* (New York and Nashville, 1943), 123. The brackets are the bishop's.

2. The relevant literature includes: Peter Drucker, *Concept of the Corporation* (New York, 1972; original edition, 1946); Kenneth Boulding, *The Organizational Revolution. A Study in the Ethics of Economic Organization* (New York, 1953, with comments by Reinhold Niebuhr); Samuel P. Hays, *The Response to Industrialism, 1885–1914* (Chicago, Ill. 1957); Alfred D. Chandler, *Strategy and Structure: Chapters in the History of the Industrial Enterprise* (Cambridge, Mass., 1962); Robert Wiebe, *The Search for Order. 1877–1920* (New York, 1967); Kenneth A. Thompson, *Bureaucracy and Church Reform; the Organizational Response of the Church of England to Social Change 1800–1965* (Oxford, 1970); Clifton K. Yearley, *The Money Machines: The Breakdown and Reform of Governmental and Party Finance in the North, 1860–1920* (Albany, N.Y., 1970); James Willard Hurst, *A Legal History of Money in the United States. 1774–1970* (Lincoln, Nebr., 1973); Benjamin M. Primer, *Protestants and American Business Methods* (Ann Arbor, Mich., 1979); Larry Berman, *The Office of Management and Budget and the Presidency, 1921–1979* (Princeton, N.J., 1979); Edward P. Kantowicz, "Cardinal Mundelein of Chicago and the Shaping of Twentieth-Century American Catholicism," *The Journal of American History*, 68 (1981): 52–68; and Stephen Skowronek, *Building a New American State: The Expansion of National Administrative Capacities, 1877–1920* (Cambridge and New York, 1982).

3. A good example is John Wesley's use (and subsequent American Methodist use) of the local church trust deed as a legal strategy to enforce the connectional authority of appointing ministers. The intention here was to prevent wealthy local church trustees from controlling what the minister preached and so to preserve the distinction between church and society. This strategy deserves further historical study.

4. "Report of the World Service Commission and the Co-operative Work of the Benevolence Boards," in Methodist Episcopal Church, *Journal of the General Conference* (1928), 1127. Journals of the General Conference will be cited hereafter as: *JGC* (year).

5. Committee on Foreign Missions, Report No. 4, *JGC* (1908), 567; "Episcopal Address," *JGC* (1912), 196–202; Committee on Temporal Economy, Report No. 4, ibid., 747–48; Harvey Reeves Calkins, "A General Conference Incident," *Men and Money*, 2, number 12 (May 1920): 5–6, on the origins of official support for tithing; "Report of the World Service Commission and the Co-operative Work of the Benevolence Boards," *JGC* (1928), pp. 1127–28; George A. E. Salstrand, *The Story of Stewardship in the United States of America* (Grand Rapids, Michigan, 1956), 47–49.

6. "Report of the Commission on Finance," *JGC* (1920), 1369.

7. Harvey Reeves Calkins, "Stewardship and the Commission on Finance," *Men and Money*, 1, number 1 (December 1917): 45–46; "Report of the Commission on Finance," *JGC* (1920), 1368–70.

8. Ibid., 1371–74.

9. Ibid., 1374–82.

10. See generally on the history of the Centenary, Alonzo E. Wilson (comp.), "Methodist Centenary Celebration" [1919?], typescript, Garrett-Evangelical Theological Seminary library; "Centenary Reports and Historical Data," *JGC* (1924), 1791–1824; "Report of the Joint Centenary Conservation Committee," ibid., 1825–60; and John Lankford, "Methodism 'Over the Top': The Joint Centenary Movement, 1917–1925," *Methodist History*, 2 (1963): 27–37.

11. "The Stewardship Alliance," *Men and Money*, 1, number 3 (May 1918): 108–109; "Report of the Commission on Finance," *JGC* (1920), 1368–77.

12. Charles M. Stuart Collection, Garrett-Evangelical Theological Seminary Library, Box 6, folder 6.

13. "The Stewardship Alliance," *Men and Money*. 1, number 3 (May 1918): 108–9; Tyler Dennett, "The Man Behind the Machine," ibid., 2, number 2 (June 1919): 24–26; Wilson (comp.), "Methodist Centenary Celebration"; "Report of the Board of Foreign Missions", *JGC* (1924), 1183; "Journal of the General Conference," ibid., 242, 387.

14. "Report of the Council of Boards of Benevolence," *JGC* (1924), 1145–81; "Report of the World Service Commission and the Co-operative Work of the Benevolence Boards," *JGC* (1928), 1128–31. On the crisis in the Methodist Episcopal Church, South, see Elmer T. Clark, *The Task Ahead; the Missionary Crisis of the Church* (Nashville, Tenn., 1925).

15. *Christian Advocate* (New York), July 20, 1922, 905; March 15, 1923, 337; May 24, 1923, 670; November 15, 1923, 1409; December 20, 1923, 1590; January 31, 1924, 124, 140–41; "Report of the Council of Boards of Benevolence," *JGC* (1924), 1172–77;

Methodist Episcopal Church, *The Daily Christian Advocate*, May 23, 1924, 546, 562. This last-named periodical will be cited hereafter as *DCA*.

16. Committee on Temporal Economy, Report No. 4, *JGC* (1924), 561–71, constitutes the majority report. The minority report was tabled 465 to 292, *DCA*, May 24, 1924, 574. *DCA* does not record the ayes and nays on the majority report, but one infers that the margin was at least as great as the vote on tabling the minority report.

17. *DCA*, May 23, 1924, 542, 543, 546, 559–60; May 24, 1924, 578–81, 582–83.

18. Ibid., May 24, 1924, 574.

19. Ibid., May 24, 1924, 572.

20. Ibid., May 23, 1924, 541–42.

21. Ibid., May 23, 1924, 560.

22. Ibid., May 23, 1924, 560, 566–67. In American Methodist legal vocabulary "amenable" referred to the duty of one person or agency to conform to instructions from another person or agency.

23. This combination of central financial control and decentralized decision-making resembled the development of multi-divisional corporate structure in some large American business during the 1920s and 1930s. See Chandler, *Strategy and Structure*. I have found, however, no evidence for influence in either direction.

24. Methodist Episcopal Church, Colorado Annual Conference, *Minutes* (1912), 50–51; *Minutes* (1913), 207; *Minutes* (1914), 327–28; *Minutes* (1915), 383; *Minutes* (1916), 11; *Christian Advocate* (New York), March 15, 1923, 337; *JGC* (1924), 136, 1803–4; World Service Commission, *Annual Report* (1924), 77–96. The minutes of the first meetings of the World Service Commission in 1924, included in this last citation, suggest some delay in the election of a treasurer but give no hint as to the reasons.

25. See G. Bromley Oxnam, "Ethical Standards for Investment of Church Funds," in [Orrin Auman (ed.),] *Annuity Agreements: Their Promotion and Management* (Chicago, 1926); and World Service Commission, *Annual Report* (1928), 48–50, a set of organizational charts in the treasurer's report that points to Auman's role in conceptualizing the work of the World Service Commission.

26. See the periodical, *Missiles for Methodist Minute Men* (1919–1920).

27. James J. Billingsley, *The Methodist Steward: A Study in Church Finance, with Special Reference to Ministerial Support* (Cincinnati, 1890).

28. *Men and Money*, 2, number 6 (October 1919): 23–27.

29. Ibid., 2, number 7 (December 1919): 22–28.

30. Ibid., 1, number 6 (October 1918): 7. This editorial was initialed and so represented something less than an official position of the magazine.

31. Ibid., 1, number 4 (June 1918): 168.

32. Committee on Temporal Economy, Report No. 9, *JGC* (1920), 560; "Was the Organist Irreverent—or Was It the Minister?" *Men and Money*, 1, number 4 (June 1918): 164.

33. Committee on Temporal Economy, Report No. 19, *JGC* (1912), 630–31; Committee on Temporal Economy, Report No. 9, *JGC* (1920), 561–62. The stewardship principles adopted in 1920 conflated Methodist Episcopal Church, *Doctrines and Discipline* (1916), paragraph 71, and "The Principles of Christian Stewardship," *Men and Money*, 1, number 1 (December 1917): 47.

34. Harris Franklin Rall, *A Christian's Financial Creed* (Chicago, [1914]), especially pp. 9–10; *idem*, "A Stewardship Creed," *Northwestern Christian Advocate*, January 21, 1920, 106. William J. McCutcheon's bibliographical study in his *Essays in American Theology: The Life and Thought of Harris Franklin Rall* (New York, 1973), 239, cited the Colorado imprint as the original of *A Christian's Financial Creed*. The Harris Franklin Rall Collection, Garrett-Evangelical Theological Seminary Library, Box 3, folder 9, contains a copy of the Commission on Finance imprint with the words, "revised edition," printed on the title page.

35. "The Principles of Christian Stewardship," *Men and Money*, 1, number 1 (December 1917):47; Harvey Reeves Catkins, "Stewardship Foundations and How to Teach," ibid., 1, number 5 (July 1918):216–21.

36. Catkins, *A Man and His Money* (New York and Cincinnati, 1914), 196. The theory of the origin of value in a collective mental process has considerable antiquity in Christian thought. See Marjorie Grice-Hutchinson, *The School of Salamanca; Readings in Spanish Monetary Theory 1544–1605* (Oxford, 1952); Raymond de Roover, *La pensée économique des scolastiques, doctrines et méthodes*, (Montreal and Paris, 1971), 46–75; *idem, Business, Banking, and Economic Thought in Late Medieval and Early Modern Europe*, ed. Julius Kirshner (Chicago and London, 1974), 15–36, 273–305, 306–35; and Odd Langholm, *Price and Value in the Aristotelian Tradition; A Study of Economic Sources* (Bergen, Oslo, and Troms, 1979). None of these works, however, explored the sources of Catkins' theological argument that the image of God in human beings consisted in their capacity to value.

37. Francis J. McConnell, *Church Finance and Social Ethics* (New York, 1920), 123.

38. *Men and Money*, 2, number 4 (August 1919): 15. My interpretation of this poem draws also on Cushman's "An Every-Morning Prayer," ibid., 2, number 7 (December 1919):2.

## Chapter 28
### Dunlap, *The United Methodist System of Itinerant Ministry*

1. *The Methodist Magazine*, Vol. XXV, 1843, 278. Quoted by James David Lynn, *The Concept of Ministry in the Methodist Episcopal Church, 1784–1844* (Ann Arbor: University Microfilms, 1978), 223.

2. Abel Stevens, *An Essay on Church Polity: Comprehending an Outline of the Controversy on Ecclesiastical Government, and a Vindication of the Ecclesiastical System of the Methodist Episcopal Church* (New York: Lane & Tippetts, 1847), 172f.

3. John Wesley, *The Letters of the Rev. John Wesley, A.M.*, John Telford, editor. Volume 3 (London: Epworth, 1931), 192.

4. John Wesley, *The Works of the Rev. John Wesley, A.M.*, Thomas Jackson, editor. Vol. VIII (London: John Mason, 1829), 311.

5. Ibid., 227. (See all of Part III, 201–47.)

6. Ibid., 313.

7. Ibid., 310.

8. Wesley, *Letters*, Vol. 3, 195.

9. A. B. Lawson, *John Wesley and the Christian Ministry* (London: S.P.C.K., 1963), 103–4.

10. James David Lynn, *The Concept of Ministry in the Methodist Episcopal Church 1784–1844* (Ann Arbor: University Microfilms, 1973), 81ff.

11. Frederick A. Norwood, "The Church Takes Shape, 1784–1824," *The History of American Methodism*, Vol. I, Emory Stevens Bucke, editor (New York: Abingdon, 1964), 469.

12. Frederick A. Norwood, "The Americanization of the Wesleyan Itinerant," *The Ministry in the Methodist Heritage*, Gerald O. McCulloh, editor (Nashville: The Board of Education of The Methodist Church, 1960), 44.

13. Quoted by Abel Stevens, *op. cit.*, 140f, from *1798 Discipline*.

14. Stevens, *op. cit.*, 1.

15. Horace Greeley Smith, "The Itinerant Ministry," *Methodism*, William K. Anderson, editor. (Cincinnati: The Methodist Publishing House, 1947), 161–66.

16. Francis Asbury, *The Journal and Letters of Francis Asbury*, Vol. I, Elmer T. Clark, J. Manning Potts, and Jacob L. Payton, editors (Nashville: Abingdon, 1958), 16.

17. Ibid.

18. Frank Baker, *From Wesley to Asbury: Studies in Early American Methodism* (Durham: Duke University Press, 1976), 120.

19. Ibid., 122.

20. Norwood, "The Church Takes Shape," *op. cit.*, 486–87.

21. Smith, *op. cit.*, 167.

22. Norwood, "The Shaping of the Methodist Ministry," *op. cit.*, 346f.

23. Robert W. Goodloe, *The Principles and Development of Church Government with Participation Application to Methodism* (Nashville: Cokesbury, 1932), 233. (Quoting Coke and Asbury's *Notes to the Discipline*.)

24. Norwood, "The Church Takes Shape," *op. cit.*, 469.

25. Ibid.

26. Quoted in Norwood, "The Americanization of the Wesleyan Itinerant," *op. cit.*, 50.

27. James A. Hensey, *The Layman in the Itinerancy* (New York: The Methodist Book Concern, 1919), 153f. Italics in the original.

28. Cited in Norwood, *The Story of American Methodism, op. cit.*, 137.

29. Ibid., 138.

30. Norwood, "The Shaping of Methodist Ministry," *op. cit.*, 342.

31. Norwood, "The Church Takes Shape. 1784–1824," *op. cit.*, 437.

32. Smith, *op. cit.*, 167.

33. Norwood, "The Americanization of the Wesleyan Itinerant," *op. cit.*, 36f.

34. F. Gerald Ensley, "American Methodism: An Experiment in Secular Christianity," in Bucke (ed.), *The History of American Methodism*, Vol III, 622.

35. Asbury, *op. cit.*, Vol. II, 288.

36. Norwood, "The Americanization of the Wesleyan Itinerant," *op. cit.*, 42f.

37. Harmon, *op. cit.*, p. 51. (Quoting from Coke and Asbury's *Notes*, p. 34.)

38. Norwood, "The Church Takes Shape, 1784–1824," *op. cit.*, 469. (Quoting from Asbury's Journal for February 1, 1809.)

39. Don W. Holter, "Some Changes Related to the Ordained Ministry", *Methodist History*, Vol. XIII, No. 3, April, 1975, 183f. (Quoting from W. W. Sweet, *Virginia Methodism, A History*, Richmond, 1955, 155.)

40. Ibid., 132.

41. Ibid., 183f. (Quoting from W. W. Sweet, *The Methodists, Religion on the American Frontier, 1783–1840*, Vol. IV, 50.)

42. Norwood, *The Story of American Methodism, op. cit.*, 139.

43. Ibid.

44. Lynn, *op. cit.*, 94. (quoting *The Address of the Bishops to the General Conference*, 1844, 11.)

45. Thomas B. Neely, *The Bishops and the Supervisional System of the Methodist Episcopal Church.* (Cincinnati, Jennings and Graham, 1912), 93f. (Quoting the answer to Question 26. What is the office of a Superintendent? from the *Discipline* of 1785.)

46. Harmon, *op. cit.*, 98f.

47. Buckley, *op. cit.*, 153ff.

48. Harmon, *op. cit.* (Citing *Journals of the General Conferences, 1796–1836*, New York, Carlton and Phillips, 1855, 56).

49. Norwood, *The Story of American Methodism, op. cit.*, p. 144. See also Smith, *op. cit.*, 169.

50. Harmon, *op. cit.*, 9.

51. Norwood, "The Americanization of the Wesleyan Itinerant," in *op. cit.*, 38.

52. Buckley, *op. cit.*, 134.

53. Charles T. Thrift, Jr. "Rebuilding the Southern Church," in Bucke (ed.), *The History of American Methodism*, Vol. II, 277.

54. Harmon, *op. cit.*, 9f.

55. Buckley, *op. cit.*, 134.

56. Harmon, *op. cit.*, 16.

57. Thrift, *op. cit.*, 277.

58. *Doctrines and Discipline of The Methodist Church* (New York: The Methodist Publishing House, 1939), Par. 400.1, 118.

59. *Doctrines and Discipline of The Methodist Church* (New York: The Methodist Publishing House, 1940), Par. 332.1, 99.

60. Frederick E. Maser, "The Story of Unification, 1874–1939," in Bucke (ed.), *The History of American Methodism*, Vol. III, 477.

61. Judicial Council Decision No. 111, 1954 *General Minutes*, 633–34, cited in Murray H. Leiffer, "United Methodism, 1940–60," in Bucke (ed.), *The History of American Methodism*, Vol. III, 514.

62. *Doctrines and Discipline of The Methodist Church* (Nashville: The Methodist Publishing House, 1948), Par. 432.1, 122.

63. *Doctrines and Discipline of The Methodist Church* (Nashville: The Methodist Publishing House, 1964), Par. 431.2, 176.

64. *The Book of Discipline of The United Methodist Church* (Nashville: The Methodist Publishing House, 1968), Par. 391.1, 143.

65. *The Book of Discipline of The United Methodist Church* (Nashville: The United Methodist Publishing House, 1972), Par. 391.1, 183.

66. *The Book of Discipline of the United Methodist Church* (Nashville: The United Methodist Publishing House, 1976), Pars. 527–531, 228–30.

67. Lynn, *op. cit.*, and Norwood, "The Americanization of the Wesleyan Itinerant," *op. cit.*

68. Lynn, *op. cit.*, 25f.

69. Norwood, "The Americanization of the Wesleyan Itinerant," in *op. cit.*, 53. His theses are stated on p. 35.

70. Goodloe, *op. cit.*, 237.

71. Cited by Lynn, *op. cit.*, 226.

72. Thomas B. Neely, *The Minister in the Appointive System* (New York: Fleming H. Revell Company, 1914), 89.

73. Gerald F. Moede, *The Office of Bishop in Methodism. Its History and Development* (New York: Abingdon, 1964), 115f.

### Chapter 29

Heitzenrater, *A Critical Analysis of the Ministry Studies Since 1948*

1. *The Methodist Ministry in 1948; Its Composition and Training and the Recruitment Needs of the Church* (Chicago: Methodist Publishing House, 1948), 63 pp.

2. *Report of The Commission to Study the Ministry* (n.p. [1952]), 16 pp.

3. *Daily Christian Advocate*, hereinafter cited as *DCA* (April 28, 1956), 17–24 (137–44).

4. *DCA* (May 1, 1956), 30 (250).

5. (Nashville: Board of Education, 1960), 143 pp.

6. *The Study of the Ministry, 1960–1964* (Nashville: Board of Education, 1964), 3; see also *DCA* (May 7, 1960), 61 (525), and *Journal of the General Conference*, hereinafter cited as *Journal*, (1964), 392.

7. *Journal* (1964), 397.

8. Ibid., 741.

9. Ibid., 737–38.

10. *DCA* (Nov. 11, 1966), 39 (935).

11. *DCA* (May 6, 1968), 67 (763).

12. *Journal* (1968), 624–25.

13. Ibid.

14. *DCA* (May 3, 1968), 21 (573).

15. *Journal* (1972), 1711–31.

16. Ibid., 1730–31.

17. "General ministry" was used by Fred Wertz in his report on the floor of the 1968 General Conference, but the report itself had used the term "ministry of the baptized." *Journal* (1968), 624; *DCA* (Apr. 30, 1968), 55 (391).

18. *Journal* (1976), 255.

19. Ibid., 256.

20. Ibid.

21. *DCA* (1976 Advance Ed.), G-12.

22. *Journal* (1976), 2162.

23. Ibid., 2161.

24. Ibid., 2158.
25. Ibid., 2162–66.
26. Ibid., 2166–67.
27. *DCA* (1980 Advance Ed.), E-25.
28. Ibid.
29. Ibid., E-25–26.
30. Ibid., E-28.
31. *Journal* (1980), 1110.
32. *DCA* (1984 Advance Ed.), E-22.
33. Ibid., E-23, D-189.
34. Ibid., E-23–24.
35. Ibid., E-26–27.
36. Ibid., E-24.
37. *DCA* (May 8, 1984), 69 (453).
38. *DCA* (1984 Advance Ed.), E-24–25.
39. *DCA* (May 5, 1984), 11 (267).
40. Vol. 11 (No. 1, Jan. 1987): 3–6.
41. *DCA* (May 8, 1984), 69–70 (453–54), 73 (457).

## Chapter 30
Deschner, *United Methodism's Basic Ecumenical Policy*

This chapter contains no notes.

## Chapter 31
White, *Methodist Worship*

1. Leslie Church, *The Early Methodist People* (London: Epworth, 1948), 222–62.
2. See *John Wesley's Sunday Service for the Methodists in North America*, Bicentennial Edition (Nashville: United Methodist Publishing House, 1984).
3. "Minutes of the Conferences," in *John Wesley*, ed. Albert C. Outler (New York: Oxford University Press, 1964), 144.
4. *Works of John Wesley*, ed. Albert C. Outer (Nashville: Abingdon, 1984), I, 381.
5. "The Rules of the United Societies," *John Wesley*, 179.
6. *Works of John Wesley*, III, 428–29.
7. John C. Bowmer, *The Sacrament of the Lord's Supper in Early Methodism* (Westminster: Dacre, 1951), 55.
8. Church, *Early Methodist People*, 155–60.
9. John Bishop, *Methodist Worship in Relation to Free Church Worship*, ([New York]: Scholars Studies, 1975), 92–94.
10. Frank Baker, *Methodism and the Love-Feast* (London: Epworth, 1957).
11. See excerpts for these by Laurence H. Stookey in *Seasons of the Gospel* (Nashville: Abingdon, 1979), 109.
12. David Tripp, *The Renewal of the Covenant in the Methodist Tradition*, (London: Epworth, 1969), 12–15.
13. *John Wesley's Sunday Service*, 139–61.

14. See John D. Grabner, "A Commentary on the Rites of 'An Ordinal,' The United Methodist Church" (unpublished Ph.D. diss., University of Notre Dame, 1983), 1–40.

15. George W. Dolbey, *The Architectural Expression of Methodism* (London: Epworth, 1964), and Paul N. Garber, *The Methodist Meeting House* (New York: Board of Missions, 1941).

16. Outler, *Works of John Wesley*, I, 13–29.

17. *John Wesley's Sunday Service*, 138.

18. *John Wesley's Sunday Service*, letter appended and dated Sept. 10, 1784.

19. See J. Ernest Rattenbury, *The Eucharistic Hymns of John and Charles Wesley*, (London: Epworth, 1948), 14–19.

20. Ibid., 195–249.

21. William N. Wade, "A History of Public Worship in the Methodist Episcopal Church" (Ph.D. diss., University of Notre Dame, 1981), 146–52.

22. Jesse Lee, *A Short History of the Methodists*, facsimile of 1810 ed. (Rutland, Vt.: Academy, 1974), 107.

23. William Chazanoff, *Welch's Grape Juice* (Syracuse, N.Y.: Syracuse University Press, 1977).

24. Thomas O. Summers, *The Golden Censer* (Nashville, 1859).

25. Andrew Trimen, *Church and Chapel Architecture* (London, 1849).

26. See the demographics in Whitney R. Cross, *The Burned-Over District* (New York: Harper & Row, 1965), 55–77.

27. See Peter Cartwright, *Fifty Years as a Presiding Elder* (Cincinnati, 1871), also *Autobiography*, intro. by Charles L. Wallis (Nashville: Abingdon, 1956).

28. Melva Wilson Costen and Darius Leander Swann, eds., "The Black Christian Worship Experience: A Consultation," *Journal of the Interdenominational Theological Center*, 14 (Fall 1986-Spring 1987).

29. Mechal Sobel, *The World They Made Together* (Princeton, N.J.: Princeton University Press, 1987), 204–13.

30. *The Wesleyan Camp Meeting Hymn Book* (Wendell, Mass., 1829), nos. 12 and 86.

31. See William T. Ward, *Variety in the Prayer Meeting* (Cincinnati: Methodist Book Concern, 1915).

32. Joseph E. Gould, *The Chautauqua Movement: An Episode in the Continuing American Revolution* (Albany, N.Y.: State University of New York Press, 1961).

33. Charles Johnson, *The Frontier Campmeeting* (Dallas: S.M.U. Press, 1955), 41–48.

34. Bernard Ruffin, *Fanny Crosby* (Philadelphia: United Church, 1976).

35. J. Jefferson Cleveland, "A Historical Account of the Hymn in the Black Worship Experience," *Songs of Zion* (Nashville: Abingdon, 1981), 1–4.

36. See Elbert Conover, *The Church Builder* (New York: Interdenominational Bureau, n.d.), *Building the House of God* (New York: Methodist Book Concern, 1928), and *The Church Building Guide* (New York: Interdenominational Bureau, 1946).

37. *The Christian Year* (New York: Federal Council of Churches, 1937 and 1940).

38. Nolan B. Harmon, *The Rites and Ritual of Episcopal Methodism* (Nashville: Publishing House of the M. E. Church, South, 1926).

39. Wilbur P. Thirkield and Oliver Huckel, *Book of Common Worship* (New York: E. P. Dutton, 1932).

40. Johnston Ross, *Christian Worship and Its Future* (Nashville: Abingdon, 1927).

41. Fitzgerald Parker, *The Practice and Experience of Christian Worship* (Nashville: Cokesbury, 1929).

42. David L. Taylor, "The Order of St. Luke and the *Versicle*," *Doxology* III (1986), 48–56.

43. Stephen W. McNierney, *Underground Mass Book* (Baltimore: Helicon, 1968).

44. These were all published in Nashville by United Methodist Publishing House or Abingdon, 1972–88.

45. *The United Methodist Hymnal* (Nashville: United Methodist Publishing House, 1989).

46. *An Ordinal* (Nashville: United Methodist Publishing House, 1980).

47. *Common Lectionary* (New York: Church Hymnal Corp., 1983).

48. *The Methodist Service Book* (London: Methodist Publishing House, 1975).

49. *Hymns and Psalms* (London: Methodist Publishing House, 1983).

## Chapter 32

Richey, *History as a Bearer of Denominational Identity: Methodism as a Case Study*

1. This essay is inspired by, though it heads in slightly different directions than, Kenneth E. Rowe's "Counting the Converts: Progress Reports as Church History," (Richey and Rowe, 1985: 11–17).

2. The propositions take most expressive form in mid-nineteenth century Methodist histories. Typical and illustrative of this first belief are these words of M. L. Scudder, affirming that the hand of providence has been continually at work in Methodism: "Have you never thought that Methodism is *providence philosophically illustrated*? 'It is the glory of God to conceal a thing'; and providence always implies concealment. But true philosophy is wisdom applying proper means to secure an end. The means that have opened before us our entire progress as a people have been so wisely ordered, that I say Methodism is providence philosophically illustrated" (Scudder, 1868: 270).

Scudder viewed "the whole economy of Methodism," as "a harmonious, well-arranged, and well-balanced ecclesiastical polity," "actively working in 'spreading scriptural holiness over the land'" (363).

3. According to Scudder, "Methodism claims to be of God, not only by his ordinary and general permission or supervision of all events, but by his assistance and direction in its own particular history. It claims that the specific work of the Spirit on the hearts of its members, renewing them, and changing them from a death in sin to a life of righteousness, is an oft-repeated attestation of God's presence in the church. It claims that there are unmistakable evidences of the intervention of the divine hand in the peculiar phases of its existence, that this power has accompanied its agencies, and has supported and given succor to its workmen. And it claims also, that the opportune introduction of Methodism, when the condition of the Protestant Church, the moral degeneracy of society, and the peculiar wants of the New World, demanded just such an

evangelical movement as Methodism introduced, is sufficient proof that its origin and design was from God" (Scudder, 1868: 521). This chapter treats "The Opportune Advent of Methodism."

Scudder continued, "Methodists claim, that, while God has been with the itinerants, making their word the power of God unto salvation, and has graciously directed the minds of the leaders of Methodism to adopt measures that have proved an efficient evangelical working system, he has also been introducing, by all these, a grand reforming agency, to fulfil his gracious designs, and an agency, too, of inestimable value, because it met the imperative necessities of the age" (523).

"There is a sense in which it may be said that Methodism was sent 'in the fullness of time.' . . . because it was adapted to meet the exigencies or wants of all" (524).

4. Scudder argued for Methodism's role in formation of American society on the premise that "The general character of the nation, its form of government, its enterprise, and its moral condition, are mainly the formations of its religious agencies. The introduction of Methodism was at a time when the wants of the nation demanded just such characteristics in its religion as Methodism supplied."

"First of all, there was a great need of a religion of the heart,— . . . a new religious life . . . " (529–30).

"The churches of America, at the time of the introduction of Methodism, needed reformation in their creed as well as in their religious experience . . . (531)." Calvinism, he thought, produced apathy, indifference to religious duty and fatalism, while Arminianism supplied and Methodism modeled activity for salvation. Methodism addressed itself also to "Infidelity—the alternative to Calvinism" through its doctrine of universal redemption (532). Methodism also showed "the superiority of a church independent of the patronage or the support of the state" (532).

Methodism was appropriate for the new nation: "It needed a religion, in its sentiments, its activity, and its hopes, corresponding to the mind and energies of the nation itself. It found that religion in Methodism. The doctrines of the freedom of the will, of a universal atonement, of the equal privilege of all men to be saved, of personal responsibility to obey the divine law, and of the duty of men to advance in the knowledge and practice of holiness,—were all corollaries morally applied, of the political doctrines of the new republic. . . . The new nation introduced a new epoch in the political governments of the world; and Methodism, congenial in its spirit with the nation, was opportunely at hand to introduce a new epoch, and to begin a new evangelical movement in the progress of Christianity in the world" (534).

5. For Scudder, "[H]e that to-day declares that Methodism is to be the future controlling religious power of this nation, and that it will be multiplied in its numbers, and increased in its influence, so that upon it will devolve a large responsibility in determining what shall be the religious character of the American people, would only be stating prospective facts, the truth of which might be presumed by every principle of reasoning from a known cause to a legitimate result. The resources and present position of Methodism warrant such a declaration" (Scudder, 1868: 569).

6. For reasons of control, the paper will focus upon The Methodist Episcopal Church, its successor The Methodist Church and its successor The United Methodist Church. For the most part, the generalizations apply, but with important variations, to the experience of The Methodist Protestant Church, The Methodist Episcopal Church,

South, the United Brethren in Christ and The Evangelical Association as well as to members of the Wesleyan family of denominations not contributory to United Methodism.

7. It is not the place of this paper to chart policy for the denomination, but one cannot help but wonder if the time has not arrived for the leaders to quit blaming themselves and the church for losing membership and to expend some time quietly inspecting the structural damage.

8. The inclusion of Methodist history within the required reading in the training of Methodist ministers provides part of the rationale for taking history seriously as a statement of Methodist identity. That requirement also serves as an important criterion in determining which histories to take seriously. Beginning in 1816, candidates for the ministry in the Methodist Episcopal Church followed a prescribed "course of study," a reading list initially elaborated and supervised on the regional "annual conference" level, eventually operated as a kind of national college. With the exception of Jesse Lee and James M. Buckley, whose histories claimed preeminence on other grounds, the individuals given attention here figured prominently in the course of study, thus constituting an important formative influence on successive generations of Methodist ministers. In most cases, the individual histories enjoyed a long life on the course. Abel Stevens' *History of the Methodist Episcopal Church* appeared on the course in 1864, 1868, 1880, 1896, 1890 and then again in 1932; his compressed version thereof, *A Compendious History of American Methodism* remained on from 1872 to 1908, with only a curious gap of 1900, when another of his works took its place. The historians and their histories will be treated in chronological order: Jesse Lee, Nathan Bangs, Abel Stevens, Matthew Simpson, James M. Buckley, the team of Halford E. Luccock and Paul Hutchinson, William Warren Sweet and Frederick A. Norwood. Each provided the major statement about Methodist history in his own day. Lee wrote the first Methodist history and in many ways set the terms for the genre. Buckley's effort appeared in the prestigious American Society of Church History series (Bowden, 1977).

9. For the criteria of selection see the reference to the course of study in the prior note. This argument relies upon L. Dale Patterson whose "The Ministerial Mind of American Methodism: The Course of Study for the Ministry of the Methodist Episcopal Church, the Methodist Episcopal Church, South and the Methodist Protestant Church, 1876–1920," (Ph.D. dissertation, Drew University) carefully identifies the literature of the course and the years each item was used. The historians are, as a prior note indicates, representative of The Methodist Episcopal tradition.

10. That saga, and particularly the declaration of independence by a group of the 'southern' preachers through presbyterial ordination thereby splitting the American movement, has been typically written from the Asbury side of the split, a side which sought to remain loyal to Wesley and not separate from him or the Church of England. Here as elsewhere Lee's handling of the story evidences his eagerness to show the American contours of the Methodist story. In so doing, however, he does not formally link church to nation.

11. Bangs prefaced this four volume statement with a discussion of his sources. Among them, he acknowledged "Bancroft's 'History of the Colonization of the United States'" for his initial discussion. He defended his decision to make "Bishop Asbury the

principal hero of the narrative" (I: 6). He also indicated his respect for Lee and dependence upon Lee's *History* (I: 7).

12. "In addition to the direct influence which Christian principles were thus brought to exert on the heart and life, the itinerating mode of preaching had a tendency in the natural order of cause and effect, to cement the hearts of our citizens together in one great brotherhood. . . . What more calculated to soften these asperities [state and sectional rivalries], and to allay petty jealousies and animosities, than a Church bound together by one system of doctrine, under the government of the same discipline, accustomed to the same usages, and a ministry possessing a homogeneousness of character, aiming at one and the same end—the salvation of their fellow-men by means of the same gospel, preached and enforced by the same method—and these ministers continually interchanging from north to south, from east to west, everywhere striving to bring all men under the influence of the same 'bond of perfectness'? Did not these things tend to bind the great American family together by producing a sameness of character, feelings, and views?" (II: 148–49)

Bangs noted that the church in its General Conference recognized that "a general itinerating superintendency [episcopacy] would "prevent local interests and jealousies from springing up, and tend most effectually to preserve that homogeneousness of character and reciprocity of brotherly feeling by which Methodism had been and should be ever distinguished" (III: 54–55).

This is a point which Donald Mathews has elaborated into a general theory concerning the second Awakening (1969) and C. C. Goen into a theory of the cause of the Civil War (1985).

13. The most frequent reference here will be to the condensed (608 pp.) of Stevens's versions—his *Compendium History*. This appeared on the Course of Study for the quadrenniums of 1872 to 1908 with the sole exception of 1900. That year his *Supplementary History of American Methodism* (New York: Eaton & Mains, 1899), which had just appeared, took its place. The course also featured Stevens's four volume treatment of American Methodism (1864–67) in 1864, 1868, 1880, 1896, 1900 and again interestingly in 1932. His work covering the whole Wesleyan tradition, *History of the Religious Movement Called Methodism* (1858–61), enjoyed the longest, most sustained tenure on the Course, continuously from 1860 to 1928, with the sole exception of 1884. That 72 year reign, 1860 to 1932 (when the work dropped off), attests the great influence enjoyed by Stevens.

14. Stevens's four volume *History of the Methodist Episcopal Church* (1864–67) begins with the same scene but lacks the chapter title. His *Religious Movement* (1858–61) gave only incidental attention to American developments and so did not lend itself to this vignette. Stevens achieved the same point there, the providential fitting of Methodism for America, with different staging and assertion. (1858–61, II: 434–37).

15. We have noticed above (notes 1–4), M. L. Scudder's enunciation of these axioms (1868). The viewpoints become a staple of Northern Methodist belief during and after the Civil War. Simpson's volume is the first history featuring such views that figured on the Course of Study. It did not displace Stevens but was put on a different segment of the Course, the reading list for local preachers. It first appeared there in 1876 and remained for three more quadrennia (1876, 1880, 1884, 1888).

16. A work that appeared at roughly the same time as Stevens's, Jesse Peck's *The History of The Great Republic* (1869), much more decidedly reflected the church's investment in the nation. Here Methodism self-consciously enunciated the public theology of a Christian America. Peck proclaimed that "the theory of this book is, that God is the rightful, actual sovereign of all nations; that a purpose to advance the human race beyond all its precedents in intelligence, goodness, and power, formed this Great Republic; and that religion is the only life-force and organizing power of liberty" (2, the above appeared in italics). See also pp. 693, 707.

17. From the very earliest days of the movement, interpreters of Methodism have found statistics, particularly comparisons of American Methodism with its British counterpart, with other denominations and with the population as a whole to have almost revelatory force. Statistical assessments of the movement abound. For instance, Goss (1866: 159) affirmed: "The moral influence of Methodism is at least commensurate with its numerical strength. In no department of Christian effort are Methodists behind their sister denominations." Then he demonstrated that with respect to Sunday schools, tract distribution, Bible circulation, home missions, foreign missions and publishing.

18. The editor was Philip Schaff, who argued strenuously that it was the church historian's office and responsibility to discern the activity of God in human affairs. Schaff was a major, perhaps the major, figure in the emergence of the discipline of church history (Bowden, 1971). The inclusion of Buckley's volume in his series gave it great prominence. It was certainly frequently reprinted or republished, twelve times according to Rowe (1975-, II: 209–10). First published in 1896, Buckley's history went through six editions as a part of the ASCH series, the 6th appearing in 1907. Another version was reprinted in a 3rd edition in 1909. The first edition was again reprinted in 1973. It is because of the importance of this series and of Buckley's inclusion in it, that we include Buckley in this study. His work apparently did not appear on the Course of Study.

19. See, for instance, a volume contemporaneous to Buckley's, Henry Wheeler's *One Thousand Questions and Answers concerning the Methodist Episcopal Church* and especially questions 1 and 66 (1, 16).

20. "But it is his duty to display their words and actions, and the utterances and deeds of those who antagonized them, so far as possible as they would present them. These, with the results of the conflict, will enable those who read to estimate the relation of events to human and divine providence—the factors in the development of every form of Christianity" (xviii).

21. Luccock and Hutchinson's *Story of Methodism* appeared on the Course of Study from 1932 through 1956. For all of those quadrennia except 1944, it was collateral reading. In 1944, it was required for admission on trial.

22. Illustrative, perhaps, is this statement concerning the crowds who heard Wesley: "Clearly the hand of God was in this, for here were myriads—the word is Wesley's own—of people who never darkened a church door brought to hear a word that was again proving its ancient power" (19). Or again, "Whether he realized it not, John Wesley returned to his great task in England at the moment when the movement of world forces had marked that 'tight little island' for a spiritual shaking. . . . England was ringed round with revival. It was time something burst loose" (73).

Of the sending of missionaries to America: "It was a prophetic moment at which Boardman and Pilmoor sailed" (142). And, "Methodism did not spring to life in America without long years of preparation. There is always a background for spiritual marvels, even when it is least apparent" (172).

Of the events of 1784: "The ordinations of Methodism are entirely outside the mechanical realm. They derive their authority from the fact that their originator, John Wesley, was a man whose ministry was evidently approved of God. And if ever the time comes when the ordaining ministry of Methodism is not thus approved, it will be time to scrap the whole thing, and start again from another life with self-authenticating powers" (158).

A comparison of the shadows of two men on horseback, Napoleon Bonaparte, on Europe and Francis Asbury, on America: "It is still easy to trace in the affairs of the United States the influence of this single man, Francis Asbury—Methodism's man on horseback. God send us such another" (232)!

23. Their predecessors, even Lee, attempted to be scholarly according to the expectations of the day. Luccock and Hutchinson made no such effort. The volume footnoted only where cited material was protected by copyright. (See, for instance, their references to Ezra Squier Tipple's *Francis Asbury, The Prophet of the Long Road*, 236, 241, 242.) They also offered no bibliography.

24. "The characteristic answer of Methodism to the war was the Centenary. Long before the United States entered the war the church had planned to celebrate with a program of missionary expansion. . . . Then, as the extent of the needs became more clear, home missions was included, and later the war relief work. . . . Finally, practically all the work which the Methodists of America, both north and south, planned to do outside their local congregations during the five years following 1919 was made a part of the Centenary's interest. The cost of this five years of work was fixed at more than one hundred million dollars" (485).

"It is still too early to judge the Centenary fully. . . . But it is possible to see that some things were accomplished. In the first place, American Methodists were helped to think of their religious enterprise in world terms at precisely the same time that Americans were being called on to think of all their other enterprises in those terms. . . . Standards of giving were raised. Young life was called to the service of the church with much the same enthusiasm as had recently been employed in recruiting for the nation's service. New buildings were erected, new enterprises begun, both in America and on other continents" (486–87).

25. Sweet's volume appeared on the Course of Study for the quadrennia beginning 1932, 1936, 1940 and 1944, for the first three as a requirement for admission on trial and for the last as collateral reading.

26. Sweet employed this, in a more generalized form, as his organizing principle in *Religion in the Development of American Culture* (1952).

## References for Chapter 32

**Discipline**

1787: *A Form of Discipline, For the Ministers, Preachers and Members of the Methodist Episcopal Church in America*. New York: n.p.

1988: *The Book of Discipline of the United Methodist Church.* Nashville: United Methodist Publishing House.

**Asbury, Francis**
1958: *The Journal and Letters of Francis Asbury.* 3 vols. London: Epworth; Nashville: Abingdon.

**Bangs, Nathan**
1837: *An Original Church of Christ.* New York: T. Mason and G. Lane.

1860: *A History of The Methodist Episcopal Church.* 4 vols., 6th edition. New York: Carlton & Porter; 1st ed. 1838–1841.

**Bercovitch, Sacvan**
1978: *The American Jeremiad.* Madison: University of Wisconsin Press.

**Bowden, Henry W.**
1971: *Church History in the Age of Science: Historiographical Patterns in the United States, 1876–1918.* Chapel Hill: University of North Carolina Press.

**Buckley, J. M.**
1900: *A History of Methodists in the United States,* 4th ed., American Church History Series. New York: Scribner. [First published in 1896.]

**Crooks, George R.**
1891: *The Life of Bishop Matthew Simpson.* New York: Harper & Brothers.

**Goen, C. C.**
1985: *Broken Churches, Broken Nation. Denominational Schisms and the Coming of the American Civil War.* Macon: Mercer University Press.

**Goss, C. C.**
1866: *Statistical History of the First Century of American Methodism.* New York: Carlton & Porter.

**Handy, Robert T.**
1984: *A Christian America. Protestant Hopes and Historical Realities.* 2nd ed., New York: Oxford University Press.

**Harmon, Nolan B.**
1974: *The Encyclopedia of World Methodism.* 2 vols., Nashville: The United Methodist Publishing House.

**Hermann, Richard E.**
1973: *Nathan Bangs: Apologist for American Methodism.* Ph.D. Diss., Emory University.

**Lee, Jesse**
1810: *A Short History of the Methodists.* Baltimore: Magill and Clime. Facsimile edition, Rutland, Vt: Academy, 1974.

**Lee, Leroy M.**
1848: *The Life and Times of The Rev. Jesse Lee.* Charleston: John Early for The Methodist Episcopal Church, South.

**Luccock, Halford E. and Paul Hutchinson**
1926: *The Story of Methodism.* New York: Methodist Book Concern.

**Mathews, Donald G.**
1969: "The Second Great Awakening as an Organizing Process, 1780–1830," *American Quarterly*, XXI, 23–43. Also in *Religion in American History*, John M. Mulder and John F. Wilson, eds. Englewood Cliffs: Prentice Hall, 1978.

**Mead, Sidney E.**
1975: *The Nation with the Soul of a Church.* New York: Harper & Row, Publishers.

**Moore, R. Laurence**
1986: *Religious Outsiders and the Making of Americans.* New York: Oxford University Press.

**Noll, Mark A.**
1988: *One Nation under God?* San Francisco: Harper & Row, Publishers.

**Norwood, Frederick A.,**
1974: *The Story of American Methodism.* Nashville: Abingdon.

**Norwood, Frederick A., ed.**
1982: *Sourcebook of American Methodism.* Nashville: Abingdon.

**Peck, Jesse T.**
1869: *The History of The Great Republic, Considered from a Christian Standpoint.* New York: Broughton and Wyman.

**Pilkington, James Penn**
1968: *The Methodist Publishing House: A History.* Vol. I (Beginnings to 1870). Nashville: Abingdon.

**Richey, Russell E. and Kenneth E. Rowe**
1985: *Rethinking Methodist History.* Nashville: Kingswood.

**Richey, Russell E.**
1989: "History in The Discipline," *Quarterly Review* 10 (Winter 1989), 3–20.

**Rowe, Kenneth E.**
1975: *Methodist Union Catalog: Pre-1976 prints.* Multi-volume series, in process. Metuchen, N.J.: Scarecrow.

**Scudder, M. L.**
1868: *American Methodism.* Hartford: S. S. Scranton.

**Shalhope, Robert E.**
1982: "Republicanism and Early American Historiography," *William and Mary Quarterly*, 39 (April), 334–56.

**Simpson, Matthew**
1876: *A Hundred Years of Methodism*. New York: Nelson & Phillips.

**Stevens, Abel**
1858–61: *The History of the Religious Movement of the Eighteenth Century Called Methodism*. 3 vols. New York: Philips & Hunt.
1864–67: *A History of The Methodist Episcopal Church*. 4 vols., New York: Carlton & Porter.
1868: *A Compendious History of American Methodism*. New York: Eaton & Mains, n.d. but 1868/67.

**Sweet, William Warren**
1952: *Religion in the Development of American Culture, 1765–1840*. New York: Scribner.
1953: *Methodism in American History*. Rev. ed. New York: Abingdon. [First published in 1933.]

**Thrift, Minton**
1823: *Memoir of the Rev. Jesse Lee. With Extracts from his Journals*. New York: Published by N. Bangs and T. Mason for the Methodist Episcopal Church.

**Tigert, Jno. J.**
1908: *A Constitutional History of American Episcopal Methodism*. 3rd ed., rev., Nashville: Publishing House of the Methodist Episcopal Church, South.

**Wheeler, Henry**
1898: *One Thousand Questions and Answers Concerning the Methodist Episcopal Church*. New York: Eaton & Mains.

**Wilson, John F.**
1979: *Public Religion in American Culture*. Philadelphia: Temple University Press.